Jewish Radicalisms

**Europäisch-jüdische Studien
Beiträge**
European-Jewish Studies
Contributions

Edited by the Moses Mendelssohn Center
for European-Jewish Studies, Potsdam

Editorial Manager: Werner Treß

Volume 39

Jewish Radicalisms

Historical Perspectives on a Phenomenon of Global Modernity

Edited by Frank Jacob and Sebastian Kunze

DE GRUYTER
OLDENBOURG

ISBN: 978-3-11-054345-2
e-ISBN (PDF): 978-3-11-054575-3
e-ISBN (EPUP): 978-3-11-054352-0
ISSN 2192-9602

Library of Congress Control Number: 2019950211

Bibliographic information published by the Deutsche Nationalbibliothek
The Deutsche Nationalbibliothek lists this publication in the Deutsche Nationalbibliografie; detailed bibliographic data are available on the Internet at http://dnb.dnb.de.

Druck und Bindung: CPI books GmbH, Leck

www.degruyter.com

Table of Contents

Section II Religious Radicalisms

Section III Cultural Radicalisms

Sebastian Kunze and Frank Jacob

Introduction

Thoughts on Jewish Radicalism as a Phenomenon of Global Modernity

Some people are just radical, according to their contemporaries. Radicalism, of course, can be expressed in many ways, e.g. politically, religiously, socially, but whether it is perceived as radical depends largely on how such acts are evaluated according to existent norms. Therefore, it is almost not surprising that what Merriam-Webster defines as "the quality or state of being radical" or "the doctrines and principles of radicals"[1] does not suffice in explaining the phenomenon. Furthermore, it is not easy to define radicalism because different and often overlapping forms of it, with varying levels of radical intensity, can exist at the same time. For example, as Italian sociologist Massimo Rosati (1969–2014) has shown in his discussion of Émile Durkheim's (1858–1917) radicalism, social radicalism "does not [only] consist in escaping social norms [or] roles. It does not consist in an affected opposition to every norm rule, or simply in criticizing their repressive and coercive role, but in being able to dance on the razor's edge between the two poles."[2] What is constituted as radical is consequently, as has been said before, usually based on accepted norms in the societies in which said radicals live.

In 2016, we discussed the idea of editing a volume on something we initially called "Jewish radicalism", which was not too specific at that time. However, a quick survey of the literature containing "Jewish" and "radicalism" in its titles highlighted two main problems: 1) they usually draw an implicit (and sometimes explicit) connection between being "radical" and being "leftist" (in any variation of its meaning) in the context of Jewish radicalism, and 2) there is far less explicit literature on this issue than expected, especially those that count as part of the research on "radicalism". To approach this topic's primary issues, as well as to display the vast body of research discussing it, we decided to edit a volume on Jewish radicalism as a phenomenon in global modernity.

It is important to understand that Jewish radicalism was not only a phenomenon that many Jews were a part of, but also that it was the backbone of many

1 "Radicalism," in *Merriam-Webster Online Dictionary*, accessed February 15 2018, https://www.merriam-webster.com/dictionary/radicalism.

2 Massimo Rosati, "Forms of Radicalism: Theoretical and Social Radicalism in Durkheim," *Durkheimian Studies*, New Series 10 (2004): 13.

https://doi.org/10.1515/9783110545753-001

left-wing organizations on both sides of the Atlantic.[3] However, this does not mean that the radicals' Jewishness was a precondition for their political radicalism.[4] Jewish radicalism is also not limited to the political arena or to left-wing individuals. There are different forms of Jewish radicalism, and these forms will be highlighted in the present volume.

When we call it a phenomenon of global modernity, we seek to emphasize that Jewish radicalism can often not be understood as a local phenomenon; it must be considered in a broader context. While Jewish communities live in a global diaspora, they remain in close contact with each other. This is why radicalization stemmed from places besides Eastern Europe's *shtetls* where Jews were often victims of pogroms, but also took place in urban centers of the modern world, such as Berlin, London, New York, Paris, Rome, etc.[5] As such, the evolution of Jewish radicalism is global and relevant to modernity, which is considered the time after the French Revolution of 1789. Following Benedict Anderson's (1936–2015) claim that print capitalism stimulated the formation of imagined communities,[6] it was the availability of transnationally read newspapers and journals, as well as their "global" distribution, that allowed Jewish radicals to establish a broad communication network in which ideas, radical or not, could be exchanged.[7] Another aspect that makes Jewish radicalism a modern global phenomenon is the transnational mobility of its actors, who very often could look back on different lives in different places. Their radicalism was therefore the product of a multi-spatial global modernity, as the actors of Jewish radicalism were not locally radicalized, but radicalized according to their transnational experiences.[8] Many Jews left Eastern Europe between the 1880s and 1920s to find new homes abroad, where they would either become radicalized

---

3 Jack Jacobs, "Introduction," in *Jews and Leftist Politics: Judaism, Israel, Antisemitism, and Gender*, ed. Jack Jacobs (Cambridge/New York: Cambridge University Press, 2017), 1. For Eastern Europe, see Alain Brossat and Sylvia Klingsberg, *Revolutionary Yiddishland: A History of Jewish Radicalism*, trans. David Fernbach (London/New York: Verso, 2016).

4 Frank Jacob will discuss this issue in more detail in his chapter within the present volume.

5 One example of such a transnational perspective is discussed in Philip Mendes, "From the Shtetl to the Monash Soviet: An Overview of Jewish Radicalism in Australia," *Australian Journal of Jewish Studies* 14 (2000): 54–77.

6 Benedict Anderson, *Imagined Communities: Reflections on the Origin and Spread of Nationalism* (London: Verso, 1991).

7 One relevant case study on this transnational network of communication and print capitalism is Tony Michels, "Exporting Yiddish Socialism: New York's Role in the Russian Jewish Workers' Movement," *Jewish Social Studies: History, Culture, Society* n.s. 16, no. 1 (2009): 1–26.

8 With regard to the relation between Jews and Anarchism see Amedero Bertolo, ed. *Juifs et anarchistes: Histoire d'une rencontre* (Paris: Eclat, 2008).

by the local preconditions or spread radical ideas they had acquired prior to emigrating.[9] Consequently, the global nature of their transportation and communication not only created modernity, but also a possibility for transnational radicalism on a global scale.[10]

Because different forms of Jewish radicalism post-1789 have been global phenomena, we have chosen to provide a panorama of case studies that showcase the scope of this volume and its contributions. This will not only provide critical insight into current academic discourse, research, and various topics from multiple fields, but also highlight the diversity of Jewish radicalism. However, discussions about Jewish radicalism are not limited to the topics in the present volume. They should be further investigated from their local, national, and global perspectives. We hope that the discussions of the topics as they appear in the present volume will stimulate further research in the field. Comparing Jewish radicalism and its developments in different national contexts would also be helpful. However, since it is, as we tried to highlight before, not always clear what the term "Jewish radicalism" refers to, we will discuss it further here.

Jewish Radicalism

Over the last forty years, books have been written about Jewish radicalism and Jewish radicals. Most of these published works draw an implicit connection between being radical, being leftist, and being Jewish. For many authors, a right-wing radical could obviously not be Jewish, or a right-wing Jew radical. In 1973, Jack Porter and Peter Dreier edited the volume *Jewish Radicalism: A Select-*

---

9 S. Robert Lichter and Stanley Rothman, "Jewish Ethnicity and Radical Culture: A Social Psychological Study of Political Activists," *Political Psychology* 3, no. 1/2 (1981/1982): 118; Kenyon Zimmer, "Saul Yanovsky and Yiddish Anarchism on the Lower East Side," in *Radical Gotham: Anarchism in New York City from Schwab's Saloon to Occupy Wall Street*, ed. Tom Goyens (Urbana/Chicago/Springfield, IL: University of Illinois Press, 2017), 34–35.

10 Emily S. Rosenberg, *A World Connecting, 1870–1945* (Cambridge, MA: Belknap Press of Harvard University Press 2012) provides a detailed analysis of the advances that "shortened" distances and made the movement of large numbers of people possible. For further discussions of these developments, see Peter Puntis, Candrika Kaul, and Jürgen Wilke, eds., *International Communication and Global News Networks: Historical Perspectives* (New York: Hampton Press, 2011); Richard Tames, *The Transport Revolution in the 19th Century: A Documentary Approach* (London: Oxford University Press, 1970); Dwayne Winseck and Robert M. Pike, *Communication and Empire: Media, Markets, and Globalization, 1860–1930* (Durham, NC: Duke University Press, 2007).

ed Anthology.[11] In their introduction, they make it clear what their volume is about: the Jewish left as a "movement of dissent."[12] The two scholars explicitly focus their anthology on the Jewish left during the 1960s, which they identify as a radical movement. In addition, Porter and Dreier trace this current movement back in time: "The early part of this century saw the simultaneous rise of two mass movements among Jews – a Jewish labor movement and a Jewish radical political movement."[13] Although Porter and Dreier dedicated their anthology to a Jewish radical leftist movement, they also observed another "mainstream" movement on the rise – they added an interview and discussion about the *Jewish Defense League* and the ideas of Meir Kahane (1932–1990), but in doing so, the editors excluded Kahane and his disciples as radicals:

> Yet we should not overlook a decidedly nonradical approach which has attracted growing numbers of young Jews, particularly in working-class areas of New York. This is the other side of the ideological coin, the right-wing Zionism of the Jewish Defense League and Betar, and their own hero, Zev [sic] Jabotinsky [...] The Jewish Left is ambivalent toward Rabbi Meir Kahane and his followers. Most radical Jews are critical of the J.D.L.'s strategy [...][14]

Although Porter and Dreier included Kahane in their book, they did not recognize him as a radical. This means they viewed Jewish radicalism as a category to be attributed exclusively to the political left and to the Jews who identified as such. Consequently, the editors drew an implicit but strong connection between being radical and belonging to the Jewish left, which is also connected to the self-perception of Jewish leftists as radicals.

This connection is also observed in Percy S. Cohen's study *Jewish Radicals and Radical Jews* (1980), in which the British scholar traces the historical connection of being Jewish and being radical, focusing solely on the political left. He states that:

> The term radical, as used throughout this book, means 'left-wing radical'; the existence of right-wing radicalism is neither denied nor even questioned. Thus when certain forms of radicalism are characterized or explained, these characterizations and explanations are directed to left-wing radicalism (or radicals) or to Jewish left-wing radicals or radicalism.[15]

---

11 Jack N. Porter and Peter Dreier, eds., *Jewish Radicalism: A Selected Anthology* (New York: Grove Press, 1973).

12 Ibid., xlv.

13 Ibid., xvii.

14 Ibid., xxxii.

15 Percy S. Cohen, *Jewish Radicals and Radical Jews* (London/New York: Academic Press 1980), 11.

While Cohen recognizes that there are more possible connections beyond being radical and being left-wing, he concentrates on Jewish left-wing radicalism; forms of right-wing radicalism are thus invisible in his work. Nevertheless, Cohen also highlighted that one must distinguish between Jewish radicals and radical Jews, and these categories are based on the "Jewishness" of the radical identity in question.[16]

A decade later, Jaff Schatz published *The Generation: The Rise and Fall of the Jewish Communist of Poland* (1991)[17] in which he frames the Jewish communist as the role model of Jewish radicalism. He writes about "Polish-Jewish radicals"[18] and adds that "[i]n modern times, radical Jews caught the attention of the world," even though "compared to their peers, [they were] the most radical of all radical Jews."[19] At the same time, "it is important to keep in mind that extreme radicals formed but a tiny minority among Jews as a whole."[20] Schatz writes a great deal about Jewish radicals and has equated being a Jewish radical with being active in the political left, particularly in communist organizations. The association between being radical and left-wing has also been demonstrated in more recent studies by different authors, such as Gerben Zaagsma in 2010: "I use the word 'radicals' as a catch all phrase for those of Jewish descent who were active in the socialist and communist movements of the time and not to denote the existence of something called 'Jewish radicalism'."[21] Tony Michels and Philip Mendes are two other examples. The former edited a volume on Jewish radicals in 2012 and focused mainly on Jewish-American socialist history, outlining his approach to radicalism in the book's introduction: "Our discussion of Jews and radicalism has, so far, focused on immigrants, but the story does not end with them. Socialism also held strong appeal for second-generation American born and raised Jews [...]."[22]

Mendes' approach was different. He did not study Jewish radicals, but rather the connection between Jews and left-wingers. His 2014 study *Jews and the Left: The Rise and Fall of a Political Alliance* does not examine connections between

---

16 Ibid., 9.

17 Jaff Schatz, *The Generation: The Rise and Fall of the Jewish Communist of Poland* (Berkeley/Los Angeles: University of California Press, 1991).

18 Ibid., 11.

19 Ibid., 12.

20 Ibid., 13.

21 Gerben Zaagsma, "Transnational Networks of Jewish Migrant Radicals–The Case of Berlin," in *Transit und Transformation: Osteuropäisch-jüdische Migranten in Berlin 1918–1939*, ed. Verena Dohrn and Gertrud Pickhahn (Göttingen: Wallstein Verlag, 2010), 218, note 1.

22 Tony Michels, "Introduction: The Jewish-Socialist Nexus," in *Jewish Radicals: A Documentary History*, ed. Tony Michels (New York: New York University Press, 2012), 11.

being radical and being left-wing, but makes connections between Judaism and the political left. However, even Mendes uses the phrase "Jewish radical," and in doing so, he equates these concepts. He admits though that "the phenomenon of Jewish radicalism seems to have been seriously under-researched by both general study of sociology and history, and Jewish studies specialists."[23] However, his own approach does not offer different insights on past works. In the context of his introduction, Mendes also connects the concept of being radical with the idea of being leftist.

In sum, the majority of the relevant research purports that there is a connection between being radical and being left-wing in the context of Jewish radicals. Some of the mentioned authors tried to explain this connection; there are several explanations, such as the Jews' marginal position in society, antisemitism, Messianism, self-hatred, other psychological reasons, and urbanism.[24] The key problem is that most studies do not define Jewish radicalism or properly indicate what they mean by it. Statements usually refer to left-wing radicalism, but a proper definition of radicalism is rarely found in studies dealing with Jewish radicalism.

For example, Zaagsma refers to radicals as people – in our case, Jews – who were active in socialist or communist movements of their time.[25] The same is true for Tony Michels' approach, who writes about the Jews' inclination toward socialist and communist movements in general, such as Jewish involvement in the history of the American socialist movements, without defining certain terms.[26] Philip Mendes maintains that his title *Jews and the Left* does not define radicalism; he uses the expression as a synonym for someone he positions on the left.

Taking everything into account, the only concrete definition of radicalism so far is a political stance that seeks to achieve fundamental change within society. However, this implies that anyone interested in change, specifically political change following left-wing ideas, would be considered radical. If this radical is a Jew, he or she would then qualify as a Jewish radical. Obviously, such a definition is rather shortsighted. In the cases presented by previous research, the

23 Philip Mendes, *Jews and the Left: Rise and Fall of a Political Alliance* (Basingstoke: Palgrave Macmillan, 2014), 2.

24 Among others, these explanations are presented by Schatz, *The Generation*, 13–18; Mendes, *Jews and the Left*, 5–17.

25 Zaagsma, "Transnational Networks," 218, note 1.

26 Michels, "Introduction," 1–3.

changes demanded by radicals are for a more equal society.[27] However, we should also examine the other side of the political spectrum; there is also a radical Jewish right, even though the literature on this subject is minimal. One exception is Eran Kaplan, who uses the term "radical" in the title of his book about revisionist Zionists and their apparently radical view of Jewish history.[28] Moreover, the radical Jewish right also desires fundamental societal change, as the Kahanists, the extremist followers of Rabbi Kahane, did.

Jewish radicalism is not easily defined. To obtain a proper definition, two things should be explained: first, we need to clarify what "Jewishness" or "Jewish identity" means to us. The traditional religious definition is that someone is a Jew if born to a Jewish mother or if they have converted to Judaism properly (what "properly" means is up for debate in the Jewish community). However, to properly observe the phenomenon in all its possible manifestations, we have decided to apply a broad definition of who is considered as Jewish, especially to address the changes within Judaism after the Enlightenment and within modernity.[29] Therefore, we also decided to go along with Philip Mendes' definition of being Jewish: "the principal criteria used to define a person as Jewish will be: 1) Self-definition; 2) Definition by significant others such as political peers whether friendly or hostile; 3) Having one or both parents who define themselves as Jewish."[30] This definition allows us to include several figures in our study without judging how "Jewish" they are. It also gives the contributors of this volume the freedom to apply their own definitions and categories and thereby to provide different and more pluralistic perspectives on Jewish radicalism.

As a second step, levels of radicalism must be explained. That said, the definition of radicalism itself seems to have changed. In 1906, James Shea wrote that "radicalism is characterized less by its principles than by the manner of their application. Its political doctrine is that of democracy, and as a general thing liberal men will approve of it."[31] He then defines what radicalism means

---

27 E.g. Mendes, *Jews and the Left*, 4; in our understanding, by scrutinizing different explanations of the possible connection between Jews and radicalism, Schatz implies that radicalism aims at fundamentally altering society, especially to fight inequality. Schatz, *The Generation*, 11–19.

28 Eran Kaplan, *The Jewish Radical Right: Revisionist Zionism and Its Ideological Legacy* (Madison, WI: The University of Wisconsin Press, 2004).

29 For a discussion of Jewish "identity," see David Harry Ellenson, *Tradition in Transition: Orthodoxy, Halakhah, and the Boundaries of Modern Jewish Identity* (Lanham, MD: University Press of America, 1989).

30 Mendes, *Jews and the Left*, 3.

31 James E. Shea, "Radicalism and Reform," *Proceedings of the American Political Science Association* 3 (1906): 161.

to him: "Radicalism, speaking loosely, is hatred of class privilege. It is a sentiment which is fanned by discontent."[32] For Shea, "radical views are dangerous because they nurture a spirit of discontent, of morbid excitement, of restlessness and change."[33]

Today, radicalism also seems to be connected with being anti-democratic and with being right-wing. A recent study by Domonkos Sik, called *Radicalism and Indifference*, states that "radicalism is inseparable from modernity [...] In this sense, emancipation and radicalism have been opposing potentials of modernization throughout the history of European countries."[34] Sik introduces radicalism in contrast to emancipation and, as such, to democracy. In his study on Eastern European right-wing politics, he raised the question of the "preconditions of the emergence of an antidemocratic political culture."[35] In his study, he also equates radicalism with being anti-democratic and with being right-wing. This shows us how the discourse on radicalism, as well as its meaning, has changed over time. Moreover, Sik refers implicitly to the religious roots of modern radicalism as presented by Shmuel Noah Eisenstadt, who wrote on this subject (e.g. in his article "Religious Origins of Modern Radicalism").

Eisenstadt also determined that the French Revolution, regardless of its common perception, was not free from religion: "Modernity, modern civilization, the cultural and political programs of modernity, have often seen as epitomizing a break from religion... It is the major argument of this essay that the roots of modern Jacobinism in their different manifestations are to be found in the transformation of the visions with strong Gnostic component and which sought to bring the Kingdom of God to earth."[36] He then mentions America as well as the French Revolution. This religious notion within secularized politics produces "Jacobinism";[37] he does not equate this with radicalism, but he identifies such totalistic tendencies with radicalism. That said, he never concretely defines the term – he simply discusses its meaning at length.

Therefore, radicalism means nothing more than belief in a totalistic, i.e. close-minded, view of the world.

---

32 Ibid., 165.

33 Ibid., 168.

34 Domonkos Sik, *Radicalism and Indifference: Memory Transmission, Political Formation and Modernization in Hungary and Europe* (Frankfurt/Main: Peter Lang Verlag, 2016), 7.

35 Ibid., 271.

36 Shmuel Noah Eisenstadt, "Religious Origins of Modern Radicalism," *Theoria: A Journal of Social and Political Theory* 106 (2005): *Fundamentalism, Authority and Globalization:* 51.

37 Ibid.

Regarding the discussion above, one might think there would be a more proper definition of Jewish radicalism. However, Jaff Schatz is right when he writes that it is a question of “concrete people involved in the concrete, complex, and changing circumstances of their time and society.” This is why for Schatz, “there exists no particular ‘Jewish radicalism’ and, consequently, that a category of ‘Jewish radicals,’ which it implies, is a chimera.”[38] Radicalism develops within specific space-time continua and is expressed by specific people who live within them. Due to this precondition, specific instances of radicalism can be related to political, social, or religious aspects of Jewish modernity. That is another reason why we only present a working definition of Jewish radicalism and approach the topic pluralistically, since such radicals existed in various temporal and geographical contexts.

Our working definition suggests that Jewish radicalism is an approach by those who, according to our definition above, either identify as Jewish or could be considered Jewish and wish to achieve one of the following goals:

1) Answer fundamental questions raised by modernity, such as the question of identity.
2) Fundamentally change their contemporary society.
3) Approach societal issues without compromise and with a totalistic worldview (in the sense of Eisenstadt).
4) Address social problems and solve them at their roots (radicalism can be traced back to the Latin *radix* which means root).
5) Consider their own religious, political, or social opinion as the *ultima ratio* for society’s protection and/or advancement.

Our goal is not to offer a coherent and fixed definition of Jewish radicalism; instead, we want to stimulate a discussion about this topic. We think that with this volume we can open up a discourse again, that seems to be necessary in these times, in which we do speak of radicals, radicalism, fundamentalism, and so on rather vaguely. We need to engage in a debate to clarify what this phenomenon is or could be. We want to be as open as possible, even though we have criticized others for being unspecific. However, our aim is to question the current ideas of Jewish radicalisms.

A common denominator or a common element in the cases in our volume is also the idea of a utopia or dystopia that is related to all forms of radicalisms as they are discussed in the present volume. As well as a critique of their current societies, all Jewish radicals discussed a specific utopian element of their

38 Schatz, *The Generation*, 19.

thoughts. The etymological origin of utopia stems from the Greek words '*ou*' and '*topos*', which mean 'no-place' or 'anywhere'; however, as Thomas Schölderle points out, this composition is wrong, as '*ou*' is used to negate sentences, not adjectives or nouns. For Thomas Morus (1478–1535), who first coined the term, '*ou*' was homophonic to the Greek '*eu*', which means good. So, one can read utopia as 'no-place' or as 'good place'.[39] In the research on utopian ideas we find the assumption that this is a "rational fiction of human societies, which are juxtaposed with a critical intention to current grievances."[40] We do agree on the critique on social grievances, however it is not clear why the alternatives have to be rational fiction. Richard Saage reads utopian ideas as phenomena of resonance which react to grievances of their specific era; therefore, it is a historical phenomenon and a social construct.[41] The ideas of dystopia, by contrast, as Saage states, keep the utopian intention implicitly in their critique of society or their exaggeration of current grievances into a dominant factor of the portrait of society.[42] Schölderle draws on Saage and states that a '*Utopie*' needs critique, resonance, and a sociopolitical alternative. He writes that "the critique on historical circumstances, is not only crucial for the prototype by Morus, but also has to be constitutive for all utopias."[43] At the same time, they are also phenomena of resonance of social crises and the imagined (better) world, which is implicitly or explicitly drawn as an alternative means for a relativization of the status quo.[44] For the Jewish radical, criticism of the existent world is consequently based on a utopian idea as a *sine qua non* for his actions and radical beliefs.

We do, however, need to make a differentiation here. It is important to emphasize that utopias were space related until the eighteenth century and only

---

39 Thomas Schölderle, *Geschichte der Utopie* (History of Utopia), 2nd edition (Vienna/Cologne: Böhlau, 2017), 10–11. In his dissertation Schölderle not only gives an historical account on Utopia; he also explains the current state of research in this field. See Thomas Schölderle, *Utopia und Utopie. Thomas Morus, die Geschichte der Utopie und die Kontroverse um ihren Begriff* (Utopia and Utopie. Thomas Morus, the History of Utopia and the Controversy of the Term) (Baden-Baden: Nomos, 2011). For utopia as a field of research see also the works of Richard Saage.

40 Schölderle, *Geschichte der Utopie*, 17 ((Als Utopien gelten fortan) "rationale Fiktionen menschlicher Gemeinwesen, die in kritischer Absicht den herrschenden Missständen gegenüber gestellt sind.", own translation).

41 Richard Saage, *Utopische Horizonte. Zwischen historischer Entwicklung und aktuellem Geltungsanspruch* (Utopian Horizons. Between Historical Development and Contemporary Claim of Validity) (Berlin: LIT Verlag, 2010), 18.

42 Ibid., 28.

43 Schölderle, *Utopia und Utopie*, 31 ("Die Kritik an den realhistorischen Verhältnissen etwa, ist nicht nur für Morus' Prototyp grundlegend, sondern muss auch für jede weitere Utopie als konstitutiv gelten," own translation).

44 Ibid.

later did time move in as a factor. That means utopias do not exist now in a remote place, but maybe at a time in the future and will therefore become the aim of Jewish radicalism.[45] That is important, because, as Kurt Lenk pointed out, myths are looking for a "compensation of meaning in a long gone, usually imagined past, which should be awakened."[46] Lenk refers to the ideas of a "golden age" which should be recreated in the present. For him, these are myths and not a utopia, which can be understood as crucial to differentiate between positive or even emancipatory utopias (which will exist in the future) and a society which relies on an oppressive system. However, it is not clear why this, which seems to be a dystopia, should be qualified as a myth. It is probably because the term is not clear and fixed, but also because, implicitly it seems, a utopia should indeed have an emancipatory element in itself. At the intersection of myth and utopia there is another element of interest: the messianic idea. Although a utopia inevitably does not have a religious notion, it is a messianic concept and therefore shares some common ground with the latter.

Gershom Scholem, for instance, creates a theoretical framework for what he calls the messianic idea. Within rabbinic Judaism he sees three main powers in place: a conservative one, which tries to keep the status quo; a restorative one, which tries to restore an imagined "golden past"; and finally, a utopian element, which strives for an unknown (but better) future. These forces are seen by Scholem to be in place around the problem of Messianism in historical Judaism.[47] This is interesting because it gives us the opportunity to think about the idea of a more open and more complex utopia.[48] According to Scholem, the restorative and utopian elements are the only ones that bring about the messianic idea, which consequently also contributes to Jewish radicalism in the sense that there is some kind of messianic utopian belief involved in its formation: "Both tendencies are intertwined and yet at the same time of a contradictionary nature; the

---

45 Schölderle, *Geschichte der Utopie*, 11.

46 Kurt Lenk, "Utopie und Mythos – Zur Differenzierung ihrer Begrifflichkeit," (Utopias and Myth – A Differentiation of Terms) in *Dimensionen der Politik: Aufklärung – Utopie – Demokratie: Festschrift für Richard Saage zum 65. Geburtstag* (Dimensions of Politics: Enlightenment – Utopia – Democracy. Commemorative Publication for Richard Saages' 65th Birthday), ed. Axel Rüdiger et al. (Berlin: Duncker & Humblot, 2006), 363.

47 Gershom Scholem, "Toward an Understanding of the Messianic Idea in Judaism," in *The Messianic Idea in Judaism and Other Essays on Jewish Spirituality*, ed. Gershom Scholem (New York: Schocken Books, 1971), 3.

48 Of course, this idea seems to be very similar to what research calls intentional or socio-psychological utopia, but with Scholem the connection also to Judaism is stressed and, so, he marries two strands of thought. For intentional utopia see e.g. Thomas Schölderle, *Utopia und Utopie*.

Messianic idea crystallizes only out of the two of them together."[49] Both the '*Restauration*' and the '*Utopie*' bear within them elements of each other. Scholem writes that "even the restorative force has a utopian factor, and in utopianism restorative factors are at work."[50] Utopia, Scholem clarifies,

> can take on the radical form of the vision of a new content which is to be realized in a future that will in fact be nothing other than the restoration of what is ancient, bringing back that which has been lost; the ideal content of the past at the same time delivers the basis for the vision of the future. However, knowingly or unknowingly, certain elements creep into such a restoratively oriented utopianism which are not in the least restorative and which derive from the vision of a completely new state of the Messianic world.[51]

So, there is a strand of argument which connects a vision of the future with the past.

In conclusion, we can connect the classical research on utopia with Scholem's ideas on messianism. That means utopias are criticizing the current society and implicitly or explicitly developing an alternative society, which should come in the future and have elements of long gone imagined "golden eras" as well as elements which have never been seen before. Of course, our contributors may disagree with us, but this is also part of the discussion we are aiming for. It is also clear that not every critique of society is to be labeled radical; however, every radical must be considered a utopian critic. In the discussed cases, the critique is usually related to the protagonist's arguments or actions, which are crucial enough to see them as radical.

All in all, we would like to open the discussion to develop an idea of what Jewish radicalism can be. We argue for an openness, which has its downsides; however, the positive sides outweigh these for us, as we can trace different possibilities of critique. That means criticizing the status quo and implicitly or explicitly developing an idea of what a better society can look like is a radical approach, especially if it deals with fundamental questions of the time, whether it be the question of killing non-Jews, an emancipatory pedagogy to fuel social change, or a psychedelic Judaism in order to overcome the economical and ecological challenges we face as mankind.

Why do we draw this conclusion? It will hopefully become clearer when we exemplify this using some cases from our volume as proof of the concept. Afterwards, we are open and very happy to engage in a discussion. In her chapter on

---

49 Scholem, *Messianic Idea*, 3.
50 Ibid., 4.
51 Ibid.

religious radicalism, Ofira Gruweis-Kovalsky presents the perspective of ultra-orthodox members of the Jewish society in Mandatory Palestine to the creation of the State of Israel. The fundamental critique her protagonists have on their society is that they reject the "modern" phenomena (possible after religious enlightenment and legal emancipation) of what they see as a desecration of Shabbat and the sexual relationship between Jews and non-Jews. These are crucial threats to their community and to their idea of a utopian good society. They aim at a Jewish society in their image of a utopia; therefore, they act as "watchdogs of religion and religious observance in the pre-state Jewish community."[52]

A somewhat different approach can be seen in the idea of the emancipatory education of Janusz Korczak. Anne Klein writes in her chapter on Jewish community action in Warsaw that Korczak's pedagogy plays a crucial role, because he wants to educate the youth to become critical and engage "citizens" – he wanted to empower young Jews to fight for social justice. It is clear that if someone educated youngsters in that way, the educator and the educated are excluded from social justice and political participation. His critique is obvious in his education. Korczak sees education as a tool to democratically change society into a better version; he dreamed of a utopia in which Jews have the opportunity to participate in society and politics.

Zalman Schachter-Shalomi's idea of psychedelic Judaism is presented by Morgan Shipley. Schachter-Shalomi wants to heal the world for a better future with the help of a joyous Judaism. He criticized consumption in modern capitalist societies as well as its destructive tendencies. Schachter-Shalomi imagined a renewed world, where mankind is oriented towards a sustainable lifestyle; his critique is fundamental as well as his idea of a society and a Judaism which "seeks egalitarianism and all this demands economically, culturally, and a level of identity; that works toward environmental justice, seeing nature as manifesting the divine and Divine responsibility; and that understands all of this at the expression of faith, both their own, and of all peoples (believer and non-believers alike)."[53]

Next to the political, educational and religious sphere, we included the idea of a cultural radicalism in this volume. Peter S. Lederer analyzes *The Producers* (1968) by Mel Brooks as a form of subversive cabaret. Brooks' film is presented as a critique of authority and of the taboos of a specific community within American society. Brooks takes a minority, to which he himself belongs, and reflects on

52 See chapter by Gruweis-Kovalsky in this volume.
53 See chapter by Morgan Shipley in this volume.

authority within society and states the idea of free individualism as well as its creation of an image of freedom by subverting all forms of tyranny.

Very different is the argument of the text *The King's Torah*, which is scrutinized by Federico Dal Bo. The text in question explores, in an apparently "classical" way of rabbinical reasoning, the possibility of justifying the killings of non-Jews. It aims at establishing new cultural and ethical values, where Israel is above all other states, peoples, and religions. It draws "an extreme right-wing vision of Israeli society and therefore mobilized against Jewish liberalism."[54] It displays a dystopian idea of a future for everyone outside the "proper" community; however, it is a vision of a new future, but in a non-liberal state with obviously non-liberal politics.

In contrast to this exclusionary utopia, Hannah Peaceman asks if radical diversity is a form of Jewish radicalism. By analyzing articles from the nineteenth century newspaper *Sulamith*, she is able to show that the critique was aimed at anti-emancipatory, anti-Jewish elements of the Enlightenment. Her protagonists showed the contradictions which bourgeois society inherently bears and that Jews were excluded from their ideals of freedom and equality. This critique tended to transcend their society and envisioned a future where not only freedom and equality apply universally to Jews and everyone else, but also where universalism achieved a new quality in that there could be a universalism as a reconciliation of differences.

We could go on to cite every chapter, but these examples should prove our idea; we see the fundamental critique as well as the implicit or explicit formulation of a (utopian) better future as essential factors for Jewish radicalism. This is the connecting element which binds the chapters together. Of course, there is room for debate, which we would like to encourage. From the presented cases it also becomes clear that Jewish radicalism is a relational term, as we mentioned earlier, as it is dependent in its context in time and space. However, we think it is a flexible category and if it is analyzed in its specific historical and sociological contexts, one can shed light on globally connected phenomena.

These phenomena present themselves in different aspects or perspectives. As we have preliminarily identified three fields in which our cases can be placed, that means all of them are aimed at criticizing the status quo of society and wish to change it to a fundamentally different one. The path of their change is either political, through direct actions or institutions; cultural, through education, film, and literature; or, finally, through religion by altering the belief system of Juda-

---

54 See chapter by Federico Dal Bo in this volume.

ism or deploying new terms or values through religious argument and settings. These three fields also structure our volume.

The Contributions

The first section on political radicalism is opened by Roman Vater, who traces the intellectual origins of post-Zionism to the thinking of Revisionist Zionism founder Ze'ev Jabotinsky (1880 – 1940). By analyzing several post-Zionist organizations created by Jabotinsky's disciples during the 1940s-1950s, Vater's chapter asserts that "first-generation" post-Zionism must be understood as a realization of Jabotinsky's "monism" principle and is therefore a manifestation of secular right-wing liberalism in Israeli public life. Peter Bergamin also emphasizes that right-wing radicalism should be closely examined in the context of Jewish radicalism, and he examines the degree to which Aba Ahimeir (1897–1962) understood, utilized, and embraced the concepts of fascism and revolution from 1924 – 1934, the period in which he was most politically (and notoriously) active. Jan Rybak then highlights the interconnections between Zionism and Jewish class consciousness, providing a detailed discussion on the Poale Zion in the years of the Russian Revolution (1917–1920). Amir Locker-Biletzki offers a different approach, discussing the role of nationalism, colonialism, and imperialism in Moshe Sneh's (1909 – 1972) and Emil Touma's (1919 – 1985) ideologies. Since the 1920s, Jewish and Palestinian communists have radically negated Western imperialism and Zionist colonialism in Palestine/Israel. Frank Jacob's chapter analyzes the radical trinity of being an anarchist, a Jew, and a New Yorker at the beginning of the twentieth century. The case of Isidore Wisotsky (1895–1970), a young Jewish immigrant who was radicalized in New York City, is discussed to highlight the American perspective on Jewish radicalism and to what extent an anarchist individual's radicalization in the US metropolis is related to Jewishness. Tal Elmaliach completes the section on political radicalism with his study on the youth organization haShomer haTza'ir and its maneuvering between Zionism and the Jewish New Left between 1967 and 1973.

The second section deals with religious case studies of Jewish radicalism. Morgan Shipley analyzes the role of psychedelic Judaism in post-war America. He therefore focuses on Zalman Schachter-Shalomi (1924 – 2014), one of the most important representatives of the Jewish renewal movement in the United States, and his role in a "Radical Religiosity of LSD Consciousness". Federico Dal Bo and Hayyim Katsman deal with contemporary Jewish radicalism. The former provides insight on nihilism and extremist religious radicalism in contemporary Israel by focusing on the Torat haMelkh, while Katsman highlights the role of religious Zionism as it is represented in contemporary Israel by people like Rabbi Yitzchak Ginsburg. Ofira Gruweis-Kovalsky completes the discussion by providing a detailed insight regarding the Zionist right and the ultra-orthodox community, particularly with regard to its role during the establishment of the State of Israel.

The final section deals with cultural Jewish radicalism. After Anne Klein's discussion of the radical pedagogy of Janusz Korczak (1878–1942), Peter Lederer provides a study of "Mel Brooks' Subversive Cabaret" when he analyzes *The Producers* (1968) for its elements of Jewish radicalism. Sebastian Kunze then discusses what it means to be a Jewish radical and provides a case study of the famous anarchist Gustav Landauer (1870–1919) to show how radicalism and Jewishness were interrelated. Hannah Peaceman concludes the volume with her analysis of the connection between the "Jewish question" of emancipation in the nineteenth century in relation to the evolution of Jewish radical ideas in this period.

All these contributions are case studies of Jewish radicalism. They demonstrate that there are numerous forms of radicalism that deserve to be included in a broader study of the subject. They also show that the phenomenon is not limited to a specific geographical area and applies on a global scale. As such, to conclude this introduction, Jewish radicalism can and should only be understood as a phenomenon of a global modernity.

Transliteration

Sometimes it is hard to determine whether a common transliteration should be used or if there should be a special one. We tried in this volume to find a balance between the established "English" transliteration of Hebrew and a different way to reproduce the sound of Hebrew words. Looking back, it was a problematic experiment; however, we could not ask our contributors to change everything, which is why we decided to reproduce our Hebrew transliteration style sheet in this volume. This will enable the reader to understand the transliterations. Some terms are so common in English that they were not transliterated by all of the contributors, which was a compromise that we made. In the end, we are convinced that the transliterations are readable and coherent; therefore, it should not be overly problematic to identify the Hebrew words.

Stylesheet for Hebrew transliteration

English	Hebrew
According to the vowel or disregarded	א
b, v	בּ, ב
g	ג
d	ד
h	ה
w	וּ, וו
z	ז
ch	ח
dt	ט
y	י
k, kh	כּ, כ
l	ל
m	מ
n	נ
s	ס

English	Hebrew
’	ע
p, f	פּ, פ
tz	צ, ץ
q	ק
r	ר
sh	שׁ
s	שׂ
t, t	תּ, ת
a	◌ָ, ◌ַ, ◌ֲ
e	◌ֶ, ◌ֵ, ◌ְ(-mobile)
i	◌ִ
o	וֹ, ◌ֹ, ◌ֳ
u	◌ֻ, וּ

For indicating the definite article or a definite prefix, please use the following formula:

haBayit, baAretz

Ayn: ' with vowel
haShomer haTza'ir

Shwa mobile
leMashal

Dugmot
גברים מזרחיים Gevarim Mizrachiyim
צָהֳרַיִים Tzohorayim
אֵיזֶה Eyzeh

Works Cited

Anderson, Benedict. *Imagined Communities: Reflections on the Origin and Spread of Nationalism*. London: Verso, 1991.

Brossat, Alain, and Sylvia Klingsberg. *Revolutionary Yiddishland: A History of Jewish Radicalism*, translated by David Fernbach. London/New York: Verso, 2016.

Cohen, Percy S. *Jewish Radicals and Radical Jews*. London/New York: Academic Press, 1980.

Eisenstadt, Shmuel Noah. "Religious Origins of Modern Radicalism." *Theoria: A Journal of Social and Political Theory* 106 (2005): *Fundamentalism, Authority and Globalization:* 51–80.

Ellenson, David Harry. *Tradition in Transition: Orthodoxy, Halakhah, and the Boundaries of Modern Jewish Identity*. Lanham, MD: University Press of America, 1989.

Jacobs, Jack. "Introduction." In *Jews and Leftist Politics: Judaism, Israel, Antisemitism, and Gender*, edited by Jack Jacobs, 1–28. Cambridge/New York: Cambridge University Press, 2017.

Kaplan, Eran. *The Jewish Radical Right: Revisionist Zionism and Its Ideological Legacy*. Madison, WI: The University of Wisconsin Press, 2004.

Lenk, Kurt. "Utopie und Mythos – Zur Differenzierung ihrer Begrifflichkeit." (Utopias and Myth – A Differentiation of Terms) In *Dimensionen der Politik: Aufklärung – Utopie – Demokratie: Festschrift für Richard Saage zum 65. Geburtstag* (Dimensions of Politics: Enlightenment – Utopia – Democracy. Commemorative Publication for Richard Saages 65. Birthday), edited by Axel Rüdiger and Eva-Maria Seng, 361–370. Berlin: Duncker & Humblot, 2006.

Lichter, S. Robert, and Stanley Rothman. "Jewish Ethnicity and Radical Culture: A Social Psychological Study of Political Activists." *Political Psychology* 3, no. 1/2 (1981/1982): 116–157.

Mendes, Philip. "From the Shtetl to the Monash Soviet: An Overview of Jewish Radicalism in Australia." *Australian Journal of Jewish Studies* 14 (2000): 54–77.

Mendes, Philip. *Jews and the Left: Rise and Fall of a Political Alliance.* Basingstoke: Palgrave Macmillan, 2014.
Michels, Tony. "Exporting Yiddish Socialism: New York's Role in the Russian Jewish Workers' Movement." *Jewish Social Studies: History, Culture, Society* 16, no. 1 (2009): 1–26.
Michels, Tony. "Introduction: The Jewish-Socialist Nexus." In *Jewish Radicals: A Documentary History*, edited by Tony Michels, 1–24. New York: New York University Press, 2012.
Porter, Jack N., and Peter Dreier, eds. *Jewish Radicalism: A Selected Anthology.* New York: Grove Press, 1973.
Puntis, Peter, Candrika Kaul, and Jürgen Wilke, eds. *International Communication and Global News Networks: Historical Perspectives.* New York: Hampton Press, 2011.
"Radicalism." In *Merriam-Webster Online Dictionary.* Accessed February 15 2018. https://www.merriam-webster.com/dictionary/radicalism.
Rosati, Massimo. "Forms of Radicalism: Theoretical and Social Radicalism in Durkheim." *Durkheimian Studies*, New Series 10 (2004): 10–18.
Rosenberg, Emily S. *A World Connecting, 1870–1945.* Cambridge, MA: Belknap Press of Harvard University Press, 2012.
Saage, Richard. *Utopische Horizonte: Zwischen historischer Entwicklung und aktuellem Geltungsanspruch* (Utopian Horizons. Between Historical Development and Contemporary Claim of Validity). Berlin: LIT Verlag, 2010.
Schatz, Jaff. *The Generation: The Rise and Fall of the Jewish Communist of Poland.* Berkeley/Los Angeles: University of California Press, 1991.
Schölderle, Thomas. *Utopia und Utopie. Thomas Morus, die Geschichte der Utopie und die Kontroverse um ihren Begriff* (Utopia and Utopie. Thomas Morus, the History of Utopia and the Controversy of the Term). Baden-Baden: Nomos, 2011.
Schölderle, Thomas. *Geschichte der Utopie* (History of Utopia), 2nd edition. Vienna/Cologne: Böhlau, 2017.
Scholem, Gershom. "Toward an Understanding of the Messianic Idea in Judaism." In *The Messianic Idea in Judaism and Other Essays on Jewish Spirituality*, edited by Gershom Scholem, 1–36. New York: Schocken Books, 1971.
Shea, James E. "Radicalism and Reform." *Proceedings of the American Political Science Association* 3 (1906): 158–168.
Sik, Domonkos. *Radicalism and Indifference: Memory Transmission, Political Formation and Modernization in Hungary and Europe.* Frankfurt/Main: Peter Lang Verlag, 2016.
Tames, Richard. *The Transport Revolution in the 19th Century: A Documentary Approach.* London: Oxford University Press, 1970.
Winseck, Dwayne, and Robert M. Pike. *Communication and Empire: Media, Markets, and Globalization, 1860–1930.* Durham, NC: Duke University Press, 2007.
Zaagsma, Gerben. "Transnational Networks of Jewish Migrant Radicals–The Case of Berlin." In *Transit und Transformation: Osteuropäisch-jüdische Migranten in Berlin 1918–1939*, edited by Verena Dohrn and Gertrud Pickhahn, 218–233. Göttingen: Wallstein Verlag, 2010.
Zimmer, Kenyon. "Saul Yanovsky and Yiddish Anarchism on the Lower East Side." In *Radical Gotham: Anarchism in New York City from Schwab's Saloon to Occupy Wall Street*, edited by Tom Goyens, 33–53. Urbana/Chicago/Springfield, IL: University of Illinois Press, 2017.

Section I
Political Radicalisms

Roman Vater

Pathways of Early Post-Zionism

Introduction[1]

When does a post-Zionism start? This seemingly simple question calls for a seemingly simple answer: when Zionism has run its course, or, in Eric Cohen's formulation, has undergone "routinization."[2] This in turn raises a question much less straightforward: *when* precisely does Zionism run its course?

The primary objective of this chapter is to challenge two strongly entrenched assumptions concerning post-Zionism as a salient political and intellectual feature of Israeli public life, and to shatter the scholarly consensus built around them. The first is that post-Zionism is a relatively recent phenomenon, which has developed gradually over the two decades since Israel's victory in the June 1967 war, with the attendant transitions in the make-up and self-definition of Israeli society, only to reach its full bloom following the conclusion of the Oslo accords between Israel and the PLO in 1993.[3] The second is that post-Zionism, by mounting a challenge to Israeli ethno-nationalism, is inherently "progressive," perforce "left-wing."[4] The following pages will endeavor to demonstrate that these two assumptions are deficient in the extreme, since they do not take into account the broader scope of post-Zionist thinking, preaching, and activity,

---

1 I am grateful to Prof. Derek Penslar (Harvard University), Margalit Shinar (daughter of Adya Horon), and Dr. Karny Rubin (daughter of Eri Jabotinsky) for their assistance with research for this chapter. I also acknowledge with gratitude the support of the Israel Institute (Washington DC), which funded my postdoctoral fellowship at the Oxford Centre for Hebrew and Jewish Studies in 2015–2017, and of the Leverhulme Trust and the Isaac Newton Fund, which fund my early career fellowship at the Faculty of Asian and Middle Eastern Studies in Cambridge in 2018–2021.

2 Eric Cohen, "Israel as a Post-Zionist Society," *Israel Affairs* 1, no. 3 (1995): 203–214.

3 For examples of various aspects of this approach see Nadia Abu el-Haj, *Facts on the Ground: Archaeological Practice and Territorial Self-Fashioning in Israeli Society* (Chicago and London: University of Chicago Press, 2001), 272–276; Alain Dieckhoff, *The Invention of a Nation: Zionist Thought and the Making of Modern Israel* (New York: Columbia University Press, 2003), 270–271; Baruch Kimmerling, *The Invention and Decline of Israeliness: State, Society, and the Military* (Berkeley – Los Angeles – London: University of California Press, 2005); Ephraim Nimni, ed., *The Challenge of Post-Zionism: Alternatives to Israeli Fundamentalist Politics* (London and New York: Zed Books, 2003).

4 Nimni, *The Challenge of Post-Zionism*; Uri Ram, *Israeli Nationalism: Social Conflicts and the Politics of Knowledge* (London and New York: Routledge, 2011), 111–115; Chaim Isaac Waxman, "Critical Sociology and the End of Ideology in Israel," *Israel Studies* 2, no. 1 (1997): 194–210.

https://doi.org/10.1515/9783110545753-002

in terms of history and content, and concomitantly ignore what I believe are the genuine intellectual sources of post-Zionism.

To own the truth, students of post-Zionism have on occasion betrayed their awareness of the insufficiency of this paradigm. Laurence Silberstein, in the introduction to his quite exhaustive study of post-Zionism, remarks that

> The current usages of the term postzionism [sic!] are by no means the first. Prior to the 1990s, one encounters scattered uses of the term. For the most part, it served to indicate that zionism [sic!], having established a refuge for the Jewish people and effecting a renewal of a Hebrew national culture, had fulfilled its goal of normalizing the existence of the nation. Insofar as zionism had attained two of its basic goals, the establishment of a Jewish state and the normalization of Jewish life, zionist institutions were no longer necessary. Now, postzionism means something very different. In its current usage, postzionism is the product of a crisis in Israeli life.[5]

Silberstein's evident fascination with the "current usage" of "post-Zionism" means that he is not at all interested as to *when*, *how*, and *why* the term was used "prior to the 1990s." His discussion is heavily focused on the closing decades of the twentieth century, though he does give a fair share of attention to both liberal and radical critiques of Zionism enunciated from the 1960s onwards, without, however, looking earlier. In a manner different from Silberstein's, Daniel Gutwein offers an interpretation of the 1990s post-Zionism as a *right-wing* phenomenon by pointing out that it was promulgated by the ascendant middle class of Israel, which looked for an ideological justification to dismantle the collectivist practices of Labor Zionism by attacking its core collectivist ethos and tenets. Post-Zionism, Gutwein writes, "make[s] use of the category of 'the Jew' in order to dismantle Israeli collective identity as defined by 'the Zionist'" and "employ[s] arguments from the arsenal of the politics of identity to undermine the hegemony of Labor Zionism."[6]

Gutwein's is a class analysis ensconced within a Marxist perspective, which he frankly admits. Without denying the merits of Gutwein's insight, my argument will be of a different nature, as it will draw upon the methodological framework of intellectual history. That is, my key proposal will be that if post-Zionism can indeed be viewed as rightist, this is so not because it dissented from Zionism by abandoning nationalist worldview, but because it *upheld* it.

---

5 Laurence J. Silberstein, *The Postzionism Debates: Knowledge and Power in Israeli Culture* (New York and London: Routledge, 1999), 8.

6 Daniel Gutwein, "Left and Right Post-Zionism and the Privatization of Israeli Collective Memory," in *Israeli Historical Revisionism: From Left to Right*, ed. Anita Shapira and Derek J. Penslar (London/Portland: Frank Cass, 2003), 34.

This chapter will thus fill in the gaps left by Silberstein, Gutwein, and others who dealt with contemporary post-Zionism, by arguing that a comprehensive critique of Zionism's philosophy and policy was formulated in circles deeply immersed in Zionism's development and implementation as early as in the mid-1940s, that is, *before* the establishment of the state of Israel. It will further demonstrate that the intellectual sources of this critique are to be traced to the radical flank of rightist Revisionist Zionism; that this critique has in many senses anticipated the 1990s post-Zionism, yet at the same time remained strongly committed to principles of national self-determination, making its relationship with the 1990s post-Zionism a dialectic one; that, in consequence, the latter should be more accurately viewed as "second-wave" or "second-generation" post-Zionism, whereas the 1940s-1950s post-Zionism ought to be redefined as "first generation." Below I will offer a detailed exploration of a number of organizations that sprung on the margins of Revisionist Zionism during the 1940s-1950s in the United States and in Israel. Among them some are better known, like The "Hebrew Committee of National Liberation," and some are less known or not known at all, such as the "Kedem Club" or "Club 59." Scrutinized together, they show that the post-Zionism that accompanied the establishment of Israel constituted a concerted and continuous effort by a solid group of Jabotinskian political thinkers and activists, who by abandoning their Zionist-Revisionist upbringing attempted to put forward a *raison d'état* that would detach Israel from Zionism and re-establish it on different moral and political foundations inspired by American and French republicanism. In the course of their activity iconoclastic assessments were made concerning Zionism, the Jewish nation, and the policy of Israel during the first decade of its existence; all of them will be exposed and discussed in this chapter. I will conclude by assessing the similarities and differences between first-generation and second-generation post-Zionism and will ponder the reasons for the former's demise since the 1960s and its potential for re-emergence.

Stage One: The Hebrew Committee of National Liberation

On December 10 1947 the *New York Herald Tribune* ran on one of its inner pages a short article styled as a letter to the editor, signed by "Peter H. Bergson, Chairman, Hebrew Committee of National Liberation, Washington DC." The article, titled "Post-Zionism," was dated to December 4 1947, less than a week after the

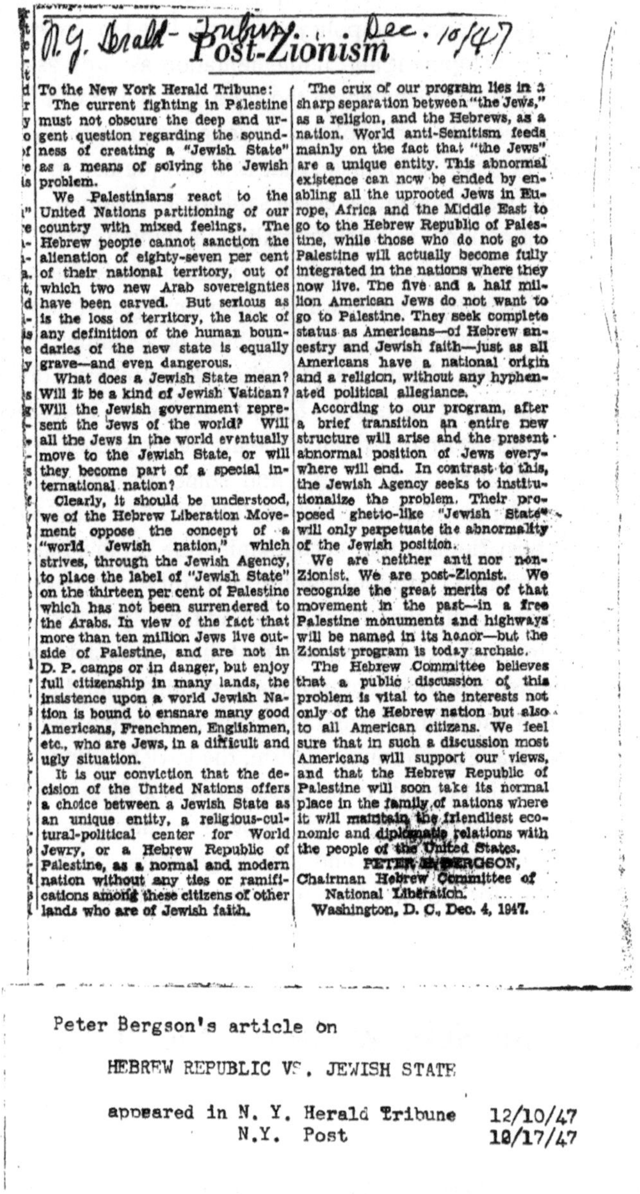

N.Y. Herald-Tribune Dec. 10/47

Post-Zionism

To the New York Herald Tribune:

The current fighting in Palestine must not obscure the deep and urgent question regarding the soundness of creating a "Jewish State" as a means of solving the Jewish problem.

We Palestinians react to the United Nations partitioning of our country with mixed feelings. The Hebrew people cannot sanction the alienation of eighty-seven per cent of their national territory, out of which two new Arab sovereignties have been carved. But serious as is the loss of territory, the lack of any definition of the human boundaries of the new state is equally grave—and even dangerous.

What does a Jewish State mean? Will it be a kind of Jewish Vatican? Will the Jewish government represent the Jews of the world? Will all the Jews in the world eventually move to the Jewish State, or will they become part of a special international nation?

Clearly, it should be understood, we of the Hebrew Liberation Movement oppose the concept of a "world Jewish nation," which strives, through the Jewish Agency, to place the label of "Jewish State" on the thirteen per cent of Palestine which has not been surrendered to the Arabs. In view of the fact that more than ten million Jews live outside of Palestine, and are not in D. P. camps or in danger, but enjoy full citizenship in many lands, the insistence upon a world Jewish Nation is bound to ensnare many good Americans, Frenchmen, Englishmen, etc., who are Jews, in a difficult and ugly situation.

It is our conviction that the decision of the United Nations offers a choice between a Jewish State as an unique entity, a religious-cultural-political center for World Jewry, or a Hebrew Republic of Palestine, as a normal and modern nation without any ties or ramifications among these citizens of other lands who are of Jewish faith.

The crux of our program lies in a sharp separation between "the Jews," as a religion, and the Hebrews, as a nation. World anti-Semitism feeds mainly on the fact that "the Jews" are a unique entity. This abnormal existence can now be ended by enabling all the uprooted Jews in Europe, Africa and the Middle East to go to the Hebrew Republic of Palestine, while those who do not go to Palestine will actually become fully integrated in the nations where they now live. The five and a half million American Jews do not want to go to Palestine. They seek complete status as Americans—of Hebrew ancestry and Jewish faith—just as all Americans have a national origin and a religion, without any hyphenated political allegiance.

According to our program, after a brief transition an entire new structure will arise and the present abnormal position of Jews everywhere will end. In contrast to this, the Jewish Agency seeks to institutionalize the problem. Their proposed ghetto-like "Jewish State" will only perpetuate the abnormality of the Jewish position.

We are neither anti nor non-Zionist. We are post-Zionist. We recognize the great merits of that movement in the past—in a free Palestine monuments and highways will be named in its honor—but the Zionist program is today archaic.

The Hebrew Committee believes that a public discussion of this problem is vital to the interests not only of the Hebrew nation but also to all American citizens. We feel sure that in such a discussion most Americans will support our views, and that the Hebrew Republic of Palestine will soon take its normal place in the family of nations where it will maintain the friendliest economic and diplomatic relations with the people of the United States.

PETER H. BERGSON,
Chairman Hebrew Committee of National Liberation.
Washington, D. C., Dec. 4, 1947.

Peter Bergson's article on

HEBREW REPUBLIC VS. JEWISH STATE

appeared in N. Y. Herald Tribune 12/10/47
N.Y. Post 12/17/47

Fig. 1: Hillel Kook's article "Post-Zionism," New York Herald Tribune, December 1947. Reproduced by permission of the Ben-Gurion Research Institute for the Study of Israel and Zionism.

United Nations General Assembly voted to partition the British Mandate of Palestine into an Arab and a Jewish state. This is how Bergson commented on this fateful event:

> The current fighting in Palestine must not obscure the deep and urgent question regarding the soundness of creating a "Jewish State" as a means of solving the Jewish problem [...] What does a Jewish State mean? Will it be a kind of Jewish Vatican? Will the Jewish government represent the Jews of the world? [...] Clearly, it should be understood, we of the Hebrew Liberation Movement oppose the concept of a "world Jewish nation," which strives, through the Jewish Agency, to place the label of "Jewish State" on the thirteen per cent of Palestine which has not been surrendered to the Arabs[7] [...] It is our conviction that the decision of the United Nations offers a choice between a Jewish State as a unique entity, a religious-cultural-political center for World Jewry, or a Hebrew Republic of Palestine, as a normal and modern nation without any ties or ramifications among these citizens of other lands who are of Jewish faith. The crux of our program lies in a sharp separation between "The Jews," as a religion, and the Hebrews, as a nation [...] We are neither anti nor non-Zionist. *We are post-Zionist.* We recognize the great merits of that movement in the past – in a free Palestine monuments and highways will be named in its honor – but the Zionist program is today archaic.[8]

A week later the *New York Post*, which had for several years offered its sympathetic pages to the Hebrew Committee, published a more extensive essay by Bergson, in which the author went as far as to question the basic principles of the Zionist program and called for the disestablishment of the main political bodies responsible for its implementation:

> We say that whatever the term "Jewish people" means, whatever may be its religious, cultural or historical significance, one thing is certain: it cannot possibly be defined as a political entity which has a state [...] Thus we propose the creation not of a "Jewish State" but of the Hebrew Republic of Palestine, in which Jewish, Christian and Moslem [sic!] citizens will have fullest equality, and opportunity under the law of the land [...] We want to forge, in these coming months, a normal, modern and liberal Hebrew Republic, and not a religious, cultural and political center for "World Jewry" called the "Jewish State" or "Judea" [...] We therefore propose that the Jewish Agency should be dissolved [...] the World Zionist Organization, and particularly the Zionist Organization of America, should

---

7 This calculation is based on the inclusion of Trans-Jordan in Palestine.

8 Hillel Kook Archive (hereinafter HKA), file 25; HKA/30 (emphasis added); Rebecca Kook ("Hillel Kook: Revisionism and Rescue" in *Struggle and Survival in Palestine/Israel*, ed. Mark LeVine and Gershon Shafir (Berkeley – Los Angeles – London: University of California Press, 2012), 157, 167) erroneously dates this article to 1945.

become a movement of friends of Palestine and should accordingly cease to be a sectarian organization.[9]

How did it come to pass that only days after Zionism's greatest political achievement to date such a scathing attack was launched on it by none other than the nephew of Avraham Yitzhak HaCohen Kook (1865–1935), the chief Rabbi of Palestine under the Mandate and the main theoretician of religious Zionism? Furthermore, how has the significance of the first-ever appearance in print of the term *post-Zionism* – and thus a landmark in the intellectual and political history of Zionism (despite its contemporary low visibility) – evaded scholars who have otherwise devoted a great deal of attention to the Hebrew Committee of National Liberation and its leader?

"Peter H. Bergson" (more often simply "Peter Bergson") was the political pseudonym adopted by Hillel Kook (1914/1915–2001) when he arrived in the United States in 1940 at the behest of the founder and leader of Revisionist Zionism, Zeev Jabotinsky (1880–1940). His role was to lead the American delegation of the ETZEL (Hebrew acronym of "National Military Organization") Palestinian underground militia, of which Jabotinsky was the nominal commander. Kook explained later that the surname "Bergson" was adopted in deference to his father (to signify "(rabbi Dov) Ber [Kook's] son"), while "Peter" was chosen after Piotr Strassman, son of a prominent Zionist-Revisionist activist in Poland, Lilia (Alicja) Strassman (1908–1959). Kook had become intimately acquainted with the Strassman family during his stay in Europe in the late 1930s while he was coordinating Jewish illegal immigration to Palestine on behalf of ETZEL.[10] Having grown in a religious household in Jerusalem, Kook lost his faith as a teenager and devoted himself instead to Jewish nationalist politics. He joined the splinter *Haganah B*, which broke off from the mainstream *Yishuv* militia, the *Haganah* in 1931, and remained with it after a second split in 1937, when it became the ETZEL and acknowledged the leadership of Zeev Jabotinsky. During the early 1930s Kook also belonged to a student fraternity in the Hebrew University of Jerusalem, the *Ṣuḥbah* (Arabic for "Brotherhood"), where he came to know some of the future leaders of Palestinian Revisionism and its breakaway groups, such as David

9 HKA/50 (published version); HKA/25; Jabotinsky Institute Archive (hereinafter JIA), file 7/1/4ח (typescripts). The essay was also reprinted in *Congressional Record* (80th Congress, first session; HKA/25), thanks to Bergson's exceptional lobbying skills, of which more will be said below.
10 Hillel Kook's interview to the Division of Oral Documentation at the Institute of Contemporary Jewry in the Hebrew University, 1968 (HKA/34). Piotr Strassman's brother Andrzej (now Gabriel) became a well-known Israeli journalist.

Raziel (1910–1941), Avraham Stern (1907–1942), and Uriel Heilperin (1908–1981).[11]

Kook's achievements in Europe made him the senior ETZEL member outside Palestine. It was thus natural for him to assume command over the organization's delegation to the United States, dispatched there at the beginning of the war to lobby for a Jewish army alongside the Allies and to create a political base in a country heretofore largely neglected by Zeev Jabotinsky's movement. Under Kook's leadership the "cut-off battalion" (an expression of Jabotinsky's that symbolized the delegation's loss of contact with ETZEL in Palestine due to wartime circumstances, but which acquired additional meaning after Jabotinsky's death in August 1940[12]) quickly developed into an independent body, both politically and, what is more significant, ideologically. By the time he made his repudiation of Zionism public in 1947, Kook headed the Hebrew Committee of National Liberation, the latest of the several organizational transmutations the ETZEL delegation went through. The Committee consisted of just seven members: apart from Kook, they were Zeev Jabotinsky's only son Eri (1910–1969); the veteran Revisionist activists Shmuel Merlin (1910–1994) and Arieh Ben-Eliezer (1913–1970); the former head of the naval school run by the Revisionist youth movement *Beitar* in the Italian harbor of Civitavecchia in the 1930s, Yirmiyahu Halpern (1901–1962); the Chicago archaeologist Pinchas (Pierre) Delougaz (1901–1975); and the Palestinian–American businessman Theodore Bennahum (1906–1972). This membership only partially overlapped with the original membership of the ETZEL delegation constituted in 1940, and Ben-Eliezer's role in it was purely nominal, since in 1943 he was delegated to Palestine, quickly arrested by the British, and never returned to the United States.

---

11 Raziel was killed in combat in Iraq while heading the ETZEL; Stern was killed by the British police in Tel Aviv while in hiding as the leader of the so-called "ETZEL in Israel" (which after his death became the LEHI, Hebrew acronym of "Fighters for the Freedom of Israel"); Heilperin, who changed his surname to Shelach but was better known under the literary pseudonym Yonatan Ratosh, became a poet, a political thinker on his own right, and the leader of the anti-Zionist "Canaanite" movement, of which more will be said below. He also edited the *Haganah B*'s weapons manual, *haEqdach* (*The Pistol*, 1935), whose clandestine printing was arranged by Kook. See Kook, "Hillel Kook," 161–162; Orna Miller, "'HaBatalion heChatukh' weHantiyot ha'-Kna'aniyot' baETZEL uviTenu'at haCherut – me'haWa'ad ha'Ivri' ad 'LaMerchav': Opozitziya le-Hanhagat haETZEL we'Cherut'" ("'The Cut-Off Battalion' and the 'Canaanite' Tendencies in the ETZEL and the Cherut Movement – From the 'Hebrew Committee' to 'LaMerchav': An Opposition to the Leadership of the ETZEL and 'Cherut'"), *'Iyunim biTequmat Israel* 14 (2004): 156; Monty Noam Penkower, "Vladimir (Ze'ev) Jabotinsky, Hillel Kook-Peter Bergson and the Campaign for a Jewish Army," *Modern Judaism* 31, no. 3 (2011): 2.

12 Penkower, "Vladimir (Ze'ev) Jabotinsky," 10.

The activities of the "Bergson group" (as it commonly became known; alternatively the "Bergson boys") and its various affiliates, which included such lobbying bodies as the Committee for an Army of Stateless and Palestinian Jews, the Emergency Committee to Save the Jewish People of Europe, the American League for a Free Palestine, and the Hebrew Committee, have been well researched.[13] Most scholars have chosen to concentrate on the wartime activity of the group, when it led a vocal public campaign first for the formation of a separate Jewish army to battle Hitler, and then, after the Holocaust had become public knowledge in the United States in November 1942, for the salvation of Nazism's not yet exterminated Jewish victims. The post-war period has received less attention, though, as I shall argue in this chapter, it was a no less important stage in the short history of the Bergson group, and intellectually probably the most captivating.

It remains beyond doubt that in several respects the work of Hillel Kook and his associates was highly innovative. Scholars have pointed out that they were probably the first Jewish political organization to foresee that following the Second World War the global geopolitical center of gravity would shift from Europe to North America;[14] they realized in real time that the Holocaust was a yet un-

---

13 A non-exhaustive but representative sample is Eran Kaplan, "A Rebel with a Cause: Hillel Kook, Begin and Jabotinsky's Ideological Legacy," *Israel Studies* 10, no. 3 (2005): 87–103; Kook, "Hillel Kook"; Rafael Medoff, *Militant Zionism in America: The Rise and Impact of the Jabotinsky Movement in the United States, 1926–1948* (Tuscaloosa and London: University of Alabama Press, 2002); Rafael Medoff and David Wyman, *A Race Against Death: Peter Bergson, America, and the Holocaust* (New York: New Press, 2002); Miller, "'HaBatalion heChatukh'"; Monty Noam Penkower, "In Dramatic Dissent: The Bergson Boys," *American Jewish History* (March 1 1981): 281–309; Penkower, "Vladimir (Ze'ev) Jabotinsky"; Louis Rapaport, *Shake Heaven and Earth: Peter Bergson and the Struggle to Save the Jews of Europe* (Jerusalem: Gefen Press, 1999); Arye Bruce Saposnik, "Advertisement or Achievement? American Jewry and the Campaign for a Jewish Army, 1939–1944: a Reassessment," *Journal of Israeli History* 17, no. 2 (1996): 193–220; Avi Shilon, "Milchemet Sheshet haYamim wehit'orerut haRa'ayon haKna'ani" ("The Six-Day War and the Resuscitation of the Canaanite Idea"), *'Iyunim bitequmat Israel* 11 (2017): 102–129; Judith Tydor Baumel, *The "Bergson Boys" and the Origins of Contemporary Zionist Militancy* (Syracuse, NY: Syracuse University Press, 2005); Judith Tydor Baumel, "The IZL Delegation in the USA 1939–1948: Anatomy of an Ethnic Interest/Protest Group," *Jewish History* 9, no. 1 (1995): 79–89; David S. Wyman, "The Bergson Group, America, and the Holocaust: a Previously Unpublished Interview with Hillel Kook," *American Jewish History* 89, no. 1 (2001): 3–34. Some reports on the Bergson group activities reached Palestine in real time through the periodical *haChevra* (*Society*), edited by the Revisionist Yaacov Weinschel (see various issues of the journal in 1944–1947). It is easy to observe that English-language literature on the topic significantly outweighs the Hebrew-language literature: food for thought.

14 Medoff, *Militant Zionism in America*, 46–47, 55.

seen, unique, and *collective* Jewish experience, a view that has taken root in the West only since the 1960s; they pioneered the use of public relations and effective marketing to the general American society to advocate Jewish and Zionist causes by tapping into the anti-British sentiment present in the American national consciousness since the American Revolution and enhanced by the presence of a large Irish diaspora there; having quickly mastered this feature of American public life, they effectively transgressed the sectarian politics of established Jewish-American political organizations;[15] they were also a precursor of the numerous ethnic advocacy groups that made their presence felt in the United States during the 1950s and 1960s.[16] All this is certainly true and adds a lot to our understanding of the issue at stake; however, my take on the Bergson group, and especially the Hebrew Committee of National Liberation, will be different. I shall approach it from the methodological vantage point of the history of ideas, my purpose being to trace and investigate the path of these initially radical Zionists toward the ultimate repudiation of Jewish nationalism in favor of a self-declared post-Zionist worldview.

Kook's article "Post-Zionism" was an expression of the sentiments that overtook members of the Hebrew Committee in the wake of the United Nations' decision on the partition of Palestine on November 29 1947. An ideological maximalist yet political pragmatist, Kook realized that rejection of the decision (as advocated by Shmuel Merlin, who succeeded Kook as the head of the Committee in early 1948) was politically unsound. In a letter of December 3 1947, Kook urged his fellow members of the Committee to accept the partition as the lesser evil and attempt to utilize it in order to disseminate their ideas regarding the shape and *raison d'état* of the state about to be established. He emphasized that the UN decision created an advantageous momentum for post-Zionism:

> Immediately after the U.N. vote there has developed a tremendous swing in favor of our basic ideology and structure – that of establishing a Hebrew republic of Palestine as a normal and modern nation as distinct from an international "Jewish State" [...] We feel it is our duty to play a leading role in the shaping of the character of the "Jewish State" and transform it into a small Hebrew republic of Palestine so that the treachery of the [Jewish – R. V.] Agency will be limited solely to a territorial loss, while today partition differs from our program also in basic principles.[17]

---

15 Baumel, *The "Bergson Boys,"* 52, 88, 98, 130 – 131, 258 – 259; Kaplan, "A Rebel with a Cause," 91; Kook, "Hillel Kook," 165; Medoff, *Militant Zionism in America*, 88.

16 Baumel, "The IZL Delegation in the USA."

17 HKA/5.

This was therefore Kook's tactical reason for declaring himself openly a post-Zionist at that crucial point of time. This "coming out," unsurprisingly, caused a tempest in a teapot within the Zionist American press. The "Bergson boys" were used to being vilified by both mainstream Zionist and Revisionist-Zionist speakers in the United States, who sidestepped their usual feuds to denounce them as fraudsters and renegades (and were obviously paid in kind; a huge part of Kook's archive is a documentation of his paper battles against established Zionism in America).[18] This time, however, the attacks were more severe and qualitatively new: Kook was lumped together with such prominent religious anti-Zionists as Rabbi Elmer Berger (1908–1996). One of Kook's detractors was the Revisionist Eliyahu Ben-Horin (1902–1966), who came to the States together with Kook and worked closely with him in the early days of the ETZEL delegation. While Ben-Horin was unable to accept (or, to judge by his letter to the *New York Herald Tribune* of December 11 1947, even to grasp) Kook's new conceptualization of Jewish identity, he remained in agreement with him regarding the need to maintain liberal standards in the future state – which, given David Ben-Gurion's domination in the "organized *Yishuv*," was far from obvious.[19] Another chasm was simultaneously opening between the Hebrew Committee and ETZEL in Palestine, which had been led since 1943 by Menachem Begin (1913–1992). The Committee played a very important role in appointing Begin to the position – this was one of the reasons for Arieh Ben-Eliezer's departure to Palestine – yet Begin proved himself not the pawn Kook half-expected him to be. Although Kook claimed later that it was under his influence that Begin's ETZEL replaced in its statements "Jew" with "Hebrew" as the agent of the anti-British struggle, finding in this distinction, in the words of Eri Jabotinsky, "a deep moral truth,"[20] Begin's worldview remained steadfastly Jewish and Zionist.[21] I will revisit the effects of

---

18 See, for instance, HKA/19 (repudiation of the Hebrew Committee by the (Revisionist) New Zionist Organization of America, November 1945) and HKA/23 (repudiation by the Jewish National Council, December 1946).

19 HKA/50. Ben-Horin, of note, never moved to Israel and passed away in the United States. Another early Revisionist ally of Kook, Ben-Zion Netanyahu (1910–2012; father of the current prime minister of Israel), wrote a lengthy article attacking the Hebrew Committee very shortly after its formation ("The Fiasco of the Hebrew Committee," *Zionews*, July 1944 [HKA/15]). As mentioned above, the ETZEL delegation was from the outset institutionally independent from the Revisionist Party, which was an early cause of frictions.

20 Eri Jabotinsky, "Jews and Hebrews" (a series of articles, 1947, JIA/3/13/410).

21 HKA/34; HKA/63; Baumel, *The "Bergson Boys,"* 174–177; Kaplan, "A Rebel with a Cause," 87, 92–93; Miller, "'HaBatalion heChatukh'," 155, 158–159; Colin Shindler, *The Rise of the Israeli Right: From Odessa to Hebron* (New York: Cambridge University Press, 2015), 6; Sasson Sofer,

this conflict between ETZEL and its "cut-off battalion" in post-1948 Israeli politics in the next section.

Kook's stay in America from 1940 to 1948 was for him a formative experience. By his own account, before coming to the United States "he had expected American Jewry to be simply *one more* Jewish community, not significantly different from those he had encountered in Warsaw [...] Paris and London." However, Kook's daughter points out, "what he encountered [...] was a Jewish community of a vastly different type."[22] This community, Kook discovered, was made up of *Americans* of Mosaic faith. Penkower specifies: "Once in America [...] the Bergsonites came to realize that many of the country's five million Jews had become fully integrated into the United States as citizens. Accepting the American separation of state and religion, most American Jews maintained in varying degrees their religious heritage but were completely indifferent to their former national origins."[23] Reflecting this new realization, the Hebrew Committee declared that

> The five million Jewish citizens of the United States [...] are Americans who wish to remain Americans. Like all other Americans they have a national extraction (in their case Hebrew) quite apart from, and in addition to, their religious affiliation, which is Jewish [...] It is therefore inaccurate, unjust and presumptuous to speak of these Jews, citizens of free countries, as if they were part of an existing national entity, loosely referred to as "the Jewish Nation" or "the Jewish People."[24]

In other words, the ETZEL delegation discovered civic national identity. What in America was the foundation of public life was hardly known in Eastern Europe and the *Yishuv:* national identities in this part of the world were predominantly (though *not* universally) built on the premises of ethno-nationalism. An undated statement by the American League for Free Palestine (one of the Hebrew Committee's satellite organizations) encapsulated this worldview simply and elegantly: "[A nation] is merely the decision of groups of everyday men; a fusion of men resulting from common interests and ideals, reacting upon economic, political environments."[25] The dilemma faced by the ETZEL delegation now presented it-

Zionism and the Foundations of Israeli Diplomacy (New York: Cambridge University Press, 1998), 228–231.

22 Kook, "Hillel Kook," 164 (original emphasis).

23 Penkower, "In Dramatic Dissent," 299.

24 HKA/19.

25 American League for Free Palestine, *The Survival and Freedom of the Hebrew Nation is your Concern!* (HKA/29). See also ALFP, *The Right of Stateless and Palestinian Jews to Nationhood* (HKA/36).

self in the following way: how to reconcile American Jews' loyalty to their nation with advocacy on behalf of the anti-British national liberation struggle in Palestine. With their entire activity re-framed in such terms, Kook and his associates were compelled to reconsider their own Zionism. Kook's daughter points to the solution they arrived at: "[T]he tragedy of European Jewry [Kook reasoned – R. V.] was that they were denied the liberty of choosing their nationality and were frequently not accepted into the body politic. The entire *raison d'être* of Zionism became clear to Hillel: *to grant this freedom of choice to Jews*."[26] To this needs to be added that once Kook realized that such a solution was impossible within the ideological framework of Zionism, whose core ethno-nationalistic principles were an inherent contradiction to civic liberalism, he decided to abandon Zionism entirely.

What, then, is the intellectual mainspring of the worldview of which Hillel Kook holds the copyright by naming it "post-Zionism?" I argue that it was a radical reinterpretation of Zeev Jabotinsky's fiercely secularist brand of Zionism (to which Kook claimed to adhere till his last day), a reinterpretation inspired by a synthesis of the principles of civic nationalism with a historical vision that contradicted the Zionist master narrative of Jewish history. This vision was supplied by Adya Gur Horon – a half-forgotten though highly significant figure of twentieth-century Hebrew intellectual history. Horon (real name Adolphe Gourevitch, 1907–1972) was one of the first associates of Jabotinsky to break with Zionism back in 1935, when he realized that Zionism's political program was not based on what he considered a firm historical-ideological platform. Horon, by profession a scholar of the history and languages of the ancient Near East, went on to develop his own historiography of Hebrew antiquity, which, translated by himself and his disciples into modern nationalistic terms, formed an alternative national idea to Zionism. This idea, known as the "Young Hebrews" ideology, or "Canaanism," was most enthusiastically taken up by Hillel Kook's acquaintance Uriel Heilperin (Yonatan Ratosh), who in 1939 established in Tel Aviv the "Committee for the Consolidation of the Hebrew Youth."[27] This committee advocated a native Hebrew territorial–linguistic national identity within the framework of the Levant (the Land of Kedem or the Land of Euphrates, in "Canaanite" terminology), which would be connected with Jewish heritage only biologically – but *not* morally, ideologically, or politically. Ultimately, "Canaanism" became a strong and intellectually consistent challenge to Zionism within Israel – a *nationalist*

26 Kook, "Hillel Kook," 166 (emphasis added).
27 Yehoshua Porath, *Shelach we'Et beYado: Sippur Chayaw Shel Uriel Shelach (Yonathan Ratosh) (The Life of Uriel Shelah (Yonathan Ratosh))* (Tel Aviv: Zmora, 1989), 186.

anti-Zionism that haunted the state of Israel till it gradually died out in the 1970s and 1980s, with the passing away first of Horon, then of Ratosh.[28]

The Hebrew Committee of National Liberation, and especially Hillel Kook, Shmuel Merlin, and Eri Jabotinsky (who was Horon's lifetime friend), belonged to the wider orbit of "Canaanism"; that is, they were influenced by, and accepted major parts of, Horon's theories, but never in such a radical way as Ratosh – they rather evinced what Avi Shilon terms "moderate Canaanism."[29] As explained by Rebecca Kook, "Hillel, who had close relationships with leading members of what came to be known as the Canaanite movement, drew upon the secular and political elements of the Hebrew idea but saw the Hebrew nation as the natural, historical development of the Jewish nation rather than a *new* nation distinct from the earlier Jewish one."[30] Saved from occupied France by the American diplomat Varian Fry (1907–1967), Horon arrived with his family in the United States in late 1940, where he took up a job as a lecturer of Semitics at the French expatriate higher education institution, the École Libre des Hautes Études in New York. Horon was never a formal member of the Hebrew Committee, though his role as the *éminence grise* behind the Committee's departure from Zionism was openly acknowledged. Speaking before the Committee in April 1945, Horon stated:

> As I mention the Committee, I must say a word about my own position regarding this Committee. It is rather peculiar. I am not a member of it, yet I am not a real outsider either. Some of the most active men in this movement I have known for years, some of them I may call my friends and comrades-in-arms. Yet I had no part whatsoever in the creation of the Committee, and no influence on the shaping of its policies, for which I cannot feel responsible. *And yet I feel very much responsible for the very name of this Committee, for the name of Hebrew, and for the ideology which should be connected with such a name.*[31]

In the same lecture Horon developed at length his ideas regarding Hebrew history, Jewish history, and their meaning for the contemporary political struggle

---

28 For an extensive discussion of Horon's historical studies and their connection to "Canaanism" see Romans Vaters, "'A Hebrew from Samaria, not a Jew from Yavneh': Adya Gur Horon (1907–1972) and the Articulation of Hebrew Nationalism" (PhD diss., University of Manchester, 2015).

29 Shilon, "Milchemet Sheshet haYamim."

30 Kook, "Hillel Kook," 166 (original emphasis). See also Baumel, *The "Bergson Boys,"* 203; Penkower, "In Dramatic Dissent," 300.

31 A. Horon, "Hebrews and Jews: A Lecture Delivered in April 1945, New York, to the Leadership and Secretariat of the Hebrew Committee of National Liberation and the American League for Free Palestine" (HKA/36; JIA/4/52פ (emphasis added)).

and nation-formation in Palestine. A striking feature of his talk, delivered in the closing days of the Second World War, as well as of other talks given to the Committee, was Horon's deep historical pessimism regarding Jewry and Judaism in the twentieth century. With the Holocaust in Europe and assimilation elsewhere taking their toll, Horon claimed that Judaism had died a social death:

> [Jews] are the followers of Judaism, members of the Jewish church-community [...] Jewry, in scientific terms, is a caste [...] During the 19th and 20th centuries, [the Jewish caste] broke up and actually ceased to exist as a distinct social body. We are now witnessing the last chapter in the history of Judaism: the more or less complete, more or less final assimilation of the Jews, in one part of the world, as well as their physical extermination under the pretext of "racialism," in another part of the world [...] Today, Jewry is in the process of complete disintegration [...and] has become merely an abstract notion [...][32]

Zionism, therefore, is a non-starter for a national liberation movement. "The organs of Zionism do not express and cannot express the Hebrew national movement," Horon told his audience, since

> The failure of Zionism, so obvious today, is due to the constant confusion of the two terms and of the two conceptions – Hebrew and Jew [...] Zionism, which was founded on the false assumption that Jewry is a national entity, has become an unworkable compromise between the superstitions of a "racial" or religious Judaism and the realities of the Hebrew rebirth in the Hebrew land.[33]

In consequence,

> The Hebrew movement [...] is, and must be, something entirely different from Zionism, and something which by its very nature denies the possibility of a Jewish nationalism or a Jewish nation [...] For half a century, Zionist thought feeds on the Jewish conception of our past, and is therefore trying to do something self-contradictory, I mean – *to build a territorial nation and a state on the philosophy of a church* [...] *Zionism is not a first effort of the Hebrew revival, it is rather the last attempt of Judaism to outlast itself, to gain a new lease on life.* Certainly, something Hebrew is being born in Palestine, – but the forces which bring about this birth are hemmed by Zionism rather than strengthened by it.[34]

The Hebrew Committee of National Liberation was officially formed in protest against the 1943 Bermuda Conference's failure to address the urgent needs of Hit-

---

32 (A. G.) Horon, "The Hebrew Movement: An Outline," January 1947 (HKA/36; JIA/4/52כ).

33 Horon, "The Hebrew Movement."

34 Horon, "Hebrews and Jews" (second emphasis added).

ler's Jewish victims,[35] and in that sense was a direct continuation of the previous incarnations of the ETZEL delegation – the Committee for a Jewish Army of Stateless and Palestinian Jews and the Emergency Committee to Save the Jewish People of Europe – though within a novel theoretical framework suggested by Horon. Kook reasoned that the Bermuda debacle was due to the Allies' lack of understanding of European Jews' radically changed collective status, defined by persecution and extermination. The Allies continued to view Jews as citizens of their respective countries – including those where their civil rights were stripped off as a precursor to genocide. Jews were thus considered alien nationals, not formally different from their oppressors, in contradiction to their factual position and elementary logic. The Hebrew Committee reproached itself for initially following the same train of thought, which it now saw as the reason for its failure to raise a Jewish army, and re-conceptualized European Jewry as a newly-formed fate community, whose vested interest was in joining the Allies as a separate national entity with no national, sentimental, or formal allegiance to the states that had become their killing fields. This, for the Committee, meant a default choice to join the Hebrew nation in Palestine as the only national society to which the Jews of Europe could offer their allegiance due to existing cultural and often familial connections. Once the Committee had reached this conclusion, it introduced a principal innovation in its vocabulary, from now on terming the persecuted Jews of Europe Hebrews, in acknowledgement of their new national status and in distinction from the Jews of the free world, whose Judaism was regarded as having no national meaning or consequence. *Jews* became a term signifying religious-communal identity separate from, and not implying, any national identity, whereas *Hebrews* became a term signifying the already established national community of the *Yishuv* in Palestine, as well as those Jews whose national identity was considered by the Committee to express itself in a desire to join the *Yishuv.* Adya Horon delineated the new operational terminology as follows:

> "The Hebrews" comprise today:
>
> a. The Hebrew settlers already rooted in the Hebrew land, forming there the nucleus of a reviving nation,
> b. Those who want to join the Hebrew nation through an act of free choice and will,

---

35 See Baumel, *The "Bergson Boys,"* 138–141. Baumel also notes that the formation of the Committee took place simultaneously with ETZEL's declaration of revolt against the British Mandate authorities, which means that the Committee was supposed to function as the legal political arm of the paramilitary underground organization, a kind of overseas "Sinn Féin" to ETZEL's "IRA" (Baumel, *The "Bergson Boys,"* 200).

c. Those who are in need of a Hebrew republic, and who must join the Hebrew nation as their only means of physical and spiritual salvation. This category includes mainly the hundreds of thousands, indeed the millions of oppressed or uprooted Jews and so-called "Non-Aryans" for whom there is no more room in the world outside the Hebrew nation – since nationhood is the law of the modern world. For every man and woman in this category the liberation of the Hebrew land and the creation of a Hebrew Republic is a question of life and death.[36]

The implications of this shift for the political philosophy espoused by the Hebrew Committee were far-reaching. As stated by Eran Kaplan, "Kook had made this distinction [between the Jewish religion and the Hebrew nation – R. V.], for the first time, into the centerpiece of a political worldview"[37] that assumed that emancipated Jews did not, and could not, have any national aspirations beyond those of their general non-Jewish society, whereas persecuted Jews' only chance of being admitted into the family of nations battling Hitlerism was the assumption of a new national identity centered around a territory with which they (still) had no tangible connection. Zionism's refusal to adopt this distinction between a national and a religious-communal identity was understood by Horon and the members of the Hebrew Committee as its biggest weakness and internal contradiction, which put emancipated Jews in peril in their home countries while doing nothing to assist oppressed Jews in Europe:

> Between the Jews and Hebrews as defined above, there is no strong bond of common interests. Yet there would be no necessity of conflict, if the two terms were as clearly separated as are the realities which they define. In that case, there might even be a common meeting ground: the Jews cannot dwell in peace where they are unless the Hebrews in exile leave and go to their country on the eastern shores of the Mediterranean; and the revival of the Hebrews cannot come about unless they relinquish their present status as Jews and renounce the claim to a double nationality.[38]

The American League for Free Palestine drew the line even farther by stating that such ideo-terminological framework will have the benefit of "absolv[ing]" [sic!] Americans of Jewish ancestry "from Jewish nationhood."[39]

The materials of the Hebrew Committee abound in critical discussions of Zionism's intellectual inconsistency and resulting political impotence, the most detailed and eloquent of which is Hillel Kook's open letter to the president

---

36 Horon, "The Hebrew Movement."

37 Kaplan, "A Rebel with a Cause," 93.

38 Horon, "The Hebrew Movement."

39 American League for Free Palestine, *The Right of Stateless and Palestinian Jews to Nationhood.*

of the World Zionist Organization (and future president of Israel), Haim Weizman (1874–1952), dated April 1945 and published by the American League for Free Palestine.[40] Making his starting assumption that the difference between Hebrew and Jew is "the difference between a nationality and a religion," Kook goes on to deconstruct Zionism's intellectual foundations and political program. In many senses, this is a truly prophetic document, foretelling three years before the establishment of Israel all the difficulties a "Jewish State" would encounter, and therefore merits being discussed at some length:

> When you speak of a Jewish Commonwealth [the ultimate objective of Zionism as defined in the May 1942 Biltmore Program – R. V.], are you proposing the establishment of a theocratic state? [...] It is impossible to deny that Jews constitute a religious group [...] The term "Jewish Commonwealth" therefore inevitably denotes the suggestion of a theocratic state, precisely such as would be denoted by the term "Catholic Commonwealth" [...] Let us imagine that your proposed "Jewish Commonwealth" has been established. A number of questions will demand answers.

Kook then goes on to pose to Weizman these questions, pertaining to what he defined as the "human boundaries" of the future state and to whom precisely the state would represent in its sovereignty. He ponders in particular the nature of the envisaged relation of the "Jewish Commonwealth" vis-à-vis the Jews of the world, its non-Jewish citizens, and the worldwide Jewish–Zionist bodies, whose future fate and role called for re-consideration. Then he concludes:

> The insistence of Jewish leaders that there exists a universal Jewish people which makes it possible for a "Jew" to be a member of the American, the Russian, the Argentine, or, for that matter, the German nation, and simultaneously also be a member of the "Jewish people" is utterly unrealistic and politically meaningless [...] We say, therefore, that it is impossible and unnecessary to maintain in 1945 in the United States the same principles of organization and objectives of a movement which was organized in 1886 in Czarist Russia...
>
> What we propose is to abandon this undemocratic and impractical point of view which calls for arbitrary enforcement of a certain status against the will of the individual [...] It can thus be made clear that there is a Hebrew nation to which adhere only those who wish to adhere to it (as is the case with any other nation) and not a "Jewish nation," which involves every Jew whether he wants it or not. We want Palestine, therefore, as a free state and not "a Jewish state." We must with cold sobriety realize the fact that the Hebrew nation is not composed of all the people in the world who are commonly referred to as Jews

40 Note the change in name: the previous non-Jewish satellite organization of the ETZEL delegation was called "American Friends of a *Jewish* Palestine." Avi Shilon ("Milchemet Sheshet haYamim," 119) notes that Menachem Begin objected to this new naming since it undermined for him the Jews' religious attachment to the Land of Israel.

> [...] We must realize that we cannot have a free state in Palestine and an international "Jewish people" at the same time...
>
> There will be the State of Palestine (or whatever name this self-governed country might call itself): *the national territory of the Hebrew nation.* Here will live several million people adhering to the Jewish, Christian, Moslem and a variety of other religions [...] Palestine will have no state religion [...] In many countries of the world there will be people professing the Jewish Religion, but these will be *purely religious* communities.[41]

Anticipating the tortured debates on "Jewish democracy" that would plague Israeli public discourse from the first day of the state, the Hebrew Committee observed that

> The Zionist spokesmen have tied themselves into knots trying to define a "Jewish State." But however they twisted and turned and evade it, it still boils down to something very suspiciously like a theocratic state. And so they switched. What they wanted they said was a "democratic Jewish State" [...] Either it is a "Jewish State" in which case the citizens of the state are Jews, and non-Jews are something else but not first class citizens. Or else it is a democratic state and it doesn't matter whether its citizens are Jews or non-Jews. And if it is a democratic state and all citizens enjoy full equality under the law regardless of whether they are Jews or not, what on earth makes it Jewish?[42]

Eri Jabotinsky asserted that this new thinking was in fact directly derived from the conceptions of both his father and the founder of political Zionism Theodor Herzl (1860 – 1904), who differentiated between assimilated and persecuted Jews in a way resembling that of the Hebrew Committee. Without attempting a critical discussion, Jabotinsky wrote off-handedly that what the two meant by "Jews" was now expressed by "Hebrews." In effect, he projected his own philosophy back to the older theoreticians of Zionism, and credited Adya Horon with polishing the terminology.[43]

We should not, however, take Jabotinsky at face value and ought to examine how far indeed the Hebrew Committee departed from Zionism; in other words, to what extent was the post-Zionism of Hillel Kook *et consortes* really an anti-Zionist phenomenon?

Firstly, as suggested above, an American-style civic secular nationalism adopted by the Hebrew Committee was incompatible with Zionist ideology, nourished as it was in the conceptual world of East European ethno-nationalism. The Hebrew Committee came to regard the Hebrews (at least in Palestine, less so in

41 *A Blueprint for Hebrew Freedom: A Letter from Peter H. Bergson to Dr. Ch. Weizman* (HKA/29, original emphases). For similar utterances see HKA/5; HKA/19; HKA/50; HKA/63; JIA/3/13/410.
42 HKA/25.
43 Jabotinsky, "Jews and Hebrews."

war-torn Europe) as a *voluntary* national community, while Zionism persisted in treating Jews as a community of *pre-determined* destiny. For example, Herzl considered Jews united by religious origin and anti-Semitic persecutions, whereas Eri Jabotinsky contradicted him directly by writing that "anti-Semitic persecutions constitute neither a positive definition nor an effective bond."[44] On a deeper and more general level, the Hebrew Committee made the implicit claim that insofar as a "Jewish problem" existed, it could be solved *only* through assimilation, either in the free world or in Hebrew Palestine, which by following the western democratic standards would form an egalitarian republic without any collective privileges being conferred upon a particular religious or ethnic group. In both cases, Jewish identity would ultimately dissipate within a different identity, therefore Jews *as* Jews had no part in the Hebrew project of national liberation. Kook drew practical conclusions from this principle, writing that the Hebrews about to be repatriated to Palestine numbered only two and a half million, whereas "the Zionist formulae of a 'Jewish people' may rightly or wrongly be interpreted as applying to about twelve or fourteen million people."[45] Thus, Kook did away with the essential Zionist principle of the "Ingathering of the Exiles."

Secondly, whenever the Hebrew Committee mentioned in its documents (both internal and public) its ideological adversaries, it invariably referred to them as "Zionists," and admitted that to all intents and purposes their ways parted ideologically and practically.[46] In this sense the formation of the Hebrew Committee was the apex of a process the ETZEL delegation had been undergoing from the early days of its existence, and especially since Zeev Jabotinsky's death in August 1940. Rafael Medoff cites Yitzhak Ben-Ami (1913–1985), a founding member of the delegation, as recalling that "Jabotinsky's passing severed our last links with traditional Zionism"[47] (Medoff, who goes very little toward concealing his pro-Zionist-Revisionist sympathies, seems entirely oblivious to the true significance of this statement).

---

44 Jabotinsky, "Jews and Hebrews." These words are actually a quotation from Horon's "The Hebrew Movement."

45 HKA/19.

46 See, for example, a letter to Mark Waldman, December 17 1947 (unsigned, probably written by Kook or Harry Louis Selden, head of the American League for Free Palestine): "We have not in the past devoted a great deal of effort to fighting the Zionist movement. We were travelling more or less the same road... Now, however, we have come to a parting of the ways" (HKA/5).

47 Medoff, *Militant Zionism in America*, 65. Yitzhak Ben-Ami's son Jeremy currently heads the Jewish-American liberal Zionist organization J Street (https://jstreet.org/about-us/staff/jeremy-ben-ami/; accessed November 13 2018).

Thirdly, the Hebrew Committee openly challenged the authority and *raison d'être* of mainstream Zionist bodies. It dismissed the Jewish Agency as a "voluntary organization of very fine Jewish gentlemen,"[48] who had no legitimate right to make any ruling impacting the Hebrew inhabitants of Palestine, whom they supposedly did not represent, let alone to agree to the severance of Transjordan from Palestine in 1946 (which the Hebrew Committee vociferously protested, mobilizing the support of sympathetic congressmen) and to the additional partition of Palestine the following year. It accused the Agency of striving to create a "truncated [...] precarious 'Jewish State' on the small beachhead around Tel Aviv,"[49] which stood no chance of survival and would perpetuate the "Jewish anomaly." The Hebrew Committee's alternative objective was "one nation [...] <u>one single Republic</u> – the Hebrew Republic. This Republic will accept all those individuals who want to be part of it, and will grant a status of complete civil equality to every group, religious or other, that would prefer to retain its moral, social, cultural autonomy."[50] This, significantly, included the Arab-speaking population of Palestine, which was invited to partake in the building of the Hebrew state on an equal footing.

Finally, the very name "Hebrew Committee of National Liberation" was styled after the names used by the exiled governments of states occupied by Nazi Germany (e.g. the French/Yugoslav/Greek committees of national liberation), which meant that the ETZEL delegation in its final incarnation saw itself as the Hebrew exiled government-in-the-making. It was thus a rival to established Zionist representative bodies such as the Jewish Agency, the World Zionist Organization, the New [Revisionist] Zionist Organization, and the World Jewish Congress, all of whom supposedly represented the Jews the world over, but not the Hebrews (another effect was the implicit equivalence between Nazi rule in Europe and British rule in Palestine). In this capacity the Committee (unsuccessfully) solicited a place among the various national delegations to the October 1945 San Francisco conference that founded the United Nations. In its ultimate form, Horon proposed, "[t]he [Hebrew] Provisional Government must comprise spokesmen of all the Hebrews in the country and abroad [...] These

48 "Text of a Statement by the Hebrew Committee of National Liberation on the United Nations Resolution of Palestine, December 2, 1947" and the following document (title page missing, HKA/25). See also "The Case against the World Zionist Organization and the Jewish Agency" (National Convention of the American League for Free Palestine, February 1947; HKA/23); "Statement Issued by Mr. Peter H. Bergson, Chairman of the Hebrew Committee of National Liberation, at Lake Success, New York, October 15, 1947" (HKA/25).
49 Jabotinsky, "Jews and Hebrews."
50 Letter to Waldman; HKA/19 (original emphasis).

spokesmen can and should belong not only to the Jewish denomination, but also to other religious communities – Christian, Moslem, etc."[51]

At the same time, the Hebrew Committee's outlook did not conform entirely to the "Canaanite" ideology, at least not in the form professed by Yonatan Ratosh and his followers. Firstly, no notion of the Land of Kedem/Euphrates was present in the Committee's publications; it insisted very strongly on the inseparability of the east and the west banks of the Jordan, but had no wider geopolitical aspirations. Secondly, the relationship between Hebrews and Jews as envisioned by Hillel Kook differed strongly from orthodox "Canaanism." As explained by his daughter, Kook saw the Hebrew nation as "the modern, nationalist embodiment of the historic Jewish people,"[52] and the Committee's publications asserted a direct continuity between Jews and Hebrews, in antiquity as well as in modernity. This contradicted the "Canaanite" concept of the Hebrews as a territorial-linguistic nation whose very existence denied the Jewish communal way of life and could not be reconciled with an arbitrary "admission" into the Hebrew nation of all European Jews suffering under Hitler. From his home-base in Tel Aviv, Ratosh strongly denounced the Hebrew Committee for considering as Hebrew "any immigrant, any refugee, any stateless person [...] that has no choice but to move to this country",[53] and Horon never returned to this idea in his other political writings. In a letter written several years afterwards he pointed that a tension existed between the ideological and the tactical in the Committee's platform: "The 'Hebrew Committee' [...] restricted the definition of 'Hebrews' (*for obvious tactical reasons*) to the Jews residing in Palestine and the inmates of European concentration camps."[54] Horon severed his relations with the Committee after a harsh quarrel with Hillel Kook, on matters probably related more to finances than to ideology, as his daughter Margalit Shinar suggested in an email message to me on November 8 2009. Eri Jabotinsky, however, hinted at differences on matters of principle as well, reporting in his memoirs on a conversation he held with Horon in 1946, in which the latter claimed that Kook would never achieve any prominence, since he was not an ideologue. To this Jabotinsky sardoni-

51 Horon, "The Hebrew Movement."

52 Kook, "Hillel Kook," 167.

53 Yonatan Ratosh, *Reshit HaYamim: Petichot 'Ivriyot* (*The First Days: Hebrew Introductions*) (Tel Aviv: Hadar, 1982), 171. All translations from Hebrew are my own.
[כל מהגר וכל פליט וכל מחוסר מולדת (...) וכל אשר אין לו ברירה אלא להגר לארץ הזאת]

54 Letter to Eri Jabotinsky and Shmuel Rosoff, February 10 1956 (HKA/32, emphasis added).

cally replied that Kook didn't need to be one, since he had ideologues on his payroll, which upset Horon.[55]

The proposal that Kook's attitude to ideas and ideologies was above all instrumental is reiterated by the Israeli journalist-politician Uri Avnery (1923–2018), who knew both Ratosh and members of the Hebrew Committee well (and occasionally published short stories and articles in the Committee's journal *The Answer*). In his memoirs Avnery portrayed Kook as a person of exceptional talents in the sphere of networking and public relations, not exactly matched by intellectual prowess.[56] It can be admitted that the Hebrew Committee's insistence on a shared national identity between Palestinian Hebrews and Jewish Holocaust survivors languishing in DP camps in Europe was quite artificial. The Committee, for one, hardly ever produced any empirical evidence that "stateless Jews" were in fact stateless or were willing to renounce their citizenship in order to join their "brethren" in Palestine. This claim, incidentally, had the polemical advantage of permitting the Committee to argue that Hebrews ("stateless Jews" included) outnumbered Palestinian Arabs and thus constituted a democratic majority that legitimized the Hebrew Committee's stated aim of becoming the representative Hebrew government-in-exile.[57]

Despite the above, I believe that the foregoing discussion demonstrated that the Committee's position was strongly influenced by profound ideological considerations. It is therefore misguided to argue, as Medoff does, that the differentiation between Hebrews and Jews was no more than a tactical trick designed to allay American Jews' fears of "double loyalty";[58] to claim so is to blind oneself to a very elaborate intellectual dynamic that formed the background to the Committee's repudiation of Zionism. Such an approach results in some remarkable manifestations of ignorance; for example, Medoff apparently has no idea who Horon was,[59] while Judith Baumel confuses him with Eliyahu Ben-Horin,[60] whose hostility to Kook's post-Zionism was mentioned earlier. Even more outrageously, Baumel and David Wyman both assert that the Hebrew Committee of National

---

55 Eri Jabotinsky, *Avi, Zeev Jabotinsky* (*My Father, Zeev Jabotinsky*) (Tel Aviv: Steimatzky, 1980), 79.

56 Uri Avnery, *Optimi* (*Optimistic*) (Tel Aviv: Yedi'ot Acharonot, 2014), 157. Avnery considered Shmuel Merlin, who held a degree from the Sorbonne, the true "mind" behind the Committee.

57 HKA/19; Jabotinsky, "Jews and Hebrews." Menachem Begin was also not averse to employing these quite creative statistics to argue a similar point, though, of course, to him those were "Jews" and not "Hebrews" (Shindler, *The Rise of the Israeli Right*, 226).

58 Medoff, *Militant Zionism in America*, 112–117.

59 Medoff, *Militant Zionism in America*, 247, n. 36.

60 Baumel, *The "Bergson Boys,"* 203.

Liberation and the American League for a Free Palestine were Zionist organizations that struggled for a Jewish state in Palestine.[61]

Stage Two: "LaMerchav" and the "Kedem Club"

The Hebrew Committee of National Liberation disbanded shortly after the establishment of Israel in 1948. Hillel Kook arrived in Israel simultaneously with the ETZEL ammunitions ship *Altalena* in June 1948 (whose sailing was co-organized by the Hebrew Committee) and was immediately arrested, thus winning the dubious honor of being one of the first political prisoners of the new state. He was released a few weeks later and, together with Eri Jabotinsky, Arieh Ben-Eliezer, and Shmuel Merlin, ran for the Cherut ("Liberty") party, established and led by Menachem Begin on the base of ETZEL, in the Israeli Constituent Assembly elections in January 1949, when it won fourteen seats. The Israeli declaration of independence provided that the Assembly's purpose was to write a constitution, yet at its second session on February 16 1949 the deputies voted to form a parliament and to postpone the constitution question indefinitely, thus turning a temporary body into a permanent one without meeting the threshold condition. Kook, who saw this as an illegal usurpation of power by Ben-Gurion (whose party had the plurality), reportedly stood up and shouted: "This is a putsch!" We have no documentation of this event: his daughter explained that his interjection was expunged from the record, so we are left only with Kook's own testimony. In an interview given two decades later he stated that he still considered this step illegitimate and expressed his regret for not having resigned from the Israeli parliament immediately.[62]

The trio, Kook, Jabotinsky, and Merlin, were the parliamentary vanguard of an oppositional faction within the Cherut, formed in December 1950, called "LaMerchav" ("To the Region/Area"). Its name, inspired by the vocabulary of the "Canaanites" (with whom the three used to meet during their parliamentary tenure), expressed a position strongly at odds with Begin's politics of *yiddishkeit*.

---

61 Baumel, *The "Bergson Boys,"* 190; Baumel, "The IZL Delegation," 84; Wyman, "The Bergson Group," 7.

62 Kaplan, "A Rebel with a Cause," 93; Kook, "Hillel Kook," 168; Kook's interview to the Division of Oral Documentation. For the broader debate (and controversy) over the issue of a written constitution for Israel in the wake of its establishment see Nir Kedar, "Ben-Gurion's Opposition to a Written Constitution," *Journal of Modern Jewish Studies* 12, no. 1 (2013): 1–16; Orit Rozin, "Forming a Collective Identity: The Debate over the Proposed Constitution, 1948–1950," *Journal of Israeli History* 26, no. 2 (2007): 251–271.

Orna Miller compellingly demonstrates that "LaMerchav" was the Hebrew Committee's political afterlife in the Israeli parliamentary system, though not all of its members originally belonged to, or shared views of, the Committee.[63] The political platform of "LaMerchav" was by and large identical to that of the Hebrew Committee, with adjustments to the realities of a state that was no longer theoretical but existed in practice. The most salient element of the position taken by "LaMerchav" was explicit post-Zionism: the assertion that Israel's victory in the independence war had put an end to Zionism, as opposed to both Ben-Gurion's and Begin's understanding of Zionism as a kind of "permanent revolution." This keystone tenet shaped all other stipulations raised by members of the faction both in the parliament (the *Knesset*) and in Cherut's internal debates. "LaMerchav" demanded the disestablishment of the World Zionist Organization and the Jewish Agency, which had now outlived their usefulness; it demanded a written constitution for Israel that provided for the separation of religion and the state, as well as opposed a centralized economy under the grip of political-economic bodies affiliated with the ruling party.[64] In terms of Israel's regional geopolitical role, it advocated an alliance with the non-Arab peoples (or those it considered non-Arab) in the Middle East, in order to break Pan-Arabism's hold over the region and thus end Britain's indirect domination over it; this was to be replaced with a democratic federation of the Levant that had Hebrew Israel and Maronite Lebanon as its leading elements, for which purpose an alliance with the USA might be considered.[65] Simply put, "LaMerchav" advocated a civic secular and liberal nationalism in a state led by its leaders in an ethno-nationalist direction.

"LaMerchav" members of the *Knesset* also struggled for their principles individually. Jabotinsky reportedly demanded that the Israeli parliament's buffet be non-kosher.[66] He repeatedly advocated the completion of the Constituent Assembly's abandoned task, arguing that as long as Israel remained without a written constitution, it would not be able to disentangle itself from the three existential paradoxes inherited from what he called "the Zionist stage" of Hebrew history: Israel's relations with its religious Jewish citizens, with Diaspora Jewry, and

63 Miller, "'HaBatalion heChatukh'."

64 See a memorandum by Shmuel Merlin ("Towards Collapse or Prosperity; Problems of Israel's Economic Independence – Analysis and Outline of a Solution," May 12 1949; HKA/8).

65 Miller, "'HaBatalion heChatukh'," 155, 168–184.

66 See Yehoshua Porat's talk at a memorial event on the occasion of the fortieth anniversary of Eri Jabotinsky's death, held at the Jabotinsky Institute in Tel Aviv on June 18 2009 (https://www.youtube.com/watch?v=0gPLFhjrhZo; accessed October 26 2017).

with the Arabs.[67] Jabotinsky, following his father and his "Canaanite" friends, professed a very strong hostility to Arab nationalism in all forms, and stated openly that for him Arabic was a foreign language whose usage must not be permitted in a Hebrew parliament.[68] He declared his belief in the ultimate equality between Arabs and Jews within a Hebrew secular state, but also revealed that he considered it necessary to temporarily limit Arab citizens' rights in Israel until this particular paradox has been solved. Most vocally, he objected to granting Arabic-speaking Israelis collective rights as a national minority, fearful of the replay of the pre-war "minorities' question" in Europe, which brought down more than one state. In his insistence on the Arabs' ultimate assimilation into Hebrew society, Eri Jabotinsky deviated from his father's position, who was in favor of cultural-national autonomy for the Arab citizens of the future Jewish state.[69] At the same time, Jabotinsky championed in the *Knesset* the struggle of the Arabic-speaking Maronite citizens of Israel to return to their village of Bir'am on the Lebanese border, from which they had been evicted by the Israeli army in 1948 under a fraudulent pretense of security and with a promise to be allowed to return shortly, which was never kept.[70]

The challenge of "LaMerchav" to Menachem Begin was short-lived. The leader of the Cherut mastered enough votes in a party plenum to push the faction members away from positions of influence. By the time of the elections to the second *Knesset* in July 1951, both Kook and Jabotinsky functioned as solitary parliamentarians, having resigned their membership of the Cherut. Neither they nor Merlin got re-elected to the *Knesset*, and they retired from public life. Jabotinsky devoted himself to an academic career as a lecturer of mathematics at the Technion (apart from 1963–1965, which he spent at the Haile Selassie University of Addis Ababa, a choice echoing the positions taken by "LaMerchav"). Kook and Merlin returned to the United States, where Kook became an investment broker and financed the "Institute for Mediterranean Affairs," co-chaired with

---

67 Eri Jabotinsky's speech in the *Knesset*, May 8 1950 (JIA/5/13/410).

68 To drive home his point that the absence of a constitution meant that in Israel there was no legal requirement to use only Hebrew in the *Knesset*, Jabotinsky concluded one of his speeches in French. According to contemporary press reports, his words were literally drowned in a tumult (JIA/5/13/410). Notably, when making this speech, Jabotinsky conceded that he was speaking in his own name only, demonstrating the tensions between "LaMerchav" and Cherut's leadership.

69 See Rafaella Bilski Ben-Hur, *Kol Yachid Hu Melekh: HaMachshava hachevratit wehaMdinit shel Zeev Jabotinsky* (*Every Individual a King: The Social and Political Thought of Zeev Jabotinsky*) (Tel Aviv: Dvir, 1988), 281–291, 329–332.

70 See Jabotinsky's memorandum on behalf of the Bir'am refugees (HKA/32). According to Hillel Cohen (*'Aravim Tovim* (*Good Arabs*; Jerusalem: 'Ivrit, 2006), 135), the Bir'am cause was taken up by the Cherut party as a whole.

Merlin. During the 1950s he attempted to reprise his Hebrew Committee glory days by founding a "Committee to Save the Middle East from Communism," but was dissuaded from further action by the Israeli legation.[71] The purge initiated by Begin against "LaMerchav" brought the already strained relations between him and Kook to the point of hatred. Uri Avnery writes that Kook had held Begin in deep contempt ever since the late 1930s in Poland when he was active as an ETZEL emissary and Begin was the local head of Beitar. When Begin was elected to the premiership in May 1977, Kook reportedly said that he would not have trusted Begin to run a grocery store, let alone a state.[72] In an interview from 1968, Kook openly called Begin "a liar."[73] There were certainly personal motives behind this conflict, along with deeper ideological schisms; in the words of Orna Miller, the demise of "LaMerchav" signified "the end of a 'Canaanite' stream that developed in the Revisionist movement in the preceding two decades" and the reversal to a Jewish political worldview and mentality.[74] Nonetheless, the failure of "LaMerchav" should not obscure a very significant aspect to its brief lifespan: it was the first, and as of yet also the last, case of post-Zionism gaining official ground and a voice in the Israeli parliament. No other instance of post-Zionism, either historically or today, can boast of such an achievement.

Shortly after his departure from the *Knesset* Eri Jabotinsky summed up his unsuccessful fight for a constitution for Israel (in the drafting of which he solicited Horon's help)[75] in an article he published in 1952 in a brochure put out in the United States by the "Levant Club" – an expatriate Maronite-Lebanese organization with which Horon closely cooperated.[76] This article has the historical value of probably being the second occurrence of the explicit term "post-Zion-

---

71 HKA/30; Miller, "'HaBatalion heChatukh'," 182.

72 Avnery, *Optimi*, 157. Avi Shilon ("Milchemet Sheshet haYamim," 124) confirms that Kook was unhappy with Begin's electoral victory.

73 Kook's interview to the Division of Oral Documentation (also Baumel, *The "Bergson Boys,"* 235). Nonetheless, in all relevant materials of the ETZEL delegation Begin is lionized as a Hebrew liberation warrior.

74 Miller, "'HaBatalion heChatukh'," 185.

[סיומו של זרם 'כנעני' שהתפתח בתנועה הרוויזיוניסטית בעשרים השנים הקודמות]

The Jewish–American Zionist Medoff misses, as usual, the entire point: "During their first term in parliament [...] Kook and Merlin quarrelled with Begin over a variety of ideological and personal issues, and soon they opted to withdraw from the political scene and return temporarily to the United States" (Medoff, *Militant Zionism in America*, 214).

75 Eri Jabotinsky's letter to Horon, November 6 1950 (JIA/4/4–4א).

76 Eri Jabotinsky, "Israel and Zionism: Why Israel has no Constitution," *The Levant: Behind the Arab Curtain* (HKA/36).

ism," and the first after the establishment of the state.[77] In it Jabotinsky dismisses the notion that the absence of a constitution in Israel is due to the coalition calculations of Ben-Gurion, and asserts that it reflects a deeper existential problem – the lack of a defined relationship between the state and Zionist ideology on the one hand, and the world Jewish diaspora on the other:

> It is today no secret that the liberation of Israel from Britain was brought about by forces acting outside the Zionist Organization or even against it [...] Yet these were all aspects of a conflict that belonged to the "Zionist period." *Today Zionism as such has ended by achieving fulfilment. We are now in what should be called the "post-Zionist period" in Hebrew history.* Zionists who refuse to disband or to re-organize, deny this [...] In the main, it can be said that the people of Israel are moving farther and farther away from Zionism and more and more towards an integrated Hebrew nationhood, based on a territory and a language, thus considering as foreigners all those, *whatever their religion or race*, who are not joining it [...] Psychologically and politically, the population of Israel today is formed by a very different type of people than those who are the rank and file of the Zionist Organization outside Israel...
>
> It is mainly because of this conflict between Israel and Zionism that Israel, after four years of existence, still has no Constitution [...] The real reason that prevented the drafting of the Constitution was the ever growing perception that Israel is but a beginning – that it is only a beachhead, an ideological and material beachhead of civilization on a vast new continent [...] The discovery that the Middle East is populated by groups and peoples who are in fact second-rate citizens in their own countries is what makes it possible to conceive of Israel spreading its ideals over the adjacent lands [...] This is the new conception that Israel (*not* Zionism) is bringing to the Middle East, and this is the sense in which Israel feels to be a beachhead [...] In fact, the very name "Israel" is restrictive. It is a compromise between the Zionist past, which would have called it "Zion" or "Judea," and the Hebrew future where it will sound somewhat like "Hebrewland."[78]

Jabotinsky's position after 1948 consists, as the above quote demonstrates, of two essential elements: that the Israeli national identity is a new one, not Jewish but not completely detached from Jewish heritage, on the one hand; and that Israel has a regional "manifest destiny" on the other. This is what Jabotinsky means when he hints that the name "Israel" is transitory; back in 1948 the American League for a Free Palestine expressed a similar dislike of the name "the

---

77 This assessment does not include private correspondence between ex-members of the Hebrew Committee and "LaMerchav," where, one might assume, references to "post-Zionism" were quite ubiquitous (see, for instance, Eri Jabotinsky's letter to Hillel Kook, December 6 1949; JIA/13/4–4א).

78 Jabotinsky, "Israel and Zionism" (first emphasis added). This article was reprinted in Hebrew in the "Canaanite" periodical *Alef*, though, curiously, with the paragraph on post-Zionism omitted (Eri Jabotinsky, "Israel wehaTziyonut: Madu'a Ein Techiqa leIsrael?," *Alef*, September 1952, 3–4, 15).

State of Israel," which brought associations with *l'État Français* ["French State"], the official name of the Vichy statelet in France during World War II (its suggested alternative was "the Republic of Israel").[79] These two interrelated principles were developed into a complete program by a political club established by Eri Jabotinsky in his home city of Haifa in the mid-1950s, the "Kedem Club" (its full name was "Kedem: a Hebrew Liberal Club," later changed to "the Israeli Liberal Club," much to the dissatisfaction of Adya Horon). This seems mainly to have been a one-man project, since apart from Jabotinsky, the only other Club member whose identity is known is Shmuel Rosoff (1900 – 1975) – an important Haifa architect who has left several landmarks in the city, son of one of the first Russian Zionists Israel Rosoff (1869 – 1947) and a childhood friend of Vladimir Nabokov (it was Rosoff who lent the future author of *Lolita* his high school diploma to enable Nabokov to enroll at the University of Cambridge).[80] The main objective of the club was to formulate and advance a new *raison d'état* for a post-Zionist Israel, based on the assumption that the establishment of the state meant the fulfillment and closure of Zionism's historical purpose. The club's statute described its aims in the following way:

> To contribute to the progress of the Levant by developing, clarifying and propagating the following basic ideas:
>
> a. Integration of the State of Israel into a Levant freed from Pan-Arab domination over the various peoples of this region, including the Moslem Arabs themselves, who are being incited by their leaders to Holy War and to the subjugation of other peoples.
> b. Moulding of an Israeli nation firmly rooted into the soil of its ancient homeland.
> c. Liberalization of the State of Israel – separation of State and Church, development of a civilized, progressive society, ensuring for the individual a life of freedom and dignity.[81]

To achieve these ends a deep transition was advocated both in Israel's internal and external policy, in accordance with Jabotinsky's view that Israeli national identity could not be expressed by Zionist moral and political vocabulary,

---

79 Editorial, *The Answer*, December 17 1948, 4 (HKA/62).
80 Brian Boyd, *Vladimir Nabokov: the Russian Years* (Princeton, NJ: Princeton University Press, 1990), 166. In a letter to Horon from December 8 1955 Rosoff states that the Club "consists of a nucleus of 5 or 6 men surrounded by 40 or 50 'well-wishers'" (JIA/4/4 – 4א), but he doesn't name them.
81 JIA/2/12/4א (the statute of the Club is reproduced in four languages: Hebrew, Arabic, French and English).

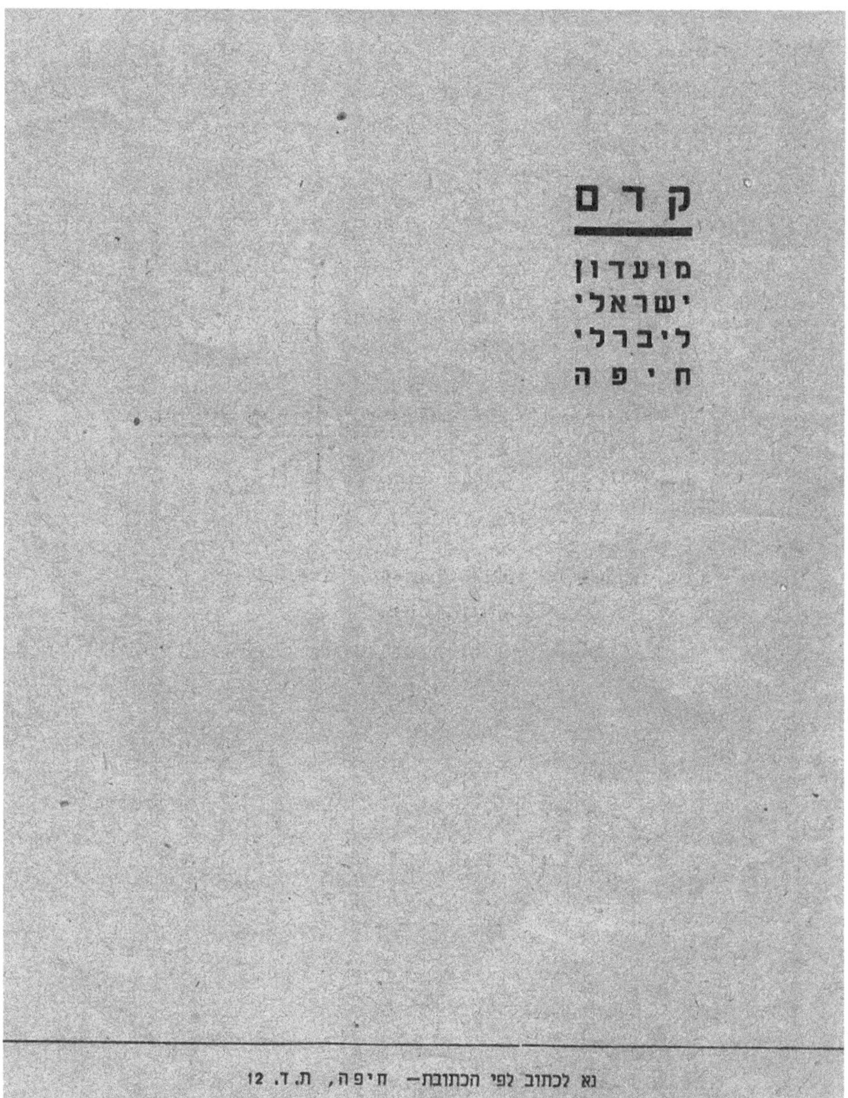

ק ד ם

מ ו ע ד ו ן
י ש ר א ל י
ל י ב ר ל י
ח י פ ה

נא לכתוב לפי הכתובת– חיפה, ת.ד. 12

Fig. 2: Statute of Kedem Club.
Reproduced by permission of the Jabotinsky Institute in Israel.

לקדום ארץ הקדם...

«קדם» מועדון ישראלי ליברלי.

1. מטרת המועדון.

לתרום לקדום ארץ הקדם על-ידי הבהרה, פיתוח והפצה של הרעיונות היסודיים האלה:—

(א) שילוב מדינת ישראל באזור הקדם המשוחרר מהשתלטות פן-ערבית על עמי האזור ועל הערבים-המוסלמים עצמם, הנגררים על-ידי מנהיגיהם להרפתקאות של דיכוי עמים וג׳יהאד דתי.

(ב) גיבוש האומה הישראלית, המשרשת בארצה כבימי קדם.

(ג) ליברליזציה של מדינת ישראל, הפרדה בין דת למדינה ויצירת חברה נאורה ומתקדמת, המבטיחה חיי חופש וכבוד לפרט.

2. חברות במועדון.

כחבר יכול להתקבל כל אזרח מדינת ישראל, ללא הבדל דת, גזע ומין, בתנאי שמועמדותו תוצג ע״י שני חברים לפחות ותאושר ע״י האסיפה הכללית. אולם לא יתקבל אזרח ישראלי, שהוא גם נתין מדינה זרה.

החברות במועדון אינה נוגדת השתייכות לכל מפלגה פוליטית או ארגון דתי.

3. פעולות המועדון.

ייסוד מועדוני «קדם» בערים שונות. עריכת פגישות חברתיות, הרצאות, קורסים וסיורים; הפצת דברי דפוס.

המועדון ישתף בעבודתו מומחים לבעיות טכניות, גיאוגרפיות ואתניות של האזור.

המועדון יחפש דרך לפתרון בעית הפליטים הפלשתינאים.

בעיקר יתמסר המועדון לעריכת תכנית לארגון מדיני של עמי ארץ הקדם. בעריכת תכנית זו ישותפו אישים בני כל אומות האזור.

• כתבינו בארצות הברית:

LEVANT CLUB 37 Wall St.
New York, N.Y.

LEVANT CLUB 10214 Charlevoix Ave.
Detroit, Mich.

Pour le progrès du Levant . . .

« KEDEM », Club liberal israelien.

1. But du club.

Le club entend contribuer au progrès du Levant par l'étude, le développement et la diffusion des principes idéologiques suivants:—

(a) Intégration de l'état d'Israel dans un Levant libéré de l'emprise pan-arabe, qui opprime les différents peuples de la région, y compris les arabes-musulmans eux-mêmes, que leurs dirigeants incitent à la guerre sainte et aux conquêtes.

(b) Consolidation de la nation israelienne dans le pays de ses ancêtres.

(c) Création d'un régime libéral; séparation de l'Eglise et de l'Etat; développement d'une société civilisée et progressive sauvegardant la liberté et dignité de l'individu.

2. Admission au club.

Tout citoyen israelien, sans distinction de race ou de religion, peut devenir membre du club. Sa candidature doit être présentée par deux membres au moins et approuvée par l'assemblée générale.

Ne sera pas admis comme candidat un citoyen israelien, ayant une seconde nationalité.

Les membres du club sont libres d'appartenir à n'importe quel autre groupe politique, social ou religieux.

3. Activités du club.

Création de clubs similaires dans des villes diverses. Organisation de réunions, conférences, cours et excursions. Publication et diffusion de brochures et pamphlets.

Le club s'assurera le concours d'experts qualifiés pour l'étude des problèmes techniques, géographiques et ethniques du Levant.

Le club cherchera une solution au problème des réfugiés palestiniens.

Le club se consacrera surtout à la mise au point d'un project de réorganisation politique des peuples du Levant.

Ce project se fera en collaboration avec des personalités appartenant à tous les peuples de la région.

نحو تقدم المشرق . . .

« قدم » نادي اسرائيلي حر

١ • اهداف النادي

المساهمة في تقدم هذه البلاد العريقة في القدم عن طريق بث وتنمية وايضاح المبادىء الاساسية التالية :

(أ) ادماج دولة اسرائيل في هذه المنطقة العريقة في القدم محررة من تحكم اي سيطرة عربية في شعوبها وفي عربها المسلمين انفسهم المنساقين وراء زعمائهم الذين يطوحون بهم ن الجهاد الديني وفي مغامرات من شأنها اضطهاد الشعوب.

(ب) تطوير الامة الاسرائيلية وتثبيت اقدامها في بلادها كما كانت في القدم.

(ج) نشر المبادىء الحرة للتسامح في الدولة والفصل بين الدين والدولة وايجاد مجتمع راق متقدم يؤمن للفرد حياة حرة كريمة.

٢ • العضوية في النادي

يقبل عضواً في النادي كل مواطن اسرائيلي بقطع النظر عن دينه او عنصره او جنسه بشرط ان يرشحه عضوان على الاقل ويوافق النادي على عضويته في اجتماع عام ولاتقبل عضوية أي شخص يحمل جنسية اسرائيلية وجنسية اخرى.

٣ • ايجاد اندية في المدن المختلفة وعقد اجتماعات ذات صيغة اجتماعية والقاء محاضرات وتنظيم دورات دراسية ورحلات وبث منشورات لهذه الغاية.

يهتم النادي بصورة خاصة بضم خبراء في الشؤون الفنية والجغرافية وفي اصول الامم مما يتعلق بالمنطقة ويسعى النادي — في ضمن مساعيه المختلفة — للبحث عن طريق لحل مشكلة اللاجئين الفلسطينيين.

وسيتفرغ النادي بصورة خاصة لوضع مشروع لتنظيم شعوب هذه المنطقة العريقة في القدم تنظيماً سياسياً يشترك في وضعه جميع شعوب المنطقة.

Correspondents in U.S.A.:

LEVANT CLUB 37 Wall St.
New York, N.Y.

LEVANT CLUB 10214 Charlevoix Ave.
Detroit, Mich.

"KEDEM", The Israeli Liberal Club.

1. Aim of the Club.

To contribute to the progress of the Levant by developing, clarifying, and propagating the following basic ideas:—

(a) Integration of the State of Israel into a Levant freed from Pan-Arab domination over the various peoples of this region, including the Moslem Arabs themselves, who are being incited by their leaders to Holy War and to the subjugation of other peoples.

(b) Moulding of an Israeli nation firmly rooted into the soil of its ancient homeland.

(c) Liberalisation of the State of Israel—separation of State and Church, development of a civilized, progressive society, ensuring for the individual a life of freedom and dignity.

2. Membership.

Every Israeli citizen irrespective of race or religion is eligible for membership, provided he has been proposed by at least two members and has been approved by a General Meeting.

An Israeli citizen having a second nationality is not eligible for membership.

Members of the Club may belong to any political group or party, or religious organization.

3. Activities of the Club.

Sponsoring the establishment of "KEDEM" Clubs in various towns; conducting of regular meetings, lectures, courses and excursions; publishing and distributing printed matter.

The Club will endeavour to enlist the participation in its work of experts on the technical, geographical and ethnographic problems of this region.

The Club will strive towards the formulation of a plan for the solution of the Palestine refugee problem.

The Club's main endeavour will be the drafting of a plan for the political reorganization of the peoples inhabiting this region.

This draft plan will be worked out jointly with persons belonging to the various peoples of the Levant.

which did not accept that national identity was a matter of free self-definition.[82] Moreover, Jabotinsky saw in the continued existence of Zionism an unmediated danger to Israeli sovereignty: "Shaking off the unnatural bonds with the voluntary ghettoes inhabited today by the Jews of the free world," Jabotinsky wrote in an April 1954 memorandum prepared for the Kedem Club, is "a simple security imperative: today the world regards us as just another Jewish community, and the world knows perfectly well what is to be done with Jewish communities." He further says that this peril is perpetuated by the Israeli government, which, by clinging to Zionist principles, is mainly preoccupied with survival and hesitates to announce Israel's geopolitical and strategic objectives in the Middle East. This, according to Jabotinsky, foments internal decay and invites external attack.[83]

The Kedem Club defined Israel's regional aim as working to establish a federation modelled after the United States (with "extensive State rights [...] more so than in the U.S.A., because of the ancient character and deep tradition of the peoples involved"),[84] united by a secular constitution and allegiance to the Hebrew historical and cultural legacy, whose global significance would be in defeating and rolling back Pan-Arabism in the Eastern Mediterranean: "Our overall purpose in the coming period is the transformation of the Levant into a political Federation of States and Territories, each of which is to be endowed with its own ethnic and cultural flavor," the Club program stated.[85] Not a global superpower, but "a regional power of the size of France", rhapsodized Eri Jabotinsky, whose suggested name would be "Ha-'Ever" ('העבר', "The Country" in Hebrew), "Levant Union" or "Semitic Federation." In this federation all Middle

---

82 Jabotinsky wrote the following on this matter: "[My approach to national self-definition] is based on the principle of a person's right to define himself. This principle means that if you wish to know to which nation one belongs, go and ask him: if he says he's a Frenchman, you ought to believe him, since the right to determine this is exclusively his own"
[הגדרה זו (...) מבוססת על יסוד זכות ההגדרה העצמית של האדם. פירוש יסוד זה הוא שאם ברצונך לדעת לאיזו אומה משתיך אדם מסוים, לך ושאל אותו: והיה ואמר לך כי צרפתי הוא, תאמין לו, כי לו ואך לו הזכות לקבוע דבר זה]
(Eri Jabotinsky, "Memorandum" [HKA/32; a truncated version of the same memorandum is found in JIA/1/12/4א]).

83 Jabotinsky, "Memorandum."
[ההתנערות מהקשרים הבלתי טבעיים עם הגיטאות-מרצון בהם חיים יהודי העולם החופשי כיום יש לה חשיבות בטחונית פשוטה: אנו נראים כיום בעיני העולם כאחת הקהילות היהודיות ואת אשר עושים עם קהילות יהודיות יודע העולם היטב]

84 "Tentative Formulation for a Program of Action," Haifa, November 19 1956 (HKA/32; JIA/3/12/4א).

85 "Tentative Formulation."

Eastern nations currently oppressed by Pan-Arabism would enjoy self-determination; this included first and foremost the Hebrews of Israel and the Maronites of Lebanon, but also Kurds, Druze, Shiites, and all non-Arab ethnic and religious minorities scattered throughout the Levant, whose legacy in the land went deeper than the Arab–Muslim presence. A space would be left for future colonization by migrants (preferably, but not necessarily, Jewish), who would create their own separate states within the federation. Taking his cue from the autonomy of the Mormons of Utah, Jabotinsky conceded that "an Arab state or two may also come into existence", along with a theocratic Jewish state. The latter would serve as a laboratory for the functioning of religion in public life, and would thus be released from the requirement to separate state and religion, a principle that would otherwise be enforced on the federal level. The Federation's liberal principles would be enshrined in a constitution that would ensure full equality and autonomy to citizens both personally and collectively, with its overall Hebrew character preserved by federal legislation.[86]

The idea that a Hebrew state's existential *sine qua non* would be a *mission civilatrice* in the Middle East, incompatible with inward-looking Zionism, had appeared back in 1947 in Eri Jabotinsky's series of articles "Jews and Hebrews," cited above. When discussing Israel's historical role as a barrier to Pan-Arabism and Pan-Islamism, Jabotinsky slips into outlandish conspiracy theories, describing Great Britain as the mastermind behind a global project of a Pan-Islamic caliphate stretching from Indonesia to Morocco:

> [The idea is] to establish a Muslim federation from the periphery of Australia in the Pacific Ocean, through to Indonesia, Pakistan, south-central Soviet republics of Middle Asia, Afghanistan, Persia and the "Arab World" to the Atlantic Ocean. *En route*, the plan is to swallow up Burma, India and Israel, and to deliver Turkey, the Muslim areas of Europe and even central Africa back to Islamdom [...] This plan is sustained – financially, militarily and politically – by England and the United States [...] The US sees in this plan a chance to stir up unrest in the Soviet Muslim republics [...] [while] England [...] probably wishes to restore the British Empire on novel foundations [...] [which will provide] a route back to India, to Israel and to the eviction of the French from North Africa.[87]

---

86 Jabotinsky, "Memorandum."

]מעצמה מסוגה של צרפת[
]ואף בודאי מדינה ערבית אחת או שתיים[

87 Jabotinsky, "Memorandum."

]פקיסטן היא המרכז של תכנית פן איסלמית שכונתה להקים פדרציה מוסלמית שתשתרע ממבואות אוסטרליה באוקינוס השקט, דרך אינדונזיה, פקיסטן, הריפובליקות של דרום מרכז אסיה שבברית המועצות, אפגניסטן, פרס ו"העולם הערבי" עד לאוקינוס האטלנטי. בדרך, התכנית הזו מתכונת לבלוע את בורמה, הודו, וישראל ולהחזיר לאיסלם את תורכיה ואת החבלים המוסלמיים של אירופה ואף את מרכז אפריקה (...) התכנית הזו נתמכת – בכסף, נשק וסעד מדיני – ע"י אנגליה וארה"ב (...) ארה"ב רואה בתכנית אפשרות להתסיס את הריפובליקות

To stem this grandiose design, Jabotinsky suggested making inroads into India in order to achieve there a regime change toward one that was more nationalistic and hostile to Pakistan, which he regarded as an illegitimate Muslim sectarian state (Jabotinsky even proposed that Israel might be interested in tightening relations with radical Hindu nationalists faithful to the legacy of the pro-Nazi Chandra Bose); to challenge the United States openly on the world diplomatic stage; to derail Soviet influence in the Middle East by assisting a (probably imaginary) underground movement in the USSR that looked to overthrow the Communist Party or by organizing illegal Jewish immigration from there drawing from the Zionist experience of the 1930s; to lend full support to France in its struggle against the Algerian independence movement; and to actively recruit supporters and followers in neighboring Middle Eastern states, on whose ruins the Hebrew Federation was supposed to rise. Jabotinsky was very explicit about the latter: he stated that Israel must sow dissent and internal discord in its hinterland by manipulating and mobilizing non-Muslim minorities in the Arab League states, so that they would eventually be able to cooperate fully and equally with Israel and Lebanon in the establishment of the Federation.[88]

To attract these minorities to Israel, it must first "constitute a laboratory and a framework for the envisaged Federation. The modification has to be both in the direction of liberalization [...] and that of the separation of state and church."[89] In practice, says Jabotinsky, this will mean the complete de-Zionization of the state and the termination of Zionist institutions at home and abroad. Other steps include "personal representation in the Knesset, abolition of military government [which ruled the Arab-Palestinian citizens of Israel and was ultimately abolished only in 1966], nationalization of the Sick-Funds, opening of Labor Unions to full membership of all citizens regardless of race, nationalization of the Qeren Qayemet. *A clear distinction between Israelis and Jews of foreign countries.*"[90]

המוסלמיות של ברה"מ (...) אנגליה (...) יש כאן כנראה רצון לחדש את האימפריה הבריטית על יסודות חדישים (...) זוהי גם דרך לחזור להודו, לישראל ולגרש את הצרפתים מצפון אפריקה]

88 Jabotinsky, "Memorandum."

89 "Tentative Formulation."

90 "Tentative Formulation" (emphasis added). In the Hebrew version of the same document (which is more extensive but similar in essentials to the English version) Jabotinsky also emphasizes the importance of a secular unitary education. A fatal mistake he identifies in Israel's internal policy is the treatment of all non-Jewish minorities as "Arabs" instead of differentiating them according to ethno-religious identity and even playing up these differences artificially by offering preferred treatment to Christians and Druze (Jabotinsky, "Memorandum").

The last sentence is key, and Jabotinsky in his "Memorandum" meticulously detailed the terminological and ideological differences between Jews and Hebrews, which would be the principal cornerstone for a post-Zionist Israel:

> Regarding the confusion concerning the terms Jewish, Zionist, Hebrew and Israeli, the [self-] definition mentioned above means the following: A) an Israeli is any person who due to certain circumstances is a citizen of Israel. This is exclusively a formality and has no bearing on this person's opinions, feelings or origin. B) A Jew is any person throughout the world that belongs in one way or another to the Jewish religion and Judaism without any bearing on this person's patriotic sentiments. C) A Zionist once meant a person who wished to abandon Diaspora life in order to come to this country and live like a Hebrew. It was a Hebrew-in-the-making. Today the adjective has lost its precision and is applied to a foreign (non-Israeli) Jew who is positively disposed toward Israel without any intention of joining it. (*I believe that today, after the Zionist period has come to an end by accomplishing its objective, we must not employ the hollow word Zionist*). D) A Hebrew is a person that sees himself part of the renewed nation. His being Hebrew is dictated exclusively by his internal feeling. This is not similar to his being a Jew: most of the Jews, even in the free world, do not tie their own fate or the fate of their children to our fate and have no plans to do so in the future. This is not similar to his being an Israeli, since there are many Israelis who do not regard themselves as part of the sovereign Hebrew nation (and this includes both Jewish and non-Jewish elements – especially among the orthodox and the communists) [...] The confusion surrounding the problems of Jews and Hebrews must be terminated also, and perhaps especially, because there is no possibility to implement all the plans above as long as our leaders see themselves as emissaries and agents of world Jewry. In order to succeed (and survive) we must integrate psychologically and spiritually with the area in which we live [...] Clear things must be said to the Jews of the world: we the Hebrews are interested in immigrants. We are interested above all in a Jewish *'Aliyah* and therefore the gates of our country stand open to you, on the condition that you become Hebrews by disconnecting yourselves from the countries to which you now belong. With Jews who refuse to do so we shall continue to maintain good relations subject to our interests but maintaining awareness that those are foreigners.[91]

91 Jabotinsky, "Memorandum" (emphasis added).
[לגבי התסבוכת שבין המושגים יהודי, ציוני, עברי וישראלי הרי פירוש ההגדרה הנ"ל הוא זה: א. ישראלי הנו כל אדם שעקב התפתחות מסוימת הנו אזרח ישראל. דבר זה הוא פורמלי בלבד ואינו קשור בדעותיו והרגשותיו ומוצאו. ב. יהודי הוא כל אדם בעולם המשייך את עצמו בצורה זו או אחרת לדת היהודית וליהדות ללא כל הבדל של הרגשותיו הפטריוטיות. ג. ציוני היה פעם אדם שרצה לעזוב את חיי הגולה לבא לארץ ולהיות כאן עברי. זה היה מין עברי בדרך. היום טושטש הדבר והתואר ציוני נתן ליהודי נכרי (לא ישראלי) הרוכש[sic!] ידידות למדינת ישראל בלי כונה להצטרף אליה. (לי נראה כי אסור להשתמש היום, לאחר שהתקופה הציונית נסתימה מתוך השגת מטרתה, במלה ציוני שהתרוקנה מתכנה). ד. עברי הוא אדם הרואה את עצמו שותף לאומה המחודשת שהוקמה. היותו עברי תלויה אך ורק בהרגשתו הפנימית. הדבר איננו זהה עם היותו יהודי: רוב רובם של היהודים אפילו בעולם החפשי, אינם משתפים את גורלם ואת גורל ילדיהם עם גורלנו ואינם מתכונים לעשות זאת גם בעתיד. הדבר איננו זהה עם היותו ישראלי מכיון שיש ישראלים רבים אשר אינם רואים עצמם כחלק של האומה העברית הרבונית (וזה כולל כאחד אלמנטים לא יהודיים ויהודיים – ביחוד בין האדוקים והקומוניסטים) (...) יש לשים קץ לבלבול השורר בקשר לבעיות היהודים והעברים גם, ואולי אפילו ביחוד מפני שאין כל אפשרות להגשים את

These principles were defended very emphatically by Shmuel Rosoff in his letter to Shmuel Merlin of November 18 1956, in which he wrote that the point he considered "of greatest importance" (perhaps more than Jabotinsky) is "the necessity to underline and proclaim the *anti-Jewishness* of Israel".[92]

One of the issues the Kedem Club tackled (apparently at the insistence of Shmuel Rosoff) was the Palestinian refugee question. Defining it as a question of priority that "stands in our way as a great obstacle to any further progress," in Rosoff's words to Merlin, the Club envisioned the liquidation of the Hashemite Kingdom of Jordan (an "artificial Kingdom [...] which today is on the eve of being partitioned by its neighbors" and a bastion of British imperialism in the Middle East) and the resettlement of the refugees there, so that in time they might join the Hebrew Federation and thus reestablish their status as free and equal citizens:

> The rehabilitation of the Refugees should be accomplished within the boundaries of "Jordan" under the international control but by an Israeli authority. A large chunk of the budget of Israel should be allocated to the project. After 5 years, the territory should be allowed to decide whether it wishes to federate with Israel (thus returning to the Palestine Refugees a stake in the whole of Palestine) or not. Simultaneously during this period, any refugee desiring to forego his rights to resettlement and wishing to swear allegiance to the State of Israel will be permitted to do so and be given a full compensation for his lost property and be admitted to Israel.[93]

This peculiar version of the "Right of Return" was advocated back in 1949 by Shmuel Merlin, who wrote that "there are about three hundred thousand Arab refugees [sic!], most of whom will probably return and take up their place both in the society and economy of the country."[94] This position was opposed by Horon, who from the United States served as a liaison between the Kedem Club and the Lebanese-Maronite expatriate "Levant Club," in whose activities he was deeply involved and to whose publications he constantly contributed.

התכניות הנ"ל כל עוד מנהיגנו יראו את עצמם כשליחי יהדות בין לאומית ועושי רצונה. בשביל להצליח (ואף בשביל להתקיים) עלינו לעבור תהליך של אינטגרציה נפשית ורוחנית עם האיזור הגיאוגרפי בו אנו יושבים (...) ליהודי העולם צריך לאמר דברים ברורים: אנו העברים מעונינים במהגרים. בראש וראשונה אנו מעונינים בעליתם של מהגרים יהודים ולכן שערי ארצנו פתוחים בפניכם בתנאי כי תפסיקו את השתיכותכם לארצות להן אתם משתיכים ותהיו לעברים. עם היהודים המסרבים לעשות זאת נקיים גם להבא יחסים טובים בהתאם לאינטרסים שלנו, אולם מתוך ידיעה כי נכרים הם]

92 HKA/32 (emphasis added).

93 "Tentative Formulation."

94 Merlin, "Towards Collapse or Prosperity" (he calls the refugee numbers cited by Arab and British sources "an exaggerated atrocity propaganda").

The Kedem Club was in fact supposed to be the Levant Club's opposite number within Israel, working towards the aligned goals of releasing Israel from Zionism and of releasing Lebanon from the yoke of Pan-Arabism (the US correspondence addresses given in the Kedem Club brochure are those of the Levant Club in New York and Detroit). Therefore, in his extensive correspondence with Eri Jabotinsky and Shmuel Rosoff in 1955–1956,[95] Horon warned against adopting policies that might seem reasonable in the narrow Israeli context but would repel potential allies among nationally-minded Maronites both in Lebanon and the American diaspora. For this reason he decried the change of the Club's designation from "Hebrew" to "Israeli," since this might be interpreted as a forfeiture of the Hebrew regional expansive vision in favor of a parochial Israeli-centered outlook (from an American angle, he also questioned the wisdom of using the designation "liberal," despite Rosoff's strong defense of the term).[96] Horon particularly objected to making the Palestinian refugee question into a central matter for the Club and to the Club's insistence on a strict separation of religion and state. The former he wanted to solve within a general federative framework in the Levant instead of pushing it to the front of the stage. The latter, he explained, would be unacceptable to Maronites, whose feeling of national identity was strongly shaped by Christianity; he also had personal reasons for protesting enforced irreligiosity, not being an atheist himself, and he denounced the "communist atheism"' advocated by the 'Canaanites'.[97] In addition, both issues – the separation of religion and state and the solution to the Palestinian refugee problem – were raised by left-wing circles in America, Jewish and non-Jewish alike, whose society, or even association with, Horon wished to avoid at all costs.

The envisaged joint activity of the Kedem and the Levant clubs fits into a much longer history of ideological and practical cooperation between Hebrew settlers in Palestine and nationalist anti-Arab Maronites in Lebanon.[98] The latter took a sympathetic view of Zionism, and thus, Horon warned, the differentiation between "Jews," "Hebrews," and "Israelis" was meaningless to them. This might be the chief reason for the ultimate failure of the cooperation between Israeli post-Zionists or "Canaanites" and the Levant Club.

---

95 HKA/32; JIA/4/4–4א.

96 Rosoff's letter to Merlin.

97 Letter by Horon to Eri Jabotinsky, February 5 1955 (JIA/4/4–4א).

98 For a participant's contemporary evidence see Eliahu Elath, "'Phoenician Zionism' in Lebanon," *The Jerusalem Quarterly* 42 (Spring 1987): 38–56. See also Kristen E. Schulze, *Israel's Covert Diplomacy in Lebanon* (Basingstoke: Macmillan, 1998).

Stage Three: "Club 59" and Afterwards

The Kedem Club was not post-Zionism's swansong during the 1950s, despite Zionism's growth in power by the end of the decade. A very vocal post-Zionist organization, yet completely unconnected to the people of the Hebrew Committee or "LaMerchav," was "Semitic Action" established by Uri Avnery and the veteran co-leader of the LEHI, Nathan Yalin-Mor (1913–1980), in protest against Israel's support for France in Algeria and its collusion with France and the UK against Egypt in 1956. The pro-Arabism of "Semitic Action" ruled out any potential cooperation with ex-members of the Kedem Club, but in other respects *The Hebrew Manifesto* published by "Semitic Action" in two editions in 1958–1959 followed quite faithfully the principles of Kook's and Jabotinsky's post-Zionism. These included the affirmation of the existence of a Hebrew–Israeli nation, separate from world Jewry though not to the extent advocated by the "Canaanites," the essentiality of a written constitution, separation of religion and state, abolition of the Jewish Agency and the World Zionist Organization, secularization of state education, release from bondage to both the USSR and the USA, etc. The *Manifesto* also called for Israel to integrate with the region instead of serving as a proxy state for world imperialism, the first step being the solution of the refugee problem by establishing a Palestinian state instead of the Kingdom of Jordan that would federate with Israel. This was probably the first non-communist political document in Israeli history that spoke of the Palestinians as a nation deserving self-determination and offering a path to it.[99]

All in all, "Semitic Action" is a relatively well-known episode in the history of early post-Zionism, one that was extensively described in political memoirs and analyses, not least by Uri Avnery himself. However, another post-Zionist society formed a number of years after "Semitic Action" remains totally in the shadows. During the early 1960s a "Club 59" (so called after the year of its establishment) organized a series of talks and political meetings to promote post-Zionist ideas. The charter of the Club laid out its principles in the following manner:

i. The State of Israel is the first imperfect expression of the Hebrew national rebirth;
ii. Israel must develop as a national Hebrew state, perforce multi-racial and multi-denominational, and not as a glorified Jewish ghetto;
iii. The mission of Israel is twofold: – to guide as many as possible among the dispersed Jewish people toward the normalcy of national Hebrew existence, – and to free from

---

99 Avnery, *Optimi*, 510–529; http://uriavnery.com/he/publications.html (accessed April 17 2019). Materials related to "Semitic Action" and *The Hebrew Manifesto* are preserved in Uri Avnery's archive deposited in Israel's National Library.

oppression as much as possible of the Levant (wherein lies the historic Hebrew territory);

iv. The appeal of Israel must therefore be directed not only to its own citizens, and not only to the Jews; but also to the oppressed "minorities" in the Levant and to all those forces in the world, particularly the Mediterranean world, which are threatened by Panarabism, or by Communism, or both.

These aims were to be achieved in the following ways:

a. To strengthen, deepen and broaden the Hebrew national outlook and movement in Israel, among its Jewish as well as non-Jewish population;
b. To seek understanding, friendship and support for this movement abroad, both in the East and the West – especially in the Mediterranean world and quite particularly within Israel's own neighbourhood, i.e. in the Levant area;
c. To help raise the cultural standards of human relations, while resisting all forms of bigotry, chauvinism or discrimination inimical to such standards;
d. To further the development of an intellectual, social and political elite capable of providing guidance and leadership for the stated ends...[100]

I have not been able to ascertain the membership or the extent of the Club's activity, though it is fair to surmise that its members were probably supporters of the Cherut or the Liberal Party, keen to advance civic-democratic concepts of nationhood, in opposition both to Begin and Ben-Gurion. Its statute, which is preserved in both typescript and handwritten form in Adya Horon's archive (which suggests that he was one of the Club's founders immediately after his move to Israel in 1959), displays some tension between "Canaanite" and Zionist tendencies.[101] The questions that Horon jotted down during his lectures for the Club also demonstrate that at least some of his listeners were not ready to embrace "Canaanite" anti-Zionism.

"Club 59" was perhaps the last organized instance of the first generation of post-Zionism: the one whose intellectual mainspring was right-wing liberal nationalism, embodied in Zionism by Zeev Jabotinsky's political thinking with its emphasis on secular national identity, and strongly filtered through "Canaanite" influence that detached it from Zionist principles. Neither the "Canaanites" nor first-generation post-Zionists succeeded in leaving a strong imprint on the Israeli society within which they lived, and by the 1960s their significance had waned almost completely. Hillel Kook returned to Israel in 1969, yet never managed to

100 All materials pertaining to "Club 59" (most of them in English) are located in Adya Horon's private archive.

101 For example, paragraph three of the draft constitution of the Club stated that "any Jew" could become a member, but this was amended by hand to "any person."

gather a following in a manner even remotely resembling his "stardom" days in wartime Washington. In the late 1960s he attempted with Eri Jabotinsky to form a think tank in Israel that would mirror his American "Institute for Mediterranean Affairs," but the initiative was cut short by Jabotinsky's untimely death in the summer of 1969. In 1975 Kook, together with Shmuel Merlin (who remained in the United States until his death in 1994), submitted a memorandum to the Israeli government, which detailed their proposals for breaking the political and strategic impasse Israel found itself in following the October 1973 war. When the memorandum yielded no official reaction (the prime minister then was Yitzhak Rabin (1922–1995), a faithful follower of Labor Zionism), they published it as a full-page advertisement in a number of Israeli dailies. The close-typed ad called for the adoption of a new *raison d'état* for Israel based on the assumption that Zionist ideology had no role to play after 1948, and that perpetuating its principles and mechanisms had a corruptive influence on the Israeli body politic:

> Following the declaration of the State there should have been opened a new page in our history, a new period of national independence. This new page is yet to be turned over [...] A transitional period [...] morphed into a permanent way of life. Emergency missions were routinized and justified by ideologies of false Zionism. Matters pertaining to sovereignty were abandoned [...] as if the great national revolution did not take place at all. After almost thirty years it is time to put an end to this anachronistic situation, which twisted all notions, terms and expressions of sovereign political life and rendered principles of a just society meaningless [...] This radical shift in philosophical, psychological and political approach assumes that the State of Israel is no longer the beginning of the realization of Zionism. The opposite is truth: the establishment of the State signified the end of Zionism as a national liberation movement [...] This assumption leads to the conclusion that Israel must no longer be regarded as an instrument and avant-garde of the world Zionist movement...[102]

---

102 Hillel Kook, Shmuel Merlin, "Hatza'a leWikuach Leumi" ("Proposal for a National Debate"), *Haaretz*, April 18 1975, 5. See also Miller, "'HaBatalion heChatukh'," 187–188; Shilon, "Milchemet Sheshet haYamim," 120–124.

[עם הכרזת המדינה, צריך היה להיפתח דף חדש בהיסטוריה שלנו, ולהתחיל עידן חדש של עצמאות לאומית. דף חדש זה עדיין לא נפתח (...) תקופת מעבר (...) הפכה מתקופת מעבר להווי פרמננטי. משימות של שעת חירום הפכו למצב רגיל, ויצרו אידיאולוגיות של ציונות כוזבת כדי להצדיקו. ענייני המדינה הסוברנית הוזנחו (...) כאילו המהפכה הלאומית הגדולה לא התחוללה כלל וכלל. לאחר תקופה של שלושים שנה כמעט, הגיע הזמן לשים סוף למצב אנכרוניסטי זה שבתוכו כל המושגים, המונחים והבטויים של חיים מדיניים עצמאיים התעוותו, ועקרונות של חברה מתוקנת והגונה סורסו (...) השינוי הרדיקלי בגישה פילוסופית, פסיכולוגית ומדינית זו מושתת על ההנחה שמדינת ישראל איננה יותר שלב התחלתי של הגשמת הציונות. אלא להפך: שהקמתה של המדינה היוותה סיומה של הציונות בתור תנועת שחרור לאומי (...) המסקנה מהנחה זו היא שאין לראות יותר במדינת ישראל מכשיר וחיל חלוץ של התנועה הציונית העולמית...]

The most sensational element of the ad, which demonstrates how far Kook and Merlin had moved forward since their Hebrew Committee days, is the idea that Israel's transition into a sovereign liberal state was dependent upon comprehensive peace with the Palestinians. At a time when even publicly mentioning the Palestinian issue in Israel bordered on blasphemy, Kook and Merlin echoed the *Hebrew Manifesto* (in the composition of which they had played no part whatsoever) by declaring that the Palestinian nation existed beyond any doubt, that it deserved its own independent state, and that peace with this state was an urgent existential need for Israel. More than half of the ad is an exhaustive blueprint of Israel's future relations with the Palestinians: the authors envisioned free representative elections on both banks of the Jordan and Gaza, followed by negotiations between Israel and the Palestinian Constituent Assembly, with the aim of establishing a Palestinian state on *both banks of the Jordan* that would ultimately merge with Israel into a confederation, and thus, in accordance with the old ETZEL ideology, the Land of Israel would once again be united. Kook and Merlin wrote frankly that one of their objectives was the elimination of the PLO from the political process, since they regarded it as a non-representative usurper of the Palestinian cause and a pawn of the Pan-Arabist regimes that blackmailed the entire world with their oil.

The idea that the Palestinian problem could be solved by the elimination of the Kingdom of Jordan was not new; as we saw above, twenty years earlier it was raised by the Kedem Club. Uri Avnery in the mid-1950s also considered Jordan as the main enemy to Israel by being the obstacle to Palestinian independence,[103] enough to include its obliteration in the *Hebrew Manifesto*. Yet how distant this was from the Hebrew Committee's publications only thirty years earlier, which, if mentioning the Arab Palestinians at all, assured the American public that they were no enemies to the Hebrews and would gladly take part in the Hebrew nation-building since they had no national identity of their own.[104]

The part of the ad relating to Israel's inner reform reflects Kook's worldview after 1948, summarized by Eran Kaplan in the following way: "To Kook [...] the modern state of Israel was an anomaly: a nation-state without a nation [...] The source of this anomaly, according to Kook, was the absence of a constitution that would define the parameters of Israeli nationalism."[105] Israel, according to Merlin and Kook, must redefine itself as the sovereign state of the *Israeli nation* (a

---

103 Avnery, *Optimi*, 478–480.

104 See HKA/19 (the Hebrew Committee also presciently warned against expelling the Palestinians, as did Zeev Jabotinsky in the late 1930s (Shindler, *The Rise of the Israeli Right*, 144)). For Kook's updated ideas see also Kaplan, "A Rebel with a Cause," 97–98.

105 Kaplan, "A Rebel with a Cause," 94.

new term that replaces the "Hebrew nation") and renegotiate accordingly its relations with Diaspora Jewry; it must adopt a new and liberal immigration law that would replace the Law of Return;[106] it must separate religion and state; it must abrogate its treaty with the Jewish Agency; it must finally adopt a written constitution that would enshrine all those principles and ensure Israel's continued existence as an *Israeli* state.[107]

Although Eri Jabotinsky, who died in 1969, did not live to see the transition in Kook's worldview, in his last years he too had the opportunity to re-examine the views he had held since the days of the Hebrew Committee. A staunch secularist, Jabotinsky was nonetheless enamored by Israel's capture of Temple Mount in the 1967 war, and joined the "Movement for Greater Israel," which advocated holding on to the captured territories. In a letter to the Palestinian mayor of Hebron he wrote that for him "the Temple Area constitute[d] the symbol and quintessence of Hebrew Nationhood."[108] Furthermore, he might have started to doubt his previous dismissal of Zionism as obsolete. In an email dated March 8 2017 his daughter Karny Rubin informed me that very shortly before his death, when the first Jewish immigrants from the USSR started to arrive in Israel (in what eventually became the 1970s *'Aliyah*), Jabotinsky admitted to his wife Aviva, who had always insisted that Zionism still had a role to play, that she was right and he was in error. Although in his 1954 "Memorandum" Jabotinsky made a passing reference to the "numerous Hebrews still trapped in the communist world" [יש גם עברים רבים הכלואים בתוך העולם הקומוניסטי], he confessed that he had not believed that the Soviet Union would ever liberalize. If so, first-generation post-Zionism rested on two assumptions that are unrelated only at first sight: that Jordan was an unviable state and that the Soviet Union was there to stay. Both assumptions, as we know in hindsight, proved wrong.

Conclusion

By probing the essential principles of Kookian post-Zionism we can finally approach the guiding question of this chapter: how is it possible that post-Zionism intellectually originated in the most right-wing and militant margins of Zionism? How can we account for Kook's insistence that in making the claim for Zionism's obsolescence he was actually following faithfully in the footsteps of Zeev Jabo-

106 See also Kaplan, "A Rebel with a Cause," 96.
107 Kook and Merlin, "Hatza'a leWikuach Leumi."
108 JIA/4/4 – 4א.

tinsky? As mentioned briefly above, this chapter wishes to demonstrate that first-generation post-Zionism was a case of a radical reinterpretation of Jabotinsky's teachings coupled with a strong "Canaanite" input in terms of future vision. Eran Kaplan is particularly adamant that Hillel Kook's ideological journey away from Zionism was the logical consequence of his allegiance to Jabotinsky:

> [Kook] believed that Jabotinsky's legacy meant that war [for national liberation] [...] was to be confined to the revolutionary phase of Zionism – but once independence had been won, Israel should have focused its energies solely on creating a civil society rather than continuing to fight battles that were motivated by a false historical sense [...] Following Jabotinsky, Kook saw Zionism as a revolutionary liberation movement with a single purpose: to free the Jewish people from their exilic condition by creating a nation-state. Once the state was created, however, Kook believed, the mission of Zionism ended.[109]

We cannot understand Kook's re-interpretation of Jabotinsky without taking into account the latter's principle of "monism" (single aim), over which he broke ranks with Labor Zionism. Sasson Sofer explains that monism meant for Jabotinsky and his followers the rejection of

> [A]ny ideology other than Zionism, which it perceived as constituting a perfect and complete ideal [...] monism appears as absolute loyalty to one aim, "a state with a Jewish majority on both sides of the River Jordan" [...] everything was subordinated to the need to attain the aim. Nothing could dwell alongside it or come between it and the ultimate objective [...] In [monism], political Zionism was regarded as a value which stood on its own, having no need of universal values to support it. The supreme aim of political sovereignty subordinated everything and towered above all else [...] It has been claimed that [monism] relates to the absolute supremacy of the nation and national considerations, regarding the national will as the highest motivating force in history. Another view links monism with the "corporate" view of Revisionism in which, through the demand for national unity, social and economic interests are subordinated to the interests of the nation...[110]

Finally, and most significantly, Sofer says, monism meant that "Jabotinsky deferred making any decision about the character and values of the future Jewish society to the period which would follow independence." Herein lies the key: Jabotinsky, who died in 1940, did not live to see the State of Israel come into life, but his followers and disciples from the Hebrew Committee, "LaMerchav" and the

---

109 Kaplan, "A Rebel with a Cause," 94, 98. Penkower ("Vladimir (Ze'ev) Jabotinsky," 35, n. 10) argues that Kaplan overlooks the differences between Kook and Jabotinsky and over-emphasizes the affinities, but I still consider Kaplan's analysis valid. After all, Kook's position was shared by Eri Jabotinsky who, of all people, can hardly be accused of misunderstanding his own father.
110 Sofer, *Zionism and the Foundations of Israeli Diplomacy*, 211–213. For a more detailed discussion of 'monism' consult Bilski Ben-Hur, *Kol Yachid Hu Melekh*, 227–334.

Kedem Club *did*. And the conclusion they drew from this fact, as noted by Kaplan above, was that the "monism" stage was over and the time was ripe to re-examine the character and values of the state, as bequeathed to them by their teacher. Having drawn inspiration from the American version of political society, they wished to apply what they regarded as the most advanced, liberal, and effective solutions in Israeli public life. For this purpose, they brokered an ideological alliance with the anti-Zionist "Canaanites," who had developed their own vision for a Hebrew–Israeli society based on shared principles and values. Therefore, post-Zionism is grounded in Zeev Jabotinsky's philosophy only with regards to the *past*; with regards to the *future*, however, it was "Canaanism" that supplied the answer.

This answer is diagnosed by Uri Ram, a contemporary post-Zionist thinker in his own right, as the "normalization" stage that Israeli society entered having achieved its ideological objective. Normalization means that the ideology that had led to the formation of the state becomes redundant by victory, but is nonetheless perceived as legitimate and necessary at the preceding historical stage. When victory is achieved, preservation of the ideology becomes a hindrance to the normal functioning of the society and might even develop into an existential danger. In this sense, first-generation post-Zionism is what Ram calls a "post-ideological" approach to questions of Israel's *raison d'état*.[111]

Hillel Kook, who died in 2001, lived long enough to see second-generation post-Zionism burst onto the Israeli social and political stage with renewed force after the late 1980s and especially after the signing of the Oslo Accords with the PLO in 1993. "Beginning in the 1980s," writes Assaf Likhovski,

> [T]wo groups, the "new historians" and the "critical sociologists," revolutionized the study of Israeli history and society, seeking to undermine the "founding myths of Israel." These two groups produced a very impressive and influential body of works [...] The arguments made by the new historians and critical sociologists produced heated debate in Israel. Questions were raised about the factual accuracy, theoretical underpinnings, and claims of novelty of the Post-Zionist paradigm [...] [M]any of the arguments of the Post-Zionist paradigm have been accepted and assimilated by the Israeli academia and, to a certain extent, even by Israeli popular culture.[112]

---

111 Uri Ram, "Post-Tziyonut: He'Asor haRishon – Sotziologia Shel 'Ir'ur 'al Hegemonia Leumit" ("Post-Zionism: The First Decade – A Sociology of Questioning the National Hegemony"), in *Chevra weKhalkala beIsrael: Mabat Histori we'Akhshawi* (*Society and Economics in Israel: Historical and Contemporary Perspectives*), ed. Avi Bareli et al. (Jerusalem – Beer Sheva: Yad Yitzhak Ben Zvi, Ben-Gurion Institute for the Study of Israel, 2005), 820–822.

112 Assaf Likhovski, "Post-Post-Zionist Historiography," *Israel Studies* 15, no. 2 (summer 2010): 4. The two most comprehensive English-language book-length treatments of second-generation

Likhovski's words demonstrate that second-generation post-Zionism is hugely different from its first-generation counterpart, which remained an isolated voice on the margins of Israel's political discourse during the first decade of the state's existence. Analysis of the second generation is way beyond the limits of the present chapter, and I have no pretense of doing justice to it within a few concluding paragraphs of a work whose main purpose was to bring back to memory a radical critique of Zionism enunciated on the eve of the state's establishment. It would be a truism to state that current post-Zionism, which Likhovski characterizes as using "a moralizing and judgmental framework [...] in which there were heroes and villains, the Zionists playing the role of the villains,"[113] constitutes a major element of contemporary Israel's political culture and discourse. It has become, as suggested by David Ohana, a state of mind for many Israelis wary of an ideology that some of them regard as outdated and – fewer still – as outwardly criminal.[114] It also encompasses many more spheres than first-generation post-Zionism, which was limited to the political sphere: second-generation post-Zionism re-examines critically Israel's history, including its founding ideological myths; its sociology and society-making processes; its civic versus religious identity; its literature and culture, etc. In addition, with regards to post-Zionism in the academia, it is strongly influenced by late twentieth-century Western modes of critical thinking, with their challenging of established narratives, values, and epistemological tools that starkly contrast with the first generation's outspoken positivism.[115] Above all, first-generation post-Zionism originated in the internal logic of Zionism (or a certain current thereof), while second-generation post-Zionism attests to a dynamic mixture of influences from within and without Israel.

Another notable difference between first-generation and second-generation post-Zionism is that the latter is strongly identified (at least at a superficial glance) with the Israeli left-wing camp, whereas the former, as demonstrated above, originated in the Zionist right wing. First-generation post-Zionism re-

post-Zionism remain Nimni, *The Challenge of Post-Zionism*, and Silberstein, *The Postzionism Debates*; both, however, take a very sympathetic view of post-Zionism.

113 Likhovski, "Post-Post-Zionist Historiography," 13.

114 David Ohana, *The Origins of Israeli Mythology: Neither Canaanites nor Crusaders* (New York: Cambridge University Press, 2012), 21.

115 Silberstein in fact makes a case in his book that "genuine" post-Zionism is inherently "postmodernist," while all forms of critical thinking on Israel that preceded it are *ipso facto* "incomplete" and valuable only insofar as milestones to the "*telos*" of deconstructionist post-Zionism. This is hardly an original approach: one can identify it in the Bolshevik interpretation of world history.

nounced Zionism in order to replace it with an alternative national ideology, whereas second-generation post-Zionism is in most cases anti-nationalist, or at least post-nationalist. It is therefore a melancholy albeit not surprising fact that in analyses of modern-day post-Zionism the influence of Hillel Kook and his associates is mentioned even more rarely than that of the "Canaanites." Uri Ram, whose article cited above concentrates solely on 1990s' post-Zionism, does acknowledge in brief "the legacy of Hillel Kook" in the historical development of post-Zionism, and is also aware of the connections between post-Zionism and "Canaanism," though he qualifies (correctly) the latter as a strongly nationalist phenomenon.[116] More knowledgeable appears to be Yosef Gorny, who in 1990 defined second-generation post-Zionism as a "post-Canaanite liberalism":

> The term "post-Canaanite liberalism," whose purpose is to define the various viewpoints that aspire to the "general normalization" of the Jewish existence, which arose with renewed force during the 1980s, points to the continuity and change within this phenomenon. On the one hand, it takes that the "Canaanite" ideology of the 1940s–1950s – as a cultural–romantic myth and as a political utopia connected to the Semitic space – is obsolete. On the other hand, the liberal element that views citizenship and nationality according to the US example, which became more pronounced in Canaanite thought after the establishment of the state, remains powerful and existent. This means that we observe here a new phenomenon in Jewish public thought, which aspires to define the nation neither by fusing religion and people, according to the Zionist belief, nor by Semitic cultural legacy, according to the first "Canaanites," but by territorial–political basis, as practiced in Western countries. In this sense, this approach is both directly and indirectly influenced by Hillel Kook's worldview, for which he struggled forty years ago, on the eve of the state's establishment.[117]

---

116 Ram, "Post-Tziyonut," 809.

[מורשתו של הלל קוק]

117 Yosef Gorny, "HaLiberalizm haBetar-Kna'ani – Gishot 'Akhshawiyot biSh'elat haNormalizatziya Shel haQiyum haLeumi biMdinat-Israel" ("Post-Canaanite Liberalism – Contemporary Approaches to the Issue of Normalizing the National Existence in the State of Israel), *Kiwunim* (*Directions*) 1 (March 1990): 46.

[המונח "ליברליזם בתר-כנעני", הבא להגדיר את ההשקפות השונות השואפות אל ה"נורמליזציה הכללית" בקיום היהודי, שנתחדשו בשנות השמונים, מתכוון להצביע על הרציפות והשינוי שבתופעה זו. כלומר, מצד אחד, הוא מבקש לומר, כי האידיאולוגיה ה"כנענית" של שנות הארבעים והחמישים – כמיתוס רומנטי-תרבותי וכאוטופיה מדינית שהיתה קשורה במרחב השמי – עבר זמנה. מצד שני, היסוד הליברלי כתפיסת האזרחות והלאומיות על פי הדוגמה של ארה"ב, שבלט בהגות הכנענית אחרי קום המדינה, נשאר שריר וקיים. כלומר אנו עדים כאן לתופעה חדשה במחשבה הציבורית היהודית, המבקשת להגדיר את הלאום לא על סמך הצירוף שבין עם לדת, כפי שחשבו הציונים, ולא על פי המורשת התרבותית השמית, כפי שגרסו ה"כנענים" הראשונים, אלא על יסוד טריטוריאלי-מדיני כמקובל בארצות המערב. מבחינה זו, גישה זו מושפעת במישרין ובעקיפין מהשקפתו של הלל קוק שעליה נאבק לפני ארבעים שנה, ערב הקמת המדינה]

Insofar as a "Canaanite" background was acknowledged by scholars of second-generation post-Zionism, they largely concentrated on *National Reckoning*[118] by the Israeli journalist and public intellectual Boas Evron (1927–2018), who in his youth was briefly a member of the "Canaanite" movement and later was one of the authors of *The Hebrew Manifesto.* This thick book, which passed almost without notice in Israel – a telling fact in itself – is a meticulously researched demolition of Zionism's intellectual basis, value-world, and policy. Evron, unsurprisingly, referred to himself as "post-Zionist" ['בתר-ציוני'], which for him meant "desir[ing] a state indifferent to its citizens' religious and national affiliations, which has no binding institutional links to the Jewish Diaspora, all of whose citizens are legally equal in theory and practice – and which does not regard itself as a body loyal to a certain ideology or mission, but its only obligations are towards its citizens".[119] Evron's position as a member of both the "Canaanite" movement (a membership that lasted, according to his testimony, only three months)[120] and of first-generation post-Zionism, and as one of the intellectual precursors of second-generation post-Zionism, in which he took a lively part until shortly before his death, makes him a unique link between the three and a *memento* of their rarely-acknowledged philosophical sources in right-wing Zionist liberalism. As stated by Laurence Silberstein, "[i]f Canaanism can be said to represent an early effort to construct a post-Zionist ideology for the generation of the 1940s and 1950s, Boas Evron [...] offers a lucid formulation of a post-Zionist ideology for the generation of the 1980s and 1990s."[121]

Despite the silencing and marginalization, Hillel Kook's legacy lives on, as does the legacy of "Canaanism." Both, ironically, live in the fact of Zionism's cur-

---

118 Boas Evron, *HaCheshbon HaLeumi* (*National Reckoning*) (Tel Aviv: Dvir, 1988); Boas Evron, *Jewish State or Israeli Nation?* (Bloomington and Indianapolis: Indiana University Press, 1995). For a discussion of Evron see Gabriel Piterberg, *The Returns of Zionism: Myths, Politics and Scholarship in Israel* (London and New York: Verso, 2008), 105–110; Israel Segal, *Israeliyut Ezrachit:* HaCheshbon HaLeumi *Shel Boas Evron* (*Civil Israel: Boas Evron's* National Reckoning) (Jerusalem: Carmel, 2018); Silberstein, *The Postzionism Debates*, 69–84.

119 Boas Evron, "HaMa'ase – uVavuato haAqademit" ("The Deed – And its Academic Reflection"), *Yedi'ot Acharonot*, March 2 1984, 20–21.
[הרוצה במדינה אדשה מבחינת הדת והלאום של אזרחיה, שאין לה קשרים מוסדיים המחייבים מבחינה ממלכתית עם התפוצה היהודית, ושכל אזרחיה שווים להלכה ולמעשה לפני החוק – ושאינה רואה במדינה גוף שיש לו אידיאולוגיה כלשהי או כנושא בשליחות כלשהי, אלא שחובותיו היחידות הן כלפי אזרחיו]

120 Boas Evron, "Ra'ayonot Mediniim weGilgulehem: 'Otobiografia Post-Tziyonit'" ("Political Ideas and their Transmutations: 'A Post-Zionist Autobiography'"), www.hagada.org.il, September 30 2008, accessed May 14 2017.

121 Laurence Silberstein, "*The New Hebrew Nation: A Study in Israeli Heresy and Fantasy* by Yaakov Shavit; *The Slopes of Lebanon* by Amos Oz; *Jewish Theocracy* by Gershon Weiler; *HaHeshbon HaLeumi* by Boas Evron," *IJMES* 23, no. 4 (1991): 688.

rent triumph; as long as the "Jewish State" has not moved to solve the paradoxes exposed by first-generation post-Zionism and "Canaanism," their critique will continue to resound at every existential turn Israel might experience. It lives in the output of one of Israel's most controversial philosophers, Joseph Agassi (b. 1927), who, like Kook, comes from a religious background, and whose meetings with Kook in the late 1970s inspired him to wage his own struggle for a secular liberal Israel.[122] It lives in the satiric articles of *Haaretz* publicist Doron Rosenblum (b. 1947), who interviewed Kook in the late 1970s and throughout his journalistic career struggled in the name of "normal down-to-earth" Israelis against the toxic mysticism of the "transcendental People of Israel."[123]

The newest evidence for the vitality of post-Zionism is the lawsuit submitted to the Israeli Supreme Court in 2003 by the 'I am an Israeli' association, to recognize the Israeli nation by the authorities as Israel's only *staatsnation*. The plaintiffs, among whom we find Uri Avnery, Yosef Agassi, and Hillel Kook's widow Nili Kook and daughter Rebecca Kook, consider the Israeli nation a territorial–linguistic reality, much in line with the Hebrew Committee's original definition of the Hebrew nation. The association is led by 'Uzzi Ornan (b. 1923), the only living member of the "Canaanite" circle of founders. Shortly after the lawsuit was filed Uri Ram wrote that it "opens the second decade of post-Zionism".[124] The second decade closed in 2013 with the rejection of the lawsuit by the Supreme Court, which reaffirmed the dominant view of Israel's character as ethno-national by accepting that a civic framing of Israeli identity threatened [sic!] the foundations of the state.[125] We are now in the middle of the "third decade," according to Ram's calculations. What will it bring?

---

122 Joseph Agassi, *Liberal Nationalism for Israel: Towards an Israeli National Identity* (Jerusalem: Geffen, 1999), especially Part 2, where he discusses at length Hillel Kook and the Hebrew Committee.

123 Kaplan, "A Rebel with a Cause," 97–99; Miller, "'HaBatalion heChatukh'," 188; Doron Rosenblum, *Tugat haIsraeliyut* (*Israel Blues*) (Tel Aviv: Am Oved, 1996); Shilon, "Milchemet Sheshet haYamim," 123.

124 Ram, "Post-Tziyonut," 840.

[תביעת 'אני ישראלי' פותחת את העשור השני של הפוסט-ציונות]

125 For 'I am an Israeli' see Nili Osheroff, *Yotze Min haKlalim – Uzzi Ornan: Sipur Chayim* [*Uzzi Ornan's Life Story*] (Jerusalem: Carmel, 2015): 125–131, 136–140; Ram, "Post-Tziyonut," 837–841.

Works Cited

Archives

Adya Horon Archive, Carmei Yossef.
Jabotinsky Institute Archive (JIA), Tel Aviv.
Hillel Kook Archive (HKA), Sdeh Boqer.

Dissertation

Vaters, Romans. "'A Hebrew from Samaria, not a Jew from Yavneh': Adya Gur Horon (1907–1972) and the Articulation of Hebrew Nationalism." PhD diss., University of Manchester, 2015.

Books and articles

Abu el-Haj, Nadia. *Facts on the Ground: Archaeological Practice and Territorial Self-Fashioning in Israeli Society.* Chicago & London: University of Chicago Press, 2001.

Agassi, Joseph. *Liberal Nationalism for Israel: Towards an Israeli National Identity.* Jerusalem: Geffen, 1999.

Avnery, Uri. *Optimi.* Tel Aviv: Yedi'ot Acharonot, 2014.

Bilski Ben-Hur, Rafaella. *Kol Yachid Hu Melekh: HaMachshava haChevratit wehaMdinit shel Zeev Jabotinsky.* Tel Aviv: Dvir, 1988.

Boyd, Brian. *Vladimir Nabokov: the Russian Years.* Princeton, NJ: Princeton University Press, 1990.

Cohen, Erik. "Israel as a Post-Zionist Society." *Israel Affairs* 1, no. 3 (1995): 203–214.

Cohen, Hillel. *'Aravim Tovim.* Jerusalem: 'Ivrit, 2006.

Dieckhoff, Alain. *The Invention of a Nation: Zionist Thought and the Making of Modern Israel.* New York: Columbia University Press, 2003.

Elath, Eliahu. "'Phoenician Zionism' in Lebanon." *The Jerusalem Quarterly* 42 (spring 1987): 38–56.

Evron, Boas. *HaCheshbon HaLeumi.* Tel Aviv: Dvir, 1988.

Evron, Boas. "HaMa'ase – uVavuato haAqademit." *Yedi'ot Acharonot,* March 2 1984.

Evron, Boas. *Jewish State or Israeli Nation?* Bloomington and Indianapolis: Indiana University Press, 1995.

Evron, Boas. "Ra'ayonot Mediniim weGilgulehem: 'Otobiografia Post-Tziyonit'." www.hagada.org.il, September 30 2008, accessed May 14 2017.

Gorny, Yosef. "HaLiberalizm haBetar-Kna'ani – Gishot 'Akhshawiyot biSh'elat haNormalizatziya Shel haQiyum haLeumi biMdinat-Israel." *Kiwunim* 1 (March 1990): 45–57.

Gutwein, Daniel. "Left and Right Post-Zionism and the Privatization of Israeli Collective Memory." In *Israeli Historical Revisionism: From Left to Right*, edited by Anita Shapira and Derek J. Penslar, 9–42. London/Portland: Frank Cass, 2003.

Jabotinsky, Eri. *Avi, Zeev Jabotinsky.* Tel Aviv: Steimatzky, 1980.

Jabotinsky, Eri. "Israel wehaTziyonut: Madu'a Ein Techiqa leIsrael?" *Alef*, September 1952.

Kaplan, Eran. "A Rebel with a Cause: Hillel Kook, Begin and Jabotinsky's Ideological Legacy." *Israel Studies* 10, no. 3 (2005): 87–103.

Kedar, Nir. "Ben-Gurion's Opposition to a Written Constitution." *Journal of Modern Jewish Studies* 12, no. 1 (2013): 1–16.

Kimmerling, Baruch. *The Invention and Decline of Israeliness: State, Society, and the Military.* Berkeley – Los Angeles – London: University of California Press, 2005.

Kook, Hillel, and Shmuel Merlin. "Hatza'a leWikuach Leumi." *Haaretz*, April 18 1975.

Kook, Rebecca. "Hillel Kook: Revisionism and Rescue." In *Struggle and Survival in Palestine/Israel*, edited by Mark LeVine and Gershon Shafir, 157–169. Berkeley – Los Angeles – London: University of California Press, 2012.

Likhovski, Assaf. "Post–Post–Zionist Historiography." *Israel Studies* 15, no. 2 (summer 2010): 1–23.

Medoff, Rafael. *Militant Zionism in America: The Rise and Impact of the Jabotinsky Movement in the United States, 1926–1948.* Tuscaloosa and London: University of Alabama Press, 2002.

Medoff, Rafael, and David Wyman. *A Race Against Death: Peter Bergson, America, and the Holocaust.* New York: New Press, 2002.

Miller, Orna. "'HaBatalion heChatukh' weHantiyot ha'Kna'aniyot' baETZEL uviTenu'at haCherut – me'haWa'ad ha'Ivri' ad 'LaMerchav': Opozitziya leHanhagat haETZEL we'Cherut'." *'Iyunim biTequmat Israel* 14 (2004): 153–189.

Nimni, Ephraim, ed. *The Challenge of Post-Zionism: Alternatives to Israeli Fundamentalist Politics.* London and New York: Zed Books, 2003.

Ohana, David. *The Origins of Israeli Mythology: Neither Canaanites nor Crusaders.* Translated by David Maisel. New York: Cambridge University Press, 2012.

Osheroff, Nili. *Yotze Min haKlalim – Uzzi Ornan: Sipur Chayim.* Jerusalem: Carmel, 2015.

Penkower, Monty Noam. "In Dramatic Dissent: The Bergson Boys." *American Jewish History* (March 1 1981): 281–309.

Penkower, Monty Noam. "Vladimir (Ze'ev) Jabotinsky, Hillel Kook–Peter Bergson and the Campaign for a Jewish Army." *Modern Judaism* 31, no. 3 (2011): 1–43.

Piterberg, Gabriel. *The Returns of Zionism: Myths, Politics and Scholarship in Israel.* London and New York: Verso, 2008.

Porath, Yehoshua. *Shelach we'Et beYado: Sippur Chayaw Shel Uriel Shelach (Yonathan Ratosh).* Tel Aviv: Zmora, 1989.

Ram, Uri. *Israeli Nationalism: Social Conflicts and the Politics of Knowledge.* London & New York: Routledge, 2011.

Ram, Uri. "Post–Tziyonut: He'Asor haRishon – Sotziologia Shel 'Ir'ur 'al Hegemonia Leumit." In *Chevra weKhalkala beIsrael: Mabat Histori we'Akhshawi*, edited by Avi Bareli, Daniel Gutwein, and Tuvya Friling, 803–854. Jerusalem – Beer Sheva: Yad Yitzhak Ben Zvi, Ben-Gurion Institute for the Study of Israel, 2005.

Rapaport, Louis. *Shake Heaven and Earth: Peter Bergson and the Struggle to Save the Jews of Europe.* Jerusalem: Gefen Press, 1999.

Ratosh, Yonatan. *Reshit HaYamim: Petichot 'Ivriyot.* Tel Aviv: Hadar, 1982.

Rosenblum, Doron. *Tugat haIsraeliyut.* Tel Aviv: Am Oved, 1996.

Rozin, Orit. "Forming a Collective Identity: The Debate over the Proposed Constitution, 1948–1950." *Journal of Israeli History* 26, no. 2 (2007): 251–271.

Saposnik, Arye Bruce. "Advertisement or Achievement? American Jewry and the Campaign for a Jewish Army, 1939–1944: A Reassessment." *Journal of Israeli History* 17, no. 2 (1996): 193–220.

Schulze, Kristen E. *Israel's Covert Diplomacy in Lebanon.* Basingstoke: Macmillan, 1998.

Segal, Israel. *Israeliyut Ezrachit:* HaCheshbon HaLeumi *Shel Boas Evron.* Jerusalem: Carmel, 2018.

Shilon, Avi. "Milchemet Sheshet haYamim wehit'orerut haRa'ayon haKna'ani." *'Iyunim biTequmat Israel* 11 (2017): 102–129.

Shindler, Colin. *The Rise of the Israeli Right: From Odessa to Hebron.* New York: Cambridge University Press, 2015.

Silberstein, Laurence. "*The New Hebrew Nation: A Study in Israeli Heresy and Fantasy* by Yaakov Shavit; *The Slopes of Lebanon* by Amos Oz; *Jewish Theocracy* by Gershon Weiler; *HaHeshbon HaLeumi* by Boas Evron." *IJMES*, 23, no. 4 (1991): 686–693.

Silberstein, Laurence J. *The Postzionism Debates: Knowledge and Power in Israeli Culture.* New York and London: Routledge, 1999.

Sofer, Sasson. *Zionism and the Foundations of Israeli Diplomacy.* New York: Cambridge University Press, 1998.

Tydor Baumel, Judith. *The "Bergson Boys" and the Origins of Contemporary Zionist Militancy.* Translated by Dena Ordan. Syracuse, NY: Syracuse University Press, 2005.

Tydor Baumel, Judith. "The IZL Delegation in the USA 1939–1948: Anatomy of an Ethnic Interest/Protest Group." *Jewish History* 9, no. 1 (1995): 79–89.

Waxman, Chaim Isaac. "Critical Sociology and the End of Ideology in Israel." *Israel Studies* 2, no. 1 (1997): 194–210.

Wyman, David S. "The Bergson Group, America, and the Holocaust: a Previously Unpublished Interview with Hillel Kook." *American Jewish History* 89, no. 1 (2001): 3–34.

Peter Bergamin

Revolutionary Fascist or Fascist Revolutionary

Abba Ahimeir and the Success of Revolutionary Zionism

Introduction

In November 1927, the young journalist Abba Ahimeir (1897–1962) wrote an article for the *Yishuv* newspaper, *haAretz*, which took as its title the well-known quotation attributed to Hillel the Elder, "*Im Ein Ani Li – Mi Li?*" (If I am not for myself, who will be for me?)[1] In the article, Ahimeir bemoaned the fact that, in the ten years since the issuing of the Balfour Declaration, not even the minimum expectations of the Zionist project had been realized.[2] Not only had a Jewish national homeland not yet come into existence, but, indeed, the whole process towards statehood had become deadlocked in a political-bureaucratic quagmire; an unhappy reality for which Ahimeir blamed both the conservative style of British rule and the immaturity of the Zionist administration in Mandate Palestine. At this stage, for him, the only apparent viable way out of this complacency was offered through the politico-territorial solutions of the relatively new Revisionist Zionist movement, led by Ze'ev Jabotinsky, an unsurprising statement for anyone familiar with the historical trajectory of Revisionist Zionism during the interwar years.[3] In the article, Ahimeir speaks out against the *Yishuv* leadership's complicity with the British administration, and calls upon the Zionist movement to con-

---

1 Abba Ahimeir, "Im Ein Ani Li – Mi Li?" *haAretz*, November 15 1927. [All translations of Ahimeir's articles are mine]. Hillel the Elder was a Jewish religious leader active in the first century BCE. See Pirkei Avot 1:14. *Yishuv* refers to the Jewish community in British Mandatory Palestine.
2 Ibid.
3 Ze'ev Jabotinsky (1880–1940) was a Russian journalist who founded the Revisionist Zionist Alliance in 1925. He had resigned from the Executive Council of the World Zionist Organisation in 1923, due to ideological differences over the organization's reaction to the Churchill White Paper (1922), which appeared to renege on promises made in the Balfour Declaration for the establishment of a Jewish national home in Palestine. The party sought a "revision" of General Zionist Policy that saw a return to the hope, and expectation, of establishing a Jewish national home on all of the biblical land of Israel, on both sides of the River Jordan. The establishment of the Revisionist Party represented the beginning of the Zionist Right as a political force, and its ideological trajectory leads to the present-day Likud Party in Israel.

https://doi.org/10.1515/9783110545753-003

sider Hillel's motto, and, like Sinn Féin in Ireland, to adopt both the attitude and means of other national liberation groups.[4] He declares that the age of Zionist Pioneering is now over, and advocates, instead, an embrace of the ideology of Revolution. Again, for anyone familiar with Ahimeir's history as a leader of the radical Maximalist arm of the Revisionist Party in the *Yishuv*, such bellicosity comes with little shock. What might give pause for reflection is the fact that Ahimeir penned the article while still a member of the moderately-socialist Zionist party, *haPoel haTza'ir* (The Young Worker), a party that glorified the Zionist Pioneer "worker-intellectuals" who were determined to establish themselves in Palestine through agricultural enterprise, which sought to regenerate the Jews' attachment to both physical labor and working the land.[5] Perhaps more notable still is the fact that Ahimeir had been engaging intellectually – and with increasingly positive conclusions – with not only the concept of revolution, but also those of dictatorship and Fascism, already from the time of his doctoral thesis and first publications, in 1923.[6] By 1928 – and now as a staunch supporter of the Revisionists – he was calling on his party to model itself after Mussolini's National Fascist Party, and implored Jabotinsky to assume the mantle of its *Duce*.

This chapter examines the degree to which Ahimeir understood, utilized, and embraced the concepts of Fascism and revolution during the period that he was most politically – and notoriously – active, from 1924–1934. Ahimeir stood at the vanguard of Zionist anti-British resistance; he referred to the British Mandatory government as both "Perfidious Albion" and a "foreign occupier" in print, already in 1929.[7] The following year, he founded the first anti-British resistance group in the *Yishuv*, *Brit haBiryonim*, and eventually went to prison, in 1934, for his involvement.[8] The passage of time, and the particular unfolding of world events since 1934, have led to a perhaps undue amount of focus on Ahimeir as a Fascist. Indeed, within a year of Ahimeir joining the Revisionist Party, Jabotinsky himself had referred to his younger colleague as "talented but too much a fascist," and this is perhaps the way in which Ahimeir is most often re-

4 Ahimeir, "Im Ein Ani Li – Mi Li?"

5 "Worker-intellectual" is Gideon Shimoni's term. See Gideon Shimoni, *The Zionist Ideology* (Hanover MA: Brandeis University Press, 1995), 207.

6 I use "Fascism" (capitalized) to denote, specifically, the phenomenon of Italian Fascism under Benito Mussolini (1883–1945). In the 1940s, similar ideological streams also developed within the Arab nationalist movement.

7 Abba Ahimeir, "Gesher haBarzel" (Bridge of Iron), *Doar Hayom*, September 10 1929.

8 *Brit haBiryonim* is given a wide range of translations, which usually reflect a particular author's political leanings: i.e. "Covenant of Brigands" (Shimoni, *Zionist Ideology*, 250) or "Praetorian Guard" (the definition put forward by members of the group during their trial, in 1934 (National Archive (formerly, Public Record Office, Kew, henceforth PRO, London, CO733/266/1)).

membered, to this day.[9] He was undoubtedly a controversial figure who espoused, at times, some highly controversial ideas. Nonetheless, Ahimeir's embrace of Fascism should be understood in its historical context, and not be analyzed with a disproportionate degree of historical hindsight. Indeed, my primary contention in this chapter is that we should view Ahimeir not as a "Fascist" who coined the rather innocuous term "Revolutionary Zionism," but rather as a Zionist revolutionary who saw Fascism as the most viable *modus operandi* for effecting his revolution. I further contend that this revision in the common perception of Ahimeir begs for deeper engagement with two key questions: specifically, what was the ideological nature and trajectory of Ahimeir's concept of Revolutionary Zionism; and, more generally, did anything resembling a *de facto* revolution occur in the *Yishuv*, on its way to Jewish statehood?

Ahimeir was born Abba Gaissinovitch on November 2 1897, in Belarus, and grew up in Bobruisk. In 1912, accompanied by his older sister, the fourteen-year-old travelled to Ottoman Palestine to study at the Herzliya Gymnasium, which had opened in 1905 as the first Hebrew high school in the *Yishuv*. He returned to Bobruisk in the summer of 1914, where the outbreak of the First World War forced him to remain for an extended sojourn. In 1921, he began studies at the University of Vienna, and received his doctorate in 1924, having written on the conception of Russia in Oswald Spengler's (1880–1936) *The Decline of the West*. He finally returned to what was now British Mandate Palestine in the summer of 1924, and – as Abba Ahimeir – began to make a name for himself as a teacher and journalist. From 1924–1928, he was a regular contributor to the party journal of *haPoel haTza'ir* and the newspapers *Davar* and *haAretz*.[10] However, his increasing disillusionment with *haPoel haTza'ir* had become clear by May of 1926, and Ahimeir, along with his colleagues, the poet Uri Zvi Greenberg (1896–1981) and writer Yehoshua Yevin (1891–1970), eventually jumped ship, and joined Jabotinsky's Revisionist Party, in February 1928.

In the wake of the Arab Riots in August 1929, the trio established the Maximalist arm of the Revisionist party in the *Yishuv*. While they accepted the territorial maximalist demands of the general Revisionists, the Maximalists fought against the British government in Palestine. They rejected Jabotinsky's policy of *Havlagah* (defensive restraint) toward both Arab and British antagonism directed

9 Jabotinsky, in a letter to Shlomo Gepstein, December 10 1928, quoted in Colin Shindler, *The Triumph of Military Zionism: Nationalism and the Origins of the Israeli Right* (London, New York: I.B. Tauris, 2010), 13.

10 Gaissinovitch changed his name in 1919, as a memorial to his brother Meir, a committed Bolshevik who had fallen at the hands of the Polish army that same year. "Ahi-meir" literally means "my brother Meir," in Hebrew.

against the *Yishuv*, and called instead for active paramilitary resistance to both groups. Finally, in addition to advocating Fascism as the ideological *modus operandi* for the Revisionists, the Maximalists, rather singularly, employed pointed quasi-messianic imagery as a rhetorical device in their articles and speeches.[11] Maximalist Revisionism enjoyed a short but intense period of relative popularity – from 1929–1934 it represented the dominant stream of Revisionist Zionism in the *Yishuv* – but was dealt a death blow in the wake of the murder of the Labor Zionist leader Chaim Arlosoroff, for which Ahimeir was arrested, but later acquitted.

Ahimeir and Fascism

What was the nature of Ahimeir's embrace of Fascism? Without a doubt, he foresaw Italian Fascism as an ideological cornerstone of Maximalist Revisionism, and Mussolini as an example of a strong, effective leader. Indeed, one of his first published articles, "Some Thoughts on Fascism," written in 1923, shows an Ahimeir already enthralled with the movement and its *Duce*, although perhaps, at this early stage of his journalistic career, only subconsciously so.[12] Ahimeir later admitted as much himself when in 1933 he wrote: "for ten years I am searching for a Jewish Mussolini."[13] Furthermore, his articles in *haPoel haTza'ir* and *haAretz*, written between 1924 and 1927, focus again and again on the failure of socialism, liberalism, and parliamentarianism, and – increasingly – on the viability of Fascism as a political ideology.[14] And finally, Ahimeir's nine articles written in the autumn of 1928, and which appeared in the newspaper *Doar Hayom* (The Daily Post) under the rubric, "From the Notebook of a Fascist," make it clear that he had embraced the ideology in a manner that went far beyond mere journalistic provocation. Thus, we should take Ahimeir at his word

11 I use "quasi messianism" as per Shimoni's definition, as "messianic rhetoric not predicated on traditionalist or orthodox understanding of the messianic belief (that does not, however,) deny its mythic potency also for nonorthodox or secular Jews". Shimoni, *The Zionist Ideology*, 406, note 19.

12 Abba Ahimeir, "Ra'yonot Bodedim 'al haFashizm," (Some Thoughts on Fascism), *haToren*, August 1923, 150–155.

13 *Brit haBiryonim* member Yaacov Orenstein's testimony at the *Brit haBiryonim* trial. Exhibit Y.L. 27, B14/6/1, Jabotinsky Institute Archive.

14 See, i.e., Abba Ahimeir, "Lean Peniah shel haDemokratiah Muadot" (Where is Democracy Headed), *haPoel haTza'ir* 42 (1926), 8–9; "Sotzializmus uFashizmus" (Socialism and Fascism), *haPoel haTzair*, 20 no. 9, (1926): 11–12; "HaOlam b'Rosh HaShanah 5688" (The World at Rosh HaShanah 5688), *HaAretz*, September 26 1927.

and accept his own contention, although, to be sure, he never provides us with any clear ideological fodder other than to state that he foresaw Jabotinsky as the Revisionist *Duce*. Yet Ahimeir himself certainly identified with Mussolini the journalist, and he was undoubtedly inspired by the non-conformist man of action who had also founded *Utopia*.[15] Ze'ev Sternhell highlights the particular attractiveness of Fascism for many European intellectuals, as it reflected their own non-conformism while representing "a new ideal of the beautiful and the admirable" that at the same time sought to orient the individual within the greater community.[16] Indeed, Ahimeir had made his own non-conformist position clear in one of the "Notebook of a Fascist" articles, when he likened himself to an "ancient pessimist [who] sometimes walks westward, sometimes eastward [and who] makes heard his Zionist ethic... without becoming interested... in the opinion of the crowd."[17]

Nonetheless, acceptance of Ahimeir's Fascist leanings comes with several caveats. Above all, he differed from Mussolini and the Italian Fascists in one key ideological aspect. Mussolini viewed Fascism in the same way that Lenin viewed Marxist-socialism: in a teleological context that allowed each to see his particular politico-ideological movement, as historian Martin Malia has noted, "as a total project, aiming as it does at transcending present society completely and creating a whole new world and a new man."[18] This was never Ahimeir's intention for the embrace of Fascism in the *Yishuv*. Rather, it served merely as a viable *modus operandi* that would, in his eyes, bring about the creation of a Jewish-Zionist nation state in Palestine in the most expedient manner possible. Ahimeir advocated Fascism as the means to an end, not as the end, itself. In another "Notebook of a Fascist" article, he remarks that socialism was an option to be considered, but only after a Jewish state had come into being. Until then, the *Yishuv* should function as if under "siege mentality."[19]

---

15 Mussolini founded *Utopia: The Fortnightly Magazine of Italian Revolutionary Socialism* in 1913.

16 Ze'ev Sternhell, "Fascism: Reflections on the fate of Ideas in Twentieth Century History," *Journal of Political Ideologies* 5, no. 2 (2000): 150.

17 Abba Ahimeir, "Amor leOman sheYitzarni" (Tell the Craftsman Who Produced Me], *Doar haYom*, November 4 1928 (All translations mine, unless otherwise indicated).
[פסימיסטן הקדמון...פעם הוא הולך מערבה ופעם מזרחה...הוא נשמע למוסר הציוני שלו...מבלי התענין ב...דעת הקהל]

18 Martin Malia, *History's Locomotives: Revolutions and the Making of the Modern World* (New Haven/London: Yale University Press, 2006), 226. Although Malia is speaking only of socialism, I suggest that his observation applies also to the aims of Mussolini's Fascist project.

19 Abba Ahimeir, "Be'Inyan haVizah leJabotinsky" (In the Matter of Jabotinsky's Visa), *Doar haYom*, September 21 1928.
[מצב המצור]

Furthermore, despite Ahimeir's attempts to win Jabotinsky over to the ideological program of the Maximalists, the Revisionist Party never adopted a Fascist platform, neither ideologically nor practically. This fact should not, however, prevent us from noting some degree of ideological overlap between Jabotinsky's concept of "monism," or the ideal of serving one overriding principal – in this case the Political Zionist goal of establishing a Jewish nation state in Palestine – and Ahimeir's Fascism, which, in his eyes, represented nothing more than the practice of monism taken *ad extremum*. While perhaps radical, Ahimeir's ideological connection is certainly not illogical.[20] Nonetheless, Jabotinsky rejected outright the suggestion that he become the "Leader" of the party, in a Fascist understanding of the word.[21] In addition, Jabotinsky and Ahimeir held differing views regarding the utility of the party's youth group, *Betar*. While Jabotinsky certainly emphasized military precision and ceremony, this was done only in the name of *Hadar*, "a Hebrew word that... comprehends some dozen different concepts: external beauty, pride, manners, loyalty."[22] However, out of Jabotinsky's sight and especially in the *Yishuv*, the group could at times turn more obviously militaristic, and become rowdy, oppressive, and violent. Ahimeir doubtlessly saw the group fulfil the role of the *Fasci* in Italy when he described *Betar* as a "national guard [in which] Hebrew culture permeated... from the Zionist public, from the Jewish youth."[23]

Finally, the Revisionists never came to political rule in the *Yishuv*. We thus have no way of determining how comprehensively either Jabotinsky's more liberal and the Maximalists' more extreme ideologies may have been realized in an applied political setting. But Ahimeir was able to implement certain facets of Fascist ideology in the *Betar* youth and the Maximalists. And if, in Walter Benjamin's assessment, Fascism is the result of introducing aesthetics into political life, then Ahimeir was certainly guilty of introducing Fascist aesthetics into Revisionist political life.[24]

---

20 See Eran Kaplan, *The Jewish Radical Right: Revisionist Zionism and its Ideological Legacy* (Madison: University of Wisconsin Press, 2005), 31–32, for a discussion of fascist ideology as a result of "evolutionary monism." Kaplan, however, does not make the necessary distinction between Jabotinsky's and Ahimeir's understanding of "monism".

21 See, i.e., Shindler, *The Triumph of Military Zionism*, 125.

22 Jabotinsky, quoted in Shimoni, *The Zionist Ideology*, 245.

23 Abba Ahimeir, "*Betar* keTefisat Olam" (*Betar* as a Worldview), *Massuot*, Issue 8–9, December 10, 1928, reprinted in *Ahimeir veBetar* (Ahimeir and *Betar*), ed. Joseph Kister (Tel Aviv: A. Oren Press, 1982), 49–51.
[גוורדיה הלאומית...[שבה] התרבות העברית חדורה...מן הציבוריות הציונית, מן הנוער היהודי.]

24 Walter Benjamin (1892–1940), "The Work of Art in the Age of Mechanical Reproduction," in *Illuminations* (London: Fontana Press, 1992), 234.

Ahimeir and Revolution

National liberation movements are imbued with the idea of revolution. As Michael Walzer recently noted:

> Liberation is closer to revolutionary politics than to national aggrandizement. Like the liberationist militants, revolutionaries set themselves in opposition to established patterns of submission, accommodation, and (what Marxists call) 'false consciousness.' They aim at a radical transformation. Social revolution requires a struggle against the existing society; national liberation requires a struggle again, rather than an 'exultation' of, the existing nation.[25]

Ahimeir's revolution was one of political insurrection, which he believed to be a necessary step on the road to Jewish national liberation.[26] The fact that historians and social scientists have been unable to reach any scholarly consensus on how merely to define, let alone predict, revolution is a fact which Ahimeir – who again and again aggrandized men of "action" over "words" – would have noted with wry cynicism. The dictionary definition of "revolution" reads, simply, as "a forcible overthrow of a government or social order, in favor of a new system,"[27] and this is certainly how Ahimeir understood the term, fundamentally.

Interestingly, he dedicates a notable amount of attention to the idea of revolution already in his dissertation on Spengler, a fact that is perhaps unsurprising, as it was penned in the wake of a Russian Revolution that Ahimeir had not only experienced first-hand, but that had also claimed the life of his brother. Ahimeir arrives at three broad conclusions. First, he sees the Russian Revolution as a victory of Western over Eastern ideals, in both a specifically Spenglerian, and more generally historical-phenomenological, sense. Second, he sees all revolution as a direct consequence of centralism, a notable observation in light of the fact that a centralized British government had taken up its mandate for Palestine while Ahimeir was completing his doctoral dissertation. Third, and most notably, Ahimeir sees revolution as the deciding factor between the preservation of an ethnic culture, and its bastardization through assimilation with a more

---

25 Michael Walzer, *The Paradox of Liberation: Secular Revolutions and Religious Counterrevolutions* (New Haven, CT/London: Yale University Press, 2015), 5.

26 The use of "Zionist" and not "Jewish" is intentional. In the "Notebook of a Fascist" article quoted above, he also wrote: "We are not for free entrance of Jews to the land, but only for free entrance of Zionists. Only Zionists are necessary to us here." Abba Ahimeir, "Be'Inyan ha-Vizah leJabotinsky."

27 Henry W. Fowler and Francis G. Fowler, eds., *The Concise Oxford Dictionary of Current English* (Oxford: Clarendon Press, 1995), 1180.

dominant culture.[28] Although Ahimeir is speaking specifically of Russian vis à vis Western European culture, we need only consider the situation of the Jewish populations throughout Europe, and, indeed, in the *Yishuv* – where Ahimeir highlighted the danger of Zionist "assimilation" with other, negative, ideological influences, such as socialism and communism – to realize that he was in fact warning of a far greater danger in his dissertation.

The second important document for our understanding of Ahimeir's concept of revolution is the article mentioned above, where he declares the age and ideology of Zionist Pioneering to be over, and implores the Zionists to adopt the ideology of revolution, in the name of national liberation.[29] Ahimeir's concept of revolution, as spelled out in this article, is rather idiosyncratic. He sees revolution unfold in two stages. First, there must be a what he calls a "period of imperialism"[30]; one that would, unlike in the socialist understanding of the term, carry some form of utopian promise. For Ahimeir, this "period of imperialism" represents a revolution of *Weltanschauung*, but he notes that this "conceptual" revolution would remain unfulfilled.[31] The ideological dichotomy thus caused – between utopian promise, and imperialist self-interest – would lead, in turn, to a period of grave disillusionment that would finally – and necessarily – effect a literal, political-insurrectionary revolution. If such a description sounds familiar, it is perhaps because this is exactly the situation that the Zionists found themselves in vis à vis the British at the time that Ahimeir wrote the article, in 1927. Thus, Ahimeir's call for a revolution in Zionism was catalyzed precisely during such a period of grave disillusionment with an imperialist – in this case, a "British-imperialist" – moment.

And while Ahimeir may have described himself simply as a Zionist Revolutionary, I believe that it is possible to better nuance our understanding of the nature of Ahimeir's revolutionariness. Sternhell highlights the philosopher Thomas E. Hulme's description of Georges Sorel as "a revolutionary who is also antidemocratic, an absolutist in ethics, rejecting all rationalism and relativism, who gives great importance to the mystical element in religion which he knows

---

28 See Abba Gaissinovitch, "*Bemerkungen zu Spenglers Auffassung Russlands*" (Remarks on Spengler's Conception of Russia) (PhD diss., University of Vienna 1924), 69–79.

29 Ahimeir, "Im Ein Ani Li – Mi Li?" Ahimeir contradicts himself somewhat, however. At first, he writes that the "period of imperialism" is preceded by a revolution "in the direct sense of the word" [במובן הישר של המלה].

30 [תקופת האימפריאליזמוס.] Ahimeir contradicts himself somewhat, however. At first, he writes that the "period of imperialism" is preceded by a revolution "in the direct sense of the word" [במובן הישר של המלה].

31 Ibid.

'will never disappear', and who speaks contemptuously of modernism and *progress,* and uses a concept like *honour* with no sense of unreality."[32] Sternhell sees both Sorel and Hulme – whom Thomas S. (T.S.) Eliot (1888–1965) described as "classical, reactionary and revolutionary, the antipodes of the eclectic, tolerant and democratic mind of the last century" – as characteristic embodiments of the "classic definition of revolutionary conservatism, which in some cases is synonymous with fascism."[33] And although Ahimeir was certainly not a conscious Sorelian, there is much in his journalistic output during the 1920s that points his ideological tenor in the direction of revolutionary conservatism.

Something else to consider is the concept of counterrevolution, which, in historian Arno J. Mayer's estimation, is inextricably bound to revolution, "both as phenomenon and process," although not "recognized and theorized as such."[34] For Mayer, counterrevolution is characterized by two major elements: reaction and conservatism.[35] It is a product of the anti-Enlightenment, and its "prophets of despair" are pessimistic, decadent, and rooted in a mythic past.[36] There is much apparent ideological overlap between Mayer's "counterrevolutionary" and Sternhell's "revolutionary conservative," and I suggest that the two terms overlap enough, ideologically, to be used interchangeably. Consequently, we might better classify Ahimeir – the "ancient pessimist [who] sometimes walks westward, sometimes eastward [and who] makes his Zionist ethic heard [with no regard to] the opinion of the crowd," as noted, above – as one of the first real counterrevolutionary figures in the *Yishuv.*[37] Indeed, the fact that Mayer sees the culmination of European counterrevolution in the phenomenon of Fascism would seem to only buttress this contention.[38]

Walzer contradicts Mayer to a certain degree in his discussion of counterrevolution. For him, the conservatism and reaction in Mayer's depiction of counterrevolution is traditional-religious. Indeed, it is clear from his context that when

---

32 Thomas E. Hulme, quoted in Ze'ev Sternhell, *The Birth of Fascist Ideology* (Princeton, NJ: Princeton University Press, 1994), 241. Hulme (1883–1917) was born in the same year as Mussolini, and one wonders how he might have viewed the development of the *Duce*, in light of his comments on Sorel, had he survived to experience the phenomenon of Fascism.

33 Ibid. Georges Sorel (1847–1922) was a philosopher and revolutionary syndicalist theoretician.

34 Arno J. Mayer, *The Furies: Violence and Terror in the French and Russian Revolutions* (Princeton, NJ: Princeton University Press, 2000), 45.

35 Ibid., 52.

36 Ibid., 61–62.

37 Ahimeir, "Amor leOman sheYitzarni."

38 Mayer, *The Furies*, 67.

Walzer speaks of "Jewish zealotry in Israel" as an example of Zionist counterrevolution, he is speaking about modern-day ultra-orthodoxy:

> [T]heir first allegiance is not to the nation-state but to something more like the traditional, pre-state community. After a time, when national liberation has receded in memory, these traditionalists stage a counterrevolution; thus the rise of Islamic radicalism in Algeria (and in Palestine), of Hindutva in India and of Jewish zealotry in Israel. The religious resurgence is a shock to the national liberation elites, who had grown complacent about the victory of newness.[39]

Walzer's counterrevolutionary Jewish zealots are truly messianic, as opposed to those of Ahimeir and the Maximalists, for whom messianism was secular, rhetorical, and indeed, far more sophisticated. I wonder, however, if the main difference between Mayer and Walzer is merely generational: Mayer is discussing the French and Russian Revolutions, while Walzer focuses on post-Second World War Israel, Algeria, and India. Ideologically-speaking, Ahimeir falls somewhere between the cracks. Perhaps it would be more accurate to call him a "revolutionary counterrevolutionary," or possibly a counterrevolutionary whose counterrevolution took the form of a *de facto* revolution? While the temptation to continue splitting hairs is great, it might serve us better, at this point, to take a step backwards, and undertake a more general discussion of the phenomenon of revolution, and how it might apply as an intellectual-historical term to both Zionism and the *Yishuv* during the British Mandate.

Zionism and Revolution

As noted above, there is little scholarly consensus on what constitutes revolution. While impossible to wade into the mire of revolutionary theory in any substantial manner in such a short study, it is nonetheless necessary to engage with the issue on some level, in order to make some salient, general observations.

The attempt at formulating a general theory of revolution is usually centered in the realms of the social sciences and history.[40] Theorists are more likely to measure the validity and success of a revolution by determining its "causes," "preconditions," "immediate incidental factors," "historical crises," etc., in

39 Walzer, *The Paradox of Liberation*, 55–56.

40 Hobsbawm dedicates a paper to this very phenomenon. See Eric J. Hobsbawm, "Revolution", in *Revolution in History*, ed. Roy Porter and Mikulas Teich (Cambridge University Press: Cambridge, 1986), 5–46.

Hobsbawm's opinion – and he was no minor player in the revolutionary leagues – to the detriment of examining a revolution's outcome as the primary determinant of its success.[41] I share Hobsbawm's skepticism at the social scientist's need for a theory that will somehow function as a magic formula to be used to predict future revolutions. Indeed, it was the case that Theda Skocpol's now classic definition of "social revolution" – "basic, rapid transformation of a society's state and class structures, accompanied and in part carried out through class-based revolts from below" – was challenged almost immediately upon publication by the unfolding events of the Iranian Revolution, in 1979.[42] Charles Tilley – rather vaguely, perhaps purposefully so – sees revolution as a "special case of collective action" in the fight for "ultimate political sovereignty… in which challengers succeed at least to some degree in displacing existing power-holders."[43] However, Tilley, an anomaly in this respect, sees violent political action as a mere by-product of such collective action, and not an "object of analysis" in its own right.[44] And Hannah Arendt adds the idea of a "pathos of novelty" that is connected with the "idea of freedom" that must coincide with the "experience of a new beginning," for a revolution in the modern age.[45]

But, of course, the social scientists, in the attempt to arrive at a predictive theory of revolution, privilege the phenomenon – if not the necessity – of social, over political, change. For them, the political element is a by-product, even if a necessary one, of the social revolution, which is the focus of their analysis. Hobsbawm recognizes the tension inherent in such duality when he notes, from the historian's perspective, that:

> Lengthy though these 'revolutionary eras' may be, they are to be distinguished from the historic macro-phenomena in which they are embedded, such as the change from pre-capitalist to capitalist societies. The revolutions which interest historians lie at the intersection of

---

41 Ibid, 15.

42 Theda Skocpol, *States and Social Revolutions: A Comparative Analysis of France, Russia and China* (Cambridge: Cambridge University Press, 1979), 287. See also Theda Skocpol, *Social Revolutions in the Modern World* (Cambridge University Press: Cambridge, 1994). The fact that Hobsbawm sees the Iranian Revolution as "a 'great revolution' by any objective standards" (Hobsbawm, "Revolution" in *Revolution and History*, ed. Porter and Teich, 19), while Walzer would probably consider it – due to its radical Islamic element – as a "great counterrevolution," (Walzer, *Paradox of Liberation*, 54, etc.) highlights the array of scholarly discrepancy surrounding the intellectual-historiographical term.

43 Charles Tilley, paraphrased in Skocpol, *States and Social Revolutions*, 10.

44 Ibid.

45 Hannah Arendt, *On Revolution* (Penguin Books: London, 2006), 18–25.

> these two types of phenomena. We are unlikely to class them as revolution if they do not involve potential transfers of power in the characteristic manner.[46]

Malia reaches a similar conclusion when he notes, as one of his seven considerations regarding revolution, that "a Western revolution is in the first instance a political and ideological transformation, not a social one."[47]

Hobsbawm defines "revolutionary eras" as "a series of events, generally associated with 'revolt' and capable of transferring power from an 'old regime' to a 'new regime'."[48] However, he notes that such a transformation does not necessarily always occur. Malia likewise sees, in what he calls a "European grand revolution," a "generalized revolt against an Old Regime."[49] For Malia, however, this can occur only once in a nation's history, since it also represents the "founding event for the nation's future 'modernity'."[50] Malia, in variance to Hobsbawm, implies a necessary transfer of power as a measure of a revolution's success. Despite this apparent contradiction, I believe that both observations are noteworthy. Furthermore, Malia maintains that revolution is a European phenomenon that should be studied historically and in specifically Western terms, and that, moreover, nothing approximating a "European grand revolution" occurred outside the European cultural sphere before the twentieth century.[51] Not surprisingly, the apparent Eurocentric smugness of Malia's argument has been heftily criticized.[52] However, before completely throwing his revolutionary baby out with the bathwater, and in Malia's defense, we should note his term, "*European grand* revolution," which I imagine to be, ideologically, not such a far cry from Hobsbawm's "great revolution."[53] Malia's focus – rightly or wrongly – is on the ideological-historical revolutionary trajectory that looks back to the American and French Revolutions, which, in addition to the social changes they effected, were also responsible for the creation of "modern" nations that had the Westphalian model, in some form, as their ideal. Malia's "European grand revolution"

46 While nonetheless noting the importance of the "context of historical transformation as essential to the phenomenon." Hobsbawm, *Revolution*, 10.
47 Martin Malia, *History's Locomotives: Revolutions and the Making of the Modern World* (New Haven, CT/London: Yale University Press, 2006), 3.
48 Hobsbawm, *Revolution*, 9.
49 Malia, *History's Locomotives*, 5.
50 Ibid.
51 For a more detailed account of Malia's seven conditions for the study of revolution, see Malia, *History's Locomotives*, 2–10.
52 See, for example, Charles Tilley, review of *History's Locomotives: Revolutions and the Making of the Modern World*, by Martin Malia, *American Historical Review*, 112, no. 4 (2007): 1120–1122.
53 Emphasis mine. See Malia, *History's Locomotives*, 5.

is perhaps rather more specific a phenomenon than Hobsbawm's "great revolution," since it is not entirely clear from the latter's context whether he equates "old regime" with "ancien régime." Be that as it may, from the beginning of the twentieth century (in keeping with Malia's parameters), global political organization has been based increasingly on the modern Western nation state model, and therefore belongs, ideologically, to the European politico-cultural orbit. Thus, the Iranian Revolution of 1906, the Chinese Xinhai Revolution of 1911, and the Mexican Revolution of 1910–1920 would all qualify, to some degree, as "European grand revolutions" in Malia's understanding of the term.[54] Consequently, we might view Malia's Eurocentricity as precisely the factor that makes him interesting for this discussion, since the political end goal of Zionism was the creation of a modern "Western" nation state for the Jews. It should be remembered that Ahimeir, in his doctoral dissertation, as discussed above, saw the Russian Revolution as a victory of Western over Eastern ideals. Malia further mandates that "each revolution learns from its predecessor and escalates that pattern each time to a more intense level of radicalism," again, a not unimportant consideration for this discussion.[55] While I am well aware that these observations in no way form a comprehensive theory of revolution, I suggest, nonetheless, that they act as a springboard for the ensuing discussion, as we shift our gaze back to the question of revolution in Zionism and the *Yishuv*, and the role that Ahimeir played in each.

Before more specifically examining the question of revolution in the *Yishuv*, I want to first consider the idea of Zionism as revolution. Indeed, at every level, the very phenomenon of Zionism itself was nothing short of revolutionary for European, and eventually world, Jewry. Driven by ideology and hope, and increasingly spurred on by a "chaotic crowd" that aimed to supplant a quasi-dual ancien régime that was embodied on one hand by the Jews' host nations in *Galut* (exile), and on the other, the political, social, and religious institutions of European Jewish life, itself:

> Zionism aimed to restore to the Jews a political body they could claim as their own; national independence was seen as the way to guard the individual against physical threats and economicwant, and the collective against the menace of assimilation and disintegration… But Zionism meant more than political independence in Palestine. It promised both material and spiritual transformation… a modernized economy of and for the Jews… and the re-

54 And therefore, do not "vanish from the main argument… through definitional fiat," as Tilley states (Ibid., 1121).

55 Malia, *History's Locomotives*, 5.

> vival of the Hebrew language... Some even hoped to form a new Jew: natural assertive, self-reliant, productive, and so on.[56]

Thus, the political success of Zionism first required Jewish – eventually Zionist – cultural, psychological, and physical regeneration; consequently, it was, *a priori*, a social revolution. Its "historical crisis" was the failure of emancipation and the rise of modern antisemitism in Europe; its "revolutionary situation" was the publication of Theodore Herzl's *Der Judenstaat*, in 1896.[57] While the political element was central to its ideology, the *de facto* utopian political goal of Zionism remained unfulfilled until the Declaration of the State of Israel, in 1948. While there was, of course, much Zionist political organization in the intervening years, and while the necessary geographical shift from Europe to the *Yishuv* did occur on some level, none of these factors was sufficient to brand the Zionist project an "unqualified success" before any real political solution – i.e. statehood – was reached (and this is to say nothing of Zionism's relative lack of popularity for the majority of European Jewry, until at least the 1930s). The phenomenon of a proto-state under a Mandate-administrator – its considerable institutional infrastructure and political organization notwithstanding – represented, without a state, nothing more than a pyrrhic victory for the Zionists. Doubtless, Zionist immigration from 1880–1948 represented the beginning of a "historical revolution" in its most literal sense – i.e. from the Latin *revolvere* (to revolve) – as Europe's Jews began "to go back to the land of their fathers and regain their Statehood."[58] Nonetheless, without a political resolution, this "historical revolution" represented nothing more than a new pattern of Jewish migration.

It was to this politico-situational holding pattern – a semi-autonomous *Yishuv* proto-government that operated under the larger political and administrative umbrella of the British Mandate government – that Ahimeir returned, in 1924. The four years preceding his arrival had witnessed the foundation of some of

---

56 Eyal Chowers, *The Political Philosophy of Zionism: Trading Jewish Words for a Hebraic Land* (Cambridge: Cambridge University Press, 2012), 7.

57 See Hobsbawm, *Revolution*, 16, for a detailed discussion of the terms "historical crises" and "revolutionary situations." He defines a "revolutionary situation" as "that variant of a short-term crisis within a system with long-term internal tensions, which offers good chances of a revolutionary outcome." (Ibid., 19).

58 The wording used in the Declaration of the Establishment of the State of Israel, May 14 1948. Quoted in Itamar Rabinovich and Jehuda Reinharz, eds., *Israel in the Middle East: Documents and Readings on Society, Politics, and Foreign Relations, Pre-1948 to the Present* (Waltham: Brandeis University Press, 2008), 72.

the most archetypical Zionist institutions: the *Haganah* (The Defence), a paramilitary organization that was established to guard the *Yishuv* population and interests; the *Va'ad Leumi* (Jewish National Council), which administered communal affairs in the *Yishuv*; and the *Histadrut* (General Organisation of Workers in the Land of Israel), a kind of "super union" that combined various trade unions, oversaw industrial enterprises, and provided health insurance, an immigration office, and a bank. All of these organizations, but especially the *Va'ad Leumi* and *Histadrut*, were, in effect, controlled by members of *Ahdut haAvodah* (The Labor Unity) or *haPoel haTza'ir*. Thus, the *Yishuv* and its institutions enjoyed a marked Labor-Left hegemony. The future first Prime Minister of Israel, David Ben-Gurion, who, in 1930, would go on to lead *Mapai* – a party formed from a merge between *Ahdut haAvodah* and *haPoel haTza'ir* – was Secretary of the *Histadrut* at the time of Ahimeir's arrival. The *Histadrut*, in particular, was an almost closed club to anyone who was not a member of one of the four parties that had members on its council, and Ahimeir quickly noted this injustice, in spite of his membership in *haPoel haTza'ir*.

Indeed, Ahimeir's short marriage to the socialist party was an unhappy one, and he openly criticized what he saw as the hypocrisy in the hegemony of the Labor Left, especially within the *Histadrut*. His first appearance, in February 1928, as a member of the Revisionist Party (along with Greenberg and Yevin), was at the Conference of the Bloc for Revisionist Labor, which sought to disassociate itself from these institutions, and form an alternative "nationalist" (i. e. Revisionist) workers' bloc within the *Histadrut*. He was further frustrated with a *Yishuv* leadership that, in an effort to appease the British mandatory government, had increasingly compromised the Zionist political goal. By the time Ahimeir joined the Revisionist Party, he had eschewed any route of diplomacy with the British, and could foresee the attainment of Jewish statehood only through a necessary path of (political) revolution that used a Fascist *modus operandi*, with Jabotinsky as *Duce*.

Ahimeir's revolutionary goal was purely political. He was certainly not trying to affect a Malian "European grand revolution." Nonetheless, there is some striking overlap with the "historical crisis" in the *Yishuv* under the British Mandate and that of other European revolutions. While the traditional ancien régime in Palestine had been weakened – although by no means completely crumbled, since the hierarchical infrastructure that ranged from a Palestinian Arab landowning elite of notables to peasant *fellah* remained intact – through the fall of the Ottoman Empire, Ahimeir did view the British Mandatory government – whom, as noted earlier, he called "Perfidious Albion" and "foreign occupiers" – as a regime to be overthrown. Furthermore, the British governed in the manner of an imperial power, not least in their bureaucratic and political inefficiency and ideology of "divide and conquer," even if the latter policy was adapted to reflect their role as a Mandatory Government. Although Britain was mandated with the task of creating a modern nation state for the Jews, it carried out the administration of its mandate using imperialist methods. Not only was the form of administration and governance in Palestine determined by the Mandatory power, there was, outside of the various councils that acted as intermediaries (i.e. the *Va'ad Leumi*), no political representation through suffrage, neither for the Jewish nor Arab citizens in Palestine. All aspects of the British Mandate leadership were decided in either Whitehall or in the office of the High Commissioner for Palestine. Thus, for Ahimeir – from a political point of view – the British fulfilled the function of an ancien régime, if perhaps one that had been transposed from Europe to Palestine.

And, in addition, just as there had been a quasi-dual ancien régime to overthrow in the Zionist "social revolution," so there was for Ahimeir's "political revolution." He doubtless saw the *Yishuv* leadership – with its Labor Left monopoly over all areas in the *Yishuv* – now fulfil the role of the traditional Jewish "Old Regime" that the Zionist "social revolution" had sought to supplant in Europe. Indeed, for Ahimeir, the *Yishuv* leadership – which had become entrenched in partisan nepotism and bureaucratic inefficiency in only a few short years – represented nothing better than a "Nouveau Ancien Régime in the *Altneuland*": a double slap in the face for a "pure" Political Zionist like Ahimeir, and thus worthy of revolutionary supplantation. In his 1926 essay, "The Scroll of the *Sicarii*," he is clear that he sees the "existing regime" as the focal point for the terror to be waged by the *sicarius*.[59] Indeed, he uses the term no less than nineteen times, and although he is never specific in the essay, which remained unpublished until it was used as evidence at the *Brit haBiryonim* trial in 1934, it is very likely that "existing regime" refers to both the British and *Yishuv* leaderships, *in toto*.

I keep returning to Malia's contention, noted earlier, that "each revolution learns from the experience of its predecessor and escalates that pattern each time to a more intense level of radicalism," and which I find noteworthy. All of European and *Yishuv* Jewry – Zionist and otherwise – had been affected by the last "European grand revolution," the October Revolution, in 1917; some, like Ahimeir, negatively, others less so (cf. *Ahdut haAvodah's* ultimate rejection of Marxism, in spite of the party's socialist character), and some positively (cf. the Marxist Zionist party, *haShomer haTzair* (The Young Guard)). Had this not

59 [המשטר הקיים.] Abba Ahimeir, "Megillat HaSikrikin," in *Brit haBiryonim* (Shamgar Press: Tel Aviv, 1972), 217–233. The historical *sicarii* were understood to be the extremists among the Zealots, active at the time of the destruction of the Second Jewish Temple, and named for the daggers – *sicae* – concealed beneath their clothing.

been the case (and again, in view of Malia's contention), it would have been *a priori*, "historically" impossible for *Ahdut HaAvodah* and the *Haganah*, in 1945, to join the Hebrew Resistance Movement, and to also eventually resort to violence against the British. It would also explain, theoretically at least, why Fascism, building as it did upon Marxism – whether positively, as per theoreticians like Ze'ev Sternhell, or negatively, as a revolt against Communism – was the most logical political ideology to serve as the *modus operandi* for what Ahimeir hoped would lead to a political revolution in Palestine. Not only was it more radical, but also – certainly in the eyes of its proponents – more ideologically evolved than Leninist-Marxism. Indeed, if we accept Malia's contention, then Ahimeir would have had no choice *but* to accept Fascism as the *modus operandi* for his revolution; as the most current of the political "isms," it could be his only choice if revolution does in fact evolve teleologically, and intensify in both means and execution, as Malia claims.

Malia's claim is further buttressed, from a different ideological perspective, by Ahimeir's embrace of Oswald Spengler. Like his mentor, Ahimeir viewed Bolshevism as the epitome of "Megalopolitan" *Über*-civilization, a status quo which, in Spenglerian theory, signified that a societal "culture" was in decline, and approaching the end of its life cycle. Thus, in Ahimeir's eyes, Bolshevism could not serve as a viable *modus operandi* for a successful Zionist revolution in Palestine. This observation may also explain some of Ahimeir's ideological inconsistencies, for example, the fact that he could speak of the need for "our own 1917" while, nonetheless, rejecting the ideological core of Bolshevism.[60] Furthermore – and rather notably, from an ideological perspective – it seems that Ahimeir, the Spenglerian, saw his Zionist political revolution as being "morphologically contemporaneous" with the Jewish Revolt, from 66–70 CE.[61] Both the *Biryonim* and *Sicarii* hail from this period. Ahimeir's appropriation of both terms for his modern-day purposes suggests – again, if we remember that Ahimeir was a Spenglerian – a very specific identification with both the nature and function of each group, i.e.,

60 Shindler, *The Triumph of Military Zionism*, 156.

61 In Spenglerian theory, parallel events that occur during corresponding spiritual epochs in any particular (Spenglerian) "culture" are considered "morphologically contemporaneous." Thus, in Spenglerian analysis, Plato and Goethe were – morphologically-speaking – contemporaries, despite having lived 1,500 years apart. Each fulfilled a similar historic function in his particular culture (Classical/Apollonian and Western/Faustian, respectively, in the cases of Plato and Goethe). A Spenglerian "culture" has, like any other biological organism, a finite life cycle, which has four main periods that correspond roughly to childhood/youth/adulthood/old age. In the final period, a culture became a "civilization": ossified, in decline and at the end of its life.

revolutionaries who revolted against both the Roman regime and the Jewish moderates who were sympathetic to it. For Ahimeir the Spenglerian, the British Mandatory government was morphologically contemporaneous with the Roman regime in Judea, and the Labor Left *Yishuv* leadership with the ancient Pharisees. Of course, the Jewish Revolt had ultimately failed; Ahimeir as both Spenglerian and historian expected his revolution to learn from the past, and succeed.

Malia further observes that it was due to "Communism's pretension to be the culmination of human progress, beyond which there is nothing but counterrevolution and the 'restoration of capitalism'" that led to the phenomenon of "revolution-as-regime."[62] I suggest that this observation may partially explain the unsatisfactory holding pattern of the *Yishuv* leadership vis à vis the British, regarding the formation of a Jewish state.[63] As proponents of socialism – to varying degrees, to be sure – they were simply unable to successfully affect the Zionist political end-goal since their 'permanent revolution' remained on the social level. Perhaps then, only a cynical and vehement opponent of Bolshevism and socialism, such as Ahimeir, could even entertain the thought of sparking a Zionist 'political revolution' that would achieve the political goals of the Zionist project. And of course, Fascist ideology espoused no less the concept of revolution, but did so, rather, in the name of national – and not international – socialism.[64]

Thus, by the time of Ahimeir's article in *haAretz*, in November 1927, in which he calls for the need for political revolution, the "historical crisis" in the *Yishuv* was represented by a British Mandatory government that was not fulfilling the conditions of its mandate: the unfulfilled "imperialist moment" that Ahimeir describes. The "revolutionary situation" in the *Yishuv* was equal to what Ahimeir calls a "period of disillusionment", and which he saw as the necessary catalysis for a literal revolution. In Ahimeir's case, this disillusionment stood on one hand with the Mandatory government, and, on the other, with the *Yishuv* leadership's apparent policy of compromise in every direction: with the British and their inability or unwillingness to achieve the Zionist political end goal, and as socialists who sought to imbue Zionism with their own self-interests. In the wake of the 1929 Arab riots, both of these situations had only intensified, which led to more intense action on Ahimeir's part: to push the ideology of Fascism in order to effectuate his political revolution.

Despite the cult status that he had achieved by the early 1930s – through his involvement with the Revisionist youth group *Betar* and teacher at the *Betar*

---

62 Malia, *History's Locomotives*, 256.

63 Ibid.

64 Although the nationalist-socialist nature of Fascism rendered the Marxist need for "permanent revolution" obsolete. Indeed, Ahimeir never uses the term himself.

Leadership Training School, as an outspoken journalist and, not least, as a notorious political activist – Ahimeir's political life in the *Yishuv* was cut short, in June 1934, due to his arrest in connection with the Arlosoroff murder. Thus, Ahimeir played no active part in any political revolution in the *Yishuv*, other than as an ideologue and agitator. However, the question remains as to whether Ahimeir's call for revolution remained nothing more than empty rhetoric, or whether it found some form of political expression. At this point, I suggest we reconsider the traditional historiographical approach that is taken when tracing the trajectory that culminated with the founding of the State of Israel, on May 14 1948, and which may be summarized as follows. In the wake of increasing resistance and violence on the parts of both the Palestinian Arab and *Yishuv* populations, Britain decided that it could no longer fulfil its role as originally set out in the League of Nations Mandate, and turned to what was now the United Nations for counsel, in April 1947. The United Nations Special Committee on Palestine (UNSCOP), which was convened specifically to deal with Britain's request, suggested – in UN Resolution 181 – the partition of Palestine into separate Jewish and Palestinian states, with Jerusalem to be administered by an international body. The resolution was passed on November 29 1947, which led immediately to a period of civil war between the Palestinian and Jewish populations, and which the British sought to mediate less and less as time went on. On the day that Britain pulled out of Palestine – May 14 1948 – the *Yishuv* leader David Ben-Gurion declared the foundation of the State of Israel, with himself as Prime Minister. The ensuing war with an invading Arab army made up of fighters from Egypt, Syria, Lebanon, Iraq, and Jordan – the Arabs had, unlike the Zionists, rejected the terms of Resolution 181 – led not only to victory for the new state, but also territorial and demographic gains that it had not foreseen. Although there is much debate, scholarly and otherwise, over details within this historiographical framework, historians nonetheless do not consider the succession of historical events that led to the Israeli War of Independence and Palestinian *Nakba* as constituting a political revolution. However, I would like to suggest that an application of the revolutionary filters discussed above to the events in the *Yishuv* from November 1927 to 1948 – i.e., from Ahimeir's first call for a revolution in the *Yishuv* and the end of the British Mandate to the subsequent Declaration of the State of Israel – may lead to some rather interesting conclusions.

The Big Picture

If we first consider the whole period before November 29 1947, we note that it began with the relatively moderate civil disobedience of *Brit haBiryonim*, which Ahimeir founded in 1930, and eventually reached a climax that was characterized by anti-British violence on the parts of all three *Yishuv* paramilitary groups – *Lehi*, the *Irgun*, the *Haganah* (and its elite unit, the *Palmakh*) – in the form of the "Hebrew Resistance Movement." Working in tandem, the groups waged campaigns of terror against the British, including the "Night of the Trains," on November 1 1945, where the railway infrastructure was blown out at one hundred and fifty-three points, and the "Night of the Bridges," in June 1946, when bridges that connected Palestine with its neighboring countries were destroyed. Although the *Haganah* and *Palmakh* discontinued their participation in terrorist acts in the wake of the King David Hotel bombing, on July 26 1946, they continued to work against the British by helping to secure illegal immigration and settlement for Jewish refugees from Europe.

During the period between the passing of UN Resolution 181, on November 29 1947, and the British withdrawal from Palestine, which was complete by May 14 1948, the intensity of both anti-British terrorist activity (by the *Irgun* and *Lehi*) and illegal immigration (aided by the *Haganah* and *Palmakh*) only intensified. Meanwhile, the beginning of the civil war with the Palestinian-Arab population and breakdown of British desire for controlling the increasing instances of violence between the two populations (unless these were directed against the British themselves) served only to spiral the situation out of control. Thus the events that occurred in the *Yishuv* were not only characterized by the "breakdown of sovereignty" and the chaotic element that Mayer sees as "the essential precondition for the escalation of revolt into revolution,"[65] but also – certainly by the end of the Second World War, in the wake of the Holocaust – by what Arendt called the "notion of irresistibility": the cumulative, eventually exponentially-so, accrual of force that would render a revolt unstoppable "beyond human power… and hence a law unto itself," that would transform it into a revolution.[66] Ahimeir himself recognized such a phenomenon when he noted that "the commencement of a revolution is like a small river and its end like [a] big ocean."[67] In the case of the *Yishuv*, there was continual forward motion in this respect. It should be remembered that almost every inhabitant who was old enough belonged to one of the *Yishuv* paramilitary groups, certainly by the beginning of the period of the Hebrew Resistance Movement. The chaotic crowd element, with the cumulative accrual of force that was necessary for a political revolution, was absolutely present in the *Yishuv*.

---

65 Mayer, *The Furies*, 35.

66 Arendt, *On Revolution*, 37–38.

67 Abba Ahimeir, undated letter. Exhibit Y.T. 9, *Brit haBiryonim* Trial, B 14/6/1, Jabotinsky Institute Archive.

Finally, we should not forget the outcome of our hypothetical Zionist "political revolution," which, in consideration of the fact that the British did pull out of Palestine, and that a Jewish nation state was, in fact, declared on the heel of their withdrawal, becomes less hypothetical, and suggests success. The fact that the civil war with the Palestinian-Arabs introduced a different dimension to the conflict, and that the British withdrawal was sanctioned by the UN, should not deter us from recognition of the fact that Britain pulled out of Palestine having not fulfilled the terms of its mandate, and indeed, with its tail between its legs.

Of course, the Labor-Left *Yishuv* leadership – the other half of Ahimeir's "existing regime" – was not only *not* supplanted by revolution, but became the *de facto* regime that took power in the new state. This fact should not concern us too greatly. The measure of success for such a protracted struggle for national liberation should be its finality, not its ideological perfection. For Ahimeir, who was above all an ardent Zionist, the overriding goal of his political revolution had been achieved. Indeed, the fact that all groups in the *Yishuv* eventually worked together to supplant the British, and to protect the new state against foreign invasion, is perhaps the best proof of the success of the revolution that Ahimeir first called for, in 1927. There was no attempt at Jewish civil war in the *Yishuv* once the new state was declared, and the majority of the *Yishuv* community accepted the new government if perhaps only begrudgingly so. While the Revisionists, under Begin, continued to oppose the Labor Left, they did so now as the official opposition party in the new state. The political revolution in the *Yishuv* spanned twenty years of increasing "general crisis" with the British. It was a slow process that occurred in fits and starts, and that changed its character throughout its long life. As Hobsbawm suggests, "the concept of 'general crisis' is useful as a reminder that particular revolutions or other ruptures occur within systems, which pass through periods of breakdown and restructuring."[68] The "general crisis" in the *Yishuv* spanned the whole period under discussion here, and ended only on May 14 1948, with the Declaration of Independence of the new state of Israel.

Conclusion

If a Zionist political revolution did, in fact, occur in the *Yishuv* – and let us assume for the sake of this argument that one did – we should further seek to determine the magnitude of its success. Hobsbawm notes that very rarely are the

---

68 Hobsbawm, *Revolution*, 17.

"system-carrying forces" in place at the beginning of most "protracted revolutions."[69] In this respect, the Zionists enjoyed a distinct advantage to other national liberation groups. A proto-state, with all its requisite political and civil institutions, had been carefully cultivated by the Zionists in the *Yishuv* since the 1920s. Once statehood was declared, they needed only to "convert" this already existing infrastructure into an official state apparatus. There was not even a need to physically supplant the British from their administrative institutions: the Zionists had their own, waiting in the wings, so to speak, and were thus able to circumvent such action that is so common to other political revolutions.

The Zionist "social revolution," discussed above, only really flourished after the foundation of the State of Israel. With the legitimacy of a new state – now recognized by the UN and riding on a crest of victory in the face of Arab invasion – the Zionist social project now had not only a spiritual-geographical, but also an official-political focal point. Arguably, no other single aspect of the Zionist "social revolution" did more to regenerate and heal the damaged Jewish psyche than the *de facto* situation of having a modern democratic nation state that was recognized by the majority of the international community. The ensuing decades have witnessed Jewish immigration to Israel from all corners of the globe, and approximately fifty percent of world Jewry now resides there. The "Zionist" has become "Israeli," and the "social revolution" has taken on a cultural dimension, as we speak now of music, art, food, literature, cinema, scholarship, research, etc. that is no longer merely "Jewish," but distinctly "Israeli."

Likewise, the Zionist "historical revolution" flourished only after the foundation of the State of Israel. Not only did a large portion of the world's Jewish population "return" to a modern Israel that was situated in part of "ancient" Israel, but Judaism itself – in various modern and political forms, to be sure – returned to become the dominant religion in the land from where it had originated.

Thus, Zionism was an amalgam of a tripartite revolution: a social revolution within Judaism, a political revolution in the *Yishuv*, and a historical revolution that reached out globally. While there was a symbiotic relationship between the three, the ultimate successes of both the social and historical revolutions could be measured only against the success of the political revolution. We need only to measure the "success" of the policy of "Practical" Zionist settlement in the *Yishuv*, before 1948 – which privileged "historical" over "political" revolution – to support this claim. Zionism was, at once, a revolution "backwards" to an ancient historical homeland and "forwards" to nation state modernity; it harked back to an ancient "Hebrew" cultural past, but used modern

69 Ibid., 22.

methods to do so. The social revolution within Zionism was, on its own, not enough to render the whole project a "great revolution." A clear political goal was also necessary. The "political revolution" in the *Yishuv*, which catalyzed the foundation of the Jewish political state, and the accompanying "historical revolution" that it effected, were both necessary components for a Zionist "great revolution." We need merely to consider a counter-factual scenario that would see a territorial polity created for the Jews anywhere else but in their "ancient homeland," and without the concomitant "social revolution" – i. e. if *shtetl* borders were merely politically demarcated, or the *shtetl* itself transplanted to its own neutral territorial polity – to see that the social regenerative element was a necessary component of the Zionist revolution. The synergy of the "social," "political," and "historical" revolutions was necessary, and I would even cautiously suggest that the retrospective success of all three revolutionary components *in toto* is sufficient to render the revolution that occurred in Zionism a Malian "European grand revolution." Indeed, the Jews' "hunger" for their own national polity was as acute as the French hunger for bread in the riots that preceded the French Revolution.[70]

Of course, I am not suggesting that Ahimeir was responsible for leading, executing, or even effecting, a revolution in British Mandate Palestine. Nonetheless, what did occur in the *Yishuv*, from the time of Ahimeir's article in 1927 until the British pulled out of Palestine on May 14 1948, was certainly a revolution by Ahimeir's understanding of the term. Indeed, the cynic might see Menachem Begin's (1913–1992) call, at the Third World Convention of *Betar* in 1938, to usher in a new period of "Military Zionism" as nothing more than an opportunistic repackaging of Ahimeir's concept of "Revolutionary Zionism" from ten years earlier.[71] Hobsbawm cites the relevance of the "date when the first adult generation of 'children of the revolution' emerge on the public scene, those whose education and careers belong entirely to the new era."[72] The original "children" of Ahimeir's revolution came of age with the eventual

70 In his testimony to the Peel Commission, Jabotinsky spoke in terms of Jewish "starvation" for national sovereignty. See Joseph Heller, "Weizmann, Jabotinsky and the Arab Question: The Peel Affair," *The Jerusalem Quarterly* 26 (1983): 109–126. Weizmann had threatened the Commission that if the Jews felt they were "about to be sacrificed," they would either seek to leave, or "they would revolt." Ibid., 115.

71 See Shindler, *The Triumph of Military Zionism*, 7–8, 17, and 205–212. Begin's "Military Zionism" was meant to supplant the earlier periods in Zionist history, "Practical Zionism" and "Political Zionism". See also Joseph Heller, *The Stern Gang: Ideology, Politics and Terror, 1940–1949* (London: Frank Cass, 1995), 41.

72 Hobsbawm, *Revolution*, 32.

election of Begin as Prime Minister of Israel, in 1977. Yet, by the time of Begin's speech in 1938, Ahimeir's political revolution had been gaining ground for almost a decade, even if it was not yet recognized as such. The fact that the first ideological proponent of political revolution in the *Yishuv* was neither its leader nor executor should not mitigate the fact that Abba Ahimeir played a decisive role in the genesis of what we should well consider to be a political revolution in Palestine, and which was responsible for the end of the British Mandate and foundation of the State of Israel.

Works Cited

Ahimeir, Abba. "Amor leOman sheYitzarni." *Doar HaYom*, November 4 1928.
Ahimeir, Abba. "Be'Inyan haVizah leJabotinsky." *Doar HaYom*, September 21 1928.
Ahimeir, Abba. "*Betar* keTefisat Olam," in *Ahmeir veBetar*, edited by Joseph Kister, 49–51. Tel Aviv: A. Oren Press, 1982, originally published in *Massuot*, Issue 8–9, December 10 1928.
Ahimeir, Abba. *Brit haBiryonim*. Tel Aviv: Shamgar Press, 1972.
Ahimeir, Abba. "Gesher haBarzel." *Doar haYom*, September 10 1929.
Ahimeir, Abba. "HaOlam beRosh HaShanah 5688." *haAretz*, September 26 1927.
Ahimeir, Abba. "Im Eyn Ani Li – Mi Li?" *haAretz*, November 15 1927.
Ahimeir, Abba. "Lean Peniah shel haDemokratiah Muadot." *haPoel haTza'ir* 42 (1926): 8–9.
Ahimeir, Abba. "Ra'yonot Bodedim 'al haFashizm." *haToren*, August 1923, 150–155.
Ahimeir, Abba. "Sotzializmus uFaschizmus." *haPoel haTza'ir* Year 20, no. 9 (1926): 11–12.
Arendt, Hannah. *On Revolution*. London: Penguin Books, 2006.
Benjamin, Walter. *Illuminations*. London: Fontana Press, 1992.
Chowers, Eyal. *The Political Philosophy of Zionism: Trading Jewish Words for a Hebraic Land*. Cambridge: Cambridge University Press, 2012.
Fowler, H. W., and F. G. Fowler, eds. *The Concise Oxford Dictionary of Current English*. Oxford: Clarendon Press, 1995.
Heller, Joseph. *The Stern Gang: Ideology, Politics and Terror, 1940–1949*. London: FrankCass, 1995.
Heller, Joseph.. "Weizmann, Jabotinsky and the Arab Question: The Peel Affair." *The Jerusalem Quarterly* 26 (Winter 1983): 109–126.
Hobsbawm, Eric J. "Revolution." In *Revolution In History*, edited by Roy Porter and MikulasTeich, 5–46. Cambridge: Cambridge University Press, 1994.
Kaplan, Eran. *The Jewish Radical Right: Revisionist Zionism and its Ideological Legacy*. Madison: University of Wisconsin Press, 2005.
Malia, Martin. *History's Locomotives: Revolutions and the Making of the Modern World*. New Haven and London: Yale University Press, 2006.
Mayer, Arno J. *The Furies: Violence and Terror in the French and Russian Revolutions*. Princeton: Princeton University Press, 2000.
Rabinovich, Itamar, and Jehuda Reinharz, eds. *Israel in the Middle East: Documents and Readings on Society, Politics, and Foreign Relations, Pre-1948 to the Present*. Waltham: Brandeis University Press, 2008.

Shimoni, Gideon. *The Zionist Ideology.* Hanover MA: Brandeis, 1995.
Shindler, Colin. *The Triumph of Military Zionism: Nationalism and the Origins of the IsraeliRight.* London, New York: I.B. Tauris, 2010.
Skocpol, Theda. *Social Revolutions in the Modern World.* Cambridge: Cambridge University Press, 1994.
Heller, Joseph. *States and Social Revolutions: A Comparative Analysis of France, Russia and China.* Cambridge: Cambridge University Press, 1979.
Sternhell, Ze'ev. "Fascism: Reflections on the Fate of Ideas in Twentieth Century History."*Journal of Political Ideologies* 5, no. 2 (2000): 139–162.
Tilley, Charles. Review of *History's Locomotives: Revolutions and the Making of the ModernWorld,* by Martin Malia. *American Historical Review* (October 2007): 1120–1122.
Walzer, Michael. *The Paradox of Liberation: Secular Revolutions and Religious Counterrevolutions.* New Haven and London: Yale University Press, 2015.

Jan Rybak

The Radical (Re-)Interpretation of Jewish Class and Nation

Poale Zion and the Revolutions of 1905 and 1917

> "Our national consciousness is negative in that it is emancipatory. If we were the proletariat of a free nation, which neither oppresses nor is oppressed, we would not be interested in the problems of national life."[1]

> "The social revolution is no dream any more, but an existing fact that needs to be reckoned with. But if the revolution has become a fact and socialism is not a utopia any more... what does one need Palestine for now?"[2]

Introduction

When the delegates of the World Union of Poale Zion ("Workers of Zion") gathered for their fifth world congress in Vienna in July 1920, everybody was aware that this would be a decisive moment in the history of the socialist-Zionist movement and the Jewish labor movement in general. Already in May 1919, the international leadership had written to Shlomo Kaplansky (1884–1950), one of its key figures: "The conference is a vital necessity for us. Our Union is threatened by a severe split. Certain parties of the East have come under undesirable influences and demand a complete reconstruction of our Union or the formation of a new one in order to fight the current one."[3] The "undesirable influences" the letter

1 Ber Borochov, "Our Platform (1906)," in *Class Struggle and the Jewish Nation: Selected Essays in Marxist Zionism*, ed. Mitchell Cohen (New Brunswick and London: Transaction Books, 1984), 89.

2 *Freie Tribüne*, November 22 1919, 3 ("Die soziale Revolution ist doch kein Traum mehr, sondern eine reale Tatsache, mit der gerechnet werden muß. Wenn aber die Revolution eine Tatsache geworden ist und der Sozialismus nicht mehr irgendwo in Utopia liegt, ... wozu braucht es jetzt Palästina?" Translation Jan Rybak).

3 Verbandsbureau des Allweltlichen Jüdischen Sozialistischen Arbeiterverbandes Poale Zion, *Letter to Shlomo Kaplansky, Stockholm*, May 24, 1919, Israel Labor Party Archive (Beit Berl), 1–10–1919–108 ("Die Konferenz ist eine Lebensnotwendigkeit für uns. In unserem Verbande droht eine schwere Spaltung einzutreten. Gewisse Parteien des Ostens sind unter ungewünschte Einflüsse geraten und wünschen völlige Umgestaltung unseres Verbandes oder die Gründung eines neuen zur Bekämpfung des gegenwärtigen." Translation JR).

https://doi.org/10.1515/9783110545753-004

referred to were connected to the European revolutionary processes, in which many activists of Poale Zion participated, and which often entailed dynamics that brought many of them to reassess their understanding of key elements of socialist-Zionist theory. Several scholars have discussed the split within the socialist-Zionist movement in the context of the Russian Revolution, focusing on both local cases of radicalization and differentiation, as well as the discussions between the left Poale Zion and the Communist International.[4]

This chapter analyzes the evolution of socialist-Zionist ideology in the context of the two defining revolutionary experiences in 1905 and 1917 and the following years. It juxtaposes the traditional socialist-Zionist understandings of the Jewish nation, the Jewish working class, and its relations, both with the wider labor movement and the national project in Palestine, as they had developed in the context of the 1905 revolution, with those new approaches, emerging out of the experiences of the new European revolutionary processes. This contribution asks what meanings activists attributed to the concepts of nation and territory and how the two related to the Jewish working class and its supposed revolutionary and national tasks. In many regards, the two quotations above represent the transformation of many socialist-Zionists' approach to the questions of Jewish nationality and territory. Both statements had been made in the context of major revolutionary events that had dramatic consequences for the Jewish populations in the affected regions. However, the conclusions the two authors, who were both activists of the same political movement, drew, were radically opposed to one another, with one arguing for the national program, the other questioning it. This chapter contextualizes the emergence of Poale-Zionist ideology during the first Russian Revolution of 1905, and its radical re-interpretation during the major revolutionary wave in Europe from 1917 onwards.

4 Amongst others: John Bunzl, *Klassenkampf in der Diaspora: Zur Geschichte der jüdischen Arbeiterbewegung* (Vienna: Europaverlag, 1975); Mario Keßler, *Zionismus und internationale Arbeiterbewegung 1897 bis 1933* (Berlin: Akademie Verlag, 1994); Mario Offenberg, *Kommunismus in Palästina: Nation und Klasse in der antikolonialen Revolution* (Meisenheim am Glan: Verlag Anton Hain, 1975); Sondra Miller Rubenstein, *The Communist Movement in Palestine and Israel, 1919–1984* (Boulder and London: Westview Press, 1985), 53–69; Thomas Soxberger, *Revolution am Donaukanal: Jiddische Kultur und Politik in Wien (1904–1938)* (Vienna: Mandelbaum, 2013), 112–138.

The Jewish Labor Movement

The traumatic experiences during the revolution of 1905 and subsequent turmoil in the Russian Empire led several actors to search for new political responses. Some of them eventually formulated an ideological synthesis of Jewish nationalism and socialism. Traditionally, such ideas had remained rather fringe phenomena in both the wider labor movement and in Jewish politics.[5] Whereas several activists, especially those organized in the *Algemeyner Yidisher Arbeter Bund* ("General Jewish Labor Bund"), founded in 1897, played a crucial role in the development of a distinctly Jewish labor movement, the references to Jewish national identity, and especially to the Yiddish language, remained largely instrumental for a long time. The nation and its claims were usually not perceived as ends in themselves. Only later, particular Jewish national concepts, especially Yiddishism, gained importance.[6]

The economic conditions of the Jewish population were decisive factors for the evolution of the Jewish labor movement and its political programs. The Jewish economy in the Russian Pale of Settlement, and to a lesser extent in Habsburg Galicia, was dominated by small-scale businesses, relegated to the lowest strata of the economic process.[7] In Russia, those conditions worsened in the last quarter of the nineteenth century, with the Jewish population and economy experiencing a decline and further marginalization.[8] Modern capitalist production rapidly destroyed the economic basis of many Jews and forced significant parts of the working population into low-level production, mostly of consumer goods, which mainly required manpower and little investment in constant cap-

5 Several authors have discussed Moses Hess as a pioneer of socialist Zionism. For example: Shlomo Avineri, *Profile des Zionismus: Die geistigen Ursprünge des Staates Israel – 17 Portraits* (Gütersloh: Gütersloher Verlagshaus, 1998), 53–64; Julius H. Schoeps, *Pioneers of Zionism: Hess, Pinkser, Rülf* (Berlin and Boston: De Gruyter, 2013), 11–33. Due to a lack of space and for the sake of a more coherent argument, I will refrain from discussing his influence, as well as that of Nachman Syrkin.

6 Amongst others: Jonathan Frankel, *Prophecy and Politics: Socialism, Nationalism, and the Russian Jews, 1862–1917* (Cambridge: Cambridge University Press, 1984), 207–208; Keßler, *Zionismus*, 51; Enzo Traverso, *The Marxists and the Jewish Question: The History of a Debate 1843–1943* (New York: Humanity Books, 1994), 97.

7 Yoav Peled, *Class and Ethnicity in the Pale: The Political Economy of Jewish Workers' Nationalism in Late Imperial Russia* (New York: Palgrave Macmillan, 1989), 5–30.

8 Antony Polonsky, "The New Jewish Politics and its Discontents," in *The Emergence of Modern Jewish Politics: Bundism and Zionism in Eastern Europe*, ed. Zvi Gitelman (Pittsburgh: University of Pittsburgh Press, 2003), 39; Jerry Z. Muller, *Capitalism and the Jews* (Princeton: Princeton University Press, 2010), 203–205.

ital (i.e. machines) to be produced.[9] The subsequent squeezing of Jewish industry by large-scale production led to a peculiar situation of small-scale industry with an excessive exploitation of the workforce. These circumstances were crucial for the fact that Jewish workers were amongst the first to organize against their employers.[10] Henry Tobias refers to three elements that led to the formation of the Jewish labor movement in the Pale: the anti-Jewish and economically regressive state, the large-scale economic competition and anti-Semitic sentiments by the gentile population, as well as the tight-knit but socially fragmented and authoritarian-led Jewish communities.[11] He argues: "The necessary catalyst was provided when developments in Russia caused the old relationships to break down, forcing a search for new responses and opening new horizons in the process."[12] However, the struggles of Jewish workers against their co-religionist employers often had the character of a "conflict of 'pauper and pauper'," as John Bunzl put it,[13] often with no or little gains, not least due to the poverty of the employers themselves. While the emerging Jewish socialist movement played a crucial part in the formation of the wider labor movement in the Russian Empire, its limitations soon became clear.[14]

The revolutionary events of 1905 put the Jewish labor movement in Russia in the contradictory position of both leading regional struggles and simultaneously being largely excluded from the central course of events. With the revolution's fate being decided outside the Pale of Settlement, Jewish revolutionary activism, as radical and as self-sacrificing as it was, could not influence the outcome of the revolution in a decisive way.[15] Even more important was the wave of anti-Semitic

---

9 Ezra Mendelsohn, *Class Struggle in the Pale: The Formative Years of the Jewish Workers' Movement in Tsarist Russia* (London and New York: Cambridge University Press, 1970), 4–7.

10 Ben Halpern and Jehuda Reinharz, "Nationalism and Jewish Socialism: The Early Years," *Modern Judaism* 8, no. 3 (1988): 220; Mendelsohn, *Class Struggle*, 28–29; Inna Shtakser, *The Making of Jewish Revolutionaries in the Pale of Settlement: Community and Identity during the Russian Revolution and its Immediate Aftermath, 1905–07* (New York: Palgrave Macmillan, 2014), 33–47; Scott Ury, "The Generation of 1905 and the Politics of Despair: Alienation, Friendship, Community," in *The Revolution of 1905 and Russia's Jews*, ed. Stefani Hoffman and Ezra Mendelsohn (Philadelphia: University of Pennsylvania Press, 2008), 104–105.

11 Henry J. Tobias, *The Jewish Bund in Russia: From its Origins to 1905* (Stanford: Stanford University Press, 1972), 1–6.

12 Ibid., 6.

13 Bunzl, *Klassenkampf*, 65 ("ein Konflikt zwischen 'Pauper und Pauper'" Translation JR).

14 Abraham Brumberg, "Anniversaries in Conflict: On the Centenary of the Jewish Socialist Labor Bund," *Jewish Social Studies*, New Series 5, no. 3 (1999): 197; Frankel, *Prophecy*, 207–208.

15 Bunzl, *Klassenkampf*, 97; Jonathan Frankel, *Crisis, Revolution, and the Russian Jews* (Cambridge: Cambridge University Press, 2009), 61–63; Simon Rabinovitch, *Jewish Rights, National Rites: Nationalism and Autonomy in Late Imperial and Revolutionary Russia* (Stanford: Stanford

pogroms that swept through the Pale in the aftermath of the revolution. Jewish self-defense became an important experience for many young revolutionaries who had to defend their communities, returning to their *shtetlekh* and neighborhoods, fighting on behalf of their community, defending Jews as Jews, rather than being engaged in a universal emancipatory struggle alongside gentile workers. Inna Shtakser showed how Jewish revolutionaries often remained the only ones defending the communities, with only occasional support from their gentile comrades, leading to disillusionment and a strengthening of their Jewish identities.[16] Eventually, the collapse of the revolution, the ineffectiveness of Jewish revolutionary activities, the pogroms, and Jewish self-defense not only led to the subsequent collapse of many organizations but forced several activists to rethink their traditional approach towards Jewish revolutionary activism.[17]

The Jewish Worker and the "Strategic Base" in Palestine

According to Jonathan Frankel, it was this experience during the revolutionary and counter-revolutionary phase of 1905–1907 that led Ber Borochov (1881–1917) to develop his concept of socialist-Zionism.[18] In contrast to romantic nationalists, Borochov formulated what he regarded as a materialist explanation and argument for proletarian Jewish nationalism.

Borochov saw the underlying problem of the Jewish workers' movement that while it could play an important political role in the Jewish street, its economic impact, due to the structure of Jewish economy, was as weak as its overall political impact.[19] Reflecting on this marginalization, he wrote in 1905: "The Jewish worker is not exploited by *gross Kapital;* his exploiter is the small capitalist whose role in the production is negligible. When the Jewish worker does go on

University Press, 2014), 85–87; Tobias, *Jewish Bund*, 299; Richard Wortman, "Nicholas II and the Revolution," in *The Revolution of 1905 and Russia's Jews*, ed. Stefani Hoffman and Ezra Mendelsohn (Philadelphia: University of Pennsylvania Press, 2008), 41.

16 Shtakser, *Making*, 131–141.

17 Vladimir Levin, "The Jewish Socialist Parties in Russia in the Period of Reaction," in *The Revolution of 1905 and Russia's Jews*, ed. Stefani Hoffman and Ezra Mendelsohn (Philadelphia: University of Pennsylvania Press, 2008), 112–117.

18 Frankel, *Prophecy*, 329–330.

19 Bunzl, *Klassenkampf*, 99; Keßler, *Zionismus*, 80–82.

strike against the industry which exploits him, he does not appreciably disturb the equilibrium of the country."[20]

Borochov and his comrades undertook the task of formulating an economic analysis of the Jewish people's conditions in order to demonstrate the necessity of concentrated emigration to Palestine. The key argument in his main 1906 work *Our Platform* was that due to the lack of a territory of its own, the Jewish economy was incapable of developing in a way that could provide a stable environment for the political and social life of the Jewish masses.[21] This was interpreted as a national problem, which required a national response. He opened his argument by declaring that "The national problem arises when the development of the nation's forces of production conflicts with the state of conditions of production."[22] According to him, these abnormal conditions (not primarily the political system of the Russian Empire) were responsible for Jewish misery and could only be overcome on a national basis by radically transforming the living conditions of the people.[23] The peculiar economic conditions of the Jews allegedly made it impossible for the Jewish proletariat to struggle successfully. It would, according to Borochov, first need to acquire a national "strategic base," by which he meant a national Jewish economy:

> The worker who is bound by his economic insecurity to the work place so that he cannot use it as a strategic base, is not in a position to carry on independent political action and can play no historical role. He is not master of his own fate. But when we speak of the proletariat as a class, we must exclude workers' competition for employment and imply only unconditional class solidarity in the struggle against capital. The worker is concerned with the place of work only insofar as he has not succeeded in entirely severing his relations with the proletarizing masses, to which he formerly belonged and into which he may be thrust again at some future time. The interests of the proletariat as a class are related

---

20 Ber Borochov, "Our Platform (1906)," in *Class Struggle and the Jewish Nation: Selected Essays in Marxist Zionism*, ed. Mitchell Cohen (New Brunswick and London: Transaction Books, 1984), 90. Emphasis here and in all following quotations in the original.

21 According to Yitzhak Ben-Zvi (1884–1963; the second president of the State of Israel), "Our Platform" was more a product of collective discussion than of Borochov's personal efforts. He remembered that after Poale Zion's founding conference at Poltava in 1906, party members gathered to discuss the program. While Borochov delivered drafts, they collectively discussed and changed the text, which later came to be known as "Our Platform". See: Izchak Ben-Zvi, "Labor Zionism in Russia," in *Russian Jewry (1860–1917)*, ed. Jacob Frumkin, Gregor Aronson, and Alexis Goldenweiser (London: Thomas Yoseloff, 1966), 215–216.

22 Borochov, *Our Platform*, 74.

23 Ibid., 75–78. Enzo Traverso has pointed out that while Borochov had taken the concept of conditions of production from Karl Marx, this had been only a minor element in Marx's overall work but became the key factor for him. Traverso, *Marxists*, 115.

> only to the strategic base – to those conditions under which it carries on its struggle against the bourgeoisie.
>
> The development of the forces of production of the masses who are forced to proletarization compels them to find a place to work; the development of the forces of production of the proletariat demands a normal strategic base for an effective class struggle.[24]

Borochov argued that without a stable national economy, productive forces could not develop and successful class struggle was impossible, since the workers would be incapable of carrying out effective industrial actions.[25] The competition between the workers of various nationalities was perceived as a given, unchangeable fact, implicitly ruling out the potential of multi-ethnic workers' organizations. In this regard, Borochov saw the national development and the development of the working class and its struggle as a uniform process. The goal was the "normalization" of the national conditions (i.e. the acquirement of a "strategic base") as a precondition for the development of effective class struggle.[26] However, Borochov at no point fully explained what "normality" ought to be. It is worth noticing, however, that the aim to "normalize" the conditions was not only prevalent amongst the Zionists, who wanted to "normalize" the Jewish people,[27] but the quest for "normalization" was a common trope amongst many Eastern-European socialists at the time.[28] The more Western European states, France, the United Kingdom, and especially Germany, seemed to

24 Borochov, *Our Platform*, 88.

25 Ibid., 81. It is quite striking – and can possibly be traced back to negative experiences during the 1905 revolution and the pogroms – that Borochov at no point discussed the idea of cross-national class-based solidarity or joint action. While he problematized "the Jewish worker's inability to face the competition of the non-Jewish worker" (Ibid.) he only saw a national solution to this problem and never discussed the potentials and limitations of multinational workers' organizations

26 Most explicitly: "Only with the proletariat is the national problem closely allied with the same strategic base, with the same imperatives of the class struggle upon which its class consciousness is built." Ibid., 89

27 Formulated the earliest and clearest by Leon Pinsker, *Auto-Emancipation! Mahnruf eines Stammesgenossen von einem russischen Juden* (Berlin: Kommissions-Verlag W. Issleib, 1882), 36.

28 Originally, Marx and Engels had assumed that the revolution would prevail "in all civilized countries, i.e. at least in England, America, France and Germany" ("in allen zivilisierten Ländern, d.h. wenigstens in England, Amerika, Frankreich und Deutschland" Translation JR), Friedrich Engels, "Grundsätze des Kommunismus," in *Karl Marx Friedrich Engels Werke*, Vol. 4 (Berlin: Dietz Verlag, 1959), 374. Following this assumption, Eastern-European followers of Marx and Engels put a lot of emphasis on the question of Russian backwardness and the necessity to overcome it; to "normalize" the situation, if you will. Most explicit in Vladimir I. Lenin, "Was sind die 'Volksfreunde' und wie kämpfen sie gegen die Sozialdemokraten," in W. I. Lenin, *Werke*, Vol. 1, 6th ed. (Berlin: Dietz Verlag, 1971), 119–338.

have been the role models, probably also because the German labor movement was the most developed, politically leading force in the Socialist International.

For Borochov, the shared economic situation of the Jewish people must necessarily lead to a shared national identity of all the members of a nation.[29] For him, "the proletariat is immediately related to nationalism and national property – to the territory. Since the proletariat participates in the production process, it must have an interest in the conditions of production. Therefore, there needs to be a specific type of proletarian nationalism."[30] Only once the question of territory and "strategic base" was solved would class-consciousness be able to develop and the nation's working class be able to struggle successfully.[31] According to Borochov, the non-proletarian classes also had a vested interest in establishing this "strategic base" to be able to compete with the capitalists of other nations. Eventually, the specific conditions of non-territorial and not independent nations would lead to a united form of nationalism, encompassing all classes. Even more: "Under such abnormal conditions, the interests of the classes of this nation become harmonious."[32] However, the standard-bearers of "real nationalism" could only be the proletariat and those classes closely connected to it. By struggling for national rights, they would fulfil a task on behalf of the entire nation:

> *Real nationalism* emerges amongst the progressive elements of an oppressed nation: real nationalism does not dream about maintaining traditions, does not make them bigger than they are, is not blinded by supposed national unity, understands the society's class structure, and does not try to gloss over the real interests of the various groups. Its only goal is the real liberation of the nation, the normalization of its modes and conditions of production.[33]

---

29 Ber Borochow, "Das Klasseninteresse und die nationale Frage (1905)," in *Klasse und Nation: Zur Theorie und Praxis des Jüdischen Sozialismus*, ed. Weltverband Hechaluz (Berlin: Hechaluz, 1932), 18.

30 Ibid., 21 ("das Proletariat steht in einer unmittelbaren Beziehung zum Nationalismus und zum nationalen Besitz – zum Territorium. Weil das Proletariat an der Produktion teilnimmt, muß es sich für die Produktionsbedingungen interessieren. Es muß deshalb ein gewisser proletarischer Typ des Nationalismus existieren." Translation JR).

31 Ibid., 37. In this context, Borochov also advocated for restrictions on labor migration.

32 Ibid., 43–44 ("Bei derartig anomalen Bedingungen werden die Interessen der Klassen dieser Nation harmonisch" Translation JR).

33 Ibid., 44–45)"Der reale Nationalismus entsteht bei den fortschrittlichen Elementen einer unterdrückten Nation: realer Nationalismus träumt nicht von der Erhaltung der Traditionen, macht sie nicht größer als sie sind, läßt sich von der scheinbaren nationalen Einigkeit nicht täuschen, versteht die Klassenstruktur der Gesellschaft und versucht nicht, die realen Interessen der verschiedenen Gruppen zu vertuschen. Sein Ziel ist allein die reale Befreiung der Nation, die Normalisierung der Produktionsbedingungen und -verhältnisse." Translation JR).

For Poale-Zionists, the key to reaching the national goal of "normalization" was the transformation of Jewish economic conditions towards a "productive life" in a national territory. In a series of articles published in 1916, Borochov discussed the problem of Jewish economic conditions as being estranged from natural resources (i.e. land) from which, according to him, economic potency and independence originated.[34] He argued that "history was driving the Jews further and further away from soil and nature and higher and higher into the insubstantial ether of social stratification"[35] and concluded: "The landlessness of the Jewish people is the source of its malady and tragedy. We have no territory of our own, hence we are by necessity divorced from nature."[36] From this analysis, Borochov derived the necessity to return to the soil in order to make Jewish labor productive. Although he put it in quasi-Marxist terminology and insisted on the materialist character of his analysis, the conclusion eventually resembled that of romantic nationalist Aaron David Gordon (1856–1922), who characterized the Jewish people as such in 1911:

> A people, completely torn away from nature, for millennia imprisoned behind walls; a people used to all kinds of life but a natural life of work by and for itself – cannot become a living, natural, working people without all of its willpower. We are lacking the most important thing: labor – not forced [labor] but [labor] to which man is organically and naturally connected to, through which the people can connect to his soil and to its culture, which is rooted in soil and labor.[37]

This emphasis on the soil, nature, and agricultural labor, which appears "natural" in the organic-nationalist, anti-modernist context of Gordon, seems somewhat misplaced in the strictly orthodox-Marxist self-perception of Borochov's

---

34 Ber Borochov, "The Economic Development of the Jewish People (1916)," in *Class Struggle and the Jewish Nation: Selected Essays in Marxist Zionism*, ed. Mitchell Cohen (New Brunswick and London: Transaction Books, 1984), 169–171.

35 Ibid., 173.

36 Ibid., 175.

37 Aaron David Gordon, "Arbeit," in *A.D. Gordon Erlösung durch Arbeit: Ausgewählte Aufsätze* (Berlin: Jüdischer Verlag, 1929), 65 ("Ein Volk, das ganz von der Natur losgerissen ist, das jahrtausendelang hinter Mauern eingesperrt war; ein Volk, das an alle Arten des Lebens gewöhnt war, nur nicht an eine natürliche, an ein Leben der Arbeit aus sich heraus und für sich, – kann nicht ohne Anspannung seiner ganzen Willenskraft, wieder ein lebendiges, natürliches, arbeitendes Volk werden. Uns fehlt das Wesentliche: die Arbeit, – nicht die aus Zwang, sondern die, mit der sich der Mensch organisch und natürlich verbunden fühlt durch die das Volk mit seinem Boden und seiner in Boden und Arbeit wurzelnden Kultur verwachsen kann." Translation JR).

Poale Zion.[38] How far arguments suggesting that the future development of capitalism would increase the importance of agriculture were actually inspired by materialist considerations is secondary, insofar as they served to legitimize the argument for the national project: that only through the acquisition of a "strategic base" (i.e. land and a national economy) in Palestine could the Jewish workers gain agency as a class.[39] The eventual argument for Zionist agrarian labor, colonization, and national rebirth, brought forward here by Leon Chasanowich (1882–1925), a leading member of Poale Zion's World Union, equaled that of Gordon:

> The agriculture of no country ... fits the Jewish people's character as well as the intensive agriculture of Palestine, which demands a lot of intellectual but little physical effort from the settlers (which is important for a people of the city that is gradually transforming), it additionally allows living together closely which is an important precondition for the flourishing of Jewish colonization.[40]

In order to obtain the supposedly required 'strategic base', the Jews would need to acquire their own territory through concentrated emigration. Borochov argued that emigration without a well-directed development of a Jewish national economy would not solve the problem since "the Jewish problem migrates with the Jews."[41] The only way to develop a strategic base for the Jewish working class would be the gathering of Jews in one territory. In regard to the migratory process, however, Borochov remained rather vague. He argued that migration of labor would always follow the migration of capital[42] and capital would currently be interested in investing in underdeveloped regions, since "international capital

38 Zeev Sternhell, *The Founding Myths of Israel: Nationalism, Socialism, and the Making of the Jewish State* (Princeton: Princeton University Press, 1999), 25. Traditionally, Marxists had emphasized the general tendency that agriculture would lose its economic importance while modern industry would increasingly become the absolute dominant force in capitalism.

39 Leon Chasanowitsch, "Ziele und Mittel des sozialistischen Zionismus," *Sozialistische Monatshefte*, July 1914, 962–973.

40 Ibid., 970 ("Die Landwirtschaft keines der ... Länder so sehr dem jüdischen Volkscharakter angepaßt ist wie die intensive Agrikultur Palästinas, die wohl große Ansprüche an die Intelligenz der Ansiedler stellt, dagegen weniger physische Anstrengungen erfordert (was für das physisch sich nur allmählich umbildende Stadtvolk von Bedeutung ist), ferner ein enges soziales Zusammenleben erlaubt und damit eine wichtige Voraussetzung für das Gedeihen einer jüdischen Kolonisation erfüllt." Translation JR).

41 Borochov, *Our Platform*, 82.

42 Aside from Borochov's (incorrect) reference to Marx (on page 93), Amos Perlmutter has pointed out that concepts which were developed in the so-called Mikhailovsky school of sociology and economics in Russia had great influence on him. See Amos Perlmutter, "Dov Ber-Borochov: A Marxist-Zionist Ideologist," *Middle Eastern Studies* 5, no. 1 (1969): 40.

began to look for new investment channels and turned to financing agricultural projects."[43] He was convinced that all the necessary conditions for such an investment could be found in Palestine:

> The country in which Jews immigrate will not be highly industrial nor predominantly agricultural but rather semi-agricultural. Jews alone will migrate there, separated from the general stream of immigration. This country will have no attraction for immigrants from other nations, and will be the only one available to the Jews ... It will be a land of low cultural and political development. Big capital will hardly find use for itself there, while Jewish small and middle capital will find a market for its products in both this country and its environs. The land of spontaneously concentrated Jewish immigration will be Palestine.[44]

The main task of the national movement was therefore to direct Jewish migration to Palestine,[45] although he insisted that he had not chosen the region because of national emotions: "Our Palestinianism is not a matter of principle, because it has nothing to do with old traditions."[46] Borochov, at least at this point, argued for Palestine as the most practical territory with a low population density and no strong economy that would pose a threat to Jewish businesses – and therefore to the "strategic base".[47] With the development of the Zionist labor movement, some aspects of Borochov's theory, especially those related to Palestine and the definition of the Jewish nation, were abandoned rather quickly. Whereas Borochov had applied a very rigid economic concept, Shlomo Kaplansky, the leader of Poale Zion in the Habsburg Empire at the time and key figure of the party's World Union, developed the economic aspect towards a general-national one, as he stated: "The Jewish nation is situated in many countries... yet nevertheless is united nationally by the common conditions of development of its productive life, as well as by its history, traditions and culture."[48] This argument shows that for many activists the nation and its territory were often more than just an instrumental aspect on the way to socialism, but increasingly a value in itself.

One of the key dilemmas socialist-Zionism faced throughout its existence was balancing between its nation- and its class-based aims. Although Borochov

---

43 Borochov, *Our Platform*, 96.

44 Ibid., 98.

45 Ibid., 93–98.

46 Ibid., 100.

47 Ibid., 98–99.

48 Shlomo Kaplansky, "HaTazkir haRishon leMisrad haInternatzional haSotzialisti (1907) (The First Memorandum to the International Socialist Bureau)," in *Hazon veHagashma* (*Vision and Fulfillment*), ed. Shlomo Kaplansky (Merhavia: Sifriyat HaPoalim, 1950), 135, quoted in Gideon Shimoni, *The Zionist Ideology* (Hanover, NH: Brandeis University Press, 1995), 191.

in a 1905 essay had portrayed the various classes' approaches to nationalism and had stated that it was only the proletariat which could – through class struggle – fulfil Zionism and socialism,[49] problems occurred on a practical level; however, this was the essence of socialist-Zionism. Borochov wrote:

> "We are Social Democrats and we are Jews." Our national consciousness is negative in that it is emancipatory. If we were the proletariat of a free nation, which neither oppresses nor is oppressed, we would not be interested in the problems of national life. Even now, when under the pressure of national conflicts, we have acquired national consciousness, spiritual culture concerns us less than social and economic problems. Ours is a realistic nationalism, free from any "spiritual" admixture.[50]

He therefore regarded Zionism as a "minimal program," a necessary precondition for the final goal, socialism.[51] While Poale Zion regarded the class-based struggles in the Diaspora to be important, at least in theory, they had to remain somewhat subjugated to the national aims, which were of course not defined by spiritual or emotional desires, but their fulfilment was necessary for achieving meaningful goals. This theory implicitly excluded the possibility of successful class struggles by Jewish workers before the "minimal program" had been fulfilled.

Over the years, the materialist-economic argument put forward by proletarian-Zionism Borochov had evolved. While the traditional theory was upheld, practical considerations turned the national "strategic base" in Palestine increasingly into an end in itself. In a 1917 essay, probably with the original title "Palestine in Our Program and Tactics,"[52] Borochov argued for more ideological

---

49 Borochow, *Klasseninteresse*, 27–39.

50 Borochov, *Our Platform*, 89.

51 Ber Borochov, "Die Grundlagen des Poale-Zionismus," in *Die Grundlagen des Poale-Zionismus*, ed. Dan Diner (Frankfurt: Borochov-Press, 1969), 72–73. This part is not included in the English-language edition of the text by Cohen.

52 Ber Borochow, "Palästina in unserem Programm und unserer Taktik," in *Sozialismus und Zionismus: Eine Synthese*, ed. Mendel Singer (Vienna: Verlag Zukunft, 1932), 255–259. Mendel Singer, who edited the text in 1932 on behalf of the Austrian Poale Zion, used the term "Palästina." The collection of texts published by the *Hechaluz* ("pioneer") group in Berlin in the same year also uses the term "Palästina". See Ber Borochow, "Palästina in unserem Programm und in unserer Taktik (1917)," in *Klasse und Nation: Zur Theorie und Praxis des Jüdischen Sozialismus*, ed. Weltverband Hechaluz (Berlin: Hechaluz, 1932), 99–103. Other editors used the phrase "Eretz Israel in Our Program, and Tactics" as a title, replacing "Palästina" with "Eretz Israel" throughout the text, thereby suggesting a more romantic-Zionist tone. For example: Mitchell Cohen and Ber Borochov, "Eretz Israel in Our Program and Tactics (1917)," in *Class Struggle and the Jewish Nation: Selected Essays in Marxist Zionism*, ed. Mitchell Cohen (New Brunswick

flexibility and an increased openness to nationalist feelings, since the materialist-economic concept had allegedly already been introduced to a wider public: "Henceforth, it is required to use a new, richer terminology. We are allowed to and must speak in an emotional terminology. Now we can and must employ an emotional language, now we can and shall say: 'Palestine. A Jewish home!'"[53]

The harmonious unity between nationalism and socialism, Palestine and the Diaspora, which had always been proclaimed by Poale Zion, turned out to be a rather tense relation, when clear decisions for either one side were required. In practice, the problem of the relation between socialism and nationalism could not simply be dismissed, as Borochov did, by saying "We are 100 percent socialist and 100 percent Zionist."[54] The problem became most obvious at election times in the Habsburg Empire. While it was easy when notorious anti-Semites, such as the Ernst Schneider (1850–1913) in Vienna or Karel Baxa (1863–1938) in Prague were standing against Social Democrats in the elections to the *Reichsrat* ("Imperial Council") in 1907, when all Jewish organizations unanimously endorsed the latter,[55] other cases turned out to be a lot more difficult and sparked internal debates. When a non-Jewish or non-Zionist Social Democrat was standing against a bourgeois Zionist, Poale Zion's activists had to make a clear decision between their class-based and their national affiliations. In 1907, the party mostly opted to endorse the Zionist candidates. In Galicia, they explicitly called to vote for the Jewish National Party against the candidates of the Social Democrats, accusing their candidate Herman Diamand (1860–1931) of "assimilationism" which was perceived as treacherous.[56] This decision for a bourgeois Zionist

---

and London: Transaction Books, 1984), 201–203. Cohen's translation is based on a collection of Borochov's writings, which was published in Yiddish by Berl Locker in New York in 1928. The essay's title therein is "Erets Israel in undzer program un taktik." It can be found in: Berl Locker, ed., *Ber Borochov: Geklibene Shriftn* (*Selected Writings*) (New York: Astoria Press, 1928), 271–274.

53 Borochow, *Palästina*, 256 ("Nunmehr gibt sich das Bedürfnis kund, in einer neuen, reicheren Terminologie zu sprechen. Wir dürfen und müssen uns jetzt auch der Gefühlssprache bedienen, jetzt können und dürfen wir sagen: Palästina. Eine jüdische Heimstätte!" Translation JR). Cohen's translation differs slightly, especially the final words: "Eretz Israel – a Jewish home!" Borochov, *Eretz Israel*, 201–202.

54 Ber Borochov, "The Socialism of Poale Zion Here (1915)," in *Class Struggle and the Jewish Nation: Selected Essays in Marxist Zionism*, ed. Mitchell Cohen (New Brunswick and London: Transaction Books, 1984), 155–162. Prior to that, Borochov had criticized those of his comrades who described themselves as 85 percent Zionists and 15 percent Socialists. Ibid., 158.

55 Adolf Gaisbauer, *Davidstern und Doppeladler: Zionismus und jüdischer Nationalismus in Österreich 1882–1918* (Vienna: Böhlau Verlag, 1988), 371. Ernst Schneider lost the elections by a margin of 0.3 percent; Karel Baxa was elected.

56 Joshua Shanes, *Diaspora Nationalism and Jewish Identity in Habsburg Galicia* (Cambridge: Cambridge University Press, 2012), 220–221, 245–246.

against a socialist candidate in return led to massive criticism within the party and forced it to change its tactics. The elections to the *Reichsrat* in 1911 saw the party's endorsement of the prominent Social Democrat Friedrich Austerlitz (1862–1931)[57] against the leading bourgeois Zionist Robert Stricker (1879–1944) in the Vienna-Leopoldstadt constituency.[58]

Similar problems, although with less political ramifications, often arose when Jewish workers went on strike against Jewish entrepreneurs who often belonged to the Zionist movement. This was the case, for instance, when in October 1904 Jewish shop workers went on strike to reduce working hours. In the East Galician city of Stanislau/Stanisławów/Stanyslawiw, a number of shop owners were members of Zionist organizations. Still, the striking workers were supported by Poale Zion.[59] When in early 1914 printers, many of them Jewish, some even members of Poale Zion, went on strike in East Galicia, they found themselves in direct opposition to the general-Zionists, whose paper, the *Togblat* ("Daily Paper") in Lemberg/Lwów/L'viv continued to be published. Poale Zion attacked the paper's editor-in-chief Moshe Frostig (1887–1928), as a leading strike-breaker, and accused the entire bourgeois-Zionist leadership as being anti-working-class agitators.[60] This delicate balance between national- and class-oriented identities and political practices was profoundly shaken by the revolutionary upheavals of 1917 and the following years, leading many activists to rethink and reinterpret their programmatic concepts.

The Second Revolution: Class and Nation Reconsidered

Although Poale Zion's program regarded the establishment of a "strategic base" to be a precondition for the development of a potent Jewish revolutionary movement, Poale Zionists in the Diaspora constantly participated in strikes and pro-

57 Austerlitz had a Jewish background but had officially renounced his religious affiliation in 1898. He was chief editor of the Social Democratic Labor Party's central daily *Arbeiterzeitung* ("Workers' Paper").

58 Gaisbauer, *Davidstern*, 404–405.

59 Ibid., 400. The same happened again in 1911. See the Ministry of Interior's report: Präsidium des k. k. Ministeriums des Inneren, *Bericht Strafsache: Ausschreitungen bei Streik/Demonstration der Handelsangestellten in Stanislau*, November 5, 1911, Austrian State Archive (Vienna), Allgemeines Verwaltungsarchiv, Inneres MdI Präsidium A2114.

60 Anonymous, "Das Lemberger Tagblatt und der Druckerstreik," *Neuer Weg: Jüdische sozialistische Zeitschrift*, February 1914, 7.

tests in their respective home countries. This activism reached its climax during the revolutionary upheavals in Russia and then throughout Central and Eastern Europe from 1917 onwards.[61] In Russia, Poale Zion was the only Jewish party whose majority came out in full support of the Bolsheviks, as early as late spring 1917.[62] The party later even founded a Jewish-only battalion, the "Borochov-Unit", mainly made up of members of Poale Zion, which was part of the Red Army.[63] The Russian party eventually split into a Social-democratic and a communist organization.[64] In some regions of the Habsburg Empire, local activists of Poale Zion played a certain role in the organization of the major strike wave that shook the country in January 1918.[65] From late October onwards, the movement came to be an integral part of the Austrian workers' councils' movement and developed close links with other – non-Jewish, and non-Zionist – revolutionary actors on the ground.[66] Similar radicalization processes could be observed in Latvia[67] and Poland,[68] as well as slightly later in Czechoslovakia[69] and Bukovina.[70] In the Viennese party's paper, which came to be the mouthpiece of the radical left within Poale Zion, an activist appealed to the city's Jewish workers:

---

61 See the special issue: *Arbeit – Bewegung – Geschichte: Zeitschrift für Historische Studien* 2 (2017): *Judentum und Revolution: Der Weltverband der Poale Zion zwischen Zionismus und Kommunismus.*

62 Poale Zion, *Dray Rezolutsiym* (Three Resolutions) (Warsaw: Farlag Arbeiterheim, 1918).

63 Oleg Budnitskii, *Russian Jews Between the Reds and the Whites, 1917–1920* (Philadelphia: University of Pennsylvania Press, 2012), 369–371; Baruch Gurevitz and Dominique Négrel, "Un cas de communisme national en Union Soviétique Le Poale Zion: 1918–1928," *Cahiers du Monde russe et soviétique* 15, no. 3/4 (1974): 342.

64 Zvi Y. Gitelman, *Jewish Nationality and Soviet Politics: The Jewish Section of the CPSU, 1917–1930* (Princeton: Princeton University Press, 1972), 215–217.

65 Bunzl, *Klassenkampf*, 125–128; David Rechter, *The Jews of Vienna and the First World War* (Oxford: The Littman Library of Jewish Civilization, 2008), 58–59.

66 Hans Hautmann, *Geschichte der Rätebewegung in Österreich 1918–1924* (Vienna: Europaverlag, 1987), 369, 370, 519; Soxberger, *Revolution*, 112–171.

67 Ebreju sociāldemokrātiskā strādnieku partija "Polei-Zion" Riga, *Letter to Ignatz Kornfeld*, November 27 1918, Israel Labor Party Archive (Beit Berl), 1–1–1917–3.

68 Ignatz Kornfeld, *Letter to Berl Locker*, May 20 1919, Israel Labor Party Archive (Beit Berl), 1–10–1918–117.

69 Josef Reiss, *Letter to Verbandsbureau der der Jüdisch-sozialistischen Arbeiterpartei Poale Zion*, September 11 1920, Israel Labor Party Archive (Beit Berl), 1–3–1919–22.

70 Jüdische Sozialistische Arbeiterpartei "Poale-Zion" Czernowitz, *Letter to Verbandsbureau der Jüdisch-sozialistischen Arbeiterpartei Poale Zion in Berlin*, March 14 1920, Israel Labor Party Archive (Beit Berl), 1–10–1917–120.

> The old [order] is dead. We want to dig a deep grave for it. But together with the old [order] its accomplices must perish from the stage of history. The new generation must create a new world in its own image, and this is why the German-Austrian Social Democracy's second revolutionary act should not have been a bourgeois-reactionary National Assembly but a socialist-revolutionary workers' council. Those men who were elected before the war and who are responsible for it will not lead the people into the Promised Land! No! Freely elected representatives of the working class must take the people's destiny in their own hands in this historic moment. Never again shall a capitalist system which has brought such a catastrophe for the people come to power! No! Only the proletariat, which had warned of the war, fought and bled, it alone has the right to build a society where there is no master and no slave and where there will never be war again. And the proletariat not only has the right but the power to do that. That is why: All power to the freely elected workers' councils![71]

Not only would the old Social-democratic leadership not be able to lead the masses into the "promised land", but the "promised land" itself was now discussed as something completely different; not Palestine, but a – geographically not defined – socialist society. This radicalization process, reflected in the Viennese party's paper, generally entailed the shift of attention towards the European revolution, and away from Palestine.[72] Contrary to the years 1905 to 1907, activists found themselves at the heart of the revolution, often struggling alongside the workers of other nationalities, and – most importantly – they seemed to succeed in their revolutionary efforts.[73] In Soviet Russia, the revolution had abolish-

---

71 Alexander Serpow, "Der Weg der Revolution," *Freie Tribüne*, February 7 1919, 2 ("Das Alte ist tot. Wir wollen ihm ein tiefes Grab schaufeln. Mit dem Alten müssen aber auch alle seine Helfershelfer von der historischen Bühne verschwinden Das neue Geschlecht muß sich selbst seine neue Welt in eigener Gestalt schaffen und deshalb hätte der zweite Revolutionsakt der deutschösterreichischen Sozialdemokratie nicht eine bürgerlich reaktionäre Nationalversammlung sein dürfen sondern ein sozialistisch-revolutionärer Arbeiterrat. Nicht jene Männer, die vor dem Kriege gewählt wurden und für diesen mitverantwortlich sind, werden das Volk jetzt in das gelobte Land führen können. Nein! Freigewählte Vertreter der Arbeiterklasse haben in diesem großen historischen Moment das Schicksal des Volkes in ihre Hand zu nehmen. Es soll nie wieder das kapitalistische System, das das Volk in eine solche Katastrophe verwickelt hat, zur Macht kommen. Nein. Das Proletariat, das vor dem Kriege gewarnt hat, kämpfte und blutete, nur dieses allein hat das Recht, eine Gesellschaftsordnung aufzubauen, in der es weder arm noch reich, weder Herr noch Knecht, und daher auch keine Kriege geben wird. Und das Proletariat hat nicht nur das Recht, sondern auch die Macht, es zu vollziehen. Deshalb: die ganze Macht dem freigewählten Arbeiterrate!" Translation JR). The article had already been written in November 1918.

72 Christian Dietrich, "Zwischen Sowjetrussland und Eretz Israel: Die Radikalisierung des österreichischen Arbeiterzionismus 1918 bis 1920," *Arbeit – Bewegung – Geschichte: Zeitschrift für Historische Studien* 2 (2017): 49–64.

73 See for example the memoirs of Hersch Mendel, then a member of the Bund, recalling the joint struggle of Jewish (including Poale Zionist) and non-Jewish revolutionaries, both in Russia

ed all anti-Semitic laws, the Bolsheviks regarded anti-Semitism as a criminal counterrevolutionary act, and – at least formally – granted autonomous rights to Jewish (Yiddishist) groups. During the civil war, the Red Army often came to be the only force not systematically engaging in pogroms, often the only force that could protect Jews.[74]

Eventually, an increasing number of Poale Zionists asked themselves whether the triumphant revolution in Europe did not in fact disprove the Borochovist paradigm. Could nationalism or the acquisition of a strategic base still be considered a precondition for socialism? Already in November 1919 an anonymous author raised doubts in the *Freie Tribüne* ("Free Tribune", the paper of the Viennese Poale Zion):

> The social revolution is no dream any more, but an existing fact that needs to be reckoned with. But if the revolution has become a fact and socialism is not a utopia any more... what does one need Palestine for? We never wanted it because of our love and admiration for Grandmother Rachel's grave as a precondition for socialism, which proclaims the right to work. Now, are the motives of "non-industrialization" and "national competition" [the problems that required the "strategic base"; JR] not losing their importance, especially now since the Jewish bourgeoisie will not be able to build the national home since it has lost its function as the bearers of capitalism?[75]

In March 1920, M. S., probably Malke Schorr (1885–1961), one of the few leading female activists in the Austrian Poale Zion, asked whether now, in the situation of the unfolding socialist revolution, the old idea of building Palestine could still be seen as precondition for the participation of the Jewish working class in the

---

and in Poland. Hersch Mendel, *Erinnerungen eines jüdischen Revolutionärs* (Cologne: Neuer ISP Verlag, 2004).

74 Budnitskii, *Russian Jews*, 95; Gitelman, *Jewish Nationality*, 105–139; Kenneth B. Moss, *Jewish Renaissance in the Russian Revolution* (Cambridge: Harvard University Press, 2009), 262–263; Peter Kenez, "Pogroms and White Ideology in the Russian Civil War," in *Pogroms: Anti-Jewish Violence in Modern Russian History*, ed. John D. Klier and Shlomo Lambroza (Cambridge: Cambridge University Press, 1992), 300–301; David Shneer, *Yiddish and the Creation of Soviet Jewish Culture, 1918–1930* (Cambridge: Cambridge University Press, 2004), 41–43.

75 "Der proletarische Palästinismus im Lichte der sozialen Revolution," *Freie Tribüne*, November 22 1919, 3 ("Die soziale Revolution ist doch kein Traum mehr, sondern eine reale Tatsache, mit der gerechnet werden muß. Wenn aber die Revolution eine Tatsache geworden ist und der Sozialismus nicht mehr irgendwo in Utopia liegt, [...] wozu braucht es jetzt Palästina? Wir wollen es ja nicht aus Liebe und Verehrung für Urmutter Rachels Grab sondern als Vorbedingung für den Sozialismus, der das Recht auf Arbeit dekretiert. Es müssen doch also auch die Motive der 'Nichtindustrialisierung', der 'nationalen Konkurrenz' u.s.w. fortfallen und vor allem kann doch nicht jetzt die jüdische Bourgeoisie das Zentrum schaffen, da sie ja als Trägerin des Kapitalismus ihre Funktion verloren hat?" Translation JR).

struggle for socialism: "If additionally, one takes into account the fact that once the social revolution has begun, the Palestinian settlement as a precondition for future class struggle completely loses its relevance, [then] the problem of the colonization of Palestine remains only current insofar as it can serve as one assembly point for potential migratory movement."[76] At the fifth congress of the World Union of Poale Zion, which was held in Vienna in July 1920, the contradicting understandings of Jewish nationalism and its role in the revolutionary process clashed in its most open form. Alexander Chaschin (Zvi Auerbach; 1888–1938), a delegate of the Russian Jewish Communist Party (Poale Zion), stated: "First, I want to make it clear that as far as the Jewish question is a political [one] and not an economic question or of a certain cultural development, it had been liquidated completely in Soviet Russia. In a political sense, there is no Jewish Question within the borders of Soviet Russia."[77] He insisted that it was very likely that the remaining economic and cultural questions could be solved within Soviet Russia, for example through the establishment of Jewish agricultural colonies in the country.[78] One of his comrades insisted on the need of transforming Jewish economic life, making it "productive", especially after the destructions of the civil war, but suggested this could also be done in the Soviet state: "The massive destruction is just a transitional phase. We are sure that as soon as... everyone has returned from the front, the Jewish masses and parties will recognize the importance [or concept; JR] of Jewish economic work. It is our task to make those masses productive."[79]

For many, the idea of the transformation of the Jewish masses, to make them "productive", remained a central feature of their ideology. However, the context

---

76 M(alke) S(chorr), "Revisionismus? Palästina in unserem Programm," *Freie Tribüne*, March 6 1920, 3 ("Wenn man aber außerdem die Tatsache in Betracht zieht, daß im Moment, als die soziale Revolution ihr Werk begonnen hat, die palästinensische Siedlung als Voraussetzung für den künftigen Klassenkampf vollständig gegenstandslos würde, verbleibt das Problem der Kolonisation Palästinas nur insoferne aktuell, als dieses Land als einer der Sammelpunkte für die eventuelle Wanderung in Betracht kommt." Translation JR).

77 *Minutes of the Fifth World Congress of the World Union of Poale Zion in Vienna*, July 1920, Pinhas Lavon Institute Archive (Tel Aviv), III 11–1–36, 283 ("Zuerst möchte ich feststellen, dass die jüdische Frage in Räterussland, soweit sie eine politische ist und keine Frage der Ökonomik oder einer gewissen kulturellen Entwicklung vollständig liquidiert worden ist. Politisch existiert innerhalb der Grenzen Räte-Russlands keine Judenfrage." Translation JR).

78 Ibid., 284–285.

79 Ibid., 252 ("Der gewaltige Zerstörungsmoment ist nur eine Übergangszeit. Wir sind sicher, dass [...] wenn alles von der Front heimkehren wird, werden die juedischen Massen und Parteien das Moment der juedischen ökonomischen Arbeit anerkennen müssen. Unsere Aufgabe ist es jetzt jene Massen zu produktivieren." Translation JR).

in which this was imagined, and the political conclusions drawn from it were radically different. No longer could this transformation only take place in the context of an acquired "strategic base" in Palestine, and more importantly, it was no longer a precondition for participation in the revolution, but rather an anticipated outcome of it. The same was true for Palestine itself. Hardly any of the Central and Eastern European parties had been engaged in Palestine-oriented work during the revolutionary period, a fact for which they received heavy criticism from their comrades in other countries.[80] A delegate complained that the Austrian party had told him that as long as British imperialism had not been thrown out of Palestine, they would not want to have anything to do with it.[81] The Palestinian delegates of Achdut haAvodah ("Unity of Labor") suspected those Eastern European parties of boycotting the work in Palestine for the sake of the struggle against imperialism and for the communist revolution. Yitzhak Tabenkin (1888–1971) denounced "this Eastern Jewish politics as what it is; treason to our cause."[82] Nahum Rafalkes (Nir; 1884–1968) from Poland replied: "Com[rade] Tabenkin does not care about anything that is happening throughout the world, he only sees Palestine. The entire world needs to be transformed in the way the comrades in Palestine would like it."[83]

While Borochov had traditionally assumed that a Jewish homeland was a precondition for successful struggle, now the successful revolution was regarded by many as the precondition for an independent Jewish commonwealth in Palestine, as *Freie Tribüne* suggested: "The active struggle of the Jewish proletariat for the proletarian world revolution, a self-conscious global Jewish workers' organization, and our World Union as its vanguard, are the means and the way that lead us to the realization of proletarian Zionism."[84] This did not only relegate the idea of Palestine to a lesser important part of the program, but funda-

80 Ibid., 46–48. According to a delegate, the Austrian activists were actively discouraging members from leaving for Palestine, telling them about high unemployment and malaria in the country.

81 Ibid., 68.

82 Ibid., 367 ("Die juedische Politik im Osten muss klargestellt werden. Sie ist ein vollständiger Verrat unserer Sache." Translation JR).

83 Ibid., 369 ("Den Gen. Tabenkin kuemmert wieder ueberhaupt nicht, was in der Welt vorgeht, er sieht nur Palästina. Alles in der Welt muss umgebaut werden, wie die Genossen in Palästina es wollen." Translation JR).

84 Anonymous, "Probleme der jüdischen Arbeiterbewegung: VII Die Realisierung des Zionismus," *Freie Tribüne*, April 3 1920, 2. ("Aktiver Kampf des jüdischen Proletariats für die proletarische Weltrevolution, eine auf sich selbst vertrauende jüdische Arbeiter-Weltorganisation und unser Weltverband als zielbewußte Vorhut derselben, das sind in großen Umrissen Mittel und Weg, die uns zur Realisierung des proletarischen Zionismus führen." Translation JR).

mentally changed the construction of socialist-Zionist self-definition in relation to territory and the ability to struggle. At the congress, the members of the movement's more right-wing faction, such as Aharon Reuveni (1886–1971), a delegate from Palestine, strongly refuted this revision of concepts: "He [Chaschin] thinks that later if there will be a Soviet government, it will use its assets to build a Jewish home in Palestine. This is a belief which reminds us of the pious Jews who are waiting for the messiah."[85] Similarly, Ignacy Schiper (1884–1943) criticized his fellow Polish comrades for what he saw as revolutionary overenthusiasm: "The Polish comrades are currently at the heart of a struggle where every perception of reality gets lost, a struggle fought with blindfolded eyes, which confuses the psyche and in which everyone is throwing around phrases about the social revolution."[86] Perceiving the world revolution as a precondition for the creation of a Jewish home in Palestine and not vice versa, as a delegate from the Social-Democratic Russian Poale Zion party argued, would mean to "lose the Poale-Zionist ground and add putschism to it."[87]

As it has been mentioned above, the experience of successful joint struggles of Jewish and gentile revolutionaries alongside each other essentially questioned the necessity of a distinct national solution for the specific conditions of the Jewish working class. A Russian delegate argued: "The Jewish proletariat is not the leader of the Russian Revolution. But it marches alongside the Russian proletariat in one front, in all its revolutionary tasks and appearances."[88] For him, this entailed a reformulation of the relations between the concepts of class and nation, overturning the classical understanding of this relation, arguing, that the (proletarian) nation would be constituted after the victory of the revolution:

> Whereas the working class is liberated, it also needs to be liberated as a national class. The working class [then] constitutes itself as the nation ... The Jewish working class must be part of the III. International. Because it will [then] have more influence, because there is

---

85 *Minutes of the Fifth World Congress of the World Union of Poale Zion in Vienna*, 291 ("Er denkt später, wenn die Sowjetregierung sein wird, wird mit ihren Mitteln und ihrer Kraft eine juedische Heimat in Palästina aufgebaut werden. Das ist eine Vorstellung, welche uns erinnert an den Gedanken der frommen Juden, die auf den Messias warten." Translation JR).

86 Ibid., 196 ("Die polnischen Genossen stehen im Brennpunkt des Kampfes wo jeder Blick fuer die Wirklichkeit verloren geht, ein Kampf in dem man mit verbundenen Augen geht, wo die Psyche verwirrt wird, wo alles nur mit Phrasen der sozialen Revolution herumwirbelt." Translation JR).

87 Ibid., 60 ("Sie... verlieren dabei aber ihren poalezionistischen Boden und fuegen noch Putschismus dazu." Translation JR).

88 Ibid., 204 ("Das juedische Proletariat ist nicht der Fuehrer der russischen Revolution. Es geht aber mit dem russischen Proletariat in einer Front in allen seinen revolutionären Arbeiten und Auftritten." Translation JR).

no other way, because there is no way back. The grandeur of the victory of the working class is also the grandeur of our victory.[89]

Some, such as Yitzhak Ben-Zvi from Palestine, saw this new approach, which had developed in many of the member parties, as subjugation to foreign interests, since "we are not a section of the Russian, German-Austrian, English or American proletariat, but we are an independent body with an independent cause, such as the Russian or German working class."[90] This is why he argued one should adopt a policy of neutrality towards the British rulers in Palestine and the Third International alike.[91] Evidently, it were mainly the delegates from Palestine who insisted on upholding the classical Borochovist approach during this debate. David Ben-Gurion (1886–1973) argued:

> In these times, when we are marching towards the dictatorship of the proletariat ... we Jewish socialists find ourselves in the tragic situation that in contrast to all other peoples, we have far less healthy elements, the real power, the working masses, which due to their own force in their own economy could become a real power within their people and create the basis to revolutionize and rebuild Jewish life.[92]

Following this classical Borochovist paradigm about the lack of a "strategic base," he also rejected the idea of "subordination" to the working classes of other nations: "If we take the social revolution seriously, it cannot be a perspective for us to play a role as a small group on the backs of the German, English or Russian proletariat. The Jewish working class must play its own role according to

89 Ibid., 259 ("Und soweit die Arbeiterklasse als Klasse befreit wird, muss sie auch als nationale Klasse befreit werden. Die Arbeiterklasse konstituiert sich als Nation. ... Die juedische Arbeiterklasse muss in der 3. Internationale stehen. Weil sie mehr Einfluss haben wird, weil ein anderer Weg nicht da ist, weil es ein zurueck nicht mehr gibt. Die Grösse des Sieges der Arbeiterklasse ist auch die Grösse unseres Sieges." Translation JR).
90 Ibid., 51 ("Wir sind keine Sektion des russischen, deutschösterreichischen, englischen oder amerikanischen Proletariats sondern sind ein selbständiger Körper mit selbständigem Zweck, wie die russische und deutsche Arbeiterklasse." Translation JR).
91 Ibid., 52.
92 Ibid., 274–275 ("In der Zeit, wenn wir der Diktatur des Proletariats entgegenschreiten... finden wir juedische Sozialisten uns vor einer so tragischen Situation, dass weit weniger als in allen Ländern und Völkern, bei uns das gesunde Element, die reale Kraft, die arbeitenden Massen, vorhanden sind die Dank ihrer eigenen Kraft in ihrer eigenen Wirtschaft eine wirkliche Macht im Volke werden könnten und die Grundlagen und im juedischen Volksleben revolutionieren und auf eine neue Basis stellen sollen können." Translation JR).

its constructive force."[93] In accordance with the party's classical theory, he made his main point:

> Our part in the social revolution must first and foremost be to create possibilities in Palestine for the creation of a great, Jewish, working Yishuv which shall be the bearer of the social revolution. We as Jewish socialists under no circumstances can make peace with the idea that we are simply the object of the revolution. We must its subject as well (big tumult). I do not think one can disrupt me with scandals. [apparently referring to the delegates' protests; JR] We think that through the constructive socialist work in Palestine, by strengthening the position of the Jewish worker, by creating a workers' economy, by strengthening the political forces of the working class, and especially by bringing new workers and work-seeking masses to Palestine, into the socialist or semi-socialist economy, that this is our most important preparatory work for the coming social revolution.[94]

For many activists who had been engaged in revolutionary activism throughout Central and Eastern Europe since 1917, this argument seemed unacceptable. Could they wait for their comrades' "preparatory work" in Palestine? They had often been part of joint struggles alongside non-Jewish workers, often regarded them as successful, and could not accept giving up this newly won agency for the sake of first building a strong working Yishuv, fulfilling a task on behalf of the entire nation. In this revolutionary situation, even an implicit cooperation with the bourgeoisie for the sake of the nation seemed unthinkable, or as a Russian delegate put it: "The Jewish bourgeoisie is no better than any other. Jewish counterrevolution is the same as any other. Therefore, there can be no coopera-

---

93 Ibid., 275 ("Wenn wir es aber ernst meinen, mit der sozialen Revolution, so ist es fuer uns keine Perspektive, dass eine kleine Gruppe sie auf dem Ruecken des deutschen, englischen oder russischen Proleatriats mitmacht und dort eine Rolle spielt. Die juedische Arbeiterschaft muss dort mit ihrer eigenen Kraft und schöpferischen Möglichkeit ihre eigene Rolle spielen." Translation JR).

94 Ibid., 276–277 ("Dass unser Anteil an der sozialen Revolution sich zuerst darin ausdruecken muss, dass wir in Palästina Möglichkeiten schaffen, fuer die Verwirklichung eines grossen, juedischen, arbeitenden Jischubs, welcher der Träger der sozialen Revolution werden soll. Wir als juedische Sozialisten koennen auf keinen Fall mit dem Gedanken Frieden schliessen, dass wir bloss das Objekt der Revolution sein sollen. Wir muessen auch ihr Subjekt sein (grosser Lärm) Ich denke durch Skandale wird man mich nicht stören. Wir denken, dass durch die schöpferische, sozialistische Arbeit in Palästina dass durch das verstärken der Positionen der juedischen Arbeiter, durch unseren Aufbau der Arbeiterwirtschaft, durch die Verstärkung der politischen Kräfte der Arbeiterschaft und besonders durch das Hereinbringen neuer Arbeiter und arbeitssuchender Massen nach Palästina, in die sozialistische und halbsozialistische Wirtschaft, dass das unsere wichtigste Vorbereitungsarbeit ist fuer die kommende soziale Revolution." Translation JR).

tion with the Jewish bourgeoisie."[95] The most radical break with this concept was formulated by Alexander Chaschin, who rejected the paradigm of the working class fulfilling a task on behalf of the nation:

> The time has come to liquidate the old on all fronts. We have to liquidate all the semi-, quarterly, and three quarterly fighters, Klal Yisroel. Now the moment has come for a working Klal Yisroel. There is no other for us. The time has come, that we cannot rely on any other classes in the name of Klal Yisroel anymore ... We have come with the hope that we liquidate, and such as capitalism destroys the fatherlands and unites them in great capitalist bodies, now the time has come for us to build a universal homeland, to build the fatherland of the social revolution.[96]

He clearly rejected any concept of a national homeland of the Jews as a precondition for the revolution but saw the revolution as the solution for the "Jewish question": "The Jewish interests, the interests of the entire world are now bound to the social revolution and this is why we need to support it."[97] In his perspective, the role of Palestine in this revolutionary process was not to make the Jews productive and capable of fighting but it would be at best a later outcome of the world revolution. In the meantime, the "fatherland" seemed to have been located somewhere else, while any cooperation with general-Zionism or the national bourgeoisie for the sake of the nation was ruled out.

The Jewish Revolutionary and Palestine

Analyzing the development of Poale Zion's understanding of the relation between the Jewish working class, the nation, and Palestine requires a look at the circumstances in which these ideologies emerged. Ber Borochov's concept

---

95 Ibid., 205 ("Die juedische Bourgeoisie ist nicht besser, wie eine andere, die juedische Konterrevolution ist ebenso wie die andere. Deshalb gibt es kein Zusammenarbeiten mit der juedischen Bourgeoisie." Translation JR).
96 Ibid., 208 ("dass der Augenblick gekommen ist, wo wir, das Alte an allen Fronten liquidieren muessen. Wo wir liquidieren muessen mit den ganzen halben, viertel, und dreiviertel-Kämpfern, mit Klall-Jisroel, das jetzt das Moment gekommen ist, wo geschaffen worden ist ein arbeitendes Klall-Jisroel. Ein anderes gibt es fuer uns nicht. Dass jetzt die Zeit gekommen ist, wo wir nicht im Namen von Klall Jirsoel diese oder jene Klasse stuetzen duerfen, ... Wir sind mit der Hoffnung gekommen, dass liqudiert wird und dass, ebenso wie der Kapitalismus Vaterländer vernichtet und neue in grosskapitalistischen Organen vereinigt, jetzt fuer uns die Zeit gekommen ist eine allgemeine Heimat, ein Vaterland aufzubauen, das der sozialen Revolution." Translation JR).
97 Ibid., 209 ("Die juedischen Interessen, die Interessen der ganzen Welt liegen in der sozialen Revolution und wie muessen sie daher stuetzen." Translation JR).

of the Jewish proletariat's common interests, shared harmoniously with the nation as well as his demand for a "strategic base", were direct results of the experiences he had made during the revolutionary and counter-revolutionary events in Russia in the years 1905 to 1907. As the Jewish labor movement seemed incapable of determining the course of events and enduring the worst of the reaction's violence, he saw the core problem in the general economic conditions in which the Jewish working class lived in the Empire. His argument, that the acquisition of a "strategic base" was necessary to give the Jewish working class revolutionary agency, was therefore both an explanation of the recent defeat and a programmatic claim for future activities. He created a causal chain for revolutionary activism: without a territory, the workers would not be able to struggle; through the acquisition of such a territory, successful participation in the revolution would be enabled. According to this line of argument, the nation was the defining factor for the evolution of a potent working class; the working class could not struggle without prior national emancipation. The Jewish worker as a revolutionary subject was therefore inherently defined through their relation to the territory, Palestine, that was eventually not only the cause of the working class but its acquisition of a national cause for the sake of the Jews as a nation.

While all members of Poale Zion formally accepted this paradigm, this revolutionary causal chain was practically undermined by many daily struggles in the Diaspora. As long as Poale Zion would not be the dominant party, it had to take almost daily decisions, navigating between its socialist-revolutionary and its national-Zionist program.

However, the biggest challenge to the socialist-national synthesis came with the revolutionary wave in Europe, unfolding after the Russian Revolution of 1917. The different assessments of the situation, the different interpretations of the party's program, were determined by local and regional conditions under which the various activists lived. It was not only polemics when at the World Congress Leon Chasanowich of Poale Zion's international leadership attacked the revolutionary enthusiasts as "high-tide socialists, communists as long as the Bolsheviks are standing 100 kilometers before Warsaw."[98] Many of his (soon to be former) comrades in Central and Eastern Europe had gone through a revolutionary experience that contradicted the party's traditional class-nation-paradigm. Some were fighting in the very same Bolshevik army that was approaching Warsaw, others were leading mass strikes of Jewish and non-Jewish

98 Ibid., 385 ("Das sind Konjunktursozialisten, Kommunisten wenn die Bolschewiken 100 km von Warschau entfernt sind." Translation JR). He referred to the recent advance of the Red Army in its war against Poland.

workers or had been elected to workers' councils. In the eyes of many activists, all these achievements had been reached despite the lack of a "strategic base." The Jewish workers' agency, which many of Poale Zion's activists had hitherto seen as dependent on the national project in Palestine, was visible on a daily basis in the Diaspora and many of the activists were unwilling to give it up for the sake of programmatic principles. This reinterpretation of the class-nation-territory paradigm in their view did not necessarily make them less Zionist. However, they not only re-shifted their priorities from Palestine to the struggles in Europe, but also reversed the connection between Jewish revolutionary activity and the establishment of a national home in Palestine. After the revolution, the Jews would be granted the right to the land: "Over the heart of worldwide reaction, there will fly the red flag of the social revolution, while on Mount Moriah, the red flag of the Jewish Communist Party will be raised."[99] While this suggests that an ideological, or maybe emotional, connection with Palestine persisted even amongst the most radical activists, the prospective rejection of Zionism as a concept itself is already visible in this line of argument. The land was not perceived as a "necessity" derived from materialist analysis any more, rather a distant wish that would be fulfilled by the world revolution in the future; however, there was no longer any causal connection to the Jewish proletariat's development. It is unsurprising that a number of the activists that made this argument later abandoned Zionism entirely and often joined the communist parties of their respective countries.

Works Cited

Avineri, Shlomo. *Profile des Zionismus: Die geistigen Ursprünge des Staates Israel: 17 Portraits*. Gütersloh: Gütersloher Verlagshaus, 1998.

Ben-Zvi, Izchak. "Labor Zionism in Russia." In *Russian Jewry (1860–1917)*, edited by Jacob Frumkin, Gregor Aronson, and Alexis Goldenweiser, 209–218. London: Thomas Yoseloff, 1966.

Brumberg, Abraham. "Anniversaries in Conflict: On the Centenary of the Jewish Socialist Labor Bund." *Jewish Social Studies* New Series 5, no. 3 (1999): 196–217.

Budnitskii, Oleg. *Russian Jews Between the Reds and the Whites, 1917–1920*. Philadelphia: University of Pennsylvania Press, 2012.

Bunzl, John. *Klassenkampf in der Diaspora: Zur Geschichte der jüdischen Arbeiterbewegung*. Vienna: Europaverlag, 1975.

99 Ibid., 209 ("Auf dem Herzblatt der Weltreaktion die rote Fahne der sozialen Revolution wehen wird, während auf dem Berg Moria die Fahne der juedisch kommunistischen Partei aufgezogen sein wird." Translation JR).

Dietrich, Christian. "Zwischen Sowjetrussland und Eretz Israel. Die Radikalisierung des österreichischen Arbeiterzionismus 1918 bis 1920." *Arbeit – Bewegung – Geschichte: Zeitschrift für Historische Studien* 2 (2017): 49–64.

Frankel, Jonathan. *Crisis, Revolution, and the Russian Jews.* Cambridge: Cambridge University Press, 2009.

Frankel, Jonathan. *Prophecy and Politics: Socialism, Nationalism, and the Russian Jews, 1862–1917.* Cambridge: Cambridge University Press, 1984.

Gaisbauer, Adolf. *Davidstern und Doppeladler: Zionismus und jüdischer Nationalismus in Österreich 1882–1918.* Vienna: Böhlau Verlag, 1988.

Gurevitz, Baruch, and Dominique Négrel. "Un cas de communisme national en Union Soviétique Le Poale Zion: 1918–1928." *Cahiers du Monde russe et soviétique* 15, no. 3/4 (July-December 1974): 333–361.

Halpern, Ben, and Jehuda Reinharz. "Nationalism and Jewish Socialism: The Early Years." *Modern Judaism* 8, no. 3 (1988): 217–248.

Hautmann, Hans. *Geschichte der Rätebewegung in Österreich 1918–1924.* Vienna: Europaverlag, 1987.

Kenez, Peter. "Pogroms and White Ideology in the Russian Civil War." In *Pogroms: Anti-Jewish Violence in Modern Russian History*, edited by John D. Klier and Shlomo Lambroza, 293–313. Cambridge: Cambridge University Press, 1992.

Keßler, Mario. *Zionismus und internationale Arbeiterbewegung 1897 bis 1933.* Berlin: Akademie Verlag, 1994.

Levin, Vladimir. "The Jewish Socialist Parties in Russia in the Period of Reaction." In *The Revolution of 1905 and Russia's Jews*, edited by Stefani Hoffman and Ezra Mendelsohn, 111–127. Philadelphia: University of Pennsylvania Press, 2008.

Mendelsohn, Ezra. *Class Struggle in the Pale: The Formative Years of the Jewish Workers' Movement in Tsarist Russia.* London and New York: Cambridge University Press, 1970.

Moss, Kenneth B. *Jewish Renaissance in the Russian Revolution.* Cambridge: Harvard University Press, 2009.

Muller, Jerry Z. *Capitalism and the Jews.* Princeton: Princeton University Press, 2010.

Offenberg, Mario. *Kommunismus in Palästina. Nation und Klasse in der antikolonialen Revolution.* Meisenheim am Glan: Verlag Anton Hain, 1975.

Peled, Yoav. *Class and Ethnicity in the Pale: The Political Economy of Jewish Workers' Nationalism in Late Imperial Russia.* New York: Palgrave Macmillan, 1989.

Perlmutter, Amos. "Dov Ber-Borochov: A Marxist-Zionist Ideologist." *Middle Eastern Studies* 5, no. 1 (January 1969): 32–43.

Polonsky, Antony. "The New Jewish Politics and Its Discontents." In *The Emergence of Modern Jewish Politics: Bundism and Zionism in Eastern Europe*, edited by Zvi Gitelman, 35–53. Pittsburgh: University of Pittsburgh Press, 2003.

Rabinovitch, Simon. *Jewish Rights, National Rites: Nationalism and Autonomy in Late Imperial and Revolutionary Russia.* Stanford: Stanford University Press, 2014.

Rechter, David. *The Jews of Vienna and the First World War.* Oxford: The Littman Library of Jewish Civilization, 2008.

Rubenstein, Sondra Miller. *The Communist Movement in Palestine and Israel, 1919–1984.* Boulder and London: Westview Press, 1985.

Schoeps, Julius H. *Pioneers of Zionism: Hess, Pinkser, Rülf.* Berlin and Boston: De Gruyter, 2013.

Shanes, Joshua. *Diaspora Nationalism and Jewish Identity in Habsburg Galicia.* Cambridge: Cambridge University Press, 2012.
Shneer, David. *Yiddish and the Creation of Soviet Jewish Culture, 1918–1930.* Cambridge: Cambridge University Press, 2004.
Shimoni, Gideon. *The Zionist Ideology.* Hanover: Brandeis University Press, 1995.
Shtakser, Inna. *The Making of Jewish Revolutionaries in the Pale of Settlement: Community and Identity during the Russian Revolution and its Immediate Aftermath, 1907–07.* New York: Palgrave Macmillan, 2014.
Soxberger, Thomas. *Revolution am Donaukanal. Jiddische Kultur und Politik in Wien (1904–1938).* Vienna: Mandelbaum, 2013.
Sternhell, Zeev. *The Founding Myths of Israel: Nationalism, Socialism, and the Making of the Jewish State.* Princeton: Princeton University Press, 1999.
Tobias, Henry J. *The Jewish Bund in Russia: From Its Origins to 1905.* Stanford: Stanford University Press, 1972.
Traverso, Enzo. *The Marxists and the Jewish Question: The History of a Debate 1843–1943.* New York: Humanity Books, 1994.
Ury, Scott. "The Generation of 1905 and the Politics of Despair: Alienation, Friendship, Community." In *The Revolution of 1905 and Russia's Jews*, edited by Stefani Hoffman and Ezra Mendelsohn, 96–110. Philadelphia: University of Pennsylvania Press, 2008.
Wortman, Richard. "Nicholas II and the Revolution." In *The Revolution of 1905 and Russia's Jews*, edited by Stefani Hoffman and Ezra Mendelsohn, 31–45. Philadelphia: University of Pennsylvania Press, 2008.

Sources

Anonymous. "Das Lemberger Tagblatt und der Druckerstreik." *Neuer Weg: sozialistische Zeitschrift*, February 1914, 7.
Borochov, Ber. "Our Platform (1906)." In *Class Struggle and the Jewish Nation: Selected Essays in Marxist Zionism*, edited by Mitchell Cohen, 75–103. New Brunswick and London: Transaction Books, 1984.
Borochov, Ber. "The Socialism of Poale Zion Here (1915)." In *Class Struggle and the Jewish Nation: Selected Essays in Marxist Zionism*, edited by Mitchell Cohen, 155–162. New Brunswick and London: Transaction Books, 1984.
Borochov, Ber. "The Economic Development of the Jewish People (1916)." In *Class Struggle and the Jewish Nation: Selected Essays in Marxist Zionism*, edited by Mitchell Cohen, 167–177. New Brunswick and London: Transaction Books, 1984.
Borochov, Ber. "Eretz Israel in Our Program and Tactics (1917)." In *Class Struggle and the Jewish Nation: Selected Essays in Marxist Zionism*, edited by Mitchell Cohen, 201–203. New Brunswick and London: Transaction Books, 1984.
Borochov, Ber. "Die Grundlagen des Poale-Zionismus." In *Die Grundlagen des Poale-Zionismus*, edited by Dan Diner, 25–116. Frankfurt: Borochov-Press, 1969.
Borochow, Ber. "Das Klasseninteresse und die nationale Frage (1905)." In *Klasse und Nation: Zur Theorie und Praxis des Jüdischen Sozialismus*, edited by Weltverband Hechaluz, 8–45. Berlin: Hechaluz, 1932.

Borochow, Ber. "Palästina in unserem Programm und unserer Taktik (1917)." In *Klasse und Nation: Zur Theorie und Praxis des Jüdischen Sozialismus*, edited by Weltverband Hechaluz, 99–103. Berlin: Hechaluz, 1932.

Chasanowitsch, Leon. "Ziele und Mittel des sozialistischen Zionismus." *Sozialistische Monatshefte*, July 1914, 962–973.

Ebreju sociāldemokrātiskā strādnieku partija "Polei-Zion" Riga. *Letter to Ignatz Kornfeld*, November 27 1918. Israel Labor Party Archive (Beit Berl), 1–1–1917–3.

Engels, Friedrich. "Grundsätze des Kommunismus." In *Karl Marx Friedrich Engels Werke*, Vol. 4, 361–380. Berlin: Dietz Verlag, 1959.

Gordon, Aaron David. "Arbeit." In *A.D. Gordon Erlösung durch Arbeit: Ausgewählte Aufsätze*, 62–76. Berlin: Jüdischer Verlag, 1929.

Jüdische Sozialistische Arbeiterpartei "Poale-Zion" Czernowitz. *Letter to Verbandsbureau der Jüdisch-sozialistischen Arbeiterpartei Poale Zion in Berlin*, March 14 1920. Israel Labor Party Archive (Beit Berl), 1–10–1917–120.

Kornfeld, Ignatz. *Letter to Berl Locker*, May 20 1919. Israel Labor Party Archive (Beit Berl), 1–10–1918–117.

Lenin, Vladimir I. "Was sind die 'Volksfreunde' und wie kämpfen sie gegen die Sozialdemokraten." In *W. I. Lenin Werke*, Vol. 1, 6th ed., 119–338. Berlin: Dietz Verlag, 1971.

Locker, Berl, ed. *Ber Borochov: Geklibene Shriftn*. New York: Astoria Press, 1928.

Mendel, Hersch. *Erinnerungen eines jüdischen Revolutionärs*. Cologne: Neuer ISP Verlag, 2004.

Minutes of the Fifth World Congress of the World Union of Poale Zion in Vienna. July 1920. Pinhas Lavon Institute Archive (Tel Aviv), III 11–1–36

Pinsker, Leon. *Auto-Emancipation! Mahnruf eines Stammesgenossen von einem russischen Juden*. Berlin: Kommissions-Verlag W. Issleib, 1882.

Poale Zion. *Dray Rezolutsiym* (Three Resolutions). Warsaw: Farlag Arbeiterheim, 1918.

Präsidium des k. k. Ministeriums des Inneren. *Bericht Strafsache: Ausschreitungen bei Streik/Demonstration der Handelsangestellten in Stanislau*, November 5 1911. Austrian State Archive (Vienna), Allgemeines Verwaltungsarchiv, Inneres MdI Präsidium A2114.

Reiss, Josef. *Letter to Verbandsbureau der Jüdisch-sozialistischen Arbeiterpartei Poale Zion*, September 11 1920. Israel Labor Party Archive (Beit Berl), 1–3–1919–22.

Serpow, Alexander. "Der Weg der Revolution." *Freie Tribüne*, February 7 1919, 2.

Verbandsbureau des Allweltlichen Jüdischen Sozialistischen Arbeiterverbandes Poale Zion, *Letter to Kaplansky*, May 24 1919. Israel Labor Party Archive (Beit Berl), 1–10–1919–108.

Amir Locker-Biletzki

The Settler, the Native and the Communist

Nationalism, Colonialism, and Imperialism in Moshe Sneh's and Emil Touma's Ideology, 1953 – 1973

Introduction

From the early 1920s Communists resisted the presence of the British Empire, the United States, and the Zionist colonial practices in Palestine/Israel. Jewish and Palestinian radicals attempted to navigate the stormy waters of the escalating national conflict and offer a vision of a socially equal and politically sovereign society in Palestine/Israel.[1] The purpose of this chapter is to present the ideological concepts that underlay the visions of Jewish and Palestinian Communists. The cornerstone of this text is an argument that on the face of it sounds paradoxical. It is maintained here that Jewish and Palestinian Communists, using the Marxist-Leninist conceptualizations – interlaced with local Marxist influences – in regard to nationalism and imperialism, actually created local national identities. It will also be contended here that as radical as the negation of Zionism by Jewish Communists was, they – to an extent – failed to grasp the settler-colonial logic of Zionism, in contrast to the more nuanced understanding of the colonial practice and essence of Zionism exhibited by Palestinian Communists. In that

1 From its formative stages in the early 1920s the Communist Party was ideologically and practically anti-imperialist. A 1923 pamphlet called the British "occupiers" [כובשים] ("LePo'aley Palestina", To the Workers of Palestine), in Leon Zahavi, *lechud O beyachad: Yehudim veAravim be-Mismachey Haqomintern 1919 – 1943* (Apart or Together: Jews and Arabs in Palestine according to Documents of the Comintern, 1919 – 1943) (Jerusalem: Keter, 2005), 42 (translation mine). This principle of Party ideology was a constant element that was repeated again and again, for instance a Communist youth educational guide for the Israeli Independence Day from the early 1960s asserts that the Arab-Israeli conflict will continue as long as "Imperialism will exploit it and meddle with it." [האימפריאליזם ינצל ויבחש בו] ("Milchemet haAtzmaut" (The War of Independence), Yad Tabenkin Archives, File #2). Peace is dependent on "saving Israel from the dependency on the imperialism" [להציל את ישראל מן התלות באימפריאליזם] (Ibid (translation mine). In practice, the Party waged an unarmed struggle against imperial influence in Palestine/Israel confined mainly to political means. On a few occasions Palestinian Communists fought against the British as part of Arab armed groups during the 1936 – 1939 Arab Revolt. See Shmuel Dothan, *Adumim: haMiflaga haqomunistit beEretz-Israel* (Reds: The Communist Party in Eretz-Israel) (Kfar Sava: Shvana Hasofer Publishing, 1991).

https://doi.org/10.1515/9783110545753-005

sense, this text is about the limitations and possibilities of radical thought – in both the Israeli-Jewish and Palestinian contexts. The argumentations featured in this chapter will be analyzed through the texts of Moshe Sneh[2] (1909–1972) – a maverick Israeli politician and theoretician – and Emile Touma (1919–1985) – one of the leading intellectuals of the Party and the Palestinians in Israel.

The Settler

Moshe Sneh casts a long shadow over the history of the Israeli anti-Zionist left. By far one of the most important political figures to cross the lines from Zionism to Marxist anti-Zionism – and back again – his political and theoretical moves from the mid-1950s to the mid-1960s were the subject of deeply emotional controversy. The aim of this section is not to try to solve the "mystery" around Sneh – meaning understanding his political twists and turns – but to try to understand his theories as one of the leading Marxist thinkers in Israel of the 1950s.

The main text to be examined in this section is the book cumbersomely named *On the National Question: Conclusions in the Light of Marxism-Leninism.*[3] The book is characterized by one former member of MAKI (Hebrew acronym for The Israeli Communist Party) and Banki (Hebrew acronym for The Young Israeli Communist League) as "written in a dense Marxist style, accompanied by many citations from the 'scriptures',"[4] and at the same time "his prose is fluent, as is usual in Sneh's writing"[5] while it prefigured his rejection of Zionism in favor of Marxist anti-Zionism.

---

2 Moshe Sneh was an Israeli politician and thinker. He started his political career as a liberal Zionist in Poland. After arriving in Palestine in 1940, he was one of the key figures in the leadership of the *Yishuv*, mainly in the Haganah (Hebrew defence. the main Jewish military underground organization in Palestine). In this period he started to lean to the left and led the left wing of MAPAM (United Workers' Party). He broke away from it in 1952, joining MAKI in 1954. In 1965 he played a key role in the splitting up of the MAKI and led the Jewish MAKI until his death in 1972.

3 Moshe Sneh, *Sikumim bashela haLeumit: leOr haMarqsizem-Leninizem* (On the National Question: Conclusions in the Light of Marxism-Leninism) (Tel Aviv: The Left Socialist Party Publication, 1954).

4 Nessia Shafran, *Shalom Lecha Qomunizm* (Farewell Communism) (Tel Aviv: Hakibbutz Hameuchad, 1983), 133. (translation mine).

[כתוב בסגנון מרקסיסטי כבד, ובליווי ציטאטות רבות מן הכתובים.]

5 Ibid., 133.

[עם זאת הרצאתו קולחת, כדרך המאפיינת את כתיבתו של משה סנה.]

The book was written as an ideological text for Sneh's party[6] and sums up the positions he would bring in when he joined MAKI. The main thrust of the book is disproving some of the basic fundamentals of Zionism. However, by rejecting Zionism using the terms of Marxism-Leninism, Sneh creates the ideological possibility of an Israeli-Jewish national identity, and one that is detached from Zionist contents.

The basic ideological premises on which *On the National Question* is based derive from Vladimir Ilyich Lenin's understating of national self-determination and imperialism as well as Joseph Stalin's conceptualization of the nation. In his 1916 theoretical text *Imperialism: The Highest Stage of Capitalism*,[7] Lenin outlines the spread of European empires as originating in a change in the formation of capital itself. Lenin's short tract on imperialism was part of a flurry of writings by mostly Marxist critics of late nineteenth century European expansion into the non-European world. In many ways Lenin summarizes, criticizes, and elucidates the more elaborate analysis of other theoreticians.[8]

In his *Imperialism*, Lenin based himself on economic data, arguing that the concentration of production in the hands of the banks that deploy their control by granting or withholding credit had made them "powerful monopolies,"[9] ushering in a new stage in the development of capitalism, different from the one in Marx's days. Instead of "the old capitalism, when free competition prevailed" and where "the export of *goods* was the most typical feature [...] under modern capitalism, when monopolies prevail, the export of *Capital* has become the typical feature."[10] In place of the individual captains of industry and manufacturing, e.g., countries like England that traded goods with world markets, "in the

---

6 Between the time of Moshe Sneh's split from MAPAM in 1952 and his followers' assimilation into MAKI in 1954 he formed the Left Socialist Party, or, in short, the Left. Those who followed him to MAKI were thus dubbed the "Left men."

7 Vladimir Ilyich Lenin, *Imperialism: The Highest Stage of Capitalism* (New York: International Publishers, 1985).

8 The basic concepts that underlie this section are taken from Murray Noonan's thesis work. See Murray Noonan, "Marxist Theories of Imperialism: Evolution of a Concept" (PhD thesis., Victoria University, 2010). Lenin on his part was influenced by liberals like John A. Hobson and a wide range of Marxists from the reformist Karl Kautsky and Rudolf Hilferding to the radicals Nikolai Bukharin and Rosa Luxemburg. See Nikolai Bukharin, *Imperialism and World Economy* (The Merlin Press: London, 1972); Rudolf Hilferding, *Finance Capital: A Study of the Latest Phase of Capitalist Development* (Routledge and Kegan Paul: London, 1981); J. A. Hobson, *Imperialism: A Study* (Memphis: General Book, 2012); Rosa Luxemburg, *The Accumulation of Capital* (London: Routledge, 2003); and Karl Kautsky, "Ultra-Imperialism," *Die Neue Zeit*, September 11 1914, accessed February 28 2017, https://www.marxists.org/archive/kautsky/1914/09/ultra-imp.htm,

9 Lenin, *Imperialism: The Highest Stage of Capitalism*, 31.

10 Ibid., 62.

last quarter of the nineteenth century [...] monopolist capitalist combines" in "a few rich countries"[11] had proliferated. This reconfiguration of wealth and control had resulted, Lenin argues, in "an enormous 'superabundance of capital'"[12] that had accumulated in the advanced countries. This excess financial capital was then exported into overseas colonies, as the big imperial powers divided the world between them.

The rise of nationalism with its integrative message, which was meant to bond together all classes of a given society under one national identity, stood in contrast to Marxism. Marx and Engels left no systematic understanding of the nation and national movements. This unintentional gap[13] in Marxist theorization was soon filled by a group of thinkers associated with the Second International. Socialists of different hues proposed different solutions to the rise of nationalism in Europe. Ranging from different forms of national autonomy suggested by the Astro-Marxists and the cultural nationalism of the Bund (General Jewish Labor Bund of Lithuania, Poland, and Russia) to the outright rejection of nationalism by Rosa Luxemburg, Marxists struggled to formulate their understanding of nationalism in Eastern and Central Europe.[14]

---

11 Ibid.

12 Ibid.

13 Marx and Engels were conscious of the power of nationalism and supported oppressed national movements like the Irish and the Poles. However, at the same time they never thought systematically of nationalism and in some cases advocated sub-national identities. For example, during the 1848 Revolution Marx preferred to stoke the flames of Rhineland resentment of Prussian rule over pan-German nationalism. There is no doubt that at the core of Marx and Engels' thought was an internationalist element; however, their extensive interest in oppressed peoples in Europe, India, and Algeria points to the fact that nationalism was present in Marxism from its origins. See Jonathan Sperber, *Karl Marx: A Nineteenth-Century Life* (Liveright: London, 2013); Tristram Hunt, *The Frock-Coated Communist: The Revolutionary Life of Friedrich Engels* (Penguin: New York, 2009); and Karl Marx and Friedrich Engels, *On Colonialism; Articles From the New York tribune and Other Writings* (International Publishers: New York, 1972). For a concise survey of Marx and Engels' reflections on nationalism, see Michal Löwy, "Marxists and the National Question," *New Left Review* 1 (1976): 81–85.

14 For the history of the Bund and the development of its national polices see Jack Jacobs, ed., *Jewish Politics in Eastern Europe: The Bund at 100* (New York: New York University Press, 2001). For the Astro-Marxists see Löwy, *Marxists and the National Question*; for Rosa Luxemburg's understanding of nationalism mainly in its Polish context see Rosa Luxemburg, "Foreword to the Anthology: The Polish Question and the Socialist Movement," in *The National Question*, ed. Horace B. Davis (New York: Monthly Review Press, 1976), 60–100.

In this context, the Russian Bolsheviks – confronted with the Russian Empire's multinational makeup[15] – fashioned their own understanding of nationalism. Their understanding was based on Lenin's reaffirmation of the concept of self-determination and Stalin's definition of the nation.

Both Lenin and Stalin[16] viewed the nation as the product of concrete historical and economic processes. Lenin phrases it thus: "the categorical requirement of Marxist theory in investigating any social question is that it be examined within *definite* historical limits."[17] He then places nationalism in a social context. Lenin – like Luxemburg – differentiates between two epochs of capitalism. The first was the rise of a new social system out of the ruins of feudalism and absolutism. This period was characterized by "the formation of the bourgeois-democratic society and state, when the national movements for the first time became mass movements and in one way or another drew *all* classes of the population into politics."[18] Spurred on by the appearance of mass media, the press, and representative democracy, nations sought national independence.[19] The second, contemporary era of developed capitalism is "the period of fully formed capitalist states with a long-established constitutional regime and a highly developed antagonism between the proletariat and the bourgeoisie."[20] In this age, the different nations, drawn more closely together by commerce, will "intermingle to an increasing degree," bringing "the antagonism between internationally united capital and the international working-class movement into the forefront."[21] Lenin goes on to place nationalism in the context of autocratic Czarist Russia

---

15 A fine illustration of this almost mindboggling diversity can be found in Luxemburg's analyses of the Western parts of the Russian Empire – mainly Poland and Lithuania – Caucasia and Siberia. See Rosa Luxemburg, "The National Question and Autonomy," in *The National Question*, ed. Horace B. Davis (New York: Monthly Review Press, 1976), 265–284.

16 For Stalin's understanding of Marxism in its Russian context and the Western roots of his thought, see Erik van Ree, "Stalin as a Marxist: The Western Roots of Stalin's Russification of Marxism," in *Stalin: A New History*, ed. Sarah Davies et al. (New York: Cambridge University Press, 2005), 159–180. For his complex construction of his own national persona, see Alfred. J. Rieber, "Stalin, Man of Borderlands," *The American Historical Review* 106 (2001): 1651–1691.

17 Vladimir Ilyich Lenin, *The Right of Nations to Self-Determination* (Moscow: Progress Publishers, 1997), 11.

18 Ibid.

19 Lenin's words bear some resemblance to later Modernist scholars of nationalism. However, in contrast to such Modernists as Benedict Anderson or Ernest Gellner who tried to look at the nation's endurance, Lenin as an internationalist Marxist tried to think beyond the nation. See Benedict Anderson, *Imagined Communities* (London: Verso, 1983); Ernest Gellner, *Nations and Nationalism* (Oxford: Basil Blackwell Ltd., 1983).

20 Lenin, *The Right of Nations*, 11.

21 Ibid.

of the early twentieth century. He argues that the Russian Empire's archaic structure stands in contrast to the more developed capitalism of Poland. Therefore – in sharp dissent from Luxemburg – the economic gap between the countries does enable Polish nationalism and self-determination.[22]

Comparable argumentation can be found in Stalin's 1913 work *Marxism and the National Question.*[23] Much like Lenin, he places the nation in a historical and socioeconomic context, stating: "a nation is not merely a historical category but a historical category belonging to a definite epoch, the epoch of rising capitalism."[24] While nations formed nation-states in advanced capitalist Western Europe, in Eastern Europe "multi-national states were formed."[25] These states, most characteristically Russia and Austro-Hungary, are the product of feudal systems. As Stalin phrased it, "this peculiar method of formation of states could take place only where feudalism had not yet been eliminated."[26] When capitalism did penetrate the East, awaking the small nations of the multinational empires, those small nations clashed with the dominant nations.[27]

Besides the particular contexts in which Stalin places national movements, earlier in the text he conceptualizes a model of the nation. Opening with the question "What is a nation?",[28] he answers by describing it as "primarily a community, a definite community of people."[29] However, continues Stalin, a multilingual empire like Russia is also a stable community. He replies to this query ("What is a nation?") by stating that what distinguishes a national community is one national language: "*community of language* is one of the characteristic features of a nation."[30] Nonetheless, different nations communicate at times in the same language, as the English-speaking British and Americans attest to. What separates them, then, according to Stalin, is territory. A separate nation is therefore characterized by "*a community of territory.*" Yet linguistic and territorial unity are not all that defines a nation. This, says Stalin, "requires [...] an internal economic bond which welds the various parts of the nation into a single

22 Ibid., 12.

23 For the circumstances of the writing of the book and the way he dealt with nationalism in later works, see Erik van Ree, "Stalin and the National Question," *Revolutionary Russia* 7 (1994): 214–238.

24 Josef .V. Stalin, *Marxism and the National Question* (Moscow: Foreign Languages Publishing House, 1945), 17.

25 Ibid.

26 Ibid.

27 Ibid., 18.

28 Ibid., 7.

29 Ibid.

30 Ibid., 8.

whole."[31] At this point he turns from the materialistic to the cultural fundamentals of the nation. Stalin argues that nations are formed by their "dissimilar conditions of existence,"[32] which lead to the development of different spiritual features. While these traits may be hard to delineate, the process "manifests itself in a distinctive culture common to the nation."[33] After summing up the discrete aspects of a nation, Stalin defines it as "*a historically constituted, stable community of people, formed on the basis of a common language, territory, economic life, and psychological make-up manifested in a common culture.*"[34] Using this theoretical classification, Stalin disproves the nationalist understandings of the Austro-Marxists. He argues that the Austro-Marxists' and the Bund's emphases on just one part of his national equation disqualify their ideas about nationalism.

While Stalin's and Lenin's understandings of nationalism are at times mechanical and reflect more of an internationalist creed ill at ease with unbridled nationalism, they had an immense impact on Israeli Communists. The application of these Leninist and Stalinist concepts to Palestine/Israel opened a space for local identities.

In his 1954 text – written on the eve of his and his followers' entry to the MAKI – Sneh refutes Zionism in order to justify a local Israeli national identity detached from Zionism. Right at the outset, he contends that the book will "help to understand, on the one hand, the bourgeois, reactionary nature of Zionist ideology, and on the other hand to understand our affinity to the motherland as Israeli patriots, as the guardians of national independence." [35]

Sneh starts with a sweeping survey of the development of the nation in Marxist terms from prehistory to modernity. When he gets to the section titled *The Bourgeois Nation*, he follows Stalin's and Lenin's readings. This is clearly evident in the following words: "the nation was historically formed as a result of the territorial, linguistic, economic and cultural association of a stable community of people; as an outcome of capitalist development."[36]

31 Ibid., 9.

32 Ibid., 10.

33 Ibid.

34 Ibid., 11.

35 Sneh, *On the National Question*, 8 (translation mine).
[תעזור גם להבנת מהותה הבורגנית של הציונות מצד אחד ומצד שני להבנת זיקתנו למולדת כפאטריוטים ישראלים – נאמני העצמאות הלאומית]

36 Ibid., 13 (translation mine)
[כך התהוותה באופן היסטורי האומה כתוצאה משותפות; טריטוריאלית, לשונית, כלכלית ותרבותית של ציבור אנשים קבוע; כתוצאה מן ההתפתחות הקפיטלסטית]

In the transition from a feudal to a capitalist system the formation of nations is not yet completed. Mainly in the colonial world, where capitalism is not fully formed, feudal relations still survive.[37]

Moving on from the more theoretical parts of his analysis, Sneh approaches the history and national development of the Jews. After asserting that "Jewish history is like the history of any people: the history of the social-economic formations that the people went through during its development,"[38] he proceeds to chart a Marxist history of the Jews. His detailed analysis culminates with a disavowal of the Jewish and Zionist national idea of an extraterritorial eternal nation. Here, again, Sneh uses Stalinist language:

> Any talk about all contemporary Jews worldwide as one nation is a mockery of reality, truth and common sense. Historical materialism has proven that only the combination of four shared markers historically formed in a stable community – territory, language, economy and culture – creates the nation.[39]

From the arguments about the globalist nature of Jewish nationhood, he turns to the main target of his polemics: Zionism. In a chapter titled *Zionism – The Means of the Jewish, Israeli and Imperialist Bourgeoisie*, Sneh uses Leninist analyses of imperialism as his theoretical weaponry against Zionism. He opens with a class definition of Zionism. It is, he proclaims, "the principal nationalist reactionary ideology of the Jewish bourgeoisie."[40] He then launches into an extensive historical survey of the Zionists' dealings with various powers. He first defines imperialism according to the basic Leninist outline, with the development of capitalism to its monopolistic stage, then to imperialism as the second phase of the national question. In this era of high imperialism, the Western nation-states, such as England, France, Italy, and the U.S., have established their rule over colonial peoples. National oppression in this phase is one of the forms of exploitation of finance capital that is spreading beyond its national borders, seeking

---

37 Ibid., 15.

38 Ibid., 62 (translation mine).
[ההיסטוריה היהודית היא כמו ההיסטוריה של כל עם, ההיסטוריה של התצורת החברתיות- כלכליות שעברו עליו בהתפתחותו.]

39 Ibid., 72 (translation mine).
[כל דיבור על כלל היהודים בעולם בימינו כעל עם אומה אחת, הוא לעג מר למציאות, לאמת, לשכל הישר. המטריאליזם ההיסטורי הוכיח כי רק צירוף של ארבע סימני-היכר משותפים, שהתהוו היסטורית אצל ציבור קבוע – טריטוריה, לשון, משק, תרבות – יוצר את האומה.]

40 Ibid., 85 (translation mine).
[האידאולוגיה הלאומנית הראקציונרית העיקרית של הבורגנות היהודית.]

more markets, raw materials, and fuel, and more places in which to invest capital and land (export capital).

From this basic Leninist definition, Sneh goes on to chart a historical narrative of the links between Zionism and imperialism. He argues for links between Zionism and the Ottoman, French, German, Russian, and British empires. As regards French imperial intentions in the Levant, he claims that the Baron de Rothschild, while in effect turning the Jewish colonies in Palestine into "underdeveloped farms or plantation farms built on cheap labor," actually meant to use them "as a channel for French capital and influence in Eretz-Israel and the Near East."[41] Still, the most "preferred of all other political links of the Zionist movement"[42] was the one with Britain. Recounting the history of Zionist-British relations, Sneh asserts that "the Zionist movement, from its origins, offered itself as a tool to different imperialist powers, and became at the end of World War I and afterwards a tool in the hands of British imperialism."[43] As British business interests moved into Palestine, "the Zionist movement and its leadership merged as subordinates with British imperialism."[44] When the dependency was no longer possible, the Zionist movement "increased its links" with American imperialism, subordinating Israel to it after 1948.[45] At the end of this line of argumentation, Sneh manages – in keeping with his ideological preferences – to disavow Zionism and its underlying assumptions as a legitimate national movement. But at the same time as he disavows one form of nationalism, Sneh accords acceptability to another.

In a segment titled *Aliya, Settlement, Independence – This is not Zionism*, he rejects the notion that Zionism is the prime mover behind the building of the *Yishuv* and Israel, seeing this idea as "a false perception borrowed from idealistic thinking." He sets out to prove that "not the Zionist idea 'created' the *aliya*, settlement, defence and independence." Rather, it "was formed by the class needs

41 Ibid., 94 (translation mine).

[למשק-איכרים מפגר או משק פלאנטאטורי בנוי על עבודת-פועלים זולה.]

[צינורות להחדרת הון צרפתי והשפעה צרפתית לארץ-ישראל ולמזרח הקרוב]

42 Ibid., 108 (translation mine).

[קשרים אלה נעשו לעדיפים על כל שאר הקשרים המדיניים של התנועה הציונית]

43 Ibid., 116 (translation mine).

[התנועה הציונית שמראשית קיומה הציעה את עצמה כמכשיר למעצמות אימפריאליסטיות שונות, נעשתה בשלהי מלחמת-העולם הראשונה למכשיר בידי האימפריאליזם הבריטי.]

44 Ibid., 117 (translation mine).

[התנועה הציונית והנהגתה התמזגו עם האימפריאליזם הבריטי מיזוג של כפיפות.]

45 Ibid., 120 (translation mine).

[גוברת ההתקשרות]

of the haute bourgeoisie." [46] The immigration to Palestine was not ideologically motivated, nor was it an answer to the Jews' plight in the form of the Zionist Ingathering of the Exiles; it is part of the larger sweep of Jewish and global migration mainly from Europe to the New World.[47] Sneh sees the economic growth of the Jewish presence in Palestine as the result of a capitalist development. In this schema – written in Leninist-inspired language – Zionism was used to channel British imperialist capital and Jewish private capital to fuel the country's economy, meanwhile exploiting the emerging Jewish working class. The import of foreign investment – mainly American after 1948 – was "stifling Israel's manufacturing and development" and preventing the "development of the Israeli national industry"[48], in effect curbing Israel's economic independence. The end product of Sneh's argument is a non-Zionist Israeli local nationalism. This crucial element is evident already earlier in the text when Sneh, while rejecting the extraterritorial nature of Jewish peoplehood, adds: "the Communist movement 'acknowledges' the nation that has been formed in Israel." [49] He further elaborates on the point later in the text. In a piece aptly called *The Struggle for Independence*, he outlines concisely how this new nation was formed:

> The capitalist development of the Jewish *Yishuv* in part of Eretz-Israel is the one that caused the development of the nation. The British imperialist rule restricted the development of the forming nation and subjected her to a regime of national oppression and colonial exploitation.[50]

---

46 Ibid., 133 (translation mine).

[תפיסה כוזבת זו הריהי שאולה מאורח- המחשבה האידיאלסטי.]
[לא הרעיון הציוני הוא ש'יצר' את העליה, ההתישבות, הביטחון והעצמאות]
[נוצר ע"י הצרכים של הבורגנות הגדולה]

47 Ibid., 133. This explanation echoes the Zionist-Marxist thinker Dov Ber Borochov's theory about the "stychic process" which will drive Jewish immigration to Palestine. However, Sneh uses his mechanistic description to disprove Zionism and not provide a Marxist base for it. For Borochov's theories, see Dov Ber Borochov, *Ktavim Nivcharim Kerech 1* (Selected Works, First Volume) (Tel Aviv: Am Oved, 1944); *Ktavim Kerech Rishon* (Works, Vol. 1) (Tel Aviv: Hakibbutz Hameuchad, 1955); *Ktavim Kerech Shlishi* (Works Vol. 3) (Tel Aviv: Hakibbutz Hameuchad, 1966).

48 Sneh, *On the National Question*, 138 (translation mine).

[משתק את הייצור והפיתוח של ישראל]
[התפתחות התעשייה הלאומית הישראלית]

49 Ibid., 76 (translation mine).

[התנועה הקומוניסטית 'מכירה' באומה המתהווה בישראל]

50 Ibid., 144 (translation mine).

[התפתחות קפיטליסטית זו של הישוב היהודי על חלק מהשטח של ארץ-ישראל, היא אשר גרמה לתהליך התפתחותו לאומה. השלטון האימפריאלסטי הבריטי הגביל את אפשרויות התפתחותה של האומה המתהווה והטיל עליה משטר של דיכוי לאומי וניצול קולניאלי.]

Thus, utilizing a combination of Stalinist and Leninist understandings, Sneh denationalizes the Jewish people and nationalizes the Jews in Israel. By using Leninist readings of late nineteenth century imperialism to disavow Zionism, Sneh creates a local Israeli identity.

Sneh's theorizing into existence a local Israeli nation had deep roots in the history of Communism in Palestine/Israel, in the form of Yishuvism. This doctrine was developed between 1924 – the year the PKP (Palestine Communist Party) was admitted to the Comintern – and 1928, as the Soviets, in the wake of their 1927 debacle in China – when the Kuomintang headed by Chiang Kai-shek massacred his Communist allies – turned against aligning with non-Communist colonial nationalist movements. It was developed by the foremost leader of the Party in the 1920s, Wolf Averbuch, and was "basically 'pro-Palestinian' covered with extreme anti-Zionism" [51] The Communists did not just reject Zionism because it was "reactionary, bourgeois, nationalist and allied with imperialism"[52] but also because it was a hindrance to the economic development of the country. According to the adherents of this ideology, the emigration of Jews to Palestine was a deterministic process, an "objective necessity, the result of the political and economic conditions under which the Jewish masses in Eastern Europe live."[53] Affluent as well as poor Jews were thus arriving in Palestine, giving rise to a Marxist process of class differentiation and capital accumulation. This capitalist project was hindering Zionism as a result of two contradictions. One was the fact that Zionism needed "feudalism, which enables it to purchase lands and create a separate Jewish economy." However, the emigration of Jews together with the creation of the *Yishuv* "instigates an economic development that destroys the feudal conditions." [54] At the same time, Zionism's alliance with the British colonial ruler – which wanted to make Palestine a colonial market for British goods by enacting heavy tariffs and taxes in order to inhibit the development of local manufacturing – was stifling the development of Jewish industry.[55] Therefore, it was seen that the Jewish *Yishuv* should abandon the Zion-

---

51 Nachman List, "Tzadaq haQomintern [Daled]" (The Comintern was Right D.) *Qeshet* 6-D (1964), 112 (translation mine).

['פרו-פלשתנאיות' ביסודן אם גם בכסות של אנטי-ציונות חריפה]

52 Ibid., 112 (translation mine).

[ראקציונית, בורגנית, לאומנית ובעלת-בריתו של האימפריאליזם]

53 Ibid., 112 (translation mine).

[כורח אובייקטיבי, תוצאת התנאים המדיניים והכלכליים אשר בהם חיים המוני היהודים בארצות מזרח-ארופה]

54 Ibid., 114 (translation mine).

[לפ'אודליזם, המאפשר לה לרכוש אדמות ולהקים משק יהודי נבדל]

[התפתחות כלכלית ההורסת את התנאים הפ'יאודליים]

55 Ibid.

ist nationalist project and join hands with the Arabs of Palestine in an anti-imperialist and anti-Zionist struggle for political and economic independence. In practice, Yishuvism enabled the PKP to draw a dividing line between the *Yishuv* and Zionism, and thus to continue participating in the autonomous institutions of the Jews in Palestine – it was an "endorsement of the Zionist program and its accomplishments [...] and at the same time, a rejection of the tenets of Zionist nationalism."[56]

Those historians that have dealt with Yishuvism attributed it to the cultural isolation of the mostly Jewish Party members from the Palestinian majority, the inherent contradiction between their being part of the European colonial minority (i. e. the *Yishuv*), and their need to side with the Palestinian anticolonial struggle.[57] Here I would like to suggest another explanation, one that focuses on the creation of national identity. It is true – as will be shown on the following pages – that the inconsistency between the fact that the Jewish Communists were part of the Zionist settler-colonial project and their Jewish-Arab politics resulted in a degree of colonial unknowing. However, the ideological answers the Party came up with time and time again throughout its history, as Musa Budeiri pointed out,[58] should be seen as an attempt at non-Zionist national indigenization. To prove this argument, one need only to go back to List's own understanding of the theory he agitated for in the 1920s. He defines it as "Zionism without Zionism" and "a Palestinian solution to the Palestinian crisis." [59] These words point to the national content of this doctrine and its local nature, embodying an attempt – much like Sneh's – to use Marxist ideology in order to create a local national identity.

---

56 Jacob Hen-Tov, *Communism and Zionism in Palestine: The Comintern and the Political Unrest in the 1920s* (Cambridge: Schenkman Publishing Company, 1974), 110.

57 See Avner Ben Zaken, *Qomunizem keImperyalizem Tarbuti: Haziqa beyn haqomunizem haEretz-Israeli laqomunizem haAravi 1919 – 1948* (Communism as Cultural Imperialism: The Affinities between Eretz-Israeli Communism and Arab Communism, 1919 – 1948) (Tel Aviv: Resling Publishing, 2006); Johan Franzén, "Communism Versus Zionism: The Comintern, Yishuvism, and the Palestine Communist Party," *Journal of Palestine Studies* 36 (2007): 6; and Ran Greenstein, *Zionism and its Discontents: A Century of Radical Dissent in Israel/Palestine* (London: Pluto Press, 2014).

58 Musa Budeiri, *The Palestine Communist Party 1919 – 1948: Arab & Jew in the Struggle for Internationalism* (Chicago: Haymarket Books, 2010), 9.

59 Nachman List, "Tzadaq haqomindtern [Hey]" (The Comintern was Right E.), *Keshet* 7-C (1965): 80 (translation mine).

[ציונות-ללא-ציונות]
[פתרון פלשתינאי למשבר פלשתינאי]

Sneh makes a radical argument that subverts many fundamentals of Zionism. It theorizes into existence an Israeli identity detached from Zionism. However, it is manifestly an Israeli-Jewish identity that accepts many elements of the Zionist project. He is cognizant of the effects of Zionist settler-colonialism on the Palestinians and his political stands are radical for their time. Sneh calls for Palestinian self-determination in an independent state and the return of refugees.[60] His understandings of class formation and capital transfer in Palestine/Israel are not divorced from the historical realties. However, he lacks a comprehensive understanding – which other Communists had – of the colonial logic of Zionism. Communist ideology decreed that at the root of the hostility between Jews and Arabs lies the malevolent scheming of imperialism. Loyal to this article of faith, Sneh attributes the colonial polices of Zionism to Western (i.e. British and American) imperialism. As he tellingly phrases it,

> The British imperialist rule tried by any means possible to direct the Arab movement away from itself and against the Jewish *Yishuv* [...] The Zionist leadership did, on its part, everything to help the British rulers fan the flames of hostility between Arabs and Jews according to the old principle of 'divide and rule.' Every case of dispossession of tenant *fellahin* from the land; every picketing of '*Avoda Ivrit*' (Hebrew Labor), which prevented workers from being employed at a Jewish proprietor; the clause in the 'Jewish National Fund' constitution that bars Arabs from working its lands; the systematic abstention from any Jewish-Arab co-operation in the political, economic, cultural and social fields... all that helped British imperialism to provoke Jews and Arabs.[61]

Despite that, Sneh asserts that Palestinian nationalism lacks an anticolonial context and national agency. He names it the "national liberation movement of the Arab People in Eretz-Israel,"[62] defining it as an agrarian reform movement which also sought national independence. The Palestinians in Israel are seen in this context as the subject of a struggle which is in essence for civil rights. Sneh's followers – soon to be MAKI members – are encouraged "to bitterly struggle against Jewish nationalism, as our Arab comrades struggle against Arab nation-

---

60 Sneh, *On the National Question*, 153 – 154.

61 Ibid., 140 (translation mine).

[השלטון הבריטי השתדל בכול האמצעים להטות את התתנועה הערבית שלא תכוון נגדו כי-אם נגד הישוב היהודי [...] ההנהגה הציונית עשתה מצידה הכל, כדי לסייע בידי השלטון הבריטי ללבות את האיבה בין ערבים ליהודים בהתאם לעיקרון העתיק 'הפרד ומשול', כל מקרה של נישול פלחים אריסים מן הקרקע; כל פעולה של משמרות 'העבודה העיברית', שמנעו מפועלים ערבים עבודה אצל מעביד יהודי; הסעיף בחוקת 'הקרן הקיימת', האוסר לערבים לעבד את אדמותיה; ההימנעות השיטתית מכל שיתו-פעולה יהודי-ערבי בשטח הפוליטי,הכלכלי, התרבותי והחברתי; [...] כל זה עזר לאימפריאליזם הבריטי לסכסך בין הערבים ליהודים]

62 Ibid. (translation mine).

[תנועת השחרור הלאומי של העם הערבי בארץ-ישראל]

alism."[63] Why did Sneh not construct an Israeli identity that would not be so manifestly Israeli-Jewish and would be able to include the Palestinians in Israel? Why could he not comprehend the colonial logic of Zionism? Part of the answer is to be found in the theoretical tools he used, as Marxism-Leninism did not develop a more nuanced understanding of settler-colonial situations. Clearly Sneh cannot be blamed for not understanding historical realties with theories that are outside his time (i.e. settler colonialism), even though other MAKI ideologists did grasp aspects of Zionist colonialism. The better part of the answer lies in Sneh's consciousness of his text's intended audience. The people that he is talking to in the context of an emerging Israeli far left are the product of the Zionist settler project, as the following portrayal of his followers makes evident: "those were young people that came to the Party straight from the mainstream of Israeli society. Most of them were native born, veterans of the youth movements, kibbutz members, in short – people that came from the heart of the *Yishuv*." [64] These young men and women – many of whom fought in the 1948 war in the elite *Palmach* (Striking Units) – brought the Zionist settler-colonial project to its culmination, a national settler state. Sneh in his text thus reflects their understanding of the historical reality they themselves and he took part in. While their understanding differed radically from Zionist conventions, it still failed to fully understand Zionism and its impact on the Palestinian natives of the land.

The Colonized

Emile Touma was one of the most influential intellectuals to come out of the Communist Party. The Palestinian Israeli poet and journalist Salem Jubran described him as "one of the most varied and important figures in the intellectual, cultural and political life of the Arab Palestinian people," adding that "the fact that he was an Israeli citizen since 1948 until his death in 1985 enabled him to have a central role in the life of the Arab population in Israel." [65] Born in 1919 in

63 Ibid., 156 (translation mine).
[הננו נאבקים מרה נגד הנאציונליזם היהודי, כשם שחברינו הערבים לוחמים כנגד הנאציונליזם הערבי]

64 Nessia Shafran, *Farewell Communism*, 134 (translation mine).
[אלה היו אנשים צעירים, שהגיעו אל המפלגה הישר מן הזרם המרכזי של החברה הישראלית. רובם ילידי הארץ,חניכי תנועות הנוער,בוגרי קיבוץ, בקצרה – אנשים שצמחו מלב לבו של הישוב]

65 Emile Touma, *haTnua haLeumit haFalasṭinit vehaOlam haAravi* (The Palestinian National Movement and the Arab World) (Tel Aviv: Mifras Publishers, 1990), 7 (translation mine).
[אחת הדמויות החשובות והעשירות בחיי ההגות והעשיה הפוליטית בקרב העם הערבי הפלסטיני.]

Haifa to a Greek-Orthodox (Rum-Orthodox) family, he was part of a cohort of young middle class Palestinian intellectuals who joined the PKP in the 1940s. They became the backbone of the leadership of the Party until the 1980s,[66] following in the footsteps of the first generation of working class Rum-Orthodox youths that joined the PKP in the 1920s.

This group of new converts were described both by historians of the Party and by contemporaries as lacking in their ideological understanding of Communism. This is clear from the words of another Communist leader, of the first generation of Rum-Orthodox Palestinians who joined the Party, Bullas Farah:

> The comrades that came from the national movement with no fixed world view and no clear ideology were only revolutionary patriots. It was not possible to see in them the social facet and they were not interested in social problems. Most of them came from the middle class […] They had only heard about Marxist ideology and the Soviet Union, but knew nothing about Marxism and the social, political and economic structure of the Soviet Union.[67]

Similarly, Musa Budeiri, the historian of the Party's Palestinian section, asserts that the new converts were

> disillusioned with the traditional leaders and were drawn not so much by the party's advocacy of communism, but by its support of the Arab independence struggle, its modernity and methods of organization … [and] the identification of the party with the Soviet Union whose growing prowess in the war was attracting enthusiastic admirers among the educated youth.[68]

[עובדת היותו אזרח ישראל מ-1948 ועד ליום מותו ב-1985 איפשרה לו למלא תפקיד מרכזי בחיי האוכלוסיה הערבית בישראל]

66 The Greek-Orthodox community in Palestine had a longtime connection to Russia. It supported the attempts of the Palestinian members of the community to Arabize the Greek-controlled hierarchy of the church and had an extensive educational network. The relations continued after the October Revolution, as the anti-clerical rebellion of some of the young members of the community made them susceptible to Communist ideology emanating from Soviet Russia. See Merav Mack, "Orthodox and Communist: A History of a Christian Community in Mandate Palestine," *British Journal of Middle Eastern Studies* 42 (2015): 384 – 400.

67 Bullas Farah, *mehaShildton haOtmani laMedina haIvrit: Sipur Chayav shel Qomunist vePadtriyodt Palastini 1910 – 1991* (From Ottoman Rule to the Hebrew State: The Life Story of a Communist and Palestinian Patriot 1910 – 1991) (Haifa: published by Udi Adiv, 2009), 68 (translation mine).
[החברים שהגיעו מן התנועה הלאומית ללא השקפה מבוססת וללא אידאולוגיה ברורה היו רק פטריוטים מהפכנים, אך לא היה אפשר להבחין אצלם בפן החברתי והם לא התעניינו בבעיות החברה. רובם באו מקרב המעמד הבינוני[…] הם שמעו על האידאלוגיה המרקסיסטית ועל ברית המועצות, אך למעשה לא הכירו את המרקסיזם ואת המבנה החברתי,הפוליטי והכלכלי של ברית המועצות.]

68 Musa Budeiri, *The Palestine Communist Party 1919 – 1948: Arab & Jew in the Struggle for Internationalism* (London: Ithaca Press, 1979), 97.

However, a more nuanced analysis of Touma's early intellectual development reveals a more complex reality. Of critical importance to his development was his meeting, during his high school years in Jerusalem, with the Lebanese Marxist thinker – and fellow Greek-Orthodox – Raif Khoury. His impact is described by one of Touma's classmates and a future Communist leader, Taufik Toubi (1922–2011): "The outbreak of The Great Socialist October Revolution, and the coming together of the political, national and social ideas – happened under the influence of the Arabic language and literature teacher, the writer and thinker Raif Khoury."[69] The ideas that he transmitted to his students consisted of a universalism inspired by the values of the French Revolution, Marxist anti-imperialism, and anti-colonial nationalism. In 1938, as a representative of the Arab youth at the International Youth Conference in New York, Khoury drew notice for "his strong objection to British policies in Palestine and his critique of Zionism as a colonial movement."[70] His stay in Palestine coincided with the fateful years of the Arab Rebellion (1936–1939). During that period, he penned, in 1937, a short pamphlet titled *Jihad Filastin* (Jihad of Palestine), in which he "explicitly argues that popular Arab resistance was directed against the British authorities and Zionism, but not against the local Jewish population."[71] These ideas, coupled with a passionate commitment to anti-Fascism, and a conviction that "only Bolshevik Russia was able to realize the liberation of humanity,"[72] led to Touma's ideological baptism into Communism.

These ideas – taught against the background of the resurgence of social activism and nationalist upsurge of the Great Arab Revolt years – served to enhance Touma's, and his friends', "national consciousness, class solidarity and socialist ideology."[73] So when Khoury's teachings were supplemented with the Marxist-Leninist ideology of the Communist Party, Touma formed an anticolonial view of Zionism intermingled with anti-imperialism. In a short booklet published in 1970 – an English reprint of an article by Touma in *Zo Ha'Derech* (That is the Way), Rakah's (New Communist List) Hebrew newspaper – Touma takes on the question of the existence of a localized Israeli-Jewish nation. The article was

---

69 Taufik Toubi, *beDarko* (In His Way) (Haifa: Raya Publishing House, 2012), 14 (translation mine).
[פריצתה של מהפכת אוקטובר הסוציאליסטית, וההתחברות אל הרעיונות המדיניים, הלאומיים והחברתיים יחד – התרחשו בהשפעתו של המורה לשפה ולספרות ערבית, הסופר והוגה הדעות ראיף ח'ורי.]

70 Götz Nordbruch, "Defending the French Revolution during War Word II: Raif Khoury and the Intellectual Challenge of Nazism in the Levant," *Mediterranean Historical Review* 62 (2006): 223.

71 Ibid., 234.

72 Merav Mack, *Orthodox and Communist*, 396, 226.

73 Ibid., 396.

written in order to disprove the claims of Arab left-wingers outside Israel that doubted the existence of a Jewish nation in Israel, and to promote the idea of a Palestinian nation-state. Paradoxically, in order to justify such a state, Touma needs to assert the existence of Israel as a nation-state without Zionism.

In the text, Khoury's old distinction between Zionism and the Jews of Palestine is rephrased in the Marxist-Leninist dogma of the Communist Party. Using heavily Stalinist language, Touma severs the link between the Jews in Israel and the Jews of the world: "It is correct, first of all, that the Jewish communities in the world do not constitute one nation, as Zionism alleges."[74] However, he does acknowledge a localized Israeli nation: "but it is also true that the Jews who came to Palestine in the time of the Mandate, and to Israel after its establishment, crystallized and are crystallizing as an Israeli nation." Motivated by the memory of the Holocaust and helped along by the spread of mass media, the Jews in Israel "have built a common economy, have started developing a defined culture [...] have lived in a common territory. In this way they have acquired the characteristics of a nation."[75]

Zionism is delegitimized due to its links to Western imperialism and the bourgeoisie: "It must be emphasized that Zionism, in spite of some traits particular to it, resembles every bourgeois-imperialist ideology."[76] As such, it is bound to disappear, leaving Israel as a peaceful and non-Zionist state coexisting beside a Palestinian one.

As for Palestinian nationalism, Touma sees it as arising from Israel's colonial policies of ethnic cleansing and Western geopolitics. Palestinian nationalism as an anti-colonial and anti-imperialist struggle against Britain and Zionism was inculcated in Touma and his classmates by Khoury. Reminiscing about his schooldays, Taufik Toubi recalls how the newly minted young radicals, filled with indignation at social class inequality and patriotic zeal, went "to demonstrate in the city streets, throwing stones at the British soldiers and policemen." He adds: "we were part of a just struggle."[77]

While Touma stayed loyal to Party doctrine – viewing imperialism as the root of the Zionist-Palestinian conflict – he exhibits a more in-depth understand-

---

74 Emile Touma, *About the Idea of a Palestinian State* (New Outlook Publishers: New York, 1970), 3.

75 Ibid., 3.

76 Ibid., 7.

77 Tom Segev, "Daddy did not Teach me to be a Communist," *Qoteret Rashit*, December 4 1985, 4 (translation mine).

[היינו יוצאים להפגנות לחוצות העיר, זורקים אבנים על החיילים ועל השוטרים הבריטיים]

[היינו חלק ממאבק צודק]

ing of Zionist colonialism. This sensitivity to the colonial logic of Zionism is clear in a speech delivered on the occasion of the sixtieth anniversary of the October Revolution in Baku, USSR. Here he adheres to Party doctrine – viewing Zionism as an organic part of Western Imperialism:

> The fact is that Zionism, which emerged at the end of the 19th century, was conceived as a colonialist venture. Until the '20s of this century, its leaders looked on colonial settlements in Algeria and Tunisia as models to be improved upon. The Zionists, led by their prophet Herzl, have worked consistently to integrate with imperialism. From the Balfour Declaration in 1917 until the '40s of this century, the Zionists colluded with British imperialism. But since the establishment of the State of Israel – notwithstanding the West European imperialist countries (Britain, France, West Germany) – they have gravitated toward U.S. imperialism and fused their policy with its global strategy.[78]

Touma also accords real agency to Palestinian nationalism, specifically among the Palestinians in Israel. This view is very much interlaced with the Leninist formulation of the national right to self-determination. In his Baku speech, Touma links Zionist anti-Communism to the Leninist right to self-determination. Zionists reject the Soviet Union because "the country of October supports the legitimate national rights of the Arab peoples, and foremost of the Palestinian people." They "generate anti-Soviet incitement notwithstanding the fact that the Soviet Union adheres to the principle of self-determination for all peoples, including the Israeli people."[79]

In his analysis of the 1948 War and the reasons behind it, imperialism is perceived as the prime mover of events. For instance, Touma states: "this war was not just a Palestinian or regional war; it was dictated by the rivalry between England and the United States."[80] Loyal to the Leninist view of imperialism as the force behind local actors and the inevitability of rivalry between imperial predators, Touma argues that in struggling for spheres of influence, "Britain acted through the Trans-Jordanian King Abdullah to safeguard its holdings in the Arab East [...] the United States supported the Zionist leadership while courting the reactionary Arab regimes in Egypt and Saudi Arabia."[81] However, this ideo-

---

78 Emile Touma, "The October Revolution and the Struggle against Zionism," *Jewish Affairs* 7 (1977): 6.

79 Emile Touma, "The October Revolution and the Struggle against Zionism II," *Jewish Affairs* 7 (1977): 7.

80 Emile Touma, *hatTnua haLeumit haFalasṭinit vehaOlam haAravi* (The Palestinian National Movement and the Arab World) (Tel Aviv: Mifras Publishers, 1990), 10 (translation mine).
[זו לא היתה מלחמה פלסטינית או אזורית בלבד;היא הוכתבה גם על-ידי התחרות בין אנגליה וארצות-הברית.]

81 Ibid. (translation mine)

logical Communist norm is interwoven with an awareness of the effects of Zionism on the Palestinian people. Weakened by an ineffective traditional leadership and the Arab states' disregard for their national rights, the Palestinian people had fallen victim to Zionist ethnic expulsion.[82] This is obvious in these words: "it is evident today that the Zionist leadership, which became the Israeli government after the state's establishment on 15 May 1948, deliberately planned the cleansing of the area it occupied from the Arab-Palestinian people."[83]

While he continues to chart the tortuous history of the Palestinians outside Israel, Touma also portrays the history of those that were left in the Jewish state. Here his account interlaces nationalism with an understanding that colonial ethnic purging was still in effect. The narrative Touma constructs for the Palestinians in Israel is one of national revival. The conditions the Palestinians in Israel found themselves facing were impossible. Besides discrimination against them, they also had to contend with the fact that the Israeli authorities were "not reconciled to the presence of this very small Arab national minority."[84] He astutely observes the continuation of settler-colonial pre-1948 policies meant to control labor and land into the new era:

> It institutionalized the classic Zionist policy – the conquest of land – by promulgating laws and administrative orders to confiscate Arab land and thus deprive the Arab inhabitants – who were mainly farmers – of their means of livelihood. In this way, the Israeli Land Administration gradually seized over one million dunams of land belonging to Israel's Arab citizens, reducing Arab land ownership to an average of one dunam per head, whereas during the British Mandate period the average had been sixteen dunams per head. Lastly, it implemented measures intended to force stagnation on Arab economic, social and cultural life.[85]

Above all, the Israeli state had not given up its main objective: the complete cleansing of the remnants of the Palestinians in Israel.[86] While the Palestinians in Israel were demoralized, alienated, and traumatized by the military defeat and the *Nakba*, they had risen from the ashes to become a national minority.

[בריטניה פעלה באמצאות המלך עבדאללה מלך עבר-הירדן, כדי להבטיח את מאחזיה במזרח הערבי [...] ארצות-הברית תמכה בהנהגה הציונית, ובו-בזמן חיזרה אחר המישטרים הראקציונריים במצריים ובסעודיה]

82 For Israeli polices in the 1948 war and the mass deportation of Palestinians, see Benny Morris, *Leydata shel beayat haPlidtim haFalestinim 1947 – 1949* (The Birth of the Palestinian Refugee Problem, 1947 – 1949) (Tel Aviv: Am Oved Publishers, 1991).

83 Emile Touma, *The Palestinian National Movement*, 11.

84 Emil Touma, "The Political Coming of Age of the 'National Minority'," *Journal of Palestine Studies* 14 (1985): 75.

85 Ibid.

86 Ibid.

This act of resurrection was the result of the coming together of popular struggle and a new leadership. Discounting notions that the Palestinians in Israel were politically passive until 1967, Touma states that "wide-scale circles of that public rose independently to defend the rights of the Arab Palestinian people and end the national persecution."[87] However, the Palestinian masses did not conduct their anti-colonial struggles leaderless. Since the discredited traditional leaders had been physically removed from the scene, the Communist Party was able to take over and lead the fight:

> The Jewish-Arab Communist Party of Israel was able to fill the vacuum left by the failure of the traditional Arab national leadership. Its Arab members, strongly backed by the Jewish members, mobilized the Arab population and stood in the vanguard to resist the Zionist policy of uprooting and expulsion.[88]

The process of renewal was not confined to political struggle, but also extended to the cultural realm. The Palestinians in Israel "have built up their identity, and they have been able to abort the attempt to spread national nihilism. They have generated a stratum of educated people, intellectuals, writers, poets."[89]

Conclusion

What is the reason for the difference between Sneh and Touma? Its roots lie in the respective audiences they are addressing. Touma is ever aware of his Palestinian compatriots: even when he writes in Hebrew in the Communist press, he refers to Palestinians and to their place as the colonized people. It can be said, then, that Touma stands for the consciousness of the colonized, while Sneh represents the consciousness of the – indeed progressive and radical – settler. In the case of Touma this difference is obvious if one looks at his initial reaction to the 1947 Partition of Palestine. In sharp difference to his comrades in the NLL[90] he

87 Emile Touma, *The Palestinian National Movement*, 30.

88 Emil Touma, "*The Political Coming of Age of the 'National Minority*,'" 75.

89 Emile Touma, Lynne Barbee, and Margaret Chiari, "Emile Touma," *Journal of Palestine Studies* 13 (1983): 16.

90 The NLL (National Liberation League) was founded in 1943 after the split of the bi-national PKP. The organization was active among the growing Palestinian working class and its unions. With the 1947 Partition the organization split between those who supported the UN plan and those who objected to it, while the fighting and the deportation of most of the Palestinians broke its base of power. For a detailed history of the NLL and a debate on its nature see Yehosua

objected to the partition of Palestine. While leaders like Emile Habibi and Taufik Toubi integrated into the newly formed Arab-Jewish MAKI (Israeli Communist Party) and supported the Jewish state,[91] Touma was forced to perform self-criticism recanting his previous stands and his way to the top leadership of the Party was blocked until the early 1960s when he gradually assumed leadership roles.[92] His initial rejection of the new Party line – that entailed a support for the Jewish nation settler state largely on the expense of the Palestinians – is translated in text penned by him to an understanding of the colonial aspects of Zionism beyond the imperialist dogma that permeated Communist ideology.

Emil Touma's understandings of nationalism and imperialism were shaped not only by Marxism-Leninism but by his indigenous Marxist teachings as

---

Porat, "The National Liberation League: Its Rise, Its Essence and Fall (1943–1948)," *The New East* 14 (1968); Budeiri, *The Palestine Communist Party 1919–1948.*

91 The 1947 U.N Partition Resolution split the NLL. Most of its leadership had supported the creation of two states. They opposed the Arab armies' invasion of Palestine and taking over parts allocated for the Palestinian state. The NLL requested the Palestinian masses "to understand the war in Palestine as part of the global struggle against Western imperialism" (Avner Ben Zaken, *Qomunizem kelmperyalizem Tarbuti: haZika beyn haqomunizem haEretz- Israeli laqomunizem haAravi 1919–1948* (Communism as Cultural Imperialism: the Affinities between Eretz-Israeli Communism and Arab Communism, 1919–1948) (Tel Aviv: Resling Publishing, 2006), 174). In a handbill named *Nada Lgon'd el-Arab* (Call to the Arab soldiers), the Arab soldiers of the invading armies were called upon "to go back to your countries, aim your fire at the heart of imperialism and its servants" (Ibid., 178). The text argues "that the war did not serve the Arab interest, but the interests of Western imperialism." The anti-imperialist ideological language seen here was shared by Palestinian and Jewish Communists and used by them to justify their political decisions. As for the Palestinians, who were losing a war against a far superior enemy, their society disintegrating, "those elements were for the most part Arabs disconnected from reality and outrages" (Ibid., 174). The Palestinian Communists did not directly support the Jewish Communists' efforts on behalf of the Israeli war effort; however, they did see the forces of the IDF "not as enemies but as allies in the struggle to achieve a shared goal – two states for two nations" (Ibid., 180). The role the Palestinian Communists played in the 1948 War came under increasing criticism in recent years by Palestinian historians. They argue that – in contrast to the heroic role as the defender of the Palestinians left in Israel's borders painted by the Party – the Palestinian Communists cooperated with the Jewish side in the war glossing over the large-scale ethnic cleansing of their people. For these allegations savagely denied by the present day Communist Party see Ahmad.H.Sa'di, "Communism and Zionism in Palestine-Israel: A Troubled Legacy," *Holy Land Studies* 9 (2010): 169–183. A more elaborate argumentation can be found in the work of Adel Manna that recognizes the complexity of the stand of the Party as she moved from a full support in 1948 to a growing confrontation with the Israeli state during the 1950s: see Adel Manna, *Nakba veHistardut: Sipuram shel haFalaltinim shNisharu beHaifa veBagalil. 1948–1956* (Nakba and Survival: The Story of the Palestinians Who Remind in Haifa and the Galilee, 1948–1956) (Tel-Aviv: Hakibbutz Hameuchad, 2017).

92 Shafran, *Farewell Communism*, 162; Manna, *Nakba and Survival*, 141.

well. He outlines two distinct national entities, the first a Jewish-Israeli non-Zionist national identity. In the theorization of this local Israeli nation, he shares with Mosh Sneh the same ideological underpinnings. Both use the Stalinist categorization of the nation as sharing a common language, territory, economy, and cultural traits. They use these distinctions as a way to separate the Jews of Israel from the Jewish people and argue for a distinctive national identity. Both of them place the development of nationalism and national conflict in the context of global imperialism. Understanding the British and American presence in Palestine/Israel according to Leninist analysis, they use Zionism's longstanding links with Western empires – as well as being an expression of the Jewish propertied class – to discredit it as an authentic national movement. Also, in accordance with Party ideology, they identify imperialism as the root cause of the Middle Eastern conflict. However, at this point the two Communist theorists diverge.

Sneh subsumes colonialism and imperialism, viewing British imperialism as the oppressive force that propelled Jewish independence in Eretz-Israel. As a result, while he was mindful of the repression of the Palestinians in Israel and the mass deportation during the 1948 War, he failed to fully understand their national agency. In contrast, Touma's narrative of the Palestinians in Israel is imbued with anti-colonial nationalism. Now pursued by the Israeli government, the same colonial policies of exploitation and dispossession continue. The struggle against them, led by the Communist Party, has configured the Palestinians in Israel as a local national minority. Touma takes pains to emphasize the fact that the Palestinian citizens of Israel are part of the wider Palestinian people.[93] At the same time, he portrays the differences between them as arising from different circumstances. Confronted by the "national repression and discriminatory policies of Israel's ruling circles,"[94] those in Israel had created their own Palestinian national identity.

93 "I emphasize the Palestinian Arab identity because sometimes I feel unhappy about the emphasis on "Palestinian" as opposed to "Arab." There is such a tendency among certain Arab intellectuals, unfortunately. This was one of our main objectives and remains so. That is why in our material, in our documents, in our press, we emphasize that we are part and parcel of the Palestinian Arab people." Emile Touma, *Emile Touma*, 21.
94 Emile Touma, *The Palestinian National Movement*, 29.

Works Cited

Anderson, Benedict. *Imagined Communities*. London: Verso, 1983.

Ben Zaken, Avner. *Qomunizem kelmperyalizem Tarbuti: haZiqa beyn haqomunizem haEretz-Israeli laqomunizem haAravi 1919–1948* (Communism as Cultural Imperialism: The Affinities between Eretz-Israeli Communism and Arab Communism, 1919–1948). Tel Aviv: Resling Publishing, 2006.

Borochov, Dov Ber. *Ktavim Nivcharim Kerech 1* (Selected Works, First Volume). Tel Aviv: Am Oved, 1944.

Borochov, Dov Ber. *Ktavim Kerech Rishon* (Works, Vol. 1). Tel Aviv: Hakibbutz Hameuchad, 1955.

Borochov, Dov Ber. *Ktavim Kerech Shlishi* (Works Vol. 3). Tel Aviv: Hakibbutz Hameuchad, 1966.

Budeiri, Musa. *The Palestine Communist Party 1919–1948: Arab & Jew in the Struggle for Internationalism*. Chicago: Haymarket Books, 2010.

Bukharin, Nikolai. *Imperialism and World Economy*. London: The Merlin Press, 1972.

Farah, Bullas. *meHashilton haOtmani laMedina halvrit: Sipur Chayav shel Qomunist vePadtriyodt Palastini 1910–1991* (From Ottoman Rule to the Hebrew State: The Life Story of a Communist and Palestinian Patriot 1910–1991). Haifa: Udi Adiv, 2009.

Franzén, Johan. "Communism Verses Zionism: The Comintern, Yishuvism, and the Palestine Communist Party." *Journal of Palestine Studies* 36 (2007): 6–24.

Gellner, Ernest. *Nations and Nationalism*. Oxford: Basil Blackwell Ltd, 1983.

Greenstein, Ran. *Zionism and its Discontents: A Century of Radical Dissent in Israel/Palestine*. London: Pluto Press, 2014.

Hen-Tov, Jacob. *Communism and Zionism in Palestine: The Comintern and the Political Unrest in the 1920s*. Cambridge: Schenkman Publishing Company, 1974.

Hilferding, Rudolf. *Finance Capital: A Study of the Latest Phase of Capitalist Development*. London: Routledge & Kegan Paul, 1981.

Hobson, J. A. *Imperialism: A Study*. Memphis: General Book, 2012.

Hunt, Tristram. *The Frock-Coated Communist: The Revolutionary Life of Friedrich Engels*. New York: Penguin, 2009.

Jacobs, Jack, ed. *Jewish Politics in Eastern Europe: The Bund at 100*. New York: New York University Press, 2001.

Kautsky, Karl. "Ultra-Imperialism," *Die Neue Zeit*, September 11 1914. Accessed February 28 2017. https://www.marxists.org/archive/kautsky/1914/09/ultra-imp.htm.

Lenin, V. I. *Imperialism: The Highest Stage of Capitalism*. New York: International Publishers, 1985.

Lenin, V. I. *The Right of Nations to Self-Determination*. Moscow: Progress Publishers, 1997.

List, Nachman. "Tzadaq haQomindtern [Daled]" (The Comintern was Right D). *Keshet* 6-D (1964): 103–117.

List, Nachman. Tzadaq haQomindtern (Hey) (The Comintern was Right E). *Keshet* 7-C (1965): 80–93.

Löwy, Michal. "Marxists and the National Question." *New Left Review* I/96 (1976): 81–85.

Luxemburg, Rosa. *The Accumulation of Capital*. London: Routledge, 2003.

Luxemburg, Rosa. *The National Question*. New York: Monthly Review Press, 1976.

Mack, Merav. "Orthodox and Communist: A History of a Christian Community in Mandate Palestine." *British Journal of Middle Eastern Studies* 42 (2015): 384–400.
Marx, Karl and Friedrich Engels. *On Colonialism; Articles From the New York Tribune and Other Writings.* New York: International Publishers, 1972.
Manna, del. *Nakba veHisardut: Sipuram shel haFalalstinim sheNotru beHaifa vebaGalil. 1948–1956* (Nakba and Survival: The Story of the Palestinians Who Remind in Haifa and the Galilee, 1948–1956). Tel-Aviv: Hakibbutz Hameuchad, 2017.
Morris, Benny. *Leydata shel Beayat haPlidtim haFalestinim 1947–1949* (The Birth of the Palestinian Refugee Problem, 1947–1949). Tel Aviv: Am Oved Publishers, 1991.
Noonan, Murray. "Marxist Theories of Imperialism: Evolution of a Concept." PhD diss., Victoria University, 2010.
Nordbruch, Götz. "Defending the French Revolution during War Word II: Raif Khoury and the Intellectual Challenge of Nazism in the Levant." *Mediterranean Historical Review* 62 (2006): 219–237.
Rieber, J. Alfred. "Stalin, Man of Borderlands." *The American Historical Review* 106 (2001): 1651–1691.
Segev, Tom. "Daddy did not Teach me to be a Communist." *qoteret rashit*, December 4 1985.
Shafran, Nessia. *Shalom Lecha Qomunizem* (Farewell Communism). Tel Aviv: Hakibbutz Hameuchad, 1983.
Sneh, Moshe. *Sikumim baShela haLeumit: leOr haMarqsizem-Leninizem* (On the National Question: Conclusions in the Light of Marxism-Leninism). Tel Aviv: The Left Socialist Party Publication, 1954.
Stalin, J. V. *Marxism and the National Question.* Moscow: Foreign Languages Publishing House, 1945.
Toubi, Taufik. *beDarko* (In His Way). Haifa: Raya Publishing House, 2012.
Touma, Emile, Lynne Barbee, and Margaret Chiari. "Emile Touma." *Journal of Palestine Studies* 13 (1983): 15–23.
Touma, Emile. *About the Idea of a Palestinian State.* New York: Outlook Publishers, 1970.
Touma, Emile. *haTnua haLeumit haFalasṭinit vehaOlam haravi* (The Palestinian National Movement and the Arab World). Tel Aviv: Mifras Publishers, 1990.
Touma, Emile. "The October Revolution and the Struggle against Zionism." *Jewish Affairs* 7 (1977): 4–7.
Touma, Emile. "The October Revolution and the Struggle against Zionism II." *Jewish Affairs* 7 (1977): 6–8.
Touma, Emile. The Political Coming of Age of the 'National Minority'." *Journal of Palestine Studies* 14 (1985): 74–83.
Sa'di, H. Ahmad. "Communism and Zionism in Palestine-Israel: A Troubled Legacy." *Holy Land Studies* 9 (2010): 169–183.
Sperber, Jonathan. *Karl Marx: A Nineteenth-Century Life.* London: Liveright, 2013.
Van Ree, Erik. "Stalin as a Marxist: The Western Roots of Stalin's Russification of Marxism." In *Stalin a New History*, edited by Sarah Davies and James Harris, 159–180. New York: Cambridge University Press, 2005.
Van Ree, Erik. "Stalin and the National Question." *Revolutionary Russia* 7 (1994): 214–238.

Frank Jacob

Radical Trinity

Anarchist, Jew, or New Yorker?

Introduction

Before the First World War marked Europe's cultural suicide and cut many existing global ties, particularly transatlantic political ties, New York City was, as American historian Tony Michels remarks, the "unofficial capital"[1] of both Jewish radicalism and the Jewish labor movements in the United States and on both sides of the Atlantic Ocean. For those familiar with the history of political radicalism, it is not surprising that "Jews played highly visible roles, over an extended period, in the leadership of leftist movements – including socialist, communist, and anarchist organizations – around the world,"[2] especially in New York organizations. As American political scientist Jack Jacobs highlights, "the presence of Jews and individuals of Jewish descent in the leadership of leftist movements was, at one point in time, considerable, and was regularly disproportionate to the percentage of Jews in the general populations of the countries in which these Jews were active."[3] This overrepresentation of Jews within radical political organizations led to the creation of a new Jewish image, i.e. "the Jew as radical," which "took shape in the 1890s. It was a stereotype that would gain wide currency during the Progressive Era, turn into a serious liability during World War I and the postwar Red Scare, and remain with Jews (often to their detriment) into the 1960s."[4] Because the city's history of political radicalism in the late nineteenth and early twentieth centuries pertains to Jewish immigration, this Jewish image is particularly strong and preserved in New York.

Between the 1880s and 1920s, around two million Jewish immigrants reached the shores of the United States from Eastern Europe; around a quarter

---

1 Tony Michels, *A Fire in Their Hearts: Yiddish Socialists in New York* (Cambridge, MA: Harvard University Press, 2005), 6.

2 Jack Jacobs, "Introduction," in *Jews and Leftist Politics: Judaism, Israel, Antisemitism, and Gender*, ed. Jack Jacobs (Cambridge/New York: Cambridge University Press, 2017), 1.

3 Ibid., 9.

4 Michels, *A Fire in Their Hearts*, 2.

https://doi.org/10.1515/9783110545753-006

of them stayed in New York.[5] Not all of them were active in radical political movements or even arrived as radicals in the United States, even if they later became radicals. The majority of this immigrant group "found employment in the hyper-exploitative sweatshops of the city's booming garment industry," which provided "ideal breading grounds for radicalism."[6] The working environments of the immigrants – not just the Jewish ones – stimulated a political radicalization that was unrelated to both the immigrants' Eastern European backgrounds and their religious traditions. It was a specific space-time continuum, i.e. New York City at the end of the nineteenth century, that provided an almost natural environment for political radicalization.[7] The sweatshops where the Jewish immigrants worked, as well as the tenement houses where they lived, helped forge a new variety of Jewish-American radicalism.

Contemporary political events, such as the Haymarket verdict[8], also radicalized several young Jewish immigrants.[9] To quote Tony Michels again, the Jewish labor movement "was arguably the largest, most creative upsurge in American Jewish history"[10] and might have drawn its human capital from the immigrant community, although it was forged on American soil. While the first Yiddish-speaking group of socialists was founded in New York in 1885, it took just a few years to fill socialist unions, political parties, and clubs with thousands of Jewish members.[11]

Eventually, the Jewish labor movement was one of the most successful ones on American soil, as "[n]o movement won more support or inspired greater enthusiasm among Jews during the four-decade era of mass immigration between the 1880s and 1920s."[12] Thousands of impoverished men and women hoping for a better future away from their birthplace and "who knew nothing of Karl Marx or his ideas before stepping foot on the island of Manhattan were soon marching

---

5 Kenyon Zimmer, "Saul Yanovsky and Yiddish Anarchism on the Lower East Side," in *Radical Gotham: Anarchism in New York City from Schwab's Saloon to Occupy Wall Street*, ed. Tom Goyens (Urbana/Chicago/Springfield, IL: University of Illinois Press, 2017), 33.

6 Ibid.

7 Some of the immigrants may have been radicalized in London before they went to the United States. See ibid., 34–35 and in more detail Constance Bantman, *The French Anarchists in London, 1880–1914: Exile and Transnationalism in the First Globalisation* (Liverpool: Liverpool University Press, 2013).

8 On the Haymarket Affair see, among others, Paul Avrich, *The Haymarket Tragedy* (Princeton, NJ: Princeton University Press, 1984).

9 Zimmer, "Saul Yanovsky," 34–35.

10 Michels, *A Fire in Their Hearts*, 2.

11 Ibid., 2–3.

12 Ibid., 4.

and striking and educating themselves in his name."[13] However, Jews were not the only ones who forged the American labor movement; unions and other socialist organizations were of "a multiethnic character,"[14] especially in New York. Nevertheless, as British sociologist Percy S. Cohen (1928–1999) correctly remarked, "Jews may have been prominent in the leadership of radical movements out of all proportion to their numbers in the population."[15] Leading socialists, anarchists, union leaders, and other labor activists in late nineteenth century New York were Jewish, which remained the case until the creation of the American New Left.[16] However, Jewish radicalism was not limited to socialism or anarchism; it was also expressed within the feminist movement, which is why "Jewish radicalism seen as a movement would have to embrace a wide range of radical thought and deed."[17]

There has long been a discussion to determine the importance of being simultaneously Jewish and radical in this historical context. In his work *Jews and the Left*,[18] Arthur Liebman claimed that a mix of religion, historical tradition, and the confrontation with antisemitism was responsible for radicalizing so many Jews. The role of religion in particular was critically discussed in the context of radicalization.[19] Considering that Jewish members of the US Socialist Labor Party, Socialist Party of America (SPA), and Communist Party accounted for twenty-five percent of all members and thereby formed "the backbone of each of these major radical organizations" – which were atheistic by nature – it is hard to believe that religion mattered at all. In addition, as Cohen highlighted, "most of the evidence for the connection between Jewishness and radicalism

---

13 Ibid. Marx's position towards Jews was, however, rarely discussed. Dennis Fischman, "The Jewish Question About Marx," *Polity* 21, no. 4 (1989): 756, concludes that Marx was "shockingly anti-semitic" in his discussion of the "Jewish question." For further information on the discourse about Marx's anti-Semitism, see Jacobs, "Introduction," 6, and, more broadly, Julius Carlebach, *Karl Marx and the Radical Critique of Judaism* (London: Routledge, 1978).

14 David P. Shuldiner, *Of Moses and Marx: Folk Ideology and Folk History in the Jewish Labor Movement* (Wesport, CT/London: Bergin and Garvey, 1999), 1.

15 Percy S. Cohen, *Jewish Radicals and Radical Jews* (London/New York: Academic Press, 1980), 2.

16 S. Robert Lichter and Stanley Rothman, "Jewish Ethnicity and Radical Culture: A Social Psychological Study of Political Activists," *Political Psychology* 3, no. 1/2 (1981/1982): 118.

17 Robert Wolfe, *Remember to Dream: A History of Jewish Radicalism* (New York: Jewish Radical Education Project, 1994), 7.

18 Arthur Liebman, *Jews and the Left* (New York: Wiley, 1979).

19 For example: Jonathan Frankel, *Prophecy and Politics: Socialism, Nationalism, and the Russian Jews, 1862–1917* (Cambridge: Cambridge University Press, 1981) and Nora Levin, *Jewish Socialist Movements, 1871–1917: While Messiah Tarried* (London: Routledge, 1978).

is 'impressionistic', not statistical."[20] US historian Allen Guttmann has also criticized the belief in an interrelationship between the Jewish faith and Jewish radicalism:

> The role of the American Jew – as anarchist, as socialist, as Communist – has, however, been misunderstood by anti-Semites, by celebrators of Jewishness, even by scholars determined neither to praise nor to blame. It is an unrecognized fact that American Jews who rejected the political status quo have also rejected Jehovah and Torah and Talmud. Their radicalism has involved the abandonment rather than the intensification of their faith in Judaism as a religion.[21]

However, it is important to understand that "definitions of Jewish radicalism are one-sided and partial, reflecting the author's own political preferences and priorities,"[22] and therefore do not display a clear methodology in studying Jewish radicalism.

While US author, rabbi, and peace activist Arthur I. Waskow tried to trace the Jewish radical tradition back to antiquity[23] and claimed that Shabbat was "the first general strike [and] a holy general strike,"[24] Robert Wolfe argued that socialism was considered a translation of "traditional radical ideals of the Jewish people into the language of secular thought."[25] To quote the American left-wing author David P. Shuldiner, the error of such approaches lies "in assuming that Judaism is unique in predisposing its adherents toward a particular ideology."[26] That socialism was a form of secularized Jewishness might have been the perception of radical Jews themselves.[27] I suggest following Liliana Riga's approach – which she used in the context of Jewish Bolsheviks – that "Jewishness was a social fact mediated by ethnopolitical context, and therefore a dimension of *varying significance* to their radicalism, even for those for whom Jewishness was not a claimed identity."[28] In other words, the

---

20 Cohen, *Jewish Radicals*, 2.

21 Allen Guttmann, "Jewish Radicals, Jewish Writers," *The American Scholar* 32, no. 4 (1963): 563.

22 Wolfe, *Remember to Dream*, 11.

23 Arthur I. Waskow, "Judaism and Revolution Today," in *Jewish Radicalism: A Selected Anthology*, ed. Jack Nusan Porter and Peter Dreier (New York: Grove Press, 1973), 11–12.

24 Ibid., 28.

25 Wolfe, *Remember to Dream*, 10.

26 Shuldiner, *Of Moses and Marx*, 33.

27 Ibid., 37.

28 Liliana Riga, "Ethnonationalism, Assimilation, and the Social Worlds of the Jewish Bolsheviks in Fin deSiècle Tsarist Russia," *Comparative Studies in Society and History* 48, no. 4 (2006): 763. My emphasis.

link between socialism and Judaism depended on personal perspectives, the role that Jewishness played in radicalism and vice versa, or – to reference Percy S. Cohen – whether someone was a Jewish radical or a radical Jew.[29] For the anarchists in New York, to name one example, organizing a Yom Kippur ball on the Lower East Side posed no problems, especially since the Jewish anarchist community tended to be "unapologetically Yiddish."[30]

Regardless of radicalization levels, religion was still discussed within political movements, even if discussions about Jewishness among the SPA were secondary to theological discourse about Christianity.[31] To discuss the impact of Jewishness as a sole factor in political radicalism would mean arguing that "Jews are more radical than others within the same social categories."[32] Nevertheless, socialism and other left-wing radicalism might have been particularly interesting for Jews; they demanded a new order of equality and often fought ideologically against antisemitism. Furthermore, Jewish radicalism was also an expression of generational struggles within Jewish communities that originated in Eastern Europe but found fulfillment in a geographically distant environment, i.e. the Lower East Side of New York. Regarding the intensity of religious ties, Percy S. Cohen provided three "principal ways" for Jewish radicalism to be expressed: "One such way is to ignore one's Jewishness or to treat it as an irrelevance; a second is to keep one's radicalism and one's Jewishness quite separate from each other; the third way is to fuse one's radical concerns with one's commitment to being a Jew."[33] It is safe to assume that all of those options applied in New York where Jewish radicalism neither imitated or imported ideas from Eastern Europe; instead, it came into existence because of the metropolitan environment of the late nineteenth century. It is important to accept that "to understand Jewish radicalism as a movement, it has to be understood as a movement in time"[34] and within its specific geographical context. Therefore, it makes sense to examine the Lower East Side of Manhattan where Jews not only "played an extraordinarily disproportionate role in socialism and other radical movements,"[35] but also had a

29 Cohen, *Jewish Radicals*, 9.

30 Zimmer, "Saul Yanovsky," 44.

31 For a detailed analysis of these discussions, see Dan McKanan, "The Implicit Religion of Radicalism: Socialist Party Theology, 1900–1934," *Journal of the American Academy of Religion* 78, no. 3 (2010): 750–789.

32 Cohen, *Jewish Radicals*, 4.

33 Ibid., 9.

34 Wolfe, *Remember to Dream*, 13.

35 Gerald Sorin, *The Prophetic Minority: American Jewish Immigrant Radicals, 1880–1920* (Bloomington: Indiana University Press, 1985), 1.

transnational impact on Jewish radicalism on the other side of the Atlantic. New York offers both a local and transnational perspective on Jewish radicalism.[36]

This chapter will present a general discussion of when and where Jewish radicalization occurred in late nineteenth and early twentieth century New York. In a second step, however, local perspectives will be considered by examining the life and radicalization process of Isidore Wisotsky (1895–1970), a Russian (Ukrainian) Jew who immigrated with his family to New York at age fourteen in 1910 and later became an anarchist. His story, i.e. a historical case study based on his autobiographical materials,[37] will highlight how political radicalization within the Jewish community of the Lower East Side could have looked like. I will thereby show that time and place played a more critical role in the radicalization process of the Jewish community than religion did, which is usually highlighted when discussing Jewish radicalism. If one is interested in the full story of Jewish-American radicalization in the late nineteenth and early twentieth century, one must understand Jewish radicalism beyond religiosity.

New York's Lower East Side and Jewish Radicalism

New York's Lower East Side was the perfect ground for developing Jewish radicalism in the United States. American historian Hasia D. Diner described it perfectly, referring to it as

> a warren of crowded, dirty, and mean streets. In this slum, these impoverished Jews re-created the culture of Eastern Europe, thick with the smells, sounds, tastes, and noises of life in the 'Old World.' But through the miracle of the American dream of mobility, their sons and daughters emerged from the Lower East Side as teachers, lawyers, doctors, movie mak-

36 For recent transnational approaches to American Jewish history, see Adam Mendelsohn, "Tongue Ties: The Emergence of the Anglophone Jewish Diaspora in the Mid-Nineteenth Century," *American Jewish History* 93, no. 2 (2007): 177–209; Daniel Soyer, "Transnationalism and Mutual Influence: American and East European Jewries in the 1920s and 1930s," in *Rethinking European Jewish History*, ed. Jeremy Cohen and Moshe Rosman (Oxford: Oxford University Press, 2009): 201–220.

37 Isidore Wisotsky Autobiographical Typescript (henceforth Wisotsky), TAM.071, Tamiment Library and Robert F. Wagner Labor Archives, New York University. An interview with Wisotsky from October 26 1963, in which he reveals similar stories, is also available in YIVO Archives: Interviews in Amerikaner Yiddishe Geschichte Bel-Pe, Collection 6036/002, Box 1, Folder 18–20, Kheel Center for Labor-Management Documentation and Archives, Cornell University Library.

> ers, musicians – aggressive and assertive about their rights as Americans but more ambivalent toward the nature of their Jewish legacy.[38]

As Diner continued to emphasize, it was the experience of having lived in that environment that "reflected in microcosm the broad outlines of the metanarrative of the Jewish past" with its "recurrent themes of oppression, constriction, and danger, on one hand, followed by the expansiveness of liberation, on the other."[39] It could thus be rightly described as a "transitional zone"[40] for Jewish immigrants from Eastern Europe who were becoming not only Americans, but also Jewish-American radicals. Jack Jacobs already alluded to this, highlighting that

> the relationship of Jews to the left was historically contingent, specific to political, historic, and economic conditions that prevailed between the late-nineteenth and mid-twentieth centuries in Europe, and that impacted upon Jewish political opinion in the United States and other countries that received large numbers of Jewish immigrants from Europe.[41]

While Jewish identity determined emigration and immigration processes, the American environment's political and economic implications formed a radical community with a European Jewish heritage.

Regardless of these interrelations, Tony Michels warned against perceiving Jewish radicalism as too European because "New York's immigrant Jewish community was not a mere replica of eastern European Jewry."[42] The US metropolis offered far more than a place to live; it "served as a laboratory of political and cultural innovation that influenced eastern Europe in ways historians are just beginning to recognize."[43] It offered both socialism and anarchism as forms of radicalism with which to identify. To name just one example, a German American named Justus H. Schwab (1847–1900) had opened a saloon on 50 East 1st Street in 1875/76 that would become a hotspot for anarchist culture in Manhattan's Lower East Side.[44] Yet not only in anarchist saloons did radicalism spread among Jewish immigrants – a rich café culture also provided radical spatialities

38 Hasia R. Diner, *Lower East Side Memories: A Jewish Place in America* (Princeton/Oxford: Princeton University Press, 2000), 20.
39 Ibid.
40 Ibid.
41 Jacobs, "Introduction," 1.
42 Michels, *A Fire in Their Hearts*, 5.
43 Ibid.
44 Tom Goyens, "Introduction," in *Radical Gotham: Anarchism in New York City from Schwab's Saloon to Occupy Wall Street*, ed. Tom Goyens (Urbana/Chicago/Springfield, IL: University of Illinois Press, 2017), 1.

where Jewish radicals met to have discussions at Sachs', Schmuckler's, or Sholem's café.[45]

However, New York's radical potential was not limited to a national scope. Rather, it served as a transnational hub of Jewish radicalism in the late nineteenth century. Jewish socialists printed thousands of copies of radical print media in Yiddish – newspapers, pamphlets, and the like – that would then be shipped to Europe, especially to Tsarist Russia. Many Jews there would be recruited into revolutionary circles, and based on their experiences with print media, the Jewish labor movement of Eastern Europe produced and published on the other side of the Atlantic.[46] It is thus critical to understand that transatlantic ties impacted the United States and vice versa; "[b]y providing an ample supply of Yiddish publications, New Yorkers successfully exported socialism to Russian Jews."[47] The Eastern European Jewish labor movement was consequently impacted by radical communities abroad, and in further studies we must accept its transnationality instead of using an old-fashioned and Eurocentric center-periphery approach.[48] In Tony Michels' words, "The leading role of New York in exporting Yiddish socialist literature to Russia suggests the need to revise the standard view of American Jewry as an outpost of European Jewry."[49] The relationship between the radical Jewish communities in Europe and the United States saw things eye to eye; as such, Jewish radicalism should be researched as a global system.

As the language of the revolutionaries, Yiddish "moved from west to east,"[50] although it had reached the United States before as a cultural form of communication. The radicalization took place on the Lower East Side and would later spread around the globe, even finding its way back to Russia. Although Yiddish was important to the revolutionaries, it would not have had the same impact without the movement of the radicals themselves. They moved back and forth across the Atlantic, stayed in contact through correspondence, and exchanged journal and newspaper articles that helped spread the fire of the revolution around the Jewish and non-Jewish world alike. When thousands of Jewish immi-

---

45 Wisotsky, 74; Zimmer, "Saul Yanovsky," 43. For a detailed discussion, see the recently published work Shachar M. Pinsker, *A Rich Brew: How Cafés Created Modern Jewish Culture* (New York: NYU Press, 2018).

46 Tony Michels, "Exporting Yiddish Socialism: New York's Role in the Russian Jewish Workers' Movement," *Jewish Social Studies: History, Culture, Society* n.s. 16, no. 1 (2009): 1.

47 Ibid., 2.

48 Ibid., 3.

49 Ibid., 2.

50 Ibid.

grants flocked to the trade unions of New York City, helped vote left-wing politicians into office in the following decades, determined the city's radical milieu, and constituted the readership, entourage, and followers of famous socialists, anarchists, and communists, they created New York's radical culture. They established this milieu in the United States before exporting it to the "Old World," from where new followers and adherents to radical ideologies would arrive in later years, having already been radicalized by their experiences in the Eastern European Jewish labor movement.[51]

The core of the American Jewish labor movement

> consisted of three interlocking institutions: the United Hebrew Trades (an umbrella organization of Yiddish-speaking unions inspired by the United German Trades), the Arbeter Tsaytung Publishing Association (which published the weekly *Di arbeter tsaytung* and the daily *Dos abend blat*), and the Yiddish-speaking branches of the Socialist Labor Party (which sponsored the monthly *Di tsukunft*).[52]

These publications also laid the foundation for the export of Yiddish papers and journals, which were usually smuggled by "Russian Jewish émigrés, typically university students, residing in Austria-Hungary, Germany, and Switzerland."[53] The workers' movement in Russia consequently obtained many of its reading materials from US printing machines, and the formation of socialism among Jewish communities of Russia originated in New York. Yiddish was also chosen as the language of the revolutionary movements in the Tsarist Empire because it was available for distribution, since the Lower East Side radicals had used it for more than a decade for communicating their own radical ideas.[54]

Based on these transnational interrelations, it would be inappropriate to explain Jewish radicalism in the United States with the geographical, religious, and social marginalization of Eastern European Jewish immigrants.[55] From a geographical perspective, Jewish radicals in New York were everything but marginal. Religion was not required as a basis for radicalism, but it could be synthesized

51 For a more detailed discussion of Russian-Jewish immigration to the US, see Simon Kuznets, "Immigration of Russian Jews to the U.S.: Background and Structure," *Perspectives in American History* 9 (1975): 35–124.

52 Michels, "Exporting Yiddish Socialism," 8.

53 Ibid., 14. Tony Michels also describes the smuggling process in more detail: "School holidays and Jewish holidays, such as Passover, provided opportune times to transport materials back home. Smugglers would often strap contraband to their bodies or hide it under false bottoms inside their suitcases. In that way, an individual might carry as much as 20 pounds of literature inside a single bag." (Ibid.)

54 Ibid., 18.

55 On that idea and its debate, see Jacobs, "Introduction," 2–3.

into radical views. As Jack Jacobs highlighted, the Jewish faith was no obstacle for many radicals: "There were, and are, Jewish leftists who have found elements of the Jewish religion to be compatible with their political proclivities."[56] The only form of marginalization that could have impacted Jewish radicalization in New York was social, and further analyzing this point requires a closer study of the lives of the nineteenth century Jewish immigrant community in the Lower East Side.

The Community

As mentioned before, around two million Jewish immigrants reached the United States between 1880 and 1924. Yet, it would be a decade and a half before the "poor *Yidn*" were considered something besides "greenhorns."[57] While the newly-arrived community began to adjust to the American way of life, it also added "important parts of their rich and long-evolving culture, by concentrating in neighborhoods in a number of large cities, particularly the lower East Side of New York."[58] In the 1900s, they added "a variety of radical ideologies"[59] to the American Jewish labor movement. As Jack Nusan Porter and Peter Dreier stated in their introduction to their selected anthology on Jewish radicalism, this is especially true because the early twentieth century "saw the simultaneous rise of two mass movements among Jews – a Jewish labor movement and a Jewish radical political movement."[60] The second wave of Jewish immigrants no longer solely arrived from Jewish *shtetls* in Eastern Europe,[61] but rather from a "revolutionary Yiddishland,"[62] as the French scholars Alain Brossat and Sylvia Klingsberg called it.

---

56 Ibid., 3.

57 Michels, *A Fire in Their Hearts*, 1; Sorin, *The Prophetic Minority*, 1; Zimmer, "Saul Yanovsky," 33.

58 Sorin, *The Prophetic Minority*, 1.

59 Jack Nusan Porter and Peter Dreier, "Introduction," in *Jewish Radicalism: A Selected Anthology*, ed. Jack Nusan Porter and Peter Dreier (New York: Grove Press, 1973), xvii.

60 Ibid.

61 On the shtetl see Sorin, *The Prophetic Minority*, 11–18. For a more detailed analysis of *shtetl* culture see Steven T. Katz, ed. *The Shtetl: New Evaluations* (New York: NYU Press, 2009).

62 Alain Brossat and Sylvia Klingsberg, *Revolutionary Yiddishland: A History of Jewish Radicalism*, trans. David Fernbach (London/New York: Verso, 2016), xi. This "revolutionary Yiddishland" only survived in the memories and its people, or abroad, as the two scholars rightly remarked: "Having failed to achieve its hopes, its utopias, its political programmes and strategies, broken on the rocks of twentieth-century European history, Yiddishland survives,

Throughout Eastern Europe,

> the mass of Jews lived, thought, suffered and acted, a whole world, a complete society, with the requisite variety of elements – workers and intellectuals, scholars and financiers, managers and labourers, etc. At the top of the pyramid a financial bourgeoisie as in the West, but without any influence; below them a middling bourgeoisie, intellectual and commercial; and finally an immense Jewish proletariat.[63]

However, said proletariat first had to form either in the Tsarist Empire or in the United States. Determining factors during these developmental processes on both sides of the Atlantic were the same: "their family; and the social and cultural environment in which they grew up. The[n] … the originality and unity of the world in which their consciousness was formed reveals itself: Yiddishland."[64] This radical Yiddishland is a world without borders; it includes the vast territories of Eastern Europe as it does New York's Lower East Side. Nevertheless, it has religious and cultural roots in the *shtetls*.

Most Jewish immigrants from Eastern Europe who came to the US had memories of their *shtetl*, where they were poor, hunted, and often ostracized. While their class consciousness was not as strong as in industrialized cities, the *shtetls* also had their social hierarchies. Within them, "the Jews, by their act of refusal to give up their religion and culture, denied the ruling elite complete domination; this rebellion was obvious to other oppressed groups."[65] Memories of the *shtetls* were stuck to Jewish emigrants, who had no realistic worldviews living in a place that would perish as a consequence of a radical antisemitism. This was already felt in pogroms during the late nineteenth and early twentieth centuries by those who became victims of anti-Jewish violence.[66] Alongside rampant antisemitism, the *shtetl* did not offer many prospects for poor people: "Though scholarship was a pillar of status, so clearly was wealth and family background."[67] In this Jewish world, a third factor began to change hierarchical dynamics: a generational conflict consisting of young Jews who "were rebelling against their parents and parts

---

in the account of the past, as a culture, a lost treasure entrusted to antiquarian remembrance." (Ibid.)

63 Ibid., 1.

64 Ibid., 29.

65 Aviva Cantor Zuckoff, "The Oppression of America's Jews," in *Jewish Radicalism: A Selected Anthology*, ed. Jack Nusan Porter and Peter Dreier (New York: Grove Press, 1973), 31.

66 On the history of the anti-Jewish pogroms in Russia see John D. Klier and Shlomo Lambroza, eds. *Pogroms: Anti-Jewish Violence in Modern Russian History* (Cambridge: Cambridge University Press, 2004).

67 Sorin, *The Prophetic Minority*, 16.

of their parents' culture."[68] Eventually, the "family was a microcosm in which the tensions and conflicts that beset the world of Yiddishland were focused,"[69] and for many young Jews, radical ideas allowed them to dream of a better world. It is thus no surprise that many young Jews who left Eastern Europe did so hoping for a brighter future.[70] Many of them must have been disappointed by the poverty that awaited them on the other side of the Atlantic, which is another reason why they were receptive to radical ideas. The Jewish immigrants were, as American historian Gerald Sorin put it, "energetically seeking outlets for deeply felt aspirations."[71] Breaking from their own parents and culture, particularly in different political environments in the US, caused "a break with the rigidity of the traditional Jewish life that invaded every sphere of existence,"[72] as it had been dominated by rituals and obligations. The young immigrants did not want to remain *Luftmenschen* but eventually became workers, organized and unionized among the ideals of socialism. As many other immigrants in the United States before and after them, they were under steady pressure to define and redefine their own identities – not only as new US citizens but also as radicals and as Jews.[73]

During this identity-defining process, the newly-arriving Eastern European Jews dealt not only with the non-Jewish New Yorker community. They also faced an older generation of German Jewish immigrants who had reached the metropolis a few decades before them. Those arriving between 1880 and 1914 were under constant and "powerful assimilative pressures from the already established Jewish community of New York."[74] Since German Jewish businessmen had established their own wealth in the metropolis, they feared that the large number of poor Jews arriving from Eastern Europe would damage their standing in New York's society; "[a]mong the reasons behind their desire for the quick and total Americanization of the new immigrants, anti-Semitism heads the list."[75] However, the arrival of new immigrants from Eastern Europe altered the Jewish community in the United States – in 1880, there were only a quarter of a million

---

68 Ibid., 42.
69 Brossat and Klingsberg, *Revolutionary Yiddishland*, 37.
70 Ibid., 36–38.
71 Sorin, *The Prophetic Minority*, 43.
72 Brossat and Klingsberg, *Revolutionary Yiddishland*, 39.
73 Melissa R. Klapper, "'Those by Whose Side We Have Labored': American Jewish Women and the Peace Movement between the Wars," *The Journal of American History* 97, no. 3 (2010): 638.
74 Selma C. Berrol, "In Their Image: German Jews and the Americanization of the Ost Juden in New York City," *New York History* 63, no. 4 (1982): 418.
75 Ibid., 419.

Jews in America – once the pogroms in Tsarist Russia set in motion a new age of Jewish migration.[76] As American historian Selma C. Berrol describes it from an economic perspective, the two groups were adversaries:

> Russian Jews were tenants and German Jews their landlords. Even more important, German Jews were the employers of the eastern Europeans. The garment industry offers the best example. In 1885, 97 percent of the garment factories in New York City were owned by German Jews, and it was in these factories that the greatest number of Russian and Polish Jews worked. This relationship was also true in the hat, cap, fur, jewelry, textile or trimming trades. Since most of the tenements that housed these workers were also in the hands of German Jews, conflict was inevitable.[77]

Considering this economic situation, new American life did not offer much more than poor life in Eastern Europe's *shtetls*.[78] The exploitation of the Jewish workforce by rich factory owners therefore continued to stimulate radicalization within the Jewish-American community.

Its Radicalization

While radicalization happened on both sides of the Atlantic, the early arrivals were usually radicalized in the United States. Those who arrived after 1900 had the chance of being radicalized before their emigration from Eastern Europe, so they integrated with an already radical Jewish community on the Lower East Side of New York. In Eastern Europe, many Jews were members of the "three major currents of red Yiddishland: the communists, the Bund and Poale Zion."[79] For many radical Jews in Eastern Europe, "it was perfectly natural [...] [to] conceive[the] Bund and revolution as one and the same thing."[80] Eastern European radicalism was based on the experience of Jewishness in this region of the world, which, to quote Alain Brossat and Sylvia Klingsberg again,

76 Ibid., 421.

77 Ibid., 422.

78 On poverty and exploitation in the *shtetl* see Ben-Cion Pinchuk, "The Shtetl: An Ethnic Town in the Russian Empire," *Cahiers du Monde russe* 41, no. 4 (2000): *Aperçus sur le monde juif:* 495–504.

79 Brossat and Klingsberg, *Revolutionary Yiddishland*, 6. On the Bund, see Henry J. Tobias, *The Jewish Bund in Russia from its Origin to 1905* (Stanford, CA: Stanford University Press, 1972). On the Poale Zion, see Mario Keßler, "Die Komintern und die Poale Zion 1919 bis 1922: Eine gescheiterte Synthese von Kommunismus und Zionismus," *Arbeit – Bewegung – Geschichte* 2 (2017): 15–30.

80 Hersh Mendel, *Memoirs of a Jewish Revolutionary* (London: Pluto Press, 1989), 35.

> was in the early twentieth century a turbulent volcano, a social and political powder keg, a world that was constantly rumbling and moving. On top of this, in this zone of instability, the situation of the Jewish communities and populations from which they came was in most cases particularly unstable – from the pogrom at Kishinev in 1903 to the state anti-Semitism of interwar Poland. This double instability, the danger in simply being Jewish in Eastern Europe, this misery that was everyday experience of the great majority of these communities, clearly formed the roots of the availability for revolutionary commitment of a large fraction of Jewish youth in the early decades of the century.[81]

All Jewish radical organizations in Eastern Europe searched for an answer to address the basic misery of the Jews, who were not only economically suppressed and exploited, but sometimes victims of violence and perpetration. In the course of such an agenda, the organizations, its members, and the circulated radical ideas spread the word about "secular, emancipatory, rationalist values that went diametrically against the social and religious traditions of the *shtetl*."[82] The members of the Jewish Bund communities questioned and opposed "a world that was cracked and overthrown by the rise of modern capitalism to the live forces that arose from the young Jewish proletariat, open to the universal culture of the modern world,"[83] while those who followed the ideals of the Poale Zion "connected the universalism of its struggle with the rather mystical vision of an Eretz Israel that would be red and socialist."[84] Both of these organizations were particularly strong in the first two decades of the twentieth century. On one hand, Bund members demanded "political and civic equality for Jews" in the beginning, and "national and cultural autonomy for the Jews of the tsarist empire"[85] in later years. On the other hand, the Poale Zion established "a proletarian movement that sought to combine Zionism and socialism,"[86] but its influence already began to decrease after the failed revolution of 1905. For those who left Eastern Europe after 1900, it is no surprise that most of them were active in radical organizations in Eastern Europe previously.[87] Gerald Sorin assumed that a "significant majority" of those who reached the United States consequently "brought a developing radicalism with them."[88] This might be true, and since seventy percent of the Jewish immigrants who stayed in New York lived on the

---

81 Brossat and Klingsberg, *Revolutionary Yiddishland*, 7.
82 Ibid., 16.
83 Ibid.
84 Ibid., 18.
85 Ibid., 24.
86 Ibid., 26.
87 Sorin, *The Prophetic Minority*, 46.
88 Ibid.

Lower East Side, it must be considered specifically radical spatiality. David P. Shuldiner described the transformative forces the new arriving members of New York's radical society were impacted by:

> For Jewish immigrant radicals in the United States, the transformation and journey to a strange country were more than metaphorical equivalents; they were the defining features of personal and political odysseys. Caught up in a storm of revolution, war, migration, and resettlement, Yiddish radicals sought to chart a steady course through turbulent political waters.[89]

The radical Jewish identity in the United States might have been based on class and ethnicity, but the first generation of immigrants, i.e. those who arrived before having underwent a radicalization process in Europe, were probably rather radicalized due to a strong class consciousness and the exploitation in New York's sweat shops. Since the "Jewish tradition did not offer an intrinsically revolutionary outlook; nor did traditional Jewish community life provide objective conditions for the emergence of Jewish-identified Left politics,"[90] the US-based radicalization in the late nineteenth and early twentieth century was not built on religion. Rather, radicalization occurred in abstraction or opposition to religious traditions, since "the traditional religious community, as represented by rabbinical and civic authority, was historically conservative, and revolutionaries were often disowned – and sometimes banished – by the religiously observant, who felt besieged by modernity, and who saw radicals of any stripe as threats to their ever-tenuous position."[91]

Regardless of immigrants' ethnic or religious backgrounds, becoming politically active was essential for all immigrant workers to secure their economic outcome, which meant improving their income and/or working conditions.[92] Many who reached the United States to work were teenagers who had just begun developing political ideas. The garment industry became the midwife of political radicalism in New York City. It paid poorly or not at all during initial weeks of training, and the fact that "[g]arment workers also often paid for needles and electricity to run their machines, were overcharged for mistakes, and were fined for lateness"[93] helped forge radical ideas in young workers' heads. That many people with Jewish backgrounds worked in the sweatshops created a sense of community, a community that was based on the same ethnic back-

89 Shuldiner, *Of Moses and Marx*, 13.
90 Ibid., 21.
91 Ibid., 28.
92 Ibid., 1.
93 Sorin, *The Prophetic Minority*, 57.

ground, the same class consciousness and, more important, the feeling of being exploited.[94] As a consequence of these preconditions, the unionization and radicalization of garment industry workers happened almost naturally. This phenomenon must be understood in the context of its space-time-continuum; that is, the Jewish community living and working in the sweatshops of New York's Lower East Side. Gerald Sorin emphasized this when he stated that

> The biographical materials on Jewish radicalism in America suggest that the roots of Jewish radical collective action lay not in irrational responses by uprooted, atomized individuals to the strain and hardship brought by extensive social change. In their radicalism these Jews were making claims on society as a cohesive group. They were organized around articulated interests that were shaped by social change, hardship, class-consciousness, and cultural background.[95]

The garment industry's exploitative nature demanded the proletarization of the Jewish immigrant community, whose members consequently became American radicals. This led to a radical community that absorbed further radical elements from abroad after 1900. Since these elements were of Jewish origin – and therefore easy to integrate into the Lower East Side's Yiddish society – they became an important part of the US Jewish labor movement.

The new arrivals, mostly poor families who had fled from economic hardship or violence, arrived in New York and found a Jewish community that was "partially rewoven with new threads, and highly girded by social formations"[96] and provided a radical tune for the future music of Jewish unionization and political radicalization alike. The song, so to speak, was not to be performed solo:

> Residential concentration, the family, the synagogues, *landsmanschaftn*, educational alliances, theater groups, mutual aid societies, reading clubs, the workplace, the union were all important social formations – places wherein one could sustain status and identity by being part of something larger than the atomized self.[97]

From the 1890s onward, immigrants did not simply arrive to the United States. They entered a world with existing Jewish communities where people spoke Yiddish and shared their pasts in the *shtetl*. In this world, workers had established the first radical structures into which new immigrants were drawn,

---

94 Ibid., 96–97.

95 Ibid., 8.

96 Ibid., 5.

97 Ibid. Landsmanshaftn were "social, fraternal, health, and mutual aid societies whose membership was generally based on common residential origin in a shtetl or region." Ibid., 67.

since they often became a gear in the exploitative system of various US industries. This familiar milieu allowed for faster radicalization; being exposed to German radicals and their socialist traditions was once essential in this process, but many Jewish communities in New York naturally incorporated new arrivals into their existing radicalism.

While "working-class Jews and German-Americans were the twin pillars of American socialism"[98] in 1900, Jewish immigrants had learned a lot from their German role models prior to the turn of the century. They established their own radicalism alongside socialist ideas, and the German radicals in earlier years "provided financial assistance, publicity, organizations models, and ideological guidance"[99] to their Jewish comrades from Eastern Europe, who "did not become so much Americanized as German-Americanized."[100] Considering these interactions, Tony Michels' evaluation is appropriate: "Jews created their labor movement in a German image."[101] This fact is particularly important because it highlights that at the end of the nineteenth century, the Lower East Side provided a radical breeding ground for Eastern European Jewish immigrants. Their radicalization initially took place in the United States, and from there it spread back to Tsarist Russia, providing a safe haven for later radicals. Said radicals traveled to the United States from there to become part of New York's radical Jewish community.

The intellectuals among the immigrants dove into the Lower East Side's rich culture of radicalism, becoming socialists or anarchists who provided a new "eclectic stew of European ideas"[102] that itself had already been cooked with ingredients from the New World. Yet the language of their radicalism was Yiddish, which, as David P. Shuldiner correctly remarked, "is not simply a linguistic, but also a cultural code of communication."[103] Many immigrant workers spoke Yiddish, leading to the creation of a labor movement that was Yiddish at its core.[104] Radical Yiddish papers were quickly established to provide the new Jewish working class with its radical ideas for the future. However, the "radical rhetoric of … [the] labor leaders and socialists caused great alarm in the bourgeois German Jewish community."[105] This was not only because of their antagonistic demands

98 Ibid., 2.
99 Michels, *A Fire in Their Hearts*, 4.
100 Ibid., 5.
101 Ibid., 4.
102 Sorin, *The Prophetic Minority*, 73.
103 Shuldiner, *Of Moses and Marx*, 43.
104 Porter and Dreier, "Introduction," xvii.
105 Berrol, "In Their Image," 423.

of society, but because of their use of Yiddish, which was considered "a 'piggish jargon' and a reminder of the ghetto."[106] However, even Russian intellectuals could not forego learning Yiddish if they wanted their political messages to reach the masses. Many of them had to learn or relearn a language that was once considered unintellectual and backward.[107] Tony Michels highlighted the pragmatic considerations that forced radical intellectuals to embrace their Jewish, i.e. Yiddish, heritage:

> To organize Jewish workers, Russian-speaking intellectuals needed to employ Yiddish, the spoken language of nearly all eastern European Jewish immigrants. But many of the intellectuals either did not know Yiddish or had rejected it years earlier as a marker of cultural backwardness. They had to learn or relearn the zhargon, or Jewish vernacular, thousands of miles from Europe's Yiddish-speaking heartland. This return to Yiddish was initially justified as a short-term concession necessary only until immigrants learned English.[108]

Due to political demands and needs, Yiddish endured a cultural renaissance in New York's Lower East Side. From there, it spread its radical potential across the globe.

It was not long before the first Jewish workers' unions were established. In 1888, they assembled under the umbrella of the United Hebrew Trades (*Vereinigte Yiddishe Gewerkschaften*).[109] Jewish unionization was a fast process because the "horrendously oppressive conditions of the sweat-shop industry impelled workers to think about escaping"[110] their economic exploitation. By 1890, there were already twenty-seven Jewish unions with around fourteen thousand members. Delegates of the United Hebrew Trades were sent to participate in the congresses of the Second International in Paris (1890) and Brussels (1891).[111] Early on, socialism played a critical role in the worldviews of Jewish workers, since the living conditions of their communities in the United States led to socialist ideas and their discussion among workers. In 1886, the Jewish Workingmen's Verein initiated its affiliation with the Socialist Labor Party and "joined a coalition of liberals and socialists to support the New York mayoral candidacy of Henry George."[112] In contrast to Eastern Europe's past, American

106 Ibid., 429.
107 Zimmer, "Saul Yanovsky," 36.
108 Michels, *A Fire in Their Hearts*, 5.
109 On the United Hebrew Trades see United Hebrew Trades, ed. *Seventy Years: United Hebrew Trades* (1958).
110 Sorin, *The Prophetic Minority*, 78.
111 Ibid., 79.
112 Ibid.

society not only offered possibilities for emancipation, but also a real chance for political change. When socialism reached the climax of its influence in the 1910s, "Jewish socialists [that] felt that they were part of a movement that in the not too distant future could emerge victorious."[113] While Jewish membership increased over the years, the SPA's militancy was not Jewish in nature. Rather, it was represented by men like William Haywood (1869–1928), Jack London (1876–1916), and Frank Bohn (1878–1975).

Within their socialist activities, many Jews maintained their Jewish identities and found ways to deal with both their religious heritage and their status as radicals. Most of those who arrived after 1900 were already radicalized Jews, so it was unnecessary for them to redefine their identities; they could easily integrate into the American Jewish radical community as it existed in contemporary New York. There, they would read the Yiddish socialist daily newspaper *Forward*, which had reached a circulation of 200,000 copies in 1917 and was rightfully named the "largest pro-socialist newspaper in the United States."[114] The Russian radicals had found a new home where both Jewish identities and radical identities coexisted in a globally-connected hub of international radicalism.[115] Until the early 1920s, the poor Jewish migrants and intellectual elites of Eastern Europe alike entered this hub to explore new possibilities for radical action in hopes of creating a better society.[116] However, in New York, it was not only the unions and socialist organizations that gained from this steady influx of (radical) immigrants; their anarchist counterparts also benefited. As US historian Kenyon Zimmer confirmed, "Although anarchists played the second fiddle to the more numerous social democrats in the organization, their role as organizers and rank-and-file militants should not be underestimated."[117] One of these rank-and-file militants was Isidore Wisotsky, whose radicalization in the US shall be analyzed in more detail in the remaining part of this chapter. His story offers greater insight into the above-mentioned processes that took place in New York City, the capital of Jewish radicalism. I will focus on Wisotsky's early life rather than discuss his radical acts in his adulthood, since his developmental years were instrumental in his radicalization.

---

113 Ibid., 86. Socialist party membership numbers had increased from 15,975 in 1903 to 118,045 in 1912. While this increase is not solely related to immigration, the growing Jewish community was well-represented among the party members.

114 Ibid., 2.

115 Michels, *A Fire in Their Hearts*, 26–68.

116 Brian Horowitz, *Russian Idea – Jewish Presence: Essays on Russian-Jewish Intellectual Life* (Brighton, MA: Academic Studies Press, 2013), 124.

117 Zimmer, "Saul Yanovsky," 40.

The Account of Isidore Wisotsky

Isidore Wisotsky reached the United States at the age of fourteen in 1909. He was part of no radical organization in Eastern Europe before his immigration, so he can be considered a "truly" Jewish-American radical. By discussing the autobiographical materials Wisotsky wrote in 1965, I will demonstrate how and why he became a Jewish anarchist – one of the numerous Jewish radicals of New York's Lower East Side.[118] Like many other Jewish immigrants, Wisotsky was born in a *shtetl*, namely Lipovets in the Kiev district of Ukraine. It "was the birthplace of several generations of our family, who were born, who lived and who died there. It was sunk in mud and poverty. There were no streets, no layouts. The houses were built of mud and straw" (3). Wisotsky described the environment in more detail:

> You seldom saw a brick house. If you did it belonged to a rich man. A thorough-dare paved with cobblestone was the main and only street of the town, and boards nailed together for about half a mile served as a sidewalk. When the mud rose you could not find it. There were also a few kerosene lamps that lit the street at night. That was your night life, hanging around those lamps. (4)

In school, the young boy encountered a violent teacher who only spoke Russian and punished students for any form of disobedience: "He had three kinds of punishments for pupils, according to the crime. Being in the corner, was for turning around or talking to someone; for coming late, he would let the pupil go to his seat and then have him go back to the door, and back, twice... If your Homework was not done, he used his cane" (24). When his father's small business could no longer secure his family's survival and pay their debts, the "have-nots" of the *shtetl* "came together in our house for a consultation, to help out Father. The only way out was to run away to America in the darkness of the night, so he could get rid of the money lenders. In America he will make a living. In a couple of years he will take the family out" (34). Eventually, the family borrowed money from relatives and parents to leave Eastern Europe together with four children. In Latvia, they spent four weeks at an immigrant house before they were able to go on a boat to America. After having missed one ship there, they boarded the Estonia, "a small, stinky steamer, that was overcrowded with emigrants, had poor service, and food you could not eat" (2). Stocked like sardines in a can, the "few hundred passengers were stuck together – with no air

118 In the following part of the present chapter, page numbers in parenthesis will be used to refer to Wisotsky's manuscript.

or light" (3). They would survive on a diet of herring and potatoes, but the mother got sick and stayed below deck until she left the ship again. After a long time at sea, the family eventually reached the New World and moved to the Lower East Side of New York.

Suffolk Street, where the family lived, was "full of sounds and shrieks, an assortment of men, women and children, shouting, yelling screaming... a symphony of discordant noises. Everyone bent on selling his wares – from pushcart, his hand or from pieces and scraps that lay on the crowded sidewalk" (1). Like many other Jewish immigrant families, the Wisotskys would live in a tenement house, "with dark hallways, small gaslights on every floor, wooden stairs, no electricity and no steam, toilets, assigned to the living room, were strategically shared by two tenants. A big black iron stove in the kitchen used coal for cooking, for boiling the wash, and in winter, served as a heater for all the rooms" (Ibid.). As described above, the family arrived at a time when Jewish communities had already been established for more than two decades. Although they were far from Eastern Europe, the *shtetl* culture was close. Wisotsky describes one evening when *landsleit* from Lipovets visited the family (3). During this evening, people would discuss history and politics and enjoy one another's company. Wisotsky describes the friendly atmosphere within this community:

> Yes, the *landsleit* all came to greet us and brought with them gifts for the "greenhorns." Refreshments consisted of beer, salted pretzels, herring. Everyone was in a festive mood. Everyone was joyous, asking about their relatives, their wives and children whom they intended to bring over soon. (6)

His father's half-brother left a particularly strong impression upon the young boy, which is why his description of this relative shall be quoted at length:

> Suddenly half-uncle Moishe, without knocking, made his appearance. He was my father's half-brother. Round-shouldered, hoarse-voiced and glassy-eyed, a wandering drunk, Moishe had left his wife and children. He earned his living by going to [S]lavic neighborhoods throughout the country, miners' towns, and steel factories where Polish, Russians and Ukrainians worked. He spoke their language fluently and sold them portraits of their grandfathers, grandmothers, grandchildren, fathers, mothers. He would carry a large painted portrait which he would show his prospective customers as his sample. Then he would ask for a small picture of whom they would want, and make an enlarged copy. This cost them one dollar. When he brought the picture back, he would say, "You don't want this beautiful picture without a frame?" Then he charged whatever he could get. This was how Moishe earned his living, roaming from town to town. This was how he avoided the sweat shop. No bosses for him! (Ibid.)

After their initial celebrations, the Wisotskys' daily lives were determined by the need to earn an income. The father became a skirt operator after learning the trade from a cousin who owned a shop on Stanton Street. He earned four dollars for sixty to seventy hours of work every week and slept in the shop. At home, the family provided rooms for four boarders who paid one dollar each per month for rent. In addition, Wisotsky's mother would sell them supper at twenty-five cents per meal (8–9). The boarders were all *landsleit* and would often discuss politics or the newest gossip in the evening. Such were moments in which Isidore encountered stories about the harsh realities of New York's working class for the first time. They talked about union meetings and, of course, "strikes in the needle trade" (10). On one day, his father and the boarders showed up in the middle of the day and announced that they were on strike as well. Rivele, one of the boarders, made it clear: "The dogs, our bosses, must give in to the union all the demands" (12). In the evenings, the striking workers would discuss their strategies, and Gussie, "a finisher at Branfman and Sheinberg's shop where my father and our boarders were striking," visited the family. When she, "a middle-aged, well-built woman, with dark hair and black burning eyes," heard that one of the women who worked as an "underfinisher" in the shop "went up to scab," she became angry and screamed: "I would rather see her in the hospital!" (13). The next morning, Gussie went to confront the other woman. When the latter appeared, "[a] fight began, with screams. Police came. One of the scabs was running away, blood all over his clothes. When Gussie hit [the other woman] with her pocketbook, she fell to the sidewalk" (14). Gussie had put "half a brick" in her pocketbook and fulfilled her promise that she would rather see the traitor go to the hospital.

At this time, many of the struggles between workers and their employers were violent. Wisotsky witnessed many of these incidents. Strikers had to fight against the police forces of hired mobsters, since bosses sometimes tried to crush strikes instead of paying workers more (15). Families usually suffered during strikes, since even the unions did not pay the workers enough. As such, most of those on strike had to borrow money within the community. That the workers' situations were miserable was often showcased by personal miseries and tragic events, like regular suicides within the tenement houses and by events like the Triangle Shirtwaist Factory fire in 1911. During the fire, "146 girls were burned because of locked doors. On a dreary, foggy, rainy day, thousands of workers cried and marched to bring them to their last resting place" (22).

School bored Wisotsky; he preferred spending time with Rivele, attending lectures by Jewish radicals such as Saul Yanofsky (26). A lecture on "revolutionary trade unionism" (Ibid.) made sense for the young attendant, who had seen the misery of the Jewish working class at home every day. The atmosphere there and the reliability to secure a part of the family income, as Wisotsky remarked, eventually

> started to choke me... to prey on my mind... the congestion, the nagging, the misunderstanding, between me and my parents. My inability to get a half-decent job to help out the family chased me out into the street. On a hot summer evening, I left and moved into 7th Street Park, a three by three square block affair, an improvement on Hester Park. It had a couple of trees, spots of grass and a shanty where they sold a schooner of milk for one cent, and for one more penny, you could buy a salt pretzel. That made a good meal for the day. (38)

His first night after leaving home, Wisotsky slept at the docks (39) and on the next day, he began to look for a job. He would clean tables at a cafeteria during lunch hour for seventy-five cents, for which he could buy two meals and lodging for a night (40). He could also stay at his friends' places from time to time. When the winter came, it was bitterly cold:

> It took considerable stamina to contend with those icy wintery days with no overcoat, no warm underwear. The only place to shield oneself from the frost was the public library. Hence, the library on East Broadway became my shelter, my home. However, not much reading can be done on an empty stomach. Besides, the library also closed at night, and that was bad. (42)

Eventually, he became a member of a commune. With nine more of his homeless companions, Wisotsky rented a "a two-room apartment on 5th Street on the top floor. There was no heat, no toilet, no water. Everything in the hall. Of course, there was no bath and no hot water. One room was completely dark and without windows. The cost? Six dollars a month rent" (44). The "Don't Worry Group," as they called themselves (44), lived in this apartment for quite a while and debated and discussed "all kinds of subjects – socialism, anarchism, individualism, philosophy, literature, vegetarianism, and men like Nietzsche, Bakunin, Kropotkin, Marx, Zola, Maxim Gorki [sic!], Jack London, Sholom Asch, Tolstoy, Peretz, Ibsen, Raisin, Strindberg and others. The main subject was the social revolution and how to make it and these debates last till dawn, until we were all breathless and hoarse" (45).

Once Wisotsky was old enough to get his legal working papers, he started looking for a job. In Eastern Europe, he began working at the age of twelve by "turning the wheel in a printing shop" (88). There, he received no salary and nothing to eat: "For six months I worked without a salary... no money and no food, only because the boss... promised my mother to teach me a trade. There was no electric power, or steam power. Human power was the cheapest. It cost nothing, only a promise" (Ibid.). Being in the United States and legally old enough to work, Wisotsky hoped for better conditions. He checked job advertisements in the *Jewish Morning* and sought employment where he could learn a trade. However, nobody was willing to offer him such an opportunity, and would usually come home "tired, heartbroken and disappointed" (89). Selling newspapers, which he had done earlier, secured him a small income. He usually earned seventy-five cents on weekdays and a dollar on Saturday and Sunday, which was not bad compared to jobs offering $3.50 for sixty hours per week. He eventually got a job packing linings for straw hats, where Wisotsky was paid three dollars for a sixty-hour work week (Ibid.). Once hat-making season ended, he was fired and had to survive by taking almost any job:

> errand boy, bus boy, dish washer, apprentice operator on caps... I was a painter, I sold large picture paintings ... I was a waiter... I worked in a printing shop... All these jobs lasted from one day to several months and all these jobs wound up in a fight between me and the boss. I could not live in peace, with my bosses. I was a pocketbook maker, a printing salesman, too, and a labor investigator in the cloak and suit industry. (90)

Wisotsky was probably too radicalized to keep a job. Discussions at home, lectures at union and anarchist meetings, and early strike experiences made him an obstacle for every boss who wanted to exploit workers without incident. For years he drifted about, sleeping at the docks or at the headquarters of the Industrial Workers of the World (I.W.W.), and "many times ... [he] sponged on those who had jobs, sometimes a meal, sometimes a night's lodging" (91). After an accident at an ice cream shop with an open electric wire, he won a lawsuit against his employer:

> I won the case. I got enough money with which to pay some of my debts, and three months' rent. I also bought myself a new suit, new shoes, a few shirts and underwear, and I still had some money left over to live on for a few weeks. My Wobbly friends also had a good time on that money. They kibbitzed [sic] and now called me a bourgeois (94).

The exact time of his political radicalization cannot be determined, since Wisotsky had many contacts with union members, radical workers, anarchist lecturers, and the like. However, one key moment seems to have impacted the seventeen-year-old boy. In 1912, he attended a debate between the famous anarchist Emma Goldman (1869–1940) and Sol Friedman, which was chaired by William "Big Bill" Haywood. This event was like a "champion prize fight" (55) and Wisotsky eventually became a member of Goldman's entourage and an activist in the I.W.W. This opened his young mind to new ideological territory:

> I stepped into a new world of thoughts and ideas that I frankly did not understand clearly. Strange to me were the conversations, debates, discussion and words like "sabotage," "the social revolution," "Socialism," "Anarchism," "Syndicalism," "Marx," "Engels," "Prud[h]on," "Commonwealth," "Bakunin," "Kropotkin," "Direct Action," "Political Action," "Craft Unions," "Industrial Unions," "Bureaucracy," "Capitalism," etc. In order to become conversant, I began to read such I.W.W. papers as "The Industrial Worker," and "Solidarity", issued weekly. "The Call" – a Socialist daily, and "Mother Earth", an Anarchist monthly. I also read pamphlets, brochures, books in Yiddish and English on social and economic problems, and became acquainted with the world of literature, fine arts, great authors and painters. I attended debates, meetings, lectures, that were held in many East Side halls. The lecturers were people of all shades and colors. Emma Goldman became my favorite. I did not miss her lectures or debates for many years. I even volunteered to help her manager, Dr. Ben Reitman, sell the booklets she had written and her magazine "Mother Earth." On many Friday evenings, I was at the door, taking the 15-cent tickets that people bought to hear her. (57)

Unemployment became a significant issue in New York during World War I, and many I.W.W. members endured daily struggles. During the war, many protesters who spoke out against unemployment – and later against the war itself, especially during the Palmer Raids[119] – were imprisoned, and "New York was the mirror of all conflicts and struggles that went throughout the country. We reacted immediately with financial and moral help. Defense committees were organized for each individual case. Money was raised, protest mass meetings were called, demonstrations on Union Square were held" (86). Wisotsky himself participated in I.W.W. actions against the government and actions in which workers occupied churches, demanding to spend the night there and receive food (104–105). These events were also used to arouse public attention, and "in both our speeches in the churches and in our declarations in the press, we charged the city politicians as well as all politicians and social and welfare leaders with neglecting their responsibility toward the unemployed. We demanded they take positive action to help all those in the need of food and shelter" (105). Wisotsky was eventually arrested by the police and sentenced to two months in prison. There, he learned "a rich vocabulary in the English language that the criminal world uses, full of profanity, double-meaning double-talk. What a lingo!" (107). He also received letters from anarchist Alexander Berkman (1870–1936) and the I.W.W. leader William Haywood; the former wrote to Wisostky saying "that he was ready to send [him] anything [he] could use, or needed" (115). Whatever the young man needed to strengthen his position as an anarchist and I.W.W. activist, Berkman's letters offered it. Wisotsky's mind was set, and he would remain active in these circles

119 Wisotsky refers to the anti-communist raids at the end of the First World War, due to which, among others, Emma Goldman was sentenced to prison and later eviction.

for decades. What made him a radical, however, was the harsh living conditions in New York City at the turn of the century and in the two decades after 1900. Like many others, Wisotsky arrived from Eastern Europe seeking good fortune across the Atlantic, but the New World offered little less than the poverty he thought his family had left behind. As such, radicalization in New York was not based on Jewish heritage, but on the exploitation of workers by a cruel capitalist system that enslaved them.

Conclusion

The radicalization of the Jewish community in the New York metropolis at the end of the nineteenth and during the early twentieth century was not a mere replica of Eastern European radicalism, as it would lead to the establishment of the Bund or the Poale Zion in the early 1900s. It was more so a process stimulated by the contemporary space-time-continuum. New York's Lower East Side provided an ideal breeding ground for radicalism. The Jewish immigrants who arrived there at the end of the nineteenth century oriented themselves around the strong German workers' movement and created a Jewish community that was radicalized in the United States. This community spread its specific variety of Jewish-American radicalism around the globe, particularly in Tsarist Russia, using Yiddish to express themselves.

The second generation of Jewish immigrants, some of whom were already radicalized in Europe, arrived in a culturally Yiddish and politically radical community. The radicalization process itself was stimulated by the harsh working conditions in the New World, especially within the garment industry, in which many Jewish immigrants tried to work for a living. However, low pay and long working hours radicalized many workers, stimulated strikes, and furthered political radicalization. Isidore Wisotsky arrived in New York in 1909 and would be radicalized like so many before him; poverty, hunger, and the hope for a better life made him easy prey for the radical ideas of the I.W.W. members and famous anarchists on the Lower East Side. Wisotsky's case is particularly interesting; it shows that beyond his ethnic and religious background as an Eastern European Jew, his specific experiences in New York trying to navigate an exploitative labor market would cause him to become radical. As such, he was more so a radical that happened to be Jewish, but not a Jewish radical. He was a radical created by the space-time-continuum he lived in, not by his religious tradition. This is why he stands as an example for so many others who came from traditional Jewish families and ended up as radicals – not only because they wanted to break with tradition, but because they struggled with the world they lived in.

Works Cited

Unpublished Source Material

Wisotsky, Isidore. Autobiographical Typescript, TAM.071, Tamiment Library and Robert F. Wagner Labor Archives, New York University.

Published Works

Avrich, Paul. *The Haymarket Tragedy.* Princeton, NJ: Princeton University Press, 1984.

Bantman, Constance. *The French Anarchists in London, 1880–1914: Exile and Transnationalism in the First Globalisation.* Liverpool: Liverpool University Press, 2013.

Berrol, Selma C. "In Their Image: German Jews and the Americanization of the Ost Juden in New York City." *New York History* 63, no. 4 (1982): 417–433.

Brossat, Alain, and Sylvia Klingsberg. *Revolutionary Yiddishland: A History of Jewish Radicalism*, translated by David Fernbach. London/New York: Verso, 2016.

Cantor Zuckoff, Aviva. "The Oppression of America's Jews." In *Jewish Radicalism: A Selected Anthology,* edited by Jack Nusan Porter and Peter Dreier, 29–49. New York: Grove Press, 1973.

Carlebach, Julius. *Karl Marx and the Radical Critique of Judaism.* London: Routledge, 1978.

Cohen, Percy S. *Jewish Radicals and Radical Jews.* London/New York: Academic Press, 1980.

Diner, Hasia R. *Lower East Side Memories: A Jewish Place in America.* Princeton/Oxford: Princeton University Press, 2000.

Fischman, Dennis. "The Jewish Question about Marx." *Polity* 21, no. 4 (1989): 755–775.

Frankel, Jonathan. *Prophecy and Politics: Socialism, Nationalism, and the Russian Jews, 1862–1917.* Cambridge: Cambridge University Press, 1981.

Goyens, Tom. "Introduction." In *Radical Gotham: Anarchism in New York City from Schwab's Saloon to Occupy Wall Street*, edited by Tom Goyens, 1–11. Urbana/Chicago/Springfield, IL: University of Illinois Press, 2017.

Guttmann, Allen. "Jewish Radicals, Jewish Writers." *The American Scholar* 32, no. 4 (1963): 563–575.

Horowitz, Brian. *Russian Idea – Jewish Presence: Essays on Russian-Jewish Intellectual Life.* Brighton, MA: Academic Studies Press, 2013.

Jacobs, Jack. "Introduction." In *Jews and Leftist Politics: Judaism, Israel, Antisemitism, and Gender*, edited by Jack Jacobs, 1–28. Cambridge/New York: Cambridge University Press, 2017.

Katz, Steven T., ed. *The Shtetl: New Evaluations.* New York: NYU Press, 2009.

Keßler, Mario. "Die Komintern und die Poale Zion 1919 bis 1922: Eine gescheiterte Synthese von Kommunismus und Zionismus." *Arbeit – Bewegung – Geschichte* 2 (2017): 15–30.

Klapper, Melissa R. "'Those by Whose Side We Have Labored': American Jewish Women and the Peace Movement between the Wars." *The Journal of American History* 97, no. 3 (2010): 636–658.

Klier, John D., and Shlomo Lambroza, eds. *Pogroms: Anti-Jewish Violence in Modern Russian History.* Cambridge: Cambridge University Press, 2004.

Kuznets, Simon. "Immigration of Russian Jews to the U.S.: Background and Structure." *Perspectives in American History* 9 (1975): 35–124.
Levin, Nora. *Jewish Socialist Movements, 1871–1917: While Messiah Tarried.* London: Routledge, 1978.
Lichter, S. Robert, and Stanley Rothman. "Jewish Ethnicity and Radical Culture: A Social Psychological Study of Political Activists." *Political Psychology* 3, no. 1/2 (1981/1982): 116–157.
Liebman, Arthur. *Jews and the Left.* New York: Wiley, 1979.
McKanan, Dan. "The Implicit Religion of Radicalism: Socialist Party Theology, 1900–1934." *Journal of the American Academy of Religion* 78, no. 3 (2010): 750–789.
Mendel, Hersh. *Memoirs of a Jewish Revolutionary.* London: Pluto Press, 1989.
Mendelsohn, Adam. "Tongue Ties: The Emergence of the Anglophone Jewish Diaspora in the Mid-Nineteenth Century." *American Jewish History* 93, no. 2 (2007): 177–209.
Michels, Tony. *A Fire in Their Hearts: Yiddish Socialists in New York.* Cambridge, MA: Harvard University Press, 2005.
Michels, Tony. "Exporting Yiddish Socialism: New York's Role in the Russian Jewish Workers' Movement." *Jewish Social Studies: History, Culture, Society* n.s. 16, no. 1 (2009): 1–26.
Pinchuk, Ben-Cion. "The Shtetl: An Ethnic Town in the Russian Empire." *Cahiers du Monde russe* 41, no. 4 (2000): *Aperçus sur le monde juif:* 495–504.
Pinsker, Shachar M. *A Rich Brew: How Cafés Created Modern Jewish Culture.* New York: NYU Press, 2018.
Porter, Jack Nusan, and Peter Dreier. "Introduction." In *Jewish Radicalism: A Selected Anthology,* edited by Jack Nusan Porter and Peter Dreier, xv-liv. New York: Grove Press, 1973.
Riga, Liliana. "Ethnonationalism, Assimilation, and the Social Worlds of the Jewish Bolsheviks in Fin deSiècle Tsarist Russia." *Comparative Studies in Society and History* 48, no. 4 (2006): 762–797.
Rosenberg, M. J. "To Uncle Tom and Other Jews." In *Jewish Radicalism: A Selected Anthology,* edited by Jack Nusan Porter and Peter Dreier, 5–10. New York: Grove Press, 1973.
Shuldiner, David P. *Of Moses and Marx: Folk Ideology and Folk History in the Jewish Labor Movement.* Wesport, CT/London: Bergin and Garvey, 1999.
Sorin, Gerald. *The Prophetic Minority: American Jewish Immigrant Radicals, 1880–1920.* Bloomington: Indiana University Press, 1985.
Soyer, Daniel. "Transnationalism and Mutual Influence: American and East European Jewries in the 1920s and 1930s." In *Rethinking European Jewish History,* edited by Jeremy Cohen and Moshe Rosman, 201–220. (Oxford: Oxford University Press, 2009).
Tobias, Henry J. *The Jewish Bund in Russia from its Origin to 1905.* Stanford, CA: Stanford University Press, 1972.
United Hebrew Trades, ed. *Seventy Years: United Hebrew Trades* (1958).
Waskow, Arthur I. "Judaism and Revolution Today." In *Jewish Radicalism: A Selected Anthology,* edited by Jack Nusan Porter and Peter Dreier, 11–28. New York: Grove Press, 1973.
Wolfe, Robert. *Remember to Dream: A History of Jewish Radicalism.* New York: Jewish Radical Education Project, 1994.
Zimmer, Kenyon. "Saul Yanovsky and Yiddish Anarchism on the Lower East Side." In *Radical Gotham: Anarchism in New York City from Schwab's Saloon to Occupy Wall Street,* edited by Tom Goyens, 33–53. Urbana/Chicago/Springfield, IL: University of Illinois Press, 2017.

Tal Elmaliach

Jewish Radicalism as a Liminal Space

HaShomer haTza'ir between Zionism and the New Left, 1967–1973

Introduction

During the second half of the 1960s and the early 1970s, a new phenomenon became apparent in the main centers of diaspora Jewry – North America, Latin America, and Western Europe. It was defined by the people of that era, as well as scholars, as "the Jewish New Left."[1]

This term came to describe the activity of thousands of young Jews who tried to shape their particular ethnic identity, while being involved in the universal political and ideological trend called the "New Left."[2] At the same time, a local version of the New Left developed in Israel. The Israeli New Left faced similar dilemmas to the Jewish New Left regarding its loyalty to the Zionist project and the

1 Michael E. Staub, *Torn at the Roots: The Crisis of Jewish Liberalism in Postwar America* (New York: Columbia University Press, 2002), 194–240; Natan Glazer, *American Judaism* (Chicago/London: University of Chicago Press, 1972), 151–186; Riv-Ellen Prell, *Prayer & Community: The Havurah in American Judaism* (Detroit: Wayne State University Press, 1989); Arthur Liebman, *Jews and the Left* (New York: Wiley, 1979), 536–587; Yosef Gorni, *The State of Israel in Jewish Public Thought: The Quest for Collective Identity* (New York: New York University Press, 1994), 111–132; David Glanz, "An Interpretation of the Jewish Counterculture," *Jewish Social Studies* 39, no. 1/2, American Bicentennial: II (1977): 117–128; Colin Shindler, *Israel and the European Left – Between Solidarity and Delegitimization* (New York: NY, Bloomsbury Publishing, 2012), 223; Jack Nusan Porter and Peter Dreier, eds., *Jewish Radicalism: A Selected Anthology* (New York: Grove Press, 1973); Bill Novak and Robert Goldman, "The Rise of the Jewish Student Press," *Conservative Judaism* 25, no. 2 (1971): 5–19; David Twersky, "Entering the 1970s: Habonim and the Jewish Student Movement," in *Builders and Dreamers – Habonim Labor Zionist youth in North America*, eds. J. J Goldberg and Elliot King (New York: Herzl Press, 1984), 213–218.

2 Among those groups in the U.S were Jewish Liberation Project, Jewish Radical Union, Jews for Urban Justice and more; in Argentina: Baderej, Fraie Schtime, Dror, Jazit Hanoar, Hajalutz-Lamerjav, Juventud Anilevich; in France: Organisation Juive Revolutinnaire; in Britain: The British-Israel-Palestine socialist action group; in the Netherlands: the critical Zionists of Holland; in Germany: the German borokovbund. See further discussion below.

https://doi.org/10.1515/9783110545753-007

universal values with which it identified.[3] This chapter focuses on the tension between Zionism and the New Left, as it was expressed in organizations which were affiliated with one of the prominent centers of the Jewish New Left – the movement of HaShomer haTza'ir.[4] The chapter describes this phenomenon in several locations – the United States, France, Argentina, and Israel – between the years 1967–1973, when this tension reached its peak.

Current research about the Jewish New Left focuses, naturally, on the biggest center of Jewish youth in the 1960s – the United States, where there were at that time about 350,000 Jewish students. Nathan Glazer examined the prominent role of Jews in the American New Left. He described how the year 1967 marked the turn of the universal New Left against Israel as a result of the Six-Day War and the rise of a conflict between Afro-Americans and Jews in the United States. After it, he argued, Jews developed a particular Jews-only movement, although they still had some connections to the universal New Left.[5]

Yosef Gorni also studied radical Jews in the United States during those years. He claimed that at the beginning of the 1960s Jews were alienated from their Jewish roots and that their national consciousness rose as a result of the war, as well as disappointment with the New Left and the hostility of Afro-Americans.[6] Other scholars, such as Jack Nusan, Peter Dreier, Arthur Liebman, and Percy S. Cohen, also argued that until the Six-Day War Jews were involved in the New Left without a declared connection to the fact they were Jewish. They also hang the emergence of the Jewish New Left on the feelings of loneliness of Jews and the sense they were betrayed by the universal New Left during and after the war.[7]

---

3 Adi Portugez, "Tnuat Smol Israeli Hadash: Smol Hadash Be-Israel," *Israel* 21 (2013): 225–252; Tal Elmaliach, "The Israeli Left between Culture and Politics: Tzavta Club and Mapam 1956–1973," *Journal of Israeli History* 33, no. 2 (2014): 169–183.

4 See note 3 and Yair Oron, *Kulanu Yehudim Germanim – Radicalim Yehudim Be-tzarfat Be-shnot Ha-shishim Ve-ha-shivim* (Tel Aviv: Am Oved, the University of Tel Aviv and the University of Ben Gurion, 1999), 105, 107, 110; Beatrice D. Gurwitz, "From the New World to the Third World: Generation, Politics, and the Making of Argentine Jewish Ethnicity 1955–1983" (PhD Dissertation, University of California, Berkeley, 2012); Leonardo Senkman, "Repercussions of the Six-Day War in the Leftist Jewish Argentinian Camp: The Rise of Fraie Schtime, 1967–1969," in *The Six-Day War and World Jewry*, ed. Eli Lederhendler (Bethesda, MD: University Press of Maryland, 2000), 167–187; Avraham Schenker, "Progressive Zionism in America," in *Against the Stream: Seven Decades of HaShomer haTza'ir in North America*, ed. Ariel Hurwitz (Givat Haviva: Yad Yaari, 1994), 273–295; Amichai Geva, "A Time for Expansion," in Hurwitz, *Against the Stream*, 125–142.

5 Glazer, *American Judaism*, 151–186.

6 Gorni, *Collective Identity*, 111–132.

7 Liebman, *Jews and the Left*, 536–587; Nusan and Dreier, *Jewish Radicalism*, xvi-iiv; Percy S. Cohen, *Jewish Radicals and Radical Jews* (London: Academic Press, 1981), 14–84.

Rejection by the universal New Left was also perceived as the main reason for the rise of the Jewish New Left in research about the two next biggest centers of Jews in the diaspora in the 1960s – France (with 20,000 Jewish students) and Argentina (15,000).[8]

Yair Oron showed how the Six-Day War aroused Holocaust awareness among the young generation of Jewish radicals in France, and how this led to their identification with the State of Israel and the Jewish people.[9]

Paula Hyman and Judith Freidlander also described a process through which the Jewish Left in France assimilated after the Second World War, but this transformed after the Six-Day War into a Jewish pride and growing ties to the Jewish tradition.[10]

The research about the Jewish New Left in Argentina also sees it as a result of rejection, although it dates its rise to an earlier period. Beatrice Dora Gurwitz claimed that this phenomenon, which she defines as "ethno-radicalism," emerged after the wave of anti-Semitism that followed the kidnapping by Israel of Adolf Eichmann (1906–1962) from his hideout in Argentina (1960), as well as the disappointment with Latin-American hostility toward Israel during the first tri-continental conference in Havana in 1966.[11]

Another description of the role of rejection in the rise of the Jewish New Left in Argentina was made by Leonardo Senkman. Senkman saw signs of feelings of rejection as early as the 1950s, as a result of anti-Semitism in the Communist party of Argentina as well its hostility towards Israel before the Six-Day War.[12]

The historical convention about the Jewish New Left, which emphasizes feelings of rejection as the prominent source for its rise, suits the traditional convention regarding radical Jews as a broad historic phenomenon. This traditional convention says that from the early stages of the universal Left, Jews wished to be part of it, and that they could integrate inside it as long as they assimilated, or at least did not emphasize their particular Jewish origins. But the emergence of different elements of rejection – such as anti-Semitism, pogroms, or disap-

---

8 *American Jewish Year Book* 70 (1969), 73; Leon Peretz, *Matzavo Shel Ha-noar Ha-yehudi Be-Argentina*, 1961, archived in Humanities Library – the Hebrew University, Jerusalem; Oron, *Kulanu Yehudim Germanim*, 18; Tfuzot Israel – Sherut Meida Al Chayei Ha-yehudim Ba-olam, Shana Chet, Hoveret He (Jerusalem, Ha-va'ad Ha-yehudi Ha-americani Be-Israel, 1970).

9 Oron, *Kulanu Yehudim Germanim*, 131–140.

10 Judith Freidlander, "The Six-Day war and the 'Jewish Question' in France," in Lederhendler, *The Six-Day War*, 125–160; Paula Hyman, *The Jews of Modern France: Jewish Communities in the Modern World* (Berkeley: University of California Press, 1998), 193–214.

11 Gurwitz, "From the New World to the Third World," 68, 97.

12 Senkman, "Fraie Schtime."

pointment with the non-Jewish Left – stopped the process of assimilation. It forced the Jews to develop a particular framework which embraced the ideas of the universal Left and implemented them in the Jewish world. Jewish nationalism and the universal Left did not suit one another and therefore the Jewish New Left arose as a result of the clash between them.

In this chapter I wish to challenge this convention and offer an alternative explanation for the rise of the Jewish New Left. This relies on current historic research about Jewish radicalism, the theoretical discussion about the creation of ethnic identity, and a specific historic test case. My explanation sees rejection feelings, especially those that followed the Six-Day War, as a catalyst for the rise of the Jewish New Left, but not as a turning point which marked its emergence.[13]

As I will show, the Jewish New Left was another expression of a built-in combination, and not contradiction, between Jewish nationalism and the universal Left, which had been part of these movements' history since they emerged. This argument relies on a hypothesis which is based on the scholarly discussion regarding ethnic solidarity among minorities living in multi-cultural societies.[14]

It says that modernization has not made ethnic solidarity unnecessary, since it is an efficient tool to confront different challenges in modernity, such as secularization, urbanization, immigration, and political and economic instability. The combination between Jewish nationalism and the universal Left was, therefore, based on the benefits that these two movements provided to Jews. Supporting them both, as I show below, not only was not a paradox but is actually self-explanatory.

Jewish Radicals between Nationalism and Universalism

The attempt to combine a Jewish national self-definition and the ideas of the universal Left is an historic phenomenon that emerged in the mid-nineteenth century. Its first signs were seen with the activity of Jews in left-wing movements, of whom Moses Hess is considered to be the "ideal type."[15]

---

13 See Staub, *Torn at the Roots*, 131–132.

14 François Nielsen, "Toward a Theory of Ethnic Solidarity in Modern Societies," *American Sociological Review* 50, no. 2 (1985), 133–149.

15 See for example Isaiah Berlin, "The Life and Opinions of Moses Hess," in *Essential Papers on Jews and the Left*, ed. Ezra Mendelsohn (New York: New York University Press, 1997); Shlomo

In the second half of the nineteenth century, it seemed that the combination between Jewish national particularism and ideas of the universal Left, of the type that Hess and others offered, did not receive significant attention. However, at the end of the century and in the first years of the twentieth century, two mass movements based on this combination were established: the Bund and Socialist-Zionism.[16]

A third movement – the Communist movement – was cosmopolitan and clearly non-Jewish, but until the 1930s its Jewish members had the opportunity – which they fulfilled – to keep their particular culture and heritage and combine it with their involvement in the general revolutionary project.[17]

Between the three movements were significant differences regarding the "Jewish question," meaning how and where Jews should live in order to make them part of the modern world. However, they also shared the basic combination of the particular and universal and from this point of view they were somewhat similar. As a result, supporters of these movements often moved from one movement to another.[18]

Research of the relationship between Jewish nationalism and the universal Left went through several developments throughout the years. These developments can be described through three perspectives, which I define as the "contradiction thesis," the "dialectic thesis," and the "built-in combination thesis." The contradiction thesis was the traditional historiographical perspective about Jewish radicals, which was developed by historians such as Simon Dubnow, Ben-Zion Dinur, Raphael Mahler, and Shmuel Ettinger and was dominant from the beginning of the twentieth century to the 1960s. It saw a complete contradiction between Jewish nationalism and the universal Left and described a permanent struggle between them. Jews who supported the universal Left, they argued, tended to assimilate, but confronted anti-Semitism which stopped this process.[19]

Avineri, *Moses Hess: Prophet of Communism and Zionism* (New York: New York University Press, 1985).

16 For further discussion see Jonathan Frankel, *Prophecy and Politics: Socialism, Nationalism, and the Russian Jews, 1862–1917* (Cambridge/New York: Cambridge University Press, 1984).

17 Kenneth B. Moss, *Jewish Renaissance in the Russian Revolution* (Cambridge, MA/London: Harvard University Press, 2009); Benjamin Pinkus, *The Jews of the Soviet Union: The History of a National Minority* (Cambridge/New York: Cambridge University Press, 1990).

18 See for example Anita Shapira, *Ha-halicha Al Kav Ha-ofek* (Tel Aviv: Sifriyat Poalim, 2001).

19 Jonathan Frankel, "Hitbolelut Ve-Hisardut Be-kerev Yehudei Eropa Ba-Me'a Ha-19: Lekrat Historiografia Hadasha?" in *Leumiyut Ve-politica Yehudit: Prespectivot Hadashot*, ed. Gideon Shimony, Yosef Shalmon and Yehuda Reinhertz (Jerusalem: Zalman Shazar Center and Boston: Tauber institute in Brandeis University, 1996), 23–56.

Anti-Semitism was therefore the driving force behind Jewish nationalism, and in the case of Jewish radicals, behind the establishment of frameworks which combined, as a compromise, Jewish nationalism and the ideas of the universal Left.

The dialectic thesis was developed mainly by Jonathan Frankel and Michael Graetz. Although they both saw the relationship between Jewish nationalism and the universal Left as a contradiction, they were aware that there was an interaction between them. Regarding the Jewish labor movement in Eastern Europe, Frankel described a dialectic move from traditional life to emancipation and a development of a synthesis of auto-emancipation[20]; Graetz, writing on French Jewry, showed how the organized attempt to encourage the assimilation of the Jews actually developed their national awareness.[21] Although, in a comparison with the contradiction thesis, they presented a more complicated perception, they actually also explained the source of the dialectic process by the rejection that Jews experienced from the Left. Frankel argued, for example, that Moses Hess developed his Socialist-Zionism after the Damascus affair (1840) and that in Russia Jewish radicals began their affiliation with Jewish nationalism mainly after the pogroms of 1881–1882.[22]

Graetz also described, regarding Hess and his Jewish roots, a route of "alienation, rejection and returning" and argued that this comprised the common roots of many Jews in that time.[23]

The driving force behind the dialectic thesis was, therefore, that the contradiction led to a combination between Jewish nationalism and the universal Left, but not intentionally.

The contradiction thesis and the dialectic thesis are inconsistent with arguments of other scholars, who see the relationship between Jewish nationalism and the universal Left as a built-in combination. Moshe Mishkinski, for example, who studied the Jewish labor movement in Russia, claimed that "the common perception, which sees only the contradictions between these two trends, is one-sided and false. Actually, there was a constant two-way interaction between

20 Jonathan Frankel, "Ha-mashber Ke-gorem Merkazi Ba-politica Ha-yehudit Ha-modernit: 1840 and 1881–1882," in *Solidaryut Yehudit Leumit Ba-et Ha-hadasha*, ed. Biniamin Pincus and Ilan Troen, (Sde-Boker: Ben Gurion Institute, 1988), 31–46.

21 Michael Graetz, *Ha-periferia Haita Le-Merkaz: Prakim Be-toldot Yehudei TZarfat Ba-Me'a Ha-yod-tet* (Jerusalem: Bialik institute, 1987).

22 Frankel, "Ha-mashber Ke-gorem Merkazi," 32–42.

23 Michael Graetz, "Le-sheivato Shel Moshe Hess La-yahadut: Ha-reka Le-chibur 'Romi ve-Yerushalaim," *Tzion*, Mem-He, Bet (1980): 133–153.

them."[24] Phyllis Cohen Albert, who examined the Jews of France, argued that they were affiliated at the same time with their Jewish roots and emancipation, without contradiction between the two. Although Albert explains this combination as a result of the insecurity that Jews felt, he still saw it as built-in and not as some interaction between two contradictory poles. He also helped to dismantle the claim of Graetz about the common root of alienation, rejection, and returning, by showing that anti-Semitism sometimes led to further assimilation and did not necessarily emphasize the national element.[25]

The built-in combination thesis was supported by other scholars as well: Eric Hobsbawm, for example, presented Jewish nationalism not as a result of rejection but as an attempt to imitate the European national movements[26]; elsewhere, Yoav Peled argued that the Bund combined national and class perspectives as a result of the special role of Jews in the labor structure of Eastern Europe.[27]

The built-in combination thesis is also supported by the current theoretical discussion about the construction of ethnic identity. During the first decades of this discussion, ethnic identity had been perceived as a primordial and permanent cultural pattern. As such, it suited the contradiction thesis and the dialectic thesis, since they both saw Jewish particularism and the universal Left as two separate elements. However, in recent years, ethnicity has been described as undergoing constant changes and reshaping.[28]

Different scholars argued that self-definition of ethnic groups is actually flexible, so when a group (such as the Jews) face some contradiction (such as between the particular and the universal), it can eliminate it by redefining its borders and characteristics.[29]

---

24 Moshe Mishkinski, *Reshit Tnu'at Ha-poalim Be-rusia: Megamot Yesod* (Tel Aviv: Tel Aviv University and Hakibbutz Ha-me'uchad, 1981), 9.

25 Phyllis Cohen Albert, "Etniut Ve-solidaryut Yehudit Be-tzarfat Ba-Me'a Ha-19," in Shimony, Shalmon and Reinhertz, *Leumiyut Ve-politica Yehudit*, 47–73.

26 Eric J. Hobsbawm, *Nations and Nationalism since 1780* (New York: Cambridge University Press, 1990), 47–48, 76.

27 Yoav Peled, *Class and Ethnicity in the Pale: The Political Economy of Jewish Workers' Nationalism in Late Imperial Russia* (New York: St. Martin's Press, 1989).

28 Fredrik Barth, ed., *Ethnic Groups and Boundaries: The Social Organization of Culture Difference* (Boston: Little, Brown and Company, 1969); Andreas Wimmer, "The Making and Unmaking of Ethnic Boundaries: A Multilevel Process Theory," *American Journal of Sociology* 113, no. 4 (2008): 970–1022; Joane Nagel, "Constructing Ethnicity: Creating and Recreating Ethnic Identity and Culture," *Social Problems* 41, no. 1 (1994): 152–176.

29 Martin Japtok, *Growing Up Ethnic Nationalism and the Bildungsroman in African American and Jewish American Fiction* (Iowa City: University of Iowa Press, 2005), 52; Shaul Magid, *Post-Judaism: Identity and Renewal in a Postethnic Society* (Bloomington: Indiana University Press, 2013).

One way to do this is by creating a "hybrid identity," which means a new identity that includes several identities which carry a mutual relation of "that and also the other."[30]

Another way in which a new identity that combines different elements can be constructed is by establishing a "liminal space," which means "in-between" the two elements.[31]

According to the scholarly discussion that deals with the role of liminality in construction of identity, every change in the self-definition of a group includes three steps: pre-liminal, liminal, and post-liminal. The most significant stage is the liminal one, since this is where the process of change actually takes place. It relies on the creation of a social group, called *communitas*, which carries special characteristics that constitute the needed conditions for the process of change. It includes, for example, a supportive atmosphere which allows the members of the *communitas* to lose their former connections with social structures, norms, and behavioral barriers.[32]

Liminal space constitutes a proper theoretical framework for the current discussion for two reasons: it has been already used, successfully, to analyze the phenomenon of Jewish radicals[33], and it includes a tighter combination than the hybrid form, since its original elements become one and do not exist side by side. However, using the term of liminal space in this article requires some adjustments.

The classic theory of liminal space actually only suits the contradiction thesis. It presents a situation in which Jews, who are in the liminal space, lose their connections with their roots, and move towards assimilation in a linear process. Liminality, therefore, is a temporary stage in this process, which is a result of the clash between Jewish particularism and universal ideas. However, the current scholarly discussion of liminality developed the classic theory and defined a new perspective about it. It claims that in many cases the liminal space is not

30 Flocel Sabaté, *Hybrid Identities* (Bern: Peter Lang, 2014); Keri E. Iyall Smith and Patricia Leavy, *Hybrid Identities: Theoretical and Empirical Examinations* (Leiden: Brill, 2008).

31 Nic Beech, "Liminality and the Practices of Identity Reconstruction," *Human Relations* 64, no. 2 (2010): 285–302.

32 Ruth C. Hill, "Liminal Identity to Wholeness: A 'Biracial' Path to the Practice of Cross-Cultural, Jungian Psychotherapy," *Jung Journal: Culture & Psyche* 4 (2010): 16–30; Jeffrey Rubenstein, "Purim, Liminality, and Communitas," *AJS Review* 17, no. 2 (1992): 247–277.

33 Joshua Harold, "Institutionalizing Liminality: Jewish Summer Camps and the Boundary Work of Camp Participants," *Sociology of Race and Ethnicity* 1, no. 3 (2015): 439–453; Jordana Silverstein, "We're Dealing with How Do We Live and Work with this Memory and What Are We Supposed to Do About It," *Borderlands* 9, no. 1 (2010): 1–17.

a stage but becomes permanent.[34] The reason is that liminality suits the conditions of modernity, which is characterized by constant change and identity fluidity. In the specific case of Jews, it has been also claimed in research that Jews are a natural example of permanent liminality.[35]

Indeed, one can see permanent liminality as a synthesis between two former identities, as the dialectic thesis claims, but that assumes there is a contradiction between those elements, which is not always the case. As we will see, the test case of HaShomer haTza'ir reveals permanent liminality neither as a result of a contradiction nor a dialectic process, but as a built-in combination from the start.

HaShomer haTza'ir as a Case Study

HaShomer haTza'ir was the first Zionist youth movement, established in Galicia on the eve of the First World War. It constitutes a classic test case of the way in which Jewish radicals combined their national-Jewish and leftist-universal identities through permanent liminality. Indeed, in the first years of its existence, when it was only a youth movement, HaShomer haTza'ir did not yet have a clear political world view. However, it did include an educational-social liminal space. The members of the movement operated in a *communitas* and developed an independent space which rejected the traditional norms of the Jewish world. But they did not move towards assimilation. Through the liminal space they created a new identity which combined Jewish nationalism, European romanticism, and utopian socialism, all integrated in model of a "new man."[36]

In the 1920s, the first graduates of the Hashomer Hatza'ir youth movement immigrated to Palestine and soon established new kibbutzim. This was followed by a turn from romanticism and utopian socialism to Marxism. The reasons for this turn were the political organization that Marxism offered, the way it differ-

---

34 Arpad Szakolczai, "Living permanent liminality: the recent transition experience in Ireland," *Irish Journal of Sociology*, 22, no. 1 (2014): 28–50; Christian Garmann Johnsen, "'It's capitalism on coke!' From temporary to permanent liminality in organization studies," *Culture and Organization* 21, no. 4 (2015): 321–337.

35 See: Vincent Brook, ed., *You Should See Yourself: Jewish Identity in Postmodern American Culture* (New Brunswick, New Jersey and London: Rutgers University Press, 2006).

36 Matityahu Mintz, *Havley Ne'urim: Ha-tnua Ha-shomrit 1911–1921* (Jerusalem: Ha-sifriya Ha-tzionit, 1995); Rina Peled, *Ha-adam Ha-hadash Shel Ha-mahapecha Ha-tzionit Ve-shorashav Ha-eiropim* (Tel Aviv: Am Oved, 2002).

entiated HaShomer haTza'ir from other socialist-Zionist organizations, and the fact that it suited the general *Zeitgeist*.[37]

The theoretical combination of Zionism and Marxism was made possible by the thesis of Ber Borochov (1881–1917). Borochov argued that every ethnic group needs a territory in order to develop the labor relations that will constitute the basic conditions for a class revolution.[38]

His thesis was developed by the thinkers of HaShomer haTza'ir into a more detailed plan which was called "the stages theory." It was included in the platform of the Kibbutz movement that HaShomer haTza'ir established in 1927 – Hakibbutz Haartzi (the nationwide Kibbutz). It said that the Jewish people should first establish a national home, and only after that turn to class struggle, which should include cooperation of Jewish and Arab workers. Hakibbutz Haartzi also offered a plan for a bi-national state.[39]

The ideological contribution of Borochov's thesis and the stages theory to the creation of the liminal space in which HaShomer haTza'ir operated was dramatic. It actually combined the two main dreams of Jewish youth of that time: a Jewish national home and the revolutionary desire for the "world of tomorrow." This combination benefited the movement with an impressive recruitment ability: on the eve of the Second World War HaShomer haTza'ir was the biggest Jewish youth movement in the diaspora, with tens of thousands of members around the world, 20,000 of them in Poland.[40] Its branch in Palestine also included a youth movement of thousands of members and its graduates, established until 1943, as well as 39 Kibbutzim where 8,381 people lived.[41]

Jewish Radicals after the Second World War

In the years after the Second World War, a significant change took place in the way Jews integrated in the global Left. Of the movements mentioned before, two

---

37 For further discussion see Elkana Margalit, *HaShomer haTza'ir: Me-adat Ne'urim Le-marksizm Mahapchani 1913–1936*, (Tel Aviv: Hakibbutz Hemeuchad, 1971); Shapira, *Ha-halicha*.
38 Dov Ber Borochov, *Ktavim Nivharim, vol. 1, Le-heker She'elat Ha-yehudim* (Tel Aviv: Am Oved, 1943); Dov Ber Borochov, *Ktavim, vol. 1–3* (Tel Aviv: Sifriat Poalim and Hakibbutz Ha-meuchad, 1955–1966).
39 David Zayit, *Halutzim Ba-mavoch Ha-politi: Ha-tnu'a Ha-kibutzit 1927–1948* (Jerusalem: Yad Yitzhak Ben-Zvi, 1993), 13–33.
40 For further discussion see Eli Tzur, *Lifnei Bo Ha-afela: HaShomer haTza'ir Be-Polin Ve-Galitzia 1930–1940* (Sede Boker: Machon Ben Gurion; Givaat Haviva: Yad Yaari, 2006).
41 "8381 Nefesh Be-Kibbutzei Ha-kibbutz Ha-artzi," *Al Hamishmar*, May 14 1944.

almost ceased to be a framework for Jewish radicals. The Bund suffered a severe blow as a result of the destruction of the European Jewry during the Holocaust. The creation of the state of Israel, which it opposed, also reduced its relevancy dramatically. At the same time, from the early 1950s, the Soviet Union turned against Soviet Jews and the state of Israel. As a result, communism also became a less relevant alternative for Jewish radicals.[42] The combination of Jewish nationalism and socialist radicalism could exist, therefore, mainly in the only trend that not only was less harmed by the Holocaust and by the changes in the Soviet Union, but which received great prestige for establishing the Israeli state: socialist Zionism.

Since Israel was the center of operation of socialist Zionism, most of the frameworks of Jewish radicals were operated after the war by the Israeli Labor movement, and especially through the Kibbutz movement. That meant that those frameworks were receiving resources from the state, the labor union organizations (especially the Histadrut), and the Kibbutzim, which made them more capable of organizing people. HaShomer haTza'ir was the most leftist and radical segment of the Israeli Labor movement, and this, along with its organizational power, made it one of the most effective ideological and political forces among Jewish radicals. In the 1950s, after the Jewish diaspora was stabilized, it had new groups of target audience, which all wished to combine pioneer-Zionism and radical socialism without making *Aliyah* (immigration to Israel). One was of graduates of the youth movement who wished to stay in their home countries, but kept their affiliation with the HaShomer haTza'ir world view; a second was of ex-Bundists and ex-communists. They did not become full Zionists and did not think of *Aliyah*, but wished to support Israel while keeping some of their former orientations. Naturally, they found HaShomer haTza'ir the most tolerant framework for this. The third was a group who were neither communists nor Zionists, mostly American Jews, who admired HaShomer haTza'ir because of its progressiveness and its implementation in Jewish and Arab relations, cooperative economics, education and more. These groups were different from each other in many aspects, but they all shared the built-in combination thesis which saw pioneer-Zionism and universal Socialism as one.[43]

In the mid-1950s HaShomer haTza'ir began establishing new frameworks for these new target audiences. In 1953 a new organization – called "the Juventud Mordejai Anilevich" (Mordechai Anielewicz Young Brigade) – was established

---

42 For further discussion see Yirmiyahu Yovel et al., eds., *New Jewish Time: Jewish Culture in a Secular Age – an Encyclopedic View* (Jerusalem: Lmada, 2008), 2, 18–62.

43 Senkman, "Fraie Schtime"; Schenker, "Progressive Zionism."

in Latin America, operating in Uruguay, Chile, and Argentina. Its members were university students, active both in the local Left and in Zionist organization[44]; in 1954 a new organization – Americans for Progressive Israel (API) was established in the United States as a merger of two former organizations which were established in 1946–1947. It was also based on pro-Zionist and socialist Jews who did not make *Aliyah*, although it was aimed at people over 35.[45]

In the same year, a new organization – called "Le Cercle Bernard Lazare" (Bernard Lazare Circle) was established in France. It was aiming at the same public as the API, but also had a young brigade, similar to Anielewicz brigade, called *Mishmar* (Guard).[46] All these organizations were operated by emissaries of Hakibbutz Haartzi and its political party – the United Workers Party (Mapam) – in partnership with local leadership, mostly graduates of the youth movement of HaShomer HaTza'ir. They enlisted members of the local Jewish communities and operated social and cultural activity (lectures, seminars, and conferences), political campaigns related to Israel, the Jewish community and the local and global Left, and fundraising for Mapam and Hakkibutz Haartzi. These frameworks did not become mass movements and each comprised only between several dozen to a few hundred active members; however, their main significance was conceptual, since they offered a new framework of permanent liminality for Jewish radicals in the diaspora. Now it was a matter of other developments which were to introduce this built-in combination to a broader public.

Jews and the New Left

In the early 1960s the New Left became the dominant political and ideological trend among the young generation in the West. The background to this was their disappointment with communism as well as with the social-democratic

44 Noar Mordechai Anilevitz – Pirsumim Pnimi'im Hinuchi'im, no. 1, June 1953 and different reports, 1966; HaShomer haTza'ir Archive, (3029)1.17.1–2; 5–9.2., 6)12.31 ;(3)1–17.2 ;(2)1–17.2). For further discussion see Yerach Grinfeld, "Ha-hativot Ha-tzioniot Sotzialistiot Be-Argentina Be-shnot Ha-shishim: Havnayat Hashkafat Olam," (M.A thesis, Hebrew University, Jerusalem, 2006).

45 Schenker, "Progressive Zionism."

46 Correspondence between Bernard Lazar circle and the world Brit of Mapam, HaShomer haTza'ir Archive, (1405) 93.54(1), (1405) 93.54(4).

welfare state. Young Jewish radicals played a notable role in the New Left, in its leadership, and as rank and file members.[47]

Seemingly, it was a continuation of the historic connection of Jews and the Left. But, unlike in the first half of the twentieth century, Jews were now part of the surrounding society in a way that had not been seen before. This made their involvement in the New Left seem like a push to their universal identity and a blow to their Jewish one. As a result, the Zionists and the Jewish establishment became very worried. Following the contradiction thesis, they saw universalism as a slippery slope towards complete assimilation of the young generation, and as a danger to the future of the Jewish diaspora.[48]

Despite the pessimistic impression of the establishment of that time, the image of assimilation of the young generation of the 1960s in the West is controversial. First, as Michael Staub claims about the case of American Jewry, the 1960s were characterized by such a high presence of Jewish values, ideas, and figures that the whole decade can be called "the Jewish 1960s."[49]

Second, the baby boomers actually grew up in a time when the Jewish diaspora was rebuilt and flourished, and the relationship with the state of Israel was one of its main core values.[50]

Popular culture – such as the book *Exodus* (1958) and the movie based on it (1960), *the Anne Frank Diary* book (1952), play (1955), and movie (1959), and Elie Wiesel's first book *Night* (1960) – also presented Jewish history and Zionism to the Jewish masses in the Western diaspora in a way that strengthened their af-

---

47 For an overview of the research of the role of Jews in the New Left see Phillip Mendes, "'We are all German Jews': Exploring the Prominence of Jews in the New Left," *Melilah: Manchester Journal of Jewish Studies* (2009/3): 1–17.

48 Summary of the first world convention of Jewish youth (Jerusalem: department of youth and pioneers in the World Zionist Organization, 1958), 41, 152, 190; Protocols of the 26th Zionist Congress (Jerusalem: World Zionist Organization, 1964), 3, 142, 384, 643, 679; Summary of a conference for emissaries, department of youth and pioneers in the World Zionist Organization, October 10 1964, Central Zionist Archive, DD1/1267; Israeli Knesset meeting, January 12 1966. See http://main.knesset.gov.il/mk/government/documents/gov13.pdf (accessed March 1 2017); Eliezer Livneh, *Yahadut Artsot-ha-Berit ve Yisrael: ha-mifneh: sikume-biḳur, Novermber-Detsember 1966* (Jerusalem: ha-Merkaz li-tefutsot, Musad le-Keshrai Tarbut 'Im Yahadut ha-Tfutsot, 1967). See also Michael A. Agronoff, Judith Kerman, Moriss U. Schappers, "Jewish Identity: Dialog with Jewish Youth," *Jewish Currents*, July-August 1965.

49 Michael E. Staub, *The Jewish 1960s: an American sourcebook* (Waltham, Mass.: Brandeis University Press; Hanover: University Press of New England, 2004).

50 Glazer, *American Judaism*, 106–128; Emily Alice Katz, *Bringing Zion home: Israel in American Jewish culture, 1948–1967* (Albany: State University of New York Press, 2015).

filiation with their Jewish roots.[51] The Eichmann trial (1961) was another way in which Jews around the Western world became familiar with the Holocaust and the Zionist narrative.[52]

In the mid-1960s the struggle for soviet Jewry began, and the young generation in the West played a prominent role in it, showing a strong ethnic solidarity.[53]

The Jewish element was also prominent in the most universalistic struggles of the Left – such as support for Algerian independence and the civil rights movement in the United States. In both, there were Jewish leaders who claimed that their obligation to strive for freedom and equality came from the Jewish tradition and religion.[54] During those years there was also a clear expression of Jewish nationalism among Jewish radicals who were affiliated with the frameworks of HaShomer haTza'ir. The members of the Mordechai Anielewicz brigade, API, Bernard Lazare circle, and Mishmar were supporters of Israel and fellow travelers of Hakibbutz Haartzi Mapam, and at the same time participated in local and global Left campaigns.[55] Although they constituted a fear of assimilation, the early 1960s showed a growing role of the combination between Jewish nationalism and universal socialism.

From Partnership to Tension

In the mid-1960s, the first signs of tension between Jews and the New Left were seen. The background was changes in the attitude of the New Left towards Israel as well as the general radicalization it went through. In 1965 the civil rights movement in the United States, one of the main fields of activity of young Jewish

---

51 Leon Uris, *Exodus* (New York, NY: Doubleday and Company, 1958); Anne Frank, *The Diary of a Young Girl* (New York, NY: Doubleday and Company, 1952); Elie Wiesel, *Night* (New York: Hill and Wang; London: MacGibbon and Kee, 1960).

52 Hasia R. Diner, *The Jews of the United States, 1654 to 2000* (Berkeley and Los Angeles: University of California Press, 2004), 264.

53 Avi Weiss, "Student Struggle for Soviet Jewry (SSSJ)," *Encyclopaedia Judaica*, ed. Michael Berenbaum and Fred Skolnik, vol. 19. 2nd edition (Detroit: Macmillan Reference USA, 2007(, 269.

54 See the involvement of Rabbis in the Civil Rights Movement, *American Jewish Year Book* Vol. 65 (1964), 77; the early stages (1966) of what later become 'Jews for Urban Justice' (JUJ); and also the influential book of Albert Memmi, *The Liberation of the Jew* (New York: Orion Press, 1966). For further discussion see Staub, *Torn at the roots*, 45–75.

55 API report for 1965–1967, HaShomer haTza'ir Archive, 3886(1)94.3; summary of the API council, May 27–28 1967, HaShomer haTza'ir Archive, 3883(4)91.93; report of Anielewicz brigade, 1966, HaShomer haTza'ir Archive; (2)1–17.2; (3)1–17.2; (6)12.31.

radicals, started to have a separatist character. The Afro-American activists demanded the leadership of their struggle for equality themselves, and started to push out white activists, many of them Jewish. This trend worsened when, in the second half of the decade, the Afro-American activists started to attack the white majority, including the Jews. They refused to accept the Jewish attempt to cooperate as two ethnic minorities. The cooperation of the early 1960s was replaced by severe interracial tension which reached its peak in 1968.[56]

At the same time, the state of Israel also began to attract more attention from the New Left. At the end of the 1950s and the early 1960s, the Palestinian struggle movement consolidated, starting to operate attacks on Israeli targets in the mid-1960s. Against this background, as well as clashes over water sources on the northern border of Israel, the tension between Israel and its neighboring countries increased and reached a new peak in 1965–1966. The third world countries identified with the Arabs and marked Israel as an imperialist aggressor.[57]

The New Left, which saw itself as the protector of the oppressed, embraced this perspective. It defined the Palestinian struggle as guerrilla warfare against a colonial state, such as the one that took place in Algeria and later in Vietnam. It also saw the struggle of the Arab countries against Israel as part of a broad Arab revolution which aimed at the collapse of the old regime that the imperial powers had forced on the region. The radicalization of the civil rights movement, the third-world-ism ideology and the developing crisis in the Middle East created a broad front of anti-Zionists in the New Left, under which Afro-Americans, white radical socialists (some of them anti-Zionist Jews), and Arab students established a strategic alignment.[58]

The rise of the tension between the New Left and the Jews pushed HaShomer haTza'ir to action. What was seen as a growing contradiction was for them an opportunity, since young Jewish radicals now looked for a new way to combine their Jewish national sentiment and the support of the ideas of the Left. Already in 1964 the world conference of HaShomer haTza'ir decided to increase its work

56 Intergroup Relations and Tensions in the United States, *American Jewish Year Book*, Vol. 70 (1969), 71–100.

57 Benjamin Rivlin and Jacques Fomerand, "Changing third world perspectives and politics towards Israel," in *Israel in the Third World*, Michael Curtis and Susan Aurelia Gitelson, eds. (New Brunswick, N.J: Transaction Books, 1976), 325–360.

58 Liebman, *Jews and the Left*, 586; Pamela Pennock, "Third world alliance: Arab – American activists in American universities, 1967–1973," *Mashriq & Mahjar* 2, no. 2 (2014): 55–78.

with Jewish students in the diaspora[59]; however, a more significant development came in 1966, when the API decided to establish a young guard under the name of "Young Americans for Progressive Israel" (YAPI).[60] The mission statement of YAPI was to attract Jewish radicals who were not happy with the trends of the New Left, and wished to combine their activity in the Left with a pro-Israeli affiliation. This act came out of a recognition of the capability of the built-in combination thesis to enlist new supporters, at a time when it actually seemed harder.[61]

The Jewish New Left after the Six-Day War

The Six-Day War (and the waiting period before it) turned the tension between Jews and the New Left into a real rift. The anxiety that followed the threats of Arab leaders to exterminate Israel led many Jews around the world to focus their attention on Israel, and its astonishing victory gave rise to a wave of pride and support that affected many.[62] Young Jewish radicals were also part of this wave, but confronted a hostile attitude from their peers. A major sign of this came a few weeks after the war, in the first formal gathering of the American New Left. The gathering, which was called "The National Conference for New Politics," approved a resolution that condemned Israel for its responsibility in the emergence of the war.[63]

The radical Left in Western Europe and Latin America embraced a similar position.[64]

The hostility of the New Left to Israel placed Jewish radicals in what seemed a dramatic identity crisis, which was characterized even as a new "Jewish Prob-

---

59 HaShomer haTzair 5th world convention. See Levi Dror and Israel Rozenzweig, eds., Sefer HaShomer haTza'ir, vol. 3 (Merchavia: Sifriat poalim, 1964), 466.
60 Young Americans for Progressive Israel – Progress report, November 19 1966, HHA 105.93(2) 3897.
61 Background materials, Moetza Rashit, 30 March – April 2 1964; report on the semi-annual national council, May 20–22 1966, HHA 3897(2)105.93; Jewishness and Socialism: conflict or compatibility, April 27 1967, HHA 3003(1)95.1
62 Sergio Della Pergola, Uzi Rebhun, and Rosa Perla Raicher, "The Six Day war and Israel-Diaspora relations: an analysis of quantitative indicators," in Lederhendler, *The Six-Day War*, 11–50.
63 Text of the resolution of the Black Caucus adopted by the National convention for new politics, Chicago, September 1967. Hoover Institute Archive, New Left Collection, box 36, folder 2; "'New Politics' Convention Modifies Its Indictment of Israel," *Jewish Telegraphic Agency*, September 6 1967.
64 Shindler, *Israel and the European Left*, 232–241; Senkman, "Fraie Schtime."

lem".[65] On the one hand, they continued to identify with the general goals of the New Left, which in 1968 reached a new peak with the student revolt in Europe, the worsening war in Vietnam, and the Soviet invasion of Czechoslovakia; on the other hand, they refused to agree to the biased perspective of the New Left regarding the Middle East crisis. Young Jewish radicals felt under pressure from both sides: the anti-Zionist Left operated an organized campaign against Israel, describing it as a colonial state which represented the West[66]; and the supporters of Israel attacked back, blaming the New Left for being anti-Semitic and "socialism of fools". Jews who supported the New Left's criticism of Israel were often presented as "self-hating Jews."[67]

The dilemmas and troubles of the young Jewish radicals who wished to combine support of Israel and loyalty to New Left ideas pushed HaShomer haTza'ir into action again. Already before the war, emissaries from different Kibbutz movements developed a plan for encouraging the young generation in the diaspora to affiliate with Zionism and even make *Aliyah.* This was done through emphasizing the built-in combination between Jewish nationalism and the universal Left as it was expressed in the Israeli Kibbutz. The plan, called the "America plan," included dedicating more funds and emissaries to work with the target audience of young Jewish radicals. It was approved right after the Six-Day War.[68]

In addition to that, in the first months of 1968, the character of YAPI, the young brigade of "Americans for Progressive Israel," was changed. A leadership from the young Jewish activists of the New Left was recruited, and it also changed its name to "the Jewish Liberation Project" (JLP), which sounded more suitable for the new times.[69] The activities of the JLP included seasonal

---

65 Sol Stern, "My Jewish problem – and ours," *Ramparts,* August 1971. See also Nusan and Dreier, *Jewish Radicalism.*

66 See for example Hal Draper, "Zionism, Israel, & the Arabs: the historical background of the Middle-East tragedy," Independent socialist clipping books; no. 3, 1967; "Zionism and the Arab Revolution – the myth of progressive Israel," The Young Socialist Alliance, August 1967; Peter Buch, *Burning Issues of the Middle-East Crisis* (New York, NY: Merit Publishers, 1969); George Novack, *How can the Jews Survive? A Socialist Answer to Zionism* (New York, NY: Pathfinder, 1969).

67 See for example Mordechai S. Chertoff, ed., *The New Left and the Jews* (New York: Pitman, 1970).

68 Haika Grossman to Avri Fisher, June 22 1967, HaShomer haTza'ir Archive 2943(2)35.1; Ministers Mordechai Bentov and Israel Barzilai in Israel government meeting, July 2 1967, Israel State Archive, 16718/1-ג; Israel Pinchasi to Shaikeh Veiner and others, July 27 1967, HaShomer haTza'ir Archive 2943(2)35.1; Israeli emissaries letter to the Kibbutz movements centers, November 17 1967; and a letter from Israel Pinchasi and Yaakov Gali to Golda Meir, November 18 1967, Yad Tabenkin Archive, 1/6/21–5.

69 API administrative committee meeting report, September 9 1968, HaShomer haTza'ir Archive 3886(1)94.3 .

seminars and permanent study groups in which the ideas of socialist-Zionism were studied, participation in New Left campaigns against the war in Vietnam and in favor of the civil rights movement, and a close connection to the daily political life in Israel. At the end of 1968 the JLP started to publish a newspaper called *the Jewish Liberation Journal*, which soon became one of the most influential newspapers among pro-Zionist Jewish radicals. It followed a line, which was present also in the other dozens of radical-Zionist newspapers which began to be published at the same time, of a critical view of the policy of the Israeli government in several fields, while supporting the right of Israel to exist and to defend itself.[70]

The JLP was supported by the API and the Zionist establishment (under the "America plan"). Although its counter-cultural style attracted criticism from the older generation, it was clear to the establishment that the contribution of such an organization to the fight for the hearts of the young Jewish radicals, who were torn between Zionism and the New Left, was extremely valuable.[71]

Parallel to the foundation of JLP, the tactic of creating a liminal space in order to absorb the confused youngsters was fully adopted by the establishment. As part of that, the state of Israel began working through the World Zionist Organization (WZO) and the Jewish Agency in establishing and encouraging a framework similar to that of the JLP all over the diaspora.[72]

Two graduates of HaShomer haTza'ir were appointed to lead this endeavor: Mordechai Bar-On (1928-) as the head of the department of youth and pioneers in WZO and Abraham Schenkar (2017–1918) as the head of the department for *hasbara* ("propaganda") in the Jewish Agency.[73]

Bar-On and Schenkar provided the radical-Zionist groups with funds and constituted an important connection between the field activists and the establishment. This collaboration was very fruitful, and between the years 1969–1971 dozens of new groups were formed. In addition to this, a young radical-

70 *Jewish Liberation Journal* copies in Tamiment Library and Wagner Labor Archives, box: 1, folder: 32; see also Jewish Student Press Service files, American Jewish Historical Society Archive.

71 API administrative committee meeting report, December 2 1968, HaShomer haTza'ir Archive 3886(1)94.3.

72 Israel Pinchasi to HaShomer haTza'ir emissaries in North America, December 2 1967, HaShomer haTza'ir Archive, 2943(2)35.1.

73 Author interview with Mordechai Bar-on, Jerusalem, December 29 2016; Mordechai Bar-On memories, unpublished (available at Yad Ben Zvi, Jerusalem); Abraham Schenkar, *Zehut Ve-Hishtaichut* (Jerusalem: Bialik institute, 2003).

Zionist leadership was consolidated under the umbrella of The World Union of Jewish Students (WUJS).[74]

Winning the hearts of Jewish radicals by creating liminal spaces which combined support of Zionism and the Left was seen also in two other sites: France and Argentina. In France the reaction of the Jewish public to the Six-Day War was similar in many aspects to what happened in the United States. This was somewhat surprising, since the Jews of France were considered as almost completely assimilated.[75]

Indeed, in the late 1950s and the early 1960s there was a mass immigration to France of North African Jews, who were loyal to their Jewish origins and constituted many of the supporters of Israel after the war.[76]

But most of the newcomers did not participate in New Left activities. It was mainly the second generation of former immigrants from Eastern Europe, who came to France around the Second World War, who seemed to make the turn from assimilation to developing a Jewish identity.[77]

Some of them, whose turn was seemingly even more dramatic, were even activists in the French communist party. But this view was not accurate. The Bernard Lazare circle and Mishmar had already been operating for more than a decade, combining Zionism and affiliation with the global Left. Similar to what happened in the United States, the existence of the liminal space that HaShomer haTza'ir established was permanent, but its social and political role was a changing matter. That was a result of external catalysts, such as the Six-Day War.

After the Six-Day War, HaShomer haTza'ir became, in France too, the main organizer of radical Zionists. Its tactic, supported by the Zionist establishment, was similar to what was done in the United States, meaning founding new organizations to absorb confused and troubled Jewish radicals who wished to combine their affiliation with the New Left and Zionism. This was parallel to an increase in the activity of the Bernard Lazare circle and Mishmar. In 1969, the main organization for that issue was established by an emissary of HaShomer haTza'ir from Israel under the name of Organisation Juive Revolutionnaire (the Jewish revolutionary organization), or OJR. The members of the OJR, about 100 in num-

---

74 Matthew Kalman, *The Kids are alright – Chapters in the history of the World Union of Jewish Students* (Jerusalem: the World Union of Jewish Students, 1986), 46–100.

75 Shlomo Avineri, *Tnu'ot Ha-mecha'a Ba-universitaot Ve-hashlachotihe'en al Ha-kibbutzim Ha-yehudi'im* (Jerusalem: Hebrew University, 1970), 20–28; *American Jewish Year Book*, Vol. 70 (1969), 182.

76 Hyman, *the Jews of Modern France*, 193–214.

77 Judith Freidlander, "The Six-Day war and the 'Jewish Question' in France," in Lederhendler, *The Six-Day War*, 125–160.

ber, were not graduates of HaShomer haTza'ir youth movements in France, but young activists of the French Left who opposed its anti-Israel line.[78]

As in the United States, this organization was much more radical than the establishment that founded it, until there were sometimes questions as to whether it should receive support. But its effectiveness was clear and it continued. Apart from the OJR, another organization was established in France – a women's circle after the name of Haviva Reick. It was intended to organize the parents (the mothers in this case) of young Jewish radicals and teach them the foundational ideas of HaShomer haTza'ir's radical Zionism.[79]

Another framework that HaShomer haTza'ir helped to establish in France was "Le Cercle Gaston Crémieux" (Gaston Crémieux circle). It was different from the pro-Zionist groups since it was not Zionist, although supportive of Israel. It included around 150 intellectuals, some of them prominent in the Jewish community, who wished to develop the cultural aspects of Jewish life in France.[80] The fact that HaShomer haTza'ir was involved in a non-Zionist organization appeared to be surprising, but it actually suited the definition of liminal space. As we have seen, the whole meaning of this space was to contain different identities and to find new definitions to eliminate the contradictions between them.

In Argentina, HaShomer haTza'ir was operating in liminal space through the organization it established in the 1950s – the Mordechai Anielewicz young brigade. The Anielewicz brigade became one of the most prominent bodies in the Jewish New Left in Latin America after the Six-Day War. The reason that HaShomer haTza'ir did not have to establish new organizations (such as the OJR in France and JLP in the United States) in order to emphasize the combination between Zionism and New Left ideas was that the combination between nationalism and the Left was already one of the core ideas of the Latin American Left.[81]

The members of the brigade even introduced the ideas of Ber Borochov to the leaders and thinkers of the Latin American Left, seeing it as an important contribution to the connections of the Zionist and the universal Left.[82]

---

78 Oron, *Kulanu Yehudim Germanim*, 109–110.

79 Telephone Interview with Levanah Frenk, Historian and former activist in HaShomer haTza'ir in France, May 30 2017.

80 Freidlander, "The Jewish Question' in France" Hyman, *Jews of Modern France*, 200.

81 Luis Alberto Romero and James P. Brennan, *A History of Argentina in the Twentieth Century* (Pennsylvania: Penn State University Press, 2013), 181–190.

82 Leonardo Cohen, "Lectura e identidad: la teoría marxista de Ber Bórojov en el contexto del judaísmo latinoamericano (1951–1979)," *Cuadernos Judaicos*, № 29 (diciembre 2012): 1–36.

The activity of the Anielewicz brigade did not cover the whole ideological range among young Jewish radicals in Argentina after the Six-Day War. Unlike the United States and France, in which Yiddish culture and the heritage of its main political movement – the Bund – almost disappeared by the 1960s, in Argentina this trend was still present in the public. That means that similar to France, which had a vital communist party, anti-Zionist Argentinian Jews also had a political home after the Second World War.[83]

After the Six-Day War, however, many of them became supportive of Israel, and HaShomer haTza'ir was there to absorb them in its satellite organizations. It helped to establish a new organization – called Fraie Schtime (Free Voice) – which included mainly ex-members of a socialist Yiddishist non-Zionist organization which was affiliated with the communist party – Idisher Culture Farband (IUCF). These members wished to oppose the anti-Israel policy of the Argentinian Left after the war; however, they could not do so under their organization, so they established a new one. Since they were still non-Zionist, HaShomer haTza'ir was the only option for collaboration for them.[84] Like the Gaston Crémieux circle in France, it also showed the freedom that the liminal space of HaShomer haTza'ir (and following it, the Zionist establishment) allowed its members and followers.

The Israeli New Left

Israel, like the rest of the Western world, experienced the results of the baby boom in the 1960s. As an outcome, the higher education system developed significantly at that time, and the number of students in Israel reached 40,000 at the end of the decade.[85] At the same time, Israel reached a similar level of progress to the Western world with the same lifestyle.[86] Consequently, some of the Israeli young generation developed patterns which expressed normalization of life and a growing relation to the outside world. They embraced counter-cultural characters, expressed in disobeying the commands of the national leadership and in establishing new arenas of individualism. Many of the high school stu-

83 Lawrence D. Bell, "Bitter Conquest: Zionists Against Progressive Jews and the Making of Post-War Jewish Politics in Argentina," *Jewish History* 17, no. 3 (January 1, 2003): 285–308.
84 Senkman, "Fraie Schtime."
85 Statistical Abstract of Israel: http://www.cbs.gov.il/archive/shnaton/shnatonh21.pdf (accessed July 25 2017), 565.
86 Nachum Gross, "Kalkalat Israel 1954–1967," in *Ha-asor Ha-sheni*, ed. Zvi Tzameret and Hanna Yablonka, (Jerusalem: Yad Itzhak Ben-Zvi, 2001), 30–46.

dents quit participating in youth movement activities, and some of them developed a bourgeois culture which included listening and dancing to rock and roll music, and dressing in what seemed a pretentious style.[87] The older ones were eager to finish their army service and afterwards turn to university studies, professional occupation, and financial consolidation. Towards the middle of the decade, the Israeli establishment and the older generation were troubled by the effects of the "empty Western culture" and the Americanization of the youngsters.[88]

The worry about the Israeli young generation worsened as a result of the first signs of the creation of a local version of the New Left in these years. This was expressed by several phenomena, which concentrated mainly around HaShomer haTza'ir's youth movement, the Kibbutzim, and the party. In the middle of the 1960s, young people in the Kibbutzim began to criticize the social and ideological life of the Kibbutz, claiming that it was materialistic and spiritually poor.[89]

At the same time, they began to oppose the labor movement-led Israeli government for its military policy; this was accompanied by an intense struggle of the young against the movement's "historic leadership".[90]

Meanwhile, the cultural apparatus of the movement (which included magazines and cultural clubs) embraced the counter-culture and the New Left messages and methods.[91]

After the Six-Day War, the Israeli New Left reached its peak. From 1967 onward, most of Hashomer Hatzair's young generation took a radical stand against the government's policy regarding the occupied territories and criticized what seemed as a lack of will to reach a peace agreement. In 1969 Mapam established a shared list with the Israeli Labor party for the coming elections. This led to a split among its members and voters. Some of the most prominent young political activists left the party and established, along with students from Tel Aviv University and the Hebrew University in Jerusalem, a new political movement called the "New Israeli Left" (Siach – acronym for Smol Israeli Chadash).[92]

---

87 Oded Heilbronner, "Resistance through Rituals – Urban Subcultures of Israeli Youth from the Late 1950s to the 1980s," *Israel Studies* 16, no. 3, (fall 2011): 28–50.

88 For further discussion see Tal Elmaliach and Anat Kidron, "Mecha'a Tzeira Bein Tarbut Lepolitica 1967–1977," *Iyunim Bitkumat Israel* 11 (2017): 78–101.

89 Alon Gan, "Ha-siach shegava: tarbut ha-sichim ke-nisayon le-gibush zehut me-ya-chedet ba-dor ha-sheny ba-kibbutzim," (PhD Dissertation, Tel Aviv University, 2002).

90 Tal Elmaliach, "Ketz ha-hanhaga ha-historit: kalkala, chevra ve-politica ba-Kibbutz Haartzi ve-Mapam 1956–1973", *Iyunim Bitkumat Israel* 24 (2014): 306–331.

91 Elmaliach, "Tzavta."

92 Portugez, "smol Israeli."

Siach struggled mainly against the Israeli occupation through demonstrations, gatherings, and pamphlet distribution, later joining a political list called "Moked" which ran in the 1973 elections. Siach had a close relation with Jewish radicals around the world, especially with members of the JLP in the United States, OJR in France, and Anielewicz Brigade in Latin America, who saw it as their twin movement.

Although the Israeli and the diaspora Jewish New Left that was affiliated with HaShomer haTza'ir had the same ideology of radical Zionism, the attitude of the establishment towards them was completely different. While the establishment encouraged the operation of the Jewish New Left organizations in the diaspora and was tolerant of the liminal character of their ideology and politics, it did not allow the same for Israeli youth. From its first day, Siach was under a constant process of de-legitimization, as were the other expressions of the Israeli New Left.[93]

One of the greatest fears of the national establishment was that a student revolt would emerge in Israel, following what was happening in the United States and Europe. Siach, and the Israeli New Left in general, also received this kind of attitude among the older generation in Hakibbutz Haartzi and Mapam, who described the young rebels as no less than "traitors" and "cancer".[94]

Indeed, some of Siach's members (not from the Kibbutzim) defined themselves as non-Zionists, but this organization was far different from the main anti-Zionist movement of that era – Matzpen. While Matzpen was collaborating with the anti-Zionist campaign of the New Left, Siach was one of the forces which fought against it. Although Siach was highly critical of the Israeli government and followed many of the characteristics of the global New Left, it was still following the borders of the liminal space, which included the built-in combination of Zionism and leftist ideas. However, with regard to Israeli youth, the establishment was not willing to confront the risks, unclear attitudes, and confusion which the liminal space involved. Unlike the flexibility it showed while dealing with the Jewish New Left in the diaspora, in the case of the Israeli New Left it implemented the contradiction thesis. The counterculture and the criticism were perceived as a slippery slope towards a complete alienation of the young

---

93 See for example Menachem Arnoni, "Ha-smol Ha-chadash Ve-ha-tzivilizatzia Ha-amricanit, *Al Hamishmar*, February 6 1970; Menachem Arnoni, "Ha-smol Ha-chadash – Bna Shel Tabut Mehagrim," *Al Hamishmar*, February 13 1970. See also Elmaliach and Kidron, "Mecha'a Tzeira."
94 Mapam executive meeting, June 18 1973, HaShomer haTza'ir Archive (4)79.90. See also articles by Meir Yaari in *Al Hamishmar*, October 27 1969; Peretz Merchav in *Al Hamishmar*, July 20 1970; and Dov Bar-Nir in *Al Hamishmar*, December 4 1970.

generation from its historical role. Every troubled thought or confusion was a danger, so the New Left activists were hunted, oppressed, and silenced.[95]

Conclusion

As this chapter shows, the Six-Day War was not the beginning of the Jewish New Left and also not its main source, but was only a catalyst in its rise. As an idea that was translated to political organizations and activity, it was another phase of the historical built-in connection between Jewish national particularism and the universal leftist ideas, which also took place in the Jewish "Old" Left. What was changing with time was not the idea and its core logic, but the public support it received and its effect on new crowds.

HaShomer haTza'ir was one of the main organizers of the Jewish New Left since historically it was shaped by the built-in combination thesis and preserved it in times when the interest in it was low. This combination, as we have seen, was not a matter of synthesis, since it was not created through the tension between Zionism and the New Left. On the contrary, the tension was what raised the need in a combination which would cancel what seemed to be a contradiction. It was also not a hybrid formula, which allowed one to be Zionist and a follower of the New Left. What HaShomer haTza'ir was providing was of a deeper internal logic, which saw the two elements as one, following the stages theory.

Already in the mid-1950s HaShomer haTza'ir's people recognized the need to establish new frameworks for diaspora Jewish radicals who wanted to follow the built-in combination identity. In the 1960s, when it seemed that the young generation was assimilating during its activity in the New Left, these organizations provided the base for a further endeavor which was expressed in the establishment of YAPI in the United States. After the Six-Day War, the need to reconcile what seemed an identity crisis made the built-in combination of Zionism and the New Left even more acute, and that pushed HaShomer haTza'ir to establish new organizations such as OJR in France, and to be involved in others like the Gaston Crémieux circle and Fraie Schtime. This liminal space was supported by the HaShomer haTza'ir leadership and the Israeli and the Zionist establishment. However, in Israel the local New Left was oppressed and this shows us the differences between the way Jewish youth was perceived and treated in Israel and in the diaspora. These differences are a matter for further research.

95 Elmaliach and Kidron, "Mecha'a Tzeira."

The case study of HaShomer haTza'ir shows that the activity of Jewish radicals in the liminal space challenges the historical convention in another way. Jewish radicalism is often perceived as an attempt to "solve" the tension between particularism and universalism. However, the built-in combination thesis, which does not see any tension or contradiction, actually dismantles the term of a "problem". Jewish radicalism can be seen, therefore, not as an historical anomaly that took place as a compromise or as an unplanned synthesis during a one-directional route from particularism to assimilation, which was disrupted by rejection. On the contrary, Jewish radicalism, as a liminal space, seems to define more properly the modern existence of large segments of the Jewish people, in Israel and in the diaspora, who are in a constant situation of "in-between".

Works Cited

Albert, Phyllis Cohen. "Etniut Ve-solidaryut Yehudit Be-tzarfat Ba-Me'a Ha-19." In *Leumiyut Ve-politica Yehudit: Prespectivot Hadashot*, edited by Gideon Shimony, Yosef Shalmon and Yehuda Reinhertz, 47–73. Jerusalem: Zalman Shazar center and Boston: Tauber institute in Brandeis University, 1996.

Avineri, Shlomo. *Tnu'ot Ha-mecha'a Ba-universitaot Ve-hashlachotihe'en al Ha-kibbutzim Ha-yehudi'im*. Jerusalem: Hebrew University, 1970.

Avineri, Shlomo. *Moses Hess: Prophet of Communism and Zionism*. New York: New York University Press, 1985.

Barth, Fredrik, ed. *Ethnic Groups and Boundaries: The Social Organization of Culture Difference*. Boston: Little, Brown and Company, 1969.

Beech, Nic. "Liminality and the Practices of Identity Reconstruction." *Human Relations* 64, no. 2 (2010): 285–302.

Bell, Lawrence D. "Bitter Conquest: Zionists Against Progressive Jews and the Making of Post-War Jewish Politics in Argentina." *Jewish History* 17, no. 3 (January 1, 2003): 285–308.

Berlin, Isaiah. "The Life and Opinions of Moses Hess." In *Essential Papers on Jews and the Left*, edited by Ezra Mendelsohn, 21–57. New York: New York University Press, 1997.

Borochov, Dov Ber. *Ktavim Nivharim, vol. 1, Le-heker She'elat Ha-yehudim*. Tel Aviv: Am Oved, 1943.

Borochov, Dov Ber. *Ktavim, vol. 1–3*. Tel Aviv: Sifriat Poalim and Hakibbutz Ha-meuchad, 1955–1966.

Brook, Vincent, ed. *You Should See Yourself: Jewish Identity in Postmodern American Culture*. New Brunswick, New Jersey and London: Rutgers University Press, 2006.

Buch, Peter. *Burning Issues of the Middle-East Crisis*. New York, NY: Merit Publishers, 1969.

Chertoff, Mordechai S., ed. *The New Left and the Jews*. New York: Pitman, 1970.

Schenkar, Abraham. *Zehut Ve-Hishtaichut*. Jerusalem: Bialik institute, 2003.

Cohen, Leonardo. "Lectura e identidad: la teoría marxista de Ber Bórojov en el contexto del judaísmo latinoamericano (1951–1979)." *Cuadernos Judaicos*, Nº 29 (diciembre 2012): 1–36.

Cohen, Percy S. *Jewish Radicals and Radical Jews*. London: Academic Press, 1981.
Della Pergola, Sergio, Uzi Rebhun, and Rosa Perla Raicher. "The Six Day War and Israel-Diaspora Relations: An Analysis of Quantitative Indicators." In Lederhendler, *The Six-Day War*, 11–50.
Diner, Hasia R. *The Jews of the United States, 1654 to 2000*. Berkeley and Los Angeles: University of California Press, 2004.
Elmaliach, Tal. "The Israeli Left between Culture and Politics: Tzavta Club and Mapam 1956–1973." *Journal of Israeli History* 33, no. 2 (2014): 169–183.
Elmaliach, Tal. "Ketz ha-hanhaga ha-historit: kalkala, chevra ve-politica ba-Kibbutz Haartzi ve-Mapam 1956–1973." *Iyunim Bitkumat Israel* 24 (2014): 306–331.
Elmaliach, Tal, and Anat Kidron. "Mecha'a Tzeira Bein Tarbut Le-politica 1967–1977." *Iyunim Bitkumat Israel* 11 (2017): 78–101.
Fomerand, Jacques. "Changing Third World Perspectives and Politics Towards Israel." In *Israel in the Third World*, edited by Michael Curtis and Susan Aurelia Gitelson, 32–360. New Brunswick, N.J: Transaction Books, 1976.
Frank, Anne. *The Diary of a Young Girl*. New York, NY: Doubleday and Company, 1952.
Frankel, Jonathan. *Prophecy and Politics: Socialism, Nationalism, and the Russian Jews, 1862–1917*. Cambridge/New York: Cambridge University Press, 1984.
Frankel, Jonathan. "Ha-mashber Ke-gorem Merkazi Ba-politica Ha-yehudit Ha-modernit: 1840 and 1881–1882." In *Solidaryut Yehudit Leumit Ba-et Ha-hadasha*, edited by Pincus, Biniamin and Ilan Troen, 31–46. Sde-Boker: Ben Gurion Institute, 1988.
Frankel, Jonathan. "Hitbolelut Ve-Hisardut Be-kerev Yehudei Eropa Ba-Me'a Ha-19: Lekrat Historiografia Hadasha?" In *Leumiyut Ve-politica Yehudit]*, edited by Shimony, Shalmon and Reinhertz, 23–56.
Friedlander, Judith. "The Six-Day War and the 'Jewish Question' in France." In *The Six-Day War and World Jewry*, edited by Eli Lederhendler, 125–160. Bethesda, MD: University Press of Maryland, 2000.
Gan, Alon. "Ha-siach shegava: tarbut ha-sichim ke-nisayon le-gibush zehut me-ya-chedet ba-dor ha-sheny ba-kibbutzim." PhD Dissertation, Tel Aviv University, 2002.
Geva, Amichai. "A Time for Expansion." In *Against the Stream: Seven Decades of HaShomer haTza'ir in North America*, edited by Ariel Hurwitz, 125–142. Givat Haviva: Yad Yaari, 1994.
Glanz, David. "An Interpretation of the Jewish Counterculture." *Jewish Social Studies* 39, no. 1/2, American Bicentennial: II (1977): 117–128.
Glazer, Natan. *American Judaism*. Chicago/London: University of Chicago Press, 1972.
Gorni, Yosef. *The State of Israel in Jewish Public Thought: The Quest for Collective Identity*. New York: New York University Press, 1994.
Graetz, Michael. *Ha-periferia Haita Le-Merkaz: Prakim Be-toldot Yehudei TZarfat Ba-Me'a Ha-yod-tet*. Jerusalem: Bialik institute, 1987.
Graetz, Michael. "Le-sheivato Shel Moshe Hess La-yahadut: Ha-reka Le-chibur 'Romi ve-Yerushalaim." *Tzion*, Mem-He, Bet (1980): 133–153.
Grinfeld, Yerach. "Ha-hativot Ha-tzioniot Sotzialistiot Be-Argentina Be-shnot Ha-shishim: Havnayat Hashkafat Olam." M.A thesis, Hebrew University, Jerusalem, 2006.
Gross, Nachum. "Kalkalat Israel 1954–1967." In *Ha-asor Ha-sheni*, edited by Zvi Tzameret and Hanna Yablonka, 30–46. Jerusalem: Yad Itzhak Ben-Zvi, 2001.

Gurwitz, Beatrice D. "From the New World to the Third World: Generation, Politics, and the Making of Argentine Jewish Ethnicity 1955–1983." PhD Dissertation, University of California, Berkeley, 2012.

Harold, Joshua. "Institutionalizing Liminality: Jewish Summer Camps and the Boundary Work of Camp Participants." *Sociology of Race and Ethnicity* 1, no. 3 (2015): 439–453.

Heilbronner, Oded. "Resistance through Rituals – Urban Subcultures of Israeli Youth from the Late 1950s to the 1980s." *Israel Studies* 16, no. 3, (Fall 2011): 28–50.

Hill, Ruth C. "Liminal Identity to Wholeness: A 'Biracial' Path to the Practice of Cross-Cultural, Jungian Psychotherapy." *Jung Journal: Culture & Psyche* 4 (2010): 16–30.

Hobsbawm, Eric J. *Nations and Nationalism since 1780.* New York: Cambridge University Press, 1990.

Hyman, Paula. *The Jews of Modern France: Jewish Communities in the Modern World.* Berkeley: University of California Press, 1998.

Iyall, Keri E. Smith, and Patricia Leavy. *Hybrid Identities: Theoretical and Empirical Examinations.* Leiden: Brill, 2008.

"Mapam 1956–1973." *Journal of Israeli History* 33, no. 2 (2014): 169–183.

Japtok, Martin. *Growing Up Ethnic Nationalism and the Bildungsroman in African American and Jewish American Fiction.* Iowa City: University of Iowa Press, 2005.

Johnsen, Christian Garmann. "'It's Capitalism on Coke!' From Temporary to Permanent Liminality in Organization Studies." *Culture and Organization* 21, no. 4 (2015): 321–337.

Kalman, Matthew. *The Kids are alright – Chapters in the history of the World Union of Jewish Students.* Jerusalem: The World Union of Jewish Students, 1986.

Katz, Emily Alice. *Bringing Zion home: Israel in American Jewish culture, 1948–1967.* Albany: State University of New York Press, 2015.

Liebman, Arthur. *Jews and the Left.* New York: Wiley, 1979.

Livneh, Eliezer. *Yahadut Artsot-ha-Berit ve Yisrael: ha-mifneh: sikume-biḳur, Novermber-Detsember 1966.* Jerusalem: ha-Merkaz li-tefutsot, Musad le-Keshrai Tarbut ʿIm Yahadut ha-Tfutsot, 1967.

Magid, Shaul. *Post-Judaism: Identity and Renewal in a Postethnic Society.* Bloomington: Indiana University Press, 2013.

Margalit, Elkana. *HaShomer haTza'ir: Me-adat Ne'urim Le-marksizm Mahapchani 1913–1936.* Tel Aviv: Hakibbutz Hemeuchad, 1971.

Memmi, Albert. *The Liberation of the Jew.* New York: Orion Press, 1966.

Mendes, Phillip. "'We are all German Jews:' Exploring the Prominence of Jews in the New Left." *Melilah: Manchester Journal of Jewish Studies* (2009/3): 1–17.

Mintz, Matityahu. *Havley Ne'urim: Ha-tnua Ha-shomrit 1911–1921.* Jerusalem: Ha-sifriya Ha-tzionit, 1995.

Mishkinski, Moshe. *Reshit Tnu'at Ha-poalim Be-rusia: Megamot Yesod.* Tel Aviv: Tel Aviv University and Hakibbutz Ha-me'uchad, 1981.

Moss, Kenneth B. *Jewish Renaissance in the Russian Revolution.* Cambridge, MA/London: Harvard University Press, 2009.

Nagel, Joane. "Constructing Ethnicity: Creating and Recreating Ethnic Identity and Culture." *Social Problems* 41, no. 1 (1994): 152–176.

Nielsen, François. "Toward a Theory of Ethnic Solidarity in Modern Societies." *American Sociological Review* 50, no. 2 (1985): 133–149.

Novak, Bill, and Robert Goldman. "The Rise of the Jewish Student Press." *Conservative Judaism* 25, no. 2 (1971): 5–19.
Novack, George. *How can the Jews Survive? A Socialist answer to Zionism.* New York, NY: Pathfinder, 1969.
Oron, Yair. *Kulanu Yehudim Germanim – Radicalim Yehudim Be-tzarfat Be-shnot Ha-shishim Ve-ha-shivim.* Tel Aviv: Am Oved, the University of Tel Aviv and the University of Ben Gurion, 1999.
Peled, Rina. *Ha-adam Ha-hadash Shel Ha-mahapecha Ha-tzionit Ve-shorashav Ha-eiropim.* Tel Aviv: Am Oved, 2002.
Peled, Yoav. *Class and Ethnicity in the Pale: The Political Economy of Jewish Workers' Nationalism in Late Imperial Russia.* New York: St. Martin's Press, 1989.
Pennock, Pamela. "Third World Alliance: Arab – American Activists in American Universities, 1967–1973." *Mashriq & Mahjar* 2, no. 2 (2014): 55–78.
Pinkus, Benjamin. *The Jews of the Soviet Union: The History of a National Minority.* Cambridge/New York: Cambridge University Press, 1990.
Porter, Jack Nusan, and Peter Dreier, eds. *Jewish Radicalism: A Selected Anthology.* New York: Grove Press, 1973.
Portugez, Adi. "Tnuat Smol Israeli Hadash: Smol Hadash Be-Israel." *Israel* 21 (2013): 225–252.
Prell, Riv-Ellen. *Prayer & Community: The Havurah in American Judaism.* Detroit: Wayne State University Press, 1989.
Romero, Luis Alberto, and James P. Brennan. *A History of Argentina in the Twentieth Century.* Pennsylvania: Penn State University Press, 2013.
Rubenstein, Jeffrey. "Purim, Liminality, and Communitas." *AJS Review* 17, no. 2 (1992): 247–277.
Sabaté, Flocel. *Hybrid Identities.* Bern: Peter Lang, 2014.
Schenker, Avraham. "Progressive Zionism in America." In *Against the Stream: Seven Decades of HaShomer haTza'ir in North America*, edited by Ariel Hurwitz, 273–295. Givat Haviva: Yad Yaari, 1994.
Senkman, Leonardo. "Repercussions of the Six-Day War in the Leftist Jewish Argentinian Camp: The Rise of Fraie Schtime, 1967–1969." In Lederhendler, *The Six-Day War and World Jewry*, 167–187.
Shapira, Anita. *Ha-halicha Al Kav Ha-ofek.* Tel Aviv: Sifriyat Poalim, 2001.
Shindler, Colin. *Israel and the European Left – Between Solidarity and Delegitimization.* New York, NY: Bloomsbury Publishing, 2012.
Silverstein, Jordana. "We're Dealing with How Do We Live and Work with this Memory and What Are We Supposed to Do About It." *Borderlands* 9, no. 1 (2010): 1–17.
Staub, Michael E. *Torn at the Roots: The Crisis of Jewish Liberalism in Postwar America.* New York: Columbia University Press, 2002.
Staub, Michael E. *The Jewish 1960s: An American sourcebook.* Waltham, Mass.: Brandeis University Press; Hanover: University Press of New England, 2004.
Szakolczai, Arpad. "Living Permanent Liminality: The Recent Transition Experience in Ireland." *Irish Journal of Sociology*, 22, no. 1 (2014): 28–50.
Twersky, David. "Entering the 1970s: Habonim and the Jewish Student Movement." In *Builders and Dreamers – Habonim Labor Zionist youth in North America*, edited by J. J Goldberg and Elliot King, 213–218. New York: Herzl Press, 1984.

Tzur, Eli. *Lifnei Bo Ha-afela: HaShomer haTza'ir Be-Polin Ve-Galitzia 1930–1940*. Sede Boker: Machon Ben Gurion; Givaat Haviva: Yad Yaari, 2006.

Uris, Leon. *Exodus*. New York, NY: Doubleday and Company, 1958.

Weiss, Avi. "Student Struggle for Soviet Jewry (SSSJ)." *Encyclopaedia Judaica*, eds. Michael Bernbaum and Fred Skolnik, vol. 19. 2nd edition. Detroit: Macmillan Reference USA, 2007.

Wiesel, Elie. *Night*. New York: Hill and Wang; London: MacGibbon & Kee, 1960.

Wimmer, Andreas. "The Making and Unmaking of Ethnic Boundaries: A Multilevel Process Theory." *American Journal of Sociology* 113, no. 4 (2008): 970–1022.

Yovel, Yirmiyahu, ed. *New Jewish Time: Jewish Culture in a Secular Age – an Encyclopedic View*. vol 2. Jerusalem: Lmada, 2008.

Zayit, David. *Halutzim Ba-mavoch Ha-politi: Ha-tnu'a Ha-kibutzit 1927–1948*. Jerusalem: Yad Yitzhak Ben-Zvi, 1993.

Section II
Religious Radicalisms

Morgan Shipley

Psychedelic Judaism in a Countercultural America

Zalman Schachter-Shalomi and the Radical Religiosity of LSD Consciousness

> "When I can undergo the deepest cosmic experience via some miniscule quantity of organic alkaloids or LSD, then the whole validity of my ontological assertions is in doubt [...] the psychedelic experience can be not only a challenge but a support of my faith. After seeing what really happens at the point where all is One and God immanent surprises God transcendent and They merge in cosmic laughter, I can also see Judaism in a new and amazing light." ~ Rabbi Zalman Schachter-Shalomi, "Response." In *The Condition of Jewish Belief: A Symposium by the Editors of Commentary Magazine*
>
> (New York: MacMillan Company, 1966), 213–214.

> "Counter-culture is thus the active critique or transformation of the existing social, scientific or aesthetic paradigm. It is religious reform. It is the heresy of whoever confers a license upon himself and prefigures another church [...] Counter-culture comes about when those who transform the culture in which they live become critically conscious of what they are doing and elaborate a theory of their deviation from the dominant model, *offering a model that is capable of sustaining itself.*" ~ Umberto Eco, "Does Counter-culture exist?" In *Apocalypse Postponed*, ed. Robert Lumley
>
> (Bloomington: Indiana University Press, 1994), 115.

Introduction

Following World War II and the atrocities of the Holocaust, Judaism found itself at a crossroads. Although 1948 marked the emergence of the Jewish State, the decades that followed bear witness to a diasporic community looking for renewed grounding both within Israel and outside it, particularly in the United States.[1] As Elliot Cohen asked rhetorically in 1945, will "American Jews evolve

1 See Gulie Ne'eman Arad, *America, Its Jews, and the Rise of Nazism* (Bloomington: Indiana University Press, 2000); Henry L. Feingold, "Who Shall Bear Guilt for the Holocaust? The Human Dilemma," in *The American Jewish Experience*, ed. Jonathan D. Sarna (New York: Holmes and Meier, 1987), 274–292; Arthur A. Goren, "A 'Golden Decade' for American Jews: 1945–1955," in *The American Jewish Experience*, ed. Jonathan D. Sarna (New York: Holmes and Meier, 1987), 294–311; and Jonathan D. Sarna, *American Judaism: A History* (New Haven: Yale University Press, 2004).

https://doi.org/10.1515/9783110545753-008

new patterns of living, new modes of thought, which will harmonize heritage and country into a true sense of at-home-ness in the modern world?"[2] Debates over the coherency of Judaism as a system of faith, an ethnic marker, and a politicized identity reified traditional expressions while also leading to the emergence of orthodox, progressive, and radicalized expressions of the Jewish faith. In a sociological study of 1960s-era University of Berkeley Jewish students, Thomas Piazza concluded that "in the past, the issue of Jewish identity was not as open as it is today to individual interpretation [...] to identify oneself as Jewish can have a variety of meanings. It is possible to identify with the Jewish religion, with the ethnic group, with Jewish culture, with Jewish organizations and causes."[3] As Samuel Heilman summarizes analogously in his *Portrait of American Jews*, "what seemed more than anything else to tie the experience of American Jewry together during the last four and a half decades was that, for all of them, being Jewish was no longer simply a matter of birth, or, more precisely, a matter of irrevocable destiny. In the open society of America, being Jewish had become a matter of choice."[4] Within the immediate post-war moment, this opportunity for self-identification produced both a drive toward assimilation and acculturation, as well as growth of religious affirmation, a bolder willingness to derive meaning and direction from one's Jewish identity amidst a culture dominated by living the "American way."[5]

Like all Americans, Jews in the 1950s found themselves beholden to and trapped by an image-obsessed brand of capitalism highlighted by conspicuous consumption. With happiness wed to financial displays of excess, many grew dissatisfied with "the world," as Rabbi Zalman Schachter-Shalomi (1924–2014) broadly identified it. In his analysis of the 1960s hippie counterculture, Timothy Miller outlines the results of this condition, noting how "in the 1950s and early 1960s some Jews, typically younger ones, saw Judaism as having become overly cold and formal, characterized by large synagogues that concerned themselves with proper rituals and nice facilities but not with maintaining the warmth

2 Elliot Cohen, "An Act of Affirmation," *Commentary* I, November 1945, accessed 20 November 2018, https://www.commentarymagazine.com/articles/an-act-of-affirmation/.

3 Thomas Piazza, "Jewish Identity and the Counterculture," in *The New Religious Consciousness*, ed. Charles Y. Glock and Robert N. Bellah (Berkeley: University of California Press, 1976), 245, 247.

4 Samuel C. Heilman, *Portrait of American Jews: The Last Half of the 20th Century* (Seattle: University of Washington Press, 1995), xii.

5 As Heilman outlines, the 1950s were "a time when American Jews experienced a minimum of prejudice, when almost all domains of life are open to them, but it is also a time of extraordinary assimilation, of swelling rates of intermarriage, and of large numbers of people simply ignoring their Jewishness completely." In *Portrait of American Jews*, 5–6.

and intimacy of true Jewish community."[6] More specifically for those connected to Schachter-Shalomi and the Jewish Renewal Movement, "our dissatisfaction stems mainly from the fact that as well-adjusted members of it we would have to live as ardent consumers of goods which we do not really need but which in fact inhibit our best possible functioning in terms of *shlemuth ha'avoda.*"[7] Meaning "the perfection of our service to God," *shlemuth ha'avoda* more broadly positions the sacred core and spiritual practice for Schachter-Shalomi and his *The B'nai Or Religious Fellowship*, an early 1960s attempt to carve out a religious community and from which the Jewish Renewal Movement eventually develops. "Motivated by a wish to 'save Judaism'," Schachter-Shalomi connected mystical encounters of God consciousness with the capacity to perform sustained service, stressing how "we are concerned to realize God in this lifetime; to achieve a higher level of spiritual consciousness; to liberate such hidden forces within us as would energize us to achieve our highest humanity with Judaism."[8] Given this desire to repair a broken world (*tikkun olam*) by achieving union with God (*devekut*), the consumption-focused, material lifestyle of the post-war period more disturbingly obscured the significance of the spiritual realm. Particularly relevant for a Chasidic rabbi like Schachter-Shalomi, "not only are we dissatisfied with the secular world, we are also dissatisfied with the 'religious' world at large. That world lives under the same consumer compulsion as the secular world. Under this consumer compulsion [...] one is far too busy to obtain the means for consuming and then far too busy to consume all the means."[9] In misdirecting focus and unsettling religious certainty, capitalism plays the role of Karl Marx's opiate, proving to be the most efficient modern mechanism for preventing full spiritual growth in order to solidify a conformist mentality.[10] For Schachter-Shalomi, a solution to this spiritual malaise and secular indifference was found in communally, spiritually, and ritually reorienting Judaism, a renewal brought uniquely into focus through his experience with psychedelics.

Born in 1924 in Poland and raised in Vienna, Rabbi Zalman Meshullam Schachter-Shalomi "straddled secular and religious worlds." Attending both a secular high school and Orthodox yeshiva, Reb Zalman, as he is commonly called by followers, escaped the Holocaust along with his family through a

---

6 Timothy Miller, *The 60s Communes: Hippies and Beyond* (Syracuse: Syracuse University Press, 1999), 116.

7 Zalman M. Schachter, "Toward an 'Order of *B'nai Or*'," *Judaism* 13, no. 2 (1964): 187.

8 Schachter-Shalomi, "Toward an 'Order of *B'nai Or*'," 185.

9 Schachter-Shalomi, "Toward an 'Order of *B'nai Or*'," 187–188.

10 Karl Marx, *Critique of Hegel's 'Philosophy of Right'*, ed. Joseph O'Malley (New York: Cambridge University Press, 1970), 127.

French internment camp, leading to his first encounter with Lubavitch Hasidism in the person of Menachem Mendel Schneerson. Arriving in the United States in 1940, Schachter-Shalomi "entered the Lubavitcher Yeshiva in Brooklyn, earning *semikhah*, rabbinic ordination, in 1947."[11] After touring the college scene with fellow Jewish countercultural icon Rabbi Shlomo Carlebach (1925–1994), Schachter-Shalomi became further implicated in the secular world, serving as both Hillel director and professor of Jewish Studies at the University of Manitoba. In experiencing directly this broader world of ideas and dialogue, Schachter-Shalomi, in 1966, "graduated Chabad," a moment defined primarily by his rabbinic expulsion resulting from his open use and support of the "sacramental potential of lysergic acid [LSD]" and corresponding belief that "sixties' drug experimentation [signaled] a spiritual search."[12]

Embracing the ecstatic potentials of mystical Judaism, Schachter-Shalomi's experimentation with psychedelics and development of the Jewish Renewal Movement re-imagined Judaism from within, ultimately helping reposition Judaism as a post-war faith practiced through imperatives of responsibility as the direct result of joyously experiencing divine oneness. Believing "that the experience of the cosmic and the divine is potentially given to all men and that, depending on one's style of life, one can become a receptacle for the Grace of God,"[13] the lessons unveiled to Schachter-Shalomi through psychedelic mysticism did not lead to a rejection of Jewish religiosity, but rather unveiled a radical openness to experiment with a redefinition and reformulation of Jewish (including Chasidic and Kabbalistic) beliefs and practices. Inspired by the ecstatic experience of mystically encountering the divine – of becoming one with the All – such a perspective furthered a post-war religious sentiment grounded in tolerance, syncretism, and pluralism, while more meaningfully offering an everyday solution to actualize a life more responsive to the needs of one's self, of others, and of our natural world.

Reflecting on the spiritual tension between how one *ought* to be versus how one *is*, Schachter-Shalomi outlines what he believes to be not "the antinomian abrogation of all Law – but in a not so antinomian way of keeping it," using the following metaphor to capture the root imperatives expected of the pious:

---

11 Rodger Kamenetz, *Stalking Elijah: Adventures with Today's Jewish Mystical Masters* (New York: HarperOne, 1998), 18–19. See also "Zalman Schachter-Shalomi: Transcending Religious Boundaries," in *Higher Wisdom: Eminent Elders Explore the Continuing Impact of Psychedelics*, ed. Roger Walsh and Charles S. Grob (Albany: State University of New York Press, 2005), 195–196.

12 Kamenetz, *Stalking Elijah*, 19.

13 Schachter-Shalomi, "Toward an 'Order of *B'nai Or*'," 187.

> Hence a man cannot be a good Jew who will not fight for the game-freedom of all men, who will not safeguard the game-freedom for others, who will not insist on the 'natural law' which makes all sorts of covenants simultaneous and compatible and which pledges itself only to one basic principle – to paraphrase Hillel: 'The game you don't want to play, inflict it not on someone else'.[14]

Manifesting as structural changes that profoundly upended conventional and orthodox expressions of Judaism, including the rabbinic ordination of women, creating the "rainbow tallit" to convey openly a full acceptance of LGBTQ+ lifestyles, and a renewal of interest in ecstatic practices, including the application of meditative techniques, Schachter-Shalomi's journey from psychedelic mystic to founder of the Jewish Renewal Movement ultimately captures the radical orthopraxy of the "good deeds" God makes incumbent upon the chosen people, thereby communicating a broader perennial claim that locates compassion as the defining mark of living religiously. To understand the fullness of this commitment to *tikkun olam* (meaning to "repair the world"), and the radical edge brought uniquely into focus through psychedelic exploration, this chapter begins by contextualizing this shift within the broader frames of post-war Judaism in order to highlight the transformation inspired by Schachter-Shalomi's mystical engagement with psychedelic consciousness.

Emergence of a Countercultural Judaism and the Havurot Movement

As a distinct – and increasingly more accepted – expression of America's heightened post-war religiosity, American Jews in the late 1950s and early 1960s found themselves freer to explore their religious identity. For the first time, American Jews, as Rabbi William Rosenblum develops, sought space to use their Americanness to explore their Judaism. "What we Jews want," Rabbi Rosenblum declares unambiguously, "is what others desire, just to be let alone to enjoy life, liberty and happiness along with our neighbors."[15] Although post-war American society envisaged a religious identity designed to mirror and advance secular causes such as consumerism, the immediate post-war period, understood as "the decade of 'sober serenity'," gave "way to the turbulent 1960s," a decade

---

14 Zalman Schachter-Shalomi, "Response," in *The Condition of Jewish Belief: A Symposium Compiled by the Editors of* Commentary *Magazine* (New York: Macmillan, 1966), 210, 216.
15 Cited in Heilman, *Portrait of American Jews*, 47.

that not only shed further light on the anxiety and violence undergirding American culture, but created the conditions to explore alternative religious and spiritual expressions designed explicitly to offer countercultural solutions.[16] "We woke up from the American dream and tried to discover who we really were," explained Hillel Levine, a prominent post-war Jewish activist: "For many of us this now means turning our concerns inward into the Jewish community because we are disenchanted with the crass materialism of the larger society. Yet where can we find inspiration in the multimillion dollar Jewish presence of suburbia?"[17]

Trapped by the illusory happiness of suburbia, and spurred on by the claim that one's Jewishness signaled one's proper role as a good American, many post-war Jews, especially among the young, recognized a growing chasm between the aims of institutional American Judaism and their faith, belief in, and obligation to God. According to sociologist David Riesman, American Jews found themselves "especially prey to the two extremes of a vindictive and aggressive and contemptuous attitude towards tradition and a honeyed and sentimental one."[18] Apparently constricted from all sides, many American Jews felt torn between full secular assimilation, surface-level religious acculturation, or a return to traditional and more orthodox religious expressions. The choice, then, was between "remaining Jewish" or "becoming American," the two, at least in the 1950s, operating as mutually sustaining devices of America's post-war civil religion. Yet for those unable – and unwilling – to remain passive or active agents in a national and spiritual soap opera beyond their immediate control, a "return to religion," as Will Herberg recognized, would begin by acknowledging and seeking to understand how, in the post-war moment, "we have lost our direction and all but lost the ability to read the map that might show us how to regain it."[19] According to Richard J. Israel, a Hillel rabbi, such a return necessitated an explicit rejection of the entwining of religion and secularity. "I am no longer

16 As Jack Wertheimer develops further, "just as Jewish religious institutions enjoyed a boom period during the American religious expansion of the post-war era they were buffeted by the upheaval that shook American society during the tumultuous 1960s." In Jack Wertheimer, "The Turbulent Sixties," in *The American Jewish Experience*, ed. Jonathan D. Sarna (New York: Holmes and Meier, 1997), 330. See also Sydney E. Ahlstrom, *Religious History of the American People* (New Haven: Yale University Press, 1972), "Chapter 57: Twentieth-Century Judaism" and "Chapter 63: The Turbulent Sixties."

17 Cited in Wertheimer, "The Turbulent Sixties," 334.

18 David Riesman, "Introduction," in *Commentary on the American Scene*, ed. Elliot E. Cohen (New York: Knopf, 1953), x.

19 Will Herberg, *Judaism and Modern Man: An Interpretation of Jewish Religion* (Woodstock: Jewish Lights Publishing, 1997), 7–8.

sure," Rabbi Israel writes, "that it makes sense to sink as much into the American dream as we always have. We have some parochial Jewish needs that have to be taken into consideration as well, and not as low priority items."[20]

Not endemic to Judaism alone, the slow hemorrhaging of religious participation by the 1960s illustrates the growing lack of fulfilment resulting from the conformity expected of institutional systems of faith, the heightened anxiety of a Cold War culture, and the recognition that one's spiritual health was not wed to traditional religious orientations.[21] "The theology of the fifties," according to Stephen Whitfield's assessment, "was not so much religious belief as belief in the *value* of religion. The benefits of devotion were not seen as mystical and metaphysical, nor existential, and less psychological or ethical than political and social."[22] Limiting the expressive and felt components of religiosity, postwar faith divorced believers from the experience of religion, replacing the phenomenology of religious experience with simple markers of public identity. The notion of a "vanishing American Jew" thus seemed viable amidst a broader sociopolitical world mired in global conflict and internal disaffection. Yet if 1964 marked the height of elevating the imagined civil value *of* religion over the sacred values *within* religious living, 1967 and onward "reveal an alternative, more expressive and culturally assertive [...] American Jewish identity, a reappearing American Jew."[23] Not a rejection of faith or religious identity, "many countercultural Jews," as Mark Oppenheimer stresses accordingly, "had no intention of forsaking their people; they wished to combine their politics, their style, and their Judaism into a new, Jewish counterculture."[24] From Jewish feminists, including Trude Weiss-Rosmarin (1908–1989), Rachel Adler (1943-), or groups like Ezrat Nashim, to public intellectuals/religious activists such as Abraham Joshua Heschel (1907–1972), Max Heller (1919–2011), or Joachim Prinz (1902–1988), and the rise of youth-based movements on college campuses, the late 1960s/early 1970s witnessed the emergence of a Jewish counterculture grounded explicitly in a return to (or, at the very least, reliance on) faith. Unlike previous moments of religious reconciliation, this return rejected traditional orthodoxy, exoteric conventions, and ecclesiastical cohesion in favor of the mysti-

---

20 Cited in Heilman, *Portrait of American Jews*, 89.

21 See Wertheimer, "The Turbulent Sixties," 336–347; Hugh McLeod, *The Religious Crisis of the 1960s* (New York: Oxford University Press, 2007), 131–134; and Stephen J. Whitfield, *The Culture of the Cold War* (Baltimore: Johns Hopkins University Press, 1996).

22 Whitfield, *The Culture of the Cold War*, 86–87.

23 Heilman, *Portrait of American Jews*, 60.

24 Mark Oppenheimer, *Knocking on Heaven's Door: American Religion in the Age of Counterculture* (New Haven: Yale University Press, 2003), 102.

cal experiences, ethical imperatives, and ecstatic devotion found within the esoteric heart of Judaism.

Writing for *Response*, a post-war journal of the Jewish counterculture, the journal's first editor, Alan L. Mintz (1947-), outlines the spiritual consciousness and religious orientation directing countercultural expressions of Judaism. As Mintz writes, "a most startling discovery has been made that Judaism does not have to be identical to the scheme of middle-class values [...] a new consciousness of the past has brought us to believe that a more fundamental and nourishing Judaism existed, was discussed, and did not need a middle-class life style and its constellation of values."[25] Breaking free from the isolation of suburban existence in favor of the imperative to community and ecstatic potentialities found within Judaism (expressed, for instance, with the mystically-oriented Chasidim),[26] the havurah movement,[27] in addition to representing the initial, and most commonly discussed, countercultural response among American Jews, offered space for "close fellowship [...] independent of established synagogues."[28] In his analysis of Judaism and the 1960s counterculture, Jack Wertheimer highlights this latter significance, emphasizing how "the Jewish counterculture scorned Jewish organization life and criticized in particular the misguided priorities of the Jewish community." Against these "misguided priorities," which distracted contemporary Jews from modern injustices and social ills, "the havurah was intended as an alternative to suburban Judaism [...] if the large suburban synagogue was a gargantuan, impersonal creation, the havurah," Wertheimer counters, "would offer a 'Judaism of scale,' where Jews could pray and study

25 Cited in Wertheimer, "The Turbulent Sixties," 334.

26 In exploring the post-war renewal of Judaism, Sarna emphasizes what he calls "remnants from the Holocaust," the "more than 300,000 refugees, survivors, and 'displaced persons'" who found "refuge in the United States between 1933 and 1950." Significant for alternative, reform-oriented movements in American Judaism, including the spiritual revivalism of Shlomo Carlebach and the Jewish Renewal Movement of Schachter-Shalomi, were the "Grand Hasidic masters known as *rebbes*, the spiritual leaders of thousands of European Jews, [who] arrived, among them the Lubavitcher rebbe, Rabbi Joseph I. Schneersohn (1880–1950), who immigrated in 1940." In Sarna, *American Judaism*, 293.

27 "A havurah (the plural is havurot) is a small community of Jews who have decided to study, worship, or celebrate religious rituals together." In Oppenheimer, *Knocking on Heaven's Door*, 97. The movement itself, as Sarna develops, was "named for the separatist religious fellowships that radical Jewish pietists, mystics, and scholars had formed back in the days of the Pharisees during the late Second Temple period." In Sarna, *American Judaism*, 319. See also Riv-Ellen Prell, *Prayer & Community: The Havurah in American Judaism* (Detroit: Wayne State University Press, 1989).

28 Miller, *The 60s Communes*, 116. See also Bernard Reisman, *The Chavurah: A Contemporary Jewish Experience* (New York: Union of American Hebrew Congregations, 1977).

in intimate fellowship."[29] In search of authentic community and sincere devotion, "by the late 1960s," as Mark Oppenheimer develops similarly, "Jews dissatisfied with the institutional feel of their religion began to leave synagogues altogether, dropping out to form unaffiliated havurot – not within synagogues, but against them."[30]

Distinctly, the havurah movement illustrates two key realities directing Judaism and American Jews in the 1960s. First, it demonstrates the latent anxiety and recognized fears dominating the American psyche beneath a thin veneer of spiritual happiness, economic prosperity, and global dominance. Second, havurah exhibits how, in "fearing that it [Judaism] would not survive" post-war culture, many "sought to revitalize their own Judaism, developing bold new initiatives to show that their faith could be timely, 'with-it,' meaningful, and in harmony with the countercultural ideas of their day."[31] Thus concerned, for instance, with young disenchanted and alienated Jews, Rabbis Arthur Green (1941-) and Albert Axelrad (1938-), director of Brandeis Hillel, founded the Havurot Shalom Community Seminary in Somerville Massachusetts.[32] Established in 1968 "as an alternative seminary, it was soon transformed into an experimental community that encouraged ritual innovation and sought to avoid having a single authority or rabbi."[33] Motivated by the failure of post-war religious and secular institutions to fulfill their spiritual needs, Havurot Shalom created space to consider the fullness of Jewish identity. Relinquishing concerns of social position and a commitment to sterile ceremonial rites, members explored an embodied expression of Judaism that resulted in imperatives of engaged social concern. "Disdaining 'self-satisfied, rich suburbanites' and 'smug institutions'," Havurot Shalom, as

29 Wertheimer, "The Turbulent Sixties," 334–335.

30 Oppenheimer, *Knocking on Heaven's Door*, 97. See also Mark I. Pinsky, "'Quiet Revolution': Havurah: A New Spirit in Judaism," *Los Angeles Times*, October 11 1986.

31 Sarna, *American Judaism*, 319.

32 See Arthur Green, "Some Liturgical Notes for Havurot Shalom," in *Contemporary Judaic Fellowship in Theory and Practice*, ed. Jacob Neusner (New York: Ktav, 1972), 155–160; Bill Novak, "Havurot Shalom: A Personal Account" in *Contemporary Judaic Fellowship in Theory and Practice*, ed. Jacob Neusner (New York: Ktav, 1972), 139–148; and Joseph Reimer, "Passionate Visions in Contest: On the History of Jewish Education in Boston," in *The Jews of Boston*, ed. Jonathan D. Sarna, Ellen Smith, and Scott-Martin Kosofsky (New Haven: Yale University Press, 2005), 285–308. One of the more sustained expressions of the havurah movement is found in *The Jewish Catalog*, an "immensely popular intellectual product" of do-it-yourself instructions, a choose-your-adventure of Jewish practices including "a section describing existing havurot and giving instructions for founding new ones." In Miller, *The 60s Communes*, 116. See *The Jewish Catalog*, ed. Richard Siegel, Michael Strassfeld, and Sharon Strassfeld (Philadelphia: Jewish Publication Society of America, 1973).

33 Wertheimer, "The Turbulent Sixties," 335.

Jonathan Sarna neatly summarizes, "sought to meet the needs of 'serious young Jews [...] deeply involved in honest religious search, who are quite fully alienated from Judaism by all the contacts that they had had to date'."[34]

Spreading quickly throughout the country, and influencing the approach of many "Reform and Conservative synagogues [who] put the havurah idea to work within their own institutions to promote the 'humanization and personalization' of worship and the democratization of synagogue life," the havurah movement "in time, either disappeared, evolved into larger and more formal prayer groups, or became attached to neighborhood synagogues."[35] And, while "many alumni," according to Oppenheimer, "drifted back toward irreligion, or toward a rather undemanding affiliation with a large synagogue, the kind of institution they had held their parents blameworthy for joining," the havurah movement's "countercultural ideals, counter-aesthetic values, and relaxed decorum lived on."[36] Participants, Sarna continues, "spoke of 'religious renewal,' disdained Judaism's 'established' movements and organizations [...] and believed that through diligent efforts they could themselves 'redeem the current bleakness of American Jewish religious life.' Their aim was to recreate Judaism in their own generation's image."[37] Havurah thus opened up non-normative space, an antinomian Judaism highlighted by a return to meditative, communal, and mystical encounters with God and others. As Oppenheimer underscores, "havurot were, after all, countercultures: they existed apart from the society, in order to offer a model incompatible with the society."[38] Promoting universal fellowship, havurah's long-term impacts, for example, can be found in the Reconstructionist Movement, which became the "first [in 1993] in Judaism to declare homosexuality and heterosexuality 'normal expressions of human diversity'." Influenced both by the 1960s counterculture and Mordecai Kaplan's (1881–1983) efforts to

34 Sarna, *American Judaism*, 319. Merle Feld, "Egalitarianism and the Havurah Movement," in *Daughters of the King: Women and the Synagogue (A Survey of History, Halakhah, and Contemporary Realities)*, ed. Susan Grossman and Rivka Haut (Philadelphia: Jewish Publication Society, 2005), 245–49.

35 Sarna, *American Judaism*, 321. Oppenheimer offers a more critical assessment: "the countercultural havurah... existed from 1968 to 1975, before winding down toward ignominy. Like the synagogue havurot, these groups would often just pray, celebrate the Sabbath and holidays, and do charitable work [...] few Jews, probably no more than a couple thousand, ever joined countercultural havurot. It was not a profound experience for all of them." In Oppenheimer, *Knocking on Heaven's Door*, 97.

36 Oppenheimer, *Knocking on Heaven's Door*, 97; Sarna, *American Judaism*, 321.

37 Sarna, *American Judaism*, 319–320. See also Heilman, *Portrait of American Jews*, 90.

38 Oppenheimer, *Knocking on Heaven's Door*, 126. See also Anthony Weiss, "Countercultural Spirit Lives at Iconic 1960s Havurah," *Times of Israel*, August 9 2014.

"reconstruct" (e.g. update) Judaism, the Reconstructionist Movement offers an example of religious adaptation, broadly illustrating, as Sarna outlines, how "the havurah movement, like so many previous attempts to radically transform Judaism, produced evolution, not revolution."[39]

Awakened from a daze of religious orthodoxy and rational secularity, havurah reintroduced the aesthetic joy of devotional celebration, allowing Jews to reconnect to the most expressive elements of their faith beyond the conventional teachings and instrumentality that bound Judaism – and most twentieth century Western faiths – to traditional inflections. Whereas post-war expectations of faith often appealed to the rational mind, countercultural expressions of Judaism returned to the heart and soul, substituting ritual sterility with "meditation, theosophy, ecstasy – indeed, the whole corpus of Jewish mystical teachings, known as Kabbalah."[40] Such an emphasis on emotive experience manifests, maybe most memorably, with the "Dancing Rabbi," Rabbi Shlomo Carlebach (1925–1994; also referred to as the Singing Rabbi and the Hippie Rabbi).[41] "Regarded

---

39 Sarna, *American Judaism*, 323, 322. See also Hasia R. Diner, *The Jews of the United States, 1654 to 2000* (Berkeley: University of California Press, 2006), 345–350.

40 Sarna, *American Judaism*, 345. As with the broader 1960s counterculture, there is no absolute uniformity when it comes to Jewish inflections. In addition to figures like Carlebach and Schachter-Shalomi, or movements such as havurah or Renewal, the 1960s-era also witnessed the emergence of movements ranging from Moishe Rosen's "Jews for Jesus" to the Orthodox-leaning, "evangelical"-oriented Hineni Movement established by Esther Jungreis. See Yaakov Ariel, *Evangelizing the Chosen People: Missions to the Jews in America, 1880–2000* (Chapel Hill: University of North Carolina Press, 1999); Carol Harris-Shapiro, *Messianic Judaism: A Rabbi's Journey through Religious Change in America* (Boston: Beacon Press, 1999); Esther Jungreis, *The Jewish Soul on Fire: A Remarkable Woman Shows How Faith Can Change Your Life* (New York: William Morrow, 1982); Esther Jungreis, *The Committed Life: Principles for Good Living from Our Timeless Past* (New York: HarperOne, 1999); Juliene G. Lipson, *Jews for Jesus: An Anthropological Study* (Norwalk: AMS Press, 1990); Roy S. Neuberger, *From Central Park to Sinai: How I Found My Lost Jewish Soul* (Middle Village: Jonathan David Publishers, 2000); Ruth Rosen, *Called to Controversy: The Unlikely Story of Moishe Rosen and the Founding of Jews for Jesus* (Nashville: Thomas Nelson, 2012); and Shuly Rubin Schwartz, "Ambassadors Without Portfolio?: The Religious Leadership of *Rebbetzins* in Late-Twentieth-Century American Jewish Life," in *Women and American Judaism: Historical Perspectives*, ed. Pamela S. Nadell and Jonathan D. Sarna (Hanover: Brandeis University Press, 2001), 244–253.

41 For general background on Carlebach, see Yitta Halberstam Mandelbaum, *Holy Brother: Inspiring Stories and Enchanted Tales about Rabbi Shlomo Carlebach* (Oxford: Jason Aronson, 2002); Natan Ophir (Offenbacher), *Rabbi Shlomo Carlebach: Life, Mission, and Legacy* (Jerusalem: Urim Publications, 2014); Joanna Teinhardt, "Neo-Hasids in the Land of Israel," *Nova Religio: The Journal of Alternative and Emergent Religions* 13, no. 4 (May 2010): 22–42; and, for a more critical reflection, particularly as it relates to Carlebach's sexuality and sexual encounters,

as the foremost composer of contemporary Jewish songs," Rabbi Carlebach created, as Natan Ophir summarizes, "a new genre of storytelling intertwined with song, and innovated experiential modes of applying Hasidic values to modern life changes."[42] Along with Schachter-Shalomi, a fellow survivor of the Holocaust, Carlebach emerged onto the American scene in 1949 after being encouraged by his rebbe, Rabbi Joseph I. Schneersohn (1880–1950), to act, as Sarna develops, as "Lubavitch's traveling emissaries to college campuses" who, "as in all Lubavitch outreach activities [...sought] to bring Jews nearer to Judaism and to promote both Jewish education and the observance of the commandments."[43] Inspired by the emotive and embodied elements of Chasidic teachings, Carlebach sought to "'worship God through joy'," relying on music, dance, and song to enliven the divinity residing in each soul, to awaken "the love that everyone should have for his fellow man, for all creation, and naturally for the Creator Himself."[44] As Elie Wiesel (1928–2016) reminisces further, Carlebach helped post-Holocaust Jews "overcome the bleak intoxicants of daily life by modeling for them the spellbinding and mysterious worlds that every human being carries within himself. He would tell the Hasidic tales, giving wings to their imagination. He would show them how to discover the beauty of prayer."[45]

Driven by a sincere belief that the divine penetrates all levels of existence and types of people, Carlebach exemplified the 1960s countercultural ethos of "one love." His life's "work reflected, embodied, and advanced," Sarna highlights, "many of the central tenets of Jewish spirituality: a stress on the inner life and experiential religion; love for all human beings, particularly the oppressed and the downtrodden; gender egalitarianism; and the embrace of Hasidic and mystical forms of wisdom and worship."[46] He "saw the divine spark in every person he encountered and strove to ignite that spark until it burst into fiery flames." For the "damaged and the dispirited [...] for those who had pur-

---

see Sarah Blustain, "A Paradoxical Legacy: Rabbi Shlomo Carlebach's Shadow Side," *Lilith* 23 (March 1998): 10–17.

42 Ophir, *Rabbi Shlomo Carlebach*, 17. See also Shaul Magid, "Rabbi Shlomo Carlebach and His Interpreters: A Review Essay of Two New Musical Releases," *Musica Judaica Online Reviews* 6 (September 2010): https://mjoreviews.org/2010/09/06/rabbi-shlomo-carlebach-and-his-interpreters-a-review-essay-of-two-new-musical-releases/, accessed 20 November 2018.

43 Sarna, *American Judaism*, 346. See also Naphtali Carlebach, *Joseph Carlebach and His Generation: Biography of the Late Chief Rabbi of Altona and Hamburg* (New York: Joseph Carlebach Memorial Foundation, 1959).

44 Elie Wiesel, "Foreword," in Yitta Halberstam Mandelbaum, *Holy Brother: Inspiring Stories and Enchanted Tales about Rabbi Shlomo Carlebach* (Oxford: Jason Aronson, 2002), xviii.

45 Wiesel, "Foreword," xviii.

46 Sarna, *American Judaism*, 348.

sued nirvana with drugs, he offered the rapture of a transcendent *davening* [recitation of Jewish prayer]; he infused holiness into the ordinary and made sacred the profane," as Yitta Mandelbaum so poetically emphasizes.[47] Carlebach's joyous and enlivened approach to spiritual expression modeled how to harmonize a world predicated on discord. In overcoming the perceived chasms between the realm of holiness and our material world, Carlebach demonstrated an "undifferentiating type of love for all Jews," expressed through his efforts to "together [...] find our way to the *Ribono Shel Olam,* our Father in heaven, to study His Torah, to keep His commandments and, above all, to be His friends."[48] This communal approach manifested in his opening of the House of Love and Prayer in the heart of San Francisco's hippie scene: the Haight-Ashbury district. Offering what he called the "holy *hippalach*" (a "Yiddish term of endearment that he invented for them"), Carlebach and the House of Love and Prayer created a "much-needed haven [...] a place where they [young, disenfranchised Jews] could experiment [...] while finding their way back to Judaism under his loving tutelage."[49] In this specific way, Carlebach drew from (and relied on) the counterculture's openness to experimentation in order to re-infuse Judaism with the central elements – meditation, pluralistic exploration, ecstatic, and embodied rituals – it had abandoned, all the while directing lost souls back to the laws and commandments of God.

Important for Carlebach, then, was not simply returning Jews to lost aspects of belief and practice, but to the faith itself. His work offers insight into a distinction Stephen Kent identifies when exploring the connection between the 1960s counterculture and spiritual movements of the 1970s. Betrayed and trapped by a system beyond their immediate control, and feeling disempowered by an inability to manifest the revolutionary changes they imagined, 1960s-era radicalized Americans, according to Kent's study, shifted from projects of direct engagement to general capitulation, resulting in the emergence of a post-1960s moment in which slogans for transformative change morphed into mantras of spiritual withdrawal. As Kent argues, "where the late 1960s had been characterized by explosions of youthful protest over social issues, in the new decade [e.g., 1970s] many of those who had been protesting were turning instead to new religions or undertaking unorthodox spiritual disciplines."[50] In other words, alternative

---

47 Mandelbaum, *Holy Brothers*, xix, xxi.

48 Murray Polner, *American Jewish Biographies* (New York: Facts on File, 1982), 58.

49 Sarna, *American Judaism*, 348.

50 Stephen A. Kent, *From Slogans to Mantras: Social Protest and Religious Conversion in the Late Vietnam War Era* (Syracuse: Syracuse University Press, 2001), 1.

and new religious movements – like Carlebach or the havurah movement – offered disillusioned souls “a persuasive message that the revolutionary goals of the 1960s could still be attained – but only by abandoning direct political efforts and substituting indirect spiritual means.”[51] The very entwining of religion and American politics that threatened the progressive orientation of post-war society and emboldened secular values of consumerism and religious contexts of withdrawal reemerges in this calculation, outlining how radical agendas (both spiritual and secular) are ameliorated through religious perspectives that, while identifying the malaise and sickness governing culture, ultimately work to reduce anxiety through various expressions of withdrawal and submission to the broader system. From the full dropping-out ethos of communal living to the ecstatic space constructed by Carlebach’s House of Love and Prayer (which closed in 1977) or havurah fellowships, the historicity of countercultural spiritual movements often ends here, suggesting how a domineering orientation toward religious and political orthodoxy stifles the emancipatory potentials opened by radical and alternative expressions of faith.

Change, of course, took place as Judaism experienced a widening of its sociocultural focus, particularly as it relates to women and the LGBTQ+ community. While important in capturing how countercultural values impact religious positioning vis-à-vis moral codes and identity acceptance, more than acculturated progress occurred in the late 1960s period. Influenced by the havurah movement, Carlebach’s ecstatic celebration of faith, and the revival of mystical traditions, Rabbi Zalman Schachter-Shalomi and the Jewish Renewal Movement offered a counter to Kent-like narratives that bound the 1960s period between transformative politics and the safety of religious surrender. Yet more than this, and unlike Carlebach who ultimately sought a traditional return to God and the *mitzvoth*, Schachter-Shalomi envisioned an expression of Judaism that radically reorients the very relationships that construct and maintain the conventional monotheistic divide between humanity and divinity.

As he reflects in his personal memoir, Schachter-Shalomi, in his efforts “to find the approach and the vocabulary by which I could inspire those who had been highly acculturated to America,” ultimately developed the means to help believers “experience with more immediacy a Judaism that they could embrace.” Central to his renewal was a move away from divine-against-human binaries to a “*gaian* theology” made palatable within the frames of mystical understanding

51 Benjamin Zablocki, “Foreword,” in Stephen A. Kent, *From Slogans to Mantras: Social Protest and Religious Conversion in the Late Vietnam War Era* (Syracuse: Syracuse University Press, 2001), xii.

and expressed through a universal ecumenism.[52] As confirmed through his psychedelic exploration, Schachter-Shalomi maps a mystical understanding that grounds Judaism within its esoteric heart and places it squarely within a perennial perspective, suggesting a unitive core that links the sacred narratives of global religious culture as well as the very nature of the divine-to-human and human-to-human connections. Mysticism suggests an overcoming of our materialist visage, an experiential moment that transcends the rational and empirical by unveiling the duplicity of our binary thinking – it refers to "religious experiences corresponding to the direct cognition of a transcendent reality beyond the division of subject and object."[53] There is not material versus spiritual, nor human under divine, but rather One. To emerge out of the cave of ignorance and shadows into the light of consciousness, to borrow from Plato's allegory, is to receive true wisdom, a cleansing of perception, as Aldous Huxley (1894–1963), drawing from William Blake (1757–1827), proposes following his first psychedelic experience, in which "every thing would appear to man as it is, infinite."[54]

As showcased in Schachter-Shalomi's efforts to renew Judaism, such revelation does not discount spirituality or religiosity, but produces the conditions to ascend into the realm of the infinite. Paralleling Kabbalistic understandings of the "Four Worlds," four distinct realms of God that, as "believers explain, 'represent the great cosmic moments of creation and creativity, the slide show of God's inwardness',"[55] the infinite, as psychedelics distinctly communicate, resides directly in the here and now, illustrating how reality, regardless of one's perspective, "remains the same forever" (Eccles. 1:4) if we are only able to open ourselves fully to this recognition. In this way, the mystical encounters made possible through psychedelic experimentation substantiated the truth of Kabbalistic teachings that stress how the essence of the divine resides within individual souls, suggesting a world defined by a sacred, panentheistic[56] intercon-

---

52 Rabbi Zalman M. Schachter-Shalomi, *My Life in Jewish Renewal: A Memoir* (Lanham: Rowman and Littlefield, 2012), xii-xiii; see also 143–153 for his account of taking LSD with Timothy Leary.

53 Arthur Versluis, *Platonic Mysticism: Contemplative Science, Philosophy, Literature, and Art* (New York: State University of New York Press, 2017), 3.

54 Aldous Huxley, Epigraph to *The Doors of Perception* (New York: Harper Perennial, 2009).

55 Cited in Sarna, American Judaism, 349.

56 Where pantheism expresses the belief that the divine/God and the natural world/universe are one and the same, panentheism, also referred to as monistic monotheism, proposes that all (the universe/natural world) is *in* God, with the divine simultaneously interpenetrating and transcending all aspects of the universe.

nection as opposed to banal and restrictive distinctions. Where Carlebach and havurah offered the means to deconstruct the line dividing the sacred from the profane, Schachter-Shalomi negated the entire binary, ultimately highlighting a mystical understanding of God "as the underlying oneness of all there is."[57]

Inspired by his phenomenological encounters with psychedelic consciousness, Schachter-Shalomi challenged Jews and non-Jews alike "to find God in reality." Yet as brought into unique focus by both Jewish mysticism and psychedelic consciousness, the real challenge is in determining "which real was more real," suggesting an entwining of religion and secularity not as a means to solidify the ruling order, but rather as the perennial knowledge that all reality is sacred, infused by the holy sparks (*nitzotzin*) of a divine Godhead.[58] Isaac Luria (1534–1572), a central rabbinic figure and Jewish mystic often considered the father of contemporary Kabbalah,[59] described the process that took the divine from the unknowable and ineffable (endlessness) to the real and finite (concreteness). He describes how, at the beginning of time, "God" filled the entire universe, ultimately fashioning the conditions for creation by contracting Himself, what Luria calls *tzimtzum* (meaning, "contraction/constriction/condensation"), the process by which God retreats into Its Own Being in order to literally create an empty space (*ayin*, or no-thing-ness). Producing a condition of darkness, God, as Torah teaches, then spoke creation into being, declaring "Let there be light" (Gen. 1:3). According to Luria's reading of the *Tanakh* and Jewish mystical texts (such as the *Zohar*), the light that subsequently fills the darkness is housed originally within ten holy vessels (*sefirot*, meaning emanation), each containing the primordial light of the divine. Too fragile to contain the fullness of God's Divine Light (*Ohr Eyn Sof*), the vessels shattered, releasing throughout God's manifold creation the holy sparks contained within. Known as *shevirat ha-kelim*, the "shattering of the vessels" unveils two potentially paradoxical ideas when it comes to an infinite divine and an all-good God – how, from the infinite, can we arrive at the finite; and how, within the harmony and balance of God, can we discover the root of evil?

Although much of the light housed within the vessels returned to their divine source upon shattering, the remainder fell into the empty space created

57 Diane Winston, "Participatory Judaism: A Look at the Jewish Renewal Movement and Its Attractiveness to Lots of People," *Long Island Jewish World* (Aug-Sept 1993): 2.

58 Kamenetz, *Stalking Elijah*, 16.

59 See Yosef Eisen, *Miraculous Journey: A Complete History of the Jewish People from Creation to Present* (Southfield: Targum/Feldheim, 2004), 213; and Lawrence Fine, *Physician of the Soul, Healer of the Cosmos: Isaac Luria and His Kabbalistic Fellowship* (Stanford: Stanford University Press, 2003).

by God's contraction, often becoming attached to the broken shards of vessels. In this setting, the shards become *qelipot*, "husks" or "shells" that represent *sitra achra*, or the "other side" of evil. Yet more distinctly for Kabbalists and figures like Schachter-Shalomi, the broken shards and escaping light also signify the source for our material world, emerging as the basis for sustaining creation as well as the continuation of evil. Within this context, Luria introduces a third concept to offset both *tzimtzum* and *shevirat ha-kelim* – when the initial *Olam HaTohu* (The World of *Tohu*, or Chaos/Confusion; *Tohu* describes unformed existence, pure essence without structure) collapses through *tzimtzum* and *shevirat ha-kelim*, it is replaced with the *Olam HaTikun* (The World of *Tikun*, or Order/Rectification). More commonly associated with the phrase *tikkun olam* (meaning to repair the world, often through acts of kindness), Luria's modeling of creation (based within broader Jewish mystical writings that range from the *Sefer Yetzirah* to the *Zohar*) demonstrates how the root aim of our humanness is designed to gather and return the sparks; to repair and restore, in other words, the broken vessels in order to return creation – and thus all elements of creation from our natural world to fellow humans – back into an original and harmonious whole. From the many, as mystics often pronounce, we return to the One.[60]

To recover the divine sparks, then, is not a means to find personal salvation amidst a phenomenal world beyond our control; nor is it a tool to deaden people to the ills and violence plaguing modern living. Rather, as uniquely captured in Jewish mysticism and Schachter-Shalomi's psychedelic reflections and efforts at concrete renewal, to recover the sparks of the divine is to gain gnosis, the wisdom that, rather than disconnected from the site and source of creation, humans always already remain part and parcel of the divine. For this reason, as Rabbi Arthur Green (writing pseudonymously as Itzik Lodzer in 1968 regarding the connection between psychedelics and Kabbalah) laments, "Judaism as presented today knows nothing of God as *Eyn Sof*; it has lost the creative mystic drive which led beyond its own images into a confrontation with the Nothing."[61] For Kabbalists, *Eyn Sof* (often *Ein Sof*) signifies the Infinite God beyond and before form, an "Endlessness," as Gershom Scholem outlines in his tracing of Jewish

60 For outlines of Kabbalistic and Lurianic thought, see David Ariel, *Kabbalah: The Mystic Quest in Judaism* (Lanham: Rowman and Littlefield, 2006); Rabbi David A. Cooper, *God is a Verb: Kabbalah and the Practice of Mystical Judaism* (New York: Riverhead Books, 1997); Eliahu Klein, *Kabbalah of Creation: The Mysticism of Isaac Luria, Founder of Modern Kabbalah* (Berkeley: North Atlantic Books, 2005); and Gershom Scholem, *On the Kabbalah and Its Symbolism* (New York: Schocken Books, 1996).

61 Itzik Lodzer (pseudonym for Arthur Green), "Psychedelics and Kabbalah," in *The New Jews*, ed. James A. Sleeper and Alan L. Mintz (New York: Vintage, 1971), 185.

mystical thought and trends, who symbolizes the "Root of all Roots," an "Indifferent Unity" "perfectly simple and infinitely complex, nothing and everything," both the hidden (esoteric) and the revealed (exoteric).[62] Such an understanding deconstructs the binary between the source of creation (e. g. an active, proscriptive "creator" God) and the effects of creation (e. g. nature and humanity), suggesting a panentheistic (meaning all is in God; what Schachter-Shalomi refers to as *gaian*) and perennial notion of divinity. In fact, as Sanford Drob so astutely outlines, "God, according to Kabbalah, incarnates Himself in Man, not just one prophet or messiah but in each and every human deed that fulfills His ethical and spiritual potential. This is the inner meaning of the Kabbalistic aphorism that 'An arousal from above comes only in response to an arousal from below'."[63] Reflecting directly the mystical notion "As Above, So Below," or what Hinduism labels *Tat tvam asi,* meaning "Thou are God," *Eyn Sof* illustrates how the infinite divine, the phenomenal world, and humanity evolve continuously and mutually together, a contingency in which the self-creation of *Eyn Sof* manifests in the creative endeavors humans undertake to redeem and repair a broken world.

Rabbi Naftali Bacharach (seventeenth century; his dates of birth and death remain unknown), in his *Emeq HaMelekh*, illustrates the contingent reciprocity of this "creative arousal":

> the world could be created only by virtue of the action of the righteous, the arousal of those below. So God contemplated the good deeds of the righteous – yet to be created – and this act of thinking was enough to actualize the thought. God drew forth light from within himself and delighted himself with holy people, like those who would eventually be. This joy engendered undulation, greater delight. In this bliss of contemplating the righteous, of imagining holy people – in this fluctuation, the power to create was born.[64]

Problematically, in losing sight of the relational reciprocity intrinsic in the nature of *Eyn Sof*, contemporary Jews "have inherited," as Arthur Green decries, "a fa-

62 Gershom Scholem, *Major Trends in Jewish Mysticism* (New York: Schocken Books, 1995), 12; and Sanford L. Drob, *Symbols of the Kabbalah: Philosophical and Psychological Perspectives* (Northvale: Jason Aronson, 2000), 61. See also Rabbi Daniel M. Horwitz, *A Kabbalah and Jewish Mysticism Reader* (Lincoln: University of Nebraska Press, 2016); and Gershom Scholem, *On the Mystical Shape of the Godhead: Basic Concepts in the Kabbalah* (New York: Schocken Books, 1991).

63 Drob, *Symbols of the Kabbalah*, 100.

64 Naftali Bacharach, "Creative Arousal," selection from *Emeq HaMelekh*, in *The Essential Kabbalah: The Heart of Jewish Mysticism*, ed. Daniel C. Matt (San Francisco: Harper San Francisco, 1996), 98.

ther figure who looms so large that one dare not *try* to look beyond Him." In becoming "trapped by our image," non-mystical Judaism thus fails to see how "God-as-the-father made sense only in the context of God-as-mother, God-as-lover, God-as-bride," resulting in a condition, at least "from the perspective of [...] psychedelic/mystic insight," in which "conventional Western religion seems to have fallen prey to a psychologically highly complex idolatry," as Green concludes.[65]

Similarly emboldened by psychedelic visions of mystical oneness, Schachter-Shalomi echoes not only the condition decried by Green, but furthers Green's psychedelic response that "an alternative to the stodgy ol' Judaism of the 1960s," as Lawrence Bush describes it, begins with the recognition that "the deepest, simplest, and most radical insight of psychedelic/mystic consciousness [...is] the realization that all reality is one with the Divine."[66] For Green, as with Schachter-Shalomi, this "feeling of the true oneness of God and man," which one encounters frequently within the writings of Jewish mystics, became real through the aid of psychedelics. Permitting one to experience without mediation "union of moment and eternity, of the here and now with the everywhere and forever," psychedelics, as with mystical consciousness, signify a direct threat to "the game of Western consciousness, including most of Western religion." By challenging the "reality of the individual ego" and subsequent isolating elevation of "the separate human self," psychedelics, as Green ultimately stresses, offer a counter-vision of humanity as reciprocally-driven and divinely interconnected.[67] Also viewing contemporary Judaism and institutional religion as the manifestations of stale orthodoxy, reactionary canon, and routinized experience, Schachter-Shalomi situated the heart of Judaism panentheistically, as a religious inflection of divine immanence, relocating the transcendence of God's will within a type of collective unconsciousness that radiates through and endlessly sustains all of creation. To access this level of consciousness – which both Jewish mysticism and psychedelic exploration promise – is to recognize, as Schachter-Shalomi underscores in his conversations with Rodger Kamenetz, how "God is reality."[68]

---

65 Lodzer, "Psychedelics and Kabbalah," 185.

66 Lawrence Bush, "Drugs and Jewish Spirituality: That Was Then, This is Now," in *Hallucinogens: A Reader*, ed. Charles S. Grob (New York: Jeremy P. Tarcher, 2002), 87; Lodzer, "Psychedelics and Kabbalah," 188.

67 Lodzer, "Psychedelics and Kabbalah," 190.

68 Kamenetz, *Stalking Elijah*, 16, 7.

Reb Zalman, Psychedelic Consciousness, and Esoteric Insight

Writing in response to an August 1966 *Commentary* symposium on "The State of Jewish Belief," Schachter-Shalomi situates the value, implications, and religious perspectives unveiled through psychedelic exploration, stressing how,

> when I can undergo the deepest cosmic experience via some miniscule quantity of organic alkaloids or LSD, then the whole validity of my ontological assertions is in doubt [...] the psychedelic experience can be not only a challenge but a support of my faith. After seeing what really happens at the point where all is One and God immanent surprises God transcendent and they merge in cosmic laughter, I can also see Judaism in a new and amazing light.[69]

Suffused with both mystical imagery of "As Above, So Below" (or all in the All) and Kabbalistic understandings that situate our lower material world as mirroring and being sustained by the upper spiritual world, Schachter-Shalomi radically upends the divine versus human binary that dominates Western religious discourse and orthodox expressions of Judaism in favor of a panentheistic understanding that, most significantly perhaps, ultimately affirms the esoteric heart of (mystical) Jewish belief. Psychedelics, in exposing the reality of unitive oneness, revealed to Schachter-Shalomi that "the questions to which the Torah is the answer are recovered in *me*."[70] Such internalization of sacred wisdom replicates the divine thought (*makhshava*) by which the Infinite Endlessness of God (*Eyn Sof*) ultimately finds expression, suggesting a base reality of interconnection that necessitates a new approach to playing the game of life, one defined not by religious purity or piety, nor political hegemony, but rather the acceptance that "the citizen and the stranger do not play the same game but they have a common civic framework – a metagame that protects all games so that they do not interfere with one another." To accept this notion, what Schachter-Shalomi identifies as the "transcendental luster", realized through psychedelics, demonstrates most fully how religiosity is measured in one's capacity to act in the present moment on behalf of and for the benefit of all others.[71]

The entwining of psychedelic consciousness and Schachter-Shalomi's continued acceptance of and dedication to Torah thus illustrates a mystical unfold-

---

69 Schachter-Shalomi, "Response," 213–214.

70 Schachter-Shalomi, "Response," 214, emphasis added.

71 Schachter-Shalomi, "Response," 214–216.

ing of Judaism that necessitated an approach to religious living that bypassed traditional orthodoxy and routinized orthopraxy in favor of a radicalized expression of Judaism more in line with the "*perspective* [...] one achieves during a psychedelic session." In other words, psychedelics allow for a mystical encounter with the realm of consciousness no longer bound by dichotomous patterning or mired in egotistical thinking; it is, as Rabbi Arthur Green stresses, a moment in which "experience, consciousness and ego become detached. One comes to view the world no longer from the contextual position of the self, but rather as an outsider."[72] Reflecting three decades removed from the 1960s and his personal exploration with psychedelics and Jewish mysticism, Lawrence Bush furthers Green's connection between Jewish mystical knowledge and psychedelic consciousness, emphasizing how such a phenomenological experience of being on the outside does not remove one from the responsibilities of being part of the everyday world. Whereas the decadent – and mediated – image of the 1960s psychedelic user accentuates projects of hedonistic withdrawal, often described in the countercultural language of "dropping out,"[73] the connec-

72 Lodzer, "Psychedelics and Kabbalah," 177, emphasis in original.

73 It is important to recognize that as much as the 1960s can be defined positively by advocates of psychedelic exploration, there were just as many voices of concern, particularly by critics who sought to discount and delegitimize those who sought to establish sacramental connections between psychedelics and religious traditions. R. C. Zaehner, in a series of works directed against psychedelic proponents, and primarily Aldous Huxley and Timothy Leary, captures this general critique: "such individuals seek their beatitude in regular drug-taking, continuing to avoid the fact that their psychedelic 'illumination' is not the sign of divine or cosmic approval they suppose it to be, but rather a flight from reality." Indeed, "to the normal, rational mind," writes Zaehner, "his [Huxley] remarks [in favor of psychedelics] make no sense whatever, and might therefore be dismissed as the illusions of a lunatic" (in, respectively, R.C. Zaehner, *Zen, Drugs and Mysticism* (New York: Vintage Books, 1972), 97 and R. C. Zaehner, *Mysticism Sacred and Profane* (London: Oxford University Press, 1957), 7). Most problematically, as this line of criticism goes, is that such "a flight from reality" disconnects the psychedelic voyager from the religious and political foundations that provide moral order and ethical direction. To transcend shared reality – to become "One" with God – is to move beyond the categories of good and evil, thus leading to and allowing for, as the polemic inevitably and spectacularly concludes, figures like Charles Manson "for whom killing and being killed were identical and the same" (in R.C. Zaehner, *Our Savage God: The Perverse Use of Eastern Thought* (New York: Sheed and Ward, 1974), 15). For similar arguments and perspectives, see Harry Oldmeadow, *Journeys East: 20th Century Western Encounters with Eastern Religious Traditions* (Bloomington: World Wisdom, 2004), 266–267; John Passmore, "Paradise Now: The Logic of the New Mysticism," *Encounter* (November 1970): 8–14; and Whitall Perry, "Drug-Induced Mysticism: The Mescalin Hypothesis," in *Challenges to a Secular Society* (Oakton: The Foundation for Traditional Studies, 1996), 7. For broader histories of "acid fascism" and the threats associated with psychedelically-inspired unitive visions, see David Felton, *Mindfuckers: A Source Book on the Rise of Acid Fascism in America,*

tion between psychedelics and religious insight speaks to an unburdening that is simultaneously a sacred regrounding. Rather than heretical, psychedelics confirmed the truth of Jewish spirituality.

As Bush recalls when discussing the experience of rabbis and educators who experimented with psychedelics, rather than removed and remote, "their psychedelic experiences [...] became tightly interwoven with their Judaism and deeply influenced their professional practice."[74] In fact, as he highlights in one interview, the "piercing perception of the infinitesimal yet infinite nature of his identity was accompanied," Bush stresses, "by an overpowering infusion of faith, a certainty about there being meaning in the universe and interconnection among all life." In affirming both faith and unitive connection, such mystical encounters validate the esoteric core of Judaism, revealing, for example, how the "fact of connectedness or 'oneness' that the *Sh'ma* [*Shema Yisrael*] expresses first became clear" under the sway of "LSD."[75] Within the landscapes mapped through psychedelic consciousness, the truth of the numinous dimension becomes all too real,[76] indicating, as the *Zohar* discloses, how "the universe of ordinary consciousness [...is] *Alma-De-Shikra* or World of Deception."[77] To overcome this illusion of time and space (as well as the ego it produces) is to see "from beyond [...] from God's point of view."[78] Once achieved, the Jewish mystic can directly and without mediation experience an "overpowering sense of *devekut*, the oceanic union with God."[79] To cleave to God, as the term *devekut* denotes, is to "'see' the entire cosmos, micro and macro," indicating how the very nature of Jewish mysticism, as opposed to strictly unveiling theological doctrine or theosophical insight, expresses an esoteric truth hidden behind the traditional imagery of Jewish monotheism, the understanding, as Green emphasizes, that "if there is a 'God' [...] He is the One within the many; the changeless constant in a world of change."[80]

Including Material on Charles Manson, Mel Liman, Victor Baranco, and Their Followers (San Francisco: Straight Arrow, 1972); and Gary Lachman, *Turn Off Your Mind: The Mystic Sixties and the Dark Side of the Age of Aquarius* (New York: Disinformation, 2001).

74 Bush, "Drugs and Jewish Spirituality," 84.

75 Bush, "Drugs and Jewish Spirituality," 85.

76 In one interview, Bush recounts how a rabbi described feeling "*more* real than my daily perception of reality" through his exploration of LSD consciousness. In Bush, "Drugs and Jewish Spirituality," 84.

77 Lodzer, "Psychedelics and Kabbalah," 178.

78 Lodzer, "Psychedelics and Kabbalah," 178.

79 Bush, "Drugs and Jewish Spirituality," 84.

80 Lodzer, "Psychedelics and Kabbalah," 180.

Such a perennial and panentheistic perspective, while appearing to challenge traditional understandings of monotheism, mirrors the understanding and growth Schachter-Shalomi achieved through psychedelic experimentation. Drawn to Lubavitch Chasidism largely due to its emphasis on "meditation and prayer," the contemplation Schachter-Shalomi sought became alive and accessible through psychedelics.[81] Inspired after reading Aldous Huxley's *The Doors of Perception* in 1954, which echoed "so close the Hasidic tradition: the various levels of consciousness, the worlds to which one can go, and what 'soul' is like," Schachter-Shalomi, through the help of Gerald Heard, met Timothy Leary, who "guided me the first time" and who "showed us how to sacramentalize our relation to them [psychedelics]," as Schachter-Shalomi recalls.[82] Taken intentionally as a sacrament, the most "wonderful thing about psychedelics," Schachter-Shalomi contends, was not merely found in proving what he already believed, but in expanding his perspective, leading to a vision of Judaism as expressing but one manifestation of a foundational perennial religiosity. Through "the 'mind move' that occurred," Schachter-Shalomi gained "recognition of the fluidity of consciousness. My reality maps were no longer absolute. I used to have absolute reality maps based on traditional creeds [...] with psychedelics, I could see how all cosmologies are heuristic and it depends on what you want to do." Most distinctly then, and as explicitly developed in Schachter-Shalomi's application of this unitive wisdom through the renewal of Judaism, "the [psychedelic] experience only opens you up to greater vision. When you have the vision, you have a burden to carry that vision out. In other words, it makes demands of you."[83] In connecting these demands to universal symbols of compassion, such as "the guy at the sky light, the bodhisattva," LSD proved "the oneness and connection with God," resulting in the gained wisdom that "behind all religions, there's a reality, and this reality wears whatever clothes it needs to speak to a particular people."[84] Such a perspective, radical in reorienting the relationship between God and humanity, as well as the capacity for humanity to encounter without mediation the divine realm, confirmed for Schachter-Shalomi that "what was needed was not to restore the religion of the *shtetl* but to renew Judaism in a way that

---

81 "Zalman Schachter-Shalomi: Transcending Religious Boundaries," 195.

82 "Zalman Schachter-Shalomi: Transcending Religious Boundaries," 196–197; Zalman Schachter-Shalomi, "Climbing Jacob's Ladder," in *Timothy Leary: Outside Looking In*, ed. Robert Forte (Rochester: Park Street Press, 1999), 223.

83 "Zalman Schachter-Shalomi: Transcending Religious Boundaries," 198–199.

84 Schachter-Shalomi, "Climbing Jacob's Ladder," 224; Sarah Davidson, *The December Project: An Extraordinary Rabbi and A Skeptical Seeker Confront Life's Great Mystery* (New York: HarperOne, 2014), 93–94.

would serve people in this time and place. 'Renewal, not restoration,' he decided."[85]

Conclusion: From Psychedelic Revitalization to Compassionate Conduct

Schachter-Shalomi's experience demonstrates how psychedelics helped revitalize commitments to longstanding systems of faith, while also finding space to radically commit these systems to values more in harmony with countercultural notions of oneness and love. In this specific way, the Jewish Renewal Movement, in addition to transforming both orthodoxic and orthopraxic aspects of Judaism, also signifies an alternative to the end-of-times perspective dominating the religious and secular landscape in post-war America. Reflecting on his psychedelic encounters, Schachter-Shalomi emphasized how

> it was clear that what I'd experienced in prayer and meditation before – the oneness and connection with God – was true, but it wasn't just Jewish. It transcended borders. I was sitting in a Hindu Ashram with Tim Leary, who was Irish Catholic, and I realized that all forms of religion are masks that the divine wears to communicate with us [...] But no single point of view alone is right.[86]

Within the entheogenic (meaning substances that manifest a godly/divine/infinite experience) framing of the Jewish Renewal Movement, Schachter-Shalomi sought to actualize this sacred lesson, introducing what *Aleph: Alliance for Jewish Renewal*, the contemporary embodiment of Jewish Renewal, labels "deep ecumenism," the belief that positions our immediate conduct as value unto itself, a religious orientation no longer emphasizing the need to return to or venerate God, but rather to experience God directly through prayer, meditation, and, most expressively, through the commitment to advance and improve the well-being of others. Reverberating in Schachter-Shalomi's psychedelically-inspired unitive encounter with God, deep ecumenism

> teaches us that every religious tradition is a path to the One [...] in Reb Zalman's metaphor, each religious tradition is an organ in the body of collective humanity: our differences are meaningful, and our commonality is significant. Deep Ecumenism teaches us that we can

85 Davidson, *The December Project*, 89.
86 Davidson, *The December Project*, 93–94.

> best serve the needs of all humanity when we not only respect other religious paths, but collaborate with them in our shared work of healing creation.[87]

Such a shared and universal dedication to "healing creation" signifies the heart of the Jewish Renewal Movement, illustrating how Jewish religiosity is ultimately found not in institutional settings, but rather in its overt desire to turn Judaism (and religion broadly) away from its routinization and "after this world" emphasis to a position fully mired in the here and now. The result is a version of Judaism that accepts the divine narratives and rituals of other traditions as true; that seeks egalitarianism and all this demands economically, culturally, and at the level of identity; that works toward environmental justice, seeing nature as manifesting the divine and divine responsibility; and that understands all of this as *the* expression of faith, both their own, and of all peoples (believers and non-believers alike).

Works Cited

Ahlstrom, Sydney E. *Religious History of the American People*. New Haven: Yale University Press, 1972.

ALEPH. *Alliance for Jewish Renewal*. "Deep Ecumenism." Accessed September 16 2017. https://aleph.org/projects/deep-ecumenism.

Arad, Gulie Ne'eman. *America, Its Jews, and the Rise of Nazism*. Bloomington: Indiana University Press, 2000.

Ariel, David. *Kabbalah: The Mystic Quest in Judaism*. Lanham: Rowman and Littlefield, 2006.

Ariel, Yaakov. *Evangelizing the Chosen People: Missions to the Jews in America, 1880–2000*. Chapel Hill: University of North Carolina Press, 1999.

Bacharach, Naftali. "Creative Arousal," selection from *Emeq HaMelekh*. In *The Essential Kabbalah: The Heart of Jewish Mysticism*, edited by Daniel C. Matt, 98. San Francisco: Harper San Francisco, 1996.

Blustain, Sarah. "A Paradoxical Legacy: Rabbi Shlomo Carlebach's Shadow Side." *Lilith* 23, no. 1 (March 1998): 10–17.

Bush, Lawrence. "Drugs and Jewish Spirituality: That Was Then, This is Now." In *Hallucinogens: A Reader*, edited by Charles S. Grob, 82–93. New York: Jeremy P. Tarcher, 2002.

Carlebach, Naphtali. *Joseph Carlebach and His Generation: Biography of the Late Chief Rabbi of Altona and Hamburg*. New York: Joseph Carlebach Memorial Foundation, 1959.

Cohen, Elliot. "An Act of Affirmation." *Commentary* I, November 1945, https://www.commentarymagazine.com/articles/an-act-of-affirmation/. Accessed 2 September 2017.

---

87 "Deep Ecumenism," *ALEPH: Alliance for Jewish Renewal*, accessed September 16 2017, https://aleph.org/projects/deep-ecumenism.

Cooper, David A. *God is a Verb: Kabbalah and the Practice of Mystical Judaism.* New York: Riverhead Books, 1997.
Davidson, Sarah. *The December Project: An Extraordinary Rabbi and A Skeptical Seeker Confront Life's Great Mystery.* New York: HarperOne, 2014.
Diner, Hasia R. *The Jews of the United States, 1654 to 2000.* Berkeley: University of California Press, 2006.
Drob, Sanford L. *Symbols of the Kabbalah: Philosophical and Psychological Perspectives.* Northvale: Jason Aronson, 2000.
Eisen, Yosef. *Miraculous Journey: A Complete History of the Jewish People from Creation to Present.* Southfield: Targum/Feldheim, 2004.
Feingold, Henry L. "Who Shall Bear Guilt for the Holocaust? The Human Dilemma." In *The American Jewish Experience*, edited by Jonathan D. Sarna, 274–292. New York: Holmes and Meier, 1987.
Feld, Merle. "Egalitarianism and the Havurah Movement." In *Daughters of the King: Women and the Synagogue (A Survey of History, Halakhah, and Contemporary Realities)*, edited by Susan Grossman and Rivka Haut, 245–249. Philadelphia: Jewish Publication Society, 2005.
Felton, David. *Mindfuckers: A Source Book on the Rise of Acid Fascism in America, Including Material on Charles Manson, Mel Liman, Victor Baranco, and Their Followers.* San Francisco: Straight Arrow, 1972.
Fine, Lawrence. *Physician of the Soul, Healer of the Cosmos: Isaac Luria and His Kabbalistic Fellowship.* Stanford: Stanford University Press, 2003.
Green, Arthur. "Some Liturgical Notes for Havurot Shalom." In *Contemporary Judaic Fellowship in Theory and Practice*, edited by Jacob Neusner, 155–160. New York: Ktav, 1972.
Lodzer, Itzik (pseudonym for Arthur Green). "Psychedelics and Kabbalah." In *The New Jews*, edited by James A. Sleeper and Alan L. Mintz, 176–192. New York: Vintage, 1971.
Goren, Arthur A. "A 'Golden Decade' for American Jews: 1945–1955." In *The American Jewish Experience*, edited by Jonathan D. Sarna, 294–311. New York: Holmes and Meier, 1987.
Halberstam Mandelbaum, Yitta. *Holy Brother: Inspiring Stories and Enchanted Tales about Rabbi Shlomo Carlebach.* Oxford: Jason Aronson, 2002.
Harris-Shapiro, Carol. *Messianic Judaism: A Rabbi's Journey through Religious Change in America.* Boston: Beacon Press, 1999.
Heilman, Samuel C. *Portrait of American Jews: The Last Half of the 20th Century.* Seattle: University of Washington Press, 1995.
Herberg, Will. *Judaism and Modern Man: An Interpretation of Jewish Religion.* Woodstock: Jewish Lights Publishing, 1997.
Horwitz, Rabbi Daniel M. *A Kabbalah and Jewish Mysticism Reader.* Lincoln: University of Nebraska Press, 2016.
Huxley, Aldous. Epigraph to *The Doors of Perception.* New York: Harper Perennial, 2009.
Jungreis, Esther. *The Jewish Soul on Fire: A Remarkable Woman Shows How Faith Can Change Your Life.* New York: William Morrow, 1982.
Jungreis, Esther. *The Committed Life: Principles for Good Living from Our Timeless Past.* New York: HarperOne, 1999.
Kamenetz, Rodger. *Stalking Elijah: Adventures with Today's Jewish Mystical Masters.* New York: HarperOne, 1998.

Kent, Stephen A. *From Slogans to Mantras: Social Protest and Religious Conversion in the Late Vietnam War Era.* Syracuse: Syracuse University Press, 2001.

Klein, Eliahu. *Kabbalah of Creation: The Mysticism of Isaac Luria, Founder of Modern Kabbalah.* Berkeley: North Atlantic Books, 2005.

Lachman, Gary. *Turn Off Your Mind: The Mystic Sixties and the Dark Side of the Age of Aquarius.* New York: Disinformation, 2001.

Lipson, Juliene G. *Jews for Jesus: An Anthropological Study.* Norwalk: AMS Press, 1990.

Magid, Shaul. "Rabbi Shlomo Carlebach and His Interpreters: A Review Essay of Two New Musical Releases." *Musica Judaica Online Reviews* 6 (September 2010), no pagination, https://mjoreviews.org/2010/09/06/rabbi-shlomo-carlebach-and-his-interpreters-a-review-essay-of-two-new-musical-releases/. Accessed October 1 2017.

Marx, Karl. *Critique of Hegel's 'Philosophy of Right'*, edited by Joseph O'Malley. New York: Cambridge University Press, 1970.

McLeod, Hugh. *The Religious Crisis of the 1960s.* New York: Oxford University Press, 2007.

Miller, Timothy. *The 60s Communes: Hippies and Beyond.* Syracuse: Syracuse University Press, 1999.

Neuberger, Roy S. *From Central Park to Sinai: How I Found My Lost Jewish Soul.* Middle Village: Jonathan David Publishers, 2000.

Novak, Bill. "Havurot Shalom: A Personal Account." In *Contemporary Judaic Fellowship in Theory and Practice*, edited by Jacob Neusner, 139–148. New York: Ktav, 1972.

Oldmeadow, Harry. *Journeys East: 20th Century Western Encounters with Eastern Religious Traditions.* Bloomington: World Wisdom, 2004.

Ophir (Offenbacher), Natan. *Rabbi Shlomo Carlebach: Life, Mission, and Legacy.* Jerusalem: Urim Publications, 2014.

Oppenheimer, Mark. *Knocking on Heaven's Door: American Religion in the Age of Counterculture.* New Haven: Yale University Press, 2003.

Passmore, John. "Paradise Now: The Logic of the New Mysticism." *Encounter* (November 1970): 3–21.

Perry, Whitall. "Drug-Induced Mysticism: The Mescalin Hypothesis." In *Challenges to a Secular Society*, 7–16. Oakton: The Foundation for Traditional Studies, 1996.

Piazza, Thomas. "Jewish Identity and the Counterculture." In *The New Religious Consciousness*, edited by Charles Y. Glock and Robert N. Bellah, 245–264. Berkeley: University of California Press, 1976.

Pinsky, Mark I. "'Quiet Revolution': Havurah: A New Spirit in Judaism." *Los Angeles Times*, October 11 1986.

Prell, Riv-Ellen. *Prayer & Community: The Havurah in American Judaism.* Detroit: Wayne State University Press, 1989.

Polner, Murray. *American Jewish Biographies.* New York: Facts on File, 1982.

Reimer, Joseph. "Passionate Visions in Contest: On the History of Jewish Education in Boston." In *The Jews of Boston*, edited by Jonathan D. Sarna, Ellen Smith, and Scott-Martin Kosofsky, 285–308. New Haven: Yale University Press, 2005.

Reisman, Bernard. *The Chavurah: A Contemporary Jewish Experience.* New York: Union of American Hebrew Congregations, 1977.

Riesman, David. Introduction to *Commentary on the American Scene*, edited by Elliot E. Cohen, vii-xviii. New York: Knopf, 1953.

Rosen, Ruth. *Called to Controversy: The Unlikely Story of Moishe Rosen and the Founding of Jews for Jesus.* Nashville: Thomas Nelson, 2012.
Rubin Schwartz, Shuly. “Ambassadors Without Portfolio?: The Religious Leadership of *Rebbetzins* in Late-Twentieth-Century American Jewish Life.” In *Women and American Judaism: Historical Perspectives*, edited by Pamela S. Nadell and Jonathan D. Sarna, 235–267. Hanover: Brandeis University Press, 2001.
Sarna, Jonathan D. *American Judaism: A History.* New Haven: Yale University Press, 2004.
Schachter-Shalomi, Zalman M. “Toward an ‘Order of *B'nai Or*’.” *Judaism* 13, no. 2 (Spring 1964): 185–197.
“Response.” In *The Condition of Jewish Belief: A Symposium by the Editors of Commentary Magazine*, 207–216. New York: Macmillan, 1966.
“Climbing Jacob's Ladder.” In *Timothy Leary: Outside Looking In*, edited by Robert Forte, 223–224. Rochester: Park Street Press, 1999.
“Zalman Schachter-Shalomi: Transcending Religious Boundaries.” In *Higher Wisdom: Eminent Elders Explore the Continuing Impact of Psychedelics*, edited by Roger Walsh and Charles S. Grob, 195–205. Albany: State University of New York Press, 2005.
My Life in Jewish Renewal: A Memoir. Lanham: Rowman and Littlefield, 2012.
Scholem, Gershom. *On the Mystical Shape of the Godhead: Basic Concepts in the Kabbalah.* New York: Schocken Books, 1991.
Major Trends in Jewish Mysticism. New York: Schocken Books, 1995.
On the Kabbalah and Its Symbolism. New York: Schocken Books, 1996.
Siegel, Richard, Michael Strassfeld, and Sharon Strassfeld, eds. *The Jewish Catalog.* Philadelphia: Jewish Publication Society of America, 1973.
“The State of Jewish Belief: A Symposium.” *Commentary,* August 1 1966, https://www.commentarymagazine.com/articles/the-state-of-jewish-belief/. Accessed September 25 2017.
Teinhardt, Joanna. “Neo-Hasids in the Land of Israel.” *Nova Religio: The Journal of Alternative and Emergent Religions* 13, no. 4 (May 2010): 22–42.
Versluis, Arthur. *Platonic Mysticism: Contemplative Science, Philosophy, Literature, and Art.* New York: State University of New York Press, 2017.
Weiss, Anthony. “Countercultural Spirit Lives at Iconic 1960s Havurah.” *Times of Israel,* August 9 2014.
Wertheimer, Jack. “The Turbulent Sixties.” In *The American Jewish Experience,* edited by Jonathan D. Sarna, 330–347. New York: Holmes and Meier, 1997.
Whitfield, Stephen J. *The Culture of the Cold War.* Baltimore: Johns Hopkins University Press, 1996.
Wiesel, Elie. Foreword to *Holy Brother: Inspiring Stories and Enchanted Tales about Rabbi Shlomo Carlebach,* by Yitta Halberstam Mandelbaum, xvii-xviii. Oxford: Jason Aronson, 2002.
Winston, Diane. “Participatory Judaism: A Look at the Jewish Renewal Movement and Its Attractiveness to Lots of People.” *Long Island Jewish World,* August-September 1993.
Zablocki, Benjamin. Foreword to *From Slogans to Mantras: Social Protest and Religious Conversion in the Late Vietnam War Era,* by Stephen A. Kent, xi-xiii. Syracuse: Syracuse University Press, 2001.
Zaehner, R. C. *Mysticism Sacred and Profane.* London: Oxford University Press, 1957.
Zen, Drugs and Mysticism. New York: Vintage Books, 1972.
Our Savage God: The Perverse Use of Eastern Thought. New York: Sheed and Ward, 1974.

Federico Dal Bo

Nihilism and Extremist Religious Education in Contemporary Israel

The King's Torah and its Discontents

Introduction[1]

A representation of non-Jews as enemies is offered in the recent, marginal, and controversial text *The King's Torah.*[2] This text of Rabbinic law was published in 2009 by two controversial figures: 1) the Israeli-born Rabbi Yosef Elitzur-Hershkowitz, later involved in a series of juridical procedures for encouraging attacks against Arabs, and 2) the Israeli-born Rabbi Yitzhak Shapira, at the time serving as the head of the *'Od Yosef Chay* – a rabbinic seminary, situated in the West Bank settlement of Yitzhar and directed by the American-born and Chabad-educated rabbi Yitzhak Ginsburgh, another very controversial figure associated with right-wing religious Zionism.

I will briefly examine the content of *The King's Torah* and its reception, both in English-speaking and Hebrew-speaking media, but I will especially address some aspects concerning the Jewish relationships with non-Jews.[3] More specifi-

1 I wish to thank Dr. George Wilkes (University of Edinburgh) and Dr. David Feuchtwanger (The Hebrew University of Jerusalem) for reading a first draft of this text and providing me with a lot of suggestions and criticism.

2 Rabbi Yitzhak Shapira – Rabbi Yosef Elitzur, *Torat ha-Melekh. Dinei Nefashot bein Yisrael le-Akum* (The King's Torah: Laws of Life and Death between Jews and Gentiles) (Jerusalem: HaMachon HaTorani she-al-yad Yeshivat 'Od Yosef Chai, 2009) (= here forth mentioned as KT). All translations are my own.

3 Academic scholarship on *The King's Torah* is relatively modest and mostly focuses on the assumption that the text would mainly justify the killing of non-Jewish individuals. See, for instance, Gerschom Gorenberg, *The Unmaking of Israel* (New York: HarperCollins, 2011), 122–123; Motti Inbari (*Messianic Religious Zionism Confronts Israeli Territorial Compromises*, Cambridge: Cambridge Univesity Press, 2012), 125; Ophir Yarden, "Recent Halakhic Discourse in Israel Encouraging Racism and Violence," in *Religious Stereotyping and Interreligious Relations*, ed. Jesper Svartvik et al. (New York: Palgrave McMillan, 2013), 207–220; Menachem Kellner, "And the Crooked Shall be Made Straight," in *Rethinking the Messianic Idea in Judaism*, ed. Michael L. Morgan et al. (Indiana: Indiana University Press, 2014), 110; Menachem Kellner, "We are not alone," in *Menachem Kellner. Jewish Universalism*, ed. Hava Tirosh-Samuelsohn et al. (Leiden-Boston: Brill, 2015), 111–112; Jonathan Garb *Yearning of the Soul. Psychological Thought in*

https://doi.org/10.1515/9783110545753-009

cally, I will argue that *The King's Torah* exacerbates some trends in Talmudic literature and overtly treats non-Jews as legally marginalized categories. Recent scholarship – especially the one particularly involved in gender studies – has proven that Talmudic literature distinguishes between a number of legal subjects that are progressively marginalized from enjoying full civil and ritual rights: a Jewish male, a Jewish woman, children, servants, non-Jewish individuals, and cattle. This hierarchy of beings can be deduced more or less directly by a number of early Jewish sources and shall mostly be treated in neutral terms. The hierarchy that is so established has the main purpose of describing degrees of obligation towards the Jewish Law – whose observance is at its highest point with Jewish males and at its lowest with "cattle," namely living creatures that obviously cannot represent a valid legal subject and therefore can only be the recipients of rights but not their actors.[4]

The King's Torah appears to interpret this hierarchy in a tendentious way. Accordingly, it accounts non-Jews as expendable victims in case of war – both in consequence of direct and indirect military action. It will be evident how this controversial text deals with highly sensitive topics and yet manifests the intention of examining them in alleged neutral language. For instance, it systematically refrains from contextualizing these issues in the present and from determining who the "enemies of Israel" – so frequently stigmatized – actually are. A careful analysis will show how *The King's Torah* relies on oversimplified, binary opposition between "the just ones" (*tzadiqim*) and "the wicked ones" (*resha'im*) that perfectly overlaps with the ethnic distinction between Jews and non-Jews and that consequently maintains the necessity of a discriminatory policy on account of theological-political presuppositions. When overtly imitating Rabbinic style and pouring a mass of classical Jewish sources, *The King's Torah* implicitly raises an important point: Jewish legal texts, its commentators, and the commentators on these commentators – or, in short, the "chain of Tradition" (*shalshelet ha-Qabbalah*) – are not exempt from holding strong theological-political assumptions and most of them may sound uunacceptable at the

---

Modern Kabbalah (Chicago: University of Chicago Press 2015), n. 24, 224; Jonathan Fine, *Political Violence in Judaism, Christianity, and Islam* (London: Rowman and Littlefield, 2015), 139–141; Eugene Korn, "Extra Sinagogam Salus Est?" in *Religious Perspectives on Religious Diversity*, ed. Robert McKim (Boston: Brill, 2016), 57–58; Aaron Huges, "The Articulation of Orthodoxy," in *The Routledge Handbook of Muslim-Jewish Relations*, ed. J. Meri (London: Routeldge, 2016), 90–91.

4 For a recent discussion on this matter, see Federico Dal Bo *Massekhet Keritot. Text, Translation, and Commentary* (Tübingen: Mohr Siebeck, 2013), 200–201; and Tal Ilan *Massekhet Hullin. Text, Translation, and Commentary* (Tübingen: Mohr Siebeck, 2017), 1–24.

present time. The fundamental ambiguity in *The King's Torah* consists in simultaneously reporting these classical sources as if there were only a tradition and yet implying that they might – or even should – be applied to the present context, hopefully impacting on the contemporary Jewish life in the State of Israel. The radical nature of this text exactly consists in this: a large number of classical Rabbinic sources are interpreted unilaterally in order to hold an extreme right-wing vision of Israeli society and therefore are mobilized against Jewish liberalism.

Yet a closer examination will show that the controversial nature of this text lays deeper – in its barely expressed assumptions on political life and culture. *The King's Torah* appears to treat Israel as a political and moral entity whose nature truly is "exceptional" – in the precise sense that its existence justifies a legal "state of exception" or its legal and moral prominence with respect of non-Jews. From this point of view, *The King's Torah* appears to treat both political life and culture in extreme reactionary terms – in a most specific sense: neither politics nor culture shall be subjected to changes in time but rather perpetually adhere to traditional Jewish expectations. I will also try to draw some consequences from these theological-political presuppositions, especially relying on two fundamental notions in contemporary political theory: Carl Schmitt's[5] controversial notion of the "friend-enemy" opposition and Giorgio Agamben's[6] notion of "bare life."

Language and Content of *The King's Torah*

The King's Torah appears at first as a dense Hebrew legal text that mostly deals with the Rabbinic "laws of war," without any apparent reference to the present times.[7]

---

5 Carl Schmitt (1888–1985) was a German jurist and political theorist, associated with National Socialism and yet well received by a number of contemporary Jewish philosophers like Walter Benjamin, Leo Strauss, Jacob Taubes, Jacques Derrida, Hannah Arendt, and Avital Ronell. Particularly prominent is his notion of "political theology" postulating that all significant concepts of the modern theory of the State are secularized theological concepts.

6 Giorgio Agamben (1942) is an Italian philosopher and political theorist, whose long work *Homo Sacer* ("sacred man") currently represents the most prominent and influential philosophical text at the present time.

7 For an examination of this topic, see, for instance George Wilkes, "Teaching about 'War in Jewish Law' to Non-Lawyers in a European University Context," *Jewish Law Association Studies*, XXVI (2016): 109–126; George Wilkes, "Peace and Conflict in the Jewish Tradition," in *Ashgate Research Companion on Religion and Conflict Resolutio*, ed. Lee Marsden (Ashgate Press: Farnham, 2012), 49–66; George Wilkes, "Religious War in the Works of Maimonides and the 'Maimo-

The language is quite terse and is typically arranged in a series of argumentative steps: a concise statement on the legal issue at stake; pertinent quotations from Jewish Hebrew and Aramaic sources; a reformulation in Modern Hebrew; a summary by means of charts and tables. The exclusive use of a large number of classical sources – scripture, legal and narrative commentaries on scripture, *midrashim*, the Mishnah, the Tosefta, the Yerushalmi Talmud, the Babylonian Talmud as well as Rabbinic authorities, from the *Rishonim* to the *Acharonim*, and occasionally some Kabbalistic notions – lends this text a reassuring, sophisticated air.[8] *The King's Torah* wants to present itself as a harmless, ordinary commentary on a number of Biblical and Rabbinic sources pertaining the act of killing in both wartime and peacetime, between Jews and non-Jews. This would at first lead to a relatively finite number of juridical cases: killing between Jews and Jews in peacetime, between Jews and non-Jews in peacetime, between non-Jews and non-Jews in peacetime, between Jews and Jews in wartime, between Jews and non-Jews in wartime, and between non-Jews and non-Jews in wartime.

Yet the theological-political dimension of this text is far more complex and relies on the articulated Biblical and Rabbinical distinction between Jewish and non-Jewish individuals. It should also be emphasized that *The King's Torah* em-

---

nideans': An idea and its transit across the medieval Mediterranean," in *Just Wars, Holy Wars, and Jihads: Christian, Jewish, Muslim Encounters and Exchanges*, ed. Sohail. Hashmi (Oxford: Oxford University Press, 2012), 146–64.

8 In a private conversation, Dr. Wilkes has drawn to my attention that any selection of classical – albeit authoritative – sources obviously implies a number of omissions. Interestingly enough, *The King's Torah* appears not to question the nature of the textual and hermeneutical limits that it poses. As far as its intellectual perimeter is marked by classical Rabbinic sources, it is still unclear whether *The King's Torah* intends to exert a sort of educational or charismatic effect on its readers, introducing a sort of typological reading of Jewish Law – that would be applicable in the abstract any time, also at the verge of Messianic times. The omission of Rabbinic sources that would insist on historical, legal, and cultural limits for the application of law is probably deliberate and goes beyond what would be considered "normative" in most national religious literature on the subject. In this respect, *The King's Torah* appears to imitate Hamas' use of *Sharīʿa* by omissions, selection of sources, and presumption of permission to use power with the alleged freedom to cause damage because of the just cause and so on. For instance, there is the deliberate omission of treating several passages from Tractate *Gittin* that well describe how the obligation of charity – or supporting those who cannot be assisted by the collective system – pertains both to a Jewish and non-Jewish government, as overtly maintained in the dictum: "Our Rabbis said: We support the gentile poor ones with the Jewish poor ones, visit their sick ones with the Jewish sick ones, and bury their dead ones with the Jewish dead ones, out of the way of peace" (bGit 61a). On similar topics, see: Dan Avnon, and David Feuchtwanger, eds., *Mizug Ophakim. Mahshavah Medinat Yehudit Israelit* (Blending Hozirons. Jewish-Israeli Political Thought) (Jerusalem: Magnes Press, 2016).

ploys several terms for addressing non-Jewish individuals, relying both on Biblical and Rabbinical phraseology: "gentile" (*goy*), "son of Noah" (*ben Noach*), "resident alien" (*ger toshav*), "pious person from the people of the world" (*chasid humot ha-'olam*), and "idolater" (*'oved kokhavim*). The investigation of each of these terms obviously escapes the limits of the present chapter. Therefore, it should be sufficient to say that each of them describes a specific theological-political dimension that characterizes morally non-Jews with respect of Jews. Whereas the term "gentile" neutrally designates a specific "non-Jewish" individual, the terms "son of Noah," "resident alien," "pious person from the people of the world," and "idolater" clarify whether the aforementioned individual shares specific cultural features with Israel – namely the latter's monotheism and its associated Revelation – and therefore whether he is entitled to enjoy specific rights. More specifically, the terms "son of Noah" and "resident alien" designate a gentile who has accepted the authority of the Torah and, by implication, of the Rabbis; whereas the "son of Noah" officially accepts only the seven mandatory Noachide laws and becomes a "pious person from the people of the world," a "resident alien" does so in front of a Rabbinic court, possibly holds all the six hundred and thirteen commandments without formally converting to Judaism, and therefore enjoys specific rights in the Land of Israel. On the contrary, an "idolater" obviously is a gentile who neither follows the seven Noachide laws nor rejects idolatry all together, which thus qualifies him to be designated as a theological-political "enemy" (*oyev*) of Israel.

The King's Torah evidently pursues also a subtler goal than providing a complete casuistic of killing between Jews and non-Jews, both in war and peace. It implicitly aims to define the theological-political terms that would allow determining what specific killing is either forbidden or allowed and in so doing seeks to establish specific cultural and ethnic prerogatives. In other terms, the already sensitive topic – the nature of killing of non-Jews in war and peace – hides a sinister dimension: determining the theological-political prominence of Israel over the gentiles. At first, it seems that this prominence is justified only by means of classical Jewish sources that the author abundantly quotes: Rabbinic commentaries on scripture, the Mishnah, the Tosefta, the Yerushalmi Talmud, the Babylonian Talmud, Maimonides, and many traditional orthodox commentators on the Talmud. Yet it actually relies on a number of reactionary assumptions on the nature of war, political relationships between Jews and non-Jews, culture and, by implication, on democracy. These assumptions are particularly clear when examining the general structure of *The King's Torah*.

As anticipated, the main issue focuses on the act of killing non-Jews in both wartime and peacetime (KT 17). This issue is examined in a terse legal language and is addressed in five chapters that deal with a number of complementary issues.

The first chapter ("The prohibition of killing a gentile") (KT 17–48) addresses the prohibition of murdering a non-Jew who has not transgressed the seven Noachide laws. *The King's Torah* maintains that the Biblical commandment "you shall not murder" and the Rabbinical commandment "you shall not shed blood" impose the same prohibition not to murder – that is to say, killing outside a legally justified context – but address ethnically different legal subjects: Jews and non-Jews, respectively. Whereas the Rabbinical commandment "you shall not shed blood" addresses the relationships among non-Jews, the Biblical commandment "you shall not murder" exclusively prescribes that a Jew is forbidden to murder a fellow Jew, as maintained according to a restrictive interpretation. As examined further, it is a matter of disputation in Talmudic literature whether the prohibition of murder as expressed in Ex 20:13 equally pertains to Jews and gentiles. Most of the Rabbinic responses argue that the negative commandment ("you shall not kill") prohibits the murder of both a Jew and a gentile, whereas Maimonides argues that the murder of a gentile is not explicitly included and therefore subsidiary. The issue is simultaneously juridical and theological-political, as it involves the ethnic perimeter of scripture: do its commandments include or exclude non-Jews? Arguing that scripture inherently pertains to Jews, the *King's Torah* would argue that its commandment mostly pertains to Jews. Therefore, strictly speaking, a Jew would be forbidden to murder a fellow Jew out of a Biblical prescription and would be forbidden to murder – namely, "shred the blood of" – a gentile only by implication, as maintained also by the Tosafists (Tosfot on bAvZar 26b). The "legal reasoning" (*sevara*) would run as follows: just as a gentile is forbidden to murder a fellow gentile, so has Israel commanded the same prohibition not to kill a gentile who has not made any transgression – out of the theological-political assumption that the seven Noachide laws are not overwritten but rather supplemented or "completed" by Sinaitic Revelation (KT 18–22), bypassing the option of interpreting them, for instance, in terms of natural law.[9] It is important to emphasize the supplementary nature of this prohibition, since it posits a specific asymmetry between Jews and non-Jews. On the basis of a Talmudic source (bSanh 69a), *The King's Torah* maintains that any regulation transmitted before the Sinaitic Revelation and not stat-

9 Dr. George Wilkes was kind enough to bring to my attention how Talmudic commentators have usually refrained from relating Noachide and Sinaitic laws in terms of a developed natural theory, as they have preferred to be engaged with the idea that they are divine commandments whose rationale fully depends on an implicit theodicy: the commandments are right because they are commended by God who is the supreme Good and so on.

ed again after the Sinaitic Revelation shall pertain exclusively to Israel but not the gentiles (KT 28), whereas any prohibition commanded to a gentile will also pertain to a Jew – such as the prohibition of murdering a gentile who has not transgressed any of the seven Noachide laws (KT 32). This asymmetrical treatment clearly shows how central Jewish Revelation is in determining the theological-political relationships between Jews and non-Jews: the Sinaitic Revelation is simultaneously accounted as a "completion" of the seven Noachide laws and yet as an exclusive privilege for the Jewish people. This apparent asymmetry will have important consequences when treating the case of killing non-Jews in wartime, as evidenced further.

The second chapter ("Killing a gentile who has transgressed the Noachide laws") (KT 49–87) addresses the issue of whether a gentile or a Jew is liable to execute a gentile who has committed a crime punishable by death sentence. Whether one enjoys this liability or not is determined by a tortuous examination of several juridical sources and especially of two apparently contradicting Rabbinic injunctions, discussed in two different Talmudic tractates, that respectively prescribe, in metaphorical terms, that a gentile shall or shall not be sentenced to death by Jewish authorities, in case that he has transgressed one of the seven Noachide laws: "do not raise a gentile" (bAZ 26a-b) and "do not to let a gentile go down" (bSanh 67b). *The King's Torah* examines at first four classical solutions: Maimonides argues that the first injunction refers to a case of a gentile known to the Jewish court, whereas the second one refers to a gentile who obviously is a foreigner (Rambam on bMakk 9a) (KT 57); Ritva[10] simply argues that a Jewish is entitled to sentence a gentile transgressor to death (Rivta on bMakk 9a) (KT 58–59); Rabbenu Yonah[11] argues that scripture would allow a Jewish court to sentence a gentile transgressor to death but the Rabbis have overruled this and assumed that it is forbidden (Yonah on bSanh 57a) (KT 62); finally, *Hagahot ha-Bach*[12] and Taz[13] argue that a Jewish court would be liable to sentence a gentile transgressor only indirectly (Hagahot ha-Bach and Taz on bSanh 57a). After reviewing these options, *The King's Torah* solomonically concludes that a Jewish court is only liable and yet not commended to sentence a gentile to death if he has transgressed a Noachide law (KT 66). More specifically,

10 Yom Tov ben Abraham Asevilli (1260–1320) was a Spanish commentator on the Talmud.
11 Rabbenu Yonah ben Abraham Girondi (d. 1263) was a Catalan commentator on the Talmud.
12 Rabbi Yoel ben Samuel Sirkis (1561–1640) was a Polish commentator on the Talmud, known after his textual emendations *Hagahot ha-Bach* ("Glosses of the Bach").
13 Rabbi David ha-Levi Segal (1586–1667) was a Polish commentator on the Talmud, known after the first letters of his main work *Turey Zahav* ("Rows of Gold"), a commentary on Joseph Caro's *Shulchan Arukh*.

the case is emblematically examined while distinguishing between an ordinary "gentile" (*goy*) and a "resident alien" (*ger toshav*), the former being exempted from following the Noachide laws and the latter acknowledging both scripture and the Rabbinic authority. As an ordinary gentile is unaware of the Noachide laws and therefore can be judged by a Jewish court who appears to know him, as prescribed by Maimonides, a "resident alien" can be condemned only for a "just reason" (KT 75) if a Jewish court has effortlessly tried to make him "repent" for his deeds (KT 80). Only when no redemption has proven to be possible shall a Jewish court then be entitled to judge him and possibly sentence him to death (KT 81). The importance of this theological-political setting – clearly resonating with the conclusions of the first chapter – cannot be overlooked. In the opinion of *The King's Torah*, the Sinaitic Revelation attributes to Israel specific ethnic and theological prerogatives: on the one hand, Israel shall keep apart from these "unknown" gentiles who appear neither to follow the seven Noachide laws nor acknowledge the Rabbis' authority; on the other hand, it shall use its moral and theological authority over those gentiles who are "known" and live as "resident aliens," for the sake of justice and not out of some vantage. It should also be emphasized that this need for both separateness and assimilation reflect the same exclusivist logic anticipated earlier – Israel only has been entitled to receive the Sinaitic Revelation that includes and fulfils the Noachide one – without necessarily involving a sort of Messianic exception. *The King's Torah* can rely on them as foundations for a political theology, emphasizing their authority at the costs of neglecting the fact that they had distinctively medieval assumptions about the use of power.

The third chapter ("Martyrdom instead of murdering among the sSons of Noah") (KT 88–155) addresses the issue whether a human being may kill another human being in order to save his life under duress. This issue – clearly anticipating the later question about the Rabbinic "laws of war" – is analyzed in the form of a specific threat: "if you do not kill so-and-so, I will kill you." This specific legal case is examined from two points of view: from a Jewish and gentile perspective. At first, *The King's Torah* objects at first that a Jewish individual under duress is forbidden to kill another fellow Jew in order to save his own life. This ruling is based on the traditional assumption that a Jew is allowed to transgress scripture in favor of his life, unless he is asked to reject three fundamental principles – monotheism, incest, and murder. Yet this ruling pertains to Jews only and exempts the gentiles who then may kill a fellow gentile under duress in order to save their lives, although this principle cannot be extend to a third party – killing a second person in order to save a third one (KT 79–80). At this point, *The King's Torah* mentions two other alternative rulings from the Yerushalmi Talmud (yAZ 2:2) that seem to posit some difficulties. On the one hand, the Yerushalmi Talmud assumes that it is punishable by death sentence to kill under duress a fellow from the same social group – namely, a Jew killing a Jew or a gentile killing a gentile. On the other hand, it posits the notable exception that a Jew killing under duress a gentile shall neither be allowed nor punished to do so but rather be "exempted" (*patur*) from any form of punishment (KT 82). *The King's Torah* tries to harmonize the contradiction assuming that the Yerushalmi Talmud rules against any indirect form of killing that might involve unnecessary pain or suffering and therefore would escape the immediacy of duress, formally similar to a case of self-defense (KT 83). While reviewing Jewish medieval authorities on the matter, *The King's Torah* concludes by emphasizing two opposite rulings on the question of whether a gentile may kill a gentile under duress in order to save his life: on the one hand, Maharsha maintains that a gentile is exempted from being punished if he kills a fellow gentile under duress to save his life, as he is not commanded to sacrifice his life, as Jews on the contrary are; on the other hand, *Parashat Derakhim*[14] assumes that gentiles too are commanded to sacrifice their own lives when asked to kill a fellow gentile, as stated by the Rabbis on account of "legal reasoning" (*sevara*) (KT 116–117).

The fourth chapter ("Jewish life in front of gentile life") (KT 156–180) elaborates on the previous considerations, especially emphasizing the theological-political prominence of a Jew with respect of a gentile. While expanding on the aforementioned ruling from the Yerushalmi Talmud (yAZ 2:2), *The King's Torah* clearly assumes that the obligation of martyrdom strictly speaking pertains only to cases involving social and ethnic equality – namely, when a Jew is asked to kill a fellow Jew or when a gentile is asked to kill a fellow gentile, as prescribed in a number of sources (bSan 64a, bYom 72b, bPes 25b). Yet a case of social and ethnic inequality – and especially in the specific case when a Jew is asked to kill a gentile – requires a different ruling, especially under the "reactionary" assumption that neither historical nor social changes shall interfere in the reception of a given tradition. In the present case, *The King's Torah* never questions the given binary distinction between Jews and non-Jews but rather reinforces it by unequivocally adhering to another passage from the Yerushalmi Talmud – which allows a Jew under duress to kill a gentile in order to save his own life (yShab 14, end) (KT 157). Regardless of the possible historical reasons why the Yerushalmi Talmud might have ruled in these terms and what its possible social significance might have been, *The King's Torah* holds firmly

14 Rabbi Yudah ben Samuel Rosanes (1657–1727) was a prominent Talmud scholar from Constantinople, who wrote *Parashat Derakhim* ("On a Crossroad"), a non-legal text on various subjects.

a point: Jewish life is prominent over gentile life. Accordingly, it elaborates against the intrinsic "correlation" (*abizrayihu*) between the two aforementioned commandments – "you shall not murder" and "you shall shed blood" – and maintains that they rather refer to two socially and ethnically different legal subjects: Jews and non-Jews, respectively (KT 158). This is a crucial point in the discussion, especially for its relevance in the later discussion on the Rabbinic "laws of war": Jewish life is sorted not only with respect of gentile life but especially with respect of a "resident alien" who has accepted both scripture and the Rabbis' authority. The complex argumentation relies on a number of sources – Rashi, Rambam, and especially *Pery Megadim* ruling on bSanh 64a, bPes 25b e bYom 72b and correlated issues – that restrict the obligation of martyrdom instead of murdering exclusively to the ethnically equal case of a Jew who is asked to kill a fellow Jew (KT 158–159). The justification for excluding the "resident alien" from the obligation of martyrdom and therefore allowing his killing under duress in order to save his own life relies on a theological-political presupposition: Israel – God's chosen people – have prominence over Shabbat, whereas "resident aliens" do not, with the clear implication that Israel has prominence over any "resident alien". More specifically, whereas the Shabbat can be profaned in order to save a Jewish life, it has to be kept holy at the possible costs of non-Jewish lives, as prescribed in a Talmudic passage (bSanh 58b); as a consequence, it would be liable to expend the life of a "resident alien" in the specific case when a Jew is asked either to kill or suffer martyrdom under duress (KT 161).

The fifth chapter ("Killing gentiles in war") (KT 181–207) applies most of the previous rulings – especially the prominence of Jewish lives over non-Jewish lives and the Jewish liability of killing a non-Jew under duress – to the unfortunate case of war. The permission of killing in war and therefore its impossibility of being assimilated to murder are elaborated on a series of legal presuppositions that allow overruling the prohibition of murdering that equally pertains gentiles with respect of gentiles and Jews with respect of Jews (KT 181). Just as the prohibition of murdering between gentiles, as stipulated with the seven Noachide laws, predates the prohibition of murdering between Jews, as restated with the Sinaitic Revelation, so is Israel's permission of waging war elaborated on the gentiles' liability of killing other gentiles for the sake of their own life (KT 181). Given everyone's natural right to self-defense, *The King's Torah* does not examine the actual, anthropological, economical, and cultural reasons of war but rigidly reduces them to a binary contrast between the assaulting and the defending party – implicitly assuming that the former are "wicked" and the latter are "righteous." On account of these stiff moral and theological presuppositions, *The King's Torah* distinguishes between five different juridical cases: the "persecutor" (*rodef*) who actively wages war; the "persecutor" who incites to shed blood;[15] various transgressors of the seven Noachide laws; whoever supports a "persecutor," even under duress; and killing gentiles in war. At first, when examining the case of a "persecutor," *The King's Torah* treats the case of a Jew persecuting another Jew (KT 181–183). On the basis of multiple sources (Gen 34:25, Or ha-Hayym on Gen 34:25 and Maimonides, *Mishneh Torah*, Hilkhot Huval 10–11), *The King's Torah* rules that a "persecutor" may be killed in war even if he is "little" (*qatan*) – including "infants" (KT 199) – and if he is likely to posit a future threat (KT 182–183). The rationale for waging anticipatory war against legal subjects that do not still posit a danger is elaborated on a series of legal and philosophical presuppositions (KT 186–188). At first, it is admissible to defend himself from whoever "is going to" become a "persecutor," arguing that there is only a formal difference between actually and potentially being a threat (bAZ 10b; Tosfot on bAZ 10b; Caro, *Shulchan Arukh* 388:11) and more specifically assuming that if a gentile can kill someone who might put a danger to his own life, all the more can a Jew do so (Responsa, *Yad Eliahu* 38). Moreover, whoever intends to wage war has already intended to "shed blood" and therefore is potentially transgressing one of the seven Noachide laws – which is punishable by death and thus susceptible to be prevented from doing that by an anticipatory act of war (KT 192–193). This principle is formally justified by the assumption that Israel may be entitled to be both witness and judge of the crime of "shedding blood," as elaborated in the previous chapters.

The sixth chapter ("Intentional Injury to Innocent People") (KT 208–237) specifically addresses the issue of collateral victims – namely, individuals who cannot be ascribed to the legal category of "persecutors" and yet shall be involved in military actions and so susceptible to die (KT 209). The rationale for admitting the killing of gentiles who are neither active nor willing to wage war against Israel is justified on account of a controversial sentence from an extracanonical Talmudic text, quoted also in Maimonides, stating the liability of killing anyone in wartime in order to save his own life: "the best among the gentiles in wartime shall be killed" (bSof 15:7). *The King's Torah* seems unaware that this sentence originally stems from an early Hebrew (Tannaitic) commentary on Exodus and exhibits important variants in later Talmudic literature. *The King's Torah* is concerned neither with the issue of establishing the origin of this sentence in textual-historiographical terms nor with the issue of determining wheth-

15 On the Talmudic notion of "persecutor" from a theological-political point of view, see also Federico Dal Bo, "Du solltest dich verfolgen lassen. Eine theologisch-politische Auslegung vom Talmudischen Traktat Baba Kamma 93," in *Täter und Opfer. Verbrechen und Stigma im europäisch-jüdischen Kontext*, ed. Claudia S. Dorchain et al. (Würzburg: Verlag Königshausen & Neumann, 2014), 69–95.

er extracanonical Talmudic should be as authoritative as the canonical ones.[16] On the contrary, *The King's Torah* reads this sentence in a literal sense and assumes that any non-Jew – regardless of his moral commitment, adhesion to scripture, or activity in wartime – is susceptible of being killed, either directly or indirectly. More specifically, *The King's Torah* argues that a Jew in wartime is liable of killing even those gentiles who are actually taking part in war or are susceptible – by culture, education, and social context – to posit a future threat (KT 201–202). While elaborating on some passages from scripture and medieval commentaries thereon (Ex 14:7; Rashi on Ex 14:7; *Sefer Tzidah la-derekh* on Ex 14:7; 1 Sam 27:8–11; Radaq on 1 Cr 22:8), *The King's Torah* then concludes that those gentiles who are still underage and therefore considered legally unfit to take responsible decisions are yet to be considered liable targets in an anticipatory war. As sustained on the basis of other supplementary sources (bAZ 26a; Is. 14:21; Radaq on Is 14:21; Rashi on Is 14:21; Targ. Yonatan 14:21), *The King's Torah* assumes that those still "innocent" subjects will inevitably take the side of their "wicked" parents, once that they have grown up, as they will have been manipulated and persuaded by propaganda – namely by "persecutors" who incite to shed blood – to do so (KT 205–206 and 215).

---

16 In the present case, it is impossible to exhaustively determine the origin and dissemination of this sentence. Most obviously, it stems from a dictum from the *Mekhilta:* "the best among the gentiles shall be killed" (*ha-tov she-be-goyim harog*) (*Mekhilta*, Be-shalach, 2, on Ex. 14:7). This latter reading appears to omit the circumstance of war, only because this is implicit from the context (Ex. 14:5–7). This dictum is epigrammatically attributed to Rabbi Shimon bar Yochay and intends to state a truism in the context of war: everyone is liable to kill any enemy soldier – regardless of his moral qualities – for the sake of saving his own life. This sentence is transmitted in the name of Rabbi Shimon bar Yochay, with some lexical differences, also in the extracanonical Talmudic tractate *Soferim:* "the most fit among the gentiles in time of war shall be killed" (*ha-kasher she-be-goyim be-sha'at milchamah harog*) (bSof 15:7). It should be emphasized that *The King's Torah* reports a third variant, obviously depending on Maimonides' *Mishneh Torah* (Hilchot Rotzeach 2:11): "the best among the gentiles in time of war shall be killed" (*ha-tov she-be-goyim be-sha'at milchamah harog*). While elaborating on Maimonides rather than on the Talmud itself, it should be clear that *The King's Torah* is implicitly relying on a Rabbinic authority – Maimonides – rather than supplementing canonical Talmudic tractates with extracanonical ones. It should also be noted that *The King's Torah*'s insistence on Maimonides as an authoritative source appears to be beyond the ordinary acknowledgment of his importance in Judaism. The distinct use of Maimonides together with Talmudic sources seems to suggest that the Chabad-educated authors of *The King's Torah* tend to see him as divinely inspired, in a way that exceeds the normal traditional leading scholars. This possibly resembles the Kahanist doctrine – whose supporter also is Rabbi Dov Lior who praised the publication of *The King's Torah* (Yarden, "*Recent Halakhic Discourse*," 223).

The Reception of *The King's Torah* and its Theological-Political Tone

The King's Torah had expectedly a strong impact on public opinion, both in the Middle East and in Europe. Despite its terse language, its exclusive reference to Jewish classical sources, and its ostensive neutral language, *The King's Torah* has drawn the attention of some popular Hebrew-speaking and English-speaking Israeli newspapers.

The Israeli reporter Roi Sharon of Channel 10 has stigmatized *The King's Torah* as a "complete guide to killing non-Jews" in a detailed Hebrew article in the prominent popular newspaper *Ma'ariv*.[17] In resonance with this article, the Israeli member of the parliament from the Labor Party Ophir Pines-Paz also called on the attorney general to open a criminal investigation on the book. In addition to this, a coalition of moderate religious Zionists "The Twelfth of Heshvan" – called after the date when the Israeli Prime Minister Isaac Rabin was assassinated in 1996 – took public action against *The King's Torah* and petitioned the High Court to confiscate the book and arrest its authors Rabbis Yosef Elitzur and Yitzhak Shapira for incitement. A few months later, the journalist Matthew Wagner from the *Jerusalem Post* admitted that *The King's Torah* appeared not to refer to any actual historical condition but emphasized that it would provide "a reason to kill babies [on the enemy side] even if they have not transgressed the seven Noachide Laws because of the future danger they may present, since it is assumed that they will grow up to be evil like their parents."[18] More recently, the Israeli historian and scholar Yehudah Bauer has reviewed *The King's Torah* and called it as a "a danger to the Jewish people," as it would intend to "impose radical interpretations to all Jewish believers," specifically assuming that Jews are intrinsically superior to non-Jews and therefore enjoy the right of prominence both in context of wartime and peacetime.[19]

Despite these early negative reviews, *The King's Torah* exhibits a more ambiguous nature, both in language and content. At a very formal level, this text ostensibly imitates the language of the classical Jewish sources from which it abundantly quotes, carefully refrains from referring to the present time, and insists to appear as a theoretical if not antiquate text. As a general impression, a

---

17 Roi Sharon, "The Complete Guide to Killing non-Jews," *Ma'ariv*, November 9 2009, 2.

18 Michael Wagner, "Shapira's distinction between Jewish, gentile blood," *Jerusalem Post*, February 2 2010, https://www.jpost.com/Israel-News?id=167475.

19 Yoel Bauer, "The Racist Teaching of the Extreme Right. *Ma'ariv*, March 11 2011. https://www.makorrishon.co.il/nrg/online/1/ART2/220/777.html.

reader could even argue that this text was written centuries ago – exactly at the time when these classical Jewish authors had written their commentaries and legal texts. The overwhelming use of classical Jewish sources appears to saturate the text and its legal reasoning, especially when treating the most controversial issues. As a consequence, one could simplistically argue that *The King's Torah* intends only to provide an academic investigation on classical Jewish texts that already treat a quite sensitive topic – killing gentiles in both wartime and peacetime. One should also raise the objection that most of the outrageous statements in *The King's Torah* have actually been derived without great effort from classical Jewish legal texts; therefore, one could also argue that Jewish tradition – or that containing these texts – already exhibits a controversial, possibly extremist nature, especially with respect of contemporary scholarly etiquette. This would then raise another important issue. As far as one could argue that the choice of systematically adhering to the style of Rabbinic Hebrew implicitly serves the purpose of taming most of the controversial rulings, a more problematic dimension shall be taken into account: the authors of the *King's Torah* obviously believe that they are uncovering a deeper reality, applicable at all time, in force of a shift from theological-political to practical. As consequence, the decisive question – that the *King's Torah* omits to address directly – would then be who would have the authority to determine this switch.

Yet one should refrain from concluding this from taking into account, for instance, the legal vicissitudes of the author of *The King's Torah.* It is unquestionable that Rabbi Yitzhak Shapira had been investigated for promoting illegal actions against Arabs in the West Bank and it is obvious that he hardly appears to be a supporter of Jewish-Arab peaceful relationships.[20] Nevertheless, the question of *The King's Torah* shall not be examined *ad hominem* – on an individual basis. As far as Shapira's political opinions may eloquently be clear, *The King's Torah* still exhibits a terse, neutral language and its most controversial assumptions appear to rely on a number of classical Jewish sources. Therefore, it is necessary to address the general theological-political tone that supports this text and subject it to critical analysis.

The King's Torah is a strongly reactionary text. The deeper sense of imitating Rabbinic language and pouring a mass of Jewish sources into the text goes far beyond the most superficial purpose of seeking hermeneutical support by means of Jewish tradition. *The King's Torah* wants to draw its epistemological pe-

20 Rabbi Elitzur-Hershkowitz was suspected of racial incitement and arrested in 2010 by Israeli police, as reported by Lappin. See Yaakov Lappin, "Yizhar Rabbi Detained by Police," *The Jerusalem Post*, August 19 2010, https://www.jpost.com/Israel/Yitzhar-rabbi-detained-by-police.

rimeter exclusively within the boundaries of Jewish Orthodoxy with a clear purpose – projecting itself in a traditional past that requires neither public sphere nor democracy. The relatively marginal importance of some statements on innocent and infant victims in cases of war should not be overemphasized; they are in fact disturbing but secondary, as they depend on a much more sinister, yet pervasive metaphor. Just as the title *The King's Torah* overtly claims, the entire text is built on a main metaphor: there is a "king" (*melekh*) who enjoys the right of giving and taking life, both in wartime and peacetime. The text insists in simplifying any form of governance to a single formal model – "kingdom" (*malkhut*). Fundamental issues – such as the anthropological, economical, and cultural conflicts between powers, states, and ethnicities – are completely neglected and ignored. The only positive model is to be found in an abstract and timeless "kingdom" that provides the sole and unique parameter for determining political life, clearly resonating with a number of Rabbinic expectations that attribute only to God the ability of reigning over His own people.[21] Both Jews and gentiles are assumed to belong to potentially conflicting "kingdoms" that would eventually fight for a theological-political supremacy. In describing political life in such extremely abstract terms, *The King's Torah* manifests then a number of reactionary assumptions: those gentiles who are not "resident aliens" appear to be associated in a "kingdom" that is either "wicked" or "atheistic," posing an immediate threat to the Jews – who are obviously associated with a "righteous" kingdom.

The King's Torah justifies this stereotypical distinction among ethnicities especially under the assumption that Jews enjoy the supreme divine Revelation that bounds them to a series of commandments overlapping – but not substituting – God's moral laws, previously delivered to the "sons of Noah." Yet the presupposition that the "king" (*melekh*) is entitled to lead his own policy – sinisterly enjoying the right over life and death, in resonance with the Roman principle of *ius vitae necisque* – is strictly maintained on the account that Scripture is a true positive reality whose ontological prominence cannot be put into question. On the contrary, it is an unquestioned faith in the divine Revelation that orients

21 Dr. Feuchtwanger was kindly brought to my attention that the notion of "kingdom" might not refer to a specific form of government – monarchy – but rather resonate with the biblical assumption that God is the king (Ps 47:8) and then conform to a number of Kabbalistic metaphors employed in the text. As evidenced further, *The King's Torah* usually manifests some ambiguity with respect of a number of theological issues. In the present case, it should also be emphasized that this text addresses the institution of Biblical monarchy – either as an abstraction or practical case – but neglects the subtle polemics in Scripture between those who support and those who oppose the institution of an Israeli kingdom.

the deepest course of *The King's Torah.* More specifically, the prominence of Jewish life over gentile life – as blatantly exemplified in the ruling that exempts Jews from punishment if targeting innocent gentile victims in case of war – is structurally built on the dialectics between Rabbinic Law and Noachide laws. *The King's Torah* states more than once that the preservation of Jewish life might involve the desecration of Shabbat, whereas a gentile life cannot. This would prove that the rationale for preferring Jewish lives to non-Jewish lives is both ethnic and theological-political. This is well proven by examining the case of a "resident alien," whose life can be expended in favor of Shabbat, since the divine commandments cannot be "abolished" for his sake (KT 167). Although a "resident alien" (*ger toshav*) leads his life by the Biblical commandments, enjoying then a number of civil rights usually ascribed only to Jews, his life would still be expendable in some critical situations, exactly because he is not a "proselyte" (*ger*) and therefore does not fully belong to the Jewish people.

The way in which *The King's Torah* affirms the prominence of Jewish lives over non-Jewish lives is the strongest issue a modern democratic reader has to be confronted with. Critical theory has to face the challenge of addressing the implications of this text, without expecting that it would be sufficient to claim the need of public sphere and democracy. On the contrary, ethnic and theological privileges in *The King's Torah* have to be rebutted in a more complex way, possibly deconstructing its very theological-political presuppositions – avoiding both to oversimplify its main thesis and to abstractly appeal to democratic values. As far as it is disturbing, *The King's Torah* is neither a simple nor linear text. In truth, it builds on such a large number of Jewish classical sources that one cannot think of dismissing its most extreme assumptions without truly asking about the theological-political nature of Jewish tradition – or, at least, of a part of it.

A subtler reading requires an innovative approach from critical theory that addresses the theological-political attitude both of *The King's Torah* and its classical Jewish sources. There is no doubt that *The King's Torah* is controversial but it cannot be denied that it exhibits a neutral when not erudite nature. Only through a critical reading does this text provide a straightforward, undigested insight into the right-wing Israeli ideology and, by implication, into the right-wing Israeli policy in the West Bank that implies an agreed policy or ideology that neglects the current opposition between religious and secularist realities. When carefully examined, this text appears to hold a quite nihilistic view on culture and therefore on religious education in contemporary Israel. Dismissing this text as a "complete guide to killing non-Jews" is indeed counterproductive, as its content would dangerously be trivialized. Paradoxically enough, *The King's Torah* would appear to be only an "extremist manifesto," which would have the main, blatant purpose to allow the killing of innocent victims during wartime. The dangerous nature of this text relies on its ability of misreading, radicalizing, and manipulating sources from Jewish tradition – whose original bio-political setting is completely neglected and ignored. On the contrary, a critical reading of *The King's Torah* truly begins with examining the sources from Jewish tradition and asking about their either implicit or explicit political theology.

A Bio-Political Look into *The King's Torah* and its Sources

The King's Torah exhibits a tendentious way of reading Jewish classical sources. This is especially clear when examining how it supports most of its controversial statements – especially those ruling that Jewish lives have prominence over non-Jewish lives – by means of Jewish tradition. As anticipated above, *The King's Torah* abundantly refers to Jewish tradition and for each of its statements it provides an accurate selection from Biblical and Rabbinic sources – scripture, legal and narrative commentaries on scripture, *midrashim*, the Mishnah, the Tosefta, the Yerushalmi Talmud, the Babylonian Talmud as well as Rabbinic authorities, from the *Rishonim* to the *Acharonim*.

It is particularly relevant to note that *The King's Torah* largely refers to the two most authoritative Jewish legal compendia: Maimonides' *Repetition of the Torah* and the famous *The Set Table*, written by the Talmudist and Kabbalist Rabbi Joseph Caro.[22] In so doing, *The King's Torah* tries to present its controversial statements as an obvious, consequent reading from these classical sources. It cannot be emphasized enough how legal compendia play a major role in the eyes of *The King's Torah*, especially with respect of the ruling about Jewish lives *vis-à-vis* non-Jewish lives. For instance, it is a sparse sentence from Maimonides' *Repetition of Torah* that allows *The King's Torah* to inconvertibly assume that a Jew may kill a "persecutor," even if he is "little" (*qatan*), considering that he would possibly posit a future threat (KT 182–183). Similarly, *The King's Torah* is able to maintain the prominence of Jewish life over non-Jewish life with the support of two converging sources: Joseph Caro's *The Set Table* and more specifically its eighteenth century supercommentary *Pery Megadim*, written by the Galician Rabbi Joseph ben Meir Teomim (KT 158–159).

---

22 Joseph ben Ephraism Caro (1488–1575) was a Spanish commentator on the Talmud, and author of the prominent Talmudic compendium *Sulchan Arukh*.

The question of how *The King's Torah* has drawn controversial statements from Rabbinic literature and some of its most famous figures – Maimonides and Joseph Caro – is both hermeneutical and theological-political. On the one hand, the aforementioned legal compendia appear to support a series of discriminatory measures with respect of non-Jews. On the other hand, *The King's Torah* appears to elaborate a "complete guide to killing non-Jews" only under a number of theological-political presuppositions that essentially rely on a literal, fundamentalist reading of Jewish sources. It is especially in this latter respect that *The King's Torah* appears to be a dangerous text: it implicitly disqualifies any hermeneutics that would discuss, in theoretical-critical terms, any assumptions from Jewish tradition. It is unquestionable that both Maimonides and Joseph Caro have literally claimed that any "persecutor" may be killed, even if "little," or that Jewish lives obviously enjoy prominence with respect of non-Jewish lives. Yet the decisive point is that *The King's Torah* appears to fail to appreciate both the complex nature of these texts and especially their implicit expectations in front of their troubled historical setting. As far as some passages might support forms of discrimination against gentiles, both Maimonides and Joseph Caro had redacted their legal compendia with a specific purpose: upholding the inner consistency of Jewish communities with respect of the outer Islamic world and, by analogy, the outer Christian world.[23]

Yet such consistency required Jewish awareness, both of its legal and cultural importance. On the one hand, Maimonides' and Joseph Caro's commentaries were extensively built on the Babylonian Talmud, which was already restrictive with respect of non-Jewish populations, and aimed to offer an almost definitive set of rules to be followed. In so doing, they intended to bypass the extenuating steps of Rabbinic argumentation, as some prominent Rabbis critics of Maimonides and Joseph Caro would frequently object. On the other hand, Maimonides and Joseph Caro had also to exalt Jewish culture and found a powerful way in introducing in their texts the idea that any legal controversy between Jews and non-Jews should ideally be normed according to Jewish Law, regardless of the actual historical and social setting. This supposition obviously contrasted with the social realities of Jewish communities living both under Christian and Muslim denomination between the thirteenth and the sixteenth centuries, when Maimonides' and Caro's compendia were redacted. It is then evident that the claim to resolve any controversy between Jews and non-Jews exclusively

23 See the excellent article on which I elaborate in the next number of pages: Hans-Georg von Mutius, "The Positions of Jews and Nonjews in the Rabbinic Law of Overreaching (Ona'ah)," in *The Three Religions*, ed. Nil Cohen et al. (Munich: Herbert Utz Verlag, 2002), 49–58.

on the basis of Jewish Law would be only a legal fiction that mirrored specific theological-political expectations – the dream of cultural, social, and political independence of the Jewish people. This theological-political dream had also culminated with the elaboration of a series of rulings that virtually completed some omissions in traditional Jewish Law – the laws on damages of chattels. Whereas Talmudic tradition was somehow inconclusive on this point, both Maimonides and Joseph Caro had worked on it and succeeded in offering a clear norm that would prescribe clear rules for reconciliation. Joseph Caro proposed a simple principle, built on ethnic opposition: if an ox belonging to a Jew gored an ox belonging to a non-Jew, the former would be exempted from compensating the latter; conversely, if an ox belonging to a non-Jew gored the ox belonging to a Jew, the former would have to pay full compensation to the latter (Caro, *Shulchan Arukh*, 139b). Joseph Caro had filled a gap in traditional Jewish Law and had especially concluded with a restrictive ruling that materialized a dream of social revenge: a gentile would be either entitled to pay for causing damage to Jewish property or declared unfit to ask for compensation when his property would be damaged by a Jew.

One should insist on the theological-political tone of this ruling. As far as it is not unlikely that the collision between chattels belonging to a Jew and a non-Jew might have represented an actual, possible case of conflict in rural pre-modern societies, it is quite obvious that the urge of completing – when not supplementing – Talmudic laws on this point had served also another purpose: using some abstruse ruling on an ox goring another ox as would offer an opportunity for introducing the assumption that gentiles would somehow have to be subjected to Jewish Law and possibly be disqualified from enjoying equal social rights. It should also be noted, as Leo Strauss would certainly do, that these legal compendia apparently exhibit two dimensions of meaning – a superficial, exoteric one and a deeper, esoteric one. Whoever is familiar with Talmudic phraseology cannot fail to note that metaphors from the natural and animal world are frequently used to describe legal relationships between humans. For instance, legal subjects who are either permanently or temporarily exempted from specific obligations might be compared to animals. This comparison is not necessarily derogatory and rather serves a double purpose: designating some specific individuals as living beings and yet exempting them from any form of legal obligation, since they shall permanently or temporarily be considered *as if* they were animals.

Yet these metaphors also convey a latent derogatory implication – specific human beings would be no better than animals and therefore exempted from enjoying specific rights. The use of animal metaphors in Talmudic literature typically suffers from an epistemological ambiguity: whether they shall be treated only as legal fictions or rather also as an implicit way of derogating specific gender, social, and ethnic groups. For instance, gender studies commentaries on Rabbinic literature have recently emphasized how metaphors from the animal world serve the purpose of establishing a fixed social-ontological hierarchy. More exactly, Rabbinic literature would provide not only a set of rules for ordinary life but also the vision of an ideal Jewish society, built around a gender-specific center and then progressively moving towards a sort of social periphery – namely, passing from the central figure of a heterosexual male Jewish individual to increasingly marginal figures, such as Jewish women, Jewish children, gentiles, and finally animals.[24] With respect of this, Rabbinic literature would constantly exhibit a latent conflict between two main attitudes – a legal and a theological-political one. It is then obvious that also Maimonides' and Joseph Caro's ruling on a very specific topic – the laws on damages of chattels – should also be considered as a way of addressing cultural, social, and political relationships between Jews and non-Jews. Accordingly, their treatment of damages involving oxen would actually imply an implicit ruling about the ethnicity of their respective owners, a Jew and a non-Jew.

The King's Torah appears to be receptive of the implications from Maimonides' and Joseph Caro's rulings on damages of chattels. It deals with this piece of legislation and clearly uses it to imply that there is a substantial difference between property rights of a Jew and a non-Jew according to the letter of Jewish Law. This reading is clearly tendentious, as it does not discriminate between traditional and historical interpretations of the text but rather conflates them into a single possible option – a fundamentalist reading of Jewish tradition. As far as Maimonides and Joseph Caro complete the Talmudic rulings on damages of chattels and mobilize animal metaphors from Jewish tradition, *The King's Torah* appears to conclude that non-Jews might be considered "animals" – at least in the sense that they are likely to be and act as brutes, incapable of morality and susceptible of waging aggressive wars. Their "wickedness" (*resha'ut*) exactly consists in waging a sort of "total war" against Israel, as it would be clear from their intention of mobilizing soldiers, propagandists, auxiliaries, civilians, and even infants for any military purpose. *The King's Torah* appears to ascribe to Israel the duty of fighting back its "enemies" (*oyevim*), under the assumption that the people of God would wage only defensive – if necessary anticipatory – military actions. The "brutality" of the enemies of Israel would then consist in their ruthlessness that would transform Israel's right to security and self-defense into a mortal fight to be waged at any legitimate cost – even if

24 See above and again: Dal Bo, *Massekhet Keritot*, 200–201; and Ilan, *Massekhet Hullin*, 1–24.

this did eventually require the shedding of blood of innocent victims. Besides, Israel's "liability" of addressing innocent victims among these brutal gentiles would be justified by the same premise that they are indeed "wicked," if not "animalistic" – therefore excluded from enjoying specific rights, as explained above.

This tendentious and circular reading of Maimonides' and Joseph Caro's ruling on damages of chattels is particularly eloquent. When inserted in the greater context of *The King's Torah*, it exposes the deepest intention of this text and its theological-political assumptions. *The King's Torah* appears to rely on a sort of "biopolitics" – an understanding of policy as a way of regulating human life in every aspect and determining a specific hierarchy among the several possibilities of being.[25] "Biopolitics" does not neglect the existence of several options of living but certainly considers some of them less or more appropriate with the respect of a latent, always emerging contraposition between humanity and animality. Differently from what Greek political thought would argue, *The King's Torah* appears not to believe that man is a "political animal." On the contrary, it seems to express the conviction that the human is not a natural kind but rather something that has to be produced – specifically by taking the burden of fulfilling God's commandments, either according to the Noachide or, better, the Sinaitic Revelation. Only adequate, decent policy could fulfil the theological-political goal of educating a potentially brute human being to actual political life, devoted to God and His sanctity. With respect of this, the inhuman would exactly consist in the very "brutality" that imposes to conscript both the wicked ones and the just ones, the soldiers and the infants – eventually delivering each of them to the risk of being involved in acts of anticipatory war that Israel might be. Probably the most disturbing assumption in *The King's Torah* is his absolute "faith" in being able to determine, manage, and police the border between the human and the animal. This demarcation is then reinforced with the help of two other assumptions: the opposition between "friend" and "enemies," and the persuasion that culture has a limited impact on human beings.

The Inability of Culture in *The King's Torah*

The King's Torah believes that the fundamental terms for human relations are provided by the almost Schmittian opposition between "friend" and "enemy." Its terse juridical language prevents *The King's Torah* from describing the

25 See, for instance, Giorgio Agamben, *Homo Sacer. Edizione Integrale* (Marcerata: Quodlibet, 2018).

event of war in actually, historically, and anthropologically reliable terms but it is somehow accepted as inevitable – not because of some obscure anthropological constant in time but rather because of the ontological conditions of the gentiles who are keen to wage war against Israel. War actually appears as an event taking place from the outside and yet affecting Israel that would be reluctant in taking part in it. It is indeed quite eloquent that *The King's Torah* examines the event of war only after treating the specific legal case: a Jew who asked under duress to kill a non-Jew in order to save his life. In other terms, *The King's Torah* intends to treat war as a further specification of the same legal case – a Jew who would normally intend to hurt no one and yet is forced to kill a fellow human being out of unfavorable circumstances. Accordingly, war appears to be an event that interests Israel only forcedly and essentially as a passive, defensive subject. *The King's Torah* occasionally describes the reality of war in extremely naïve and simplistic terms, especially when it argues that the primary duty of a "kingdom" would be to protect "the weak ones" from the "strong ones," as well as "the righteous and probe ones" from the "wicked ones," while elaborating on some Rabbinic sources (bAZ 4a, mAv 3:2 and Maimondies, *Guide*, 3:40) (KT 210).

The implication of this treatment of war is substantial. From a legal standpoint, war would interest Israel only as an event that has been imposed from the outside and forces one to take any measure of security and self-defense. *The King's Torah* seems unaware that war can be motivated by a series of social, political, and economical reasons; therefore, its parameters constantly refer to a sort of ontologically frozen dichotomy between "friends" and "enemies" – the former willing to be supportive of Israel and the latter willing to attack it exclusively out of their "wickedness" (*resha'ut*). The lack of any reliable historical and anthropological investigation on the nature of war seems to find compensation in a quite discouraging assumption: gentiles would somehow be inclined to wage war against Israel that would otherwise live in peace, without intending to harm anyone. This irenic perspective is reinforced by some Kabbalistic assumptions that describe gentiles in metaphysical terms – there is evil in the world but Israel cannot take part in it due to the essential reason that God has chosen it as the recipient of His Revelation. History would then be the specific dimension in which Israel and gentiles have been entitled to two different kinds of Revelation – the Noachide and the Sinaitic ones, respectively. The Noachide Revelation would essentially be incomplete – both in legal and moral terms – with respect of the Sinaitic one (KT 43–44) and this would hardly prevent from establishing a sort of specific hierarchy in history. Yet, *The King's Torah* cannot admit that Israel would fundamentally be kept astray from non-Jewish world. Therefore, although such a difference should convey, in principle, a rigid ethnic and social distinction, Israel has admittedly aimed to "clothe" itself also with Noachide commandments, in order to be able to converse with gentiles and to successfully relate to them (KT 46).

Yet the rigid coordinates that *The King's Torah* employs for describing political life make it impossible to envision wartime in realistic terms. War essentially appears to be the inevitable outcome of an apocalyptic confrontation between Israel and the forces of evil. Notably, *The King's Torah* assumes that gentiles are associated with "husks" of impurity (*qelipot*) surrounding Israel – that is sanctity connected to God (KT 42–43). While mobilizing these Kabbalistic concepts, *The King's Torah* then admits candidly that the "gentile soul" is essentially contaminated by impurity from which Israel necessarily has to purify itself (KT 43). While purifying itself, Israel would then be able to assume upon itself the epochal task of following also the Noachide commandments and eventually leading gentiles, as traditionally prescribed by Biblical Revelation. In the end, the Noachide commandments would be only a sort of temporary measure, given especially to those who had neither direct nor indirect contact with sanctity (KT 43). This overt hierarchy between the Noachide and Sinaitic Revelation would once more reinforce *The King's Torah* in its theological-political presuppositions: Israel would enjoy both an ethnic and legal privilege especially because it spreads the Word of God in the world (KT 216). These occasional yet powerful references to the Kabbalah seem to provide the deepest rationale as to why *The King's Torah* discriminates between Jewish lives and non-Jewish lives. Jewish legal tradition would provide only the juridical terms for confirming a sort of metaphysical distinction with respect of gentiles who are essentially removed from enjoying sanctity with God. In other terms, Jewish Law would only put into legal words what has already been determined metaphysically – Israel shares sanctity with God, whereas gentiles belong to the "husks" of impurity. In consequence of this, *The King's Torah* can even reintroduce the idea that any "persecutor" may be killed in war even if he is "little" (*qatan*) (KT 182–183) or one of the "infants" (KT 199) – as he likely to posit a future threat, if raised by "wicked" parents. It is important to insist one more on this point, as it contradicts several teachings in Talmudic literature and exhibits its truest core – a nihilistic, reactionary, and deeply negative evaluation of human nature.

When *The King's Torah* relaunches some sparse Rabbinic ruling that would allow the killing of infants as they will posit, in the future, a threat to Israel, it is not simply working its way around a number of legal options that would potentially excuse soldiers from waging military actions that inevitably have collateral costs. One could even indulge in some of these assumptions, if not argue that modern military justice envisions and tolerates some "collateral damages" among civilians. With respect of this, *The King's Torah* would not say anything essentially different from arguing that military actions can have a strong impact on civilians and therefore that the traditional distinction between combative and non-combative targets should eventually be removed. Yet, *The King's Torah* exposes its nihilistic nature especially when it reinforces the assumption that civilians may be targeted during anticipatory military actions with special remarks on those "infants" who might be killed. *The King's Torah* overtly states that these children would be likely to be just like their parents and therefore potentially future "persecutors" (KT 199). The rationale of this ruling is deeply ferocious and contradicts those Talmudic narratives that indulge in the Socratic fantasy that even the sons of Israel's greatest enemies – Sennacherib, Haman, and so on – had been able to become Jewish sages, when removed from their wicked parents and made participate in Jewish culture. Whereas the Talmud supports the humanistic dream that Jewish culture – or culture in principle – can redeem everyone and even the son of wicked men, *The King's Torah* seems rather to protest against this assumption and argue the opposite: those kids will eventually be their parent's children – wicked.

While so ruling, *The King's Torah* exhibits a reactionary and untimely nature. Aside from an occasional reference to Arabs (KT 190), there is no actual reference to the outer world. The rigid perimeter of Jewish Law provides the inflexible boundaries of the world in which the reality of a Jewish "kingdom" shall exhaust its existence. Only specific circumstances – such as wars and Israel's commandment of leading gentiles to God – would be exceptional and yet confirm this aim to separateness. Yet, *The King's Torah* is built on a covert dialectics between the Jewish and non-Jewish world. These dialectics preclude from unequivocally assessing the nature of this text – whether it is a legal fantasy or a Rabbinic handbook for practical actions.

On the one hand, one could emphasize the untimely nature of *The King's Torah* and its most controversial rulings – for instance, the one allowing a Jew to target an innocent infant as possible, future threat. Its exorbitant, almost blatant tone would only prove the case that *The King's Torah* does not intend to be actual but rather untimely, especially because it promotes war neither against the "enemies" of Israel nor the "Arabs" but possibly betrays the awareness that acts of war in contemporary Israeli society are normed and negotiated by international laws of war. On the other hand, both the authors of *The King's Torah* have been charged for a series of crimes and accused of illegal actions against Arabs. Regardless of their juridical outcome, these allegations are notable: they suggest that both Rabbis Yosef Elitzur and Itzhak Shapira have tried – or were believed of trying – to put their political theology into practice. With respect of that, the difficulty of determining whether *The King's Torah* is a legal fantasy or a practical handbook would hardly be incidental. On the contrary, it would follow a specific strategy of writing under duress. In other terms, it would reflect the assumption – popularized by Leo Strauss – that controversial texts cannot but follow a double standard: they manifest a harmless nature to common readers but exhibit their truest interest in practical use to the right readers. As far as it is difficult to determine whether *The King's Torah* is presented as if complete to unlearned readers, one cannot exclude that some specific traits of this text – especially its language and medieval sources – have a specific function: using a subtle hermeneutical deception for hiding the deepest theological-political finality of the text.

Conclusion

This brief survey of *The King's Torah* can conclude with the assumption that this text actually intends not to provide any practical use for contemporary Israeli soldiers but rather to support – in much more implicit and subtle terms – a theological-political agenda. *The King's Torah* would exhibit a sort of discontent against modern civilization and then claim for a different attitude towards culture and society. As far as culture would not be able to impact on human beings deeply enough and therefore children of "wicked" parents could only develop in future "persecutors," *The King's Torah* appears to present itself as an "untimely" piece of Rabbinic scholarship – as a *traditional* commentary on Rabbinic literature that would accurately refrain from alluding to any contemporary situation or to any contemporary source but some specific Rabbinic authorities. In so doing, *The King's Torah* would offer a representation of Jewish Law that is intrinsically "removed" – as far as it is "abstract" – from the outer world and therefore it is "absolute." In other words, *The King's Torah* would intend to draw the perimeter of legitimate Jewish life exclusively within the boundaries of traditional Jewish Law, claiming to offer an incontrovertible representation of the "truest" Jewish jurisprudence.

Yet this assumption would lead to an apparent paradox – *The King's Torah* would be practical as much as it is abstract, concrete as much as it is generic, and timely as much as it is untimely, as founded on ancient Jewish laws. At the bottom of this paradox would lay, then, an unexpressed "motif" – there would be no ultimate ethical, legal horizon but the one provided by Jewish Law. Everything that did escape its perimeter would necessarily be "obsolete" in a very peculiar sense: "out of date" not because of its "antiquity" – rather because of its "novelty." In other terms, the setting of *The King's Torah* within and exclusively within the perimeter of Jewish Law would automatically disqualify any other possible legal negotiation. More specifically, its "untimely" nature would hide a nihilistic assumption – that there is no use in negotiating with the modern world either with respect to the laws of war or in treating with the "enemies" of Israel. Accordingly, *The King's Torah* would be rooted into a dangerous inversion of time coordinates because of fundamentalist religious expectations. According to *The King's Torah*, the real enemy is the liberal Jew.

This specific trait would eventually be much more dangerous to the contemporary Israeli society than blatant, ineffective statements about killing innocents in war. The untimely nature of *The King's Torah* implicitly disqualifies the modern Jewish experience of the world and supports a very dark, nihilist, and pessimistic conception of humanity. While assuming that the children of the "enemy" can be addressed as legitimate targets in reactive or even anticipatory acts of war, *The King's Torah* does not simply distort the modern notion of "collateral damages"; more radically, it manifests a deep mistrust in the ability of educating children with humanism and culture. The legal reasoning that would justify the anticipatory killing of "enemies" fundamentally implies the conviction that everything can and must be only what it essentially is – with no changes and no hope.

Works Cited

Agamben, Giorgio. *Homo Sacer. Edizione Integrale.* Macerata: Quodlibet, 2018.

Avnon, Dan, and David Feuchtwanger. *Mizug Ophakim. Mahshavah Medinat Yehudit Israelit* (Blending Hozirons. Jewish-Israeli Political Thought). Jerusalem: Magnes Press, 2016.

Bauer, Yoel. "The Racist Teaching of the Extreme Right." *Ma'ariv*, March 11 2011. Accessed March 12 2011. https://www.makorrishon.co.il/nrg/online/1/ART2/220/777.html.

Dal Bo, Federico. *Massekhet Keritot. Text, Translation, and Commentary.* Tübingen: Mohr Siebeck, 2013.

Dal Bo, Federico. "Du solltest dich verfolgen lassen. Eine theologisch-politische Auslegung vom Talmudischen Traktat Baba Kamma 93." In *Täter und Opfer. Verbrechen und Stigma im europäisch-jüdischen Kontext*, edited by Claudia S. Dorchain and Tommaso Speccher, 69–95. Würzburg: Verlag Königshausen & Neumann, 2014.

Fine, Jonathan. *Political Violence in Judaism, Christianity, and Islam.* London: Rowman and Littlefield, 2015.

Garb, Jonathan. *Yearning of the Soul. Psychological Thought in Modern Kabbalah.* Chicago: University of Chicago Press, 2015.

Gorenberg, Geschom. *The Unmaking of Israel.* New York: HarperCollins, 2011.

Kellner, Menachem. "And the Crooked Shall be Made Straight." In *Rethinking the Messianic Idea in Judaism*, edited by Michael L. Morgan and Steven Weitzman, 108–140. Indiana: Indiana University Press, 2014.

Kellner, Menachem. "We are not alone." In *Menachem Kellner. Jewish Universalism*, edited by Hava Tirosh-Samuelsohn and Aaron W. Huges, 107–118. Leiden-Boston: Brill, 2015.

Korn, Eugene. "Extra Sinagogam Salus Est?" In *Religious Perspectives on Religious Diversity*, edited by Robert McKim, 37–62. Boston: Brill, 2016.

Huges, Aaron. Theology. "The Articulation of Orthodoxy." In *The Routledge Handbook of Muslim-Jewish Relations*, edited by Jonathan Meri, 77–94. London: Routledge, 2016.

Ilan, Tal. *Massekhet Hullin. Text, Translation, and Commentary.* Tübingen: Mohr Siebeck, 2017.

Inbari, Motti. *Messianic Religious Zionism Confronts Israeli Territorial Compromises.* Cambridge: Cambridge University Press, 2012.

Lappin, Yaakov. "Yizhar Rabbi Detained by Police." *The Jerusalem Post*, August 19 2010. Accessed August 20 2010. https://www.jpost.com/Israel/Yitzhar-rabbi-detained-by-police.

von Mutius, Hans-Georg. "The Positions of Jews and Non Jews in the Rabbinic Law of Overreaching (Ona'ah)." In *The Three Religions*, edited by Nill Cohen and Andreas Heldrich, 49–58. Munich: Herbert Utz Verlag, 2002.

Shapira, Rabbi Yitzhak, and Rabbi Yosef Elitzur. *Torat ha Melekh. Dinei Nefashot bein Yisrael le Akum* (The King's Torah: Laws of Life and Death between Jews and gentile). Jerusalem: HaMachon HaTorani she-al-yad Yeshivat 'Od Yosef Chai, 2009.

Sharon, Roi. "The Complete Guide to Killing non-Jews." *Ma'ariv*, November 9 2009.

Wagner, Michael. "Shapira's distinction between Jewish, gentile blood." *Jerusalem Post.* February 2 2010. Accessed February 3 2010. https://www.jpost.com/Israel-News?id=167475.

Wilkes, George. "Teaching about 'War in Jewish Law' to Non-Lawyers in a European University Context." *Jewish Law Association Studies* XXVI (2016): 109–126.

Wilkes, George. "Peace and Conflict in the Jewish Tradition." In *Ashgate Research Companion on Religion and Conflict Resolution*, edited by Lee Marsden, 49–66. Farnham: Ashgate Press, 2012.

Wilkes, George. "Religious War in the Works of Maimonides and the "Maimonideans": An idea and its transit across the medieval Mediterranean." In *Just Wars, Holy Wars, and Jihads: Christian, Jewish, Muslim Encounters and Exchanges*, edited by Sohail Hashmi, 146–64. Oxford: Oxford University Press, 2012.

Yarden, Ophir. "Recent Halakhic Discourse in Israel Encouraging Racism and Violence." In *Religious Stereotyping and Interreligious Relations*, edited by Jasper Svartvik and Jakob Wirén, 207–220. New York: Palgrave McMillan, 2013.

Hayim Katsman

Reactions Towards Jewish Radicalism

Rabbi Yitzchak Ginsburg and Religious Zionism

Introduction

For the past four years I have been working as a car mechanic in a garage located in southern Israel. One of the things I enjoy in my work is the ability to identify trends in local public opinion based on the stickers that appear on car bumpers. For example, I could reckon the population is normally passive and tends to adopt the motto "*Trust in God*," but in times of war "*We are a firm cliff – In combat and on the home front.*" Among the customers were residents of three Religious-Zionist communities populated mostly by evacuees from Gush Katif. One day, I began to notice several red-and-yellow stickers appearing on car bumpers of drivers from the religious settlements, bearing the words "*Jews love Jews*". The implicit racism and the muted violence emanating from the stickers fascinated me, and I sought to trace their source. When I examined one sticker closely, I saw that there was an Internet address leading to the website of the "Derech-Chaim" movement. A tour of the movement's website revealed that it wishes "to bring about a fundamental change in the public sphere of the Jewish people"[1] following the vision of the movement's president, Rabbi Yitzchak Ginzburg.

Rabbi Yitzchak Ginzburg is an American-born rabbi, associated with Chabad-Hassidism. After his immigration to Israel in 1965 he got close to radical-right circles and became head of the "Od Yosef Chay" Yeshiva in Nablus (currently in the Yitzhar settlement). He is publicly known for his racist statements and his alleged support of violence towards Arabs, which resulted in several arrests and the accusation of incitement (though he was never convicted).[2] I have previously heard Ginzburg's name from references across the media that presented him as a radical and dangerous rabbi, preaching violence against Palestinians. Therefore, I was under the impression that he is a rabbi who represents only neg-

1 "Beruchim haBaim leTnu'at 'Derech Haim'" ("Welcome to 'Derech Chaim' Movement"), Derech Chaim, accessed July 28 2017, http://www.derech-chaim.org/
[תנועת דרך חיים קמה על מנת לחולל שינוי יסודי במרחב הציבורי של עם ישראל.]

2 Natan Odenheimer, "The Kabbalist Who Would Be King of a New Jewish Monarchy in Israel", *Forward*, October 14 2016, accessed July 28 2017, http://forward.com/news/352016/the-kabbalist-who-would-be-king-of-a-new-jewish-monarchy-in-israel/.

https://doi.org/10.1515/9783110545753-010

ligible radical margins of Religious Zionism, if at all. This dissonance has left me puzzled – how come these seemingly moderate customers support a political movement led by such a radical rabbi?

This experience motivated me to research the ideological and political shifts Religious Zionism has undergone during the past century, and try to understand the psychological and political processes evoking Religious-Zionist reactions to Rabbi Ginzburg.[3] In this paper, I wish to use the case of Rabbi Ginzburg to demonstrate how two seemingly contradictory theologies can lead to supporting the same modes of practical action. I intend to analyze Rabbi Ginzburg's political thought while comparing it to the Religious-Zionist political-theology of the "Merkaz haRrav" school, as well as its expressions in public statements made by key figures in the contemporary Religious-Zionist society. Although at first it may seem there are substantial disparities between Rabbi Ginzburg's theology and the viewpoints of most Religious-Zionists, I suggest a more nuanced approach, distinguishing Ginzburg's theology from the practical aspects of his thought. My analysis of Ginzburg's theology, emphasizing its Kabalistic-Hassidic origins, shows its substantial divergence from "Merkaz haRrav" theology. However, a close examination of the practical aspects in Rabbi Ginzburg's thought reveal that the modes of political action he suggests are similar to those expressed by prominent Religious-Zionist Rabbis.

The phenomenon described in this paper can illuminate extremist political trends taking place within contemporary Religious Zionism. The fact that Religious Zionism's criticism of Rabbi Ginzburg focuses on the practical aspects of his thought, rather than on his theology, suggests the existence of a displacement mechanism among Religious Zionism. Constructing Rabbi Ginzburg as an extremist plays a political role in national politics, aimed at broadening the legitimization of Religious-Zionist ideas. Therefore, the existence of the displacement mechanism indicates a political tactic used by Religious Zionism, in their struggle for hegemony in Israel.

3 Hayim Katsman, "'Pachad Yitzchak': Yachasah Shel haTziyonut haDatit laRav Yitzchak Ginzburg" ('The Fear of Isaac': The Religious-Zionist Reaction to Rabbi Yitzchak Ginzburg) (M.A. Thesis, Ben-Gurion University in the Negev, 2017).

Public Criticism of Rabbi Yitzchak Ginzburg

Due to his identification with the Israeli radical right and his alleged support for acts of violence and "price tag"[4] actions against Palestinians and security forces, Rabbi Ginzburg is the subject of severe criticism across Israeli society. He was the focus of several public storms concerning "Jewish terror." "Od Yosef Chay" Yeshiva in Yitzhar, where Ginzburg serves as its president, was closed down and held by Border Police forces in 2011, and Ginzburg himself was arrested and interrogated several times regarding accusations of incitement. For this reason, Rabbi Ginzburg is an undesirable personality in many institutions. For example, when in December 2015 Rabbi Ginzburg's followers sought to hold an event at the Tel Aviv Culture Palace, resistance arose among the city's liberal residents who protested against Ginzburg's arrival at the event. A demonstration was held at outside the venue, attended by representatives of the "Meretz" party, "Peace Now", "Free Israel", and other liberal left-wing organizations. Mickey Gitzin, a member of the Tel Aviv City Council and director of the "Free Israel" Movement, was interviewed on the radio regarding the subject and said:

> You must understand that Rabbi Ginzburg is the head of "Od Yosef Chay" yeshiva in Yitzhar, which is the place generating the "hilltop youth", the "price tag" people, and so on. Many of the most problematic activities that exist today in the territories [...] he [Rabbi Ginzburg, H.K.] is the man spiritually behind them, everyone knows it, everyone is aware of it, and yet he is accepted as any other person or as a Kabbalistic expert in the Tel Aviv Culture Palace [...] I want to ask – where do the secret services and the police stand on these issues? [...] They know exactly who Rabbi Ginzburg is. This is dangerous, it has very clear social implications for Israeli society.[5]

4 "Price tag" is the name used to describe acts of vandalism and terrorism carried out by Jewish settlers, aimed mostly against Palestinian civilians and Israeli security forces. Nadera Shalhoub-Kevorkian and Yossi David, "Is the Violence of Tag Mehir a State Crime?" *British Journal of Criminology* 56, no. 5 (2015): 839 – 841.

5 "Mankal 'Israel Chofshit' Neged HaRav Yitzchak Ginzburg: 'Hu Lo Yachol Lekabel Bama Bekol Makom'" (CEO of 'Free Israel' Movement Against Rabbi Yitzchak Ginzburg: "He Can't Get a Stage Anywhere"), Radio 103FM, originally broadcasted November 30 2015, accessed July 28 2017, http://103fm.maariv.co.il/programs/media.aspx?ZrqvnVq=GHIDMK&c41t4nzVQ=EE (Hebrew,-translation mine).
[צריך להבין, הרב גינזבורג עומד בישיבת 'עוד יוסף חי' ביצהר שבימים אלו ממש היא המקום ממנו יוצאים אותם 'נערי גבעות', אנשי 'תג מחיר' וכו'. הרבה מהפעילות הבעייתית ביותר שמתקיימת היום בשטחים... הוא האיש שבעצם עומד מאחוריה ברמה הרוחנית, כולם יודעים את זה, כולם מודעים לזה, והוא מתקבל כאחד האדם או כמקובל בהיכל התרבות בתל-אביב... אני רוצה לשאול איפה השב"כ ואיפה המשטרה בסוגיות האלה... הם הרי יודעים בדיוק מי זה הרב גינזבורג... הדבר הזה הוא מסוכן, יש לו השלכות חברתיות מאוד מאוד ברורות על החברה הישראלית]

Notwithstanding the fierce criticism from left-wing organizations and public figures, Rabbi Ginzburg is also surprisingly the object of criticism directed from the religious-messianic right, which seems to advance goals similar to his. The main accusation of the Religious-Zionists towards Rabbi Ginzburg is that he grants halakhic legitimacy to "price tag" actions, thus laying down a "theological/ideological infrastructure" for those operations. For example, Yehuda Yifrah, a resident of Ofrah Settlement and the legal correspondent of the Religious-Zionist newspaper "Makor Rishon", claims that the "price tag" acts cast a serious threat on the settlement movement, Religious Zionism's flagship enterprise:

> It happened in Yitzhar during the intermediate days of Pesach. Twenty years after the publication of the 'Baruch Hagever' booklet[6] [...] Rabbi Ginzburg sketched theological and theosophical outlines justifying the 'price tag' acts [...] This seems to be the first time that a thinker of the status of Rabbi Yitzhak Ginzburg directly refers to the specific phenomenon of 'price tag' acts and makes sense of it. Therefore, there is no real vacuum [...] For a long time now the tire-slashers, the graffiti sprayers and the mosques arsonists are using a great headache not only to the Jewish unit of the Shin Bet security service and the people of the Prime Minister's Office. Even in Yesha Council's[7] leadership, these anarchists constitute a grave and almost existential threat to the entire settlement enterprise [...] Behind the events that drive the country crazy there is a cohesive worldview with direction and purpose.[8]

In an interview I have conducted with a rabbi leading an urban-bourgeois Religious-Zionist community, he expressed criticism towards Rabbi Ginzburg and his movement and accused him of organizing the youth who carry out "price tag" actions:

6 '*Baruch HaGever*' (Baruch the Man) is a booklet based on a talk given by Rabbi Ginzburg, in which he defended the acts of Jewish terrorist Baruch Goldstein, who had massacred twenty-nine Palestinian worshippers in the Cave of the Patriarchs in Hebron.

7 Yesha Council is an umbrella organization of municipal councils of Jewish settlements in the West Bank.

8 "Hamanifest HaDati Meachorei Tag Mechir: 'Chevley Leyda Shel Am Chadash'" (The Religious Manifesto Behind 'Price Tag': 'The Birth of a New Nation'), accessed July 28 2017, http://www.nrg.co.il/online/11/ART2/575/555.html (Hebrew, translation mine).
[זה קרה ביצהר בחול המועד פסח. עשרים שנה לאחר פרסומה של החוברת "ברוך הגבר"... שרטט הרב גינזבורג לראשונה קווי מתאר תיאולוגיים ותיאוסופיים להצדקת מעשי תג המחיר... נדמה שזו הפעם הראשונה שבה הוגה בסדר הגודל של הרב יצחק גינזבורג מתייחס ישירות לתופעה הספציפית של מעשי תג מחיר ומכיל אותה. אז אין באמת ואקום... המפנצ'רים, מרססי הגרפיטי ושורפי דלתות המסגדים, הם מזמן לא רק כאב ראש גדול לחטיבה היהודית בשב"כ ולאנשי משרד ראש הממשלה. גם בתפיסתה של הנהגת יש"ע מהווים האנרכיסטים איום תדמיתי ופוליטי חמור, קיומי כמעט, על מפעל ההתיישבות כולו... מאחורי האירועים שמשגעים את המדינה יש תפיסת עולם מגובשת עם כיוון ועם יעד.]

> What Rabbi Ginzburg does is collect all kinds of punks, people who lack any ability to read seriously, and he sweeps them with very impressive avant-garde statements [...] they [the Israeli society] only know the 'hilltop youth', but the hilltop youth are a bunch of unbridled criminals [...] It turns out to be a bunch of punks, 30 – 40 guys, doped to the top of their heads, their small society suffers from sexual promiscuity and antinomianism, totally discarding all values of religion and morality, and the way they justify their minimalist existence is by abusing Arabs. They are rejected by Religious Zionism, everyone sees them as a bunch of psychos [...] By the way, Rabbi Ginzburg himself will not publicly support these actions (though he probably does it secretly) because he's smart, so you see it's a fiction, there's really no avant-garde [...][9]

Maybe the most prominent Religious-Zionist opponent to Rabbi Ginzburg is Dr. Gadi Gevaryahu, founder of "Tag Meir" Forum, which brings together dozens of civil society organizations in order to "express a voice of tolerance, mutual respect and respect for neighbors, foreigners and those living within us."[10] In an broadcast about the forum on Channel 10 News, the narrator describes Gevaryahu as "A person full of contradictions, Gadi Gevaryahu. He defines himself as a Religious-Zionist, he has one son who is a key activist in 'Breaking the Silence'[11], and another son who studies in the pre-military academy 'Atzmonah'.[12] A man of God who went to war with senior rabbis, along with Arab sheikhs he considers friends."[13] In response to the reporter's question about the extent of organization behind the "price tag" actions, Gevaryahu replies unequivocally:

---

9 It should be noted that the rabbi acknowledges that the clear majority of "hilltop youth" are not identified with Rabbi Ginzburg, yet he claims that there are students of Rabbi Ginzburg engaged in "price tag" activities (although probably a minority among students). Interview with Religious-Zionist rabbi, May 2016.

[מה שהרב גינזבורג עושה זה מלקט כל מיני פרחחים, אנשים שהם חסרי הבנה, חסרי כל יכולת לעיון רציני, והוא סוחף אותם באמירות אוונגרדיות מאוד מרשימות... מה שהם (החברה הישראלית) מכירים זה את "נוער הגבעות", אבל נוער הגבעות זו חבורה של עבריינים נטולי כל רסן... הסתבר שמדובר בחבורה של פרחחים, 30–40 חבר'ה, מסוממים על הראש, שהחברה הקטנה שלהם סובלת מהוללות מינית ומאנטינומיזם, פקיעה מוחלטת של כל ערכי הדת והמוסר, והדרך להצדקת קיומם המינימליסטית היא על ידי התעללות בערבים. חברה שהציונות הדתית דוחה אותה מקרבה, כולם רואים אותם כחבורה של פסיכים... דרך אגב גם הרב גינזבורג בעצמו בפומבי לא יצהיר על תמיכה בתג מחיר (בנסתר הוא בוודאי עושה את זה), פשוט כי הוא חכם. אז אתה קולט שזו פיקציה, אין באמת אוונגרד]

10 "HaHazon Shelanu" [Our Vision], *Tag Meir*, accessed July 28 2017, / (Hebrew, translation mine).

[פורום תג מאיר נוסד בחג החנוכה תשע"ב במטרה להשמיע קול של סובלנות, כבוד הדדי ומאור פנים כלפי שכנים, זרים וגרים בתוכנו]

11 An Israeli non-governmental organization identified with the radical left.

12 An institution identified with the messianic Religious-Zionist stream.

13 "Hadatiyim Sheme'achorey 'Tag Mechir' Nechsafim" [Revealing the religious people behind 'Tag Meir'], *Channel 10 news*, broadcasted September 19 2015, accessed October 22 2017, http://news.nana10.co.il/Article/?ArticleID=1148983 (Hebrew, translation mine)

> It's true that in 2009 the first mosque set on fire in the village of Yasuf was labeled "price tag", and since then 43 mosques, churches and monasteries have been torched and/or desecrated [...] They always caught the small fish; without the permission of rabbis, it would not have been done. There is a book, there is a booklet, there is a series of talks discussing the connection between the King Messiah and revenge. To anyone who wondered why the graffiti of "Long live King Messiah!" was in Duma – there is a series of talks about it.[14]

After this statement the figure of Rabbi Ginzburg is presented, accompanied by a threatening melody, and the narrator reports: "Rabbi Yitzhak Ginzburg is considered the supreme spiritual authority from which "price tag" people derive their halakhic justification for their activities. The head of "Od Yosef Chay" yeshiva in Yitzhar is really into matters of revenge."[15]

Accordingly, in a report published by the "Tag Meir" Forum concerning incitement by religious leaders (both Jews and Arabs) Rabbi Ginzburg is characterized as a radical rabbi inciting the extreme right in Israel:

> Since 2009, Israel has been subjected to a wave of hate crimes and racism, including the desecration of Muslim and Christian prayer houses, assaults on innocent Arab passersby on the streets of Israel, and the murder of innocent Arabs [...] Rabbi Yitzhak Ginzburg is the main ideologue behind the wave of hate crimes known as 'price tag'.[16]

On these grounds, it seems there is strong criticism within Israeli society towards Rabbi Ginzburg, rejecting his political views and the violence which he allegedly advocates. The source of the Israeli left's criticism seems to be evident, since the religious-messianic right and the Israeli left have a fundamental ideological dis-

---

[אדם מלא ניגודים גדי גבריהו, הוא מגדיר את עצמו "איש הציונות הדתית, יש לו בן אחד פעיל מרכזי ב'שוברים שתיקה' ומנגד, בן אחר שלומד במכינה הקדם צבאית 'עצמונה'. איש ירא שמיים שיצא למלחמת חורמה ברבנים בכירים כשלצידו שיח'ים ערבים שאותם הוא מגדיר חברי נפש]

14 Ibid.

[נכון שב2009 היה המסגד הראשון שהוצת בכפר יאסוף וכתבו עליו "תג מחיר", ומאז 43 מסגדים, כנסיות, מנזרים הוצתו ו/או חוללו... תמיד תפסו את דגי הרקק, ללא אישור של רבנים זה לא היה נעשה. יש ספר, יש חוברת, יש סדרת שיעורים שעוסקת בקשר שבין המלך המשיח והנקמה. לכל מי שתהה מה עושה הכתובת 'יחי המלך המשיח!' בדומא – יש על זה סדרת שיעורים]

15 Ibid.

[הרב יצחק גינזבורג נחשב לסמכות הרוחנית הבכירה שממנה יונקים אנשי תג מחיר את ההצדקה ההלכתית לפעילותם. ראש ישיבת 'עוד יוסף חי' ביצהר חזק מאוד בענייני נקמה]

16 "Doch Anshei Dat Mesitim" [Report on incitement by religious figures], *Tag Meir*, Accessed October 22 2017. https://drive.google.com/file/d/0B7LRHq6GBTfwMmdKWGVGNzdJVjA/view (Hebrew, translation mine)

[החל משנת 2009 פוקד את ישראל גל של פשעי שנאה וגזענות המתבטא בחילול בתי תפילה מוסלמים ונוצרים, פגיעה ותקיפה של עוברי אורח ערבים חפי מפשע ברחובות ישראל ורצח של ערבים חפים מפשע... הרב יצחק גינזבורג, נשיא מוסדות עוד יוסף חי, הוא האידיאולוג הראשי העומד מאחורי גל פשעי השנאה המכונה תגי מחיר]

pute and the left constantly criticizes radical messianic rabbis of Rabbi Ginzburg's sort. However, the source of Religious-Zionist criticism on Rabbi Ginzburg is not clear, since, as I will demonstrate, the actions that Rabbi Ginzburg publicly calls for are not substantially different from those other Religious-Zionist rabbis call for.

Religious Zionism, the "Merkaz Harav" School, and Rabbi Ginzburg

Due to its central role in Israeli politics and its great impact on Israeli society, there is extensive academic work regarding the Religious-Zionist movement. These studies describe the historical and theological-ideological developments the movement underwent and particularly its significant transformation during the 1960s and 1970s.[17] Specifically, researchers focus on Gush Emunim, a messianic social movement formed to renew Jewish settlement in the territories occupied by Israel in the 1967 War, whose founders were Religious-Zionist activists. The movement's members were ideologically affiliated with the "Merkaz Harav" school, influenced by Rabbi Avraham Yitzhak Hacohen Kook and his son Rabbi Zvi Yehuda Kook (most of Gush Emunim's founders were his disciples), which has become the dominant ideology among Religious Zionism over the past few decades, due to Gush Emunim's success.

A comprehensive and groundbreaking study of the roots of Gush Emunim as a religious movement was carried out in a PhD dissertation written by Gideon Aran, "From Religious Zionism to Zionist Religion."[18] Aran discusses the unique religious idea promoted by the movement, along with an in-depth account of the historical events that led to its establishment and its widespread influence in Israeli politics. According to Aran, "Gush Emuni" led a theological revolution

17 Avi Sagi & Dov Schwarz, "Religious-Zionist Enterprise Facing a Modern World," in *Mea Shnot Tzionut Datit (A Hundred Years of Religious Zionism)*, ed. Avi Sagi and Dov Schwarz (Ramat Gan: Bar-Ilan University, 2003, Hebrew); Aviezer Ravitzky, *Haketz Hameguleh uMedinat haYehudim: Meshichiut, Tzionut veRadikalizem Dati beIsrael (Messianism, Zionism and Jewish Religious Radicalism)* (Tel Aviv: Am Oved, 1993, Hebrew); *Dov Schwarz, haTzionut haDatit: Toldot uPirkei Idiologia* (*Religious-Zionisim: History and Ideology*) (Tel Aviv: Ministry of Defense Press, 2003, Hebrew).

18 Gideon Aran, meTzionut Datit leDat Tzionit: Reshit Gush Emunim keTnuah Datit (From Religious Zionism to Zionist Religion: The Origins and Culture of Gush Emunim) (PhD Diss, Hebrew University, 1987); later published as Gideon Aran, *Kukism: Shorshei Gush Emunim, Tarbut haMitnachalim, Teologia Tzionit, Meshichiut beZmanenu* (*Kukism: The Roots of Gush Emunim, Zionist Theology, and Contemporary Messianism*) (Jerusalem: Carmel Press, Hebrew).

within Religious Zionism, shaped by Rabbi Avraham Yitzhak Hacohen Kook's historiosophic conception, which considers history as a dialectical process directed towards messianic redemption. Following Aran, further research was conducted regarding the influence of Rabbi Kook and his son Rabbi Zvi Yehuda Kook's theology on the practices carried out by members of Gush Emunim. These studies focus mainly on the Kook Rabbis' stand regarding the sanctity of the Israeli state and its institutions, as well as on the Land of Israel and the divine command to settle it.[19]

There is a considerable disparity between the self-image of most Religious-Zionists and the public perception of the movement as expressed in academic literature and the media. While Religious-Zionists view themselves as loyal to the institutions of the State of Israel which they sanctify, their movement is frequently presented as a religious-messianic extremist group that threatens to bring about a political, social, and moral disaster upon the State of Israel and the Jewish people. Accordingly, most academic literature has categorized Gush Emunim as a radical movement expressing modern Jewish fundamentalism.[20] These studies examine the religious infrastructure used as justification for the movement's political activity, which does not treat biblical texts as ethereal and symbolic, but rather interprets the present through them and uses them as basis for political calculation and action.[21] Furthermore, researchers have emphasized the piety of the believers stemming from an absolutist world view, their unwillingness to compromise or show pragmatism and their intentions to act violently in order to actualize their messianic goals. Gush Emunim's activities to establish Jewish settlements in the West Bank, the Sinai Peninsula, and the Golan Heights derived from their belief that messianic redemption was promoted through fulfillment of the divine com-

---

19 Michael Feige, *Shtey Mapot laGada, Gush Emunim, Shalom Achsav ve'Itzuv haMrchav beIsrael* (*One Space, Two Places: Gush Emunim, Peace Now and the Construction of Israeli Space*) (Jerusalem: Magnes Press, 2004, Hebrew); Ravitzky, *Messianism, Zionism and Jewish Religious Radicalism*; Dov Schwarz, *haTzionut Hadatit Beyn Higayon leMeshichiut (Religious-Zionism Between Logic and Messianism)* (Tel-Aviv: Am Oved, 1999, Hebrew); Gadi Taub, *haMitnahalim veHamavak Al Mashmautah Shel haTzionut* (*The Settlers and the Struggle over the Meaning of Zionism*) (Tel-Aviv: Yediot Aharonot, 2007, Hebrew).

20 Ian Lustick, *For the Land and the Lord: Jewish Fundamentalism in Israel* (New York: Council on Foreign Relations Press, 1988); Israel Shahak and Norton Mezvinzki, *Jewish Fundamentalism in Israel* (London: Pluto Press, 1999); Ehud Sprinzak, *The Ascendance of Israel's Radical Right* (New York, Oxford University Press, 1991), 109–124; Ehud Sprinzak, *Brother Against Brother: Violence and Extremism in Israeli Politics From Altalena to the Rabin Assassination* (New York: Free Press, 1999), 145–174; Peter Herriot, *Religious Fundamentalism: Global, Local and Personal* (New York: Routledge, 2009), 95–108.

21 Lustick, *For the Land and the Lord*, 72.

mandment to settle the Land of Israel and by the future establishment of "Malkhut Israel" – the Kingdom of Israel. These researchers note the movement's ambivalence towards Israeli democracy and the obligation to obey its laws if they undermine the messianic process of redemption.[22] The struggles between the pioneer settler groups and the Israeli government during the first term of Prime Minister Yitzhak Rabin (1974–1977) were characterized by direct confrontations between settlers and military forces. Later, the Israeli government's intention to withdraw from some territories it occupied in the 1967 war (the main incidents revolved around the evacuation of Sinai Peninsula in 1982, negotiations on the Oslo Accords in the early 1990s, and the withdrawal from the Gaza Strip in 2005) provoked widespread civil disobedience on the part of Religious-Zionist society. Moreover, researchers found willingness to use violence among members of the movement, which unfolded in several incidents: the shooting at the Islamic College in 1980, the terror attack against Palestinian mayors carried out by members of the "Jewish Underground" in 1983, and the intention of some of the underground's members to blow up the Dome of the Rock. In addition, members of Religious Zionism have resorted to violent actions in order to deliberately and blatantly harm the peace process between Israel and the Palestinians. Examples of this can be seen in the mass murder committed by Baruch Goldstein in Hebron in 1994, as well as the assassination of Prime Minister Yitzhak Rabin by Yigal Amir.[23]

In contrast to these researchers, some recent studies challenge the "fundamentalist" thesis presented above and claim that kind of writing represents an orientalist discourse aimed at constructing Gush Emunim as "the other" vis-a-vis the researcher's self-perception as a Western-rational-modern subject.[24] In Avinoam Rosenak's book *Cracks* he challenges the "fundamentalist" thesis, arguing it does not properly represent the theological complexities in Rabbi Kook's writings.[25] Alternatively, Rosenak emphasizes the *Achdut HaHafachim* ("Unity of the Opposites") theme in the Kookist theology. This Kabbalistic-mystical approach acknowledges the fathomless polarization between religion and modernity, while referring to the struggle between them (in which each side must maintain its principles) as a

22 Motti Inbari, *Messianic Religious Zionism Confronts Israeli Territorial Compromises* (Cambridge University Press, 2012); Sprinzak, *Brother Against Brother.*

23 Although Goldstein and Amir are not strongly associated with Gush Emunim (unlike the Jewish underground), they were both religious Zionists significantly influenced by the Gush's ideology.

24 Shlomo Fisher, "haParadigman haFondementalistit uMa Shemever La" (The Fundamentalist Paradigm and Beyond), *Theory and Criticism* 31 (2007, Hebrew): 283–295.

25 Avinoam Rosenak, *Sedakim: Al Achdut haHafacim haPoliti veTalmidei HaRav Kook* (*Cracks: Unity of Opposites, the Political and Rabbi Kook's Disciples*) (Tel-Aviv: Resling, 2013, Hebrew).

veneer blurring the mystical truth that both opposites derive from the same divine unity. Therefore, in the teachings of Rabbi Kook there is also an emphasis on the need to comprehend the role of the "other" (in this case – secular Zionism) from a point of view considering *Klal Israel* ("the united People of Israel"). Accordingly, Rosenak places a clear border between the theology of Rabbi Kook's students, who still maintain the "Unity of the Opposites" approach, and the rabbis of "Od Yosef Chay" Yeshiva in Yitzhar, who have abandoned that approach in favor of a dichotomous world view that treats ethnic minorities (as well as political rivals) as enemies. Additional studies also cast doubt on the willingness of settlers and Religious-Zionists to directly and violently confront the State of Israel in cases perceived as detrimental to the messianic redemption process. Anat Roth criticizes the studies portraying "Merkaz HaRav" school as Jewish fundamentalism.[26] According to Roth, those studies ignore the sanctity of *Mamlachtiyut* ("statism") among Religious-Zionists, or alternatively underestimate its significance by suggesting the sanctity of the state as merely instrumental to the process of redemption. Roth establishes her claim by analyzing the character of the struggles against the disengagement plan in 2005 and the demolition of nine houses in Amona settlement in 2006. Roth argues that the "statist" theology (and practice) of the "Merkaz HaRav" school was the central factor that prevented Religious-Zionists from resorting to violence during those evacuations, despite their strong opposition to their implementation. Even though some factions who took part in the struggle against the disengagement pressed for fierce opposition (and even the use of violence, excluding firearms) to the state and the security forces, Roth claims these "militant extreme-right organizations" do not represent Religious Zionism and the "Merkaz HaRav" school, but rather represent different groups – "Yitzhar people", Chabad Chassidim, and secular right-wing movements.[27]

A recent study conducted by Moshe Hellinger and Isaac Hershkowitz offers an intermediate position between the "fundamentalist" approach and its critics, presenting a complex and balanced depiction of the public views among Religious Zionism regarding issues of civil disobedience and vigilant violence.[28] Their study demonstrates how throughout the years of Gush Emunim and the "Merkaz HaRav" school's dominance, Religious Zionism has been characterized

---

26 Anat Roth, *Lo Bekol Mechir: meGush Katif Ad Amona: Hasipur Meachorey haMaavak Al Eretz Israel (Not at any Cost: From Gush Katif to Amona: The Story behind the Struggle over the Land of Israel)* (Tel-Aviv: Yediot Aharonot, 2014, Hebrew).

27 Roth, *Lo bekol Mechir*, 89–94.

28 Moshe Hellinger and Isaac Hershkowitz, *Tziut ve'i Tziut baTzionut haDatit: miGush Emunim leTag Mechir* (*Obedience and Civil Disobedience in Religious Zionism: From Gush Emunim to the Price Tag Attacks*) (The Israeli Democracy Institute, 2015, Hebrew).

by a tendency towards civil disobedience, yet it has seldom been expressed in practice due to the "theological-normative balance", which combines a civil-democratic world view with the religious faith in the State of Israel and its institutions' sanctity ("statism"). In their book, they demonstrate how this value system balances the deep and seemingly uncompromising ideological commitment of Religious-Zionists to settlement in the occupied territories.[29]

While Gush Emunim and the "Merkaz HaRav" school's loyalty to the state and its institutions raises a scholarly controversy, there is a consensus in the academic literature written about Rabbi Ginzburg's theology and the political activity of his supporters regarding his opposition to Zionism and his support for civil disobedience to the Israeli state's laws.[30] Furthermore, some studies go so far as directly linking his political thought to vigilant acts of violence towards Palestinians and the Israeli security forces, known since 2008 as "price tag" policy.[31] In the introduction to his comprehensive work on Rabbi Ginzburg's thought, Refael Sagi writes:

> It is important to note that Rabbi Yitzhak Ginzburg has a great influence on the Israeli radical right through his students [...] It is worth mentioning that Rabbi Ginzburg conceived and initiated violent activities against Arabs, such as 'price tag' acts [...] He set up institutions, such as the 'Od Yosef Chay' yeshiva [...] The yeshiva was closed down recently due to heavy accusations that "price tag" actions were carried out from it [...] This radical social political activity must be understood on the basis of his Messianic Kabbalistic-Hasidic philosophy.[32]

---

29 Ibid.

30 Motti Inbari, *Fondementalizem Yehudi veHar Habayit (Jewish Fundamentalism and the Temple Mount)* (Jerusalem: Magness Press, 2008, Hebrew); Hellinger and Hershkowitz, *Obedience and Civil Disobedience in Religious Zionism*; Yechiel Harari, Mistika keRetorika Meshichit (Mysticism as Messianic Rhetoric) (PhD Diss. Tel-Aviv University, 2005, Hebrew); Kobi Hefetz and Liat Cohen, *Ad Redet Machshachey Tehom: Mechkar Al Yeshivat Od Yoseph Chay Vekavanoteiha Klapey haHevra haIsraelit (Into the Dark Abyss: A study on "Od Yoseph Chay" Yeshiva and its intentions toward Israeli Society)* (Tel-Aviv: Dror LaNefesh, 2013, Hebrew); Chanan Moses, *From Religious Zionism to postmodern religion.* (PhD. diss. Bar-Ilan University, 2009, Hebrew); Rephael Sagi, *Radicalizem Dati beMedinat Israel: Prakim beSod haTikun haMeshichi Shel HaRav Yiyzchak Ginzburg (Messianic-Radicalism in The State of Israel: Chapters in the concept of Messianic 'Tikun' in Rabbi Yitzchak Ginzburg's Thought)* (Tel-Aviv: Gvanim, Hebrew).

31 Hellinger and Hershkowitz, *Obedience and Civil Disobedience in Religious Zionism*; Hefetz and Cohen, *Into the Dark Abyss*; Sagi, *Messianic-Radicalism in The State of Israel*; Moses, *From Religious Zionism to Postmodern Religion.*

32 Sagi, *Messianic-Radicalism in The State of Israel*, 8 (Hebrew, translation mine).
[חשוב לציין כי לרב יצחק גינזבורג השפעה רבה באמצעות תלמידיו על הנעשה בימין הרדיקלי הישראלי. ראוי להזכיר כי הרב גינזבורג כתב קונטרס הגנה בשם "ברוך הגבר" על הרוצח ברוך גולדשטיין, הגה ויזם פעילויות אלימות נגד הערבים, כגון "תג מחיר"... הוא הקים מוסדות, כגון ישיבת "עוד יוסף חי"... הישיבה נסגרה לאחרונה בשל האשמה

In a similar manner, Hefetz and Cohen's study on "Od Yosef Chay" in Yitzhar also finds a direct connection between Rabbi Ginzburg's writings on the "hilltop youth" phenomenon and "price tag" actions: "It is important to note that Ginzburg's plan is already accompanied by acts of terrorism justified by the 'right of vengeance' and fueled by hatred."[33] Furthermore, the authors examine the attitude towards Rabbi Ginzburg among the Religious-Zionist public. They suggest certain points of similarity between the views of "Od Yosef Chay" rabbis and some other Religious-Zionist rabbis, especially regarding the commandment to settle in "The Land of Israel" and the spiritual connection between the Jews and the land. However, they argue that "[t]he main dispute between the Religious-Zionist and Gush Emunim rabbis versus 'Od Yosef Chay' people revolves around two intersections: the justification for murder on behalf of a violent interpretation of Torah and Halakha; and the independence of rabbinical institutions and the laws of halakha vis-a-vis the State of Israel and its institutions."[34] Although the authors claim that the views presented by Rabbi Ginzburg and his students are far from those of most Religious-Zionist rabbis, they acknowledge that regarding certain issues, some Religious-Zionist rabbis have expressed similar views to Rabbi Ginzburg's.

The following analysis offers conclusions substantiating Hershkovitz and Helinger's work, rejecting the dichotomous view of Religious Zionism as "fundamentalista" or "statist," and attempt to demonstrate the ideological diversity that characterizes it today. In addition, the analysis reinforces preliminary studies casting doubt on Rabbi Ginzburg's unique influence on "hilltop youth."[35] However, unlike

כבדה כי יצאו ממנה פעולות "תג מחיר"... אין להבין את הפעילות החברתית הפוליטית הרדיקלית הזו אלא רק על בסיס הגותו הקבלית-חסידית המשיחית]

It should be noted that Sagi's book hardly deals directly with Rabbi Ginzburg's support for "price tag" actions, but rather discusses the concept of messianic "Tikun" in his thought, as taking place in the individual, the society, and the state. For a review of the concept of "Tikun" in the Jewish tradition, see ibid., 33–45.

33 Hefetz and Cohen, *Into the Dark Abyss*, 17.

[חשוב לציין כי תכניתו של גינזבורג מלווה כבר כיום במעשי טרור המוצדקים באמצעות "זכות הנקמה" ומלובים באש השנאה]

34 Ibid., 47.

[עיקר המחלוקת בין רבני הציונות הדתית וגוש אמונים לאנשי "עוד יוסף חי" סבות סביב שני צמתים: הפרשנות האלימה של כתבי ההלכה והתורה וההצדקה של הרג ורצח בשמם; ועצמאותם של מוסדות רבניים וחוקי ההלכה בנפרד ממדינת ישראל על מוסדותיה]

35 Shimi Friedman, Noar HaGva'ot: Beyn Mered Neurim Lehitnachalut baSfar (*The Hilltop Youth: Between Teenage Rebellion and Frontier Settlement*) (PhD Diss. Ben-Gurion University in the Negev, 2013); Assaf Harel, "Beyond Gush Emunim: On Contemporary Forms of Messianism Among Religiously Motivated Settlers in the West Bank," in *Normalizing Occupation: The*

previous studies conducted in this direction, which are based on anthropological observation, this chapter is based mostly on critical analysis of the theological and practical aspects in Rabbi Ginzburg's political thought, revealing similarities and disputes with Religious Zionism. By making a clear distinction between theological ideas and practical aspects, I am able to demonstrate how two seemingly contradictory theologies eventually lead to similar practices.

Rabbi Yitzchak Ginzburg's Theology

In this section I will review Rabbi Ginzburg's political writing, and present the theological foundations upon which his thought is based. More specifically, I will discuss his views on several central issues – his conception of Messianic redemption and possible ways to promote it, and the resulting position regarding the theological status of the Zionist idea and the State of Israel. A cursory review of those positions presents these perceptions as fundamentally different from the "Merkaz HaRav" concept of redemption held by Religious-Zionist public. As I illustrate in this section, Rabbi Ginzburg's philosophy is based mainly on the basic writings of Chabad Hasidism. Contrarily, contemporary Religious Zionism (particularly the "Merkaz HaRav" school) derives its theological foundations mainly from the writings of Rabbi Zvi Yehuda Kook, who identifies the establishment of "The State of Israel" as actualization of the messianic redemption. Later, however, I will critically analyze the practices espoused by Rabbi Ginzburg (and which, in fact, generate most criticism from Religious Zionism), and show how these in fact demonstrate fundamental similarities to those of "Merkaz HaRav." By reflecting on the similarities in practice between "Merkaz HaRav" and Rabbi Ginzburg, I substantiate my position that contradicting theologies may lead to similar practices. This point is important, since it indicates there are sociopolitical considerations stirring up the Religious-Zionist criticism of Rabbi Ginzburg and his presentation as a radical figure. Furthermore, it can shed light on social and discursive processes through which 'radicalism' is produced.

Rabbi Ginzburg's concept of messianic redemption is influenced by Chabad Hasidism, which seeks to promote the redemption by bringing Divine Presence to

Politics of Everyday Life in the West Bank Settlements, ed. Ariel Handel et al. (Indiana: Indiana University Press, 2017). It is also claimed these youngsters do not tend to accept any absolute rabbinic authority whatsoever. See Tessa Satherly, "'The Simple Jew': The 'Price Tag' Phenomenon, Vigilantism, and Rabbi Yitzchak Ginsburgh's Political Kabbalah," *Melilah* 10 (2013): 57–91.

the "lower world" (concrete reality). Rabbi Shneur Zalman of Liadi, the founder of Chabad Hasidism, wrote in *Tanya*[36]:

> In a well-known statement, our Rabbis declared that the purpose for which this world was created is that the Holy One, blessed be He, desired to have an abode in the lower realms [...] and it is known that the Messianic era, especially the period after the resurrection of the dead, is indeed the ultimate purpose and the fulfillment of this world. It is for this [purpose] that [this world] was originally created.[37]

Accordingly, the Chabad Hasidim hold a teleological conception of reality, according to which human history is a deterministic process directed towards messianic redemption, in which God will be revealed in the concrete reality and the whole world will recognize the uniqueness of God and his creation. For this purpose, it is necessary that the People of Israel create an infrastructure that will enable God to reveal himself – *Dira BaTachtonim* (an abode in the lower realms). This goal is achieved by the return of each of the People of Israel to faith in God. This obligation is incumbent upon the entire Jewish people, and therefore Chabad Chassidim take upon themselves the task of actively promoting the return of the Jewish People to God. Rabbi Ginzburg cites the Lubavitcher Rebbe's statements that the current generation is the one in which the redemption will take place, while emphasizing the People of Israel's responsibility for promoting it: "I did what I can [...] from now on, do as much as you can to actually bring the pious messiah right away."[38] Subsequently, Rabbi Ginzburg clarifies the Rebbe's description of the means to promote the coming of the Messiah: "The direct, easy and quick way to act in order to promote the Messiah's revelation is by studying the subjects of redemption and Messiah in the Torah."[39] In his writings, Rabbi Ginzburg deals extensively with the messianic *Tikun* (Rectification) of the individual.[40] The personal *Tikun* of each individual will eventually lead to the healing of the society and the promotion of redemption. This perception, which emphasizes the change in private consciousness, has led many research-

---

36 *Tanya* is Chabad Hasidism's foundational book. The Chabad Hasidim sees great importance in studying and disseminating the book, and memorizing it or parts of it is a Chabad custom.
37 Rabbi Shneur Zalman of Liadi, *Tanya*, 90.
[והנה מודעת זאת מאמר רבותינו ז"ל שתכלית בריאת עולם הזה הוא שנתאווה הקב"ה להיות לו דירה בתחתונים...
ונודע שימות המשיח ובפרט כשיחיו המתים הם תכלית ושלימות בריאות עולם הזה שלכך נברא מתחילתו]
38 Quoted in Yitzchak Ginzburg, *Be'Ita Achishena* (*When the time comes I will hurry it*) (Kfar-Chabad: Gal Einai, 2003), 9.
[אני את שלי עשיתי.. מכאן ואילך עשו אתם ככל אשר ביכולתכם להביא את משיח צדקנו בפועל תכף ומיד ממש]
39 Quoted in ibid., 10.
[הדרך הישרה, הקלה והמהירה כדי לפעול להתגלות וביאת המשיח היא לימוד ענייני גאולה ומשיח בתורה]
40 See footnote 26. Sagi, *Messianic-Radicalism in The State of Israel*, 33–45.

ers to view him as a key figure in the New Age culture,[41] although other researchers also see it as a practical demand that is required collectively from believers.[42]

Rabbi Ginzburg follows a Kabalistic tradition perceiving the redemption of the People of Israel as the metaphoric fulfillment of a spousal relationship between the male active essence of God and the passive feminine nature of *Kenesset Yisrael* (the Congregation of Israel), representing the collective consciousness of all souls of the People of Israel. According to this approach, in order to achieve redemption, the People of Israel must adopt a collective "feminine" and passive consciousness. This collective consciousness is an aggregation of all individual consciousness and therefore the emphasis must be on changing the individual's consciousness. The small personal change that will occur among each member of the Jewish people will ultimately lead to a collective change.[43]

According to Rabbi Ginzburg, the outcome of God's mating with *Knesset Yisrael* is the birth of King Messiah, which reflects the characteristics of both parents: on the one hand, the Messiah feels responsibility for actively redeeming Israel, and on the other hand identifies with the people's demand for redemption on the part of God.[44] Redemption will occur when all individuals within the Jewish people will adopt a "feminine" consciousness in the manner of God's service. Ginzburg illustrates the desired relationship between man and God, by comparing it to an axis of femininity (daughter-wife-mother). At the lower level, "daughter," the individual feels he is enslaved to God – he fulfills his commandments as he understands them and turns to him in prayer when he needs assistance. However, in this state of consciousness one believes he is capable of perceiving God's will (as well as his own needs) and therefore fulfills his "commands" properly. Therefore, the changes God will make in that person's life will be small and gradual, since they are also subject to the limitations of his human intellect. Contrarily, Rabbi Ginzburg calls for raising consciousness to the level of "mother," in which the individual completely abolishes his own personality and will. He works with all his effort to bring redemption but does not false-

41 Boaz Huss, "The New Age of Kabbalah," *Journal of Modern Jewish Studies* 6 (2009): 107–125; Julia Schwarzman, "Rabbi Yitzchak Ginsburgh and his Feminine Vision of the Messianic Age," *Journal of Modern Jewish Studies* 12 (2013): 52–70; Assaf Tamari, "The Place of Politics: The Notion of Consciousness in Rabbi Yitzchak Ginsburgh's Political Thought," *Israel Studies Review* 29 (2014): 78–98.

42 Sagi, *Messianic-Radicalism in The State of Israel*; Inbari, *Jewish Fundamentalism and the Temple Mount*; Harari, *Mysticism as Messianic Rhetoric*.

43 Tamari, *The Place of Politics*; Schwarzman, *Rabbi Yitzchak Ginsburgh and his Feminine Vision of the Messianic Age*.

44 Ginzburg, *Be'Ita Achishena*, 227–229.

ly believe he is capable of conceiving its meaning and has no assurance he is entitled to it or that his actions are in the right direction. The desire for active messianic action, while completely abolishing oneself in the face of God, is the ultimate state of consciousness, that once becomes collective will enable God's revelation in the lower realms.[45]

Therefore, we can conclude that regarding the concept of messianic redemption, there are substantial disparities between Rabbi Ginzburg's Kabalistic-Chabad-Hassidic theology and the "Kookist" theology characterizing the "Merkaz HaRav" School. The Kook rabbis' historiosophic approach interpreted the Jewish people's history throughout the early twentieth century (particularly the rise of the Zionist movement and the 1967 war) as evidence for the actual realization of the messianic redemption. Accordingly, contemporary Religious-Zionists continue to interpret topical political events as expressions of the progress of the redemption process and its actual realization. These interpretations lead to political activism, contrasting Rabbi Ginzburg's preaching to passiveness.[46]

The State of Israel's Theological Status in Rabbi Ginzburg's thought

Rabbi Ginzburg is well known for his militant opposition to Zionism and the State of Israel. In his books, he categorically rejects the ideas of liberal democracy and calls for the establishment of *Malkhut Israel*, a Jewish monarchy over all the Greater Land of Israel,[47] headed by King Messiah. Rabbi Ginzburg criticizes democratic regimes for favoring the well-being of the individual, since they reject the possibility of an absolute divine truth, and therefore must acknowledge the rights of cultural and ethnic minorities. According to Ginzburg, the desired re-

---

45 Ibid., 269–271.

46 For example, see Rabbi Shmuel Eliyahu, "Eych Ha'olam Nirah miLemala?" (How Does the World Seem from Above), *Olam Katan*, September 13 2015, 5. Accessed July 28 2017, https://www.flipsnack.com/79987ECF8D6/466.html?pn=12 (Hebrew). For elaboration on the aspect of activism in Religious-Zionist thought see Schwartz, *Religious-Zionism Between Logic and Messianism*; Ravitzky, *Messianism, Zionism and Jewish Religious Radicalism*; Feige, *One Space, Two Places*.

47 Rabbi Ginzburg presents several possible interpretations for this term, though even the minimalist interpretation includes the lands of Judea and Samaria. Yitzchak Ginzburg, *Malkhut Israel Vol. 1* (*Kingdom of Israel*) (Kefar-Chabad: Gal Einai, Vol. 1, 1999; Vol. 2 2000; Vol. 3, 2005, Hebrew), 135–144.

gime is an absolutist state led by King Messiah, who fulfills the "general will" in each individual.[48]

In addition to his criticism of the regime type in the State of Israel, Rabbi Ginzburg also criticizes Israeli government institutions for not being directed by the Torah, but rather influenced by secular ideologies. In the book *Rectifying the State of Israel* he describes the defects of the secular Zionist ideology, which, although it has a significant and necessary role in the physical reality, still lacks proper spiritual guidance:

> The light inherent in the Zionist dream – the aspiration that the Jewish People, after nearly two thousand years of exile, return to their homeland – is indeed great, but its secularly oriented vessels are small and immature. Secular Zionism has succeeded in creating material vessels, constructing buildings and roads, developing industry, and creating institutions of higher, secular education. But it has willfully neglected, or even rejected [...] the conscious intention that they serve God's purpose in creation [...] Now, we have returned to our homeland and possess a strong and skilled army. Nonetheless, our very identity as Jews [...] is in danger. The sociological phenomenon of so-called post-Zionism, even more secular in its orientation than its predecessor, the original Zionism, threatens to undermine Jewish identity by replacing it by either cosmopolitan identity or an 'Israeli' Identity, devoid of Judaism.[49]

In later texts, Rabbi Ginzburg's opposition to the State of Israel and the Zionist regime has intensified. Until the beginning of the 2000s, Rabbi Ginzburg mainly advocated passive resistance and change of inner consciousness and focused this criticism to a limited number of problems (mainly the secular legal system and the treatment of non-Jewish minorities). However, the Israeli government's intention to withdraw its forces from northern Samaria and the Gaza Strip, thereby evacuating more than eight thousand Jewish residents from their homes, led to a change in Rabbi Ginzburg's position, and he began to publicly call for an uncompromising struggle against the Israeli state and its institutions.

In the articles "Time to Crack the Nut"[50] and "The Shell Precedes the Fruit"[51], Rabbi Ginzburg described Israel's spiritual status using an allegory comparing the Israeli State to a nut. In his allegory, the nutshell has an essential role

---

48 For elaboration on Rabbi Ginzburg's "Kingdom of Israel," see Tamari, *The Place of Politics*, 90–94.

49 Yitzchak Ginzburg, *Rectifying the State of Israel: A Political Platform based on Kabbalah* (Israel: Gal Einai, 2002), 21–23.

50 Yitzchak Ginzburg, *Kumi Uri: Pirkey Maavak uTekumah* (*Rise and Shine: Chapters on Struggle and Revival*) (Kfar-Chabad: Gal Einai, 2006, Hebrew).

51 Yitzchak Ginzburg, *U'Mimena Yivashe'a* (*He will be salvaged from her*) (Kfar-Chabad: Gal Einai, 2006, Hebrew).

in preserving the fruit, but when the fruit is ripe it becomes unnecessary and even harmful. In the same way, the State of Israel and the Zionist movement played an important role in safeguarding the Jewish people by bringing many Jews to live in the Land of Israel and instilling them with the aspiration to establish a Jewish state. Today, however, the nutshells are beginning to endanger the Jewish people. In order to enable the development of the Jewish people in its land, the four "shells" suffocating it must be cracked: Zionist ideology and secular Jewish culture, which seeks to deliberately destroy the Jewish people spiritually; the Israeli legal, judicial, and educational systems ("the permanent establishment"), which are rooted in the world of liberal values; the Israeli parliament and government ("the changing establishment"),[52] who have abandoned their role to ensure the welfare of the citizens and the security of the people, and instead act out of harmful interests. Besides those three shells, there is another shell combining good and evil, representing the Israeli Army. The army is a positive factor, since it is composed of "simple people"[53] willing to sacrifice their lives for the sake of preserving the Jewish people and the land. On the other hand, the army creates negative moral failures such as men serving alongside women, non-Jews serving in the army, and the laws concerning "purity of arms", which are based on Christian morality.[54]

The transformation in Rabbi Ginzburg's views is clearly reflected in his views regarding the proper state of mind for the struggle against the establishment. In his early publications, Rabbi Ginzburg emphasized the importance of the gradual change "from within," and the activism he preached for was change of consciousness.[55] However, in his later publications, a different approach is expressed. Rabbi Ginzburg acknowledges the futility of change "from within" and calls for complete disengagement from Israeli institutions, and the establishment of alternative institutions to prepare the ground for their replacement when the time comes. Ginzburg quotes the Talmudic saying "The prisoner cannot free himself from jail"[56], and derives from it that political struggle can be effective

52 "The government should be overthrown, and when a new government rises we shall bring it down as well, and so on – until a regime based on the Torah is established," Ginzburg, *Kumi Uri*, 18.

[יש להפיל את הממשלה, ולכשתקום חדשה להפיל גם אותה, וכך הלאה – עד לכינון ממשל תורני בארץ]

53 For elaboration on "The Simple Jew" concept in Ginzburg's thought see Satherly, *The Simple Jew*.

54 Ginzburg, *Kumi Uri*, 122–123.

55 Ginzburg, *Malkhut Israel*, 183.

56 Babylonian Talmud, Berakhot 5b.

[אין חבוש מתיר עצמו מבית האסורים]

only if the state's support is cut off. The belief that every Jew has a "Divine Spark" reinforces the legitimacy of the establishment and conceals the fact that it is a "nutshell" that must be broken. Furthermore, even those who consider the establishment as merely instrumental and therefore advocate gradual change for purely tactical reasons are mistaken, since the institutions demand a total and absolute change. Therefore, limited gradual actions cannot deal with the "unchangeable establishment", and thus are futile and doomed to failure.[57]

From the above, we can clearly conclude that Ginzburg's theology is fundamentally opposed to the ideas presented by the "Merkaz HaRav" school. There is extensive academic scholarship about the "statist" approach of Religious Zionism and the "Merkaz Harav" school, which views the State of Israel as *Atkhalta Degeula* (The beginning of redemption), and therefore endowed with sanctity.[58] Moreover, Religious Zionism's flagship projects are carried out with extensive budgetary, security, and logistical support from the State of Israel. Rabbi Ginzburg's public statements, calling for disengagement from the establishment's support, could severely harm institutions of Religious Zionism: educational institutions, settlement movements, youth movements, etc. Therefore, it is clear why the "Merkaz HaRav" school is opposed to Rabbi Ginzburg on the theological level.

Practical Aspects in Rabbi Ginzburg's Thought

In this section, I will examine the practical implications Rabbi Ginzburg derives from his theology, and compare them to the practices prevalent among Gush Emunim and the Religious-Zionist movement, as well as to the writings and statements of prominent rabbis from the "Merkaz HaRav" school. In particular, I will focus on three key practical actions he discusses: the fulfillment of the "public commandments" and the establishment of the "Kingdom of Israel"; civil disobedience; and vigilant violence towards Palestinians.

57 Ginzburg, *Kumi Uri*, 212.

58 See Ravitzky, *Messianism, Zionism and Jewish Religious Radicalism*, 111–200; Aran, *Kukism*; Roth, *Not at any Cost*, 44–66.

"Public Commandments" and the Establishment of the "Kingdom of Israel"

Despite his great preoccupation with promoting the redemption following the Chabad Hasidism tradition, Ginzburg's writing calls for concrete political change that does not take place merely in the consciousness of the individual. In the "Kingdom of Israel" series of books, Rabbi Ginzburg discusses the three "public commandments" binding the Jewish People once they enter the Land of Israel, whereas in contrast to the other commandments imposed on each individual, the fulfillment of the "public commandments" is a collective responsibility of the Jewish People.[59] The three commandments Rabbi Ginzburg wishes to implement are declaring a king, the extermination of Amalek, and the building of the Temple. The fulfillment of those commandments and the establishment of the "Kingdom of Israel" are necessary conditions for the "abode in the underworld" that will enable the redemption and the descent of the Divine Presence into the lower spheres.[60]

Concretely, Rabbi Ginzburg calls for adopting several practical principles that will lead to the establishment of the "Kingdom of Israel"[61]:

- The people of Israel are endowed with a special holiness that must be spread throughout the world on three levels: geographic expansion, demographic growth, and the dissemination of the Hebrew language.
- Non-Jews should be prevented from staying in the Land of Israel: "We must make an effort, with high dedication of our body and money, to refrain, as far as possible, from any action (employment, purchase, etc.) that maintains a non-Jewish community in Israel."[62]
- Confiscation of products manufactured in Germany.
- "Kosher" Jewish education, in which secular studies will be subjected to religious studies.
- Avoidance of secular civil courts.
- Economic independence: cut off of dependence on state institutions.[63]
- Loving the nation, despite all the flaws in the existing establishment.[64]

---

59 Yitchak Ginzburg, *Malkhut Yisrael*, Vol 1.

60 Ginzburg, *Malkhut Israel*, Vol. 1, 17–20.

61 Ibid., 128–130.

62 Ibid., 130.

63 Regarding this point, which I have discussed previously, there seems to be a profound difference between Rabbi Ginzburg's stance and that of the "Merkaz Harav" school.

64 Ibid. Vol. 1, 129–130.

Although some practical aspects in Rabbi Ginzburg's political writings are racist and undemocratic, and therefore might justify Religious Zionism's critical perception of Rabbi Ginzburg as an extremist, also other Religious-Zionist rabbis have frequently expressed similar views. In the following paragraphs I will present statements made by "Merkaz HaRav" school rabbis, advocating actions similar to those Rabbi Ginzburg calls for.

The aspiration to prevent gentiles from staying in the Land of Israel is a view many Religious-Zionist rabbis share with Rabbi Ginzburg, derived from the biblical commandment: "When the Lord your God brings you into the land you are entering to possess and drives out before you many nations [...] nations larger and stronger than you [...] then you must destroy them totally. Make no treaty with them, and show them no mercy."[65] Accordingly, Religious-Zionist rabbis have signed petitions calling the public to avoid employing,[66] renting houses to,[67] and buying from[68] non-Jews.

Regarding other undemocratic points made by Rabbi Ginzburg, it seems that "Merkaz HaRav" rabbis would agree with them as well. Rabbi Zvi Yehuda Kook was known for his severe criticism of both the Israeli Judicial system and secular education, which he conceived as subject to foreign influences.[69] Accordingly, Naftali Bennett, the Israeli Minister of Education and head of the Religious-Zionist party The Jewish Home, works to introduce Jewish-orthodox content into the secular education system. In a conference held in 2016 Bennett presented his hierarchical educational approach, in which secular studies should be subjected to holy studies:

> Studying Judaism is more important to me than math or science studies, since as a high-tech superpower, we need to be a spiritual power and to export spiritual ideas to the

65 Deuteronomy 7:1–2.
[(א) כִּי יְבִיאֲךָ יְהוָה אֱלֹהֶיךָ אֶל הָאָרֶץ אֲשֶׁר אַתָּה בָא שָׁמָּה לְרִשְׁתָּהּ וְנָשַׁל גּוֹיִם רַבִּים מִפָּנֶיךָ הַחִתִּי וְהַגִּרְגָּשִׁי וְהָאֱמֹרִי וְהַכְּנַעֲנִי וְהַפְּרִזִּי וְהַחִוִּי וְהַיְבוּסִי שִׁבְעָה גוֹיִם רַבִּים וַעֲצוּמִים מִמֶּךָּ. (ב) וּנְתָנָם יְהוָה אֱלֹהֶיךָ לְפָנֶיךָ וְהִכִּיתָם הַחֲרֵם תַּחֲרִים אֹתָם לֹא תִכְרֹת לָהֶם בְּרִית וְלֹא תְחָנֵּם]

66 E.g. "Atzumat Rabanim Neged Ha'asakat Aravim" (Rabbi's Petition Against Employing Arabs), NRG, accessed July 28 2017, http://www.nrg.co.il/online/1/ART1/766/982.html (Hebrew).

67 Yaki Adamker and Eli Shlezinger, "Bil'adi – 'Mi sheMaskir Dirah leAravim Chayav beNidui' – haMichtav haMale" (Exclusive – 'Those who Rent an Apartment to Arabs Must be Ostracized' – The full letter), *Behadrei Haredim*, August 12 2010, accessed July 28 2017, https://www.bhol.co.il/news/77315 (Hebrew).

68 "Shoot Selulary" (SMS Q&A), Olam Katan, accessed July 28 2017, https://www.flipsnack.com/79987ECF8D6/553.html?pn=4 (Hebrew).

69 Aran, *From Religious Zionism To Zionist Religion*; Neriah Guttel, "Murkavut Yachaso Shel HaRav Kook Zatzal Lemimshakey Torah uMada" (The Complexity in Rabbi Tvi Yehuda's Approach Towards the Torah-Science Nexus), *Oreshet* 4 (2003): 131–156.

> world, as we did in the past when we sat on our land. This is the next chapter of our Zionist vision. This is how we will once again be a light unto the nations.[70]

Regarding the use of the secular judicial system, following Rabbi Zvi Yehuda's objection, Religious-Zionist rabbis ruled that disputes must be settled in rabbinical courts, while civil courts must be avoided.[71]

Civil Disobedience

Together with his operative plan for establishing the "Kingdom of Israel", and corresponding with his theological views, Ginzburg calls for active resistance to the current Israeli state. Regarding the issue of military insubordination, Rabbi Ginzburg's stance is unequivocal – one must assertively refuse to carry out any order contradicting the laws of the Torah, particularly orders to evacuate Jewish settlements on the Land of Israel. Rabbi Ginzburg has held this position for many years, and unlike other rabbis, he publicly expressed it decades before the declaration of the disengagement plan, and he continues to voice it consistently in his talks today, while showing no hesitation to confront "statist" rabbis and public figures.

In an article written before the evacuation of the Yamit settlements in the Sinai Peninsula as part of the Camp David Accords, Ginzburg quotes from Maimonides: "*A person who negates a king's command because he was occupied with a mitzvah, even a minor one, is not liable.*"[72] Moreover, besides the Halakhic obligation to disobey orders contradicting the Halakha, in later publications Ginzburg goes as far as considering non-violent civil resistance as a tool to dismantle the democratic regime in Israel. As explained above, Rabbi Ginzburg's attitude toward the army is ambivalent. The contaminated "nutshells" (the Zionist ideology, the permanent and changing establishments) consistently refrain from men-

---

70 Yarden Skoop and Or Kashti, "Bennet: 'Limudei Yahdut Chasuvim Yoter meLimudey Matematika uMada'im'" (Bennet: "Judaic studies are More Important Than Studying Math and Science"). Haaretz, September 12 2016, accessed October 22 2017, https://www.haaretz.co.il/news/education/1.3066279 (Hebrew, translation mine).
[לימוד היהדות וההצטיינות בה חשוב בעיניי יותר מלימודי מתמטיקה או מדעים, כי גם כמעצמת היי-טק, יצאנֵי ידע וחידושים לכל העולם, עלינו להיות גם מעצמה רוחנית ולייצא רעיונות רוחניים לכל העולם, כפי שעשינו בעבר, כשישבנו על אדמתנו]

71 See Yaakov Ariel, "Hamishpat beMedinat Israel veIsur 'Erka'ot'" (The Hebrew Law in the State of Israel and the Prohibition of 'Erka'ot)], *Techumin* 1 (1980): 319 – 328.

72 Maimonides, *Misnheh Torah* 14, "The Book of Judges, Kings and Wars," chapter 3 halakha 9.
[המבטל גזרת המלך בשביל שנתעסק במצות אפילו במצוה קלה הרי זה פטור]

tioning the name of God, or otherwise use it cynically to derive political profits. On the other hand, the army nutshell consists mostly of simple people who acknowledge God, yet do as they are ordered by their commanders. Therefore, this shell has the potential to save the People of Israel by stimulating soldiers' commitment to God and Torah. One must enlist in the army since it has a potential for change, but in any case of an order that contradicts the Torah's opinion, he must tell his commander: "*I love you, and I'm happy to fulfill the commands, but the Torah is the supreme source of authority, both mine and yours.*"[73]

The subject of civil disobedience and military insubordination has evoked one of the last major disputes within contemporary Religious Zionism. Though it is impossible to find a uniform and coherent position among Religious-Zionists, it is evident that the ongoing political struggles have led to significant shifts in the positions expressed on this matter. Hershkowitz and Hellinger discuss how despite the "statist" image of the "Merkaz HaRav" school, Rabbi Zvi Yehuda supported illegal settlement activities, while emphasizing the supremacy of the divine command over man-made laws. Another recent study, examining the interrelations between Religious Zionism and the state during the struggle against the disengagement plan, analyzes the major viewpoints of "Merkaz HaRav" Rabbis on the subject. The study shows most rabbis ruled that participation in the evacuation is prohibited, though they differed on the grounds to this stance.[74] Accordingly, another recent study shows forty percent of Religious-Zionists believe that disobeying an army order to evacuate Jewish settlements is justified.[75]

"Price Tag" and Vigilant Violence

Due to his controversial statements,[76] Rabbi Ginzburg is regularly accused of supporting "Nekamah" (vengeance) – vigilantism towards Palestinian civilians. Despite the wide scope of Rabbi Ginzburg's writings,[77] it appears that most aca-

73 Ginzburg, *Kumi Uri*, 19.

74 Roth, *Not at any Cost*, 305–317.

75 Tamar Herman et al., *Datiim? Leumiim! haMachane haDAti-Leumi beIsrael 2014* (*The National-Religious Sector in Israel 2014*) (Jerusalem: The Israeli Democracy Institute, 2014, Hebrew), 145.

76 Most notable is the publication of the booklet "Baruch haGgever".

77 Rabbi Ginzburg has published over one hundred books, discussing Kabbalah, Jewish holidays, Jewish psychology, music, business, marriage, messianic redemption, the ideal Jewish regime, and more.

demic research on Ginzburg's thought focuses on the act of vengeance.[78] Hence I will not elaborate on it, but rather focus on other statements, generally interpreted as deliberate calls to harm Palestinians' life and property, and demonstrate the complexity of his position on this issue.

I claim that it is possible to extract a complex yet coherent and consistent position on the use of violence against Palestinian civilians and Israeli security forces from Ginzburg's writing. According to Ginzburg, the use of violence by an individual is prohibited, and the proper means for struggle against the Israeli state are material and ideological disengagement from the establishment. However, if an individual Jew commits a spontaneous violent act, he should not be condemned (even though the act was not justified in the first place), since the action stems from sincere frustration caused by the existing situation.[79]

Some critics who argue that Ginzburg encourages violence quote his statements from a *Hitva'adut* ("gathering")[80] under the title *BeAra'a De'Israel Beney Chorin* ("Free on the Land of Israel"), held on April 18 2014 in the settlement of Yitzhar. During the gathering, Ginzburg used his speech in order to refer to the pressing topical events.[81] Ginzburg spoke of "Od Yosef Chay" students as going through a process taking them from slavery to freedom. Ginzburg sees

---

78 For example "Don Seeman, Violence, Ethics, and Divine Honor in Modern Jewish Thought," *Journal of the American Academy of Religion* 73 (2005): 1015–1048; Inbari, *Jewish Fundamentalism and the Temple Mount*; Shlomo Fisher, Teva, "Otentiut veAlimut baHagut haTZionit haDatit haRadikalit," (Nature, Authenticity and Violence in Radical Religious-Zionist Thought) in *Dorot, Merchavim, Zehuyot: Mabatim Achsaviim al Chevrah veTarbut belSrael (Generations, Locations, Identities: Contemporary Prespectives on Society and Culture in Israel)*, ed. Hannah Herzog, Tal Kohavi, and Shimshon Zelniker (Tel-Aviv: Ha'kibbuz Ha'Meuhad, 2007, Hebrew); Shlomo Fisher, "Bein haKlali laCharig: Yehuda Etzion veHarav Yitzchak Ginzburg," (Between the General and the Exceptional: Yehuda Etzion and Rabbi Yitzchak Ginzburg) in *Lifnim miShurat haDin: heCharig uMatzav haCherum* (*State of Exception and State of Emergency*), ed. Yehudah Shenhav, Christoph Schmidt, and Shimshon Zelniker (Tel Aviv: Ha'Kibbuz Ha'Meuhad, 2009, Hebrew); Satherly, *The Simple Jew*; Hershkowitz and Helinger, *Obedience and Civil Disobedince in Religious Zionism*.

79 See "haRav Yitzchak Ginzbur uPaneyha haRAbim Shel haEmet: Teguvah Lamevakrim" (Rabbi Yitzchak Ginzburg and the Many Sides of the Truth: Response to Critics), Bein Kodesh Le'Hol, accessed July 28 2017, https://nirmenussi.com/rabbi-yitzchak-ginsburgh-reply-to-critics/ (Hebrew).

80 An event in which a number of Hasidim gather for the purpose of singing Hassidic melodies, telling stories, and learning Torah, usually accompanied by an alcoholic drink.

81 Yitzhar is home to the "Od Yosef Chay" yeshiva, of which Rabbi Ginzburg is president; its students were accused of regular confrontations with Palestinian civilians and the security forces. As a result, the yeshiva's building was taken over by the Israeli Border Police. The "Hitvaadut" discussed here took place a week after the evacuation from the building, and, therefore, although not directly mentioned, it is interpreted as referring to the events that led to the evacuation of the yeshiva.

this process as analogous to the process of childbirth: "*When a child is born [...] both the mother suffers and the infant [...] The pain pushes him towards unregulated acts [...] Here in Yitzhar there is a special womb, and in particular there is a special womb that is the yeshiva, and the purpose of the womb is to give birth to a new nation [...] Therefore we sometimes act as gentiles.*"[82] However, although these are "acts of gentiles," he believes that the confrontations with the security forces are justified since they stem from pure motives. However, although he sees the motivations of "Od Yosef Chay" students positively (or at least does not condemn them), he considers them as immature acts representing a preliminary stage of liberation from the chains of the establishment ("labor pains"). Rabbi Ginzburg emphasizes that the desired course of action is non-violent civil disobedience.

The increasing of "price tag" activities brought fierce criticism from Religious-Zionist rabbis concerning the phenomenon.[83] Furthermore, analysis of the Religious-Zionist opposition to Rabbi Ginzburg indicates that most of the criticism of his thought revolves around his alleged advocacy of vigilant violence towards Palestinian civilians and Israeli security forces. However, organized or spontaneous acts of vigilant violence are not foreign to Religious Zionism and the settlement movement, and have received relatively broad support among the settlers.[84] The most notable case of organized violence by settlers was the formation of "The Jewish Underground," which carried out several terror attacks against Palestinian civilians, and planned to blow up the Dome of the Rock in Jerusalem.[85] Sprinzak quotes from the investigation of Shaul Nir, one of the perpetrators of the attack on the Islamic College, who claims that he personally received authorization from four rabbis. Sprinzak mentions the names of Rabbi Eliezer Waldman of Kiryat Arba and Rabbi Moshe Levinger, both of whom were

---

82 "Be'Araa De'Israel Benei Horin" (Free on the Land of Israel), Malchut Yisrael, accessed July 29 2017, http://malchuty.org/2011-01-20-01-37-36/46–q/1136-q-q-q-q-.html (Hebrew, translation mine).

[כשיש לידה יש צירים... שגם האמא סובלת וגם התינוק-העובר ודאי מרגיש ... הוא עושה מעשים בלתי מבוקרים... כאן ביצהר יש רחם מיוחד, ובפרט יש בית מיוחד של רחם שהוא הישיבה למטה, והמטרה של הרחם שיולד ממנו עם חדש... לכן עושים מעשים שהם כמו גוים]

83 Jeremy Sharon, "West Bank Rabbis Say Price Tag Attacks Contravene Torah and Ethical Behavior," *The Jerusalem Post*, January 15 2014, accessed October 22 2017, http://www.jpost.com/Diplomacy-and-Politics/West-Bank-rabbis-say-price-tag-attacks-contravene-Torah-and-ethical-behavior-338265.

84 David Weisbrud, *Jewish Settler Violence: Deviance as Social Reaction* (Pennsylvania State University Press, 1989); Sprinzak, *Brother Against Brother*; Hershkowitz and Hellinger, *Obedience and Civil Disobedience in Religious Zionism.*

85 Hershkowitz and Hellinger, *Obidience and Civil Disobedience in Religious Zionism*, 82–89.

founders of Gush Emunim and close disciples of Rabbi Zvi Yehuda. Rabbi Moshe Levinger, one of the pioneer settlers in Hebron, was accused and convicted several times of acting violently towards Palestinians.[86] Despite these convictions, Rabbi Levinger continued to gain respect among Religious Zionism until his death. Rabbi Levinger won the Moskowitz Prize for Zionism in 2013, and at his funeral (attended by over ten thousand people) was eulogized by the Israeli President, Reuven Rivlin, in addition to prominent Religious Zionist figures, including Rabbi Eliezer Waldman, Rabbi Dov Lior, Rabbi Chaim Druckman, and the Agricultural Minister Uri Ariel.

Conclusion

This chapter compares Rabbi Ginzburg's political thought to the mainstream Religious Zionist theology and ideology, as represented by the "Merkaz HaRav" school. Rabbi Yitzchak Ginzburg is well known as a radical rabbi, and is constantly criticized across Israeli society, as well as by Religious Zionists. Although academic literature discusses the fundamentalist aspects in contemporary Religious Zionist ideology, Religious Zionists self-portray themselves as moderate, law-abiding citizens. Therefore, many Religious Zionists criticize Rabbi Ginzburg's ideology, and accuse him of supporting violent "price tag" acts. However, an examination of contemporary Religious Zionism reveals support for actions similar to those Ginzburg advocates.

In order to understand the source of Religious Zionist criticism of Rabbi Ginzburg, I presented a comparative analysis of Ginzburg's political thought with Religious Zionist ideology, while making a distinction between the movement's theology and the practical aspects derived from it. This distinction reveals a substantial theological dispute between Ginzburg's theology, based mainly on Chabad Hasidism and Jewish mysticism, and the theology of the "Merkaz HaRav" school, which is influenced by the writings of Rabbi Avraham Yitzchak Hacohen Kook, his son Rabbi Zvi Yehuda Kook, and other Religious Zionist rabbis. Nevertheless, although their theologies are completely different, a close analysis reveals similarities between Ginzburg's practical mode of action and declarations made by prominent Religious Zionist figures. This paper demonstrated that similarity by analyzing three key issues in Rabbi Ginzburg's ideology: the fulfillment of the "public commandments" and establishment of the

86 Betselem, *Achifat haChok Al Ezrachim Israelim Bashtachim* (*Law enforcement on Israeli Citizens in the West Bank*) (Jerusalem, Betselem, 1994), 85–87.

"Kingdom of Israel"; civil disobedience and military insubordination; and support for violent vigilant acts. Analysis of Ginzburg's standpoint on these issues reveals they correlate with the "Merkaz HaRav" school's practices, as demonstrated in their writings, public declarations, petitions, and actions.

This paper contributes to the understanding of contemporary Jewish radicalism, and specifically political trends within Religious Zionism. The distinction made between theology and practice reveals the radical subcurrents within Religious Zionism, concealed by a moderate "statist" theology. It demonstrates how two seemingly opposed theologies, one "moderate" and the other "radical", can eventually lead to supporting the same radical practices. Furthermore, it raises questions (here left undiscussed) regarding the concept of "radicalism", and the sociopolitical processes leading to the characterization of individuals and movements as radical.

Works Cited

Aran, Gideon. "meTzionut Datit leDat Tzionit: Reshit Gush Emunim keTnuah Datit" (From Religious Zionism to Zionist Religion: The Origins and Culture of Gush Emunim), PhD diss., Hebrew University, 1987. (Hebrew)

Aran, Gideon. *Kukism: Shorshei Gush Emunim, Tarbut haMitnachalim, Teologia Tzionit, Meshichiut beZmanenu* (*Kukism: The Roots of Gush Emunim, Zionist Theology, and Contemporary Messianism*). Jerusalem: Carmel Press, 2013. (Hebrew).

Ariel, Yaakov. "Hamishpat beMedinat Israel velsur 'Erka'ot'" (The Hebrew Law in the State of Israel and the Prohibition of 'Erkaot'). *Techumin* 1 (1980): 319–328.

Betselem. *Achifat haChok Al Ezrachim Israelim Bashtachim* (*Law enforcement on Israeli Citizens in the West Bank*). Jerusalem: Betselem, 1994. (Hebrew)

Feige, Michael. *Shtey Mapot laGada, Gush Emunim, Shalom Achsav ve'Itzuv haMrchav belsrael* (*One Space, Two Places: Gush Emunim, Peace Now and the Construction of Israeli Space*). Jerusalem: Magnes Press, 2004. (Hebrew)

Fisher, Shlomo. "Bein haKlali laCharig: Yehuda Etzion veHarav Yitzchak Ginzburg" (Between the General and the Exceptional: Yehuda Etzion and Rabbi Yitzchak Ginzburg). In *Lifnim miShurat haDin: heCharig uMatzav haCherum* (*State of Exception and State of Emergency State of Exception and State of Emergency*), edited by Yehudah Shenhav, Christoph Schmidt, and Shimshon Zelniker, 421–454. Tel Aviv: Ha'Kibbuz Ha'Meuhad, 2009. (Hebrew)

Fisher, Shlomo. "Teva, Otentiut veAlimut baHagut haTZionit haDatit haRadikalit" (Nature, Authenticity and Violence in Radical Religious-Zionist Thought). In *Dorot, Merchavim, Zehuyot: Mabatim Achsaviim al Chevrah veTarbut belSrael* (*Generations, Locations, Identities: Contemporary Perspectives on Society and Culture in Israel*), edited by Hannah Herzog, Tal Kohavi, and Shimshon Zelniker, 93–107. Tel-Aviv: Ha'kibbuz Ha'Meuhad, 2007. (Hebrew)

Fischer, Shlomo. "haParadigman haFondementalistit uMa Shemever La" (The Fundamentalist Paradigm and Beyond). *Theory and Criticism* 31 (2007): 283–295. (Hebrew)

Friedman, Shimi. "Noar Hagva'ot: Beyn Mered Neurim Lehitnachalut baSfar" (The Hilltop Youth: Between Teenage Rebellion and Frontier Settlement). PhD diss., Ben-Gurion University in the Negev, 2013. (Hebrew)

Harari, Yechiel. "Mistika keRetorika Meshichit" (Mysticism as Messianic Rhetoric). PhD diss., Tel-Aviv University, 2005. (Hebrew)

Harel, Assaf. "Beyond Gush Emunim: On Contemporary Forms of Messianism Among Religiously Motivated Settlers in the West Bank". In *Normalizing Occupation: The Politics of Everyday Life in the West Bank Settlements,* edited by Ariel Handel Marco Allegra and Erez Maggor, 142–162. Indiana: Indiana University Press, 2017.

Hefetz, Kobi, and Liat Cohen. *Ad Redet Machshachey Tehom: Mechkar Al Yeshivat Od Yoseph Chay Vekavanoteiha Klapey haHevra haIsraelit* (*Into the Dark Abyss: A study on "Od Yoseph Chay" Yeshiva and its intentions toward Israeli Society*). Tel-Aviv: Dror LaNefesh, 2013. (Hebrew)

Ginzburg, Yitzchak. *Be'Ita Achishena* (*When the time Comes I will hurry it*). Kfar-Chabad: Gal Einai, 2003. (Hebrew)

Ginzburg, Yitzchak. *Malkhut Israel* (*Kingdom of Israel*). Kfar-Chabad: Gal Einai, Vol. 1, 1999; Vol. 2, 2000; Vol. 3, 2005. (Hebrew).

Ginzburg, Yitzchak. *Rectifying the State of Israel: A Political Platform based on Kabbalah.* Israel: Gal Einai, 2002.

Ginzburg, Yitzchak. *Uri: Pirkey Maavak uTekumah* (*Rise and Shine: Chapters on Struggle and Revival*). Kfar-Chabad: Gal Einai, 2006. (Hebrew)

Ginzburg, Yitzchak. *U'Mimena Yivashe'a* (*He will be salvaged from her*). Kfar-Chabad: Gal Einai, 2006. (Hebrew)

Guttel, Neriah. "Murkavut Yachaso Shel haRav Kook Zatzal Lemimshakey Torah uMada" (The Complexity of Rabbi Tvi Yehuda's Approach Towards the Torah-Science Nexus). *Oreshet* 4 (2003): 131–156.

Hellinger, Moshe, and Isaac Hershkowitz. *Tziut ve'i Tziut baTzionut haDatit: miGush Emunim leTag Mechir* (*Obedience and Civil Disobedience in Religious Zionism: From Gush Emunim to the Price Tag Attacks*). The Israeli Democracy Institute, 2015. (Hebrew)

Herman, Tamar, Yuval Lebel, Chanan Cohem, Ella Heller, Gilad Be'ery, Kalman Neuman and Chanan Mozes. *Datiim? Leumiim! haMachane haDAti-Leumi beIsrael 2014* (*The National-Religious Sector in Israel 2014*). Jerusalem: The Israeli Democracy Institute, 2014. (Hebrew)

Herriot, Peter. *Religious Fundamentalism: Global, Local and Personal,* New York: Routledge, 2009.

Huss, Boaz. "The New Age of Kabbalah." *Journal of Modern Jewish Studies* 6 (2009): 107–125.

Inbari, Moti. *Fondementalizem Yehudi veHhar haBayit* (*Jewish Fundamentalism and the Temple Mount*). Jerusalem: Magness Press, 2008. (Hebrew)

Inbari, Motti. *Messianic Religious Zionism Confronts Israeli Territorial Compromises.* Cambridge University Press, 2012.

Katsman, Hayim. "'Pachad Yitzchak': Yachasa Shel haTzionut haDatit laRav Yitzchak Ginzburg" ('The Fear of Isaac': The Religious-Zionist Reaction to Rabbi Yitzchak Ginzburg). M.A. Thesis, Ben-Gurion University in the Negev, 2017. (Hebrew)

Lustick, Ian. *For the Land and the Lord: Jewish Fundamentalism in Israel.* New York: Council on Foreign Relations Press, 1988.

Moses. "Chanan. meTzionut Datit leDatiut Post Modernit" (*From Religious Zionism to Postmodern Religion*). PhD. Diss., Bar-Ilan University, 2009. (Hebrew)

Ravitzky, Aviezer. *Haketz Hameguleh uMedinat haYehudim: Meshichiut, Tzionut veRadikalizem Dati beIsrael* (*Messianism, Zionism and Jewish Religious Radicalism*). Tel Aviv: Am Oved, 1993. (Hebrew)

Rosenak, Avinoam. *Sedakim: Al Achdut haHafacim haPoliti veTalmidei HaRav Kook* (*Cracks: Unity of Opposites, the Political and Rabbi Kook's Disciples*). Tel-Aviv: Resling, 2013. (Hebrew)

Roth, Aanat. *Lo Bekol Mechir: meGush Katif Ad Amona: Hasipur Meachorey haMaavak Al Eretz Israel* (*Not at any Cost: From Gush Katif to Amona: The Story behind the Struggle over the Land of Israel*). Tel-Aviv: Yediot Aharonot, 2014. (Hebrew)

Sagi, Avi, and Dov Schwarz. "Tzionut Datit Nokhach Olam Moderni" (Religious-Zionist Enterprise Facing a Modern World). In *Mea Shnot Tzionut Datit* (*A Hundred Years of Religious Zionism*), edited by Avi Sagi and Dov Schwarz, 9–39. Ramat Gan: Bar-Ilan University, 2003. (Hebrew)

Sagi, Rephael. *Radicalizem Dati beMedinat Israel: Prakim beSod haTikun haMeshichi Shel HaRav Yiyzchak Ginzburg* (*Messianic-Radicalism in The State of Israel: Chapters in the concept of Messianic 'Tikun' in Rabbi Yitzchak Ginzburg's Thought*). Tel-Aviv: Gvanim. (Hebrew)

Satherly, Tessa. "'The Simple Jew': The 'Price Tag' Phenomenon, Vigilantism, and Rabbi Yitzchak Ginsburgh's Political Kabbalah." *Melilah* 10 (2013): 57–91.

Schwarz, Dov. "haTzionut haDatit: Toldot uPirkei Idiologia" (*Religious-Zionisim: History and Ideology*). Tel Aviv: Ministry of Defense Press, 2003. (Hebrew)

Schwarz, Dov. *haTzionut Hadatit Beyn Higayon leMeshichiut* (*Religious-Zionism Between Logic and Messianism*). Tel-Aviv: Am Oved, 1999. (Hebrew)

Schwarzman, Julia. "Rabbi Yitzchak Ginsburgh and his Feminine Vision of the Messianic Age." *Journal of Modern Jewish Studies* 12 (2013): 52–70.

Seeman, Don. "Violence, Ethics, and Divine Honor in Modern Jewish Thought." *Journal of the American Academy of Religion* 73 (2005): 1015–1048.

Shahak, Israel, and Norton Mezvinzki. *Jewish Fundamentalism in Israel.* London: Pluto Press, 1999.

Shalhoub-Kevorkian, Nadera, and Yossi David. "Is the Violence of Tag Mehir a State Crime?" *British Journal of Criminology* 56, no. 5 (2015): 839–841.

Sprinzak, Ehud. *Brother against Brother: Violence and Extremism in Israeli Politics From Altalena to the Rabin Assassination.* New York: Free Press, 1999.

Sprinzak, Ehud. *The Ascendance of Israel's Radical Right.* New York: Oxford University Press, 1991.

Tamari, Assaf. "The Place of Politics: The Notion of Consciousness in Rabbi Yitzchak Ginsburgh's Political Thought." *Israel Studies Review* 29 (2014): 78–98.

Taub, Gadi. *haMitnahalim veHamavak Al Mashmautah Shel haTzionut* (*The Settlers and the Struggle over the Meaning of Zionism*). Tel-Aviv: Yediot Aharonot, 2007. (Hebrew)

Weisbrud, David. *Jewish Settler Violence: Deviance as Social Reaction.* Pennsylvania State University Press, 1989.

Ofira Gruweis-Kovalsky

Religious Radicalism, the Zionist Right, and the Establishment of the State of Israel

Introduction

On May 16 1951, newspapers throughout the State of Israel ran headlines proclaiming: “Extremist thugs plot Knesset bombing to sabotage debate on drafting women.” The plot was reportedly headed off by the Israeli security services, thereby “thwarting an attack on the Knesset.”[1] The perpetrators were identified as members of *Brit Qanaim* (“Covenant of Zealots”), a militant faction of the Charedi youth movement, Tze’iray Agudat Yisrael. Throughout the years, this dramatic episode has remained etched in Israeli collective consciousness and scholarship as the act of religious extremists who embraced terror in their battle to determine the country’s Jewish character.[2]

Theoretically, the battle should have ended in 1948: here was a state whose very existence defined what it meant to be Jewish, as Jews poured into the country en masse, assumed full political responsibility, and instated Jewish hegemony in the public space. However, the Jewish identity of citizens in a Jewish nation-state had been debated in political, cultural, and literary circles since the rise of the Zionist movement in the late nineteenth century. During the pre-state period, when the Jews lived under foreign rule, the question of self-identity rumbled beneath the surface, but erupted from time to time, culminating in political infighting and public expressions of discontent, such as demonstrations against Shabbat desecration in places like Jerusalem where the Jews constituted a majority. Nevertheless, the power of the Yishuv leadership, headed by the Zionist Socialists, was not diminished, and it was able to exercise its authority over

---

1 The security services thwarted the attempt to sabotage the Knesset, *A’l HaMishmar, Davar, Ma’ariv*, May 16 1951.

2 Avraham Deskal, “Non Parliamentary Oppositional Behavior in the 1950s: Brit-Kanaim and Malchut-Israel” (MA thesis, Bar-Ilan University, 1990); Shely Levin and Jonatan Erlich, *Background Document: Jewish Political Violence in Israel*, (Jerusalem: The Knesset research and information center, 2005); Ami Pedahzur, *The Triumph of Israel’s Radical Right* (PlaceOxford UK: Oxford University Press, 2012); Ehud Shprinzak, *Brothers Against Brothers: Violence and Extremism in Israeli Politics from Altalena to the Rabin Assassination* (New York, USA: New York Free Press, 1999); Ehud Shprinzak, “The Emergence of the Israeli Radical Right” *Comperative Politics* 21, no. 2 (1989): 92–171.

https://doi.org/10.1515/9783110545753-011

most of the parties and militias.[3] Jewish identity in the Yishuv was basically dictated by this administration, which stifled the voices of anyone who did not conform with its Zionist-Socialist line. In response, those who were rejected and pushed to the margins resorted to unconventional methods and even violence to convey their message, although the reality of British Mandate had a moderating influence and served to tone down and repress the political and social discord in some measure.[4] During this period, two dissenting groups in the Yishuv set themselves up as an ideological, political, and ideological alternative, splitting from the mainstream and refusing to accept the authority of the Yishuv leadership. The very existence of such groups became a radicalizing force in the Yishuv.

In the first camp were the underground organizations of the Revisionist right and large segments of the Revisionist party. While the Revisionists identified as Zionists, they clashed with the Zionist leadership on ideological issues and policy, which led to their formal resignation from the Zionist movement and pursuit of independent activity in the underground.[5] In the second camp were the Charedim, a community of many subgroups that openly declared war on Zionism and those at its helm. At the same time, some of the leading rabbis were moderates who found ways of cooperating with the Yishuv leadership and the Zionist movement. Within these two camps were pockets of extremists who held radical views on a variety of subjects, including the definition of Jewish identity. Their actions fueled the flames and deepened the Yishuv's mistrust of the two groups as a whole.[6]

After the establishment of the State of Israel, Etzel and Lechi, the radical underground organizations of the Revisionist right, agreed to disband and join the Israel Defense Forces. In Jerusalem, however, due to the unresolved international status of the city which left it outside the bounds of Israeli sovereignty, these organizations continued to operate autonomously. Suspicion and mistrust of the

3 Itzhak Galnoor and Dana Blander, *The Political System of Israel, Formative Years; Institutional Structure; Political Behavior; Unsolved Problems; Democracy in Israel* (Tel Aviv: Am-O'ved, 2013), 42.

4 Moshe Lissak, *Studies in Israeli Social History* (Jerusalem: Bialik Institute Press, 2009), 217–341.

5 Colin Shindler, *The Triumph of Military Zionism, Nationalism and the Origins of the Israeli Right* (London: I.B. Tauris, 2006); Eran Kaplan, *The Jewish Radical Right, Revisionist Zionism and its Ideological Legacy* (Wisconsin: The University of Wisconsin Press, 2005), 3–30.

6 Binyamin Braun, The Ultra-Orthodox Jewry and the State, Yedidia Z. Stern et al., eds., *When Judaism Meets the State* (Tel Aviv: MISKAL-Yedioth Ahronoth Books, 2015), 79–63; Yossef Pund, *Separation or Participation, Agudat Israel Confronting Zionism and the State of Israel* (Jerusalem: The Magnes Press, 1991).

Revisionists and the Revisionist underground ran deep, hampering communication with the State of Israel leadership and ending in violent skirmishes such as the *Altalena affair.* It was hence not surprising that the political parties established by former members of Etzel and Lechi were seen as illegitimate by the Israeli politics.[7]

While the leaders of the Charedi and national-religious communities also signed an accord with the Ben-Gurion administration, known as the status quo agreements, the character of Israeli public sphere remained a bone of contention. The dispute revolved mainly around Shabbat observance, military service for women and education, specifically the education of immigrant children. In Jerusalem, the conflict was particularly bitter, triggering violent protests and demonstrations. The Charedim and national-religious communities, feeling that they were being pushed to the sidelines, joined forces. In the lead-up to the elections of the Constituent Assembly in January 1949, the two Charedi parties, Agudat Yisrael and Poaeli Agudat Yisrael, formed a political bloc with the two religious Zionist parties. This bloc became part of the legitimate political establishment of the State of Israel upon joining the coalition headed by Ben-Gurion. Among the Charedim were groups of extremists who opposed this move by the Charedi mainstream. Embracing fringe views, they broke away from the community and aligned themselves with the far right and Neturei Qarta.

Studies of Jewish radicalism in the 1950s generally portray the two groups – Charedi radicals and the radical right of the Lechi and Revisionist school – as not connected to one another.[8] In this paper, I argue that there were ties despite the fact that the Charedim bowed out of Israeli politics and did not join the political right. The Israeli government's use of its intelligence services to exert political pressure on the Charedi leadership turned out to be counterproductive. It led to the radicalization of Charedi leaders and the social and cultural rejection of both the far right and the Charedim, who became pariahs in the State of Israel. The liminal geographic space of Jerusalem and the political status of the city, which remained unclear after the establishment of the state, further contributed to the radicalization of these groups.

7 Ofira Gruweis-Kovalsky, "Between Ideology and Reality: Menachem Begin and the Jerusalem Question, 1948–1949," *Israel Studies* 21, no. 3 (2016): 99–125.

8 Mudde Cas, *Populist Radical Right Parties in Europe* (Cambridge USA: Cambridge University Press, 2007); Kaplan, *The Jewish Radical Right*; Pedahzur, *The Triumph*; Shlomo Shpiro, "The Intellectual Foundations of Jewish National Terrorism: Avraham Stern and the Lehi," *Terrorism and Political Violence* 25, no. 4 (2013): 606–620; Shprinzak, *The Emergence*; Shprinzak, *Brothers against Brothers.*

The Right-Wing-Charedi Alliance

Ze'ev Jabotinsky (1880–1940) and the ideologues of the Revisionist movement were secular, non-practicing Jews. At the same time, they harbored an emotional attachment to Judaism and Jewish tradition that fluctuated between tolerance and nostalgia. Active primarily in Eastern Europe until World War II, the Revisionists' demographic and political support base was religious and Charedi. These communities saw Revisionist ideology and activism as a way of restoring Jewish dignity, while the Revisionists regarded this diverse sector as part of the Jewish plurality they sought to represent. Although monism was one of the principles of Revisionist thinking (using the Hebrew term *chad ness*, literally "a single banner"),[9] the Revisionists had no problem welcoming pious Jews into their ranks: religion was seen as a private affair, not a hostile alternative ideology that would sidetrack them from their primary goal. Religious observance and Revisionism were not *shatnez* (i.e., the biblical prohibition on weaving together linen and wool),[10] as Jabotinsky put it, using religious terminology himself.[11] This approach contrasted sharply with that of the Zionist workers' parties, which publicly proclaimed their opposition to religion. Agudat Yisrael emphasized this point later on to explain its affiliation with the Revisionists and their political successors.[12]

From an ideological, administrative, and political standpoint, the Charedi sector is a complex society spanning a whole spectrum of social groupings, organizations, and doctrines.[13] On the eve of Israeli statehood, the Charedim could be roughly divided into three main streams. For the purpose of this article, the difference between them was in their attitude toward the Jewish state. The moderate Charedi camp, largely represented by Poa'lei Agudat Yisrael, viewed the establishment of the state as a positive development, but one which did not change their Charedi ethos in any way. The centrist camp, represented by Agudat Yisrael, held diverse opinions and included splinter groups such as Histadrut Tze'iray Agudat Yisrael.[14] Israel's establishment was seen not as a reli-

---

9 Kaplan, *The Jewish Radical Right*, 31–50.

10 Judith Tydor Baumel, "Strange Bedfellows: The Revisionist Movement and Agudath Yisrael during the Holocaust," *Iyunim Bitkumat Israel* 12 (2002): 465–492.

11 Svetlana Natkovich, *Among Radiant Clouds: The Literature of Vladimir (Ze'ev) Jabotinsky in Its Social Context* (Jerusalem Magnes Press, 2015): 219.

12 M. K. Rabbi Menachem Porush, *Koll Israel*, 40 (1982).

13 Cahaner Lee, Nikola Yozgof-Orbach and Arnon Sofer, eds., *The Haredim in Israel – Space, Society, Community* (Haifa: Chaikin Chair In Geostrategy, University of Haifa, 2012), 8–33.

14 Pund, *Separation or Participation*, 242.

gious commandment but as a threat to Jewish tradition, although there was no call for a boycott. For the third stream, made up of the Satmar Chasidim, the E'da Charedit in Jerusalem and Neturei Qarta, the very existence of a state was illegitimate because it was a declaration of Jewish sovereignty before the coming of the Messiach. This group boycotted anything connected to the state and continues to do so until today.[15] It consciously seeks to build walls between itself and Israeli society, and lives as an enclave within an enclave. On the other hand, it is a tiny minority that constitutes only three percent of Israel's Charedi population.[16]

In the period leading up to the founding of the state, Agudat Yisrael rejected secular Zionism but strongly supported the settlement of the Land of Israel as a Torah commandment. It even endorsed the establishment of new colonies like *B'nai- Barak* by members of the community,[17] although its approach was more on the passive side.[18] Agudat Yisrael's problem with Zionism was the character of the Jewish center that the Zionists sought to build.[19] Nevertheless, political ties grew up between Agudat Yisrael and the Revisionist movement and they aided one another in their battle against the Zionist establishment. The rabbis of Agudat Yisrael were fully aware of the critical differences between the Zionist right and other political camps, and saw the Revisionists as neutral and even sympathetic toward the religious cause. The Aguda-Revisionist partnership in the late 1930s and 1940s stemmed from this image of religious tolerance, the readiness of both groups to employ unconventional tactics if necessary, and a sense of brotherhood between groups that perceived themselves as victims of discrimination.[20] This political collaboration influenced Charedi thinking, all the more so in view of its endorsement by the rabbis, and a mutual alliance grew up between the two camps. The Charedim were prepared to listen to and consider the ideological arguments of the Revisionists, and the Revisionists, unlike the Zionist labor parties, did not reject the Charedi community out of hand.

This special empathy for the Revisionists extended to its attitude toward the underground movements. For the centrist Charedi leadership, there was a direct connection between repudiating Zionism and repudiating clandestine activity

---

15 Braun, *The Ultra-Orthodox Jewry*, 80 – 81.

16 Menachem Keren-Kratz, "Ha-E'dah Ha-Haredit in Jerusalem in 1948 – 1973," *Cathedra* 161 (2017): 139 – 174.

17 Pund, *Separation or Participation*.

18 Rabbi Yitzhak Meir, *On the Walls of B'nai- Barak – the first Decade of B'nai- Barak* (B'nai-Barak: The society for research the history of B'nai- Barak Press, 1989).

19 Gershon C. Bacon, *The Politics of Tradition: Agudat Yisrael in Poland, 1916 – 1939* (Jerusalem: Magnes Press, 2005), 50.

20 Tydor Baumel, *Strange Bedfellows*.

carried out in its name, by Etzel, Lechi, or the Haganah. These two components did not stand alone: if one was rejected, so was the other. On the other hand, the contention of Etzel and Lechi that organized resistance to an illegitimate regime and its illegitimate actions meshed with Jewish political tradition was an argument that the Charedi public could understand to some degree.[21] It was this rationale that enabled the Revisionists to make headway in Charedi circles. At the same time, the leaders of Agudat Yisrael openly opposed the terror tactics of Etzel and Lechi, and some claim that the party's stance was the impetus for Ben-Gurion's decision to launch "the Saison."[22]

A number of rabbis accepted by both the Charedi and national-religious public gave the stamp of approval to affiliation with the Revisionists. One was Aryeh Levin (1885–1969) of Jerusalem, known as the "rabbi of the prisoners." Reb Aryeh, a Gur chassid who had been in contact with Jabotinsky even before the Revisionist movement, was born as one of the rabbis who lobbied for Jabotinsky's release after his incarceration by the British in 1920.[23] Levin's ties with members of the underground who became active in Israeli political life continued after the establishment of the state.[24] Another rabbinical figure from the Charedi world who maintained ties with the Revisionist movement was Rabbi Yitzhak Yedidya Frenkel (1913–1986) of Tel Aviv's Florentin neighborhood, known as the "rabbi of the neighborhoods." Frenkel, also a Gur hassid, was a disciple of the Imrei Emet and close to Rabbi Kook and Rabbi U'ziel.

From the early twentieth century, the Charedim in Jerusalem began staging protests against Shabbat desecration. Holding soccer matches and operating public transportation on the Jewish day of rest were the core issues of the time.[25] During the British Mandate, groups of young Charedim inspired by Etzel and Lechi also organized in secret to enforce religious observance through violence. Two groups known to have taken part in this activity were *Irgun Lochamei Yahadut* (Fighters for Judaism), which planted bombs in cafes that opened on the Shabbat, and *Bnei Pinchas* (Sons of Pinchas), which targeted women in

---

21 Hilda Schatzberger, *Resistance and Tradition in Mandatory Palestine* (Bar-Ilan University, 1985), 84.

22 Pund, *Separation or Participation*, 184–185.

23 Rabbi Kook letter, 1920. *Meged Yerachim*, 16. 2001.P 3.

24 Letter from Noach Zevoluni to Aba Achimeir, May 8 1949, Aba Achimeir Archives, Ramat-Gan.

25 Menachem Friedman, *The Origin of the Haredi Society, Orientation and Process* (Jerusalem: Jerusalem Institute for Israel Studies, 1991), 63.

relationships with non-Jews.[26] Aside from the fact that these groups hailed from the Charedi community, they were both in contact with the Revisionist underground and their operational base was mainly at Jerusalem.[27]

Jerusalem as a Liminal Sphere

Following the establishment of the state, Jerusalem became the operational hub of the far right and the assembly point for activists of Lechi and Etzel.[28] The underground took shape there, because the city had not been declared part of the state. Until August 1948, Israel did not proclaim any form of sovereignty over Jerusalem and thereafter proclaimed conditional sovereignty. The clandestine military organizations that operated during the British Mandate became militias charged with the defense of the Jewish population when the British withdrew and war broke out.[29] The uncertainty of the future Jerusalem led to the radicalization of the population, which was expressed in their support for the Revisionist organizations. Lechi and Etzel maintained several bases in Jerusalem and their presence impacted greatly on life there.[30] Isser Halperin-Harel (1912–2003), who was responsible for surveillance of Jewish political organizations in Jerusalem and later became head of Israel's security services, testified that "the insurgents, Etzel and Lechi, took over Jerusalem and asserted their control through sheer terror. Even the police were terrified of them. None of the inhabitants would act against them, not out of support but out of fear."[31]

To describe the cooperation of Jerusalemites with Etzel and Lechi as the product of fear not only attests to a partial understanding of what was going on in the city, but to the vested interests of someone who sought to vilify the rival political camp and win points for his own side. The people of Jerusalem were enthusiastic backers of these groups and worked with them willingly. The

---

26 Menachem Friedman, "ELI: Jewish Religious Underground during the British Mandate," in *Milestones, Essays in Jewish History Dedicated to Zvi Yekutiel*, ed. Immanuel Etkes, David Assaf, and Yosef Kaplan (Jerusalem: The Zalman Shazar Press, 2016), 379–396.

27 Summary of the police activity against the members of Brit Qanaim, written by the Jerusalem Police commander, Israel State Archives, file 2/75/5/6.

28 Avraham Vered, *A Burning Bush on Fire – Epic of War and Conquest* (Tel Aviv, 1950), 16.

29 Mordechai Bar-On and Nir Mann, "An Interview with the Fifth President Yitzhak Navon," *Aley Zait Vacherev* (Olive Leaves and Sword) 13 (2013): 13–30.

30 Ofira Gruweis-Kovalsky, "The Attitude of the Revisionists Right Wing toward Jerusalem in the War of Independence," *Aley Zait Vacherev (Olive Leaves and Sword)* 13 (2013): 140–174.

31 The Swedish Attorney General Special Report on the murder of Count Bernadotte, ISA, file: A-7668/6, 37.

data bears this out: perhaps the most telling statistic of all with respect to the cultural and political inclinations of the locals is the fact that the majority of Jerusalem children attended religious schools,[32] even though secular schools were available and highly recommended by the Yishuv leadership. Analyzing the outcome of the municipal elections in 1950 confirms this view of the Jerusalem public and highlights the disparity between the attitude of the national leadership and the locals. The Jerusalemites were a conservative-minded bunch who voted in the Constituent Assembly and municipal elections as directed by their rabbis. Hence the Religious Front, a merger of Agudat Yisrael, Poa'lei Agudat Yisrael Hamizrachi, and Hapoe'l Hamizrachi, was very popular in Jerusalem and played an important role as a united front in the general elections and as individual parties in the municipal elections.[33] In the mayoral elections the local and national religious parties formed a coalition with the Herut movement, which again testifies to the solid backing enjoyed by religious organizations and the Revisionist right in Jerusalem.[34]

The radicalization of the Jerusalem public and its link to the far right is also attested to by the growth of Lechi in Jerusalem after UN Resolution 181. The underground was joined by people from every sector, from Charedi anti-Zionists to Communists.[35] The numbers of Ultra-Orthodox who sought membership was so large that Lechi opened a religious unit in Jerusalem. This unit operated under the aegis of the rabbis and served as an ideological bridge between religious and secular messianic doctrines. Most of those who joined the religious unit in Jerusalem, which had over fifty members,[36] do not appear on the official Lechi membership roster.[37]

Lechi in Jerusalem thus incorporated in its ranks a distinct, self-standing unit of non-Zionist Charedim, and there is evidence that this unit was in contact

---

32 Twenty-five percent of the Jerusalem children were registered at the Worker Wing Schools, *A'l HaMishmar*, April 29 1951.

33 Pinhas Alpert and Dotan Goren, eds., *Diary of a Muchtar in Jerusalem – The History of the Beit Yisrael Neighborhood and its Surroundings in the Writings of Rabbi Moshe Yekutiel Alpert (1938–1952)* (Bar-Ilan University Press, 2013), 174.

34 Yechiam Weitz, The Jerusalem Municipality Elections, Arnon Golan, Amnon Ramon, eds., *Jerusalem* (Jerusalem: Yad Ben-Zvi, forthcoming).

35 Joseph Heller, *Lehi-Ideology and Politics 1940–1949* (Jerusalem: Zalman Shzar Press, 1989), Vol. 2, 388; Nadel Baruch, *Bernadotte Murder* (Tel-Aviv, 1968), 96; Hadas Regev-Yarkoni and Ofer Regev, *Jerusalem's Liberation Fighter, the Memories of Yehoshua Zetler* (Tel-Aviv: Porat Press, 2007), 121; Yisrael Eldad, *The First Tithe – Memories Episodes and Moral* (Tel-Aviv, third edition, 1975), 367.

36 The estimated number of the Lechi members in 1948 was one thousand members.

37 Association for Lehi legacy Memorialization, http://lehi.org.il/?page_id=125.

with Rabbi Avraham Yesha'ya Qarlitz, known as the Chazon Ish.[38] These ties with the Chazon Ish are of considerable significance in view of his lofty status in Charedi circles and the State of Israel. Tze'iray Agudat Yisrael, and especially its Jerusalem members, looked up to the Chazon Ish as a spiritual leader of the first degree. However, it is hard to know exactly what he thought about the political parties in Israel and the Religious Front, as many conflicting statements were issued in his name.[39]

It was this combination of politically and culturally shunned groups operating behind the scenes, apocalyptic messianic doctrines and a tempestuous political situation, inside the Yishuv and on an international scale, that fueled extremism. Jerusalem, as a place where nationalist, messianic, and theological doctrines converged, became a hot spot of instability during the period in question, which only heightened the apocalyptic premonitions of far right fringe groups in the national-religious and Charedi sectors. The fact that Jerusalem was physically divided between the State of Israel and the Kingdom of Jordan, and the sites holiest to Jews were in non-Jewish hands and off-limits to Jewish worship, helped to strengthen messianic groups calling for action. On top of this was the sense of many right-wingers and religious groups that they were being pushed to the margins of society and excluded from politics in the newly-established state.[40]

Messianic Doctrine and Radicalism

Traditional Jewish messianism is bound up with the concept of redemption and the two are ultimately inseparable.[41] Redemption is linked in Judaism to the ingathering of the exiles in the Promised Land, reinstating the House of David, renewing the religious rituals of worship in the Temple in Jerusalem, and establishing a society governed by Jewish religious law. Religious Zionists took pains not to identify Zionism as a messianic movement, whereas the Charedi

---

38 Rabbi Avraham Isaiah Karelitz, 1878–1953.

39 Zvi Wineman, *From Katovitz to He Be-Iyyar – Chapters in the History of Agudat Yisrael, and the Ultra-Orthodox Jews New Perspectives* (Jerusalem: Vatikin Press, 1995), 159–165.

40 Amir Goldstein, *Heroism and Exclusion: The Gallows Martyrs and the Israeli Collective Memory* (Jerusalem: Yad Izhak Ben-Zvi, 2011); Ofira Gruweis-Kovalsky, *The Vindicated and the Persecuted – The Mythology and the Symbols of the Herut Movement* (Sede-Boker: The Ben-Gurion Research Institute, 2015); Udi Lebel, *The Road to the Pantheon-Etzel, Lehi and the Borders of Israeli National Memory* (Jerusalem: Carmel Publisher, 2007).

41 Friedman, *The Origin of the Haredi Society*, 19

fear of Zionism was related in part to this very issue. However, of all the traditional values of Judaism, the messianic idea was the one that secular Zionists tried hardest to preserve. Prior to the establishment of the state, the goal of rebuilding the Land of Israel by secular Jews had distinct messianic overtones. All streams of Orthodox Judaism found themselves up in arms with Zionism over the interpretation of basic religious concepts in the context of messianism.[42] The secular character of the Zionist enterprise was clearly a source of theological discomfort in the Orthodox world, although religious Zionist leaders rationalized their partnership with non-religious groups on the grounds that Jews must unite in times of emergency. World War II and its consequences for the Jews led Agudat Yisrael to accept the reality of settlement in the Land of Israel and join the debate over the character of a future Jewish state.[43]

In the interim period between the two world wars, some Agudat Yisrael rabbis interpreted the chaos in the world as the "birth pangs of the Messiach" and a sign that redemption was on its way. This messianic frame of mind spread beyond Agudat Yisrael and permeated the thinking of other Haredi groups, such as Chabad under the leadership of the Lubavitcher Rebbe,[44] and the disciples of the Munkacs Rebbe, who were sworn enemies of Zionism (and also of Agudat Yisrael).[45]

The shock of World War II, together with the birth of a Jewish state, provided further impetus for the emergence of messianic thought that combined religious and secular elements. The messianic ideas that developed in the Chasidic courts were a complex ideological and theological brew. Traces of messianism were even perceptible in the Gur dynasty from which Agudat Yisrael sprang.[46] A year before the establishment of the state, the Gerrer Rebbe, Imrei Emet, spoke of the times as the "era of the footsteps of the Messiach," although these remarks were subsequently downplayed by his son and successor.[47]

Viewing the world through a theological lens forced the Charedi rabbis to delve deeper into the spiritual significance of redemption. Some Aguda leaders

---

42 Friedman, *The Origin of the Haredi Society*, 19.

43 Chaim Shalem, *A Time to Take Action to Rescue Jews, Agudat Yisrael in Eretz Israel Confronting the Holocaust 1942–1945* (Sede-Boker: Ben-Gurion University of the Negev Press, 2007), 286.

44 Gershon C. Bacon, *The Politics of Tradition: Agudat Yisrael in Poland, 1916–1939* (Jerusalem: Magnes Press, 2005), 58–59.

45 Motti Inbari, "Messianic Activism in the Work and Thought of Chaim Elazar Shapira (the Munkacser Rebbe) in the Interwar Period," *Cathedra* 149 (2014): 77–104.

46 Mendel Piekarz, "The Inner Point of the *Admorim* Gur and Alexander as a Reflection of their Ability to Adjust to Changing Times," in *Studies in Jewish Mysticism Philosophy and Ethical Literature*, ed. Joseph Dan and Joseph Hacker (Jerusalem: Magnes Press 1986): 569–592.

47 Braun, *The Ultra-Orthodox Jewry*, 96.

looked askance at the enthusiasm with which Israel's founding was greeted. They saw the state as a danger to Judaism and feared that it would become a rubber stamp for secularism. Other rabbis of the movement hailed the creation of a Jewish state as an act of divine providence that would actually strengthen Charedi/religious society. In the words of Rabbi Jacob Rosenheim, one of leading proponents of this view, "only a blind person could say that what is unfolding now… in the Holy Land is mere history or the result of human design or natural causes, and not see that the birth of the Jewish state is the metaphysical outcome of sweeping Jewish self-sacrifice!"[48] Some of the leading Charedi rabbis and yeshiva heads joined the religious Zionist leadership in signing a joint proclamation that portrayed the achievement of statehood as *atchalta degeula* (beginning of salvation).[49] Agudat Yisrael's official bulletin said much the same thing.[50] Directly or indirectly, reading such material drove the message home, even if some of the undersigned rabbis, and those who succeeded them, later changed their tune. Maybe it was even over-influence that led them to backtrack and wage war on those who rejoiced over Israeli statehood, like Rabbi Soloveitchik, the Brisqer Rebbe,[51] who bemoaned the fact that "so many good people are being swept up by the masses and infected by the virus of enthusiasm for autonomous Jewish rule in Eretz Israel."[52] Indeed, many Charedi leaders avoided contact with the Zionist movement after the establishment of the state, while others refused to voice an opinion on the subject.

The publications and public statements of Histadrut Tse'iray Agudat Yisrael attest to the theological confusion in Charedi circles on the subject of Israeli statehood: sometimes they took one approach and sometimes another. On the eve of the Constituent Assembly elections towards the end of 1948, members of the all the Charedi youth movements handed out flyers that portrayed Israel's establishment as a miracle: "The miracle of the victory of the few over the many has been reenacted before our eyes."[53] Two years later, with the elections for the Second Knesset around the corner and Agudat Yisrael wracked by infighting, the party's youth wing passed a resolution at its annual convention that veered in the opposite direction: "In view of the emotional turmoil and disagreement

48 Pund, *Separation or Participation*, 214–215; Jacob Rosenheim, "Al Domi Lach," (Do not remain silent) *Hamevaser*, Elul 28 1949.

49 Braun, *The Ultra-Orthodox Jewry*, 96.

50 Pund, *Separation or Participation*, 223.

51 Shimeon Josef Meller, *The Rabbi of Brisk Book* (Jerusalem: Feldhaim Press, 2004), Vol. 2, 516–517.

52 Shimeon Josef Meller, *The Rabbi of Brisk Book* (Jerusalem: Feldhaim Press, 2004), Vol. 3, 325.

53 'United Religious Front' Pamphlet, Zionist Religious Archives, file 1 (in Hebrew).

over the issue of the establishment of the state, which has also affected the Charedi Jewish community, we hereby declare that Zionism in all its variations constitutes a grave spiritual and physical danger to the Jewish people."[54] The fact that the party leaders and rabbis needed to clarify that they were still opposed to Zionism shows that many were eager to become part of the state and acknowledged the miraculous nature of its birth.

The triple alliance of the far right, the religious Zionists, and the Charedim was thus another factor in the mounting radicalization in the 1950s, as political secular messianism joined up with theological religious messianism. Jerusalem was the hub in this context not only because of its theological significance but because the formation of many of these groups took place in the city. The Jerusalem branches of Poa'lei Agudat Yisrael and Histadrut Tse'irey Agudat Yisrael were of particular note.

Religious Zionist thinkers contributed indirectly to the radicalization process by portraying the military conflicts and apocalyptic world wars of the time as their own battle and as a confrontation of the Messiach and those on his side against the forces of evil. A handful of Jewish legal scholars tried to put together a system of laws for military engagement and soon after the state was founded, work began on a code of military ethics. The spirit of revolution permeated many factions of the Religious Zionist movement. In this context, there were a number of rabbinical figures from the heart of the religious establishment whose authority was accepted by both the Religious Zionists and Charedim. One was Rabbi Ben-Zion Meir Chai Uziel (1880–1953), who recognized the founding of the state as a sign of messianic times, as borne out by his correspondence. He believed that the existence of a state would lead to the demise of secularization, a view shared by Rabbi Tzvi Yehuda Kook (1891–1982), Rabbi Ze'ev Gold (1889–1965), and Rabbi Joseph Soloveitchik (1916–1981) Achieving statehood was perceived as a "revealed miracle." For Rabbi Chaim David HaLevy (1924–1998), the state was the first stage in the realization of the divine promise.[55] Israel's establishment in 1948 made the link between Jewish nationalism and messianism even clearer.[56] Religious Zionist thinkers were careful not to engage too deeply or openly in such apocalyptic thinking, but they tried hard to preserve the idea of the miraculousness of Israeli statehood as opposed to the modern day conception of coming into being naturally. After the Holocaust there was a grow-

---

54 From the decisions of Tse'iray Agudat Yisrael, *Herut*, October 2 1950. "This Year's Slave," *Davar*, April 26 1950.

55 Dov Schwartz, *Religious Zionism between Logic and Messianism* (Am-Oved Press Tel-Aviv, 1999), 31–37, 94–96.

56 Inbari, *Zionism in the Thought.*

ing sense that the return of secular Jews to their roots was close at hand, and this feeling strengthened as the Jewish homeland became a reality. Many drew a link between the birth of the state and the Holocaust, and regarded the two as part of a single divine plan.[57] The upshot was that members of the Yishuv were influenced by a medley of ideas and ideologies, and drew validation for their activism from a blend of Charedi and religious Zionist rabbinic sources as well as discussions of the dimensions of Eretz Yisrael and the State of Israel in secular sources.[58] Therein lay the roots of the concept of a secular "Kingdom of Israel" interwoven with aspects of religious messianism so fervently embraced by Lechi. The ideas of Israel Eldad)1910–1996) and Uri Tzvi Greenberg (1896–1981), which they shared in writing on the pages of *Sulam*, a monthly journal edited by Eldad, and at parlor meetings of the paper's readership, thus appealed to audiences across the religious and social spectrum – secular, religious, and Charedi.[59]

Political Strife and Extremism

The heated political battles over the character of the Jewish state that ensued after Israel declared its independence widened the gulf between the religious/Charedi sector and the secular public. The religious parties fought to instate laws that would enforce kashrut and Shabbat observance in Israel but they failed to win support for legal sanctions against those who violated the laws. As time went on, loopholes were found which enabled people to skirt the Shabbat and kashrut laws.[60] The protest demonstrations organized by the religious and Charedi camp culminated in violent clashes. Scholarship to date has studied Charedi violence in Jerusalem, but little has been written about acts of violence committed against this sector. The police used unreasonable force against this population as a matter of course and justified its actions on the grounds that the Char-

57 Schwartz, *Religious Zionism*, 91.

58 Arye Naor, *Greater Israel Theology and Policy* (University of Haifa Press, 2001), 24.

59 Ofira Gruweis-Kovalsky, "A Tale of Love and Darkness: The Radical Right Wing and the Herut Movement, 1948–1957," *Kesher (Communication)* 50 (2017): 89–99.

60 Aviad Hacohen, "The State of Israel – This is a Holy Place!: Forming a 'Jewish Public Domain' in the State of Israel," in *On Both Side of the Bridge, Religion and State in the Early Years of Israel*, ed. Mordechai Bar-On and Zvi Zameret (Jerusalem: Yad Izhak Ben-Zvi Press, 2002), 169–170.

edim were enemies of Israel who sought to destroy the state.[61] The Charedim were often the victims of retaliatory attacks by supporters of the political left. These attacks, mostly perpetrated by gangs of young people and soldiers from the socialist youth movements and kibbutzim, were reported in the newspapers and came up for discussion in the Knesset.[62]

Under these circumstances, the enthusiasm of the Charedi leaders and their flock over the birth of a Jewish state began to wane. Similar feelings arose in the national-religious sector. The cultural-theological excitement of statehood was tempered by reality. The fringe groups grew restless and agitated, especially in Jerusalem. For the city's religious and Charedi inhabitants, the battle loomed on two fronts: on the one hand, they were fighting for the character of the state, and on the other, for the character of the city. Jerusalem was a holy city with a special role in Jewish theology, but also a divided city in which the administrative system of the British Mandate no longer functioned. In addition, it was home to a population that was largely religious. A new municipal framework with a new set of bylaws was required, but because Jerusalem was not recognized as part of the state, even by Israel, the municipality that came into being would be operating outside the jurisdiction of the Israeli government.[63] The political tug of war in Jerusalem thus grew even stronger. Jerusalem became the arena for public protest – on issues of concern to the religious sector, mainly the character of public sphere, as well as issues related to the city's national and international standing. This served as the foundation for political cooperation between the Revisionist right and local religious and Charedi parties, which reached a peak with the establishment of a coalition led by Zalman Shragai of Hapoe'l Hamizrachi after the municipal elections in 1950. It was a political alliance that sprang at the core from collaborative efforts to organize protests against Shabbat desecration. The election results attested to the mounting strength of the religious right-wing and Charedi sector. This coalition, made up of parties which sat in the opposition in the national government, was greeted with suspicion and dismay by Israel's national leaders, who did all they could to cripple it. The Jerusalem city council thus became a political battleground

61 Summary of the police activity against the members of Brit Qanaim, written by the Jerusalem Police commander, ISA, file 2/75/5/6 (in Hebrew).

62 *'Divrei Haknesset* (protocol of the Israeli Parliament), Session 61, July 27 1949. "Stones and Batons in the Shabbat Wars Between Religious and Mapam," *Ma'ariv*, August 27 1950.

63 Motti Golani, "Zionism without Zion: The Position of the Pre-state and National Leadership of Israel on the Jerusalem Question 1947–1949," in *Divided Jerusalem 1948–1967*, ed. Avi Bareli (Jerusalem: Yad Ben-Zvi, 1995), 30–52.

where the local parties fought between themselves and also with the government.[64]

This internal fighting in the city council paralyzed the work of the municipality, but it was also a catalyst for radicalism. The political battles moved into the streets, sparking demonstrations and displays of militancy. Charedi organizations were established to fight Shabbat desecration that joined forces with groups from outside the Charedi world. HaMoe'tza lema'an hashabbat (Council for the Sabbath), affiliated with the Ministry of Religious Affairs in Jerusalem, then headed by Rabbi Yehuda Leib Maimon, organized outreach in secular communities to promote religious observance throughout the country. Among the leaders of Brit Hashabbat (Shabbat Covenant), which masterminded the Shabbat demonstrations, were Israel's two chief rabbis. This organization drafted the "Shabbat law" which it sought to pass as a municipal bylaw in Jerusalem.

Outside movie theaters in Jerusalem, big posters hung by the Mapai-dominated Workers' Council declared: "Anyone who defies the laws of the state or its constitution will be met with forceful resistance... Down with the appalling propaganda of the forces of darkness in the Yishuv. The community of workers, Jerusalem's intelligent majority, will join the forces of modernity to stamp out this plot."[65] The militancy of the socialist youth movements was regarded by everyone, but especially the religious and Charedi public, as an "undeclared culture war on religious Judaism in Israel."[66] This struggle strengthened ties between the religious denominations, and led to an alliance between the religious moderates and extremist groups like Neturei Qarta that were driven by a desire to incite religious-secular friction and rebellion against the state. At the same time, religious radicals were brought together with right-wing radicals under the auspices of Eldad's newspaper *Sulam*.

Zealots and the Underground

As political tension between religious and secular Jews in Jerusalem ran high, rumors began to circulate about an anti-establishment Charedi underground. These rumors were set off by a series of arson attacks targeting vehicles and places of entertainment across the country that were open on Shabbat. While the

64 Ofira Gruweis-Kovalsky, "Between National Politic to Local Politics," in *Jerusalem*, ed. Arnon Golan and Amnon Ramon (Jerusalem: Yad Ben-Zvi, forthcoming).

65 Deskal, *Non Parliamentary*, 27.

66 "From Stumbling to Stumbling," *HaModia'*, January 5 1951.

rabbis emphatically denied the existence of an underground, such claims suggested a possible link between the far right and Charedi groups in the context of Lechi terror in Jerusalem. Police reports regularly stated that the electoral success of the religious parties in the 1950 municipal elections was credited in some Charedi circles to the Shabbat demonstrations, which were accompanied by physical force.[67] Mapai's newspaper *HaDor* lay the blame for the tense atmosphere in Jerusalem on the Charedim due to their "conspiracies to win the municipal leadership."[68] The Charedim saw this as incitement against their community, which was reflected in the responses of their rabbis and newspapers.[69] Despite this talk of an underground, internal memos of the security services ruled this out and attributed the terror supposedly carried out by the religious underground in November 1950, in this case arson, to the "unpremeditated act of random individuals."[70]

That same month as the arson attacks spread to Jerusalem, the newspapers reported an attempt to set fire to the central bus station in Jerusalem. The incident, which took place early Friday morning, was said to be the work of an unknown group by the name of Brit Qana'im.

Up until this point, the young people of Tse'iray Agudat Yisrael had mainly devoted themselves to educational work with the children of Yemenite immigrants living in transit camps. A political battle was raging over what schools they would be sent to, and the Yemenites as a whole were being belittled by the establishment. According to the Jewish Agency, the Charedi activists, students from *B'nai- Barak*s Ponevetz yeshiva, were guilty of "incitement, distributing flyers, convincing the Yemenites that they were being brainwashed and religiously manipulated, and warning them against the 'eaters of carrion and non-kosher food' in whose midst they lived". At a Jewish Agency Executive meeting, it was reported that "these young people were acting on their own, without party authorization."[71] Some members of the executive demanded that they be barred from entering the camps. Despite the grave suspicions against them and the decision to track their movements and keep them under surveillance, intelligence agents discovered no evidence of an underground. None of the reported vio-

---

67 Summary of the police activity against the members of Brit Qanaim, written by the Jerusalem Police commander, ISA, file 2/75/5/6 (in Hebrew).

68 "Set Fire in Jerusalem," *Hador*, January 21 1951.

69 "HaDor falsely libel Agudat Yisrael," *HaModia*', March 20 1951.

70 Summary of the police activity against the members of Brit Qanaim, written by the Jerusalem Police commander, ISA, file 2/75/5/6 (in Hebrew).

71 Protocol of the Jewish Agency Executive, Central Zionist Archive, February 20 1950, 17 (in Hebrew).

lence, including arson, was deemed the work of a clandestine organization. The security services worried that the radicalization of the young people might lead in this direction, but in the neighborhoods of Jerusalem the acts of arson and talk of an underground were portrayed as a government conspiracy to marginalize the religious sector. According to the police, religious groups were spreading the word that the cases of arson were "a provocation by the workers parties and especially the secretary of the Jerusalem Workers Council, Moshe Bara'm" (1911–1986).[72]

In response to the tempest over religious observance in the State of Israel, groups of young Charedim across the country began to work behind the scenes in several cities at once, lobbying for change in Charedi politics and, above all, challenging the community's traditional leadership.[73] The most visible of them was the Jerusalem group, which refused to accept the authority of Agudat Yisrael. These groups were monitored by the security services, but surveillance failed to produce incriminating evidence. Intelligence reports began to note a growing flurry of activity in Jerusalem: "From time to time we receive reports, admittedly insufficiently verified, of large quantities of weapons in the possession of various bands of religious extremists in Jerusalem."[74] In January 1951, after another attempt to set buses on fire in Jerusalem, nine suspects were rounded up. According to the charge sheet, all belonged to Neturei Qarta.[75] Despite his ideological differences with this sect, Moshe Porush (1893–1983) of Agudat Yisrael, the Deputy Mayor of Jerusalem, interceded on their behalf and negotiated their release.[76] The national-religious camp was convinced that the vandalism was the work of "some group seeking to blacken the reputation of the religious public in Jerusalem."[77]

At this stage, political pressure began to be exerted on the police and security forces to stop the wave of arson attacks. The issue was brought up the Knesset when MK Reuven Shari (1903–1989) of Mapai[78] addressed a parliamentary query

---

72 Top Secret Letter from the Head of the Police General Department to the Head of the Police Investigation Department, Jannuary 21 1951. ISA, file 2/75/5/6 (in Hebrew).

73 Friedman, *The Origin of the Haredi Society*, 64; "Open crisis in Agudat Yisrael, *Ma'ariv*," December 31 1950; "Putsch against Y. M Levin Inside Agudat Yisrael," *A'l HaMishmar*, January 1 1951; *HaTzofeh*, January 1 1951; *Davar*, January 2, 1951.

74 Summary of the police activity against the members of Brit Qanaim, written by the Jerusalem Police commander, ISA, file 2/75/5/6 (in Hebrew).

75 "Shabbat Zealot set Fire Cars in Jerusalem," *Davar*, January 21 1951.

76 "7 cars were set on Fire by Shabbat Zealot," *Herut*, January 21 1951.

77 "Sin Drags Another Sin," *HaTzofeh*, January 22 1951.

78 1903–1989, Jerusalem resident, Secretary of the Jerusalem Workers Council before Moshe Baram and Deputy of the Jerusalem Mayor Daniel Auster 1948–1950.

to the Minister of Police on the subject of car-torchings.[79] The police reiterated its claim that the violence in Jerusalem was a product of the municipal elections, and the press in Israel and around the world picked it up. *The New York Times* ran a story that "Election of religious mayor stokes extremist violence."[80] The Charedi newspaper *HaModia'* stressed that the chief rabbis and the Council of Torah Sages also condemned the arsonists."[81] *HaTzofeh*, the organ of the Mizrachi movement, noted that Brit Qanaim and its actions were not part of Neturei Qarta but rather a band of "leftovers from the defunct religious wing of Lechi."[82] *A'l HaMishmar*, affiliated with Mapam, described the culprits as a "well-organized gang of thugs who probably learned their trade as insurgents back in the days of the underground."[83] Intelligence officers accused the mayor, Zalman Shragai (1899–1995), of collaboration with the Charedi underground and providing it with political backing.[84]

In May 1951, the Jerusalem police chief appeared before the top commanders of the police force to report an alleged plot by this underground: "On the evening of May 14, 1951, our informant exposed a plan to toss an incendiary device into the Knesset plenum which would ignite and fill the hall with smoke while the MKs were debating the conscription of women."[85] The police chief claimed this was part of a special operation code-named "Operation Bride" which the group envisaged as the pinnacle of its achievements.[86] From testimony gathered after the arrests, the group was to enter the visitors' gallery with the bomb and those who remained outside would shut off the electricity at the appointed time. When the hall went dark, the lit bomb would be thrown from the balcony.[87] These details were repeated by all the detainees who were interrogated. Yehuda Reider, identified as the ringleader and sentenced to prison for his part in the

79 'Divrei Haknesset' (protocol of the Israeli Parliament), Session 220, January 30 1951, 913.

80 Sydney Gruson, "Zealots in Israel Reviving Struggle; Religious Group Burns Cars in Jerusalem in its Fight for Sabbath Observance," *New York Times*, January 23 1951.

81 "The Minister of Police Informed that the Cars Lighters were Bunch of Fanatics," *HaModia'*, January 21 1951.

82 "The Religious Organizations will be Activated against Cars Lighters," *HaTzofeh*, March 7 1951.

83 "Cars were set on fire again in Jerusalem," *A'l HaMishmar*, March 15 1951.

84 Summary of the police activity against the members of Brit Qanaim, written by the Jerusalem Police commander, ISA, file 2/75/5/6 (in Hebrew).

85 Summary of the police activity against the members of Brit Qanaim, written by the Jerusalem Police commander, ISA, file 2/75/5/6 (in Hebrew).

86 "The Dangerous Underground Waked up," *Ma'ariv*, March 26 1952.

87 Summary of the police activity against the members of Brit Qanaim, written by the Jerusalem Police commander, ISA, file 2/75/5/6. (in Hebrew).

affair, shed light on some of the actions leading up to it: "The next day we met again. We discussed the matter of entry tickets and turning off the lights. I was the one who wrote up the minutes of this meeting." While he outlined all stages of the operation as intended, he pointed out that the original plan was dropped a day before they went into action.[88] Other group members who stood trial confirmed the cancellation of the plan in its original form, and the report of the chief of police supports this:[89]

> As luck would have it, the bomb was found in the possession of the Shin Bet informer, who was trying to pass it on to another group member, without knowing that this member was also an informer. So these two informers were trying as best they could to get one another to take the bomb (and get the other person arrested). The district commander took both of them into custody on the spot, as they clutched the bomb, along with the other fellows in the gallery and around the Knesset, followed by a sweeping round of arrests.[90]

So, the Jerusalem police chief claimed that the bomb was smuggled into the Knesset by a Shin Bet operative who was instructed to hand it to another person in order to implicate the group as a whole and wipe it out once and for all. It is hard not to reach the conclusion that the security establishment was manufacturing evidence on the assumption that this community was behind the torching of the cars. In the wake of this episode, some fifty Haredi Jews were rounded up and deported to Camp Jallame in the north of the country on charges of membership in an underground. The basis for these arrests was Regulation 111 of the 1945 Palestine Defense Emergency Regulations. All the detainees were Charedi men affiliated with Agudat Yisrael. The police were severely reprimanded for their rough treatment of the suspects, leading to the first parliamentary commission of inquiry in the history of the State of Israel.[91] The commission found that the allegations of severe police brutality were true: "The brutality in Jallame was planned, not coincidental or the impulsive, random behavior of an individual police officer or sergeant."[92] Four suspects were brought to trial for treason but the proceedings ended in a whisper. In spite of the gravity of the charges, none of the accused was sentenced to more than a few months in jail, and all were pardoned before serving time.

---

88 "Testimony of the Police Inspectors," *HaTzofeh*, June 1 1951; *Herut*, June 1 1951.

89 "New discoveries on "Operation Bride," *Davar*, June 1 1951.

90 Summary of the police activity against the members of Brit Qanaim, written by the Jerusalem Police commander, ISA, file 2/75/5/6 (in Hebrew).

91 'Divrei Haknesset', (protocol of the Israeli Parliament), Session: 256 – 259, May 28 – 30 1951.

92 'Divrei Haknesset', (protocol of the Israeli Parliament), Report of the parliamentary committee of inquiry on the issue of the detainees in the Jallame camp. August 3 1951, 2209.

Conclusion

The radicalization of the right-wing and the Charedi sector can be traced back to the unending battle over the character of Jewish public sphere in the newly-founded state. For political reasons, two groups were pushed to the sidelines: the Revisionist right and the ultra-Orthodox community. Jerusalem was home to a large concentration of Charedim and supporters of the right. The city's unresolved international status added fuel to the flames of the debate and played a part in the radicalization of these two groups. In contrast to the image projected by these groups and the perceived ties between them, they followed different directions. For the right and left-wing extremists who belonged to Lechi before the establishment of the state, terrorism was seen as a legitimate tool for achieving political goals. Thus, as the situation grew more chaotic, they leaned even more towards radicalism. The Charedi radicals cut themselves off from Israeli politics. This was true not only for Neturei Qarta, but also for the ultra-Orthodox mainstream, Agudat Yisrael, which ran in the Knesset elections. It was a total walkout from the political system and the state: They refused to join the coalition at any price, the young people declined to serve in the army, and the Charedi community became a "society of learners".

The results of the Jerusalem municipal elections strengthened the Charedi/religious right and the right wing in Jerusalem. The coalition that was formed, which was on the opposite side of the political divide, was seen as a threat by the national government, which did everything possible to strew obstacles in its path. The Jerusalem city council became a political battlefront plagued not only by fighting between coalition partners but between the municipality and the government. In addition to bringing the work of the municipality to a standstill, the discord was a catalyst for radicalism: the political disputes moved into the streets, sparking demonstrations and acts of violence. As the concerns specific to Jerusalem merged with matters of national import, the local aspect of the battle took a step back, whereas the core issue, with its explosive power for the country as a whole, intensified. The round of events that followed the news of a Charedi underground operating in Jerusalem only increased Charedi hostility toward the state, encouraged insularity, and stoked religious fanaticism. At the same time, the acts of terror continued, largely because it was not this community that was behind them. In retrospect, one might even say that the events of this period solidified the alliance of outcasts that took shape in earnest after the political upheaval of 1977.

Works Cited

Archives

Aba Achimeir Archives, Ramat-Gan.
Centeral Zionist Archives, Jerusalem, (CZA)
Israel State Archives, Jerusalem, (ISA)
Zionist Religious Archives, Ramat-Gan

Newspapers

A'l HaMishmar
Davar
HaDor
HaModia'
HaTzofeh
Herut
Ma'ariv
New York Times

Secondary Sources

Alpert, Pinhas, and Dotan Goren, eds. *Dairy of a Muchtar in Jerusalem – The History of the Beit Yisrael Neighborhood and its Surroundings in the Writings of Rabbi Moshe Yekutiel Alpert (1938–1952).* Ramat-Gan: Bar-Ilan University Press, 2013. (in Hebrew)

Bacon, Gershon C. *The Politics of Tradition: Agudat Yisrael in Poland, 1916–1939.* Jerusalem: Magnes Press, 2005. (in Hebrew)

Bar-On, Mordechai, and Nir Mann. "An Interview with the Fifth President Yitzhak Navon." *Aley Zait Vacherev* (Olive Leaves and Sword) 13 (2013): 13–30. (in Hebrew)

Braun, Binyamin. "The Ultra-Orthodox Jewry and the State." *When Judaism Meets the State,* edited by Yedidia Z. Stern et al. Tel-Aviv: MISKAL – Yedioth Ahronoth Books, 2015. (in Hebrew)

Cahaner, Lee, Nikola Yozgof-Orbach, and Arnon Sofer, eds. *The Haredim in Israel – Space, Society, Community.* Haifa: Chaikin Chair In Geostrategy, University of Haifa, 2012. (in Hebrew)

Cas, Mudde. *Populist Radical Right Parties in Europe.* Cambridge USA: Cambridge University Press, 2007.

Deskal, Avraham. "Non Parliamentary Oppositional behavior in the 1950s: Brit-Kanaim and Malchut-Israel". MA thesis, Bar-Ilan University, 1990. (in Hebrew)

'Divrei Haknesset', protocol of the Israeli Parliament (1949–1951). (in Hebrew)

Eldad, Yisrael. *The First Tithe – Memories Episodes and Moral.* Tel-Aviv, third edition, 1975. (in Hebrew)

Friedman, Menachem.

-*The Origin of the Haredi Society, Orientation and Process.* Jerusalem: Jerusalem Institute for Israel Studies, 1991. (in Hebrew)
-ELI: "Jewish Religious Underground during the British Mandate". In *Milestones, Essays in Jewish History Dedicated to Zvi Yekutiel*, edited by Immanuel Etkes, David Assaf, and Yosef Kaplan, 379 – 396. Jerusalem: The Zalman Shazar Press, 2016 (in Hebrew)
Galnoor, Itzhak and Dana Blander. *The Political System of Israel, Formative Years; Institutional Structure; Political Behavior; Unsolved Problems; Democracy in Israel.* Tel-Aviv: Am-O'ved, 2013. (in Hebrew)
Goldstein, Amir. *Heroism and Exclusion: The Gallows Martyrs and the Israeli Collective Memory.* Jerusalem: Yad Izhak Ben-Zvi, 2011. (in Hebrew)
Golani Motti. "Zionism without Zion: The Position of the Pre-state and National Leadership of Israel on the Jerusalem question 1947 – 1949." In *Divided Jerusalem 1948 – 1967*, edited by Avi Bareli. Jerusalem: Yad Ben-Zvi, 1995, 30 – 52. (in Hebrew)
Gruweis-Kovalsky, Ofira. *The Vindicated and the Persecuted – The Mythology and the Symbols of the Herut Movement.* Sede-Boker: The Ben-Gurion Research Institute, 2015. (in Hebrew)
Gruweis-Kovalsky, Ofira. "The Attitude of the Revisionists Right Wing toward Jerusalem in the War of Independence." *Aley Zait Vacherev (Olive Leaves and Sword)* 13 (2013): 140 – 174. (in Hebrew)
Gruweis-Kovalsky, Ofira. "Between Ideology and Reality: Menachem Begin and the Jerusalem Question, 1948 – 1949." *Israel Studies* 21, no. 3 (2016): 99 – 125.
Gruweis-Kovalsky, Ofira. "'A Tale of Love and Darkness'": The Radical Right Wing and the Herut Movement, 1948 – 1957." *Kesher (Communication)* 50 (2017): 89 – 99. (in Hebrew)
Gruweis-Kovalsky, Ofira. "Between National Politic to Local Politics." In *Jerusalem*, edited by Golan Arnon and Ramon Amnon. Jerusalem: Yad Ben-Zvi, forthcoming. (in Hebrew)
Hacohen, Aviad. "The State of Israel – This is a Holy Place!: Forming a 'Jewish Public Domain' in the State of Israel". In *On Both Side of the Bridge, Religion and State in the Early Years of Israel*, edited by Bar-On Mordechai and Zameret Zvi, 169 – 170. Jerusalem: Yad Izhak Ben-Zvi Press, 2002. (in Hebrew)
Heller, Joseph. *Lehi – Ideology and Politics 1940 – 1949.* Jerusalem: Zalman Shazar Press, 1989. (in Hebrew)
Inbari, Motti. "Messianic Activism in the Work and Thought of Chaim Elazar Shapira, the Munkacser Rebbe, Between Two World Wars." *Cathedra* 149 (2014): 77 – 104. (in Hebrew)
Kaplan, Eran. *The Jewish Radical Right, Revisionist Zionism and its Ideological Legacy.* Wisconsin: The University of Wisconsin Press, 2005.
Keren-Kratz, Menachem. "Ha-E'dah Ha-Haredit in Jerusalem in 1948 – 1973". *Cathedra* 161 (2017): 139 – 174. (in Hebrew)
Lebel, Udi. *The Road to the Pantheon – Etzel, Lehi and the Borders of Israeli National Memory.* Jerusalem: Carmel Publisher, 2007. (in Hebrew)
Levin, Shely, and Jonathan Erlich. *Background Document: Jewish Political violence in Israel.* Jerusalem: The Knesset research and information center, 2005. (in Hebrew)
Lissak, Moshe. *Studies in Israeli Social History.* Jerusalem: Bialik Institute Press, 2009. (in Hebrew)
Meir, Yitzhak (Rabbi). *On the Walls of B'nai- Barak – the First Decade of B'nai- Barak.* B'nai-Barak: The society for research the history of B'nai- Barak Press, 1989. (in Hebrew)
Meller, Shimeon Josef. *The Rabbi of Brisk Book.* Jerusalem: Feldhaim Press, 2004. (in Hebrew)

Nadel, Baruch. *Bernadotte Murder.* Tel-Aviv, 1968. (in Hebrew)
Naor, Arye. *Greater Israel Theology and Policy.* Haifa: University of Haifa Press, 2001. (in Hebrew)
Natkovich, Svetlana. *Among Radiant Clouds: The Literature of Vladimir (Ze'ev) Jabotinsky in Its Social Context.* Jerusalem: Magnes Press, 2015. (in Hebrew)
Pedahzur, Ami. *The Triumph of Israel's Radical Right.* Oxford, UK: Oxford University Press, 2012.
Piekarz, Mendel. "The Inner Point of the *Admorim* Gur and Alexander as a Reflection of their Ability to Adjust to Changing Times." *Studies in Jewish Mysticism Philosophy and Ethical Literature*, edited by Joseph Dan and Joseph Hacker, 569–592. Jerusalem: Magnes Press, 1986.
Porush, Menachem (M.K. Rabbi). *Koll Israel* 40 (1982). (in Hebrew)
Pund, Yossef. *Separation or Participation, Agudat Israel Confronting Zionism and the State of Israel.* Jerusalem: The Magnes Press, 1991. (in Hebrew)
Regev-Yarkoni, Hadas, and Ofer Regev. *Jerusalem's Liberation Fighter, the Memories of Yehoshua Zetler.* Tel-Aviv: Porat Press, 2007. (in Hebrew)
Schwartz, Dov. *Religious Zionism between Logic and Messianism.* Tel-Aviv: Am-Oved Press, 1999. (in Hebrew)
Shalem, Chaim. *A Time to Take Action to Rescue Jews, Agudat Yisrael in Eretz Israel Confronting the Holocaust 1942–1945.* Sede-Boker: Ben-Gurion University of the Negev Press, 2007. (in Hebrew)
Shindler, Colin. *The Triumph of Military Zionism, Nationalism and the Origins of the Israeli Right.* London: I.B. Tauris, 2006.
Shpiro, Shlomo. "The Intellectual Foundations of Jewish National Terrorism: Avraham Stern and the Lehi." *Terrorism and Political Violence* 25, no. 4 (2013), 606–620.
Shprinzak, Ehud. "The Emergence of the Israeli Radical Right". *Comparative Politics* 21, no. 2 (1989): 92–171.
Shprinzak, Ehud. *Brothers Against Brothers: Violence and Extremism in Israeli Politics from Altalena to the Rabin Assassination.* New York: Free Press, 1999.
Tydor, Baumel Judith. "Strange Bedfellows: The Revisionist Movement and Agudath Yisrael during the Holocaust." *Iyunim Bitkumat Israel* 12 (2002): 465–492. (in Hebrew)
Vered, Avraham. *A Burning Bush on Fire – Epic of War and Conquest.* Tel Aviv, 1950. (in Hebrew)
Weitz, Yechiam. "The Jerusalem Municipality Elections." In *Jerusalem*, edited by Arnon Golan and Amnon Ramon. Jerusalem: Yad Ben-Zvi Jerusalem (forthcoming). (in Hebrew)
Wineman, Zvi. *From Katovitz to He Be-Iyyar – Chapters in the History of Agudat Yisrael, and the Ultra-Orthodox Jews New Perspectives.* Jerusalem: Vatikin Press, 1995. (in Hebrew)

Section III
Cultural Radicalisms

Anne Klein

Education, Citizenship, Social Justice

Janusz Korczak and Jewish Community Action in Warsaw at the Beginning of the Twentieth Century

Introduction

> "The hero the story discloses needs no heroic qualities [...]"[1]

At the beginning of the twentieth century, in all European countries the so-called "social question" was closely linked to women's emancipation, recognition of minorities, and children's rights.[2] The process of modernization had torn families and communities apart. Under the influence of Marxist analyses, the need for the workers' class to establish networks of support had become quite obvious during the last quarter of the nineteenth century. Although imperialist Germany under Bismarck had strategically undermined the socialist urge for a just redistribution of common goods,[3] the German workers' insurance and the state-run social welfare served as an inspiring example for social movements all over Europe.

The situation in Central Eastern Europe was quite different, especially for the large Jewish minority that for centuries lived in this geographical region. Social inequality induced by a rigid industrialization went together with fierce oppression on the political level. Although there was a strong Jewish upper and also middle class, economic hardship and anti-Semitic discrimination were intertwined. The Polish and Yiddish language were subdued by the Tsarist regime and school education was organized in a military-like discipline with the consequence that a lot of children did not go to school at all. In order to produce a critical knowledge that linked personal empowerment to the awareness of social inequality, Jewish intellectuals in Eastern Europe started to act as inspiring lead-

1 Hannah Arendt, *The Human Condition* (Chicago/London: University of Chicago Press, Second Edition 1998), 186.

2 Robert E. Blobaum, "The 'Woman Question' in Russian Poland, 1900 – 1914," *Journal of Social History* 35, no. 4 (2002): 799 – 824.

3 Lucjan Blit, *The Origins of Polish Socialism: The History and Ideas of the First Polish Socialist Party, 1878 – 1886* (London/New York: Cambridge University Press, 1971); Albert A. Lindemann, *A History of European Socialism* (New Haven, CT: Yale University Press, 1983); Michael Newman, *Socialism: A Very Short Introduction* (Oxford: Oxford University Press, 2005).

https://doi.org/10.1515/9783110545753-012

ers of emancipation. Warsaw as one of the main cities in Eastern Europe was a quite specific place with its vivid communal life and transcultural activism. As a foremost urban phenomenon, Jewish welfare circles of support succeeded in attenuating the most evident forms of poverty.[4]

Born as the son of a Jewish couple in 1878, Janusz Korczak (1878/1879 – 1942) belonged to the assimilated middle class of Warsaw. After the early death of his father, the family experienced economic hardship and instability. Although the Jewish community was very secular and socially active, it was a very new idea to establish secular educational institutions. When thirty-four-year-old pediatrician Henryk Goldszmit decided to become a pedagogue in a home for Jewish orphans in 1912, he had in mind to empower the younger generation to fight against anti-Semitism and social inequality. In his opinion, the growing gap between poor and rich endangered to split the Jewish community itself. Working as a doctor between 1905 and 1912, Korczak had profited from his rich patients. But he resigned this privilege in order to become a social worker and pedagogue for the rest of his life. The decision to devote his life to support the most vulnerable members of the Jewish community did not come overnight and was not only situational. Korczak had in mind to develop a pedagogical concept substantiated by empirical research. His aim was to generate reliable information on how to arrange educational settings adequate for the oncoming political transition towards a democratic society.

Being able to profit from an extensive research on Korczak's life and his written *oeuvre* published in Poland, Germany, the United States, and Israel,[5] this chapter is a case study on Jewish community action in Warsaw in the first quarter of the twentieth century. Dealing with specific aspects of Janusz Korczak's life and work, I want to illustrate what can be understood as "Jewish radicalism" or, as Korczak researcher Marc Silverman has put it: "radical humanism"![6] I will prove the thesis that Jewish radicalism was not merely based on ideas but ex-

4 Anthony Polonsky, ed., *The Jews of Warsaw, Polin 3* (London et al.: Littman Library of Jewish Civilization, 2004); Glenn Dynner and François Guesnet, eds., *Warsaw, the Jewish Metropolis: Essays in Honor of the 75th Birthday of Professor Antony Polonsky* (Amsterdam: Brill, 2015).

5 German readers have access to a sixteenth volume edition of Korczak's writings, translated into German. Janusz Korczak, *Sämtliche Werke* (*Collected Works*), eds. Erich Dauzenroth, Friedhelm Beiner et al. (Gütersloh: Gütersloher Verlagshaus, 1996 – 2010).

6 Marc Silverman, "Korczak's Road to Radical Humanism," in *A Pedagogy of Humanist Moral Education* (New York: Palgrave Macmillan, 2017), 19 – 70, accessed July 17 2017, doi https://doi.org/10.1057/978-1-137-56068-1_2.

pressed by critical interventions into the everyday life of a Jewish community.[7] Korczak's engagement aimed at bridging the gap of social inequality by empowering marginalized Jewish youth through participative educational practices. His pedagogical ideas were based on concepts of a radical democracy that focused on consciousness-raising. Experiences of self-efficacy and democratic discourse should enable the children and youth to speak up for their rights and to transcend the barriers of structural exclusion. Social justice education wanted to empower especially those who because of their social background had no access to economic, social, and cultural capital. In the face of rapid capitalist progress, Korczak put forward his idea to tackle the root causes of the "social question" by education. Democratic settings were seen as an important trajectory towards a just society. Korczak hoped that those who were raised in the spirit of active citizenship would have the power to construct a democratic Poland without anti-Semitism.

In the first section, I will describe some central aspects of Jewish life in Warsaw under Russian occupation at the beginning of the twentieth century in order to make intelligible the relevance of this specific historical context for Jewish community action. In the second section, I will highlight Korczak's social and intellectual engagement as a student and young doctor between 1900 and 1912. The third section will give a closer insight into the contemporary European debate on educational reforms. The fourth section focuses on the development of Korczak's pedagogical theory and practice, after he had taken over the management of the Jewish orphanage Dom Sierot in 1912. In the fifth section, I will provide evidence to Korczak's radicalism by a theory-led reflection on "humanity in dark times."[8] In evaluating courageous acts, German-Jewish philosopher Hannah Arendt reminds us of the fact that human beings are foremost moral and political subjects who challenge old truths and create new realities, thus leaving traces in the course of history to posterity. The conclusion points to the fact that for us today, ideas of social justice and democracy reinforce the relevance of Janusz Korczak's radical intervention into social community life for future political action.

---

7 For a sociological approach to the link between the history of ideas and personal action see Robert J. Brym, *The Jewish Intelligentsia and Russian Marxism. A Sociological Study of Intellectual Radicalism and Ideological Divergence* (London and Basingstoke: The Macmillan Press, 1978).
8 Hannah Arendt, "On Humanity in Dark Times: Thoughts about Lessing," in *Men in Dark Times*, ed. Hannah Arendt (New York: Harcourt, Brace & World, 1968), 3–31.

Jewish Culture in Warsaw at the Beginning of the Twentieth Century

"Change is constant, inherent in the human condition, but the velocity of change is not."[9]

How can a Jewish life be reconstructed in the midst of political turmoil and under rapidly changing circumstances in Eastern Central Europe at the beginning of the twentieth century? Historians can only access the traces people have left in the form of images or written documents whose transmittance through history is always connected to questions of power. Many lives have disappeared, are forgotten, and therefore will not have a meaning for further generations. Historiography after the Shoah has to deal with an enormous destruction of Jewish sources, but with a rich heritage and memory at the same time.[10] The work of Simon Dubnow[11] (1860–1941) is crucially important as well as that of Emanuel Ringelblum (1900–1944) and his colleagues, who collected an extensive amount of written information on Jewish social history.[12] The staff of the *Yidisher visnshaftlekher institut* (YIVO) founded in 1925 in Vilnius (Lithuania) had transferred documents to archives in New York early enough to preserve them from Nazi aggression. Tens of thousands of photographs, taken by Roman Vishniac (1897–1990), Alter Kacynze (1885–1941), and others, deposited at the YIVO-*Institute for Jewish Research* in New York, give a striking impression of the vivid and diverse Jewish culture in Poland between 1864 and 1939.[13] Similar to the material of the Warsaw Ghetto archive, the so-called Ghetto diary of Janusz Korczak has survived hidden by his scholar Igor Newerly (1903–1987) in the "Aryan" quartier of Warsaw.[14] Thus a lot of documents of the Jewish com-

9 Hannah Arendt, "Civil Disobedience," in *Crisis of the Republic*, ed. Hannah Arendt (New York: Harcourt Brace Jovanovich, 1969), 78.

10 Natalia Aleksiun, Brian Horowitz and Antony Polonsky, eds., *Writing Jewish History in Eastern Europe, Polin 29* (Oxford, Portland, Oregon: The Littman Library of Jewish Civilizations, 2017).

11 Semjon Markowitch Dubnow, *Jewish History: An Essay on the Philosophy of History* (Philadelphia: The Jewish Publication Society, 1903).

12 Samuel D. Kassow, *Who Will Write Our History? Rediscovering a Hidden Archive from the Warsaw Ghetto*, Reprint Edition (New York: Vintage Books, 2009).

13 Lucjan Dobroszycki and Barbara Kirshenblatt-Gimblett, *Image before my Eyes: A Photographic History of Jewish life in Poland, 1864–1939* (New York: Schocken Books, 1977).

14 Betty Jean Lifton, "Who was Janusz Korczak," in *Janusz Korczak, Ghetto Diary*, with an introduction by Betty Jean Lifton, first published by the Holocaust Library (New Haven and London: Yale University Press, 2003), XXIII-XIV.

munities in the Warsaw region could be transmitted to the post-Shoah generation.

Korczaks's written heritage encompasses twenty-four books, over one thousand professional articles, numerous radio features, contributions to schoolbooks and pedagogical statements. His complete work has been published over a period of fifty years in Polish, translated already during Korczak's lifetime into many languages, particularly into Yiddish and even Esperanto.[15] Research into Korczak's work deals with his biography, his pedagogical theories, and his educational practices. Often, his life is presented by underlining his heroic behavior, because he did not take the chance to evade the Warsaw Ghetto. During the deportation procedure at the *Umschlagplatz*, a German Gestapo man offered Korczak to deliver only the children and to stay back himself. With inner contempt, Korczak commented that he – as a human being – did not want to become as corrupt as the Nazis were. Because of this act of solidarity, Korczak is honored in Yad Vashem as Righteous among the Nations.[16] At the age of sixty-four, he was deported to Treblinka, leaving behind a life's work that to this day represents an elaborate concept of Jewish democratic culture and education.[17]

Korczak always defined himself as a Polish citizen. However during his lifetime, the Polish state had only existed twenty-one years until it was attacked and occupied by the German army in September 1939.[18] Besides travelling because of medical studies and pedagogical trainings in European cities like Paris, London, Zurich, and Berlin, Korczak also visited Palestine several times during the 1930s. Demonstrating a certain readiness to learn from life, Korczak enunciated ideas and points of view that reflected no national or otherwise predetermined boun-

---

15 Friedhelm Beiner, preface to *Janusz Korczak, Themen seines Lebens: Eine Werkbiographie* (*Janusz Korczak. Themes of his Life: A Biography based on his Oeuvre*) (Gütersloh: Gütersloher Verlagshaus, 2011), 13.

16 Moshe Gilad, "Righteous among the Nations – and Much More," *Haaretz*, July 30 2012. Accessed March 3 2017. http://www.haaretz.com/israel-news/culture/leisure/righteous-among-the-nations-and-much-more-1.454502.

17 Michael Kirchner, "Das Lebenswerk von Janusz Korczak," in *Pionier der Kinderrechte. Ein internationales Symposium*, ed. Manfred Liebel ("The Lifework of Janusz Korczak," in *Pioneer of Children's Rights. An international Symposium*) (Berlin, Münster, Wien, Zürich, London: LIT Verlag, 2013), 13.

18 Alexander B. Rossino, *Hitler Strikes Poland: Blitzkrieg, Ideology, and Atrocity* (Lawrence: University Press of Kansas, 2003); Bogdan Musial, "The Origins of 'Operation Reinhard': The Decision-Making Process for the Mass Murder of the Jews in the General Government." *Yad Vashem Studies* 28 (2000): 113–153. The Molotov-Ribbentrop Pact had led to the division of Poland already in August 1939.

daries. Korczak was cosmopolitan who fused openness to the world with loyalty to local roots and practices in Warsaw. Because of migration movements, the urban conglomeration was one of the most vivid centers of Jewish life in Central Eastern Europe. In this multicultural environment, Jewish individuals developed quite diverse understandings of what it meant for them to be Jewish.[19] When Janusz Korczak was born on July 22 1878 or 1879 – his parents did not register him for an official birth certificate[20] – the impressive Great Synagogue built by the Warsaw's Jewish community since 1875 had just opened at Tłomackie street, at the south-eastern tip of the district in which the Russian Imperial authorities had allowed Jews to settle. The Korczak family adhered to the secular branch of the Jewish community. Józef Goldszmit, a lawyer, was well-known for his publications on the liberalization of divorce. He had also publicly argued for the integration of the Jewish community into Polish society and addressed the Jewish bourgeoisie to institutionalize secular public schools.[21] Efforts to mediate between the Jewish and the Christian communities and the engagement for a civic, not religious, understanding of society appeared to be a family heritage. The young Korczak preferred to define himself as someone relating to different lifestyles, in the midst of a hybrid construction of being Polish and Jewish. He felt like a citizen of a prospective democracy and a cosmopolitan Jew at the same time. In the first instance, Korczak saw himself as a political defendant of a secular society. His motivation was based on a strong moral obligation, such that he transformed into an intellectual habitus combined with a strong urge for social action. Although he personally preferred the Polish national option to the Zionist idea of a Jewish state in Palestine, he sympathized with the Zionist movement, was befriended by many Zionists, visited Palestine, and received visitors from the Kibbutzim-movement, where European social progressivism had found a new home.[22] Facing the growing anti-Semitism of the 1930s, even Korczak considered to migrate to Palestine.[23]

---

19 For the history of Warsaw see the website of the Jewish Virtual Library, a project by AICE, accessed March 30 2017, https://www.jewishvirtuallibrary.org/warsaw-poland-2.

20 Korczak, *Themen seines Lebens*, 15.

21 Ibid., 16.

22 Ludwig Liegle and Franz Michael Konrad, eds. *Reformpädagogik in Palästina: Dokumente und Deutungen zu den Versuchen einer 'neuen' Erziehung im jüdischen Gemeinwesen Palästinas, 1914–1948* (*Reform Education in Palestine: Documents and Interpretations of Experiments with 'new' Education in Jewish Community Life in Palestine, 1914–1948*) (Frankfurt a. M.: dipa-Verlag, 1989).

23 In 1934 and 1936, Korczak visited Palestine. In 1938, he was in close contact to the emissary of the Kibbutz Ejn Harod, the poet Zerubal Gilead, who visited Warsaw. Korczak, *Themen seines Lebens*, 205–210, 215–217, 225–229.

According to Norman Davies, "for most of the period 'Poland' was just an idea – a memory from the past or a hope for the future."[24] Since the so-called third division of Poland in 1795, no Polish state had existed until November 9 1918. The Warsaw region underwent a very specific political development with liberal periods but also strong oppression. As an effect of political instability and changing working conditions, between 1858 and 1897, the population of Warsaw had risen from 160,000 to 600,000.[25] Attacks and pogroms against Jews alternated with strikes of Jewish workers. The Jewish social movements were widely connected all over Eastern Europe, claiming an international approach to Jewish emancipation under the roof of solidarity. This secular idea of belonging encompassed the idea that the engagement for social justice should primarily be realized by workers' self-associations.[26] The redefinition of Polishness played a significant role in this political process and became even more decisive after the First World War.[27]

The Second Polish Republic was founded as a progressive parliamentary democracy with women granted the right to vote by a decree of Józef Piłsudski (1967–1935) on November 28 1918.[28] The landscape of political parties at this time was vast. The *Socialist General Jewish Labour Bund* (The Bund), parties of the Zionist right and left wing, and religious conservative movements were represented in the *Sejm* (the Polish Parliament) as well as in the important regional councils.[29] However, the political situation remained unstable and after the mili-

---

24 Norman Davies, *Heart of Europe: The Past in Poland's Present*, New Edition (Oxford: Oxford University Press, 2001), 139.

25 Gérard Kahn, *Janusz Korczak und die jüdische Erziehung: Janusz Korczaks Pädagogik auf dem Hintergrund seiner jüdischen Herkunft* (*Janusz Korczak and the Jewish Education: Janusz Korczak's Pedagogy in the Context of his Jewish Origin*) (Weinheim: Deutscher Studienverlag 1993), 36.

26 Isaac Deutscher, *The Tragedy of Polish Communism between the Wars* (London: Socialist Labour League, n.d.). The publication is a reprint of an article that had first appeared in *Les Temps Modernes*, March 1958 (Vol. XIII, 1632–1677) in the form of an interview between Isaac Deutscher and the Polish journalist K.S. Karol.

27 Edyta Barucka, "Redefining Polishness: The Revival of Crafts in Galicia around 1900," *Acta Slavica Iaponica* 28 (2016): 7, 76.

28 Feigue Cieplinski, "Poles and Jews: The Quest for Self-Determination 1919–1934," *Binghamton Journal of History* 3 (2002), accessed March 27 2017, https://www.binghamton.edu/history/resources/journal-of-history/poles-and-jews.html; Joseph Marcus, *Social and Political History of the Jews in Poland, 1919–1939* (Berlin/New York/Amsterdam: Mouton Publishers, 1983).

29 Zvi Y. Gitelman, *The Emergence of Modern Jewish Politics: Bundism and Zionism in Eastern Europe* (Pittsburgh: University of Pittsburgh Press, 2002); Jaff Schatz, "Jews and the Communist Movement in Interwar Poland," in *Dark Times, Dire Decisions: Jews and Communism. Studies in Contemporary Jewry*, ed. Jonathan Frankel (Oxford: Oxford University Press, 2005), 13–37. The *United Jewish Socialist Workers Party* strongly established in the Ukraine was not represented

tary coup in 1926, the social climate became even more harsh and rigid. Under the economic crisis of 1929, social conflicts increased. When General Piłsudski – the Polish dictator, as Hannah Arendt called him – died in 1935, an authoritarian constitution had just been approved.[30] Polish nationalism was now exclusively defined as being anti-Jewish. In addition, the social democrats who traditionally had propagated Jewish assimilation now wanted to reduce the political and public participation of Jews. From all Polish parties, only the socialists took a stance against anti-Semitism.[31] The everyday life of migrated Jews who lived in Poland without valid national identity papers thus became more and more difficult. Although the protection of minorities as outlined in the Paris treaties of 1919 had been adopted by the Polish constitution of 1921,[32] the Jewish situation was not particularly mentioned, meaning there did not exist any public or legal shelter against anti-Semitic discrimination.

Formative Experiences as a Student and Doctor

> "Power is what keeps the public realm, the potential space of appearance between acting and speaking men, in existence."[33]

Janusz Korczak was twenty years old when he enrolled in medical studies at Warsaw University for the winter semester 1898/99.[34] After six years of studies, he gained experience in the medical profession for another seven years, until he took over the educational management of Dom Sierot in 1912. Korczak was thirty-three years old when he decided to become an educator, strongly motivated by his social and political engagement. He was also affected by his earlier personal and intimate life experiences. In disappointing childhood episodes

---

in the Polish parliament. The party was also called *Fareynikte*, founded in June 1917 through the merger of the Zionist Socialist Workers Party (SSRP) and the *Jewish Socialist Workers Party* (SERP). It adhered to the Second Socialist International. Politically the party favored a secular, national autonomy for the Jewish community.

30 Hannah Arendt, "Rosa Luxemburg (1971–1919)," in *Men in Dark Times*, ed. Hannah Arendt, 33–56, 42.

31 Kahn, *Janusz Korczak und die jüdische Erziehung*, 49–51.

32 Dobroszycki/Kirshenblatt-Gimblett, *Image Before My Eyes*, 133; Martin Scheuermann, *Minderheitenschutz contra Konfliktverhütung? Die Minderheitenpolitik des Völkerbundes in den zwanziger Jahren (Protection of Minorities versus Prevention of Conflict? Minority Policy of the League of Nations in the 1920s)* (Marburg: Verlag Herder-Institut, 2000).

33 Arendt, *Human Condition*, 200.

34 Korczak, *Themen seines Lebens*, 28.

that he remembered, he had not been allowed to play in the streets with children from poor families. It was precisely this reminiscence of segregation and social inequality that let him delve deeper into his past. As a student and young doctor, he analyzed his biographical experiences, thus becoming convinced of the need and necessity to develop a new approach to education.

The influence of formative life-experiences on Korczak's decision to become an educator has often been underlined.[35] Besides childhood, the *Model of Productive Processing of Reality* (PPR), well known from human development studies, calls our attention to the relevance of formative learning processes during youth.[36] The idea of life passages, as outlined by biography-researcher Gail Sheehy, seems additionally helpful to understand the influence of life experiences at certain ages.[37] Following the traits of biographical formation, Sheehy differentiates between a provisional adulthood (between eighteen and thirty) and an early adulthood (thirty and forty-five), a classification that helps to structure the circle of life. Korczak's active engagement in intellectual discourses and social projects during his provisional adulthood influenced him to develop a perception of human beings – including himself – as being strongly affected by their socialization. This perspective on human subjectivity underlined the necessity of a sustainable social citizenship education for democratic participation.

Looking back at his life as expressed in a letter to a friend in Palestine, Korczak described his political engagement as bound to the decision not to start a family himself.[38] He compared his situation to that of "a slave who is a Polish Jew under Russian occupation."[39] Since Russian had become the official teaching language in 1885, Polish and Yiddish only existed in clandestine instructions.

35 Friedhelm Beiner, "Wie wurde Korczak zum 'Pionier der Menschenrechte des Kindes' – und welchen Beitrag leisteten Stefania Wilczynska und Maria Falska dazu?," in *Janusz Korczak. Pionier der Kinderrechte. Ein internationales Symposium*, ed. Manfred Liebel; *Pionier der Kinderrechte. Ein internationales Symposium*, ed. Manfred Liebel ("How Korczak became the 'Pioneer of Children's Rights' – and the Contribution of Stefania Wilczynska and Maria Falska," in *Pioneer of Children's Rights. An International Symposium*) (Münster: LIT Verlag 2013), 29–31.

36 Klaus Hurrelmann, "Adolescents as Productive Processors of Reality," in *The Developmental Science of Adolescence*, ed. Richard M. Lerner, Arthur C. Petersen, Rainer K. Silbereisen, and Jeanne Brooks-Gunn (New York: Psychology Press, 2014); 230–238.

37 Gail Sheehy, *New Passages: Mapping Your Life Across Time* (Toronto: Random House of Canada, 1995).

38 Janusz Korczak, "Brief an L. Zylbertal, 30.3.1937," in *Sämtliche Werke, vol. 15, Briefe und Palästina Reisen*, ("Letter to L. Zylbertal, 30.3.1937," in *Collected Works, vol. 15, Letters and Travels to Palestine*) (Gütersloh: Gütersloher Verlagsanstalt, 2005), 54.

39 Betty Jean Lifton, *The King of Children: The Life and Death of Janusz Korczak* (New York: St. Martin's Griffin 1988), online edition provided by the Janusz Korczak Communication Center, accessed August 18 2017, http://korczak.com/Biography.

The typing fonts of the administration had been replaced by the Cyrillic alphabet. During his studies of medicine at Warsaw University, Korczak visited the seminaries of the so-called "Flying University" (*Uniwersytet Latający*), a subversive learning structure to empower young Jews to further their emancipation.[40] Women played a substantial role in these clandestine practices that formed an effective counterculture against the authoritarian Russian regime. The curriculum of the "Flying University" covered five or six years with eight to eleven hours per week of study on five main subjects: social sciences, pedagogy, philology, history and natural sciences. Korczak underlined that his interest in education emanated from his studies at the "Flying University."[41] One of Korczak's teachers, the sociologist Ludwik Krzywicki (1859–1941), had cooperated in the translation of Karl Marx's *Das Kapital* into Polish and also edited the newsletter of the *Polish Socialist Party* (*Polska Partia Socjalistyczna*). Language skills were seen as very important. Taking a stance against the Russian monolingual habitus, the Jewish community furthered multilingual competencies and transnational communication. Korczak's Polish written publications were translated into Russian, Czech, Yiddish, and Esperanto in 1905.[42]

Jewish intellectuals of the younger generation, women and men, decided to work for the integration of Jewish children from poor families by supporting their alphabetization and social learning. Poverty was a mass phenomenon, although mostly hidden from the bourgeois perception by urban segregation. Child-work, child-neglect, depression, sexual violence, suicide, child prostitution, and trafficking were usually dealt with by police. The city council provided some provisional measurement of social hygiene and clinical expertise. However, deviant youths were medicalized or criminalized without taking into account the effects of social inequality. Facing this striking injustice, many students looked for fields of engagement, whether it might be political organization, social welfare, or public education. Jewish youths who were affected by anti-Semitic discrimination, in particular, showed a strong interest in engaged research and socialist practices. When Korczak visited the slums of Warsaw together with his friend, ethnographer Ludwik S. Licinski (1874–1908), this field study taught him a lesson for life.[43] The idea of children's rights and the obligation of a society to take care of children's dignity and well-being had already been developed during that time, but not yet been institutionalized. In Central Eastern Europe, influences

---

40 The "Flying University," sometimes translated as "Floating University," operated from 1885 to 1905 in Warsaw. Lifton, *King of Children*, 35.

41 Korczak, *Themen seines Lebens*, 29.

42 Ibid., 50; Dobroszycki/Kirshenblatt-Gimblett, *Image Before My Eyes*, 202.

43 Korczak, *Themen seines Lebens*, 30.

from the Proletkult Movement could be observed[44], but the negative experiences with the Russian occupation made most political activists in Warsaw turn towards Western trajectories of democratization. This might have been one reason why Korczak decided to go to Zurich in order to visit educational institutions that worked on the basis of the pedagogical concept of Johann Heinrich Pestalozzi. A century ago, the Suisse pedagogue had developed a humanist approach to social work at the orphanage in Stanz[45], influenced by the French Children's Rights Movement.[46]

For Korzcak, spoken and written language was a precondition of social learning and emancipation. After his return to Warsaw, he opened a public library in his little backyard flat in a worker's district.[47] In 1904, he also started to work as an educator in the summer colony *Michalówka*, organized by a welfare society in Warsaw. Korczak made friends with many of the children and youths who visited him in his flat in Warsaw the following winter. They met for reading circles or spent the Sabbath evening together, playing domino or lottery.[48] On March 17 1905, Korczak gained his degree as a doctor, but it seemed as if he was rather productive in the field of writing. Between 1904 and 1905, he published around fifty articles in the radical social journal *Głosz*. Korczak spoke up against anti-Semitism and at the same time criticized the hypocrisy of Jewish philanthropy that failed to address the economic foundations of social inequality.[49]

In the beginning of 1905, Korzcak started to work as a ward physician in the Berson-Bauman-Spital, one of the Jewish philanthropic centers in Warsaw. But the political conflicts in the city escalated because of the aggressive anti-Semitism of the National Democratic Party.[50] In July, Korczak was conscripted into

---

44 Lynn Mally, *Culture of the Future. The Proletkult Movement in Revolutionary Russia* (Berkeley, Los Angeles, Oxford: University of California Press, 1990), 181–182.

45 Rebekka Horlacher, "Schooling as Means of Popular Education: Pestalozzi's Method as a Popular Education Experiment," in *A History of Popular Education: Educating the People of the World*, ed. Sjaak Braster, Frank Simon, and Ian Grosnevor (London/New York: Routledge, 2012), 67–69.

46 Yves Denérchére and David Nigel, *Droits des Enfants au XXe Siècle. Pour une Histoire Transnationale* (*Children's Rights in the 20th Century. A Transnational History*) (Rennes: Presses Universitaires de Rennes, 2015), 210; Joseph M. Hawes, *The Children's Rights Movement: A History of Advocacy and Protection* (Boston: Twayne Publishers, 1991).

47 Korzcak, *Themen seines Lebens*, 32.

48 Ibid., 41–43.

49 Ibid., 44 and 49–50.

50 Ury Scott, *Barricades and Banners: The Revolution of 1905 and the Transformation of Warsaw Jewry* (Stanford, CA: Stanford University Press, 2012).

the army to serve as a doctor in the Russo-Japanese War, from which he returned in March 1906. The war experience had deepened his critical analyses of illness and disability. Inspired by sociological and psychoanalytic ideas, he diagnosed states of mental confusion and expressions of fear as traumatic experiences triggered by the violence of war.[51] He had also felt the hardship and distress of injured people, whom he could not help because of the lack of infrastructure. In an article in the journal *Nowa Gazeta*, he campaigned for the support of care workers who went on strike against poor resources and the mismanagement in health clinics.[52] He signed the article with Dr. Henryk Goldszmit, adding his title in order to underline the writer's authority. He also criticized his own status group of being ignorant. In his opinion, medical professionals should not function as subaltern executors of authoritarianism, but speak up in public as representatives of a future democracy.

In his studies in medicine, Korzcak had specialized on pediatrics, although there did not exist such a chair at Warsaw University. However, the European discourse was quite advanced and transnational. Many pediatricians, a lot of them Jewish, were socially engaged with a fierce interest in social medicine and structural prevention. When Janusz Korczak visited Berlin during winter 1906/07 for medical training, he met the Jewish pediatrician Heinrich Finkelstein (1865–1942), who was responsible for the child asylum in the Kürassierstraße as well as for the city orphanage.[53] In 1918, Finkelstein followed Adolf Aron Baginsky (1843–1918) as medical director of the *Kaiser- und Kaiserin-Friedrich-Kinderkrankenhaus* (Emperor- and Empress-Friedrich-Children-Hospital) in the workers district Berlin-Wedding, where Korczak had taken some practical lessons during his stay in Berlin more than ten years before. During that time, Baginski had managed a home for people with learning difficulties, a sector of the psychiatric station at the *Charité*, where Korczak also had taken a traineeship. Visiting the rehabilitation centers for so-called deviant youths, Korczak must have also met Gustav Tugendreich (1876–1948), who until his emigration from Germany in 1933 led the infant and youth welfare center of the public health department in Berlin.[54] Korczak showed himself to be impressed by these professional en-

51 Korzcak, *Themen seines Lebens*, 50.

52 Ibid., 52.

53 Konrad Weiß, "Kinderarzt und medizinischer Lehrmeister," (Pediatrician and Medical Teacher) *Aufbau* 61, no. 15 (July 21 1988): 17.

54 Max Mosse and Gustav Tugendreich, *Krankheit und Soziale Lage* (*Disease and Social Situation*), ed. Jürgen Cromm, Third Edition (Göttingen/Augsburg: Jürgen Cromm Verlag, 1994); Eduard Seidler, *Jüdische Kinderärzte 1933–1945. Entrechtet, geflohen, ermordet* (*Jewish Pediatrists 1933–1945. Deprived of Rights, Escaped, Murdered*), Second Edition (Basel: Karger, 2007).

counters as well as by the advanced infrastructure of the Prussian welfare system.[55]

However, the living conditions in Warsaw were completely different. There did not exist comprehensive public schooling, most welfare networks were privately organized and poor families could not afford medical services. Facing this striking poverty, Korczak decided to become even more socially engaged and also deepened his political affiliations. Although he was never a member of a political party, he subscribed to the publications of the *Polish Socialist Party* (PPS-Lewica) and often met with the left-wing political activist Tadeusz Rechniewski (1862–1916) who had been arrested during the 1905 conflicts and later returned to Warsaw.[56] In 1909, Korczak himself was imprisoned for a short time. Together with his old teacher from university times, sociologist Ludwik Krzywicki, also his supervisor and even friend, Korczak gave a lecture at a public meeting of a women's organization explaining the link between poverty, political oppression, and authoritarian education. This critical intervention did not please the authorities, so it was not surprising that the two activists were denounced on the grounds that their payment for the lecture should have benefitted the Socialist party.[57] Although an anti-Leftist and anti-Semitic attitude became very present in public life, Korczak held on to his idea of Jewish/non-Jewish cooperation, united in a common fight against social inequality and political intolerance with the aim to establish a sovereign Polish democracy.[58]

Korczak critically observed the different world views separating Jewish community members from each other. By confronting the respectable citizens of Warsaw with the social needs of marginalized youth, he hoped to reduce prejudices and enhance social integration. Although a humanitarian credo was part of the self-concept of the Jewish elite, signs of bourgeois hypocrisy were always present. Korczak suggested approaching problems of disintegration not with social hygiene or medicalized therapy, but socially engaged practice.[59] By establishing

---

55 Janusz Korzcak, "Eindrücke aus Berlin," in *Sämtliche Werke, vol. 8., Sozialmedizinische Schriften*, ed. Michael Kirchner and Henryk Bereska ("Impressions from Berlin," in *Collected Works, vol. 8, Essays in Social Medicine*) (Gütersloh: Gütersloher Verlagshaus 1999), 29–31.

56 Korczak, *Themen seines Lebens*, 66. See also Stefan Wiese, *Pogrome im Zarenreich: Dynamiken kollektiver Gewalt* (*Pogroms under the Tsarist Regime: Dynamics of Collective Violence*), (Hamburg: Hamburger Edition, HIS Verlag, 2016).

57 Korczak, *Themen seines Lebens*, 72–74; Beiner, "Wie wurde Korczak zum 'Pionier der Menschenrechte des Kindes'," 33.

58 Korczak, *Themen seines Lebens*, 78–79.

59 A desideratum of research is Korczak's dealing with eugenics in the context of special education. Stanislaw Rogalski, "Das Schulexperiment Dr. Janusz Korczaks," in *Von der Grammatik, und andere pädagogische Texte*, ("The school experiment of Dr. Janusz Korczak," in *About Gram-*

networks of care and education, he acted as an important mentor of Jewish emancipation. His enormous competence to deal politically with the overall presence of social inequality was connected to his non-academic, existentialist approach to life. "The reason I became an educator was that I always felt best when I was among children," Korczak told a young interviewer many years later. "The road I have chosen towards my goal is neither the shortest nor the most convenient" he said, but he underlined that he felt completely convinced by his decision, "because it is my own." And he added: "I found it not without effort or pain and only when I had come to understand that all the books I read, and all the experiences and opinions of others, were misleading."[60]

Understanding Pedagogics: A Scientific Approach to Education

> "We start with a very necessary distinction. Education is what the educator does. Pedagogy is the research and teaching, the science of this action."[61]

When Swedish civil rights activist Ellen Key proclaimed the "century of the child" in 1900,[62] efforts to liberalize education were substantiated by new arguments. Similar to reforms in the political realm, educational concepts were now closely linked to ideas of social justice and democracy. In contrast to some reform pedagogues who adhered to ideas of heredity as explanatory models of social inequality, Janusz Korczak preferred to focus on learning and socialization.[63] He felt inspired by the liberal pragmatism of John Dewey[64] and the socialist ap-

---

mar and other Pedagogical Chapters), ed. Friedhelm Beiner and Elisabeth Lax-Höfer (Heinsberg/Rhld.: Agentur Dieck, 1991), 205.

60 Lifton, *King of Children*, chapter 8, accessed 30 July 2017, http://korczak.com/Biography/kap-8.htm.

61 Siegfried Bernfeld, "Sozialistische Erziehungskritik (1926)," in *Sozialistische Pädagogik und Schulkritik*, ("Socialist Critique of Education," in *Socialist Pedagogics and Critique of Schooling*), vol. 8, ed. Ulrich Herrmann (Gießen: Psychosozial Verlag, 2016), 11. (Translation mine, "Wir beginnen mit einer sehr nötigen Unterscheidung. Erziehung ist das tatsächliche Tun des Erziehers. Aber Pädagogik ist die *Lehre*, die Wissenschaft von diesem Tun.")

62 Ellen Key, *Century of the Child* (Cambridge: Cambridge Scholars Publishing, 2009).

63 Sjaak Braster, "The People, the Poor, the Oppressed: The Concept of Popular Education through Time," *Paedagogica Historica* 27 (2011): 1–14.

64 Jim (James) Garrison, Stefan Neubert and Kersten Reich, *John Dewey's Philosophy of Education: An Introduction and Recontextualization for Our Times* (New York: Palgrave Macmillan, 2012).

proach of Anton Semjonowitch Makarenko, especially by his experiments in group-education.[65] Korczak's later secretary, Igor Newerly (1903–1987), had been engaged in the Communist Youth after the Russian Revolution and later studied pedagogics in Warsaw.[66] Korczak was extremely critical of any authoritarian style of education and concerning the hegemony of grown-ups in general. Instead, he saw children as persons – or better, personalities – who had an intuitive perception of their environment with an unmistakable idea of truth and justice. To him, children even seemed to be more sophisticated than grown-ups; Korczak was impressed by their sensitivity in dealing with dependency and practicing cooperation. It seemed as if not foremost that they had to be educated, but that the educators had to learn to be critically reflective themselves.

In Korczak's opinion, professionals had to learn from their encounters with children, and at the same time, it was their obligation to guarantee stable educational settings seen as a precondition for human growth. Korczak did not believe in a just individual by nature. Instead, he thought that justice had to be learnt by democratic processes and dialogical encounters. Finding a non-violent way to deal with conflicting exigencies and expectations seemed to be extremely necessary in times of rapid social change. The declining importance of religious traditions, according to the argument of Korczak, could only be compensated by educational networks that assured a new secular credibility, especially for those who lived at the margins of society. Korczak also sympathized with an understanding of liberty and free will as binding individuals together on the basis of moral obligations and political rights.[67] The organization of social life in Korczak's orphanages and foster homes aimed at generating confidence through democratic procedures similar to forms of self-government practiced in the institutions for Jewish youth provided by ORT (*Obchestvo Remeslenogo Truda*, the Association for the Promotion of Skilled Trades, founded in St. Petersburg in 1880), Centos (Association of Societies for the Care of Jewish Orphans, founded 1924),

---

65 Anton Semjonowitch Makarenko, *Kinderrepubliken: Geschichte, Praxis und Theorie radikaler Selbstregierung in Kinder- und Jugendheimen* (*Children's Republics: History, Practice and Theory of Radical Self-Government in Hostels for Children and Youth*), ed. Johannes-Martin Kamp (Opladen: Leske+Budrich, 1995), see chapter 20: "Makarenko u. a. in Russland und der Ukraine," ("Makarenko i.a. in Russia and Ukraine,") 467–544.

66 Konrad Weiß, "Wie Igor Newerly Janusz Korczak kennenlernte," ("How Igor Newerly got Acquainted to Janusz Korczak,") *Die Weltbühne* 83, no. 11 (March 15 1988): 339–341.

67 Michael Kirchner, "Anarchistische Spuren bei Janusz Korczak," ("Anarchical Traces in the Work of Janusz Korczak,") *Korczak Bulletin* 9, no. 2 (2000): 32–40.

or TOZ (*Towarzystwo Ochrony Zdrowia*, Society for the Safeguarding of Health, established in 1921, sponsored by the American Joint Distribution Committee).[68]

The German pedagogue Emil Dauzenroth once called Korczak "the Pestalozzi from Warsaw."[69] However, the conceptualization of childhood and youth during the eighteenth century fundamentally changed in the nineteenth century. On one hand, the prospect of work had become the central motive of governing the proletariat during industrialization. On the other hand, during the last quarter of the nineteenth century, human sciences had become much more influential with the effect that children and youth were seen as interesting study objects of medical, criminological, and psychological research.[70] Jewish children coming from the poor quarters of Warsaw belonged to this target group. Many of them lived as abandoned children, some of them foundlings right after birth, others *mamzers* from forbidden relations.[71] Making a living in the streets, along with their fellow peers, many of them resorted to beggary in order to support their mothers, sisters, and brothers with some money. In orthodox religious contexts – Catholic or Jewish – unmarried mothers were disregarded and morally despised; modern welfare states like Prussia went on criminalizing illegitimate births.[72] Poor women with an offspring from an illegitimate relation had nearly no chance to provide adequate education for their children. The situation of single mothers and orphans aggravated during the First World War, when many Polish men did not return from their war mission.[73]

---

68 Dobroszycki/Kirshenblatt-Gimblett, *Image Before My Eye*, 173–174 and 184; Marcus, *Social and Political History of the Jews in Poland*, 143.

69 Erich Dauzenroth, *Janusz Korczak – Der Pestalozzi aus Warschau* (*Janusz Korczak – The Pestalozzi from Warsaw*) (Zürich: Schweizerische Lehrerzeitung, 1978).

70 Elisabeth Wiesbauer, *Das Kind als Objekt der Wissenschaft: Medizinische und psychologische Kinderforschung an der Wiener Universität 1800–1914* (*The Child as Object of Science: Medical and psychological Research on Children at the Vienna University 1800–1914*) (Wien: Löcker, 1981).

71 A *mamzer* is a person born from certain (forbidden) relationships or the descendant of such a person, in the Hebrew Bible and Jewish religious law. In modern Jewish culture it is someone who is either born out of adultery by a married Jewish woman and a Jewish man who is not her husband, or born out of incest, or someone who has a *mamzer* as a parent. *Mamzer* status is not synonymous with illegitimacy, since it does not include children whose mothers were unmarried.

72 Teresa Dworecka, "Illegitimate Births in Selected Poviats of Northern Mazowsze in the Period of the Second Republic of Poland," *Med. Nowouzytna* 14, no. 1–2 (2007): 137–166; Percy Gamble Kammerer, "The Unmarried Mother: A Study of Five Hundred Cases," *Criminal Science Monographs* 3 (1918): 1–337; Solomon Schechter and Julius H. Greenstone, "'Foundling", *Jewish Encyclopedia*, accessed March 30 2017, http://www.jewishencyclopedia.com/articles/6255-foundling.

73 Robert Blobaum, *A Minor Apocalypse: Warsaw during the First World War* (Ithaca, NY: Cornell University Press, 2017); Robert Blobaum, "A Warsaw Story: Polish-Jewish Relations during the

However, the growing demand for justice and rights challenged the practices of denigration and exclusion, especially concerning women, youth, and dependent minors. As Hannah Arendt has explained, this new democratic thinking was linked to the concept of citizenship that should guarantee respect and equal recognition despite of economic differences, social segregation, and political exclusion. On one hand, the "right to have rights"[74] meant the right to vote and to represent oneself in public contexts. This right could be understood as the founding act of political participation that no longer was reserved to property owners. On the other hand, a "democracy in the making"[75] promised to protect its citizens against harm and violence not only by other state power, but also by the state itself. Civic education became a very important tool to bind hopes to the new democracy. Not only the emancipation of the Jewish "minority" – a numeric majority in Warsaw as in many parts in Central Eastern Europe – was now on the political agenda. The status of children and youth as well as of other vulnerable groups – for example stateless people – could no longer be ignored in the political realm. The human rights discourse started to fill the gaps of injustice that had broadened through the course of industrialization and could no longer be ignored since the First World War.[76] Defining human rights as universal, imprescriptible, and impartible meant a commitment to those who lived on the margins of society. With this promise of inclusion in mind, Janusz Korczak devoted his first articles to the rights of children.[77]

Korczak wanted to modernize society by challenging authoritarianism through democratic education. The idea of children as right-bearers had first been discussed at the international child-welfare congress in Brussels in 1913 and became effective approximately ten years later by the Geneva Declaration of the Rights of the Child, approved by the League of Nations on September 26 1924. The five points of the declaration still reflected the disastrous situation during and immediately after the First World War, addressing mainly nourishment, shelter, protection, support, spiritual, and material development and

---

First World War," in *Warsaw – The Jewish Metropolis: Essays in Honor of the 75th Birthday of Professor Anthony Polonsky*, ed. Glenn Dynner and François Guesnet (Leiden and Boston: Brill, 2015), 271–296.

74 Hannah Arendt, *The Origins of Totalitarianism* (London: André Deutsch, 1986), 277.

75 Kathleen M. Blee, *Democracy in the Making: How Activist Groups Form* (Oxford: Oxford University Press, 2012).

76 Micheline Ishay, *The History of Human Rights: From Ancient Times to the Globalization Era* (Los Angeles, California: University California Press, 2004).

77 Friedhelm Beiner, "Wie wurde Korczak zum 'Pionier der Menschenrechte des Kindes'," 29–31.

the guarantee of a basic education for children.[78] It was underlined that children "must be the first to receive relief in times of distress" and that "the needs and demands of each individual child has to be satisfied corresponding to its life situation." And it was emphasized that "the child that is backward must be helped; the delinquent child must be reclaimed; and the orphan and the waif must be sheltered and succored."[79] Korczak's social engagement was inspired by the idea of Zedaka (in Hebrew צְדָקָה, translated as "charity") and a dialogical approach to education, also well-known from the Jewish tradition that said that truth does not exist, but can only be generated by the exchange of diverse opinions.[80] According to Korczak, scientific knowledge was essential, but needed a continuous "radical revision by living research."[81] He explained his educational diagnostics as based on detailed observations and empirical data collection. To recognize structural habits – or the typology – of children was one focal point, but his main interest was to find out about forms of cooperation in social interaction. Only after thorough research, he validated conclusions for the arrangement of adequate educational settings.[82] Korczak's scientific approach qualified him as an educational advisor for the school system of the Second Polish Republic. Later, when the German authorities asked him whether his work could be judged as scientific, he answered: "Tak, obserwacje dziecka." ("Yes, I observe children.")[83]

Korczak was undogmatic, agnostic, sceptic; he identified himself as non-religious although sometimes longed for an existentialist encounter with God through prayer.[84] He did not foster a dogmatic political orientation. Deeply influenced by a humanist tradition, Korczak's reflective educational approach aimed at establishing networks of self-help and support. In his opinion, political and cultural change could only be implemented by anticipatory practices; this urge for social justice was deeply linked to ideas of a radical democracy. Korczak's idea of pedagogical professionalism referred to a concept of a conscious subject

---

78 Friederike Kind-Kovács, "The 'Other' Child Transports: World War I and the Temporary Displacement of Needy Children from Central Europe/Les déplacements temporaires d'enfants déshérités en Europe centrale pendant la première guerre mondiale," *Revue d'histoire de l'enfance "irregulière"* 15 (2013): 75–109.

79 Eglantyne Jebb, "Declaration of the Right of the Child – 19," adopted by the League of Nations in 1924, accessed October 14 2017, www.crin.org/en/library/un-regional-documentation/declaration-rights-child-1923.

80 Korczak, *Themen seines Lebens*, 31.

81 Ibid., 28.

82 Ibid., 115.

83 Ibid., 117.

84 Ibid., 145.

that showed courage for political action in a sense, which Karl Marx had underlined in his early *Reflection on the Jewish Question:* "*All* emancipation is a *reduction* of the human world and relationships to *man* himself."[85]

Formative Practices and Concepts of Education

> "One deed, and sometimes one word, suffices to change every constellation."[86]

During his time as a medical practitioner, Korczak had seen the constraints of those people who could not afford adequate medical treatment. In his opinion, not heredity or infections, but urban segregation, educational exclusion, and economic poverty caused people's maladjustment and suffering. When Korczak decided to work in the field of education, he had a clear strategy in mind. Based on his observation of children in social settings, he sympathized with the idea of creating an experimental environment. In this "laboratory of education"[87] he wanted to arrange and influence the conditions of development in order to retrieve reliable and valid information, proving his educational approach on an empirical basis. His idea was that pedagogical interventions could effectively ban illness, depression, and disease and at the same time support the development of resilience necessary to resist against the structural reproduction of poverty. For Korczak, education seemed to be the best method to explore the possibilities of acquiring alternative knowledge and life skills. Pedagogical practices were seen as a systemic intervention into the everyday life of communities, thus providing a basis for the more far-reaching democratization of society as a whole.[88]

Korczak referred to *wychowywać*, the Polish word for education derived from the word *chowac* that means protection, welfare, and support. There is a significant difference in meaning in the Anglo-American context that defines "education" as "learning" and the German concept that defines "education" as "development."[89] The word *chowac* underlines the link between dignity and advocacy,

---

85 Karl Marx, "The Jewish Question," first published 1844 in *Deutsch-Französische Jahrbücher.* Accessed July 11 2017. https://www.marxists.org/archive/marx/works/1844/jewish-question/.
86 Arendt, *Human Condition*, 190.
87 Liba H. Engel, "Experiments in Democratic Education: Dewey's Lab School and Korczak's Children's Republic," *The Social Studies* 99, no. 3 (2008): 117–121.
88 See also Daniela G. Camhy, ed., *Dialogue – Culture – Philosophy: Philosophizing with Children in Transcultural Environments* (Sankt Augustin: Academia, 2009).
89 Korczak, *Themen seines Lebens*, 223.

referring to the idea of humanity, defined as a community of individuals with their lives interconnected and embedded in networks of support. Autonomy and dependency were not constructed as oppositions or even as mutually exclusive, but as interconnected qualities of life. Similarly, Korzcak analyzed children within the context of systemic settings. Practices of everyday life should keep the young people grounded and provide a framework with rules for a "just community."[90] Korczak believed being raised in this special mindset would empower young people to confront anti-Semitism and also to overcome a precarious social position.[91]

In his first writings on education, published in 1900 in the literary revue *Wedrowiecz*, Korczak had underlined that children needed love, respect, and confidence.[92] He criticized the bourgeois style of education using the German term *Affenliebe* (monkey love),[93] indicating an over-idealization and infantilization of children. Instead, Korczak portrayed the influence of social conditions on the well-being of children with a sensitive awareness for dependency, denigration, and assertiveness. Following a materialist approach, he underwent some self-studies demonstrating that the stomach was more important than the intellect or the heart.[94] In other words, children should not feel hunger and suffer agonies, otherwise they could not become social subjects. With his public lectures, radio contributions, journal articles. and books, Korczak assumed the role of a public counselor and intellectual mentor of pedagogical approaches to society, thus influencing the philosophy of life and the mindset of the Warsaw urban community. Jewish as well as non-Jewish citizens knew Korczak as a gifted man of words right from his youth. His early public acknowledgement as a writer gave Henryk Goldszmit the impulse to use his pseudonym Janusz Korczak as his professional name. During his medical studies, Korczak had stayed in close contact with Polish and Jewish intellectuals at the "Flying University" who believed in the power of the written and spoken word. Subjective writings from the per-

---

90 Fritz K. Oser, "Towards a Theory of the Just Community Approach: Effects of Collective Moral, Civic and Social Education," in *Handbook of Moral and Character Education*, ed. Larry Nucci, Darcia Narvaez, and Tobias Krettenauer, Second Edition, (New York/London: Routledge, 2014), 201.

91 Dietrich Beyrau, "Anti-Semitism and Jews in Poland, 1918–1939," in *Hostages of Modernization: Current Research on Antisemitism*, vol. 2–3, ed. Herbert A. Strauss (Berlin: de Gruyter, 1993), 1063–1090.

92 Korczak, *Themen seines Lebens*, 33–34.

93 Ibid., 35.

94 Ibid., 39–41.

spective of children had a long tradition in Poland.[95] Korczak created a rich literature, radio speeches, and feuilletons for children and young people that related directly to their living environment.[96] Stories and narratives had several educational benefits: they developed the reading and writing ability of children and young people, enlarged their intellectual horizon, and transported socializing messages in a very unpretentious but effective way.[97]

When Korczak was appointed director of the Dom Sierot in the Krochmalnastreet 92 in October 1912, he transferred his idea of democracy into his educational practice right from the beginning. The rules regulating the social life at the orphanage were based on participative agreements and announced in written form via notice boards or poster sites. This transparency should allow new children to become familiar with the rules of common life in order to feel "at home" at *Dom Sierot* or later at *Nasz Dom*. Mentors supported the newcomers, until they felt secure and accepted.[98] The house regulations demanded respect of privacy. Some playful competitions and gambling were organized in order to further inclusion. Contemporary witnesses also remember public writing activities organized for the children and youth of Dom Sierot. The most important medium was the handwritten weekly journal that served as the central communication tool to spread issues of concern for all; the journal also functioned as an archive/"memory" of the house history.[99] Thirteen years later, in 1926, the journal – now in a

---

95 Janusz Korczak, *Das Recht des Kindes auf Achtung* (*The Children's Right to Respect*), translated from Polish by Armin Dross (Göttingen: Vandenhoeck & Ruprecht, 1970), 233; Eugenia Prokop-Janiec, "Children's Literature: Polish Literature," *YIVO Encyclopedia of Jews in Eastern Europe*, 2011, accessed October 28 2017, http://www.yivoencyclopedia.org/article.aspx/Childrens_Literature/Polish_Literature. Korczak once stated that Maria Konopnicka and Bolesław Prus had been his instructors of writing literature and theater plays for children.

96 See the articles in Janusz Korczak, *Sämtliche Werke*, vol. 13, 97–310; George Z. F. Bereday, "Janusz Korczak. In Memory of the Hero of Polish Children's Literature," *The Polish Review* 24, no. 1. (1979), 27–32; Kahn, *Janusz Korczak und die jüdische Erziehung*, 42–44. For a critical discussion on racism see Manfred Liebel, "'Weiße' Kinder – 'schwarze' Kinder. Nachdenkliche Anmerkungen zu Janusz Korczaks Kinder-Roman vom kleinen König Macius," in *Janusz Korczak. Pionier der Kinderrechte. Ein internationales Symposium*, ed. Manfred Liebel ("'White' Children – 'Black' Children. Reflexive comment on Janusz Korczak's novel on the little King Macius," in *Pioneer of Children's Rights. An International Symposium*) (Münster: LIT Verlag, 2013), 105–136.

97 Ute Frevert et al., *Learning How to Feel: Children's Literature and the History of Emotional Socialization, 1870–1970* (Oxford: Oxford University Press, 2014). The anthology presents case studies of emotional education through children's literature, but without referring to Janusz Korczak.

98 Korczak, *Themen seines Lebens*, 132–134.

99 Ibid., 88.

professional version – became an addendum to the weekly journal for the Warsaw Jewish community, *Nasz Przegląd*.[100]

After the first half year of improvised living, the newly established building of Dom Sierot was finished in March 1913. In his inaugural address before the Jewish sponsors of the orphanage, Korzcak promised that the professional educators could offer a more qualified education than traditional families.[101] He worked together with Stefania Wilczynska (1886–1942), who had been voluntarily engaged in the assistance of Jewish orphans after her return to Warsaw from natural science studies at the University of Liège. The two pedagogues now were responsible for the well-being of eighty-five children between the ages of six and fifteen. Together with Maria Falska (1877–1942), Korczak founded a second home in Pruszków that was relocated to Bielfang ten years later. *Nasz Dom* accommodated around fifty children from workers' families and carried the specific mandate to train pedagogues in the methods of group education.[102]

Seen from the distance during his military service in World War I, Korczak evaluated his pedagogical experiences with the aim to elaborate a programmatic approach to education.[103] The first part of his tetralogy *Jak kochac dziecko* (How to Love a Child) was published at Christmas 1918 with the title *Dziecko w rodzinie* (The Child in the Family); the other three parts were published two years later. In the first book, Korczak proclaimed the central rights of children. The so-called *Magna Carta Libertatis* that outlined the right to death, the right to the present day, and the right to be what you are was a passionate plea for autonomy and the freedom of children. In Polish, there are two meanings of "liberty": *swoboda* means control over body and mind, *wolnosc* means the free will to act. In Korczak's opinion, the responsibility of the educator therefore was twofold: firstly, to guarantee the rights and the freedom of the child in their current situation, and secondly, to create a future society through the means of education. The child should not feel any pressure and did not have to be perfect, but like all human beings had to learn to accept mistakes, errors, faults, and its own imperfection. The German pedagogue Friedhelm Beiner has underlined the specific relevance of esteem and dignity in Korczak's educational concept; in a Kantian sense, these qualities had no equivalent and could not be transferred into other

100 Leon Harari, "Janusz Korczak und die 'Kleine Rundschau'," in *Von der Grammatik, und andere pädagogische Texte* ("Janusz Korczak and the 'Little Review'," in *About Grammar and Other Pedagogical Chapters*), ed. Friedhelm Beiner and Elisabeth Lax-Höfer (Heinsberg/Rhld.: Agentur Dieck, 1991), 184; Korczak, *Themen seines Lebens*, 170.

101 Ibid., 86–88.

102 Ibid., 120.

103 Ibid., 109–114.

(economic) values.[104] Both characteristics were seen as deeply linked to the inviolability of body and mind. This meant dignity and esteem could not get lost by unworthy or dishonorable behavior nor be taken away from a person.[105]

Besides dialogical recognition, Korczak also encouraged free speech in a public *agora,* which he believed was central for a democratic education.[106] Pedagogical arrangements were seen as learning facilities, where children could show their readiness to assume responsibility and act in cooperation. It took Korczak approximately eight years, from 1912 to 1919/20, to conceptualize and implement three different institutions of a self-governed social justice.[107] The first institution was the fellowship court, established right from the beginning at Dom Sierot. Its first mandate was to elaborate a code of ethics and justice that could be applied to the cases treated before the court. However, most of the cases were simple and accusations could easily be redrawn.[108] The court functioned more or less like an arbitration panel or a mediation board that did not decide about punishment but suggested forms of conflict regulation.[109] In order to guarantee cooperation on an eye-to-eye level, educators could also be accused or forward a self-accusation.[110] The second institution was the council that should supervise the "alphabet of rights"[111] and decide on issues of more fundamental concern for the house community. Obligations and liabilities that functioned like a normative constitution were elaborated and decided upon by a council of five children and one educator. Those children, who wanted to do the job and had been accepted by the

104 Beiner, "Korczak," 12–13, fn. 12. Unlike Kant, who thought that one becomes human through education, Korczak underlined that a child is already human without education.

105 Christine Baumbach and Peter Kunzmann, eds., *Würde – Dignité – Godność – Dignity: Die Menschenwürde im internationalen Vergleich* (=*Ta ethika* 11) (*Human Dignity in International Perspective*) (München: Herbert Utz Verlag, 2010).

106 Hermann Giesecke, "Janusz Korczak: Das Kind als unterdrückter Mensch," in *Die pädagogische Beziehung: Pädagogische Professionalität und die Emanzipation des Kindes* ("Janusz Korczak: The Child as Oppressed Human Being" in *The Educational Relation: Pedagogical Professionalism and Emancipation of the Child*), ed. Hermann Giesecke, Second Edition (Weinheim und München: Juventa Verlag, 1999), 161–169.

107 Korczak, *Themen seines Lebens*, 30–32; Tadeusz Lewowicki, "Janusz Korczak (1878–1942)," *Prospects: The Quarterly Review of Comparative Education*, XXIV, no. 1/2 (1994): 41; Wincenty Okoń, "Janusz Korczak – ein heroischer Pädagoge," in *Lebensbilder polnischer Pädagogen* ("Janusz Korczak – Heroic Pedagogue," in *Curriculum Vitae of Polish Pedagogues*), ed. Oskar Anweiler, transl. Janusz Daum (Köln/Weimar/Wien: Böhlau Verlag, 1998), 175–178.

108 Ibid., 178. Statistics collected over one week showed that from fifty-seven accusations thirty-four were either withdrawn or mediated without a court hearing.

109 Korczak, *Themen seines Lebens*, 136.

110 Ibid., 139.

111 Okoń, "Janusz Korczak," 177.

majority of the house inmates in secret ballots, were elected to the council. The council also had a kind of executive function in dealing with problematic cases whose impact was too far-reaching in order to be decided by the court.[112] The third institution was the children's parliament, the *Sejm*, founded as the highest legislative authority, that confirmed or abrogated laws, passed resolutions, and was responsible for general decisions concerning the house community.[113] The democratic procedures also embraced the possibility of a plebiscite and the assignment of rights, for example to allow individual children to possess memory cards.[114] These memory cards were part of a reward system that signified recognition for good behavior. Many aspects and elements of Korczak's pedagogical work remind us of methods we know today from social-cognitive learning, systemic counseling, or trauma therapy.[115]

The three institutions mentioned before should assure social justice and guarantee a basic climate of respect and tolerance, cooperation, and solidarity. By these institutions, social justice, public transparency, and participative control were anchored in the center of educational practices. To experience democratic principles in a very early period of life seemed to be the best guarantee to develop a democratic personality. For Korczak, the educator was responsible for the education of children, but his main task was to implement arrangements that teach children the basic principles of a just society.[116]

---

112 Ibid., 180 – 182.

113 Korczak, *Themen seines Lebens*, 133.

114 Okoń, "Janusz Korczak," 181.

115 Christine Rothdeutsch-Granzer, Wilma Weiß, "Reformerische und emanzipatorische Pädagogik: Inspirationen für die traumapädagogische Praxis und Theoriebildung," in *Handbuch Traumapädagogik* ("Reform and Emancipation in Pedagogics: Inspirations from Trauma Therapy for Pedagogical Practice and Theory," in *Handbook of Trauma Pedagogics*), ed. Wilma Weiß, Tanja Kessler, and Silke Birgitta Gahleitner (Weinheim: Beltz Verlag, 2016), 43.

116 Korczak, *Themen seines Lebens*, 140 – 141.

"Men in Dark Times": Jewish Radicalism as Political Action

"Goodness can only exist when it is not perceived not even by its author ..."[117]

"Context is everything."[118]

For Korczak, education was a necessary consequence of his analyses of social inequality, while at the same time seen as a tool of democratic transformation. Although he legitimated his educational competence in a scientific way, his life work has mostly entered historical memory by a narrative of personal courage and integrity. Indeed, his last act of braving the German Nazis and getting deported together with the Jewish children carries an enormous symbolism. For Korczak himself, his refusal to cooperate with the Nazis was the logical consequence of his lifetime commitment. He certainly felt obliged to the children whose education and well-being had been in the center of his interest. As a pedagogue, he had acted like an advocate defending the rights and dignity of children, based on an emancipatory attitude that wanted to overcome the striking social inequality. With a radical consequence, Korczak transferred his ethical orientation into a solid educational practice. As a student of medicine and as a young doctor, he had started to support the political emancipation of the Jewish minority. In 1912, when he decided to become an educator at the age of thirty-three, he transformed his political conviction into pedagogical professionalism.

Korczak was a multitalent. He provided medical care to children, lectured at the university, wrote for radio stations and journals, worked as a hairdresser of children, engaged himself as a social politician, and spoke as an expert in court trials against young offenders. He combined clinical expertise with the knowledge of social science and practical analyses. Korczak felt inspired by theories of democracy, psychological knowledge, and philosophical reflections which deepened his insight into the necessity of constructivism, subjectivity, and inclusion.[119] Korczak did not believe that interests were the most intriguing

117 Arendt, *Human condition*, 74.

118 Yohanan Petrovsky-Shtern, "Context is Everything: Reflections on Studying with Antony Polonsky," in *Warsaw – The Jewish Metropolis: Essays in Honor of the 75th Birthday of Professor Antony Polonsky*, ed. Glenn Dynner and François Guesnet (Leiden and Boston: Brill, 2015), 613–616.

119 Kirchner, "Das Lebenswerk von Janusz Korczak," 18.

social motive but focused on the "moral grammar of social conflicts."[120] His educational practice based on dialogical elements of the Haskala[121] as well as on socialist experiences in group-education. By creating democratic realities for those on the margins of society, he turned history against the course of political events, which during this time period were unfolding rapidly, seemingly directed by an "invisible actor behind the scenes."[122]

Being honored with the Lessing-Prize in Hamburg in September 1959, German-Jewish Philosopher Hannah Arendt elaborated the concept of "men in dark times" that can serve as an analytical frame in order to get a closer insight into the cultural and historical meaning of Korczak's work.[123] With "dark times" – a metaphor borrowed from a poem by Bertold Brecht – Arendt did not refer especially to the "monstrosities of this century," but wanted to give a lecture on relatively "normal" political periods.[124] Arendt did not present Janusz Korczak in her collection of honorable men and women whose action left some kind of "illumination" to posterity. However, without doubt, if she had known him and his work in the late 1950s, she would have integrated his biography into this collection. With these biographical portraits, Hannah Arendt reminds us of the human obligation to make the world humane. Without denying psychic complexity, she suggests judging people foremost on the basis of their actions. Her concept of society is based on political dialogue, existentialist encounters, and dialectic thinking. "In acting and speaking, men ... make their appearance in the human world"[125], Arendt underlines, "where people are with other people, in sheer togetherness."[126]

Arendt differentiates between three dimensions of the "vita activa": labor (necessity), work (utility), and action (mostly referring to a language-based social engagement).[127] Action – in difference to labor and work – opens our perception for the political realm: action "always establishes relationships and therefore has

---

120 Axel Honneth, *The Struggle for Recognition: The Moral Grammar of Social Conflicts* (Cambridge: Polity Press, 1995/1992); Axel Honneth and Nancy Fraser, *Redistribution or Recognition? A Political-Philosophical Exchange* (London and Brooklyn: Verso, 2003).

121 Jan Woleńsk, "Jews in Polish Philosophy," *Shofar: An Interdisziplinary Journal of Jewish Studies* 29, no. 3 (2011). Accessed June 29 2017. https://muse.jhu.edu/article/478211.

122 Arendt, *Human Condition*, 199.

123 Hannah Arendt, "On Humanity in Dark Times".

124 Arendt, preface to *Men in Dark Times*, ix.

125 Arendt, *Human Condition*, 179.

126 Ibid., 180.

127 Ibid., 79–81; Christian Trottmann "Vita activa/vita contemplative," in *Historisches Wörterbuch der Philosophie* (*Historical Encyclopedia of Philosophy*), vol. 11 (Basel: Schwabe Verlag, 2001), Sp. 1071–1075.

an inherent tendency to transcend limitation and cut across boundaries."[128] Action is not output-directed, but boundless and unpredictable[129]; "its full meaning ... reveals itself fully only to the storyteller, that is to the backward glance of the historian."[130] That "action" can pass by rather unperceived and unacknowledged by contemporaries makes it so extraordinary. Unlike human behavior "judged according to 'moral standards' – taking into account motives and intentions on one hand and aims and consequences on the other – action can only be judged by the criterion of greatness".[131] This means that action foremost has to be understood as a political expression with the power to humanize society. Hanna Arendt states that "the popular belief in a 'strong man' who isolated against others owes his strength to his being alone is sheer superstition." She further states: "Action ... is never possible in isolation; to be isolated is to be deprived of the capacity to act."[132]

From this perspective, it is convincing to state that Janusz Korczak acted as part of the Jewish social movements in Eastern Europe at the beginning of the twentieth century. With his democratic aspiration, he gained enormous charisma and strength. He implemented democracy through radical interventions into society's everyday life. In giving voice to the experiences of a minority, authoritarian traditions were put into question. Emancipation as a code of social and cultural change was stimulated. Practical associations, public debates, the written and the spoken word, educational and social projects facilitated experiences of solidarity, thus improving the quality of life for all members of the Jewish community. Improving the cohesion of society was fundamentally important at a time when doubt had replaced religious ideas.[133] Skepticism and an inner restlessness led to the production of new knowledge. The old habits continued, but the "loss of certainty"[134] stimulated a "radical change in moral standards."[135] As Hannah Arendt underlines, "the Cartesian solution of this perplexity was to move the Archimedian point of knowledge into man himself."[136] A growing need in personal resources (not *cogito ergo sum*, but *dubito ergo sum* – not '*I think, therefore I am*', but '*I doubt, therefore I am*') became necessary. This decentering

128 Arendt, *Human Condition*, 190.
129 Ibid., 191.
130 Ibid., 192.
131 Ibid., 205.
132 Ibid., 188.
133 Ibid., 273–275.
134 Ibid., 277.
135 Ibid., 278.
136 Ibid., 284.

of perspective allowed new insights, evaluating the subjective experiences of former excluded members of the Jewish society as reference points of a new ethics.[137]

Janusz Korczak's self-reflexivity had a high intellectual quality based on a "commitment" to the world.[138] What Arendt said about Lessing – that "his attitude toward the world was ... radically critically" – can also be said about Korczak. However, it has to be doubted that Korczak, in respect to the public realm of that time, was "completely revolutionary."[139] A more convincing interpretation seems to be that his "partiality" and his "pedantic carefulness"[140] empowered him to such an extent that he really "enjoyed to challenge prejudices."[141] As for Lessing, Korczak also believed that the "essence of poetry was action."[142] Both pleaded against the dogma of the rational argument because it endangered the freedom of thought. The link of "self-thinking to action"[143] had to be improved, and therefore Korczak never intended "to communicate definite conclusions but wanted to stimulate also in others independent thought."[144] The solidarity with those at the margins of society allowed Korczak to get into contact to a world that he always had perceived as estrangement. In the Jewish community he found what Arendt calls the "warmth of human relations", a "kind of humanity" which "is the great privilege of pariah people."[145]

To fully understand "the political relevance of friendship"[146] as the uniting force of the citizens of a polis, it should be acknowledged as a "gift ... with openness to the world, and finally, with genuine love of mankind."[147] Janusz Korczak, whose engagement resulted from an inner devotion towards humanity, enjoyed a high credibility. Similar to other members of the Jewish intelligentsia during that time, he did not live as a "rootless cosmopolitan," but engaged himself as an active citizen. But instead of striving for status positions, he rather avoided them.[148] Korczak was more interested in the kind of power that "arises only where people

137 Ibid., 280 (Descartes spoke of the "certainty of the I am").
138 Arendt, "On Humanity in Dark Times," 3.
139 Ibid., 5.
140 Ibid.
141 Ibid., 6.
142 Ibid.
143 Ibid., 10.
144 Ibid.
145 Ibid., 13.
146 Ibid., 24.
147 Ibid., 26.
148 Brym, *Jewish Intelligentsia and Russian Marxism*, 111–113.

act together, but not where people grow stronger as individuals."[149] As Gérard Kahn, vice-president of the Suisse Korczak Society, has underlined, Korczak's political action was part of a Jewish secular culture directed towards emancipation, justice, and solidarity. The lifetime achievement of the Jewish pediatrist Henryk Goldsmith (Janusz Korczak) survived the Nazi Holocaust, documenting fundamental humanism and social responsibility as central qualities of an educational professionalism that also today might navigate societies into a democratic future.[150]

Conclusion

The social engagement and educational practices presented in this chapter refer to a time period when Janusz Korczak found himself in the most productive phase of his life. His social consciousness had been formed by childhood and adolescent encounters with social inequality. As a student, Korczak had been engaged in the Jewish social movements, taking care of and supervising children from poor families. Between the age of twenty and forty-five, the pediatrician gained practical experience in social justice education, thus anchoring the discourse on inclusion in the midst of Jewish community life in Warsaw. Above all, Korzak wanted to ensure that Jewish minorities could voice their experiences, thus transgressing the limits of social engagement into the political realm. The pedagogue strongly sympathized with secular and socialist ideas of a community organization. His educational institutions aimed at empowering marginalized youth to become future political leaders, making inclusion imaginable in a highly segregated urban society. Although the urge for democratization was so obvious, the Jewish struggle for recognition remained difficult after the foundation of the Polish state. Facing growing anti-Semitism all over Europe in the 1930s, Jewish youth started to organize emigration to Palestine on one hand, while on the other practicing self-defense against the violent discrimination in their European home countries. Many activists had personally profited from Korczak's democratic learning arrangement, in education or in pedagogical training. Their competence to act as democratic subjects made the subsequent resistance against Nazi violence possible, finally leading to the revolt in the Ghetto of Warsaw in April and May 1943.

149 Arendt, "On Humanity in Dark Times," 23.
150 Kahn, *Janusz Korczak und die jüdische Erziehung*, 140.

Seen in this context, it sounds convincing to state that Janusz Korczak acted as part of the Jewish social movements in Eastern Europe at the beginning of the twentieth century. Korczak's democratic aspiration and political participation allowed him a degree of credibility and radicalness that he himself was rarely aware of. Although he was a public person, well-known for his intellectual inspirations, he always acted very decently and took a back seat at public events. Korzak's charismatic personality was elucidated by a high degree of authenticity. He renounced the option to become a member of the bourgeois Warsaw middle class, and preferred instead to follow his inner convictions with radical consistency.

Korczak's pursuit of personal autonomy revealed a definition of Jewish radicalism that can well be understood with the help of Hannah Arendt's ideas on "Men in Dark Times". Arendt reflects her characters within a contextualized historical analysis, thus emphasizing the fact that the personal is always political. Korczak, together with his friends and colleagues, embodied the social consciousness of an unjust society, by implementing democracy through radical interventions into society's everyday life. By giving voice to the experiences of marginalized Jewish youth, personal emancipation was stimulated as well as social and cultural change. Janusz Korczak's pedagogics of respect and esteem could hardly guarantee the survival of the Jewish people under Fascist violence. However, the radical educational practices and the firm belief in a socially just democracy have been passed on to us today and to future generations as a heritage of Eastern European Jewish life prior to the Holocaust.

Works Cited

Aleksiun, Natalia, Brian Horowitz, and Antony Polonsky, eds. *Writing Jewish History in Eastern Europe, Polin 29*. Liverpool: The Littman Library of Jewish Civilizations, 2017.

Arendt, Hannah. "Civil Disobedience." In *Crisis of the Republic*, edited by Hannah Arendt, 49–102. New York: Harcourt Brace Jovanovich, 1969.

Arendt, Hannah. "On Humanity in Dark Times: Thoughts about Lessing." In *Men in Dark Times*, edited by Hannah Arendt, 3–31. New York: Harcourt, Brace and World, 1968.

Arendt, Hannah. "Rosa Luxemburg (1971–1919)." In *Men in Dark Times*, edited by Hannah Arendt, 33–56. New York: Harcourt, Brace & World, 1968.

Arendt, Hannah. Preface to *Men in Dark Times*, by Hannah Arendt, 1–3. New York: Harcourt, Brace and World, 1968.

Arendt, Hannah. *The Human Condition*. Chicago/London: University of Chicago Press, 1998.

Arendt, Hannah. *The Origins of Totalitarianism*. London: André Deutsch, 1986.

Barucka, Edyta. "Redefining Polishness: The Revival of Crafts in Galicia around 1900." *Acta Slavica Iaponica* 28 (2016): 71–99.

Baumbach, Christine, and Peter Kunzmann, eds. *Würde – Dignité – Godność – Dignity: Die Menschenwürde im internationalen Vergleich* (=*Ta ethika* 11) (*Human Dignity in International Perspective*). München: Herbert Utz Verlag, 2010.

Beiner, Friedhelm. "Wie wurde Korczak zum 'Pionier der Menschenrechte des Kindes' – und welchen Beitrag leisteten Stefania Wilczynska und Maria Falska dazu?." In *Janusz Korczak. Pionier der Kinderrechte. Ein internationales Symposium*, edited by Manfred Liebel ("How Korczak became the 'Pioneer of Children's Rights' – and the Contribution of Stefania Wilczynska and Maria Falska." In *Pioneer of Children's Rights. An international Symposium*), 29–52. Münster: LIT Verlag 2013.

Beiner, Friedhelm. Preface to *Janusz Korczak, Themen seines Lebens: Eine Werkbiographie* (*Janusz Korczak. Themes of his Life: A Biography based on his Oeuvre*), 12–13. Gütersloh: Gütersloher Verlagshaus, 2011.

Bereday, George Z. F. "Janusz Korczak. In Memory of the Hero of Polish Children's Literature." *The Polish Review* 24, no. 1 (1979): 27–32.

Bernfeld, Siegfried. "Sozialistische Erziehungskritik (1926)." In *Sozialistische Pädagogik und Schulkritik* ("Socialist Critique of Education.") In *Socialist Pedagogics and Critique of Schooling*), vol. 8, edited by Ulrich Herrmann, 11–16. Gießen: Psychosozial Verlag, 2016.

Beyrau, Dietrich. "Anti-Semitism and Jews in Poland, 1918–1939." In *Hostages of Modernization: Current Research on Antisemitism*, vol. 2–3, edited by Herbert A. Strauss, 1063–1090. Berlin: de Gruyter, 1993.

Blee, Kathleen M. *Democracy in the Making: How Activist Groups Form*. Oxford: Oxford University Press, 2012.

Blit, Lucjan. *The Origins of Polish Socialism: The History and Ideas of the First Polish Socialist Party, 1878–1886*. London/New York: Cambridge University Press, 1971.

Blobaum, Robert E. "The 'Woman Question' in Russian Poland, 1900–1914." *Journal of Social History*, 35/4 (2002): 799–824.

Blobaum, Robert. "A Warsaw Story: Polish-Jewish Relations during the First World War." In *Warsaw – The Jewish Metropolis: Essays in Honor of the 75th Birthday of Professor Anthony Polonsky*, edited by Glenn Dynner and François Guesnet, 271–296. Leiden and Boston: Brill, 2015.

Blobaum, Robert. *A Minor Apocalypse: Warsaw during the First World War*. Ithaca, NY: Cornell University Press, 2017.

Braster, Sjaak. "The People, the Poor, the Oppressed: The Concept of Popular Education through Time." *Paedagogica Historica* 27 (2011): 1–14.

Brym, Robert J. *The Jewish Intelligentsia and Russian Marxism. A Sociological Study of Intellectual Radicalism and Ideological Divergence*. London and Basingstoke: The Macmillan Press, 1978.

Camhy, Daniela G., ed. *Dialogue – Culture – Philosophy: Philosophizing with Children in Transcultural Environments*. Sankt Augustin: Academia, 2009.

Cieplinski, Feigue. "Poles and Jews: The Quest for Self-Determination 1919–1934." Binghamton Journal of History, vol. 3 (Fall 2002). Accessed March 27 2017, https://www.binghamton.edu/history/resources/journal-of-history/poles-and-jews.html.

Dauzenroth, Erich. *Janusz Korczak – Der Pestalozzi aus Warschau* (*Janusz Korczak – The Pestalozzi from Warsaw*). Zürich: Schweizerische Lehrerzeitung, 1978.

Davies, Norman. *Heart of Europe: The Past in Poland's Present.* New Edition. Oxford: Oxford University Press, 2001.

Denérchére, Yves, and David Nigel. *Droits des Enfants au XXe Siècle. Pour une Histoire Transnationale* (*Children's Rights in the 20th Century. A Transnational History*). Rennes: Presses Universitaires de Rennes, 2015.

Deutscher, Isaac. *The Tragedy of Polish Communism Between the Wars.* London: Socialist Labour League, n.d.

Dobroszycki, Lucjan, and Barbara Kirshenblatt-Gimblett. *Image Before my Eyes: A Photographic History of Jewish Life in Poland, 1864–1939.* New York: Schocken Books, 1977.

Dubnow, Semjon Markowitch. *Jewish History: An Essay on the Philosophy of History.* Philadelphia: The Jewish Publication Society, 1903.

Dworecka, Teresa. "Illegitimate Births in Selected Poviats of Northern Mazowsze in the Period of the Second Republic of Poland." *Med. Nowouzytna* 14, no. 1–2 (2007): 137–166.

Dynner, Glenn, and François Guesnet, eds. *Warsaw, the Jewish Metropolis: Essays in Honor of the 75th Birthday of Professor Antony Polonsky.* Amsterdam: Brill, 2015.

Engel, Liba H. "Experiments in Democratic Education: Dewey's Lab School and Korczak's Children's Republic." *The Social Studies* 99, no. 3 (2008): 117–121.

Frevert, Ute, and Pascal Eitler, Stephanie Olsen, Uffa Jensen, Margrit Pernau, Daniel Brückenhaus, Magdalena Beljan, Benno Gammerl, Anja Laukötter, Bettina Hitzer, Jan Plamper, Juliane Brauer, and Joachim C. Häberlen. *Learning How to Feel: Children's Literature and the History of Emotional Socialization, 1870–1970.* Oxford: Oxford University Press, 2014.

Garrison, Jim (James), Stefan Neubert, and Kersten Reich. *John Dewey's Philosophy of Education: An Introduction and Recontextualization for Our Times.* New York: Palgrave Macmillan, 2012.

Giesecke, Hermann. "Janusz Korczak: Das Kind als unterdrückter Mensch." In *Die pädagogische Beziehung: Pädagogische Professionalität und die Emanzipation des Kindes* ("Janusz Korczak: The Child as Oppressed Human Being." In *The Educational Relation: Pedagogical Professionalism and Emancipation of the Child*), edited by Hermann Giesecke, Second Edition, 143–171. Weinheim, München: Juventa Verlag, 1999.

Gilad, Moshe. "Righteous among the Nations – and Much More." *Haaretz*, July 30 2012. Accessed March 3 2017, http://www.haaretz.com/israel-news/culture/leisure/righteous-among-the-nations-and-much-more-1.454502.

Gitelman, Zvi Y. *The Emergence of Modern Jewish Politics: Bundism and Zionism in Eastern Europe.* Pittsburgh: University of Pittsburgh Press, 2002.

Harari, Leon. "Janusz Korczak und die 'Kleine Rundschau'." In *Von der Grammatik, und andere pädagogische Texte*, ("Janusz Korczak and the 'Little Review'." In *About Grammar and other Pedagogical Chapters*), edited by Friedhelm Beiner and Elisabeth Lax-Höfer, 181–186. Heinsberg/Rhld.: Agentur Dieck, 1991.

Hawes, Joseph M. *The Children's Rights Movement: A History of Advocacy and Protection.* Boston: Twayne Publishers, 1991.

History of Warsaw. Jewish Virtual Library, a project by AICE. Accessed March 30 2017. https://www.jewishvirtuallibrary.org/warsaw-poland-2.

Honneth, Axel, and Nancy Fraser. *Redistribution or Recognition? A Political-Philosophical Exchange.* London and Brooklyn: Verso, 2003.

Honneth, Axel. *The Struggle for Recognition: The Moral Grammar of Social Conflicts.* Cambridge: Polity Press, 1995.

Horlacher, Rebekka. "Schooling as Means of Popular Education: Pestalozzi's Method as a Popular Education Experiment." In *A History of Popular Education: Educating the People of the World*, edited by Sjaak Braster, Frank Simon, and Ian Grosnevor, 65–76. London/New York: Routledge, 2012.

Hurrelmann, Klaus. "Adolescents as Productive Processors of Reality." In *The Developmental Science of Adolescence*, edited by Richard M. Lerner, Arthur C. Petersen, Rainer K. Silbereisen, and Jeanne Brooks-Gunn, 230–238. New York: Psychology Press, 2014.

Ishay, Micheline. *The History of Human Rights: From Ancient Times to the Globalization Era.* Los Angeles/Cal.: University of California Press, 2004.

Jebb, Eglantyne. "Declaration of the Right of the Child – 1923." Adopted by the League of Nations in 1924. Accessed October 14 2017, www.crin.org/en/library/un-regional-documentation/declaration-rights-child-1923.

Kahn, Gérard. *Janusz Korczak und die jüdische Erziehung: Janusz Korczaks Pädagogik auf dem Hintergrund seiner jüdischen Herkunft* (*Janusz Korczak and the Jewish Education: Janusz Korczak's Pedagogy in the Context of his Jewish Origin*). Weinheim: Deutscher Studienverlag, 1993.

Kammerer, Percy Gamble. "The Unmarried Mother: A Study of Five Hundred Cases." *Criminal Science Monographs* 3 (1918): 1–337.

Kassow, Samuel D. *Who Will Write Our History? Rediscovering a Hidden Archive from the Warsaw Ghetto.* Reprint Edition. New York: Vintage Books, 2009.

Key, Ellen. *Century of the Child.* Cambridge: Cambridge Scholars Publishing, 2009.

Kind-Kovács, Friederike. "The 'Other' Child Transports: World War I and the Temporary Displacement of Needy Children from Central Europe/Les déplacements temporaires d'enfants déshérités en Europe centrale pendant la première guerre mondiale." *Revue d'histoire de l'enfance "irregulière* 15 (2013): 75–109.

Kirchner, Michael. "Anarchistische Spuren bei Janusz Korczak." ("Anarchical Traces in the Work of Janusz Korczak.") *Korczak Bulletin* 9, no. 2 (2000): 32–40.

Kirchner, Michael. "Das Lebenswerk von Janusz Korczak." In *Pionier der Kinderrechte. Ein internationales Symposium*, edited by Manfred Liebel ("The Lifework of Janusz Korczak." In *Pioneer of Children's Rights. An international Symposium*), 13–28. Berlin, Münster, Wien, Zürich, London: LIT Verlag, 2013.

Korczak, Janusz. *Ghetto Diary.* New Haven and London: Yale University Press, 2003.

Korczak, Janusz. "Brief an L. Zylbertal, 30.3.1937." In *Sämtliche Werke, vol. 15, Briefe und Palästina Reisen,* ("Letter to L. Zylbertal, 30.3.1937." In *Collected Works, vol. 15, Letters and Travels to Palestine*), edited by Friedhelm Beiner and Silvia Ungermann, 54. Gütersloh: Gütersloher Verlagsanstalt, 2005.

Korczak, Janusz. *Das Recht des Kindes auf Achtung* (*The Children's Right to Respect*). Translated from Polish by Armin Dross. Göttingen: Vandenhoeck & Ruprecht, 1970.

Korczak, Janusz. *Sämtliche Werke, vol. I–XVI,* (*Collected Works*), edited by Erich Dauzenroth, Friedhelm Beiner et al. Gütersloh: Gütersloher Verlagshaus, 1996–2010.

Korzcak, Janusz. "Eindrücke aus Berlin." In *Sämtliche Werke, vol. 8, Sozialmedizinische Schriften* ("Impressions from Berlin." In *Collected Works, vol. 8, Essays in Social Medicine*), edited by Michael Kirchner and Henryk Bereska, 29–31. Gütersloh: Gütersloher Verlagshaus 1999.

Lewowicki, Tadeusz. "Janusz Korczak (1878–1942)." *Prospects: The Quarterly Review of Comparative Education* XXIV, no.1/2 (1994): 37–48.

Liebel, Manfred. "'Weiße' Kinder – 'schwarze' Kinder. Nachdenkliche Anmerkungen zu Janusz Korczaks Kinder-Roman vom kleinen König Macius." In *Janusz Korczak. Pionier der Kinderrechte. Ein internationales Symposium*, edited by Manfred Liebel ("'White' Children – 'Black' Children. Reflexive comment on Janusz Korczak's novel on the little King Macius," in *Pioneer of Children's Rights. An international Symposium*), 105–136. Münster: LIT Verlag 2013.

Liegle, Ludwig, and Franz Michael Konrad, eds. *Reformpädagogik in Palästina: Dokumente und Deutungen zu den Versuchen einer 'neuen' Erziehung im jüdischen Gemeinwesen Palästinas, 1914–1948* (*Reform Education in Palestine: Documents and Interpretations of Experiments with a 'new' Education in Jewish Community Life in Palestine, 1914–1948*). Frankfurt a. M.: dipa-Verlag, 1989.

Lifton, Betty Jean. "Who was Janusz Korczak." In *Ghetto Diary*, edited by Janusz Korczak, XXIII-XIV. New Haven and London: Yale University Press, 2003.

Lifton, Betty Jean. *The King of Children: The Life and Death of Janusz Korczak*. New York: St. Martin's Griffin, 1988. Online Edition provided by the Janusz Korczak Communication Center. Accessed August 18 2017, http://korczak.com/Biography.

Lindemann, Albert A. *A History of European Socialism*. New Haven, CT: Yale University Press, 1983.

Makarenko, Anton Semjonowitch. *Kinderrepubliken: Geschichte, Praxis und Theorie radikaler Selbstregierung in Kinder- und Jugendheimen* (Children's Republics: History, Practice and Theory of Radical Self-Government in Hostels for Children and Youth), edited by Johannes-Martin Kamp. Opladen: Leske+Budrich, 1995.

Mally, Lynn. *Culture of the Future. The Proletkult Movement in Revolutionary Russia*. Berkeley, Los Angeles, Oxford: University of California Press, 1990.

Marcus, Joseph. *Social and Political History of the Jews in Poland, 1919–1939*. Berlin/New York/Amsterdam: Mouton Publishers, 1983.

Marx, Karl. "The Jewish Question." First published 1844 in *Deutsch-Französische Jahrbücher*. Accessed July 11 2017, https://www.marxists.org/archive/marx/works/1844/jewish-question/.

Mosse, Max, and Gustav Tugendreich. *Krankheit und Soziale Lage* (*Disease and Social Situation*), edited by Jürgen Cromm, Third Edition. Göttingen/Augsburg: Jürgen Cromm Verlag, 1994.

Musial, Bogdan. "The Origins of 'Operation Reinhard': The Decision-Making Process for the Mass Murder of the Jews in the General Government." *Yad Vashem Studies* 28 (2000): 113–153.

Newman, Michael. *Socialism: A Very Short Introduction*. Oxford: Oxford University Press, 2005.

Okoń, Wincenty. "Janusz Korczak – ein heroischer Pädagoge." In *Lebensbilder polnischer Pädagogen* ("Janusz Korczak – Heroic Pedagogue." In *Curriculum Vitae of Polish Pedagogues*), edited by Oskar Anweiler. Translated by Janusz Daum, 153–185. Köln/Weimar/Wien: Böhlau Verlag, 1998.

Oser, Fritz K. "Towards a Theory of the Just Community Approach: Effects of Collective Moral, Civic and Social Education." In *Handbook of Moral and Character Education*, edited by

Larry Nucci, Darcia Narvaez, and Tobias Krettenauer, 198–221. New York/London: Routledge, 2014.

Petrovsky-Shtern, Yohanan. "Context is Everything: Reflections on Studying with Antony Polonsky." In *Warsaw – The Jewish Metropolis: Essays in Honor of the 75th Birthday of Professor Antony Polonsky*, edited by Glenn Dynner and François Guesnet, 613–616. Leiden and Boston: Brill, 2015.

Polonsky, Anthony, ed. *The Jews of Warsaw, Polin 3*. Liverpool: Littman Library of Jewish Civilization, 2004.

Prokop-Janiec, Eugenia. "Children's Literature: Polish Literature." *YIVO Encyclopedia of Jews in Eastern Europe*, 2011. Accessed October 28 2017, http://www.yivoencyclopedia.org/article.aspx/Childrens_Literature/Polish_Literature.

Rogalski, Stanislaw. "Das Schulexperiment Dr. Janusz Korczaks". In *Von der Grammatik, und andere pädagogische Texte* ("The School Experiment of Dr. Janusz Korczak." In *About Grammar and other Pedagogical Chapters*), edited by Friedhelm Beiner and Elisabeth Lax-Höfer, 187–207. Heinsberg/Rhld.: Agentur Dieck, 1991.

Rossino, Alexander B. *Hitler Strikes Poland: Blitzkrieg, Ideology, and Atrocity*. Lawrence: University Press of Kansas, 2003.

Rothdeutsch-Granzer, Christine, and Wilma Weiß. "Reformerische und emanzipatorische Pädagogik. Inspirationen für die traumapädagogische Praxis und Theoriebildung." In *Handbuch Traumapädagogik* ("Reform and Emancipation in Pedagogics. Inspirations from Trauma Therapy for Pedagogical Practice and Theory." In *Handbook of Trauma Pedagogics*), edited by Wilma Weiß, Tanja Kessler, and Silke Birgitta Gahleitner, 33–43. Weinheim: Beltz Verlag, 2016.

Schatz, Jaff. "Jews and the Communist Movement in Interwar Poland." In *Dark Times, Dire Decisions: Jews and Communism. Studies in Contemporary Jewry*, edited by Jonathan Frankel, 13–37. Oxford: Oxford University Press, 2005.

Schechter, Salomon, and Julius H. Greenstone. "Foundling." *Jewish Encyclopedia*. Accessed March 30 2017, http://www.jewishencyclopedia.com/articles/6255-foundling.

Scheuermann, Martin. *Minderheitenschutz contra Konfliktverhütung? Die Minderheitenpolitik des Völkerbundes in den zwanziger Jahren (Protection of Minorities versus Prevention of Conflict? Minority Policy of the League of Nations in the 1920s)*. Marburg: Verlag Herder-Institut, 2000.

Scott, Ury. *Barricades and Banners: The Revolution of 1905 and the Transformation of Warsaw Jewry*. Stanford, CA: Stanford University Press, 2012.

Seidler, Eduard. *Jüdische Kinderärzte 1933–1945. Entrechtet, geflohen, ermordet* (*Jewish Pediatrists 1933–1945. Deprived of Rights, Escaped, Murdered*), Second Edition. Basel: Karger, 2007.

Sheehy, Gail. *New Passages: Mapping Your Life Across Time*. Toronto: Random House of Canada, 1995.

Silverman, Marc. *A Pedagogy of Humanist Moral Education*. New York: Palgrave Macmillan, 2017.

Trottmann, Christian. "Vita activa/vita contemplative." In *Historisches Wörterbuch der Philosophie* (*Historical Encyclopedia of Philosophy*), vol. 11, Sp. 1071–1075. Basel: Schwabe Verlag, 2001.

Weiß, Konrad. "Kinderarzt und medizinischer Lehrmeister." ("Pediatrician and Medical Teacher.") *Aufbau* 61, no. 15 (July 21 1988): 17.

Weiß, Konrad. "Wie Igor Newerly Janusz Korczak kennenlernte." ("How Igor Newerly got acquainted to Janusz Korczak.") *Die Weltbühne* 83, no. 11 (March 15 1988): 339–341.
Wiesbauer, Elisabeth. *Das Kind als Objekt der Wissenschaft: Medizinische und psychologische Kinderforschung an der Wiener Universität 1800–1914* (*The Child as Object of Science: Medical and Psychological Research on Children at the Vienna University 1800–1914*). Wien: Löcker, 1981.
Wiese, Stefan. *Pogrome im Zarenreich: Dynamiken kollektiver Gewalt* (*Pogroms under the Tsarist Regime: Dynamics of Collective Violence*). Hamburg: Hamburger Edition, HIS Verlag, 2016.
Woleńsk, Jan. "Jews in Polish Philosophy." *Shofar: An Interdisciplinary Journal of Jewish Studies* 29, no. 3 (2011). Accessed June 29 2017, https://muse.jhu.edu/article/478211.

Peter Scott Lederer

Mel Brooks' Subversive Cabaret

The Producers (1968)

Despite the growing attendance of the cabaret by a general public, its personnel and creators continued to be drawn from peripheral groups whose viewpoint remained ironic. The proliferation of cabarets allowed minority concerns to infiltrate popular entertainment. Throughout central and eastern Europe, a large percentage of performers, composers, authors, and impresarios were Jews; and although there were only a few exclusively Jewish cabarets, comedy and political commentary were permeated with Yiddish rhythms, attitudes, and words.[1]

Introduction: Holocaust Humor

Mel Brooks' *The Producers* (1968) is a film in which a desperate producer, Max Bialystock (Zero Mostel), convinces his bookkeeper, Leo Bloom (Gene Wilder), to take part in a fabulous scheme: receive investments for a play, produce a flop, and then rake in the money.[2] The plot is simple enough, which Brooks' films have often been criticized for being. As Beth E. Bonnstetter suggests, scholars have not paid due respect to Brooks' lowbrow humor. Although *Blazing Saddles* (1974), *Young Frankenstein* (1974), and *The Producers* are listed on the American Film Institute's top one hundred comedies, a small amount of scholarly work has been committed to Brooks' feature films.[3] Despite this, Maurice Yacowar argues that reassessing Brooks' "vulgarity" is needed.[4] After all, if intellectuals and young viewers "can figure out" what Brooks is "getting at," as the filmmaker suggests, then others doing so seems necessary.[5] As Alex Symons notes, "by assessment of the film's varied reviews in 1968, it can be illustrated that a comic reading of *The Producers* constitutes the deliberate appreciation of bad

1 Laurence Senelick, *Cabaret Performance: Volume II: Europe 1920–1940: Sketches, Songs, Monologues, Memoirs* (Baltimore: Johns Hopkins University Press, 1993), xiii.
2 *The Producers*, dir. by Mel Brooks (1968; Burbank, CA: Optimum, 2008), DVD.
3 Beth E. Bonnstetter, "Mel Brooks Meets Kenneth Burke (and Mikhail Bakhtin): Comedy and Burlesque in Satiric Film," *Journal of Film and Video* 63, no. 1 (2011): 19.
4 Maurice Yacowar, *Method in Madness: The Comic Art of Mel Brooks* (New York: St. Martin's Press, 1981), vii.
5 Yacowar, *Method in Madness*, vii-viii.

https://doi.org/10.1515/9783110545753-013

taste."[6] Furthermore, Jamie Moshin argues that Brooks leaves out "any cues of Jewish identity from his filmic protagonists," altering "the genre in *The Producers* into a Jewish 'quotidian' humor, a humor that is used for everyday purposes but without the depth of irony or empowerment."[7] This claim seems doubtful, however, since Zero Mostel and Gene Wilder clearly play characters representing distinct Jewish types. If this were not enough, plenty of other elements of the film left Jews "horrified," leading many to write "resentful letters of protest."[8] What disheartened them was not that Hitler was used comically, which American filmmakers had already done,[9] but that Jews were not treating the Shoa seriously, once again propagating self-hatred. Paul McDonald suggests that Brooks' characters personify "corrupting values": Bialystock "is an unscrupulous gigolo," while Leo Bloom is "a criminal and a purveyor of tasteless and distorted narratives; worse, they have turned him from an unassuming Jewish accountant into someone willing to collaborate with a Nazi."[10] Moreover, Andrew Sarris emphasizes that "Jewish producers" connecting themselves with "such a project" is far-fetched.[11] Jews teaming up with a former Nazi, argues Stanley Kauffmann, "seems odd"; furthermore, that "the Nazi is oblivious to the Jewishness of his producers" does not make the scenario any more believable.[12] Also revealing is Pauline Kael's criticism that *The Producers* is "amateurishly crude"; "show-business Jewish humor," she argues, took advantage of stereotypes.[13] Even more telling is Gregg Rickman's assertion that, as a television comedy writer, and "a showman capable of amazing spectacle," Brooks may simply be memorialized as someone

---

6 Alex Symons, "An Audience for Mel Brooks's *The Producers:* The Avant-Garde of the Masses," *Journal of Popular Film and Television* 3, no. 1 (2006): 24, accessed November 17 2016, http://www.tandfonline.com.

7 Jamie Moshin, "On the Big Screen, but Stuck in the Closet: What Mel Brooks' *The Producers* Says about Modern American Jewish Identity and Communicating the Holocaust," *Journal of the Northwest Communication Association* 35 (2006): 33.

8 Mel Brooks, "With Comedy, We Can Rob Hitler of His Posthumous Power," Interview with Mel Brooks, *Spiegel*, 16 March 2006, accessed September 20 2016, http://www.spiegel.de/international/spiegel/spiegel-interview-with-mel-brooks-with-comedy-we-can-rob-hitler-of-his-posthumous-power-a-406268.html.

9 Hitler is satirized in many comedies: The Three Stooges' *You Natzy Spy!* (1940), Ernst Lubitsch's *To Be or Not to Be* (1942), Disney's *Der Führer's Face* (1943), and Charlie Chaplin's *The Great Dictator* (1940).

10 Paul McDonald, "'They're Trying to Kill Me': Jewish American Humor and the War against Pop Culture," *Studies in Popular Culture* 28, no. 3 (April 2006): 25.

11 Andrew Sarris, "Films," *Village Voice*, March 28 1968, 47.

12 Stanley Kauffmann, "Zero and Others," *New Republic*, April 13 1968, 24.

13 Pauline Kael, "O, Pioneer!" *The New Yorker*, March 23 1968, 140.

"'putting on a show' [...] rather than as a satirist or performer."[14] His argument that the film is filled with "irrelevant gags,"[15] however, falls short of appreciating Brooks' larger social commentary. If Brooks is concerned with how historical events exist "in modern memory, in how people and events are remembered,"[16] then he probably has a more important point to make. How Brooks uses Jewishness in his humor to achieve this becomes necessary to explore. Unlike Rickman, I do not recognize Brooks as a "Busby Berkeley of comedy."[17] Instead, I identify his humor as a Jewish form of subversive cabaret. Distinct from a musical like *Fiddler on the Roof* (play, 1964; film, 1971), *The Producers* propagates a different message. This distinction is important, since "the notion of 'Jewish humor' immediately evokes the name of Shalom Aleichem," as Ruth Adler suggests, and Aleichem's gift "to find a jest amongst the tears and make tragic situations tolerable."[18]

Brooks once remarked that "by using the medium of comedy, we can try to rob Hitler of his posthumous power and myths."[19] While *The Producers* does not reference the Holocaust directly, it accomplishes the feat of disintegrating "the holy seriousness that always surrounded [Hitler] and protected him like a cordon."[20] Brooks' gallows humor, then, certainly has its advantages. Gallows humor is recognized by Alan Dundes and Thomas Hauschild: "Nothing is so sacred, so taboo, or so disgusting that it cannot be the subject of humour."[21] Properly, "gallows humour generally refers to jokes made about and by the *victims* of oppression. They are jokes told by those supposedly about to be hanged, not by the hangmen."[22] As Dundes and Hauschild note, "there are some anti-Semitic jokes which would rarely if ever be told by Jews,"[23] with such an example including the infamous and vulgar "Auschwitz joke": "How many Jews will fit in a Volkswagen? 506 – six in the seats and 500 in the ashtrays."[24] Such a joke would not go down well if told by a Jew, and certainly not by a Gentile. A better

---

14 Greg Rickman, ed., *The Film Comedy Reader* (New York: Limelight Editions, 2001), 302.
15 Ibid., 298.
16 Ibid., 298.
17 Ibid., 302.
18 Ruth Adler, "Shalom Aleichem's 'On Account of a Hat': Universal and Jewish Applications," in *Jewish Humor*, ed. Avner Ziv (New Brunswick, NJ: Transaction, 1998), 19.
19 Brooks, "With Comedy, We Can Rob Hitler of His Posthumous Power," no pagination.
20 Ibid.
21 Alan Dundes and Thomas Hauschild, "Auschwitz Jokes," in *Humour in Society: Resistance and Control*, eds. Chris Powell and George E. C. Paton (London: Macmillan, 1988), 56.
22 Ibid., 56 (emphasis in original).
23 Ibid., 56.
24 Ibid., 56–57.

example of an acceptable joke in the gallows humor style would be one often credited to Weiss-Ferdl, which Hillenbrand identifies: "Good evening! I'm sorry I'm so late. I've just come back from a little excursion to – Dachau! Well, you ought to see the place! Barbed-wire fence, electrified, machine-guns; another barbed-wire fence, more machine guns – but I can tell you, I managed to get in all the same!"[25] The joke, told from the perspective of a prisoner "often imprisoned" at Dachau,[26] is definitely in the Brooksian tradition. In other words, it demands certain conditions: "the situation must be absurd. [...] The more serious the situation, the funnier the comedy can be. The greatest comedy plays against the greatest tragedy."[27] Brooks can be seen perfecting the style in one of his earlier works, *The Twelve Chairs* (1970), where the dark chorus of "Hope for the Best (Expect the Worst)" is heard with a Yiddish inflection: "Live while you're alive. / No one will survive. / Life is funny. / Save your worries, spend your money. / Live while you're alive. / No one will survive. / There's no guarantee."[28]

With this in mind, then, *The Producers* can be considered to be a comedy developed in the style of the cabaret, which Brooks adored. The comparison between Brooks' humor and the performers from the Nazi era is indeed strong. Cabaret performers used satire, sexuality, and political comedy set around musical numbers. In the Weimar Republic, German nightclub entertainment was revived: "[T]he end of censorship after the fall of the monarchy in 1918 promised to pave the way to a new openness on the stage, as performers would finally be able to take a stand on contemporary issues and address the daily concerns of the audience."[29] The possibilities of sexuality became more prominent as entertainers satirized mainstream conservative themes.[30] The freedom to explore topics, however, often created "a flood of obscenity and nudity" instead of more insightful satire; the "smut" being offered to audiences was less challenging.[31] Successful, left-wing cabaret, however, could both satirically ridicule authoritarianism and

25 F. K. M. Hillenbrand, *Underground Humour in Nazi Germany, 1933–1945* (London: Routledge, 1995), 112. Weiss-Ferdl was a compère from Munich who used anti-Nazi humor. Weiss-Ferdl was once given a signed photo of Hitler, and his humorous response contained a clever double entendre: "What shall I do with it? Shall I put him in the corner or shall I hang him?" (18).
26 Hillenbrand, *Underground Humour in Nazi Germany*, 112.
27 Yacowar, *Method in Madness*, viii.
28 *The Twelve Chairs*, dir. Mel Brooks (1970; Burbank, CA: Twentieth Century Fox, 2006), DVD, 7:53–7:58.
29 Alan Lareau, *The Wild Stage: Literary Cabarets of the Weimar Republic* (Columbia, SC: Camden, 1995), 13.
30 Peter Jelavich, *Berlin Cabaret* (Cambridge, MA: Harvard University Press, 1997), 5.
31 Ibid., 13–14.

offer entertaining song and dance.[32] The entertainers providing such unique sketches and songs were mostly Jewish.[33] Understanding this creative and subversive decadence, I examine Brooks' film. My analysis will also compare Kurt Gerron's life and the Nazi propaganda documentary he made under pressure from the SS while a prisoner at Theresienstadt.

Melvin Kaminsky

Mel Brooks (Melvin James Kaminsky) was born in 1926. The anger in his comedy, Brooks realizes, in part arises from an "inability to deal with the realities of the world."[34] Brooks once worked on Sid Caesar's *Your Show of Shows* (1950–1954) with other notable writers Neil Simon and Carl Reiner.[35] While appearing sophomoric, Brooks' "nice, dirty fun," as he likes to call it,[36] shares aspects of the cabaret, particularly subversiveness. A product of New Hollywood, such Jewish comedy was given the opportunity to fully realize itself. As Brooks suggests, "every contemporary movie has its antecedents in films of the twenties and thirties."[37] Even though his films, he admits, have been influenced by the Marx Brothers, Continental Europe is where one can find the origins of Brooks' comedic style. As a World War II soldier, and a member of a family of immigrants from some of the most devastated areas, Brooks is quite aware of the history and traditions of countries in Eastern Europe: his mother had many relatives suffer the Pogroms in Ukraine[38] and his father escaped Danzig,[39] while other family members did not survive the Holocaust.[40]

While stationed in Germany, Brooks experienced life in Berlin: "When you come to Germany as a Jew you have an uneasy feeling, but I've always felt

32 Senelick, *Cabaret Performance*, xii.

33 Ibid., xiii.

34 Jerry Bauer, "Interview with Mel Brooks," *Adelina*, February 1980, accessed September 20 2016, http://www.brookslyn.com.

35 Steve Neale and Frank Krutnik, *Popular Film and Television Comedy* (London: Routledge, 2000), 232.

36 Bauer, "Interview with Mel Brooks," no pagination.

37 Ibid.

38 Philip Fleishman, "Interview with Mel Brooks," *Maclean's*, April 17 1979, accessed November 24 2016, http://www.brookslyn.com.

39 Alex Belth, "Mel Brooks is Always Funny and Often Wise in this 1975 Playboy Interview," *Daily Beast*, February 16 2014, accessed December 7 2016, http://www.thedailybeast.com.

40 "The Making of *The Producers*" in *The Producers*, directed by Mel Brooks (1970; Burbank, CA: Twentieth Century Fox, 2006), DVD, 45:10.

okay in Berlin."[41] For many years preceding the Nazi era, Berlin was "a city of enlightenment" where there was "a policy of religious tolerance which brought exceptional numbers of immigrants," including Jews.[42] In Berlin, Brooks saw *The Threepenny Opera*, the play that caused him to become infatuated with musicals, "totally crazy."[43] The "anarchic spirit" of the production results in the play's appearing as "a characteristic expression of 1920s' dissidence";[44] this black comedy is appropriately imitated by Brooks, and in *The Producers* the dark humor becomes dark 'Jewish' humor. In the hands of Brooks, however, black comedy has been misinterpreted as self-hatred despite its obvious criticisms of anti-Semitism. One example of this is Alex Symons' insistence that the film is distasteful.[45] Another comes from Moira Walsh, who states that her "mind boggled at the psychological implications in the premise that any audience would laugh at the play within the movie."[46] While these criticisms are reasonable, the knowledge that Jews have always relied on black comedy and that this does necessarily entail Jewish anti-Semitism is missing from such positions.

Out of a long history of Jewish struggle, *The Producers* eventually emerged, "an angry work, a Jewish expression of fury with the Nazi murder of European Jewry."[47] Although enlisted in the US Army, Brooks' lack of full participation in the fight against the Nazis more than likely caused "some subconscious frustration as a result of this."[48] It has been suggested that Brooks' "failure to engage the hated Huns directly apparently left him with a permanently thwarted sense of duty."[49] With this in mind, it is rather important that Brooks' protagonist, Max Bialystock, shares the name of a Polish city with historical significance. Białystok, in Poland, was home to one of largest struggles against Nazi occupation.[50] *The Producers*, though, despite its rage against Hitlerism, encoun-

41 Brooks, "With Comedy, We Can Rob Hitler of His Posthumous Power," no pagination.

42 George Colerick, *From the Italian Girl to Cabaret: Musical Humour, Parody and Burlesque* (London: Juventus, 1998), 67.

43 Brooks, n. pag. The part of Jackie "Tiger" Brown was originally played by Kurt Gerron in 1928.

44 Colerick, *From the Italian Girl to Cabaret*, 81.

45 Symons, "An Audience for Mel Brooks's *The Producers*," 27.

46 Moira Walsh, "The Producers," *America*, April 6 1968, 51.

47 Kirsten Fermaglich, "Mel Brooks' *The Producers:* Tracing American Jewish Culture through Comedy, 1967–2007," *American Studies* 48, no. 4 (Winter 2007): 67.

48 Yacowar, *Method in Madness*, 17.

49 David Desser and Lester D. Friedman, *American-Jewish Filmmakers: Traditions and Trends* (Chicago: University of Illinois Press, 1993), 118.

50 Sara Bender, *The Jews of Białystok During World War II and the Holocaust*, trans. Yaffa Murciano (Waltham, MA: Brandeis University Press, 2008), 8–9. Sara Bender notes that the city of Białystok, still two-thirds Jewish, was not as assimilated as other Polish cities in the nineteenth

ters problems because of its Jewish stereotypes. According to Michael Epp, stereotypes present "dangers," for "satire can be used as a suspicious excuse for promoting racist ideology."[51] In addition, it may "further oppress marginalized peoples,"[52] even if its intentions are the opposite. This is when the Jewish stereotypes perpetuated by Brooks become problematic. Rickman has argued that other stereotypes used by Brooks, such as the "mock hippie" and the "flamboyant gay stereotype," interfere with his comedy.[53] These images, however, match the "American-Jewish sense of always being out of place" that is crucial to Brooks' humor, which is also integral to all comedy in general.[54] It is my opinion that Bialystock and Bloom's *Springtime for Hitler* is proof enough that *The Producers* is neither anti-Semitic nor homophobic but instead propagates the opposite. To quote Fermaglich, Bailystock and Bloom are "lovable Jewish losers more aware of the dangers of Nazism than the members of the American middle class who flocked to their fascist play."[55] Therefore, I propose Brooks' cabaret humor is the film's own defense against critical attacks.

The Cabaret

The Nazis were determined to shut down the cabaret because of its subversiveness. Joseph Goebbels (1897–1945) believed that the cabaret was entertainment that opposed "the demands of good public taste."[56] More than "cheap and frivolous" entertainment, the cabaret was a danger since it attempted to undermine the "leadership" of the National Socialists.[57] Understanding that laughter is a difficult thing for any totalitarian regime to keep in check, the cabaret used comedy as an important part of resistance. Jewish performers had "artists' license to be

century. Anti-Zionist Jewish businesses, however, promoted assimilation, while Orthodox Jews considered the city "heretical" (8–9). The city was affected in 1906 with the Pogrom (14), and again in 1941 when it was turned into a ghetto (103).

51 Michael Epp, "Raising Mistrelsy: Humor, Satire and the Stereotype in *Birth of a Nation* and *Bamboozled*," *Canadian Review of American Studies* 33 (2003): 33.

52 Fermaglich, "Mel Brooks' *The Producers*," 28.

53 Rickman, *The Film Comedy Reader*, 299.

54 Geoff King, *Film Comedy* (London: Wallflower Press, 2002), 153.

55 Fermaglich, "Mel Brooks' *The Producers*," 66.

56 Joseph Goebbels, "Order Prohibiting Masters of Ceremonies and Commentary from the Stage," in *Cabaret Performance: Volume II: Europe 1920–1940: Sketches, Songs, Monologues, Memoirs*, ed. Laurence Senelick (Baltimore: Johns Hopkins University Press, 1993), 281.

57 Goebbels, "Order Prohibiting Masters of Ceremonies and Commentary from the Stage," 281.

fools" and successfully ridiculed their oppressors when possible.[58] Hitler, Gentiles in general, and even other Jews became objects of humor for Jews who performed "to audiences that were primarily Gentile."[59] These comedians, though, were targeted not only for their Jewishness but for promoting what was considered Communist propaganda.[60] They were eventually forced to immigrate to Canada, the United States, and Great Britain in 1933, after Jews found their businesses destroyed and their livelihoods threatened.[61]

There are several reasons that I consider Brooks' comedy to be inspired by the cabaret. Cabaret, as James Gavin notes, provided an environment "nearly devoid of prejudice,"[62] even facing it head-on. In Berlin, the cabaret was a show with songs, dancing, clever dialog, and humorous monologs; often, "topical issues" were dealt with in a "satirical or parodistic manner."[63] Jelavich suggests that the entertainment also included "vaudeville, nude dancing, revue, and agitprop."[64] These devices, as well as the drag show, are also used by Brooks to critique Nazism and other oppressive hegemonies (Figure 1). While Yacowar suggests that Brooks propagates "the grotesque images of heterosexuality" and "kinky instances of homosexuality,"[65] I disagree. Brooks' use of the "flamboyant gay stereotype," to which Rickman also objects,[66] requires dissection in its proper context.

Desser and Friedman call homosexuality in Brooks' films "unfortunate."[67] What they fail to note, however, is exactly how in doing so Brooks is able to critique the "cultural hegemony dominated by a white, middle-class, masculine, and decidedly gentile worldview," the very "background," they recognize, in which Brooks works.[68] The cabaret also fought this. The cabaret provided an environment for homosexuals where they could present caricatures of themselves in order to counter oppression.[69] Similar to Jews' use of self-deprecating humor, drag shows were used as much by homosexuals to expose bigotry as they were

58 Senelick, *Cabaret Performance*, 280.
59 Jelavich, *Berlin Cabaret*, 6.
60 Ibid., 3.
61 Ibid., 9.
62 James Gavin, *Intimate Nights: The Golden Age of New York Cabaret* (New York: Backstage Books, 2006), 2.
63 Ibid., 2.
64 Ibid., 3.
65 Maurice Yacowar, *Method in Madness*, 76.
66 Rickman, *The Film Comedy Reader*, 299.
67 Desser and Friedman, *American-Jewish Filmmakers*, 154.
68 Ibid., 112.
69 Gavin, *Intimate Nights*, 44.

Fig. 1: Bialystock and Bloom solicit Roger De Bris to direct *Springtime for Hitler.*

for folly. To take *Springtime for Hitler* to the stage, Max Bialystock seeks the expertise of Roger De Bris (Christopher Hewett), a cross-dressing director whose colorful assistant, Carmen Giya (Andreas Voutsinas), flaunts himself in his own unconventional attire (Fig. 1).[70] Although Hatch argues that Brooks mistreats homosexuals in a "mean" manner,[71] I suggest that Brooks uses the same humor as the cabaret entertainer in order to subvert conventionality. One should recall that African Americans and homosexuals, like Jews were part of the cabaret in several nightclubs that neither practiced nor endorsed discrimination.[72] I conclude, then, that Brooks identifies "with the outsiders in history rather than the ruling classes," bringing "a marginalized mentality to all his films";[73] by doing so, Brooks does not exclude any member of the marginalized. This may be why Brooks' film audience is among the most diverse, as nightclub crowds in Germany were; there, "cabaret survived longer than other art forms in providing a platform which vocal opposition to the régime could reach an eager public; its several forms varied from subtle innuendoes, addressed to a sophisticated audience in the capital, to more down-to-earth and often crude jokes to listeners in a Bavarian beer-cellar-cum-stage."[74] Lampooning Hitler, when possible, received

70 *The Producers*, 47:06.

71 Robert Hatch, "Films," *The Nation*, April 8 1968, 486.

72 Gavin, *Intimate Nights*, 69.

73 Desser and Friedman, *American-Jewish Filmmakers*, 134.

74 Hillenbrand, *Underground Humour in Nazi Germany*, 112.

strong reactions from audiences, as it also did in publications.[75] *The Producers* achieves the same effectiveness.

Hitler as Humor

In Germany, subversive humorists retreated to the underground where they created "contemporaneous satire about Hitler" focusing on "his background, appearance, path to power, personal traits, 'universal genius' and his decline."[76] Hitler's "egocentricity" and "megalomania" were satirized by cartoonists, as were the Führer's "play-acting" and "lack of humour."[77] Even after the war, Hitler continued to be lampooned by comedians, inevitably giving Brooks more material for his satire. Will Jordan's bit "about show-biz moguls casting a replacement for Hitler" possibly inspired *The Producers.*[78] Lenny Bruce's routine about "Hitler and the MCA," Yacowar notes, is possibly another.[79] I believe the latter explanation is more likely. The bit is one of Bruce's earliest.[80] In the routine, two producers are auditioning actors to play a dictator; suddenly they notice a painter working in the corner:

> First Agent: Oh ya . . . Zis is really veirdo! Look at dot fink mit dot mustache! Hey, you! Frenchy! Put down dot painting. You, ya, mit da hair jazz there. Put down dot painting und step around in front. Yes, you! Ve vonna look at you. Right? Ya. Alright . . . Look at zis face! Is zis an album cover? Hey, vat is your name, my friend?
>
> Painter: Adolf Schicklgruber.
>
> First Agent: You're putting us on.
>
> Painter: Hey, come on, don jerk me around, you guys. I got tree garages to paint in Prague today. I gotta finish dem up.
>
> First Agent: No von is jerking you around, dere. You ever did any show business bits?
>
> Painter: Vell, I did a Chaplin impression at a party once.[81]

---

75 Ibid., 8–12.
76 Hillenbrand, *Underground Humour in Nazi Germany, 1933–1945*, 8.
77 Ibid., 7, 16.
78 Yacowar, *Method in Madness*, 83.
79 Ibid.
80 Kitty Bruce, ed., *The Almost Unpublished Lenny Bruce* (Philadelphia: Running Press, 1984), 40. A 1949 review in *Variety* mentions this early routine (40).
81 John Cohen, *The Essential Lenny Bruce: His Original Unexpurgated Satirical Routines* (St. Albans, Hertfordshire: 1975, Panther), 222.

Further support for the argument that Bruce's material is the source of Brooks' story comes from Ioan Davies: "Bruce's point is not to turn Hitler into a hero, but to show how the media industry can use even the most horrendous stories purely for the sake of making money."[82] Brooks' Bialystock and Bloom decide on offering the role of Hitler to LSD (Dick Shawn). LSD (Lorenzo Saint DuBois) is a bratty, self-centered hippie with the tendency to throw childish tantrums.[83] LSD, however, like Hitler, does not recognize his own childishness and megalomania. During *Springtime for Hitler*, the audience sees LSD as a laughing stock, the object of ridicule in much the same way Hitler was for the subversive cabaret, even though LSD considers himself to be cool.

Considering this, Brooks' comedic style finds its origins not in the musicals of the US but in the cabarets of Germany. Even though Busby Berkeley's pre-war musicals can be considered influential – for instance, *Gold Diggers of 1933* (Figure 2) – their impact is perhaps overstated.[84] Berkeley's numbers are harmless, while Brooks' off-color choreographed bits can be seen as offensive and subversive (Fig. 3).[85] His number, although seeming to imitate the Berkeley musical, ridicules the spectacle the National Socialists relied on: for example, the Nuremberg torchlight rallies (Figure 4).[86] The small rotating swastika the dancers make satirizes Nazi theatrics. Instead of Berkeley's or Brooks' musical looking "camp," it is the Nazis' parade that seems to achieve such a feat.

Brooks' style has been called "camp."[87] Camp "has long been a central component of American musical theater," Knapp suggests; it is a tradition where "race and ethnicity [...] matter tremendously."[88] Brooks' take on "camp" turns it into a subversive form, as dangerous as the African American jazz found in the cabaret that the Nazis eventually banned. His perfection of the style was learned by performing in the Catskill Mountains.[89] With this in mind, *The Producers* becomes a complex Jewish film indeed, and *Springtime for Hitler* can be understood as critical of discrimination, no matter what it happens to look

---

82 Ioan Davies, "Lenny Bruce and the Death of Jewish Tragic Humor," *Social Text* 22 (Spring 1989): 101.

83 *The Producers*, 1:02:02.

84 *Gold Diggers of 1933*, dir. Melvyn Leroy (1933; Warner Brothers, 2003), DVD, 1:26:05.

85 *The Producers*, 1:00:27.

86 "Nazi Torch Parade," *YouTube*, 0:24, accessed June 25 2017. The Nazis preferred the "dance and spectacle" of the musical over other forms of popular entertainment (Colerick, 74).

87 Sanford Pinsker, "Mel Brooks and the Cinema of Exhaustion," in *From Hester Street to Hollywood*, ed. Sarah Blacher Cohen (Bloomington: Indiana University Press, 1983), 249.

88 Raymond Knapp, *The American Musical and the Formation of National Identity* (Princeton: Princeton University Press, 2005), 5.

89 Desser and Friedman, *American-Jewish Filmmakers*, 113.

Fig. 2: Busby Berkeley's choreographed number "The Shadow Waltz."

Fig. 3: Brooks parodies both Busby Berkeley and National Socialism.

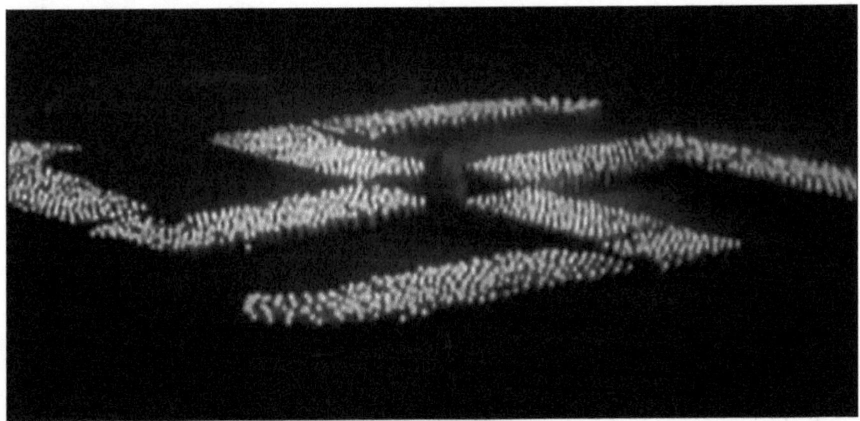

Fig. 4: Nazis imitate Berkeley's lavish productions.

like. Authoritarianism is the target, even when Germans appear to be the butt of the joke most of the time. "Mainly as a result of two world wars, we were encouraged to think of the Germans as humourless," Colerick reminds us.[90] The humorlessness of the Germans meant that they are often shown by Brooks as militaristic. As Bonnstetter stresses, however, merely "laughing at the Nazis' flaunting of their power misses the point" and itself becomes "potentially anti-Semitic."[91] The humor of *The Producers* should be understood as something more than lowbrow. To accomplish this, I will compare Max Bialystock and Kurt Gerron, the Jewish entertainer and prisoner who betrayed his people. This requires an examination of the Terezín/Theresienstadt ghetto. Furthermore, I will also analyze Gerron's documentary about life in the ghetto, which the Nazis forced him to make.

The Cabaret in the Terezín/Theresienstadt Ghetto

Jews, even in the harsh setting of the Terezín/Theresienstadt ghetto, were able to entertain one another.[92] One might call them performances of "resistance."[93]

---

90 Colerick, *From the Italian Girl to Cabaret*, 67.

91 Beth E. Bonnstetter, "Mel Brooks Meets Kenneth Burke (and Mikhail Bakhtin): Comedy and Burlesque in Satiric Film," *Journal of Film and Video* 63, no. 1 (2011): 18.

92 Peschel, *Performing Captivity, Performing Escape: Cabarets and Plays from the Terezín/Theresienstadt Ghetto* (London: Seagull Books, 2014), 1. As Peschel reminds readers, the Nazi camp where Jews were imprisoned is called both "Theresienstadt" (in German) and "Terezín" (in Czech). It is referred to as a "camp" as well as a "ghetto" by the prisoners who resided there (1).

Lisa Peschel's *Performing Captivity, Performing Escape: Cabarets and Plays from the Terezín/Theresienstadt Ghetto* (2014) describes how prisoners did not abandon culture, even in the conditions of the ghetto: "deprivation itself spurred prisoners to perform"; there, through the cabaret, Jews found "ways to manage the feelings of fear," restoring "a sense of power and control."[94] These ghetto performances allowed Jews to escape a "strange, grimly bizarre situation yet, at the same time, portray it."[95] Mel Brooks' cinematic world runs parallel. To borrow Rickman's words, Brooks' "view is at once optimistic, as it posits a cultural memory shared by all, and pessimistic, in that the events remembered are so painfully bleak." In other words, Brooks has been able to show how "hell and entertainment go together very well."[96] With this in mind, Brooks' dark humor should be compared with Kurt Gerron's own ghetto performances as well as Gerron's documentary.

Fig. 5: Gerron's extravagant personality is on display in *Prisoner of Paradise.*

Kurt Gerron (1897–1944) was a German-Jewish actor who had a small part in Josef von Sternberg's *Der blaue Engel* (1930) and performed in the premiere of Bertolt Brecht and Elisabeth Hauptmann's *The Threepenny Opera* (1928) (Figure 5). The Nazis singled out Gerron, who was a blacklisted performer like Zero Mos-

93 Ibid., 2.

94 Ibid., 4–6.

95 Ibid., 41.

96 Rickman, *The Film Comedy Reader*, 298.

Fig. 6: Bialystock carries on his showbiz ways inside prison walls.

tel; he "symbolize[d] everything they despised about the Jews."[97] Gerron was eventually sent to the Terezín/Theresienstadt ghetto, where he created his cabaret, *Karussell.* The Jewish entertainer Camilla Spira (1906–1997), who appeared on stage with Gerron, describes the ghetto cabaret: "The people who went to Auschwitz were sitting in a huge theater the night before, killing themselves with laughter at Gerron and me. It was magnificent cabaret."[98] Spira's statement confirms the tragicomedic element of Jewish thinking and performance.

The Nazis set up the Terezín/Theresienstadt ghetto as a "transit camp" where Jews would stop before transferring to "slave labor and death camps." Upper-class Jews, the elderly, and thousands of political dissidents, however, never reached their final stop.[99] Kurt Gerron was considered part of the upper echelon of Jewish society. He also was a World War I veteran, and so useful to the Nazis. The Nazis purposely imprisoned "veterans [...], artists, musicians, scholars, judges, and other members of the cream of the social and intellectual world of pre-Hitler Germany" at the Terezín/Theresienstadt camp; this "assure[d] some of the more sympathetic Germans" of the safety of their fellow citizens.[100]

---

97 *Prisoner of Paradise*, dir. Malcolm Clarke and Stuart Sender (2002; PBS Home Entertainment, 2005), DVD, 38:53–38:58.

98 Ibid., 47:16–47:29. *Todlachen* ("death-laugh") is the German word for such laughter.

99 Peschel, *Performing Captivity, Performing Escape*, 21.

100 Joel Shatzky, introduction to *Theresienstadt: Hitler's Gift to the Jews* by Norbert Troller (Chapel Hill, NC: University of North Carolina Press, 1991), xxii.

The Nazis chose Gerron, "a useful Jew," to film a documentary that would prove the pleasant conditions inside the camp.[101] The propaganda film *Terezín: A Documentary Film from the Jewish Settlement Area* (1944) is today called *The Führer Gives the Jews a City.*[102] Mostel did not want to be in *The Producers* at first;[103] this is understandable, for the characters are stereotypically Jewish. Likewise, the propaganda film the Nazis wanted Gerron to direct was also "unthinkable" from Gerron's perspective.[104] The Nazis had already tricked the Red Cross into thinking the ghetto was up to standards when it was previously evaluated.[105] They wanted to keep opinions of Terezín/Theresienstadt positive and use a film to influence this. In the film, inmates would be dressed nicely and appear happy and comfortable.[106] Gerron – a "vain" person who had an "enormous ego" – was the perfect choice for helping to put on this "hoax."[107] In many ways, he was similar to Mostel.[108] The possibilities of creating a film project all his own was appealing to Gerron, so he filmed the documentary. However, he was seen as a Nazi "puppet" or "traitor," his film making him questionable in the eyes of Jews.[109]

The documentary does not provide an accurate representation of life in the ghetto. Everyone seems to be happily participating in ghetto life; they work, play, and spend their time being productive and sociable.[110] Prisoners have hobbies, such as sculpting and sewing.[111] There is even a game of soccer, which many youngsters watch enthusiastically.[112] Everyone seems excited, as the camera pans across the crowd of onlookers. The ghetto even has its own symphony orchestra if one chooses to listen to some music.[113] For those who choose neither a sporting event nor the symphony, a library offers an additional choice of an af-

---

101 *Prisoner of Paradise*, 48:53.

102 *The Führer Gives the Jews a City*, Two Parts, dir. Kurt Gerron (Theresienstadt, 1944), *YouTube*, accessed January 27 2017.

103 "The Making of *The Producers*," 8:08 – 8:10.

104 *Prisoner of Paradise*, 1:15:40 – 1:15:48.

105 Shatzky, introduction, xxiii.

106 Ibid.

107 *Prisoner of Paradise*, 14:36, 16:44.

108 Directing *The Producers* was a "nightmare" for Brooks. According to Yacowar, even though Mostel was "an old friend," his "ego did not fit Brooks's ideal of ensemble," and so the two constantly argued (83).

109 *Prisoner of Paradise*, 1:25:47 – 1:25:53.

110 *The Führer Gives the Jews a City*, Part 1, 1:00 – 3:00.

111 Ibid., 1:30 – 2:18

112 Ibid., 5:48.

113 Ibid., Part 2, 2:41.

ternoon of quiet reading,[114] and there are pleasant gardens in which to spend some time.[115] Life in the barracks, however, is also always nice: women can write letters and knit; children may play with their favorite dolls.[116] Representations of conditions by ghetto artists, though, show quite a different reality.[117] Despite somewhat of a "vigorous cultural life"[118] – prisoners did read, write, and perform in the ghetto cabaret – Gerron's documentary only shows what the Camp Commandant, SS Major Karl Rahm (1907–1947), and Head of Jewish Deportation, SS Major Hans Günther (1910–1945), wanted viewers to see: a productive and joyous ghetto in which prisoners could live their daily lives contently.

Gerron betrayed the people in the ghetto in order to stay alive as long as possible. Bialystock and Bloom also appear to be "sell-outs" in Brooks' film. There is, however, an extraordinary difference: the producers merely want to earn profits. Furthermore, their play undermines Hitler's tyranny by making it look ridiculous, from the viewpoint of the audience at least. Gerron's film, on the other hand, betrays Jews by failing to show the ghetto as it actually was. *The Führer Gives the Jews a City* is the product of a man who seems to have deserted not only his people but also his morals, and for nothing. Gerron never made it out of Terezín/Theresienstadt alive; the Nazis murdered him. The actor, director, and cabaret entertainer would forever be seen as a traitor.

It is not Brooks' intention to use *Springtime for Hitler* to mock Jews to achieve laughs, and certainly Bialystock and Bloom saw the play as tragic and sick, as they incorrectly assumed the audience would also. What Brooks accomplishes is a moral, satiric, tragicomedic cabaret, in some ways similar to the theater in Terezín/Theresienstadt, which "oscillated between attempts to portray reality and the desire to make light of it with a smile."[119] At the end of the film, Bialystock and Bloom also do what ghetto prisoners finally did in their imprisonment, encouraging performance within what seems to be a hopeless situation. Like the entertainers in the Terezín/Theresienstadt ghetto, who satirized other Jews the best,[120] Bialystock and Bloom know how to poke fun at themselves. This sort of power, to borrow Peschel's description, is "exercised within the symbolic space of performance."[121] Brooks's ending does not differ in this regard; the

114 Ibid., 1:30.
115 Ibid., 4:53–5:50.
116 Ibid., 6:33–7:42.
117 Ibid., 1:14:05.
118 Peschel, *Performing Captivity, Performing Escape*, 2–3.
119 Ibid., 42.
120 Ibid., 42–43.
121 Ibid., 7.

film concludes with the producers and their fellow performers singing "Prisoners of Love" (Figure 6).[122] *The Producers*, then, accomplishes the feat of displaying subversive cabaret humor, through openly mocking Hitler, and performance within captivity, as those in the Terezín/Theresienstadt ghetto had done.

If comedy is an alternative way of dealing with delicate topics, as Giuliana Sorce suggests,[123] then it may also be a way to memorialize the Holocaust, as Louis Kaplan argues.[124] It is also useful to note that ridiculing Hitler is another way to regain control.[125] As Brooks proposes, ridicule is the best alternative to "invective" to counter totalitarianism.[126] *The Producers* is able to be subversive, whereas Gerron ultimately failed. Gerron died a collaborator, but Bialystock and Bloom continue to subversively entertain while imprisoned. This is the best defense for Brooks' style of Jewish humor, which is sometimes attacked for being anti-Semitic. What needs to be considered is that Brooks' comedy is liberal while still being Jewish. Liberal Jews in Nazi Germany were likely to "reject the traditional notion that Jews still formed a separate nation hoping to return to Israel."[127] Brooks' liberal Jewish humor is not so different. Understanding his New World outlook perhaps can best be understood if his comedy is compared with a quite traditional Jewish story, a popular narrative in which Zero Mostel also once acted.

The Producers Meets *Fiddler on the Roof*

Whereas *The Producers* is merely Jewish with its use of stereotypes and dependence on dark satire, *Fiddler on the Roof* offers a more traditional look at Judaism. *The Producers* was released between the premiere of the musical *Fiddler on the Roof* (1964) and the film version (1971). Zero Mostel's performance, therefore, is an important element that needs exploration, since he originally played Tevye in *Fiddler* on Broadway and was responsible for its success.[128] An ethnic musical

122 *The Producers*, 1:23:16.

123 Giuliana Sorce, "Hitler and Humor: Coming to Terms with the Past through Parody," *Global Media Journal* 5, no. 2 (2015), accessed November 17 2016.

124 Louis Kaplan, "'It Will Get a Terrific Laugh': On the Problematic Pleasures and Politics of Holocaust Humor," in *Hop on Pop: The Politics and Pleasures of Popular Culture*, ed. Henry Jenkins et al. (Durham, NC: Duke University Press, 2002), 324.

125 Sander L. Gilman, "Is Life Beautiful? Can the Shoah be Funny? Some Thoughts on Recent and Older Films," *Critical Inquiry* 26, no. 2 (2000): 279.

126 Fleishman, "Interview with Mel Brooks," 6.

127 Peschel, *Performing Captivity, Performing Escape*, 8.

128 Knapp, *The American Musical*, 184.

which seemed to have "limited appeal," *Fiddler* was in the beginning compared to the 1957 musical *West Side Story*, which was adapted for the screen in 1961.[129] *Fiddler*, however, managed to avoid backlash from critics. According to Knapp, "the characters and events of *Fiddler on the Roof* are not drawn from a verifiably inaccurate [...] past; rather, they were drawn from a people and way of life that were systematically erased from existence across the first half of the twentieth century, but which are remembered with nostalgia and deep sorrow."[130] Knapp gives credit for the musical's evading such a problem to the "Jewish presence on the creative team, and to its careful withholding of judgment on Tevye's hard-line anti-assimilationist position."[131] Joseph Stein attributes *Fiddler*'s success to its being "about people who happen to be Jewish" rather than "about Jewish people,"[132] even though Knapp believes that *Fiddler* "first and foremost *is* about Jews, however much its story may resonate with other cultures and peoples."[133] Director Norman Jewison's fear was that Mostel's performance would not transfer to film so nicely, that a good balance would not be achieved because of the actor's big, bold presence.[134] With this in mind, comparing *The Producers* and *Fiddler on the Roof* needs to be considered. Max Bialystock, a character perhaps more like Zero Mostel, is both more liberal and more intense than Tevye.

The amoral Bialystock and neurotic *schlimazel* ("unlucky person") Bloom have been considered "caricature Jewish figures" by some critics.[135] Geoff King also sees them as a "strategy [...] in comedy of a distinctive racial or ethnic slant."[136] They are part of what he calls "exaggeration to the point of absurdity of negative stereotypes."[137] This is one of the techniques of subversion in comedy. The negativity of the Bialystock character in part initiated Mostel's refusal to participate in the film. The concept of the "greedy Jew" has a long history, and one can understand why the role would have been unappealing. Abraham H. Foxman has identified the stereotype as one of three recognizable anti-Semitic figures, the other two being the Jew as "anti-assimilationist" and Christ "murder-

129 Ibid., 185.
130 Ibid., 216.
131 Ibid., 185.
132 Joseph P. Swain, *The Broadway Musical* (Lanham, MD: Scarecrow, 2002), 247.
133 Knapp, *The American Musical*, 215 (emphasis in original).
134 Norman Jewison, "'Norman Jewison': Filmmaker Documentary," in *Fiddler on the Roof*, dir. Norman Jewison (1971; MGM Home Entertainment, 2002), DVD, disc two, 14:00 – 14:15.
135 King, *Film Comedy*, 153.
136 Ibid., 152.
137 Ibid., 152.

er."[138] These "not so funny" stereotypes, Foxman suggests, may be employed by comedians humorously; however, such usage merely perpetuates the problem, according to him.[139] Reviewing how such types were used in the past for "humorous" purposes, one can better understand Foxman's argument (Figure 7).[140] Depictions of Jews of such an obvious anti-Semitic nature present problems, since these stereotypes have been for so long a part of a discourse of hate. If Max Bialystock is clearly the "boisterous conniver," as Desser and Friedman suggest,[141] then Brooks is merely perpetuating prejudice – or is he? The wolfish Bialystock at first does appear to be just another Jewish stereotype, as the big, bad "B" stitched on his smoking jacket seems to indicate (Figure 8).[142] The sign of caution, the "B", identifies what this conniving man represents. Desser and Friedman tell readers about the type: "the cunning Jew who unscrupulously fleeces others, the money-hungry Jew who sacrifices morality on the altar of immediate riches, the manipulative Jew who trades on the finer emotions of others for his own gain, the garish Jew who flaunts his wealth at the least opportunity."[143] The Jewish protagonist's manipulation of elderly ladies is certainly unethical. One can see why Mostel found the character repulsive.[144] He soon would learn, though, that Brooks' film was a proud comedic display of subversion. Brooks has openly admitted his "open anger with the crimes of Nazism,"[145] and his subversive comedy is a reflection of this: "Why should I not like the Germans? Just because they're arrogant and have fat necks and do anything they're told so long as it's cruel, and killed millions of Jews in concentration camps and made soap out of their bodies and lamp shades out of their skins? Is that any reason to hate their fucking guts?"[146] What Rickman calls the "singing-dancing dystopia" found in Brooks' films also demonstrates the alienation Jews still felt in America.[147] Brooks came to embrace his identity, though. As the angry Jewish comedian, he had an explanation for his craziness: "For every ten Jews beating their

---

138 Abraham H. Foxman, *Jews and Money: The Story of a Stereotype* (New York: Palgrave MacMillan, 2010), 43.

139 Foxman, *Jews and Money*, 179.

140 "Anti-Semitic Character on the Occasion of the Stock Exchange Crash of 1873," *Kikeriki*, May 18 1873, accessed December 4 2016, http://www.hasburger.net.

141 Desser and Friedman, *America-Jewish Filmmakers*, 147.

142 *The Producers*, 3:34.

143 Desser and Friedman, 147, 149.

144 "The Making of *The Producers*," 8:08 – 8:10.

145 Fermaglich, "Mel Brooks' *The Producers*," 68.

146 Yacowar, *Method in Madness*, 17.

147 Rickman, *The Film Comedy Reader*, 298.

breasts, God designated one to be crazy and amuse the breast-beaters."[148] The combination of Brooks and Mostel, therefore, becomes necessary to keep in mind when comparing *Fiddler* and *The Producers.*

Fig. 7: The anti-semitic magazine *Kikeriki* regularly caricatured Jews.

What Chaim Topol, an Israeli actor, brings to Tevye in *Fiddler* is quite different from Zero Mostel's interpretation of the character. The Brooklyn-born Mostel may

148 Paul D. Zimmerman, "The Mad Mad Mel Brooks," *Newsweek*, February 17 1975, accessed November 29 2016, http://www.brookslyn.com.

Fig. 8: Bialystock preys on one of his elderly financiers.

have first given Tevye the qualities with which audiences are familiar, but another missing element was needed for the film. Topol was born in Tel Aviv. As a practicing Israeli Jew, Topol does add some authenticity to the character; this religious genuineness and sincerity is not only lacking in Mostel's portrayal but also in the more liberal Max Bialystock character. The clear differences between the modern, subversive Bialystock and the conservative Tevye can be identified upon analyzing the first scenes of both films.

The opening scene in *Fiddler* confirms the Orthodox Jewish culture upon which the narrative relies. With Tevye speaking directly to the audience, he establishes his conservative religious beliefs: "And because of our traditions, every one of us knows who he is, and what God expects him to do."[149] He looks skyward and points towards the heavens, confirming the ultimate authority, the God of Judaism. He identifies himself as an Orthodox Jewish man who respects the Law. On the other hand, there is Max Bialystock, a non-observant Jew who does not report to the authority of God. His independence relies on the wealth of elderly spinsters and widows. He stores their portraits in a type of secular altar he has; he is loyal to nothing but the holy dollar. A woman's picture is only worthy to come out when she pays a visit and brings a check.

149 *Fiddler on the Roof*, dir. Norman Jewison (1971; MGM Home Entertainment, 2002), 4:31–4:40.

Tevye clings to his religion as well as the customs attached to them: families arrange marriages, men and woman cannot dance together, etc. Such traditions, however, are not favorable in a modern age. Tevye cannot win, and neither can Bialystock, a scammer who finds himself convicted of his crime. There is one fundamental difference between the two, however: the terror that comes to the Jewish village of Anatevka is a greater problem; it affects every Jewish townsperson. Bialystock's problem, though, is merely his: he is a failed and desperate producer unable to put on a successful play. Tevye's understanding of the tragedy of the Jews is steeped in history and tradition, but he deals with it through laughter that is both joyous and somber. Bilaystock, however, seems to trivialize the Jewish problems of the past to guarantee positive financial results; by doing so he intends his musical to be a successful flop. Despite his apparent lack of sympathy for the Jews, Bialystock's play becomes more than the scheme of a selfish man, however; it turns into a great humanitarian work of satire. Bialystock and Bloom's amoral musical instead appears to be greatly moral and anti-authoritarian, promoting commentary similar to Brooks' own: "The great Holocaust by the Nazis is probably the great outrage of the Twentieth Century. There is nothing to compare with it. So what can I do about it? If I get on the soapbox and wax eloquently, it'll be blown away in the wind, but if I do *Springtime for Hitler* it'll never be forgotten."[150]

Tevye, though, is intentionally moral and traditional with regard to obedience to God. Respect and cultural norms are to be honored. Tevye does not want his daughters to assimilate; he is righteous, and he regrets deeply the break-up of his family and their *shtetl*. For Tevye, Anatevka may be Zion. He yells at the Constable, "Get off my land," underlining that no other place can be his home.[151] Aviv and Shneer suggest that "the ways in which Eastern Europe has become a mythic part of the Jewish past and not an imagined mythic home in the future is central to understanding how American Jews see themselves at home in America."[152] The Old World belongs to Tevye in much the same way the New World belongs to Bialystock. Bialystock is not alone, though. Timothy Parrish argues that many liberal American Jews, especially those living in New York, no longer believe in a "Zion" but think that their homeland may simply be "a New York restaurant where Yiddish is still spoken."[153] Bialystock would

---

150 Fleishman, "Interview with Mel Brooks," no pagination.

151 *Fiddler on the Roof*, 2:33:30.

152 Caryn Aviv and David Shneer, "From Diaspora Jews to New Jews," in *Postzionism: A Reader*, by Laurence J. Silberstein (New Brunswick, NJ: Rutgers University Press, 2008), 351.

153 Timothy Parrish, *The Cambridge Companion to Philip Roth* (Cambridge, Eng.: Cambridge UP, 2007), 135.

be among these. After all, he is not faithful to anything, reliant on only his freedom and individuality, until those are taken away from him. Bloom is no different. Bialystock, as manipulator and father figure, mentors Wilder's character, showing him the path to autonomy. As a result, Bloom is as independent and liberal as Bialystock. After tricking the Nazi Franz Liebkind into handing over the rights to his musical on Hitler, the two of them throw their Nazi armbands into the trash and spit on them, rejecting not only Nazism but any form of authority. Behind Bialystock and Bloom, a flag in a window resembling the LGBT rainbow flag can be seen, giving new meaning to the 1977 film.[154] The producers' individuality is emphasized; they are their own men.

There is no doubt that *Fiddler*, in some ways, defends not only the Jewish faith but anti-assimilationism, at least from Tevye's point of view. Tevye recommends, "Each shall seek his own kind."[155] After one of his daughters decides to marry a Gentile, the belief remains the same: "Some things do not change for us; some things can never change."[156] Knapp suggests that "the taboo against mixed marriages was then [1964] still strong among Jews." During the time of the musical's release "intermarriage meant a denial of something essential to their nature."[157] In Jewish New Hollywood, however, old traditions were challenged by liberal filmmakers.

Bialystock, as written for the screen by Brooks and portrayed by Mostel, connects with modern audiences who may identify with his liberal approach to life. The character reflects the New World intricacies of being Jewish even while perpetuating a stereotype; appearing to be the immoral, avaricious Jew from anti-Semitic caricatures, Bialystock maintains his independence and Americanness. However, he is also aware of the history of Jewish struggle and the tragicomedy that has grown out of it. In one insightful shot, after failing to find a bad script to produce, Bialystock comes across Franz Kafka's *Metamorphosis*. He reads its famous opening line aloud: "'Gregor Samsa awoke one morning to find that he had been transformed into a giant cockroach.' It's too good!"[158] The statement demonstrates the moment Bialystock identifies with the tradition of Jewish writing, acknowledging its occasional darkness and absurdity. Kafka's words and

154 *The Producers*, 32:43. I compare the unidentifiable flag in the shot to the one that represents the LGBT community. Gilbert Baker designed the rainbow flag in 1978 in San Francisco ("Rainbow Flag," 100).

155 *Fiddler on the Roof*, 2:18:22–2:18:25.

156 Ibid., 2:18:42–2:18:48.

157 Knapp, *The American* Musical, 225.

158 *The Producers*, 25:23–25:33.

Gregor's reality ring too true. Bialystock's self-awareness of being a Jew is transferred to his business partner.

Bialystock takes advantage of Bloom; however, he also convinces him that he can achieve being a free individual. In the first scene with the two together, Bialystock addresses the problem: "So, you're an accountant, huh? Then account for yourself!"[159] Bloom is eventually able to overcome his old nebbish ways, demonstrating his individuality as the two sit next to the Revson Fountain in Lincoln Center. After deciding to help Bialystock with his scheme, Bloom sprints around the fountain in celebration as it shoots into the air, confirming his freedom and new identity. Until that point, the neurotic Bloom was, to use Wilder's description of the character, "the perfect victim."[160] Bloom, though, successfully overcomes the stereotype of the Jewish weakling. At that moment, he enters a new world, escaping that Kafkaesque dilemma which Gregor Samsa cannot: "I'm Leo Bloom! I'm me! I can do whatever I want! It doesn't matter! I'm Leo Bloom!"[161]

One finds the opposite situation in *Fiddler*, where tradition, Old World Jewishness, and conventionality suffocate the younger Jews' attempt to find themselves. After the Six-Day War, *Fiddler on the Roof* can arguably be seen as contesting New World Jewry. It propagates the "exaggerated pride" and "national intoxication" that David Alexander insists "strengthened the foundations of the Zionist vision." These "myths," Alexander notes, were satirized by Israeli humorists.[162] One of these satirists was Hanoch Levin, whose cabaret "made harsh proclamations about the war and its moral outcome." In Tel Aviv, however, such criticism was not appreciated; it seemed to promote irreverence.[163] After all, Israel's defeat of her Arab neighbors following the war provided "new opportunities for Israel to pursue the maximalist goals of Zion."[164] Such ambitions, though, seemed unnecessary, superfluous. Israel, having triumphed in Palestine and Sinai, "quadrupled its territory."[165] Considering this, *Springtime for Hitler* is also, in some ways, a critique of Jewishness.

---

159 Ibid., 10:09 – 10:14.

160 "The Making of *The Producers*," 16:10.

161 *The Producers*, 24:40 – 24:47.

162 David Alexander, "Political Satire in the Israeli Theatre: Another Outlook on Zionism," in *Jewish Humor*, ed. Avner Ziv (New Brunswick, NJ: Transaction, 1998), 169.

163 Ibid., 170.

164 M. Shahid. Alam, *Israeli Exceptionalism: The Destabilizing Logic of Zionism* (New York: Palgrave Macmillan, 2009), 186.

165 Alam, *Israeli Exceptionalism*, 188.

Fermaglich suggests that after the Six-Day War Jews experienced a sense of "pride"; the Holocaust was necessarily "a component of that Jewish identity."[166] Brooks' cabaret, though, is a production with a dominant American Jewishness at its center. His producers do not respect any type of authority. Furthermore, they represent individualism, not monolithic Jewishness. Such proper cabaret subverts all forms of tyranny; it is entertainment "exercised within the symbolic space of performance,"[167] and no one escapes its criticism.

Conclusion

In 1967, *The Producers* was viewed as a "threat to the Jewish community."[168] Some Jews may have showed "outrage" because of their feelings about "fascism," "anti-Semitism," and "the murder of millions of Jews during World War II."[169] However, another problem may have been that Brooks' film approaches Jewishness in general. Brooks modifies Old World stereotypes, contesting not only anti-Semitism but typical notions of Jewishness. After the Six-Day War, Jews may have worn their Jewishness as a "badge of pride";[170] however, American Jewishness as represented in *The Producers* reflects different values. Mostel and Wilder, through their performances, accomplished more than either of them set out to, thanks in part to Brooks' original script and directing. If Brooks' humor is dismissed as "tasteless," "despicable," and "dangerous,"[171] it may well be that critics have overlooked his contribution to Jewish black comedy, which, as I have shown, has a rather complicated and long history, from the German cabaret to the stages of Terezín/Theresienstadt. Such comedy has a special home in US cinema, especially for Jews who appreciate and respect the multiplicity of Jewish identities.

---

166 Fermaglich, "Mel Brooks' *The Producers*," 68.

167 Peschel, *Performing Captivity, Performing Escape*, 7.

168 Fermaglich, "Mel Brooks' *The Producers*," 77.

169 Ibid., 60.

170 Ibid., 68.

171 Ibid., 60.

Works Cited

Films Cited

The Producers. Directed by Mel Brooks. Burbank, CA: Embassy, 1968. DVD, Optimum, 2008.

Blazing Saddles. Directed by Mel Brooks. Burbank, CA: Warner Bros., 1974. DVD, Warner Bros. Home Video, 2004.

Der blaue Engel. Directed by Josef von Sternberg. Germany, UFA, 1930. DVD, Kino, 2001.

Fiddler on the Roof. Directed by Norman Jewison. Yugoslavia and Buckinghamshire, Eng.: United Artists, 1971. DVD. MGM Home Entertainment, 2004.

The Führer Gives the Jews a City. Two Parts. Directed by Kurt Gerron. Theresienstadt, 1944. *YouTube*. Accessed January 27 2017.

Der Führer's Face. Directed by Jack Kinney. Hollywood, CA: Walt Disney Productions, 1943.

Gold Diggers of 1933. Directed by Mervyn Leroy. Numbers created and directed by Busby Berkeley. Warner Bros., 1933. DVD, Warner Home Video, 2006.

The Great Dictator. Directed by Charles Chaplin. United Artists, 1936.

"Nazi Torch Parade." *YouTube*. Accessed June 25 2017. https://www.youtube.com/watch?v=D0LPWWPpTt0.

Prisoner of Paradise. Directed by Malcolm Clarke and Stuart Sender. Menemsha Entertainment, 2002. DVD, PBS Home Entertainment, 2005.

To Be or Not to Be. Directed by Mel Brooks. Burbank, CA; Twentieth Century Fox, 1983. DVD, Twentieth Century Fox Home Entertainment, 2006.

The Twelve Chairs. Directed by Mel Brooks. Universal Marion Corporation, 1970. DVD, Twentieth Century Fox, 2006.

West Side Story. Directed by Robert Wise and Jerome Robbins. New York, New York: United Artists, 1961.

You Natzy Spy! Directed by Jules White. Hollywood, CA: Columbia Pictures, 1940.

Young Frankenstein. Directed by Mel Brooks. Burbank, CA: Twentieth Century Fox, 1974. DVD. Twentieth Century Fox Home Entertainment, 2006.

Your Show of Shows. Directed by Nat Hiken and Max Liebman. Perf. Sid Caesar. NBC, 1950–54.

Works Cited

Adler, Ruth. "Shalom Aleichem's 'On Account of a Hat': Universal and Jewish Applications." In *Jewish Humor*, edited by Avner Ziv, 19–26. New Brunswick, NJ: Transaction, 1998.

Alam, M. Shahid. *Israeli Exceptionalism: The Destabilizing Logic of Zionism*. New York: Palgrave Macmillan, 2009.

Alexander, David. "Political Satire in the Israeli Theatre: Another Outlook on Zionism." In *Jewish Humor*, edited by Avner Ziv, 165–171. New Brunswick, NJ: Transaction, 1998.

"Anti-Semitic Character on the Occasion of the Stock Exchange Crash of 1873." *Kikeriki* May 18 1873. *Habsburger.net*. Accessed December 4 2016.

Aviv, Caryn, and David Shneer. "From Diaspora Jews to New Jews." In *Postzionism: A Reader*, edited by Laurence J. Silberstein, 345–368. New Brunswick, NJ: Rutgers University Press, 2008.
Bauer, Jerry. "Interview with Mel Brooks." *Adelina*, February 1980. *Brookslyn.com*. Accessed September 20 2016.
Belth, Alex. "Mel Brooks is Always Funny and Often Wise in this 1975 Playboy Interview." *Daily Beast*, February 16 2014. Accessed December 7 2016.
Bender, Sara. *The Jews of Białystok During World War II and the Holocaust.* Translated by Yaffa Murciano. Waltham, MA: Brandeis University Press, 2008.
Bonnstetter, Beth E. "Mel Brooks Meets Kenneth Burke (and Mikhail Bakhtin): Comedy and Burlesque in Satiric Film." *Journal of Film and Video* 63, no. 1 (2011): 18–31.
Brooks, Mel. "With Comedy, We Can Rob Hitler of His Posthumous Power." *Spiegel*, March 16 2006. Accessed November 17 2016.
Bruce, Kitty, ed. *The Almost Unpublished Lenny Bruce.* Philadelphia: Running Press, 1984.
Cohen, John, ed. *The Essential Lenny Bruce: His Original Unexpurgated Satirical Routines.* St. Albans: Panther, 1975.
Cohen, Sarah Blacher, ed. *From Hester Street to Hollywood: The Jewish-American Stage and Screen.* Bloomington: Indiana University Press, 1983.
Colerick, George. *From the Italian Girl to Cabaret: Musical Humour, Parody and Burlesque.* London: Juventus, 1998.
Davies, Ioan. "Lenny Bruce: Hyperrealism and the Death of Jewish Tragic Humor." *Social Text* 22 (Spring 1989): 92–114. Accessed February 2 2017. doi: 10.2307/466522.
Desser, David, and Lester Friedman. *American-Jewish Filmmakers: Traditions and Trends.* Chicago: University of Illinois Press, 1993.
Dundes, Alan, and Thomas Hauschild. "Auschwitz Jokes." In *Humour in Society: Resistance and Control*, edited by Chris Powell and George E. C. Paton, 56–66. London: Macmillan, 1988.
Epp, Michael. "Raising Mistrelsy: Humor, Satire and the Stereotype." *Birth of a Nation* and *Bamboozled*." *Canadian Review of American Studies* 33 (2003): 17–35.
Fermaglich, Kirsten. "Mel Brooks' *The Producers:* Tracing American Jewish Culture through Comedy, 1967–2007." *American Studies* 48, no. 4 (Winter 2007): 59–87.
Fiddler on the Roof. By Joseph Stein. Music by Jerry Bock. Lyrics by Sheldon Harnick. Imperial Theatre, New York. September 22 1964.
Fleishman, Philip. "Interview with Mel Brooks." *Maclean's*, April 17 1979. Accessed November 24 2016. *http://www.brookslyn.com*.
Foxman, Abraham H. *Jews and Money: The Story of a Stereotype.* New York: Palgrave MacMillan, 2010.
Gavin, James. *Intimate Nights: The Golden Age of New York Cabaret.* New York: Backstage Books, 2006.
Gilman, Sander L. "Is Life Beautiful? Can the Shoah be Funny? Some Thoughts on Recent and Older Films." *Critical Inquiry* 26, no. 2 (2000): 279–308.
Goebbels, Joseph. "Order Prohibiting Masters of Ceremonies and Commentary from the Stage." In *Cabaret Performance: Volume II: Europe 1920–1940: Sketches, Songs, Monologues, Memoirs*, edited by Laurence Senelick, 281–282. Baltimore: Johns Hopkins University Press, 1993.
Grosz, George. "Siegfried Hitler." *Die Pleite* 8, no. 1 (1923): cover.

Grunberger, Richard. *A Social History of the Third Reich.* London: Phoenix, 1983.
Hatch, Robert. "Films." *The Nation*, April 8 1968: 486.
Hillenbrand, F. K. M. *Underground Humour in Nazi Germany, 1933–1945.* London: Routledge, 1995.
Jelavich, Peter. *Berlin Cabaret.* Cambridge, MA: Harvard University Press, 1997.
Jenkins, Henry, Tara McPherson, and Jane Shattuc, eds. *Hop on Pop: The Politics and Pleasures of Popular Culture.* Durham, NC: Duke University Press, 2002.
Jewison, Norman. "'Norman Jewison': Filmmaker Documentary." In *Fiddler on the Roof*, MGM Home Entertainment, 2002, Disc two.
Kael, Pauline. "O, Pioneer!" *The New Yorker*, March 23 1968. Accessed November 23, 2016. http://www.newyorker.com/magazine/1968/03/23/o-pioneer.
Kaplan, Louis. "'It Will Get a Terrific Laugh': On the Problematic Pleasures and Politics of Holocaust Humor." In *Hop on Pop: The Politics and Pleasures of Popular Culture*, edited by Henry Jenkins, Tara McPherson, and Jane Shattuc, 343–356. Durham, NC: Duke University Press, 2002.
Kauffmann, Stanley. "Zero and Others." *New Republic*, April 13 1968.
King, Geoff. *Film Comedy.* London: Wallflower P, 2002.
Knapp, Raymond. *The American Musical and the Formation of National Identity.* Princeton: Princeton University Press, 2005.
Lareau, Alan. *The Wild Stage: Literary Cabarets of the Weimar Republic.* Columbia, SC: Camden, 1995.
"The Making of *The Producers*." In *The Producers*, directed by Mel Brooks. Optimum, 2008, DVD.
McDonald, Paul. "'They're Trying to Kill Me': Jewish American Humor and the War Against Pop Culture." *Studies in Popular Culture* 28, no. 3 (April 2006): 19–33. Accessed November 16 2016. http://www.jstor.org/stable/23416169.
Moshin, Jamie. "On the Big Screen, but Stuck in the Closet: What Mel Brooks' *The Producers* Says about Modern American Jewish Identity and Communicating the Holocaust." *Journal of the Northwest Communication Association* 35 (2006): 22–45.
Neale, Steve, and Frank Krutnik. *Popular Film and Television Comedy.* London: Routledge, 2000.
Parrish, Timothy, ed. *The Cambridge Companion to Philip Roth.* Cambridge, Eng.: Cambridge University Press, 2007.
Peschel, Lisa, ed. *Performing Captivity, Performing Escape: Cabarets and Plays from the Terezín/Theresienstadt Ghetto.* London: Seagull Books, 2014.
Pinsker, Sanford. "Mel Brooks and the Cinema of Exhaustion." In *From Hester Street to Hollywood*, edited by Sarah Blacher Cohen, 246. Bloomington: Indiana University Press, 1983.
Powell, Chris, and George E. C. Paton, eds. *Humour in Society: Resistance and Control.* London: Macmillan, 1988.
"Rainbow Flag." *The Alyson Almanac: A Treasury of Information for the Gay and Lesbian Community.* Boston: Alyson Publications, 1989.
Rickman, Gregg, ed. *The Film Comedy Reader.* New York: Limelight Editions, 2001.
Sarris, Andrew. "Films." *Village Voice*, March 28 1968: 47.
"Schlimazel." *Oxford Dictionary of English.* 3rd ed. 2010.

Senelick, Laurence. *Cabaret Performance: Volume II: Europe 1920–1940: Sketches, Songs, Monologues, Memoirs*. Translated by Laurence Senelick. Baltimore: Johns Hopkins University Press, 1993.

Shatzky, Joel. Introduction to *Theresienstadt: Hitler's Gift to the Jews*, by Norbert Troller, xviii-xxxvi. Chapel Hill, NC: University of North Carolina Press, 1991.

Silberstein, Laurence J. *Postzionism: A Reader*. New Brunswick, NJ: Rutgers University Press, 2008.

Sorce, Giuliana. "Hitler and Humor: Coming to Terms with the Past through Parody." *Global Media Journal* 5, no. 2 (2015). Accessed November 17 2016.

Swain, Joseph P. *The Broadway Musical: A Critical and Musical Survey*. Lanham, MD: Scarecrow, 2002.

Symons, Alex. "An Audience for Mel Brooks's *The Producers:* The Avant-garde of the Masses." *Journal of Popular Film and Television* 34, no. 1 (2006): 24–32. Accessed November 17 2016. http://www.tandfonline.com/doi/abs/10.3200/JPFT.34.1.24-32.

The Threepenny Opera. By Elisabeth Hauptmann. Music by Kurt Weill. Lyrics by Bertolt Brecht. Performed by Kurt Gerron. Theater am Schiffbauerdamm, Berlin. August 31 1928.

"Todlachen." Collins English-German Dictionary. Accessed February 27 2017.

Troller, Norbert. *Theresienstadt: Hitler's Gift to the Jews*. Chapel Hill, NC: University of North Carolina Press, 1991.

Walsh, Moira. "The Producers." *America*, April 6 1968.

West Side Story. By Arthur Laurents. Music by Leonard Bernstein. Lyrics by Stephen Sondheim. Winter Garden Theatre, New York. September 26 1957.

Yacowar, Maurice. *Method in Madness: The Comic Art of Mel Brooks*. New York: St. Martin's Press, 1981.

Zimmerman, Paul D. "The Mad Mad Mel Brooks." *Newsweek*, February 17 1975. Accessed November 29 2016. http://www.brookslyn.com.

Ziv, Avner. *Jewish Humor*. New Brunswick, NJ: Transaction, 1998.

Sebastian Kunze

The Cultural Heretic

Gustav Landauer as a Radical Writer

Introduction

Gustav Landauer (1870–1919), known as a Jewish-German anarchist, was not only a political critic, activist and, as he put it, an "anti-politician," but also a philosopher and a person entangled in the cultural scene in Germany. Landauer was more than just a radical anarchist, *ergo* a political figure, as this chapter will argue. His philosophical approach led him to a specific type of writing, his love of literature and theatre produced a certain kind of cultural critique, and his complex understanding of identity made him a unique person. In his time, it was not only Landauer who felt the need for self-assurance and was looking into the concept of identity, but also his contemporaries in Europe and around the world.[1]

In his novella *Arnold Himmelheber*, published in 1903, Landauer discusses the question of Jewish "identity".[2] In his novella, Landauer presents various "concepts of identity" and positions himself towards them; this gives an insight into Landauer's ideas about "Jewish identities" as well as his radical approaches, questions of self-perception, and the relationship between individual and society. I aim to identify Landauer's idea of "identity" and to distinguish it from other "identity concepts" in his time. Moreover, I am interested in Landauer as a radical writer; hence, I ask what kind of radical answer he gives to the question of modern "identity".

For this purpose, I need to explain what "radical" and "modernity" mean in this context. As John Murray Cuddihy argued, following Talcott Parsons, "modernity" is understood in this article as a process of differentiation, which is also an effect of secularization and capitalism. The differentiation, therefore, produced new situations for people who were living in the countries where this process took place: "It splits ownership from control (Berle and Means); it sep-

1 Philipp Blom, *Der taumelnde Kontinent: Europa 1900–1914 (The Reeling Continent: Europe 1900–1914)* (Munich: dtv, 2015), 12–13.

2 In this chapter I will use the terms "identity", "self-perception" and "self-identification" synonymously. For a critique of the "identity-concept" see Rogers Brubaker and Frederick Cooper, "Beyond 'Identity'," *Theory and Society* 29 (2000): 1–47.

https://doi.org/10.1515/9783110545753-014

arates church from state (the Catholic trauma), ethnicity from religion (the Jewish trauma); it produces the 'separated' or liberal state, a limited state that knows its 'place', differentiated from society."[3]

In the case of the Jewish "trauma," it raises the question of who we are. Who is a Jew and what does being Jewish mean if not being religiously observant?[4] A lot of Jews and non-Jews alike have tried in the following years to answer this question; it is still up for lively debate among Jews as well as non-Jews around the world.

Gustav Landauer approaches this question in his novella *Arnold Himmelheber.* He does this in a manner that I describe as radical. Etymologically, radical stems from the Latin word *radix*, which means "root" and in a wider sense "basis, ground, cause, origin". To use the common medical metaphor, Landauer does not want to discuss "symptoms" of the problem or question, but rather wants to combat the cause of the disease or, in our case, to give an answer concerning the causes of the posed question of modern "identity". That means, in short, Landauer uses everything he can to approach the question of Jewish "identity"; this includes the use in his story of murder, incest, and violence. This rather literal understanding of "radicalism" – i.e. getting to the root of a problem or question to resolve or answer it – provides me with a tool broad enough to scrutinize Landauer's novella.[5]

Moreover, I will analyze *Arnold Himmelheber* from this radical perspective, which enables me to read the non-conformism and taboo-breaking within Landauer's novella as part of his radical program in his search for answers. By breaking the chains of bourgeois morality, he can approach the concepts thoroughly and try to identify the self-conceptions of Jews without limitations in his thinking, for better or for worse.

I will briefly present Landauer's vita with a cultural impetus and then introduce the novella and some interpretations made by researchers in the past. Subsequently, I approach the novella through its main protagonists and neglected issues in the research; I will thereby be able to identify Landauer's perspective on identity in his time and according to his personal standpoint.

3 John Murray Cuddihy, *The Ordeal of Civility: Freud, Marx, Lévi-Strauss, and the Jewish Struggle with Modernity* (New York: Basic Books, 1974), 10.

4 On this issue there is a whole field of research; for an introduction see, for example, Michael A. Meyer, *Jewish Identity in the Modern World* (Seattle: University of Washington Press, 1990).

5 Here I utilize a rather simple but useful definition of radicalism. For an intensive discussion of this concept see the introduction to this volume.

A Cultural Intellectual in Historical Perspective

Gustav Landauer was born on April 7 1870, and lived with his family in Karlsruhe at the time of the so-called *Reichseinigung* (the German unification process, which came to an end in 1871). They belonged, as a bourgeois, rather assimilated Jewish family, to the middle class.[6] Thus, they were not only able to allow Gustav, the third son of the family, to pass his *Abitur* at the *Gymnasium* but also to study from 1888 onwards. Even as a teenager, he was interested in literature and music, which led him to his studies of philology, while also attending philosophical, economic, and literary studies seminars. Landauer began his studies in Heidelberg (1888–1889) and moved to Berlin (1889–1890; 1891–1892) as well as Strasbourg (1890–1891).[7] He did not finish his studies. Especially after the end of the *Sozialistengesetze* (Socialist Laws) (1878–1890), Landauer became increasingly politicized and engaged in the Social Democratic movement, as a lot of writers did at this time.[8] Landauer's friend Fritz Mauthner (1849–1923) introduced him to the literary circle of *Friedrichshagen*, which had a massive impact on the German cultural scene. Landauer belonged to the anarchistic circle there, whose members were influential, as anarchism was an interesting subject for most avant-garde writers.[9] Landauer was part of this intellectual circle, the *Naturalisten*, who tried to combine political activities within the social democrats with being literary intellectuals. They were part of the left-wing party opposition within the *Social Democratic Party of Germany* (SPD), which understood itself to be anarchistic. Therefore, they were excluded from the party convention in Erfurt in October 1891, which had a twofold outcome: first, the excluded founded the *Verein unabhängiger Sozialisten* (Association of Independent Socialists) in February 1892. Landauer joined them that year and positioned himself openly as an

---

6 Rolf Kauffeldt and Michael Matzigkeit, *Zeit und Geist: Kulturkritische Schriften 1890–1919 (Time and Spirit: Cultural Critic Writings 1890–1919)* (Munich: Boer, 1997), 345.

7 "Gustav Landauer Papers Nr. 7," n.d., ARCH00780, International Institute for Social History, Amsterdam.

8 Jens Malte Fischer, *Fin de Siècle. Kommentar zu einer Epoche (Fin de Siècle. Commentary on an Epoche)* (Munich: Winkler Verlag, 1978), 43.

9 Gertrude Cepl-Kaufmann, "Gustav Landauer Im Friedrichshagener Jahrzehnt und die Rezeption seines Gemeinschaftsideals nach dem I. Weltkrieg (Gustav Landauer in the Friedrichshagener Centenary and the Reception of His Community Ideas after the First World War)," in *Gustav Landauer Im Gespräch (Gustav Landauer in conversation)*, ed. Hanna Delf and Gert Mattenklott, Conditio Judaica 18 (Tübingen: M. Niemeyer, 1997), 235–236.

anarchist.[10] The second major outcome was that the intellectuals pulled out of the *Freie Volksbühne* (Free Peoples Theatre), a joint venture of the *Naturalisten* and the Social Democrats. They founded the *Neue Freie Volksbühne* (New Free Peoples Theatre) in October 1892, among them Gustav Landauer as well as well-known intellectuals such as Wilhelm Bölsche (1861–1939), Paul (1864–1945) and Bernhard Kampffmeyer (1867–1942), Fritz Mauthner and Bruno Wille (1860–1928). Landauer was part of the art committee (*künstlerische Leitung),* a position he held until 1917, even after the re-unification of the two theatres in 1913.[11]

His first novel, *Der Todesprediger* (*The Preacher of Death*), was published in 1893, and Landauer then began his work on the next novella, which was later published as *Arnold Himmelheber.*[12] During this time (1892) he corresponded with his early love Clara Tannhauser (1872–1935), who came from rural, more traditional Jewry, as did Ida Wolf (1871–1942), his girlfriend before Clara Tannhauser. In 1898 Landauer tried to employ Emile Zola's (1840–1902) tactic for a hairdresser, who had been convicted of murder but whom Landauer thought innocent. As he accused the investigating commissioner of counterfeiting evidence to obtain a resumption of the trial, Landauer was indicted. Landauer's witness, Moritz von Egidy (1847–1898), died before his testimony and Landauer was sentenced to several months' imprisonment, which he served from the end of 1899 to the beginning of 1900.[13]

During his incarceration, Landauer translated speeches by Meister Eckhart and copy-edited the first volume of his friend Fritz Mauthner's *Zur Kritik der Sprache.*[14] He also corresponded with Hedwig Lachmann (1865–1919), his later wife, whom he had met at the beginning of 1899.[15] After his imprisonment, in 1900, Landauer became involved in the *Neue Gemeinschaft* (New Community),

---

10 Barabra Eckle, "Die Berliner Jahre von 1892–1901 (The Berlin Years 1892–1901)," in *Gustav Landauer (1870–1919). Von der Kaiserstraße nach Stadelheim*, ed. Literarische Gesellschaft Karlsruhe (Eggingen: Edition Isele, 1994), 24.

11 Ibid., 26.

12 Gustav Landauer, "Der Todesprediger (The Preacher of Death)," in *Wortartist: Roman, Novelle, Drama, Satire, Gedicht, Übersetzung*, ed. Siegbert Wolf and Ausgewählte Schriften, vol. 8 (Lich/Hessen: Verlag Edition AV, 2014), 31–144; Gustav Landauer, *Arnold Himmelheber: Eine Novelle (Arnold Himmelheber: A Novella)*, ed. Philippe Despoix (Berlin: Philo, 2000).

13 Gustav Landauer, "Der Dichter als Ankläger (The Poet as Accuser)," in *Internationalismus*, ed. Siegbert Wolf, Ausgewählte Schriften, vol. 1 (Lich/Hessen: Verlag Edition AV, 2008), 62–68; Kauffeldt and Matzigkeit, *Zeit und Geist*, 349.

14 Fritz Mauthner, *Sprache und Psychologie (Language and Psychology), Beiträge zu Einer Kritik der Sprache* (Contributions to a Critique of Language), vol. 1 (Stuttgart: Cotta, 1901).

15 Kauffeldt and Matzigkeit, *Zeit und Geist*, 349–50.

a settlement project which grew out of the Friedrichshagen community, where he met Erich Mühsam (1878–1934) and Martin Buber (1878–1965), who both became good friends with Landauer, while Buber even became his literary executor.[16] Gustav Landauer left the *Neue Gemeinschaft* in 1901 and travelled with his future wife Hedwig Lachmann to England, where they lived and worked for almost a year.[17]

After returning to Germany in 1902 and, eventually, divorcing his first wife, Gustav Landauer and Hedwig Lachmann, who came from a traditional Jewish cantor family, married in May 1903.[18] In the same year, Landauer also published two books: firstly, the volume *Macht und Mächte (Power and Powers)*, which contained the novella *Arnold Himmelheber*; secondly, *Skepsis und Mystik: Versuche im Anschluss an Mauthners Sprachkritik* (*Skepticism and Mysticism: Attempts Following Mauthner's Critique of Language*).[19]

From this point on, Landauer's life began to rise intellectually. Besides his friendship with Martin Buber and his confrontation with Constantin Brunner and his philosophy, in 1907 he published, in a series edited by Buber, his *Geschichtsphilosophie* (philosophy of history), *Die Revolution.*[20] Therein Landauer drew up his philosophies of both history and revolution theory alike. Both determine his understanding of history as well as his political activities, which should lead to revolution. The basic principle of his philosophy is discontinuity. The past is continually updated according to the need and context of the act of speaking about history, and also through its speaker. History is, thus, subject to our will and our intentions: "We only know of the past what is our past; we understand of what has been only what concerns us today; we understand what has been only in the way we are; we understand it as our way."[21] The past and the future are to be understood as one, that is, the past is always shaped anew depending

---

16 Tilman Leder, *Die Politik eines 'Antipolitikers': Eine politische Biographie Gustav Landauers (The Politics of an 'Anti-Politician': A Political Biography of Gustav Landauer)*, Ausgewählte Schriften 10 (Lich/Hessen: Verlag Edition AV, 2014), 352.

17 Kauffeldt and Matzigkeit, *Zeit und Geist*, 350; Leder, *Antipolitiker*, 1: 357–64.

18 Leder, *Antipolitker*, 1: 369.

19 Gustav Landauer, *Macht und Mächte (Power and Powers)* (Berlin: E. Fleischel & Co., 1903); Gustav Landauer, "Skepsis und Mystik: Versuche im Anschluss an Mauthners Sprachkritik (Skepticism and Mysticism: Attempts Following Mauthners' Critique of Language)," in *Skepsis und Mystik: Versuche im Anschluss an Mauthners Sprachkritik*, ed. Siegbert Wolf, Ausgewählte Schriften 7 (Lich/Hessen: Verlag Edition AV, 2011), 39–128.

20 Gustav Landauer, *Die Revolution (The Revolution)*, ed. Siegbert Wolf (Münster: Unrast, 2003).

21 Ibid., 43 (translation mine): "Wir wissen von der Vergangenheit nur unsere Vergangenheit; wir verstehen von dem Gewesenen nur, was uns heute etwas angeht; wir verstehen das Gewesene nur so, wie wir sind; wir verstehen es als unseres Weg."

on the use of the past, which is subject to the intentions of the present. This changes the past, and it will become the future: "In other words, the past is not something finished, but something that is becoming. For us there is only way [i.e. process, SK], only future; the past is also future that is evolving with our moving on, that changes, that has been different."[22]

It turns out that Landauer positioned himself against the idea of progress in his time and, therefore, against a linear understanding of history, since this suggests a continuity that does not exist.[23] In his ideas, the postmodern concepts of construction and performativity resonate, but his counterproposal of the "foreign and neighboring history" is an expression of Eurocentric thinking. This suggestion, in turn, is to be understood as an expression of the connection of one's own people with others.[24]

In 1908 Landauer founded, in an attempt to realize his socialist ideas, the *Sozialistischen Bund* (Socialist Federation). Early members included Erich Mühsam as well as Martin Buber.[25] After lectures and translations in 1911, Landauer's political *Aufruf zum Sozialismus* (*Call to Socialism*) appeared,[26] in which he outlined his socialism: his starting point is the individual who must be convinced that the revolutionization of social relations is necessary. Only then could people join together in voluntary confederations and lead a socialist life.[27] Landauer relies on the peaceful change of human thought, since a violent revolution does not promise success. If people behave differently to each other, it is possible to dissolve the state, since Landauer understands the state as a social relationship between people.[28] Socialism is also a pattern of behavior which can be practiced, and is not only held together by Landauer's diffuse idea of *Geist* (spirit).[29]

22 Ibid. (translation mine): "Anders ausgedrückt heißt das, dass die Vergangenheit nicht etwas Fertiges ist, sondern etwas Werdendes. Es gibt für uns nur Weg, nur Zukunft; auch die Vergangenheit ist Zukunft, die mit unserem Weiterschreiten wird, sich verändert, anders gewesen ist."

23 Ibid., 45.

24 Ibid., 46–50.

25 Tilman Leder, *Die Politik eines 'Antipolitikers': Eine politische Biographie Gustav Landauers (The Politics of an 'Anti-Politician': A Political Biography of Gustav Landauer)*, Ausgewählte Schriften 2: 10 (Lich/Hessen: Verlag Edition AV, 2014), 421–433; 458–477.

26 Gustav Landauer, *Aufruf zum Sozialismus: Ein Vortrag (Call to Socialism: A Presentation)*, Ausgewählte Schriften 11 (Lich/Hessen: Verlag Edition AV, 2015).

27 Wolf Kalz, *Gustav Landauer: Ein deutscher Anarchist (Gustav Landauer: A German Anarchist)* (Bad Buchau: Federsee-Verlag, 2009), 176.

28 Ibid., 177–78.

29 Ibid., 178.

He aims at a federal system of voluntary associations, which he describes as a society of societies.[30]

While Europe was approaching the First World War, Landauer tried to issue warnings about the implications of a Great War. To prevent the imminent world war, Landauer engaged in the *Forte-Kreis* (Forte Circle), a circle of European intellectuals who wanted to set an example of international cooperation.[31] The circle, however, collapsed even before it was officially constituted, because of the First World War.[32]

At the request of Kurt Eisner (1867–1919), Landauer participated in the November Revolution in Bavaria as, among other things, a member of the *Revolutionary Workers' Council.*[33] Eisner's USPD (Minority-SPD) lost the elections conclusively in early 1919. On the way to Parliament on February 21, where Kurt Eisner was heading to step down as prime minister, he was assassinated by Anton Graf von Arco auf Valley (1897–1945). Gustav Landauer gave his obituary in Munich. The revolution, however, had not yet come to an end. Thus, Landauer was there when the first anarchist Soviet Republic was proclaimed on April 7 1919, in which he was to assume the office of Minister of Culture.[34] Only six days later, a communist *coup d'état* led to the establishment of a communist Soviet Republic. Landauer withdrew and lived with the widow of Kurt Eisner.[35] In the course of the conquest of Munich by counter-revolutionary government groups, Landauer was arrested on May 1 1919, and only one day later was brutally murdered by soldiers in Stadelheim prison.[36]

To sum up Landauer's life in a few pages and embed it into the historical context of the time proves to be difficult, in particular due to the diverse activities of Landauer. Therefore, this contextualization has been confined to the core data and ideas from Landauer's life and work as well as the rough historical developments of his time needed to better understand this chapter. The German Empire, which he had fought so hard against, finally perished. However, it took Landauer with it.

---

30 Landauer, *Aufruf zum Sozialismus*, 79.

31 Christine Holste, *Der Forte-Kreis (1910–1915): Rekonstruktion eines utopischen Versuchs (The Forte-Circle (1910–1915): Reconstruction of an Utopian Attempt)* (Stuttgart: M & P, 1992).

32 Kauffeldt and Matzigkeit, *Zeit Und Geist*, 352, as well as Holste, *Der Forte-Kreis (1910–1915).*

33 Leder, *Die Politik Eines 'Antipolitikers'* 2: 751–846.

34 Ibid., 2:819–24.

35 Ibid., 2:833–34.

36 Ibid., 2:840–46.

The Novella *Lebenskunst/Arnold Himmelheber*

In his novella *Arnold Himmelheber*, Gustav Landauer does not describe his own Jewish identity, instead showing his perspective on various identities, placing a strong focus on Jewish identity and exploring it. The novella is interesting as it offers an insight into Landauer's early thinking on this subject and the question of modernity manifested in the "identity question."

In research, Landauer's novella has been seldom noticed. Norbert Altenhofer only mentions it with one sentence,[37] while Thomas Regehly at least devotes a part of his article to it.[38] There is, however, an article on the novella by Lorenz Jäger from 1997,[39] as well as an epilogue written by Philippe Despoix in the 2000 revised edition of *Arnold Himmelheber.*[40] Despoix's epilogue was republished in 2015, translated into English and only linguistically adapted, in an anthology by Paul Mendes-Flohr.[41] The most recent and, to date, most extensive study of Landauer's novella is presented in Corinna Kaiser's chapter on *Arnold Himmelheber* in her book *Gustav Landauer als Schriftsteller* (*Gustav Landauer as Writer*).[42]

Reflections on the time of origin and the first publication can be found in Lorenz Jäger[43] and Philippe Despoix.[44] The time of origin is briefly mentioned

---

37 Norbert Altenhofer, "Tradition als Revolution. Gustav Landauers Geworden-Werdendes" Judentum," in *Jews and Germans from 1860 to 1933: The Problematic Symbiosis*, ed. David Bronsen (Heidelberg, 1979), 175–76.

38 Thomas Regehly, "'Stürmische Bekenntnisse.' Gustav Landauers literarische Arbeiten ('Tempestuous Confessions.' Gustav Landauers Literary Work)," in *Gustav Landauer im Gespräch (Gustav Landauer in conversation)*, ed. Hanna Delf and Gert Mattenklott (Tübingen: Max Niemeyer Verlag, 1997), 18–20.

39 Lorenz Jäger, "Der Herr des Lebens und der Anarchie. Zu Landauers Novelle 'Arnold Himmelheber' (The Master of Life and Anarchy. On Landauers Novella 'Arnold Himmelheber')," in *Gustav Landauer im Gespräch (Gustav Landauer in conversation)*, ed. Hanna Delf and Gert Mattenklott (Tübingen: Max Niemeyer Verlag, 1997), 1–10.

40 Philippe Despoix, "Konstruktion des Deutsch-Jüdischen. Gustav Landauer als Schriftsteller," in *Arnold Himmelheber: eine Novelle*, ed. Philippe Despoix (Berlin: Philo, 2000), 109–24.

41 Philippe Despoix, "Toward a German-Jewish Construct: Landauer's Arnold Himmelheber," in *Gustav Landauer: Anarchist and Jew*, ed. Paul Mendes-Flohr and Anya Mali (Berlin, Boston: De Gruyter, 2015), 121–31.

42 Corinna R. Kaiser, *Gustav Landauer als Schriftsteller: Sprache, Schweigen, Musik (Gustav Landauer as Writer: Language, Silence, Music)*, Conditio Judaica 81 (Berlin/Boston: De Gruyter, 2014).

43 Jäger, "Herr des Lebens," 1–2.

44 Despoix, "Konstruktion des Deutsch-Jüdischen," 110; Despoix, "Toward a German-Jewish Construct: Landauer's Arnold Himmelheber," 122.

in Altenhofer.[45] Corinna Kaiser not only corrects inaccuracies by the authors mentioned above but also criticizes Despoix in particular for dating the novel within Landauer's work around 1903, since this perspective neglects the years of origin between 1893 and 1895.[46]

Kaiser shows that Landauer wrote the novella or its predecessor *Lebenskunst* (*Art of Living*) during a prison term between November 1893 and September 1894; however, he could not finish it until summer 1895. Moreover, the novella was later published in a total of twenty episodes by *Der Sozialist* from October 1896 to June 1897.[47] For its publication in his volume *Macht und Mächte* (*Power and Powers*), Landauer worked on his novella, probably also in the light of the criticism of his late second wife, Hedwig Lachmann.[48] Kaiser presents the first detailed comparison of the two versions,[49] writing that in addition to minor changes, Landauer gives, on the one hand, a relativization of the incestuous relationship between Arnold Himmelheber and Lysa, as well as, on the other hand, justifications for the murder of Wolf Tilsiter, such as rape and violence in the marriage.[50] In 1903, the novella *Arnold Himmelheber* was published as part of the volume *Macht und Mächte* by publisher Egon Fleischel.[51]

In order to help the reader follow the interpretations and discussion in this article, I will provide a short summary of the novella. The text is divided into six chapters. The first two are declared to function as a prologue (*Vorspiel*) and the sixth as an epilogue (*Nachspiel*); accordingly, chapters three, four, and five can be called the main part. The individual chapters differ in their styles of writing according to the genre they are representing. Thus, the first and especially the second chapter have a very high proportion of direct speech, so that one can regard them as a drama. The third chapter, on the other hand, is very prosaic and is replaced in the fourth chapter by the form of an epistolary novel. "[I]dyllic love, [and] a phantasmagoric epilogue",[52] as Despoix puts it, follow in chapters five and six.

---

45 Altenhofer, "Tradition als Revolution," 175–76.

46 Kaiser, *Gustav Landauer Als Schriftsteller*, 204–9. Despoix, however, mentions the history of the novella in a chapter of an earlier book; see Philippe Despoix, *Ethiken der Entzauberung: zum Verhältnis von ästhetischer, ethischer und politischer Sphäre am Anfang des 20. Jahrhunderts (Ethics of Disenchantment: the Relationship between the esthetic, ethical and political Spheres at the Beginning of the 20th Century)* (Bodenheim: Philo, 1998).

47 Kaiser, *Gustav Landauer als Schriftsteller*, 208–9.

48 Ibid., 207.

49 Ibid., 362–77.

50 Ibid., 211.

51 Landauer, *Macht und Mächte (Power and Powers).*

52 Despoix, "Konstruktion des Deutsch-Jüdischen," 111.

In the first chapter, Ludwig Prinz returns home – after having passed his medical examination – to his "father" Arnold Himmelheber and his half-sister Suse, whom the father and then also Ludwig call Lysa. At the beginning of their reunion, Lysa makes him promise that he is not in love with her and imposes a ban on the love between the half-siblings. Both Arnold and Lysa Himmelheber are surprised by Ludwig's return but are happy about it.

The second chapter opens with the beginning of spring in the same year. Already retired, Arnold Himmelheber is treating a Jew from a nearby village, Schöneck, which is a two-hour walk away. Himmelheber inquires about old patients and learns about the son of a patient who has been married for eight years and has a very beautiful wife but no children. Later in the course of the chapter, Himmelheber and Ludwig have a conversation in which Ludwig talks about himself being unhappy. Himmelheber speaks a mystically encouraging speech and encourages him to enjoy his life. In the subtext, this does not rule out adultery, so at the end of the chapter, he presents him with a fake prescription: "Rec. / Youth, light-heartedness (much). / Force. / Thirst, Beauty / Aqu. vitae distillate. In the morning and evening a spoon full. / Dr. Himmelheber."[53]

This scene ends the prologue, and the third chapter, the first of the main part, tells the story of Judith Tilsiter. The village of Schöneck and its Jewish population are described with harsh words and anti-Semitic clichés. Judith lives in this place with her husband, the cattle trader Wolf Tilsiter, under whom she suffers a lot. Both belong to the Jewish population. She also remembers her childhood and, above all, her encounter with the Christian boy Ludwig Prinz, the goose shepherd and village idiot. At the end of the chapter, Judith argues with her husband and, eventually, replies to an anonymous advertisement in the newspaper, which reads as follows: "Looking for a woman. Letters poste restante / cipher 1–2–3 -Free."[54] After reading this advertisement, she dreams of her past with the goose shepherd and then decides to write.

The ensuing fourth chapter documents the correspondence between Judith and Ludwig; this is done, as the title of the chapter suggests, "in letters of new-fashioned people"[55] and thus adopts the form of an epistolary novel. In these letters, Ludwig and Judith become acquainted, though under their pseudonyms of Ludwig and Ida. In their letters, both approach each other and discover

---

53 Landauer, *Arnold Himmelheber*, 38 (translation mine): "Rec. / Jugend, Leichtsinn (viel). / Kraft. / Durst, Schönheit / Aqu. vitae destillat. / Morgens und abends ein Löffel voll. / Dr. Himmelheber".

54 Ibid., 52 (translation mine): "Eine Frau / wird gesucht. Briefe postlagernd / Chiffre 1–2–3 -Frei."

55 Ibid., 55.

similarities. Judith feels her thoughts and ideas have been understood – for the first time in her life. In the penultimate letter, Ludwig finally tells his story and reveals his full name. He describes in detail the meeting and the time spent with Judith. In the following letter, "Ida" writes very briefly and arranges a meeting in the forest. She is assured that it is her old love.

On the day of the scheduled meeting, the fifth chapter begins. At the beginning, a storm rages, which descends in the course of the chapter and then blows over at the end. Ludwig and Judith meet in the forest, where it is raining and is already stormy. Since Judith already knows about Ludwig's identity, she reveals herself to him quickly. The love of the two rekindles again immediately; they look for protection against the weather during the storm in a cave and, eventually, shelter there, after having sex. They decide to come together again, despite Judith's marriage, and that they will elope, if there is no other option. With the mutual promises made to each other, the two separate to return to their homes. Herewith the last chapter of the main part ends.

The sixth chapter, marked as an epilogue, is the climax and end point of the novel. It starts with Ludwig and Judith meeting again for the first time after their encounter in the woods. Judith waits with Lysa in the garden of Arnold Himmelheber. Wolf Tilsiter, Judith's husband, is having surgery, as he was pushed out of bed by Judith when he tried to rape her. Wolf dies during the surgery, as is described later, during the chloroforming by Arnold Himmelheber. He confesses to murder by signaling that the death of Wolf was intentional. Judith is pregnant – not by her husband, however, but by Ludwig. Still at her husband's deathbed, she asks her lover whether he is her own – Prinz affirms this, and Himmelheber marries the two.

At the end of the book, Himmelheber, Lysa, Judith, and Ludwig undress. They sit in the garden and drink wine, seamlessly following the previous action. Himmelheber (murder) and Judith (adultery) confess their sins. Lysa also expresses her relationship with her father (incest). After her confession, she is not well and eventually breaks down. That night Lysa dies, and in the morning there are two corpses in Himmelheber's home.[56]

Interpretations

Three attempts have been made so far to interpret the novella of Landauer as a whole. "Revolution" is the leitmotif of Lorenz Jäger's article. At the beginning,

---

56 Ibid., 105.

Jäger analyses the relationship between Ludwig Prinz and Judith Tilsiter, especially since both still think about each other and neither have forgotten the other. Afterwards, Jäger focuses briefly on the motif of nudity and then introduces the revolutionary motif.[57] On the one hand, Jäger shows a parallel between the nude motif and ideas on paradise through Sigmund Freud's theory of dream interpretation.[58] On the other hand, he presents Himmelheber as an impulse of life and revolution. At the center of it stands his voice, on which Jäger writes that "Landauer could not think of a revolution other than as the work of a voice which has no boundaries."[59] The novella, for Jäger, is a metaphor of a possible revolution because Landauer's book on the French Revolution is similar in its dramaturgical structure to the Himmelheber novella.[60] At the end of his analysis, Jäger comes to another subject: the language of the character Lysa. Her voice and her articulation are presented as a medicine, with which Lysa's singing and rhyming is justified in the novel.[61] In Jäger's analysis of the novella *Arnold Himmelheber*, the themes of anti-Semitism and Judaism do not play a role.

In his epilogue, which he later republished as an article, Philippe Despoix interprets Landauer's text under the premise of placing Landauer as a writer in the foreground, which was unusual.[62] His perspective on the text is one of a to be found "German-Jewishness". Despoix tries to put Landauer's novella into the context of a work-historical context and embeds it with his oeuvre into a whole Jewish generation:

> Yet *Arnold Himmelheber* is also a truly significant work, albeit for reasons which lie beyond purely aesthetic considerations. It represents a search for a genre that experiments with a blending of translation, literary prose and philosophical reflection. This singular quest links Landauer not only with his close friends Mauthner and Buber, but also with a whole generation of German-Jewish intellectuals. But the utopia of a "lawless life," the fantasy pursued in *Himmelheber*, also refers to a relationship between German and Jewish culture, which is distinctive of Landauer's work in general.[63]

---

57 Jäger, "Herr des Lebens."

58 Ibid., 3.

59 Ibid., 5 (translation mine): "Landauer [...] sich die Revolution nicht anders denken [konnte] denn als das Werk einer Stimme, vor der keine Grenzen mehr Bestand haben.".

60 Ibid., 7–8.

61 Ibid., 9–10.

62 Despoix, "Toward a German-Jewish Construct: Landauer's Arnold Himmelheber," 121.

63 Ibid., 122–123.

In addition to this context, Despoix also breaks down the genre mix of the novella and reveals that more than "the experiment with literary form, it is the choice of subject matter which makes this work unique."[64] He then highlights a profanization of Jewish and Christian religion within the novel by, on the one hand, the desecration of the name of God by its classification as a contingency and, on the other, by Landauer reversing the words of Jesus, that he and the father are one, and, in Lysa's case, that she and the mother would be one. For Despoix, these are expressions of "Landauer's *Kulturkampf* against monotheism."[65] Despoix justifies blasphemy by saying that Ludwig and Judith must be innocent in order to be able to commit themselves to a new existence.[66] Thus, it is possible for Landauer to present Wolf Tilsiter as religious and bourgeois, and Ludwig and Judith as new men. The nakedness at the end of the novella justifies and completes the ritual of the transition.[67] After this first analysis and interpretation, Despoix introduces Hedwig Lachmann's rejection of the novella and the dispute between Landauer and his late second wife. Considerations of other friends, such as Fritz Mauthner, are also presented. Landauer's naked, incestuous end of the story, in particular, offended them. It broke several taboos of its time.[68] Despoix also addressed the representation of Jews in the novella: "The strong rejection of conventional Jewish life is brought to bear exclusively on the figure of the merchant Tilsiter. Here, Landauer plays an ambiguous way with the anti-Jewish clichés of the time. Certainly no trace of his critique is to be found in the figure of Judith, who is also Jewish."[69]

Referring to the death scene of Wolf Tilsiter, Despoix describes an affirmation of his Jewish origin:

> And just when she learns of her husband's death, the midsummer's night procession and the singing of the words "Be glad, daughter of Zion," can be heard in the background. As if hallucinating, she then perceives the words "rejoice, Jerusalem." Himmelheber's words, which had been profanatory up to this point, have suddenly reversed their meaning. A joyful affirmation of life as well as of its Jewish origins is articulated here.[70]

64 Ibid., 123.
65 Ibid., 124.
66 Ibid., 125.
67 Ibid., 125.
68 Ibid., 125–26.
69 Ibid., 127.
70 Ibid., 127.

Since Ludwig is described as of "German Christian"[71] origin by Despoix, he concludes that the "prerequisite for the construction of a new human generation, then, has a definite German-Jewish connection."[72] Constellations characterized as incestuous relationships are doomed by Landauer; "there is only one feasible future constellation, namely one in which there is a pairing of feminine-Jewish and the masculine-Christian elements, and in which, both the Jewish and Christian religions are dispensed with."[73] Himmelheber is characterized as a Faustian figure, and this is also his position in the novella. The end, Despoix argues, is more an affirmation of life as it turns towards apocalyptic-messianic expectations:

> Landauer seems to have been aware of the dangerous flip-side of anomism. But he was too Nietzschean to let his depiction of the transgression of the law take on a messianic, or even apocalyptic dimension – as was the case with Dostoevsky. In Landauer, there is a positive attitude with regard to life that surpasses the pure negation of the law. The ending of *Arnold Himmelheber* is mystical in the sense that it presents *not* some collective eschatology, but rather an ecstatic, Dionysian eros as the agent of life and death.[74]

With the help of the Freudian dream interpretation, Despoix shows that Landauer turns against the motif of the classical father figure by letting Himmelheber's relationship with his daughter be incestuous and directing his violence outwards.[75] However, he poses a crucial question: how does Landauer's aesthetic utopia change after his reception of Buber's Chassidic writings? Despoix writes: "There was certainly a shift in emphasis, as Landauer now began to articulate a positive stance toward Jewish culture – without this changing in any fundamental way his view of a necessary bipolar, German-Jewish alliance."[76] Despoix thus embeds the novella in Landauer's later life, without any conclusions being drawn from the novella itself. Hence, Despoix speaks of the fact that Landauer finds in Buber's writings the counter-image of Himmelheber, and that, for Landauer, a thinking understood as "feminine" is essential for the renewal of Jewish "identity"[77]:

71 Ibid., 127.
72 Ibid., 127.
73 Ibid., 127.
74 Ibid., 127–28.
75 Ibid., 128.
76 Ibid., 129.
77 Ibid., 130.

> In positing his aesthetic utopia of a crossing of elements from the Jewish and German cultural traditions – and this was one of the reasons he distanced himself from any metaphorics of purity – Landauer took up a most singular position between Mauthner on the one hand, and Buber on the other. Landauer showed no desire to repress Jewish culture [...] Yet Judaism could not become the basic core of his identity, as it had for Buber. This also explains why Landauer distanced himself from a cultural Zionism, which might become too strongly tied to the "ground" (*Boden*).[78]

His interpretation is severely questioned by Corinna Kaiser. In particular, she argues against the fact that Judith is drawn without anti-Semitic stereotypes and instead points to the stereotype of the "'beautiful Jewess'."[79]

Kaiser concentrates on Lysa's singing and, in particular, on its claimed power to heal,[80] as well as the interdependencies between Lysa's singing and the characters of Himmelheber and Prinz.[81] Kaiser rejects the German-Jewish connection and Despoix's positive perspective on the novella:

> The language barrier between the "'beautiful Jewess'" Judith, who remains unredeemed in spite of all the education, Wagnerian concerts, and books, and the illiterate German Ludwig, who had so effortlessly succeeded within only eight years in what the emancipation of Jews in Europe had not in more than a hundred years, that is to become part of the European cultural and linguistic community with every fiber, no longer being subject to restrictions of access and discrimination, raises justified doubts as to whether sustainable means, according to Despoix, "a constellation in which the female-Jewish and the male-German pair, simultaneously dismiss the Jewish as well as the Christian religion."[82]

Hence, Kaiser moves on to analyze and interpret the character of Judith. With the name "Judith", Landauer refers to the Jewish tradition in the form of the popular apocryphal book *Judith*. Although Landauer's Judith and her husband are described as Jewish and married synagogically, they are not credited with any religiosity.

---

78 Ibid.

79 Kaiser, *Gustav Landauer als Schriftsteller*, 226.

80 Ibid., 218.

81 Ibid., 218–19.

82 Ibid., 226 (translation mine): "Die Sprachbarriere zwischen der schönen Jüdin Judith, die trotz aller Bildung, WagnerKonzerte und Bücher unerlöst bleibt, und dem illiteraten Deutschen Ludwig, dem so scheinbar mühelos in nur acht Jahren das gelang, was die Emanzipation der Juden in Europa in hundert Jahren nicht erreicht hatte, nämlich mit jeder Faser Teil der europäischen Kultur- und Sprachgemeinschaft zu werden und keinen Zugangsbeschränkungen und Diskriminierungen mehr zu unterliegen, wirft berechtigte Zweifel auf, ob als zukunftsfähig nur, wie Despoix meint, eine Konstellation [erscheint], in der sich weiblich-Jüdisches und männlich-Deutsches paare und zugleich die jüdische wie die christliche Religion verabschiedet werden."

Kaiser sees the pseudonym "Ida", which Judith uses in the letters, on the one hand as a distancing from herself as Judith and, on the other hand, with reference to an earlier chapter of her book, as a biographical reference to Landauer's early love Ida Wolf.[83] In contrast to her ancient model, Landauer's Judith did not save her people, but only wanted to save her own life. However, this Judith, in contrast to her ancient namesake, persists with an attitude of waiting, awaiting a savior who appears in the form of Ludwig Prinz and Arnold Himmelheber.[84] With regard to, among other things, the creation of a kind of new religion by Himmelheber, including Judith's "conversion", Kaiser classifies the novella as a typical conversion novel and as a beautiful Jewess text.[85] Here, however, no one converts to Christianity, but to Himmelheber's new religion.[86]

Kaiser, then, shows how Jews are portrayed in Landauer's novella and stresses at the beginning of the section that Landauer only serves anti-Semitic stereotypes.[87] Kaiser highlights this assumption with the description of the village of Schöneck, which is peppered with anti-Semitic stereotypes:[88]

> The use of anti-Semitic stereotypes and comparisons, which do not show any distancing but rather culminate in its elimination, is disturbing in this novel by Landauer, and Despoix's reference to a statement made by Landauer in 1913 in which he argued against baptism for Jews [...] is ahistorical, as he skips almost twenty years. Rather, two of Landauer's perceptions of Judaism intersect: his politically motivated critique of capitalism, for which he uses the anti-Semitic stereotype of the "trading Jew", and his confession to Judaism, which he seeks to detach from this criticism.[89]

The scene at the end of the novella, in which Lysa hears the song of the *Johannisumzug* and in her own ears the song *Tochter Zion* (Daughter Zion), is regarded

---

83 Ibid., 226–27.
84 Ibid., 228.
85 Ibid., 230.
86 Ibid., 230.
87 Ibid., 231.
88 Ibid., 232–33.
89 Ibid., 235 (translation mine): "Der Gebrauch antisemitischer Stereotype und Vergleiche, die keinerlei Distanzierung erkennen lassen, sondern in der Elimination gipfeln, verstört in dieser Novelle Landauers, und Despoix' Verweis auf eine Aussage Landauers von 1913, in der er sich gegen Judentaufen aussprach [...] ist a-historisch, da er fast zwanzig Jahre überspringt. Vielmehr treffen hier zwei Wahrnehmungen Landauers vom Judentum zusammen: seine politisch motivierte Kapitalismuskritik, für die er sich des antisemitischen Stereotyps des Börsenjudentums bedient, und sein eigenes Bekenntnis zum Judentum, das er von dieser Kritik abzuspalten sucht."

by Kaiser as the second central intermediate event of the novella.[90] The sources of the Daughter Zion song, such as the books of the prophets Zephaniah and Zechariah, are important to Kaiser's interpretation. Judith recognizes at this point "what Himmelheber had just accomplished, namely, the clearing-up of her enemy, her Jewish husband Wolf Tilsiter. Through this reference Arnold Himmelheber is, thus, called the Messiah."[91] Himmelheber is conceived as the Messiah of his new religion, which is celebrated in the final scene – naked in the garden:

> Several linguistic crises and forms of language skepticism, but also testimonies of faith in a power of language, combine in Landauer's *Lebenskunst / Arnold Himmelheber* with anti-Semitic stereotypes, represented by the "eternal Jew", Wolf Tilsiter and his wife, the "beautiful Jewess", Judith Tilsiter, born Schammes, and are also a textual as well as a structural feature of the novella.[92]

Finally, Kaiser notes that Landauer's use of anti-Semitic stereotypes reveals not only his reception of Nietzsche and Wagner but also an insecurity of the Jewish self and its position in society. Moreover, she rejects the positive interpretations of the novella by Despoix, as well as Altenhofer's assertion that there is no Jewish issue in Landauer's novella.[93]

Despite her focus on intermediality, Kaiser contributes a great deal to the deciphering and interpretation of *Arnold Himmelheber*. In particular, her distinctions from the interpretation of Despoix are not only insightful but also helpful for the subsequent interpretation of this work.

Arnold Himmelheber: An Alternative Approach

Both Despoix and Kaiser have strong and sometimes even contradictory points in their interpretations, but I think a synthesis of both approaches is possible and necessary, because, despite the anti-Semitic stereotypes, a positive attitude

90 Ibid., 235–36.

91 Ibid., 238 (translation mine): "[...] was Himmelheber soeben vollbracht hatte, nämlich das Hinwegräumen ihres Feindes, ihres jüdischen Ehemannes Wolf Tilsiter. Arnold Himmelheber wird also mittels des Verweises zum Messiah ausgerufen."

92 Ibid., 242 (translation mine): "Mehrere Sprachkrisen und Formen der Sprachbezweiflung, zugleich aber auch Zeugnisse des Glaubens an eine Sprachmacht, treffen in Landauers Lebenskunst/Arnold Himmelheber mit antisemitischen Stereotypen, repräsentiert durch den Ewigen Juden Wolf Tilsiter und seine Frau, die Schöne Jüdin Judith Tilsiter, geborene Schammes, zusammen und sind inhaltliches wie strukturelles Kennzeichen der Novelle."

93 Ibid., 245.

towards Jewish "identity" can be seen in Landauer's text. However, it is not the traditional religious way of life of rural Jewry. In addition, some details need to be elaborated, mainly because of their actuality and usability. Kaiser's study is used as the main reference. Moreover, I will point to Landauer's radicalism which can also be seen in this novella.

The starting point of my interpretation is the assumption that Landauer is looking in his text for a possible "identity" or "self-identification" for a modern Jew. Here, following the text of Despoix, Landauer was "on the search for a genre whose field of experimentation included both the transmission, the literary prose, and the philosophical reflection"[94] with a whole generation of German-Jewish intellectuals, such as, among others, Martin Buber and Fritz Mauthner.[95]

My approach is to scrutinize the characters and to use them as tools for my analysis of the novella. Five relevant characters play a major role in Landauer's novella. Arnold Himmelheber is the eponymous and main character of the novella. At the time of the story, he is sixty-two years old, strongly built, with a grey beard.[96] Ludwig Prinz describes him as a man with "a healthy redness around his cheekbones and with a brightening eye under his forehead".[97] This positive image is rounded off by a beautiful bass voice.[98] Although Himmelheber is referred to as Satan and as in league with the devil, which is mentioned in the research literature several times,[99] Prinz calls him a role model who "inhales life through all his pores and exhales happiness".[100] In addition, he uses his medical abilities at the service of people who apparently do not want to go to any other doctor; hence, he helps a Jew from the countryside who has come to him, even though he is already retired. Himmelheber also does not take any payment; he even inquired after a former patient.[101] Therefore, he appears to have a duty-minded and solidary character. It must, however, not be withheld that after his patient left, Himmelheber denounces all rural Jews as pigs.[102] There is no apparent reason for it, and no explanation is given; it is also the only direct verbal insinuation of Jews by Himmelheber. In the research literature there is a neglect-

94 Despoix, "Konstruktion des Deutsch-Jüdischen," 111.

95 Ibid., 111.

96 Landauer, *Arnold Himmelheber*, 20, 27, 72.

97 Ibid., 72 (translation mine): "[...] eine[r] gesunde[n] Röte um die Backenknochen und mit Glanzaugen unter der Stirn [...]".

98 Ibid., 19.

99 Ibid., 21, 36.

100 Ibid., 58 (translation mine): "[...] durch alle Poren Leben saugt und Glück ausatmet [...]".

101 Ibid., 25–26.

102 Ibid., 126.

ed passage of the novella, which is described shortly before the visit of his patient: "[Himmelheber] lay one afternoon in his rocking chair in the study [...] smoking and slowly thinking while reading a thick book. His body was wrapped in a dressing-gown, his head was covered by a round cap of light-green velvet, and his feet by light slippers of gritty, very thin sheepskin."[103] It becomes clear that Himmelheber himself is Jewish. In my opinion, he is wearing a *Kippah* and the "thick book" that he is reading from could easily be a *Tanakh*. It is a small detail but, in my opinion, a decisive one, as it would contradict Corinna Kaiser's assertion that Himmelheber is not Jewish.[104] Hence, it is not a non-Jew who kills the Jew Tilsiter, but rather a different, *new* Jew who does. Himmelheber is conceived by Kaiser as the Messiah of a new religion, in which the old Jew is extinguished and a new one emerges, away from Jewish tradition.[105] However, the fact that Himmelheber is himself a Jewish character shows that this new religion does not have to split off from its Jewish part or to discard it altogether. Himmelheber is rather the embodiment of a new Jewishness, a notion that Landauer later develops. Here, too, it must be pointed out that in the novella Christianity is portrayed as a community in Landauer's sense of the word, as expressed in his political writings until 1908; that means Christianity was the embodiment of a spirit between humans and, in a way, as a spiritual community. However, it is essential that the Jewish motif did not develop with Landauer's reading of Buber, but is already clearly present in the character of Arnold Himmelheber. It is important to ask what Himmelheber's function in the novella is. Certainly, his name – Himmel-heber, meaning "heaven-lifter," shows us that he is a mediator not only between the old and the new, but also between Ludwig Prinz and Judith Tilsiter. Moreover, he is the bearer of an idea for a new society. Likewise, he is the mediator between Judith and her husband Wolf – by killing the latter, he thereby completes his mediation between Ludwig and Judith.

Lysa or Suse is hardly described physically. At the end of the novel, one can read that she is "delicate and slender."[106] Moreover, the reader learns at the beginning of the novella about the intimate relationship between Lysa and her father Arnold, which is already hinted to be an incestuous relationship,[107] but Lysa

103 Ibid., 24 (translation mine): "[Himmelheber] lag eines Nachmittags in seinem Schaukelstuhl im Studierzimmer [...] rauchend und langsam-nachdenklich in einem dicken Buche lesend. Um den Leib hatte er einen Schlafrock, auf dem Kopfe ein rundes Käppchen aus hellgrünem Samt und an den Füßen leichte Pantoffeln aus grellrotem, sehr dünnem Schafleder."

104 Kaiser, *Gustav Landauer als Schriftsteller*, 233.

105 Ibid., 238.

106 Landauer, *Arnold Himmelheber*, 90 (translation mine): "zart und schlank".

107 Ibid., 23–24.

does not want to make it public.[108] Eventually, one only learns that Lysa suffers from a disease that is said to be related to the heart.[109] Moreover, she seems to be extremely devoted to her father, towards whom she cannot take any opposition and who she always wants to please. For example, when Ludwig ate all the cake, Lysa brings him cigars as a substitute.[110] Since she is a half-orphan and little is known about her, Lysa appears unhistorical, unlike Ludwig and Judith. Kaiser has written extensively on her singing and its function in the novella in her PhD thesis.[111] Here, I would like to point out that Lysa could also represent the character of a *femme fragile*, as Walter Fähnders explains: she is shown as aesthetically pleasing, pale and very delicate – qualities we find in the description of Lysa. However, her character could also be understood as a *femme enfant*, which is also constructed as being directed to the sexual seduction of men.[112]

Ludwig Prinz is a twenty-six-year-old doctor, who has just passed his final medical exam examination, unusually fast.[113] Physically, Ludwig is scarcely described; he carries a pince-nez and appears to be an averagely trained young man.[114] In addition to Judith and Wolf Tilsiter, Prinz openly talks about his religion. Born as a Christian in the countryside, whose parents died and relatives had no interest in him, he grows up in nature with a shepherd and becomes the goose-shepherd of a village.[115] The almost negligible physical description of Ludwig is opposed to the elaborate presentation of his inner world. Thus, he talks with Arnold Himmelheber about his love affair and confesses that he wants a fulfilling relationship. It turns out that Judith, the early love of Prinz, is the standard that all other women have to stand up against.[116] It is more interesting, however, that Landauer describes how Prinz, after the love of his youth left him, wanted to commit suicide. It was suddenly important to him to leave something, a letter, to Judith, that he was not able to write. He hence set out for the city, where he was picked up by Himmelheber and, eventually, trained. Through the lessons, Prinz lost the desire to die.[117] He was saved by Himmelheber, who gave him a different life: Prinz refers to it in a letter to Judith as a "second

108 Ibid., 27.
109 Ibid., 14.
110 Ibid., 27.
111 Kaiser, *Gustav Landauer als Schriftsteller*, 129–216.
112 Walter Fähnders, *Avantgarde und Moderne 1890–1933 (Avant-Garde and Modernity 1890–1933)* (Stuttgart, Weimar: J. B. Metzler, 2010), 112.
113 Landauer, *Arnold Himmelheber*, 14, 21.
114 Ibid., 77.
115 Ibid., 67–68.
116 Ibid., 31–32.
117 Ibid., 71–72.

birth", which changed him fundamentally. He was born "once as a living being, as a part of wild nature, and later as a human being, as a member of the great community of culture."[118] Nevertheless, Prinz feels excluded from Christianity, his apparent culture of origin: "Outside in the old world, there are communities; these church bells – I can no longer enjoy their sounds aesthetically since I have painfully realized that they mean something – for an infinite crowd of people who belong together, who understand each other. We, however, are excluded."[119]

Although Ludwig entered the European cultural world,[120] he is excluded. Ludwig speaks in the form of a collective "we", but as a more or less secular person; this "we" neither means Jewish nor Christian. This is especially because they hear church bells and give a certain meaning to it. Perhaps he already feels connected to a new world, a different community, which, however, does not exist yet. In my opinion, it is a premonition of the new connection with Judith and an evolving new community. Landauer will later develop this idea of a new community:[121] he will call it "a becoming nation"[122] and "grown-becoming".[123] However, the "new" does not appear to be realizable on its own, which is why Prinz needs a female counterpart, Judith, who also considers him to be her savior.[124]

Judith Tilsiter is described as a young woman whose beauty is unusual and who is getting more beautiful every year.[125] She is not described in detail; the reader only learns in the last chapter that she is "rich and full".[126] She has been married to Wolf Tilsiter for eight years and lives in a village inhabited by Christians and Jews.[127] To get out of her village, Breitenau, in which she feels

---

118 Ibid., 66 (translation mine): "[...] einmal als lebendiges Wesen, als ein Stück wilde Natur, und später noch als Mensch, als Mitglied der großen Gemeinschaft der Kultur.".

119 Ibid., 59 (translation mine): "Draußen in der alten Welt, da gibt es Gemeinschaften; diese Kirchenglocken – ich kann ihre Klänge auch nicht mehr ästhetisch genießen, seit es mir schmerzvoll zum Bewußtsein gekommen, daß sie etwas bedeuten – für eine unendliche Menschenschar, die zusammengehören, die einander verstehen. Wir aber sind ausgeschlossen."

120 Ibid., 73.

121 Gustav Landauer, "Durch Absonderung zur Gemeinschaft (Through Isolation to Community)," in *Skepsis und Mystik: Versuche im Anschluss an Mauthners Sprachkritik*, ed. Siegbert Wolf, Ausgewählte Schriften 7 (Lich/Hessen: Verlag Edition AV, 2011), 131–47.

122 Gustav Landauer, "Sind das Ketzergedanken? (Are These Heretical Thoughts?)," in *Philosophie und Judentum*, Ausgewählte Schriften 5 (Lich/Hessen: Verlag Edition AV, 2012), 365 (translation mine): "eine werdende Nation".

123 Ibid., 368 (translation mine): "Geworden-werdendes".

124 Landauer, *Arnold Himmelheber*, 76.

125 Ibid., 41.

126 Ibid., 90 (translation mine): "üppig und voll".

127 Ibid., 25, 39.

constricted, she finally marries Wolf and lives with him in the town of Schöneck, which, however, equals hers.[128] In addition, she has the urge to be different from her surroundings.[129]

Her honeymoon leads Judith to the capital, where she comes into contact with culture, especially with art and the music of Richard Wagner (1813–1883). After her return, she begins to read the books she received for her wedding. However, she hides her *Bildung* (education) from her husband.[130] Here, we see an alienation of Judith from her husband, but also from her former self. Without realizing it, she also enters the European cultural world. Judith is not depicted as particularly Jewish. She neither seems to do any particular housework in this regard, nor are her external characteristics attributed to a Jewish stereotype (regarding the motif of the beautiful Jewess, see below). It could also be argued that Landauer possibly played with the motif of a *femme fatale,* which was in quite common use at this time.[131] In a letter to Ludwig, she even appears rather arrogant: "But I will not; I do not believe in any hidden providence; not even blind coincidence."[132] As honest as she is here, she does not make any illusions about the circumstances from which she would like to break out again.[133] It is unusual that she gives herself a pseudonym when she writes her letters to Prinz. Corinna Kaiser referred to the name of Landauer's young love Ida Wolf,[134] who, in my opinion, became Judith and Wolf Tilsiter, because the pseudonym of Judith and the first name of her husband merge in the name, Ida Wolf. It is remarkable, however, that his relationship with Ida Wolf ended in 1891 and his work on the novella began two years later.[135] Thus, an image of rural Jewry, which Landauer evokes in his novel, seems for him to be closely connected with Ida Wolf.

The character of Wolf Tilsiter is depicted negatively in the novella. Wolf has been married to Judith for eight years, but they do not have children yet.[136] He is presented as Jewish and has, as Kaiser shows, a classic Jewish name for his time.[137] Wolf works as a cattle trader in the village of Schöneck and is rather

128 Ibid., 41–42.
129 Ibid., 42.
130 Ibid., 47–49.
131 Walter Fähnders, *Avantgarde und Moderne*, 111.
132 Landauer, *Arnold Himmelheber*, 56.
133 Ibid., 56.
134 Kaiser, *Gustav Landauer als Schriftsteller*, 227.
135 Ibid., 105–6.
136 Landauer, *Arnold Himmelheber*, 25.
137 Kaiser, *Gustav Landauer als Schriftsteller*, 240, footnote 157.

practically-minded, since he also uses his honeymoon to do some trade deals.[138] At the beginning, Wolf behaves differently towards Judith, as she had a positive impression of him. However, she was soon disappointed. Starting with the wedding night, Wolf is described increasingly negatively, first as "raw, silly, presumptuous, without any momentum, greedy and low",[139] then even as a "raw animal, no, worse than [an] animal, [...] [a] degenerate human being."[140] These descriptions of Wolf have rightly been characterized as anti-Semitic stereotypes in all research literature. Thus, Wolf apparently has the task, on the one hand, to be the flip side of Judith, and, on the other hand, to represent an old and uncultivated world as well as rural Jewry. In addition, he serves in the story as a justification for adultery, in particular through his violent nature, which ultimately also relativizes his murder.[141]

Kaiser not only shows that Wolf receives anti-Semitic attributions, but that his wife Judith is depicted as the reverse, representing a different, opposite stereotype. Since it is not necessary to repeat what can be read in the study of Kaiser, an attempt is made to interpret the depictions differently.[142] Despoix's solution is that a new form emerges from the combination of "the feminine-Jewish and the masculine-Christian".[143] According to Kaiser, Judith, despite her *Bildung*, still does not belong to the European cultural and linguistic community without discrimination.[144] I agree with her in this specific critique of Despoix, but the *Bildung* motif appears to be more complex and different in this novella than Kaiser's presentation suggests. Landauer seems to indicate something with the connection between Judith and Ludwig. When the two meet on the "devil's pulpit", they sleep together in the falcon cave, while also described is how they flooded "the dams of culture".[145] At the turn of the century, in around 1900, the *Lebensreformbewegung* (life-reform movement) demanded and practiced new ways of living, including free love. In literature this movement was reflected in sexual motifs, especially provocative ones. Authors wrote, for example, on incest or vi-

---

138 Landauer, *Arnold Himmelheber*, 47–48.

139 Ibid., 47 (translation mine): "roh, albern, anmaßend, ohne jeen Schwung, geldgierig und niedrig."

140 Ibid., 82 (translation mine): "mit einem rohen Tier, nein, schlimmer als [ein] Tier [...] [als ein]entartete[r] Mensch."

141 Kaiser, *Gustav Landauer als Schriftsteller*, 211.

142 Ibid., 226–35.

143 Despoix, "Konstruktion des Deutsch-Jüdischen," 118.

144 Kaiser, *Gustav Landauer als Schriftsteller*, 226.

145 Landauer, *Arnold Himmelheber*, 83 (translation mine): "über die Dämme der Kultur".

olence with a sexual background.[146] Here, we also find characteristics of Landauer's novella.

Before and during their meeting in the forest, there is a thunderstorm, which depicts the whole scene as a natural force. When the two want to leave again, the sun shines shortly before sunset. The completion of their intercourse, and the new life arising therefrom, will be revealed later. The thunderstorm passes, the social convention was broken and lost its significance, and as the weather clears, the new, shared life of Judith and Ludwig begins.[147] It is not only Judith and Ludwig who are the solution to a seemingly cultural or ethnic difference, but also their common child. On the one hand, it is clear that women play an important part in this story and development; it remains, therefore, to question if there are resemblances to the well-known conception of Johann Jakob Bachofen (1815–1887) concerning matriarchy and the position of women in society.[148] However, with Landauer's solution presented in the novella, we already witness what Landauer later explicitly suggests for combating anti-Semitism: sexual love (*Geschlechtsliebe*), ergo, mixed-marriages, which he presented in his essay "In Sachen Judentum" (On the Matter of Judaism) in 1901.[149] Landauer's position, however, has already been indicated in his novella.

Nevertheless, the criticism of Despoix, as mentioned above, persists, since the new community that Judith and Ludwig seek is represented by their child and by themselves. Their child, however, only surpasses the stereotypical attributions to Jews. At this point it could be argued that Landauer was aware of the negative stereotype of the beautiful Jewess and dissolves it with the child, but clear references to the intention of Landauer are missing here. Despite these objections, the analysis of Corinna Kaiser is impressive and should be supplemented with the arguments presented.

A neglected topic is the motif of *Bildung*, which is also a leitmotif of German-Jewish history.[150] Judith and Ludwig were rather late to cultural education, while

---

146 Walter Fähnders, *Avantgarde und Moderne*, 113.

147 On the usage of landscape and weather in literary texts, see Elizabeth George, *Wort für Wort: oder Die Kunst, ein gutes Buch zu schreiben (Word by Word: or The Art of Writing a Good Book)* (Munich: Goldmann, 2004), 49–61.

148 Johann Jakob Bachofen and Hans-Jürgen Heinrichs, *Das Mutterrecht: eine Untersuchung über die Gynaikokratie der alten Welt nach ihrer religiösen und rechtlichen Natur (The Right of Mothers: an Investigation on Gynaikokraitie on the old World according to its Religious and Juridical Nature)* (re-print) (Frankfurt am Main: Suhrkamp, 2003).

149 Gustav Landauer, "In Sachen: Judentum (In Matters of Judaism)," in *Philosophie und Judentum*, Ausgewählte Schriften 5 (Lich/Hessen: Verlag Edition AV, 2012), 341–45.

150 See for example George L. Mosse, *German Jews beyond Judaism* (Bloomington, Cincinnati: Indiana University Press, Hebrew Union College Press, 1985).

Wolf Tilsiter was not confronted by it at all. Lysa studies with her father, but her education is not discussed further. Himmelheber appears as a mediator of education and as the one who apparently had to deal with education all his life. For Ludwig and Judith, however, their education is like a new birth. Both are portrayed as "close to nature". Ludwig learns to write, and within eight years he develops from an illiterate goose shepherd to a trained physician. This is also an expression of what non-formal education can achieve in contrast to obligatory formal schooling. Judith comes into contact with modern culture through her journey to the capital, and after her return, she educates herself auto-didactically through reading. In contrast to Kaiser, who recognizes a failure of the emancipation of the Jews in the rapid rise of Ludwig, since Judith remains unredeemed,[151] it seems rather as if *Bildung* creates the precondition that both redeem themselves together, since even Ludwig does not feel a part of society[152] and when they meet again in the woods, they say: "We have both become two new human beings."[153] Education, eventually, rescues Ludwig, and Judith can escape from her marriage into *Bildung.*

It should be noted that Landauer did not develop his own theory of self-perception in this novella. For Landauer, education was the entrance ticket into society, especially for Jews. Moreover, the fact that he so intensely criticized the normative variant of Judaism (the normative variant of Christianity is also not excluded here) shows Landauer to be at the center of the discourse on identity and modernity of his time. With regard to the different "identity offers," that were self-concepts which answered the modern "Jewish question," Landauer was not interested in any of them. He presented different approaches to Jewish self-perception, and preferred neither the national-liberal nor the assimilationist nor the Zionist self-conception.[154]

Although the eponymous Arnold Himmelheber is an important character, Ludwig and Judith are the protagonists of the novella, because the story is told exclusively from their perspective, and thus they are at its core. Hence, Himmelheber is a mediator, but not too exaggerated in his role and function, for Ludwig and Judith, and even their common child, seem to signify the future of a modern community, if not of a modern Jewish "identity."

---

151 Kaiser, *Gustav Landauer als Schriftsteller*, 226.

152 Landauer, *Arnold Himmelheber*, 59.

153 Ibid., 81 (translation mine): "Wir sind beide zwei neue Menschen geworden."

154 There is vast literature on these issues; for an introduction see Steven M. Lowenstein et al., eds., *Deutsch-jüdische Geschichte in der Neuzeit (German-Jewish History in modern Times)*, 3: Umstrittene Integration 1871–1918 (München: Verlag C.H. Beck, 1997).

In his novella, Landauer especially juxtaposes rural and urban Jewry; he prefers the latter, because it appears to be more cultivated and, above all, more progressive. However, the coming together of Jews and Christians in Germany is determined by anti-Semitic discourses, as is having children appear to Landauer as liberation in the sense of overcoming prejudices as well as the "old religions." However, Landauer's radical approach to paradigms of Jewish self-perception is a concept of a kind of new religion, with nature as the common ground rather than Jewish tradition, although it is introduced by a secular Jewess and a secular Christian. This connection is also mediated and initiated by a Jew, Arnold Himmelheber, who, however, expresses revulsion towards his fellow believers; however, this rejection does not represent Landauer's standpoint.

Conclusion: Gustav Landauer as Radical Writer

By scrutinizing the novella and taking into account the research literature, I think *Arnold Himmelheber* should clearly be seen as a testimony of Landauer's search for Jewish self-identification. Despite the anti-Semitic stereotypes he reproduces,[155] it is an examination of Landauer's idea of rural as well as urban Jewry and a new form of community. Thereby, as I emphasized, the neglected point is that Arnold Himmelheber himself is Jewish.

The novella indicates some of Landauer's later positions, which is also a clue that he is on the lookout, and that the interpretations of both Kaiser and Despoix are justified. However, Landauer later develops a different individual concept of Jewish "identity" in his *Sind das Ketzergedanken?*[156] The novella indicates that Landauer approached the fundamental question of modernity quite early in his oeuvre and presented his thought process in the form of a fictional text. He does so in a rather radical style: he uses exaggerations such as anti-Semitic stereotypes to delegitimize rural Jewry as well as taboos to free himself of the stiff and narrow moral corset of his time. The outcome of this process is the idea of a new community, which he also calls religion, which overcomes and radically rejects the "old" religious and national affiliations and notions as well as the racialized attributes which came into being at the turn of the century.

The above mentioned differentiation as a core of the process of modernity is reflected in Landauer's novella as well. He deals with the question of whether

155 At this point, it is not quite clear if he does this consciously or not.
156 Gustav Landauer, "Sind das Ketzergedanken? (Are These Heretical Thoughts?)," in *Vom Judentum: Ein Sammelband*, ed. Verein jüdischer Hochschüler Bar Kochba in Prag (Leipzig: Kurt Wolff Verlag, 1913), 250–57.

Jewish self-perception should be based on religion or a non-religious concept of the "self". Landauer sides with the non-religious approach by delegitimizing rural (orthodox) Jewry as well as urban (reformed) Jewry and presenting his concept of a new community. He is, consequently, not so interested in the question of who is a Jew but rather in how to deal with the differentiation of Jews and non-Jews alike. Hence, he approaches this topic radically by pursuing the basis of the "identity-question" of modernity, rejecting the traditional communities of his time and presenting his idea of a new community. This community radically breaks with the "old world" by creating new humans who are not only physically renewed, but also stand on new moral ground. That would mean a new mankind arises and, consequently, the question of "modern identities" would be obsolete.

Works Cited

Altenhofer, Norbert. "Tradition als Revolution. Gustav Landauers 'Geworden-Werdendes' Judentum (Tradition as Revolution. Gustav Landauer's 'Grown-Becoming Judaism')." In *Jews and Germans from 1860 to 1933. The Problemativ Symbiosis*, edited by David Bronsen, 173–208. Heidelberg: Carl Winter Universitätsverlag, 1979.

Bachofen, Johann Jakob, and Hans-Jürgen Heinrichs. *Das Mutterrecht: eine Untersuchung über die Gynaikokratie der alten Welt nach ihrer religiösen und rechtlichen Natur* (*The right of mothers: an investigation on Gynaikokraitie on the old World according to its Religious and Juridical Nature*). (Re-print) Frankfurt am Main: Suhrkamp, 2003.

Blom, Philipp. *Der taumelnde Kontinent: Europa 1900–1914* (*The Reeling Continent: Europe 1900–1914*). Munich: dtv, 2015.

Cepl-Kaufmann, Gertrude. "Gustav Landauer im Friedrichshagener Jahrzehnt und die Rezeption seines Gemeinschaftsideals nach dem I. Weltkrieg (Gustav Landauer in the Friedrichshagener Centenary and the Reception of His Community Ideas after the First World War)." In *Gustav Landauer im Gespräch* (*Gustav Landauer in conversation*), edited by Hanna Delf and Gert Mattenklott, 235–278. Tübingen: M. Niemeyer, 1997.

Cuddihy, John Murray. *The Ordeal of Civility: Freud, Marx, Lévi-Strauss, and the Jewish Struggle with Modernity.* New York: Basic Books, 1974.

Despoix, Philippe. *Ethiken der Entzauberung: zum Verhältnis von ästhetischer, ethischer und politischer Sphäre am Anfang des 20. Jahrhunderts* (*Ethics of Disenchantment: The Relationship Between the Esthetic, Ethical and Political Spheres at the Beginning of the 20th Century*). Bodenheim: Philo, 1998.

Despoix, Philippe. "Konstruktion des Deutsch-Jüdischen. Gustav Landauer als Schriftsteller." In *Arnold Himmelheber: eine Novelle*, edited by Philippe Despoix, 109–124. Berlin: Philo, 2000.

Despoix, Philippe. "Toward a German-Jewish Construct: Landauer's Arnold Himmelheber." In *Gustav Landauer: Anarchist and Jew*, edited by Paul Mendes-Flohr and Anya Mali, 121–131. Berlin, Boston: De Gruyter, 2015.

Eckle, Barabra. "Die Berliner Jahre von 1892–1901 (The Berlin Years 1892–1901)." In *Gustav Landauer (1870–1919). Von der Kaiserstraße nach Stadelheim*, edited by Literarische Gesellschaft Karlsruhe, 22–37. Eggingen: Edition Isele, 1994.
Fischer, Jens Malte. *Fin de Siècle. Kommentar zu einer Epoche* (*Fin de Siècle. Commentary on an Epoche*). München: Winkler Verlag, 1978.
Fritz, Mauthner. *Sprache und Psychologie* (*Language and Psychology*). Vol. 1. 3 vols. Beiträge zu einer Kritik der Sprache (Contributions to a Critique of Language). Stuttgart: Cotta, 1901.
George, Elizabeth. *Wort für Wort: oder die Kunst, ein gutes Buch zu schreiben (Word for Word: Or the Art of Writing a Good Book*). Munich: Goldmann, 2004.
"Gustav Landauer Papers Nr. 7," no date ARCH00780. International Institute for Social History, Amsterdam.
Holste, Christine. *Der Forte-Kreis (1910–1915): Rekonstruktion eines utopischen Versuchs* (*The Forte-Circle (1910–1915): Reconstruction of an Utopian Attempt*). Stuttgart: M & P, 1992.
Jäger, Lorenz. "Der Herr des Lebens und der Anarchie. Zu Landauers Novelle 'Arnold Himmelheber' (The Master of Life and Anarchy. On Landauers Novella Arnold Himmelheber')." In *Gustav Landauer im Gespräch* (*Gustav Landauer in conversation*), edited by Hanna Delf and Gert Mattenklott, 1–10. Tübingen: Max Niemeyer Verlag, 1997.
Kaiser, Corinna R. *Gustav Landauer als Schriftsteller: Sprache, Schweigen, Musik* (*Gustav Landauer as Writer: Language, Silence, Music*). Berlin, Boston: De Gruyter, 2014.
Kalz, Wolf. *Gustav Landauer: Ein deutscher Anarchist* (*Gustav Landauer: A German Anarchist*). 2. Bad Buchau: Federsee-Verlag, 2009.
Kauffeldt, Rolf, and Michael Matzigkeit. *Zeit und Geist: Kulturkritische Schriften 1890–1919* (*Time and Spirit: Cultural Critic Writings 1890–1919*). Munich: Boer, 1997.
Landauer, Gustav. *Arnold Himmelheber: Eine Novelle* (*Arnold Himmelheber: A Novella*), edited by Philippe Despoix. Berlin: Philo, 2000.
Landauer, Gustav. *Aufruf zum Sozialismus: Ein Vortrag* (*Call to Socialism: A Presentation*). Ausgewählte Schriften, vol. 11. Lich/Hessen: Verlag Edition AV, 2015.
Landauer, Gustav. "Der Dichter als Ankläger (The Poet as Accuser)." In *Internationalismus*, edited by Siegbert Wolf, 62–68. Ausgewählte Schriften, vol. 1. Lich/Hessen: Verlag Edition AV, 2008.
Landauer, Gustav. "Der Todesprediger (The Preacher of Death)." In *Wortartist: Roman, Novelle, Drama, Satire, Gedicht, Übersetzung*, edited by Siegbert Wolf, 31–144. Ausgewählte Schriften, vol. 8. Lich/Hessen: Verlag Edition AV, 2014.
Landauer, Gustav. *Die Revolution (The Revolution)*, edited by Siegbert Wolf. Münster: Unrast, 2003.
Landauer, Gustav. "Durch Absonderung zur Gemeinschaft (Through Isolation to Community)." In *Skepsis und Mystik: Versuche im Anschluss an Mauthners Sprachkritik*, edited by Siegbert Wolf, 131–147. Ausgewählte Schriften, vol. 7. Lich/Hessen: Verlag Edition AV, 2011.
Landauer, Gustav. "In Sachen: Judentum (In Matters of Judaism)." In *Philosophie und Judentum*, 341–45. Ausgewählte Schriften, vol. 5. Lich/Hessen: Verlag Edition AV, 2012.
Landauer, Gustav. *Macht und Mächte (Power and Powers)*. Berlin: E. Fleischel & Co., 1903.
Landauer, Gustav. "Sind das Ketzergedanken? (Are these Heretical Thoughts?)." In *Vom Judentum. Ein Sammelband.*, edited by Verein jüdischer Hochschüler Bar Kochba in Prag, 250–257. Leipzig: Kurt Wolff Verlag, 1913.

Landauer, Gustav. “Sind das Ketzergedanken? (Are these Heretical Thoughts?).” In *Philosophie und Judentum*, 362–368. Ausgewählte Schriften, vol. 5. Lich/Hessen: Verlag Edition AV, 2012.

Landauer, Gustav. “Skepsis und Mystik: Versuche im Anschluss an Mauthners Sprachkritik (Skepticism and Mysticism: Attempts Following Mauthners’ Critique of Language).” In *Skepsis und Mystik: Versuche im Anschluss an Mauthners Sprachkritik*, edited by Siegbert Wolf, 39–128. Ausgewählte Schriften, vol. 7. Lich/Hessen: Verlag Edition AV, 2011.

Leder, Tilman. *Die Politik eines “Antipolitikers:” Eine politische Biographie Gustav Landauers* (*The Politics of an “Anti-Politician:” A Political Biography of Gustav Landauer*). Vol. 1. 2 vols. Ausgewählte Schriften, vol. 10. Lich/Hessen: Verlag Edition AV, 2014.

Leder, Tilman. *Die Politik eines “Antipolitikers:” Eine politische Biographie Gustav Landauers* (*The Politics of an “Anti-Politician:” A Political Biography of Gustav Landauer*). Vol. 2. 2 vols. Ausgewählte Schriften, vol. 10. Lich/Hessen: Verlag Edition AV, 2014.

Lowenstein, Steven M., Paul Mendes-Flohr, Peter Pulzer, and Monika Richarz, eds. *Deutsch-jüdische Geschichte in der Neuzeit (German-Jewish History in Modern Times).* Vol. 3: Umstrittene Integration 1871–1918. Munich: Verlag C.H. Beck, 1997.

Meyer, Michael A. *Jewish Identity in the Modern World.* Seattle: University of Washington Press, 1990.

Mosse, George L. *German Jews beyond Judaism.* Bloomington, Cincinnati: Indiana University Press, Hebrew Union College Press, 1985.

Regehly, Thomas. “‘Stürmische Bekenntnisse.’ Gustav Landauers literarische Arbeiten (‘Tempestuous Confessions.’ Gustav Landauers Literary Work).” In *Gustav Landauer im Gespräch (Gustav Landauer in conversation)*, edited by Hanna Delf and Gert Mattenklott, 11–23. Tübingen: Max Niemeyer Verlag, 1997.

Rogers, Brubaker, and Frederick Cooper. “Beyond ‘Identity’.” *Theory and Society*, no. 29 (2000): 1–47.

Walter Fähnders. *Avantgarde und Moderne 1890–1933 (Avant-Garde and Modernity 1890–1933).* Stutgart, Weimar: J.B. Metzler, 2010.

Hannah Peaceman

Jewish Radicalism as Radical Diversity?

Radical Thought in Jewish Perspectives on the Jewish Question in early Nineteenth Century Germany

Introduction[1]

The Jewish Question has accompanied the development of bourgeois society from its early stages and is still persistent today. It addressed the situation of Jews vis-à-vis modern bourgeois society and the requirements of and obstacles to their full emancipation, that is their recognition as citizens with equal rights. Moreover, the specific Jewish political interest lay in all forms of discrimination and of anti-Judaism/anti-Semitism.[2] In the following, I want to take up a specific aspect of this struggle for emancipation. My question is: What was the connection between the so-called Jewish Question[3] and Jewish Radicalism in the nineteenth century? To answer this question, we must probe the term radical in relation to Jews. First and foremost, two historic developments come to mind.

Firstly, many Jews dedicated themselves to Socialism. In this context, they defined themselves as radicals. In Eastern Europe, as immigrant workers in the United States and across the globe, they took part in revolutionary politics and movements[4]. Some were engaged in Jewish-Socialist organizations like the

1 This chapter was written during my time as a research associate at the Research Centre "Dynamics of Jewish Ritual Practices in Pluralistic Contexts from Antiquity to the Present" at University of Erfurt, accessed November 28 2017, www.uni-erfurt.de/en/max-weber-centre/projects/cooperation-projects/dynamics-of-jewish-ritual-practices-in-pluralistic-contexts-from-antiquity-to-the-present/.

2 In this essay I mostly use the term anti-Judaism as it is a broader term that includes anti-Semitism in its specificities, especially when I refer to the early nineteenth century. For a more detailed elaboration on the terms, see, for example, Gideon Botsch, "Von der Judenfeindschaft zum Antisemitismus: Ein historischer Überblick," *Aus Politik und Zeitgeschichte* 28–30 (2014): 10–17.

3 Andreas Reinke, et. al., *Die "Judenfrage" in Ostmitteleuropa: Historische Pfade und politisch-soziale Konstellationen* (Berlin: Metropol, 2015). This recent publication looks at the history of the Jewish Question in Europe.

4 Lori Shaller and Judith Rosenbaum, "Jewish Radicalism and the Red Scare. Introductory Essay," accessed November 30 2017, http://jwa.org/teach/livingthelegacy/jewish-radicalism-and-red-scare-introductory-essay.

https://doi.org/10.1515/9783110545753-015

famous "Bund".[5] Others participated in the worker's movement as part of secular (or, rather, undisclosed Christian) trade unions or the manifold revolutionary groups and parties. Their politics aimed at a radical transformation of society as elaborated in Socialist thought. However, the alliance between Socialist movements and Jews was not without tensions. Jews experienced anti-Semitism within the workers movements. Jewish-Socialist Alliances did not guarantee a solution of the Jewish Question that would decease anti-Judaism/anti-Semitism in the vision of a radically transformed society.

Zionism was a second radical answer of Jews to the Jewish Question and the difficult living conditions for Jews in Russia, Eastern Europe, and Germany. As part of the emerging nationalist movements, Zionism aimed at an own Jewish state and superseded the necessity of life in the diaspora. In comparison to a radically transformed society, this produced a national answer to the Jewish Question.

The two ideas were often intermingling. Moses Hess (1812–1875) is an example of an early socialist in Germany who became a Zionist predecessor.[6] He composed socialist manifests, claiming for example, for the abolition of class differences, and equality of women and men. His standpoint was shaped by societal, economic, and national-cultural conditions that suppressed people, including anti-Semitism. A solution of the so-called Jewish Question was part of his socialist political and radical agenda. The emergence of Zionism was a radical answer to the rise of anti-Semitism: an own (other) state which he envisioned as a Socialist state.[7] Hence, he combined the Jewish claim for emancipation and a socialist agenda in his vision of a Jewish state.

In this chapter, I show that there was a third strand of radical thinking in Jewish answers to the Jewish Question that is not usually taken as such. In my systematic approach, I argue that this radicalism was implicit in the Jewish debates on emancipation of Jews into bourgeois society. It was grounded in the mode of engagement of these thinkers with Enlightenment. These Jews did not define themselves as radicals nor are they usually understood as such. In fact, their claim for full emancipation does not seem radical, but moderate – the re-

---

5 The "Bund," the Jewish working-class movement, was founded in 1897 to especially give Russian and Polish Jewish workers a voice to express their rights. This was also an answer to the discrimination Jewish workers experienced in the Socialist movements that often preserved their Christian world view despite proclaimed secularism.

6 "Moses Hess," Jewish Virtual Library, accessed November 17 2017, http://www.jewishvirtuallibrary.org/moses-hess.

7 Moses Hess, *Rom und Jerusalem: Die letzte Nationalitätenfrage* (Rom and Jerusalem: Die last Question of Nationality) (Saarbrücken: VDM Verlag Dr. Müller, 2007).

alization of the core principle of bourgeois society. I claim, however, that their critique of the anti-emancipatory anti-Jewish moments of Enlightenment is radical because it already tends to transcend this society. By showing how ideals of freedom and equality did not apply universally to Jews, these critics hinted at the immanent contradictions of bourgeois society.[8]

I aim to dialectically enfold this Jewish critique of anti-emancipatory anti-Jewish moments in Enlightenment. I read this critique as a determinate negation of the anti-universal and of the anti-particular moments in universalism. As such, it seeks to sublate exclusionary universalism into a transformed universalism based on diversity.

My argument is based on a microstudy of two articles in the Jewish magazine Sulamith that give an insight into Jewish critique of Enlightenment. My claim is that these Jewish perspectives implicate demands for a radically transformed universalism in which Jews are not seen as external anymore: they call for the sublation of anti-particularism towards a new quality of universalism as reconciliation of differences.

Jewish In-Betweenness and Determinate Negation

Determinate negation is part of a theory and practice of critique with a history in philosophical critical thought from Spinoza to Hegel to Marx to the Frankfurt Critical Theory. The latter shared the intention, on the one hand, to radically critique societal contradictions, and, on the other hand, to make better societal circumstances thinkable. This concerned both epistemological and emancipatory questions. Wolfgang Fritz Haug summarizes this very complex mode of critique as follows:

> The point of the determinate negation is the faculty of distinction between the moments of conditions that are to be retained and those to be denied, which cannot be denoted as a mechanical next to each other, but what needs to make itself to the repeal of that what the 'negative' achieves in the critiqued condition, as was the Capital not only exploiting, but also had a productive effect.[9]

---

8 Retrospectively, their critique of Enlightenment gives evidence to the thesis that anti-Judaism coincided with Enlightenment. Historians like David Niremberg have worked on this in detail: David Niremberg, *Anti-Judaism: The Western Tradition* (New York and London: W. W. Norton & Company, 2014).

9 ["Der bN geht es um Unterscheidungsfähigkeit zwischen festzuhaltenden und zu verneinenden Momenten an den Verhältnissen, was freilich kein mechanisches Nebeneinander bezeichnet, sondern sich auch zu Aufhebung dessen machen muß, was das 'Negative' im kritisierten

The potential and challenge lie in the way to think of the relation of contradictions and the possibility to overcome them. This is not a one-dimensional line of argument but involves dialectical thought on several layers.

Characteristically for determinate negation as part of a theory and practice of critique is its basis of concrete societal circumstances, especially contradictions, as starting points for analysis.

Philosophy does not deliver abstract categories for analysis, but these are reflected through and determined by the societal circumstances. Presupposed terms may change their meaning and relation, depending on societal conditions. Hence, if determined negation is understood as an instrument of analysis, it itself develops further and changes its mode of critique. Immanent contradictions may be discovered.

In their *Dialectics of Enlightenment*, Horkheimer and Adorno detected the relation between Enlightenment and myth as dialectical. They presumed that freedom in society was inseparable from enlightening thought. At the same time, enlightening thought was entangled in socio-historical circumstances and contained the sprout of regress.[10] In terms of determinate negation this may be put as follows: the transition from myth to Enlightenment was no fundamentally new era, but continuous. Aspects of myth proceeded in Enlightenment in a developed form. Aspects of Enlightenment were already inherent in myth. Hence, Enlightenment was not a linear progress, but needed to reflect on preserved anti-emancipatory elements in an ongoing process. The reflection was the requirement to actively negate the anti-emancipatory elements by determinate change.

Adorno and Horkheimer analyzed several episodes throughout history. In particular, they reflected on the "Elements of Anti-Semitism"[11] and their persistence throughout Enlightenment in their multiple anti-emancipatory dimensions leading into the Shoah. This can be understood as a critical analysis of the Jewish Question.

With reference to Haug's definition of determinate negation one could ask what productive moments occurred in the critiqued conditions. Surely, this is not about affirming anti-Judaism, anti-Semitism or the Shoah. However, Ador-

---

Zustand leiste, wie ja das Kapital nicht nur ausbeutend, sondern auch ‚produktivierend' wirkt." (English translation by H.P.)] Wolfgang Fritz Haug, "Bestimmte Negation," [Determinate Negation] *HKWM* 2 (1995): 177–188.

10 Theodor Adorno and Max Horkheimer, *Dialektik der Aufklärung. Philosophische Fragmente* ("Dialectics of Enlightenment. Philosophical Fragments" (English translation by H.P.)) (Frankfurt: Fischer, 2010), 3.

11 Adorno and Horkheimer, *Dialektik der Aufklärung*, 177.

no's and Horkheimer's analysis of the relation between Enlightenment and anti-Judaism/anti-Semitism left out a central perspective: namely, that of the people who were affected by anti-Judaism and anti-Semitism. Productive moments could lie in the Jewish critique of anti-universal and anti-particular moments of universalism.

Non-Jewish enlighteners proclaimed that ideals like freedom and equality were universal. However, this did not apply to enlightened Jews who wanted recognition as Jews. Many bourgeois Jews saw themselves as future members of civil society. They used Enlightenment language to express their attitudes. They understood themselves as Jewish Germans or German Jews. Neither did they give up their Jewishness and completely assimilate to the German people, nor did they separate themselves as merely Jewish from the rest of society.[12] They situated themselves in-between particularity as Jews and universality as Enlighteners.

Based on this in-betweenness that was not to be dissolved in assimilation, these Jews pointed at the contradiction in Enlightenment's universalism that did not allow particularity. Their critique could be read as seeking a determinate negation of universalism and particularism towards a transformation of universalism based on differences; moments of universalism and particularism would thereby be sublated as well as preserved in a transformed way.

The most famous example and predecessor for these in-between bourgeois Jews was Moses Mendelssohn,[13] who served as a role model for Jewish-German Enlightenment. He was a protagonist of the Haskala, the Jewish Enlightenment, and involved in the discussions of the Berlin Enlightenment. This created his twofold social and political standpoint as in-between a Jewish and a German Enlightener. In his essay *Was ist Auklärung?* Mendelssohn elaborated on the potentials and threats of Enlightenment with the aim to preserve Enlightenment: "The more noble a thing is in its perfection, is said by a Hebrew author, the grislier it is in its decay."[14]

---

12 The various German-Jewish magazines of the nineteenth and early twentieth century show the different ways of situating themselves in-between.

13 Moses Mendelssohn, *Jerusalem oder über religiöse Macht im Judentum* (Jerusalem, or, on Religious Power and Judaism) (Hamburg: Meiner 2005), 29–142, and Moses Mendelssohn, "Vorrede zu, Menasse Ben Israel: Rettung der Juden'" in Moses Mendelssohn, *Jerusalem oder über religiöse Macht im Judentum* (Hamburg: Meiner, 2005), 1–28.

14 ("Je edler ein Ding in seiner Vollkommenheit, sagt ein hebräischer Schriftsteller, desto gräßlicher in seiner Verwesung." (English translation by H.P.)); Moses Mendelssohn, "Was ist Aufklärung" (What is Enlightenment?), in *Was ist Aufklärung? Thesen und Definitionen (What is Enlightement? Theses and Definitions)*, ed. Ehrhard Bahr (Stuttgart: Reclam, 1996), 7.

In his critique, Mendelssohn did not demarcate his standpoint as Jewish. But he focused on the relation between particular interests and universal ideals and pointed at the relation between abstract ideals and reality.[15] The prejudices of people needed to be overcome actively by education to realize Enlightenment ideals. The differences of humans needed to be accounted for in this realization.[16] Mendelssohn argued that the ideals of Enlightenment could not be enforced like trammels of logical necessity[17], but needed to be enacted in relation to people's needs and interests. He critiqued one-sided abstract philosophy that did not connect to people's lives.

In my reading, Mendelssohn's critique of Enlightenment aimed to preserve universal ideals of Enlightenment by sublating the discrepancy between abstract principles and reality. Simultaneously, it aimed to sublate particular prejudices of people and preserve their particular needs and interests as conditions for the realization of ideals. The discrepancy between universal abstract principle and particular reality became a source for productive moments of critique that would enable a change of conditions that stood in opposition to the ideals of Enlightenment.

My reading of Moses Mendelssohn emphasizes the implications of his critique of Enlightenment. In the following, I will look at two articles in the first German-Jewish magazine *Sulamith* that saw itself in tradition of Moses Mendelssohn's critique of Enlightenment. I will thereby show more thoroughly how their Jewish critique of Enlightenment was shaped by the in-betweenness of Jewish Enlighteners.

Sulamith, die Friedliebende, and Jewish-German Critique of Enlightenment

The first Jewish magazine in German language was *Sulamith: Zeitschrift zur Beförderung der Kultur und Humanität unter der jüdischen Nation*[18], founded in 1806 in tradition of Mendelssohn's critique of Enlightenment. The editors were David Fränkel and Joseph Wolf. *Sulamith* brought life into Mendelssohn's critique; it entailed not only discussions about Enlightenment, but also more prac-

15 Mendelssohn, *Was ist Aufklärung?*, 4.

16 Ibid., 6.

17 (Fesseln (English translation by H.P.)) Ibid., 7

18 All issues of Sulamith are available online. Accessed November 27 2017, http://sammlungen.ub.uni-frankfurt.de/cm/periodical/titleinfo/2304627.

tically on education, reform of Jewish practices, culture and progress, and the question of realization of Enlightenment for Jews and all people.

The following presents a suggestion to read the opening remarks of the magazine *Sulamith* and an article that tells a story about her name as source for productive moments of Jewish critique of Enlightenment.

Sulamith: "Content, Purpose and Title of this Journal"

The opening article of *Sulamith* was written by Joseph Wolf in 1806, entitled "Content, Purpose and Title of this Journal."[19] Wolf began the article by elaborating on the relation between "general" and the "specific."[20] The general referred to "humankind," the specific to the "national." All people shared "human's character." According to Wolf, finding the shared comities and developing culture was a question of education. Images of nature fed into his argument: there were spouts that needed to come into blossom.[21] The first two pages used a language of Enlightenment, which was common for this time.

They were followed by a historical narration about the best men that had found the real foundations of humankind and fought against illusions. Wolf explained their deeds with reference to a story from the Talmud.[22] This is the first time in the text that Judaism became a topic, and the story leads over to the history of the Jewish nation that had times of glory. Wolf described Jews as tolerant towards humankind and as very content,[23] which served as grounds for the argument that Jewish religion was a religion of humankind.[24] According to Wolf, Judaism was the source to bear the difficult conditions Jews had had to cope with afterwards. Wolf highlighted that Jews had not become miserable but were ready for new times.[25] Judaism also commanded to live for the best of every human being.[26]

---

19 Wolf, "Inhalt, Zweck und Titel dieser Zeitschrift," (Content, Purpose and Title of this Journal), 1.
20 Ibid.
21 (Keime (English translation by H.P.)), Ibid., 2.
22 Ibid., 3.
23 Ibid., 5.
24 Ibid.
25 Ibid., 6.
26 Ibid., 7.

Wolf's central questions were: How could humans find their shared humankind? How could they realize their living together? Enlightenment was to him a matter of will that must be developed in practice.[27]

> Sulamith aims to arouse deference towards religion, that means towards those truths that are worthy the name of religion, in the nation; she aims to invigorate the desperate desideratum to feel religious sentiments and imaginations; at the same time, she wants to show the truth that terms and sentences that Jewish religion compounds are neither harmful for individuals nor for civil society in any sense.[28]

Wolf followed a line of argument that can be found in Mendelssohn's essay on Enlightenment. He started with a theoretical elaboration on philosophical terms, but then connected them first to historical and then to present societal circumstances. The persecution of Jews was treated as a problem of the general, not as a specific Jewish problem. For the general to meet their own ends, Jews would have to be treated as humans. Wolf saw Judaism as a source for solving the persecution and living together based on shared humankind. He referred to and critiqued the theoretical figure of a dualism, typical for Enlightenment:[29] Theory over practice, the general over the specific, rationality over sentiments: rather than maintaining the dualisms he turned their hierarchy into an interplay by starting with the history of Jews.

Jews challenged the societal conditions by preserving their religion. They thereby questioned the status quo of the realization of humanity. Wolf referred to Jews as a religion and a nation. He did not use both as absolute categories but let them interact. They led into a conglomerate that tied into education and culture. The quoted lines express the idea how Judaism could become a lively part of the whole society.

---

27 Ibid., 8.

28 (Sulamith will Ehrerbietung gegen die Religion, d. h. gegen diejenigen Wahrheiten, welche des Namens Religion allein würdig sind, bei der Nation erwecken; sie will das dringende Bedürfniß, religiöse Empfindungen und Vorstellungen zu fühlen, von neuem beleben; sie will aber zugleich die Wahrheit zeigen, daß die Begriffe und Sätze, die in der jüdischen Religion enthalten sind, weder dem einzelnen Menschen, noch der bürgerlichen Gesellschaft im mindesten schädlich sind. (English translation by H.P.)) Ibid., 10.

29 Feminist philosophers have done a great deal of work deconstructing dualisms. See, for example, Alison Stone, "Matter and Form: Hegel, Organicism, and the Difference between Women and Men," in *Hegel's Philosophy and Feminist Thought: Beyond Antigone*, ed. Kimberly Hutchings et al. (New York: Palgrave, 2010), 211–232.

Sulamith: "Explanation of the Title Image"

The article "Explanation of the Title Image"[30] shed light on the choice of the title and the illustration on the cover of the first issue. Wolf described Sulamith, the peace bringer[31], referring to the second book of Samuel.[32] She saved king David from his traitors:

> The gentle God of peace, rationality, appears often in the middle of the worst wars, and with words of peace she disarms the increasing rage of indignant hearts, and brandished swords are lowered quickly by powerful heroes. Inspirited by the love of the homeland, Sulamith appears on first look-out and brings the covenant of peace to the field commander.[33]

Wolf introduced the story, explicitly referring to a female readership.[34] He noted that knowledge of history was important and took up the educational approach. The biblical Sulamith served in his argument as a historically exemplified role model for the "German Sulamith"[35]. She faced a similar situation: "As the other she steps out from the middle of an embattled nation and arises as mediator and peace bringer between the former and her enemies, that stand in delusion as if she was facilitating the enemy of humankind in her middle."[36]

The Jewish German Sulamith aimed to bring peace between all people. The Jewish nation was seen as an enemy by others; Sulamith hoped to bring forth community between humans and to show how the image of the Jewish enemy had been the result of hypocrisy and violence.[37]

---

30 Joseph Wolf, "Erklärung der Titelvignette," *Sulamith* 1, no. 1 (1806), 160.
31 (die Friedensstifterin (English translation by H.P.)), Ibid.
32 Original in Samuel 2.20.19. Interestingly, in this passage Sulamith is not referred to by name. Wolf seemed to have added this name. Further, the biblical story refers to enemies within Israel and not enemies outside. Both aspects indicate that Wolf's interpretation of the story of Sulamith was quite free and in accordance with his political interest of constructing a German Sulamith. In this article, I cannot critically assess this in detail. This will be part of further research.
33 (Die sanfte Friedensgöttin, Vernunft, tritt oft mitten im heftigsten Kriegsgetümmel auf, und durch Worte des Friedens entwaffnet sie die aufstrebende Wuth empörter Herzen, und die gezückten Schwerter entsinken schnell den mächtigsten Heldenarmen (English translation by H.P.)), Ibid., 163.
34 The emancipatory image of a woman in this article could be an interesting topic for further research.
35 Ibid., 164.
36 (Deutsche Sulamith (English translation by H.P.)), Ibid.
37 Ibid.

Like the first text, the story of Sulamith addressed the Jewish perspectives on Enlightenment. It underlined humankind as a shared basis and its non-realization. Wolf presented Sulamith's story not as specifically Jewish, but as universable and as a role model for peaceful living together. The importance of sentiments was expressed for rationality to come into the hearts of the people.[38] *Sulamith* explicitly marked a standpoint: a Jewish center that became part of the general. Her main aims were to connect divergent positions, emotionally and politically.[39]

Both articles reflect the modest tenor and the unpretentious approach of the editors of the magazine. The author saw himself as an Enlightener. *Sulamith* aimed to enlighten Jews and a non-Jewish public. One will not find open manifests for political emancipation of Jews in any of the issues. The language used was sophisticated and was supposed to show the potential of Jews as members of civil society. So, why and how could these – non-political, sophisticated, idealist – articles implicate a critique that pointed at a radical transformation of universal ideals?

Implications Towards a Radical Transformation of Universalism

To publish *Sulamith* was an act of deliberate public situating. Judaism was not rejected and it did not vanish in assimilation. *Sulamith* was consequently an act of self-determination. Jews situated themselves between religion, culture, and nation. This did (and does) not coincide with the category of the nation-state or pure religion. Jews that identified as in-between Jews self-defined their standpoint on a basis of shared humanity. After years of defenses, publishing a Jewish debate on universal Enlightenment opened conditions of debate at eye level. Jews set the topics from their in-between standpoint, which included showing the benefits of Jewish religion and their potential for society as a whole. Jews were not supposed to become non-Jews. Rather, society needed to change in a way that Jews would not be excluded.

The in-betweenness could be understood as a determinate negation of anti-particular and anti-universal moments in the ideals of Enlightenment. It aimed to sublate the exclusionary moments that did not allow for differences. It aimed to preserve universal ideas in accordance. Hence, it sought for a transformation

38 Ibid., 165.

39 Ibid., 164.

of the grounds on which universality is based. Which consequences would bring forth societies' emancipation as a whole? How could these be refined, using the Jewish critique of Enlightenment and the in-betweenness of this standpoint?

Jewish Critique of Enlightenment: Emancipation Towards Radical Diversity?

Firstly, the critique of anti-Jewish anti-emancipatory moments can be read as a claim for reconciliation of differences without flawing the differences. Implications for this lie in the in-betweenness. This claim contains two political and philosophical aspects: firstly, it maintains radical differences (particularity), and secondly, it demands for a radical different understanding of generality (universality) as reconciliation of differences. Adorno writes about emancipation of society and reconciliation of differences (historically retrospectively) in the *Minima Moralia* in 1951:

> An emancipated society however would be no unitary state, but the realization of the generality in the reconciliation of differences. A politics which took this seriously should therefore not propagate even the idea of the abstract equality of human beings. They should rather point to the bad equality of today ... and think of the better condition as the one in which one could be different without fear.[40]

For sure, *Sulamith* had a different temporal, societal, and political context and intention than Adorno. Still, Adorno's thought can help to elucidate productive moments for emancipation of *Sulamith* in the following way:

Joseph Wolf thought about the situation in which one could be different without fear, concretely, in which Jews could be different without fear. In both of his articles he made very clear that the explicit overall condition was that every person could be different without fear without having to give up one's particularity.[41]

Wolf's argument was rooted in an affirmative attitude towards Jewish religion and towards religion in general. Strictly viewed, this cannot be merged with critical theory. However, one aspect of his attitude towards religion could shed light on the determinate negation, while it also entailed a sublation of particularity. As indicated, the solution did not lie in the abolition of Judaism or by

---

40 Adorno, *Minima Moralia* (Frankfurt: Suhrkamp, 2014), 116. English translation, accessed November 30 2017, https://www.marxists.org/reference/archive/adorno/1951/mm/ch02.htm.
41 Wolf, "Erklärung der Titelvignette," 164.

preserving elements of anti-Judaism in a determinate negation. Wolf delivered indications of how (Jewish) particularity could be sublated as well as persevered. *Sulamith* also contained a self-criticism of Jewish religious practices, education, and lifestyles.[42] The goal was to educate a Jewish and a broader public by pointing at aspects of Jewish religion that were not limited to Jewish faith but could be fruitful for emancipation for the whole of society.[43]

Further productive moments of the critique of Enlightenment were implicit in (Jewish) practices: in his articles, Wolf introduced practices like lifelong learning in the community and disputability.[44] They referred to Talmudic traditions. Different understandings of the Thora and debates of how to realize the law never brought forth a single answer. The outcome was not a fixed solution, but the process of the dispute. It implied that there was not one person who knew the one right way. Every person could become aware of new perspectives and find his/her blind spots.

Both disputability and lifelong learning have the potential of shaping a less hierarchical debate culture which is necessary to see the many sides of a problem. Both practices could also be seen as constituting processes in which particularities, e.g. needs and interests, are transformed (sublated and preserved) in a way that they coincide universally. The hint at practices indicates that transformed universality is not a fixed result, but an ongoing process of negotiation.

With reference to Adorno, one could say that reconciliation of differences meant a procedural investigation that had roots in concrete societal circumstances that ran against people's needs. Reconciliation of radical differences would be the continual process of critique, enlightenment, and education that could bridge the discrepancy between concrete societal conditions and universal ideas of Enlightenment. This would bring particular life to the universal ideals.

Both points lead towards grounds for arguments for a living together based on radical diversity, a society in which all people should be able to be "different without fear." This is a vision that entails a radical transformation of society, but also of the understanding of universality und particularity, which sublates their anti-particular and anti-universal moments. A determinate negation also allowed to preserve Jewish radical otherness by sublating and keeping it at the

---

42 Ibid. and Wolf, "Inhalt, Zweck und Titel dieser Zeitschrift," 10.

43 This does not substitute a substantial critique of religion. In the nineteenth century, however, there was no radical attempt to abolish all religion. In this context, the question of how also religious particularity could be preserved and sublated contributes to the attempt to sublate the anti-particular elements of universalism.

44 Wolf, "Inhalt, Zweck und Titel dieser Zeitschrift," 3, 7–8.

same time, and by determining the conditions of society as based on radical diversity.

Philosophically, the previous elaborations need some more words. Objections could be raised: firstly, radical diversity could be understood as relativism. The term radical could be used to justify every perspective, for example anti-Semitic ideology. This is a contradiction to the aim of this text, and to the agenda of *Sulamith*. Even if one says the interpretation in this text went beyond the intention of *Sulamith*, she would probably admit that *Sulamith* intended an improvement of the conditions of living together and against maltreatment of people because they were different. The context of *Sulamith*, the concrete claims, set a historical and normative frame that did not allow for everything goes.

Secondly, this analysis presented a specific example under given conditions. How could it be valuable beyond its societal, religious, and temporal contexts? Practices like disputability and lifelong learning were neither merely religious nor only valuable in the past. They relied on circumstances and varied accordingly. The knowledge about them could be used in different temporal and societal contexts. This is twofold: on the one hand, a historically exemplified analysis could inform the new situation. On the other hand, it could bring about new information that in turn could change the practices themselves.

As an immanent method of critique, the determinate negation detected productive and exploiting moments in Enlightenment universalism. It shed light on how it produced contradictions in itself, as well as, respectively, ways of transforming the contradictions into a condition in which radical diversity as reconciliation of differences could be possible.

Emancipatory Power of Jewish Radicalism: An Outlook

The third strand of thinking in Jewish answers to the Jewish Question shed light on implicit radicalism in the Jewish debate on emancipation of Jews into bourgeois society. In it lay approaches to negate the anti-emancipatory moments of Enlightenment ideals, more specifically the anti-particular moments in universalism and anti-universal moments in particularism. The exclusion of Jews from supposedly universal ideals could serve as a source to detect the exclusionary moments. But it also shed light on the productive moments that sought to overcome these contradictions and transform universalism.

These Jewish Enlighteners aimed to strengthen the idea and reality of Enlightenment and universalism. Their critique was no argument in favor of particularism and would not serve as a basis for a standpoint theoretical argument; instead, it hinted at a possibility to overcome the gap in-between universalism and particularism. These Jewish perspectives served as a fruitful source for this endeavor because they were themselves situated in-between the contradictory pols. Judaism was seen as the other that could not amalgamate with the (secularized) Christian understanding of universalism.

A transformed universalism would be a societal condition, in which people would live together based on the reconciliation of differences. Reconciliation of differences would need to be understood as a process of negotiation. It could not be a fixed societal condition. Every person would be able to participate and shape the conditions and it would have to happen in a constant movement.

These thoughts go beyond the intentions of Joseph Wolf who aimed at the acknowledgement of Jews as equals in bourgeois society. Reading his texts through the lens of critical theory on the one hand allowed to detect the implicit radical thoughts of his articles. On the other hand, it enables us to consider them further, which has become a dire necessity since the emancipation of Jews into bourgeois society failed.

What potential lies in the Jewish Enlighteners' perspectives that aimed at actual Enlightenment and emancipation? What would real emancipation involve? It could not merely mean emancipation from anti-Jewish/anti-Semitic thought, as this would only initiate the process of emancipation of society. The reconciliation of differences that would allow all people to negotiate their needs and interests could not only refer to questions of identity. Consequent reconciliation of differences would imply determinate negation of economic and political societal relations.

The last point connects to the solution of the Jewish Question which Jewish Socialists aimed at in the nineteenth century (and failed as well). The Jewish Enlighteners' critique could have informed the main contradiction more thoroughly. It could have questioned how anti-particular and anti-universal moments constituted the political claims within Socialist movements. More potential for a substantial practical critique lies in the critical practices of Jewish Enlighteners. In this chapter, I highlighted lifelong learning and disputability. There has always existed a large gap between the practices of political movements and the theoretical thinking about changes in society. Lifelong learning and disputability are traditional Jewish practices which aim to bridge thought and practice (following the Jewish law). They could be further developed into practices that could constitute living together based on the reconciliation of differences, namely in the sense that they served as tools that made visible multiple perspectives, needs, and interests and sought for their connection.

The further development of radical thinking I detected in the Jewish enlighteners' perspectives could be fruitful for today's philosophical political debates on truly democratic living together, in which there exists a gap between theoretical debate and political practices.[45] It could be a fruitful endeavor to take the perspectives of groups who suffer exclusion from universal ideals as a starting point for a critical assessment of current conditions. The approach would not end by making visible their perspectives; they could be examined for moments that needed to be sublated and preserved to reconcile the detected contradictions without flawing the differences. This could produce a historically and socially concrete critique of societal relations that could unlock a potential towards a more emancipated democratic society.

The critique on Enlightenment persists within the philosophical debates. After all, anti-Judaism and anti-Semitism continue in post-Nazi democratic Germany (and throughout the world). In this sense, the Jewish Question prevails. This calls for radical thought on the continuity and the ways of de-thematization and legitimization within democratic and self-proclaimed pluralistic societies. (Jewish) radical thought could contribute socio-historically grounded perspectives to the critical reflections on society and produce insights for its change.

Works cited

Adorno, Theodor, and Horkheimer, Max. *Dialektik der Aufklärung. Philosophische Fragmente*, Frankfurt: Fischer, 2010.

Adorno, Theodor. *Minima Moralia*. Frankfurt: Suhrkamp, 2014. English translation. Accessed November 30 2017. https://www.marxists.org/reference/archive/adorno/1951/mm/ch02.htm.

Benz, Wolfgang, "Antisemitismus im 19. und 20. Jahrhundert." *Dossier Antisemitismus bpb* (2006). Accessed November 30 2017. http://www.bpb.de/politik/extremismus/antisemitismus/37948/19-und-20-jahrhundert.

Botsch, Gideon "Von der Judenfeindschaft zum Antisemitismus. Ein historischer Überblick." *Aus Politik und Zeitgeschichte* 28–30 (2014): 10–17. Accessed July 30 2017. http://www.bpb.de/apuz/187412/von-der-judenfeindschaft-zum-antisemitismus?p=all.

Dohm, Christian Wilhelm von. *Über die bürgerliche Verbesserung der Juden*. Berlin und Stettin: Friedrich Nicolai, 1781 and 1783.

Geuss, Raymond. *Philosophy and Real Politics*. Princeton: Princeton University Press, 2008.

Haug, Wolfgang Fritz. "Bestimmte Negation." In HKWM 2, 1995, Spalten 177–188.

Hess, Moses. *Rom und Jerusalem. Die letzte Nationalitätenfragen*. Saarbrücken: VDM Verlag Dr. Müller, 2007.

45 Raymond Geuss, *Philosophy and Real Politics* (Princeton, NJ: Princeton University Press, 2008).

Jewish Virtual Library. "Moses Hess." Accessed November 17 2017. http://www.jewishvirtualli brary.org/moses-hess.

Kober, Adolf. *Jewish Periodicals in Germany 1784–1938.* New York: n.p., 1966.

Marx, Karl. "Theses on Feuerbach". In *Marx/Engels Selected Works*, Volume One (2002), translated by W. Lough, 13–15. Accessed November 30 2017. https://www.marxists.org/archive/marx/works/1845/theses/theses.pdf.

Mendelssohn, Moses. *Jerusalem oder über religiöse Macht im Judentum*, 29–142. Hamburg: Meiner, 2005.

Mendelssohn, Moses. Vorrede zu "Menasse Ben Israel: Rettung der Juden" in *Jerusalem oder über religiöse Macht im Judentum*, Moses Mendelssohn, 1–28. Hamburg: Meiner, 2005.

Mendelssohn Moses. "Was ist Aufklärung." In *Was ist Aufklärung? Thesen und Definitionen*, edited by Ehrhard Bahr, 7. Stuttgart: Reclam, 1996.

Meriam Webster Dictionary. "Radicalism." Accessed November 28 2017. http://www.merriam-webster.com/dictionary/radicalism.

Niremberg, David. *Anti-Judaism. The Western Tradition.* New York and London: W.W. Norton & Company, 2014.

Reinke, Andreas, Katerina Capková, Michal Frankl, Piotr Kendziorek, and Ferenc Laczó. *Die "Judenfrage" in Ostmitteleuropa. Historische Pfade und politisch-soziale Konstellationen.* Berlin: Metropol, 2015.

Shaller, Lori, and Judith Rosenbaum. "Jewish Radicalism and the Red Scare. Introductory Essay." Accessed November 30 2017. http://jwa.org/teach/livingthelegacy/jewish-radical ism-and-red-scare-introductory-essay.

Stone, Alison. "Matter and Form: Hegel, Organicism, and the Difference between Women and Men." In *Hegel's Philosophy and Feminist Thought. Beyond Antigone*, edited by Kimberly Hutchings and Tuja Pulkkinen, 211–232. New York: Palgraves, 2010.

Wolf, Joseph. "Erklärung der Titelvignette." *Sulamith 01/01* (1806): 160–165.

Wolf, Joseph. "Inhalt, Zweck und Titel dieser Zeitschrift." *Sulamith 01/01* (1806): 1–11.

Contributors

Peter Bergamin is Visiting Scholar of the Oxford Centre for Hebrew and Jewish Studies, and Tutor for the Visiting Student Programme at Mansfield College. His *The Making of the Israeli Far Right: Abba Ahimeir and Zionist Ideology* (I.B. Tauris) will be published in 2019. His current research looks at Britain's withdrawal from the Palestine Mandate.

Amir Locker-Biletzki, a BSIA (Balsillie School of International Affairs) fellow, is a cultural historian of Communism in Palestine/Israel. His current research focuses on the way Jewish and Arab Communists created alternative Jewish-Israeli and Palestinian national identities, as well as identities formed through the Communist Party's anti-imperialist and anti-colonial political mobilizations.

Federico Dal Bo (1973) holds a PhD in Translation Studies from the University of Bologna and a PhD in Jewish Studies from the Free University of Berlin. He currently is the recipient of a postdoctoral fellowship at the University of Heidelberg at the project *Material Text Cultures*. His most recent publications are *Emanation and Philosophy of Language. An Introduction to Joseph Ben Abraham Giqatilla* (Los Angles: Cherub Press, 2019) and *Deconstructing the Talmud. The Absolute Book* (London-New York: Routledge 2019). For more information, please visit: http://www.federicodalbo.eu.

Tal Elmaliach is a Post-Doc fellow in the Center for Israel Studies, The Ben-Gurion Research Institute for the Study of Israel and Zionism, Ben-Gurion University of the Negev. He wrote his PhD dissertation at the University of Haifa on the subject of Hakibbutz Haartzi-HaShomer haTza'ir and Mapam between the Years 1956–1977. This work has been recently published in a book in Hebrew (under The Ben-Gurion Research Institute press and the Open University Press) and will soon be published in English (under Syracuse University Press). He is currently working on a new research project dealing with Radical socialist-Zionism in the United states in the 1930s and the 1960s.

Frank Jacob is Professor for Global History (nineteenth and twentieth centuries) at Nord Universitet, Norway. Before this he held positions at Würzburg University, Germany and the City University of New York, USA. He has authored or edited more than fifty books and his current main research foci include the transnational history of anarchism and Japanese history (Meiji period), as well as comparative revolutionary history.

Hayim Katsman researches messianic political extremism in Israel. He was raised in a Jewish orthodox family, and currently lives in a Kibbutz (collective agricultural community) on the Israel-Gaza-Egypt border, where he works as a car mechanic. He received his M.A. from the Department of Politics and Government in Ben-Gurion University, and is currently entering a PhD program at the University of Washington.

Anne Klein is a historian, educational, and political scientist (Ph.D.) as well as researcher and senior lecturer at the University of Cologne. Her research focus is on Contemporary History, Social Movements, Democracy Education, Holocaust/Memory Studies, and Disability Studies/History. She prefers poststructuralist/discourse critical approaches in order to remember forgotten stories and support minority representation in academic and public discourse.

Ofira Gruweis-Kovalsky Is a Senior Lecturer at Zefat Academic College and Associate Researcher at Herzl Institute University of Haifa, Israel. Her published articles include "Israeli Policy on the Foreign Consulates in Jerusalem in the Early 1950s," *Israel Studies*, 24 no. 1 (2019); and "Map as an Official Symbol and the 'Greater Israel' Ideology," *Middle Eastern Studies* 53, no. 5 (2017).

Sebastian Kunze studied Middle Eastern Studies and Political Science at the Martin-Luther-University Halle-Wittenberg as well as Jewish Studies in Potsdam, Berlin, Southampton, and Jerusalem. In the academic year 2018 / 19 he was a Leo Baeck Fellow (Studienstiftung des deutschen Volkes / Leo Baeck Institute London). He currently works as a research associate at the University of Erfurt at the Chair for Judaic Studies and is writing his PhD thesis on Gustav Landauer as a Jewish Intellectual.

Peter Scott Lederer earned his BA and MA in English from SDSU. He is now at Queen's University Belfast researching Jewish filmmakers. His works include "Presence: An Existential-Humanistic Analysis of Bodymind Unity in *The Graduate*" (*The Dovetail* 2, 2016) and *The Critical Thinker: Examining the Fallacies of Our Convictions* (BVT Publishing, 2016).

Hannah Peaceman studied philosophy in Marburg, London and Jena. She is a research assistant at the Max Weber Centre (University of Erfurt). Her PhD focuses on "Jewish traditions in philosophy in the 19th century and their potential for political philosophy today". Hannah is editor of the magazine "Jalta – Positionen zur jüdischen Gegenwart".

Jan Rybak is currently a Postdoctoral Research Fellow Art the University of York. He received his PhD in History and Civilization from the European University Institute in Florence in 2018. He previously studied at the University of Salzburg and SOAS in London and had been a GEOP Research Fellow at POLIN: Museum for the History of the Polish Jews and the Jewish Historical Institute in Warsaw.

Morgan Shipley serves as an Academic Specialist in the Department of Religious Studies at Michigan State University. Author of *Psychedelic Mysticism: Transforming Consciousness, Religious Experiences, and Voluntary Peasants in Postwar America* (Lexington, 2015), his research focuses on American religious culture and new religions.

Roman Vater is a Leverhulme Trust Early Career Fellow at the Faculty of Asian and Middle Eastern Studies in the University of Cambridge and a fellow of St. Edmund's College, Cambridge. He was an Israel Institute post-doctoral fellow at the Oxford Centre for Hebrew and Jewish Studies in 2015 – 2017 and holds a PhD in Middle Eastern history from the University of Manchester (2015).

Index